privatization programs and making already-launched programs work more effectively. However, there is much that is still not understood, and it remains unclear just how important privatization is likely to be over the next quarter century. Megginson ends by assessing what assets governments have left to sell, and predicting the likely future course of privatization.

ABOUT THE AUTHOR

Bill Megginson is Professor and Rainbolt Chair in Finance at the University of Oklahoma's Michael F. Price College of Business. He is also a voting member of the Italian Ministry of Economics and Finance's Global Advisory Committee on Privatization. Professor Megginson's research in recent years has focused on the privatization of state-owned enterprises, executed through public share offerings. His work on significant performance improvements in recently privatized companies received the Smith Breeden Distinguished Paper Awards for outstanding research published in the *Journal of Finance*. He is author or co-author of seven textbooks. He has served as a privatization consultant for the New York Stock Exchange, the OECD, the IMF, the World Federation of Exchanges, and the World Bank. He is widely published in such journals as the *Journal of Economic Literature*, the *Journal of Finance*, the *Journal of Financial Economics*, the *Journal of Financial and Quantitative Analysis*, and *Foreign Policy*. Prior to entering academia in 1986, he worked for five years as a petroleum chemist.

The Financial Economics
of Privatization

The Financial Economics of Privatization

William L. Megginson

OXFORD
UNIVERSITY PRESS
2005

OXFORD
UNIVERSITY PRESS

Oxford   New York
Auckland   Bangkok   Buenos Aires   Cape Town   Chennai
Dar es Salaam   Delhi   Hong Kong   Istanbul   Karachi   Kolkata
Kuala Lumpur   Madrid   Melbourne   Mexico City   Mumbai   Nairobi
São Paulo   Shanghai   Taipei   Tokyo   Toronto

Published by Oxford University Press, Inc.
198 Madison Avenue, New York, New York 10016

www.oup.com

Oxford is a registered trademark of Oxford University Press

Library of Congress Cataloging-in-Publication Data

Megginson, William L.
The financial economics of privatization / William Leon Megginson.
p. cm.
Includes bibliographical references and index.
ISBN 0-19-515062-7 (alk. paper)
1. Privatization. 2. Government business enterprises. 3. Finance, Public. I. Title.
HD3845.6.M44 2005
338.9'27—dc22   2004004717

9 8 7 6 5 4 3 2 1
Printed in the United States of America
on acid-free paper

*This book is dedicated to my wife, Peggy,
our son, BJ, and our daughter, Melissa.*

Contents

The Financial Economics of Privatization

The Scope of Privatization

Pivotal events in economic history often pass with an almost surreal normalcy, only rarely evoking the drama of decisive battles or the excitement of great political moments. Nonetheless, economic events can impact human affairs just as decisively. The past quarter-century has certainly witnessed its share of fundamental political change and high military drama, but a strong case can be made that the economic changes that the world has experienced since 1979 are even more profound than the political changes that ended communist rule in central and eastern Europe and the revolution in warfare displayed in the Balkans, central Asia, and Iraq. The unhappy recent history of the nation of Afghanistan illustrates this point well.

When the Soviet Union invaded Afghanistan in November 1979, state power seemed as ascendant in world economics as it clearly was in world politics. Roughly a quarter of the world's population—living in what are today 29 countries—was ruled by communist governments, most developing countries had large state sectors and pursued development strategies emphasizing state direction, and state-owned enterprises accounted for 10 percent or more of total output in many Western democracies. By the time the Taliban government was expelled from Afghanistan and a new government installed under the protection of North Atlantic Treaty Organization (NATO) troops in 2003, the Soviet Union was a dozen years gone, the statist model of economic development had been thoroughly discredited, the output of state-owned enterprises as a fraction of world gross domestic product (GDP) had been cut roughly in half, and the sole remaining major communist power was Marxist in name only. While it is far too early to say that free-market economics has decisively routed socialism, capitalism has certainly won the last quarter-century's round on points.

The political and economic policy of privatization, broadly defined as the deliberate sale by a government of state-owned enterprises (SOEs) or assets to private economic agents, has been one of the most important and visible aspects of this global trend toward greater reliance on markets to allocate resources. Since its introduction by Britain's Thatcher government in the early 1980s to a then-skeptical public (which included many economists), privatization now appears to be accepted as a legitimate—often a core—tool of statecraft by governments of more than 100 countries. Privatization has not only dramatically reduced the direct role of the state in producing goods and services, it has also massively increased the size and efficiency of the world's capital markets and fueled an unprecedented increase in the number of people who own corporate shares.

This book attempts to tell the story of how privatization rose from a radical notion to economic orthodoxy in less than a generation, and in the process changed how we view the role of government in the business of nations. The story cannot be told without presenting a measure of economic theory, but the primary focus will be on those practical actions taken by politicians, economists, businesspersons, investors, and ordinary citizens in transitioning between government and private ownership of productive enterprises, and on the concepts that have guided their actions. To understand how and why privatization emerged when it did, we begin our narrative with a brief history of the rise and fall of state ownership in the modern era. After this, we ask and seek to answer a series of basic questions: How much privatization has actually occurred? Why have so many countries adopted privatization programs? What are the costs and benefits of state versus public ownership, both theoretically and in actual practice? How do governments privatize state-owned enterprises? And, most important, has privatization worked? As we will see, the general answer to this last question is yes, but yes with many qualifiers and nuances, especially regarding the evidence from the transition economies of central and eastern Europe.

The middle part of this book examines the impact that privatization has had, and is likely to continue having, on financial markets and corporate finance practices. Cynics might call these chapters "How Governments Helped American Investment Banks Conquer the World," but the impact of privatization on global finance is a critical and largely untold story. It is also a story that I, as a finance professor, find especially fascinating. As will be discussed at length in chapters 6 and 7, the ten largest (and 30 of the 35 largest) share offerings in history have all been privatization issues, and the biggest of these (the $40.6 billion Nippon Telegraph and Telephone offering in September 1987) is also the largest single security offering of any type in the history of finance. Furthermore, while American investment banks have indeed prospered by underwriting these share issue privatizations (SIPs), and many of these issues have been sold in part to U.S. investors, this is not primarily an American story. In fact, there have been very few privatizations of American SOEs for the simple reason that state ownership has never been popular in the United States. Americans have historically preferred to use regulation (augmented by private litigation) rather than state ownership to achieve political objectives in economic affairs.

Chapters 8 through 10 of this book analyze the privatization experiences of five industries that have seen the largest number of state ownership sales—specifically, telecommunications, banking, oil and gas, electricity production and distribution, and commercial airlines. A hard lesson that the world seemingly must keep re-learning is that privatizing companies operating in industries that are (or can be made to be) competitive is far easier than privatizing companies that are at least partly natural monopolies. This is especially true for critical infrastructure and transportation assets, as well as electric, water, oil and gas, or telecommunications utilities. Virtually any utility privatization necessarily imposes on the divesting government the need to establish a regulatory regime that simultaneously protects consumers from abuse by producers and protects producers from expropriation by regulators acting on behalf of consumers. Few governments have nailed this task on the first attempt, and all governments face the temptation of selling off an intact monopoly rather than first promoting effective competition, since private buyers will naturally be willing to pay a higher price for a private monopoly.

The final chapter of this book summarizes what experience and empirical research have taught are the key lessons of privatization and also examines several unresolved issues, especially the impact of state ownership sales on employment. As it happens, researchers know a great deal—both about what works and what does not work—and we can offer decision makers useful guidance in designing future privatization programs and making those programs already launched work more effectively. However, there is much we still do not understand, and it is also unclear just how important privatization is likely to be over the next quarter-century. We can (and do) assess what assets governments have left to sell, but we cannot predict where future citizens will choose to draw the line between the public and private sectors of a given nation's economy.

A Brief History of State Ownership Until 1979

State ownership of a given business activity or organization can arise for any of five generic reasons. First, state ownership can emerge as a natural extension of royal power in feudal or tribal societies. Though not important today, the next section shows that this largely explains how state ownership evolved during antiquity and the Middle Ages. Second, state ownership can emerge as a means to commercialize complex, vital, and/or expensive new technologies. This rationale became prominent during the late nineteenth and early twentieth centuries, as the technologies spawned by the industrial revolution multiplied in scale and import. Third, states often nationalize failing private businesses, either to preserve employment or to continue producing essential goods and services, or both. This can occur either on an ad hoc basis, for an individual company, or in response to a systemic economic crisis such as the Great Depression. The fourth reason for state ownership—ideology—largely explains the rise in state-owned enterprises in the post–World War II era. At one extreme, communist governments considered private ownership of land or enterprise to be inherently exploitative, and thus prohibited private ownership entirely. Further rightward on the political spectrum, even ardently social democratic governments allowed private ownership in many areas, but insisted that the state own the "commanding heights" of the national economy. The fifth and final reason for state ownership is extreme political factionalism. In societies that are fundamentally divided by race, class, religion, or ethnicity, state ownership of key enterprises provides vast opportunities for the group in power to punish the other group(s) and favor its own members. All five of these rationales have played some role in explaining the historical evolution of state ownership, though each has been more important at different times and in different places, as we now discuss.

State Ownership in Antiquity and the Middle Ages

Throughout history, there has been a mixture of public (often including religious institutions) and private ownership of production and commerce. Sobel (1999) writes that state ownership of the means of production, including mills and metal working, was common in the ancient Near East, while private ownership was more common in trading and money lending. The Bible mentions moneylenders, who were essentially bankers [Means (2001)]. In ancient Greece, the government owned the land, forests, and mines, but contracted out the work to individuals and firms. The rise of state owned-banks also occurred in Greece at essentially the same time. In the Ch'in dynasty of China, the government had monopolies on salt and iron, but by the 1500s it had developed sophisticated markets where private parties transacted in luxury goods such as silk and tortoise shells [Means (2001)]. Ancient Egypt had state monopolies on the manufacture of various products including papyrus, beer, honey, salt, and vegetable oils. The state controlled the entire production process—planting, retailing, prices, and wages. In addition, the state severely restricted foreign imports.

Ancient Rome provides examples of both private and state ownership. Sobel (1999) notes that in the Roman Republic the "publicani (private individuals and companies) fulfilled virtually all the of the state's economic requirements" (1999, page 21). He writes that the state contracted out for "tax collection, supplying the army, providing for religious sacrifices and . . . construction." In the Roman Republic, almost all goods, whether contracted for by the state or private parties, were produced by the private sector. Some very large firms even arose, with one mining firm employing 40,000 people. Sobel goes on to discuss that the replacement of the Roman Republic with the Roman Empire led to a greatly increased role for the state in producing and distributing goods. For example, much of the grain for the empire was grown on large estates belonging to the emperor and worked by tenant farmers. Private enterprise remained, especially in the manufacturing and trading of textiles. Sobel also suggests that the great cost of the government bureaucracy was one of the reasons for the fall of Rome.

In the thousand years between the fall of Rome and the beginning of the industrial revolution, Europe's economic system evolved in various ways. Throughout this period, the Catholic Church exerted a strong influence on how commerce developed and for whom goods were produced (often for the Church). As in Imperial Rome, there were wealthy landowners and tenant farmers, and a mixture of state and private ownership. However, as time went on markets and private entrepreneurs began to arise in many different contexts. Sobel reports that by the year 1000, local knights would organize fairs that often lasted several weeks, where merchants, who had paid a fee to the knight, would sell goods they had bought from other private producers (or made themselves). At the same time, moneylenders would lend to many people, including the rulers. Many of the loans had large default risks with no enforceable collateral (especially the loans to the rulers). Thus, the moneylenders charged high interest rates and as a result were often despised, an early example of how people do not like the distribution of wealth that arises with the use of markets. Sobel notes that Dante reserved a special place for moneylenders in Hell. However, the finance industry developed, and by the 1300s the Italian city-states became major centers for monetary commerce. Markets and private ownership developed in other settings, and Rondinelli and Iacono (1996) note that by the time of the industrial revolution in the Western industrialized societies and their colonies, the private sector was the most important producer of commercial goods and was also important in providing public goods and services.

To summarize, until the late Middle Ages, state ownership arose primarily as a natural extension of royal power. In Asia, this power was generally near absolute, so there was little differentiation between "royal" and "private" property. Royal power in Europe, however, was always constrained by competition from lesser nobles, the Church, and from the eleventh century on, private merchants and entrepreneurs. As the power of the crown (and private entrepreneurs) increased relative to that of princes and the Church, truly national states emerged with vast holdings of land and with the power to tax, regulate trade, and produce goods (particularly ships and weaponry) on a national basis. The efficiency and stability engendered by this consolidation of royal power promoted much more rapid growth in trade, finance, and industry, but it was also accompanied by a significant increase in state ownership and control.

The Industrial Revolution's Impact on State Ownership

Just as the industrial revolution marked the beginning of the modern economic and industrial era, it also inaugurated the first truly "modern" debates about state versus private ownership. Many of the new technologies that emerged from European workshops after 1750 required adopters to obtain financial and organizational capital on a hitherto unprecedented scale. Furthermore, many of the emerging technologies also had decisive military applications, which spelled potential ruin for any country that could not successfully incorporate the new machines and processes into their societies. For both philosophical and practical reasons, a few countries (particularly Britain and, later, the United States) chose to allow private enterprise to take the lead role in commercializing steam power, iron and steel manufacturing, railroading, telegraph and telephone communications, chemical manufacturing, oil exploration and production, electricity production, and the other transforming new technologies. The publication by Adam Smith of *The Wealth of Nations* in 1776 also provided a strong intellectual rationale for promoting private versus state ownership of most businesses (except, famously, the mail service).

However, given the stakes of the competitive and colonizing era that emerged after the Napoleonic Wars, many national governments felt compelled to rely on state ownership and funding in order to commercialize some or all of these vital technologies. As a corollary, these same states generally prohibited private companies from competing with state-owned enterprises, which thus evolved into monopolies. Wallsten (2002) provides a clear example of how and why France, Germany, and many other European nations chose to roll out telephone communications through a state-owned monopoly, whereas Sweden, Britain, and the United States allowed private entrepreneurs to compete to deliver phone service. Even though telephone service spread far more rapidly, and with much higher quality standards, in private-ownership countries than in those dominated by state-owned enterprises, the notion that "telecoms" was a natural monopoly soon took hold, and by the early 1920s telecommunications had become a state-owned monopoly in most countries except the United States. Table 1.1 describes the organizational structure of the telecommunications industry in several countries during the early twentieth century, as well as the number of phone lines provided by government versus private operators and national teledensity — the number of phone lines per 100 people. Most of the large continental European countries had state-owned telecom monopolies, while the Scandinavian countries, the United States, and even several developing countries allowed private competition — and enjoyed much better service.

During the period leading up to World War I, and for the immediate postwar period, this pattern of heavy state ownership was repeated for the commercialization of many other basic utilities and services, particularly electricity generation and distribution, water and sewage services, and gas distribution. The massive economic dislocation that resulted from World War I also promoted state intervention, as did the success of war economy measures in many countries — including Britain and the United States. Governments frequently ended up controlling a nation's railroads (even in the United States during WWI), either by design or in response to the failure of private companies, and most ports were owned and operated by local or national governments. Full or partial government ownership also became the norm for national airlines, with the United States once more the sole important exception.[1]

On the other hand, there was much greater heterogeneity in the ownership structure chosen for other capital-intensive industrial sectors. Most large mining and manufacturing companies (even those producing weaponry) were founded by private entrepreneurs and developed under private ownership, at least until the onset of the Great Depression forced governments to nationalize failing firms during the 1930s. Oil exploration and production was more of a mixed bag. Most of the American, British, and Anglo/Dutch companies that dominated the global petroleum industry until the rise of the Organization of Petroleum Exporting Countries (OPEC) were privately owned, though the British government had purchased a large equity stake in British Petroleum prior to World War I (at the prompting of Winston Churchill, then First Lord of the Admiralty) as a way of ensuring secure oil supplies for the Royal Navy.[2]

TABLE 1.1. The Organizational Structure of Telephone Companies in the Early 20th Century

Country	Government Monopoly	Number of Telephones, January 1914		Teledensity, January 1914
		Government	Private	
United States	No	0	9,542,017	9.7
Canada	No	106,183	393,591	6.5
New Zealand	Yes	49,415	0	4.6
Denmark	No	1,586	127,691	4.5
Sweden	No	158,171	74,837	4.1
Norway	No	40,120	42,430	3.4
Australia	Yes	137,485	0	2.8
Switzerland	Yes	96,624	0	2.5
German Empire	Yes	1,420,000	0	2.1
Great Britain	No (before 1911)	780,512	0	1.7
Luxembourg	Yes	4,239	0	1.6
Netherlands	No	76,267	10,223	1.4
Finland	No	0	40,000	1.2
Uruguay	No	0	13,599	1.0
World total	—	**4,128,278**	**10,760,272**	**0.9**
Argentina	No	0	74,296	0.9
Belgium	Yes	65,000	0	0.9
France	Yes	330,000	0	0.8
Cuba	No	299	15,798	0.7
Austria	Yes	172,344	0	0.6
Chile	No	0	74,296	0.6
South Africa	Yes	28,889	0	0.5
Japan	Yes	219,551	0	0.4
Hungary	Yes	84,040	0	0.4
Italy	No	61,978	29,742	0.3
Romania	Yes	20,000	0	0.3
Russia (European)	No	157,710	162,148	0.2
Spain	No	2,722	31,278	0.2
Portugal	No	1,203	7,647	0.2
Brazil	No	1,165	38,018	0.2

Source: Table 1 (supplemented with data from Table 4) of Wallsten (September, 2002).

Note: This table details whether several Western countries organized telephony services as state-owned monopolies or allowed private ownership and competition during the formative years before World War I. The number of telephone subscribers from public and private providers and teledensity (telephone lines per 100 population) levels are also provided.

The Great Depression Spurs State Ownership

As Reviglio (2002) shows, the economic catastrophe of the Great Depression prompted many governments to take on a vastly more active role in economic management. The publication of John Maynard Keynes's book, *The General Theory of Employment, Interest and Money*, in 1934 provided an intellectual rationale for hugely increased government intervention in economic life, though the greatest impact of his teaching occurred long after his death 12 years later. In Mussolini's

Italy, the Instituto per la Rivconstruzione Italiana (IRI) was founded, also in 1934, to take over the assets of the three largest commercial banks and the industrial companies they controlled. Over time, IRI and other state-owned holding companies came to play a truly sweeping role in Italy's economic life. Figure 1.1 demonstrates the reach of IRI immediately before it launched a major privatization program in 1994.

The socialist government of Leon Blum, which came to power at the height of the Great Depression, targeted (unsuccessfully) many French industries for nationalization. However, the first truly sweeping French nationalizations occurred immediately after the end of World War II, and were prompted in no small part by the perception that French bankers and industrialists had collaborated with the Nazi occupiers. In the eyes of millions of the citizens in Western countries, the suffering caused by the Great Depression—and the inability of private business to right itself after the slump began—undermined the basic legitimacy of the capitalist system. Up to that time, most people had been willing to accept capitalism's inequality and insecurity in exchange for the dynamism, wealth, and growth that free enterprise delivered. The Depression seemed to show that only the inequality and insecurity remained. In comparison, the rosy picture of industrial growth and social progress in the Soviet Union put forward by communist propagandists appeared very attractive; the brutal nature of Stalinism and the hideous human cost of Soviet industrial "progress" would become clear only much later.

The response to the crisis of the Great Depression varied around the world, but in every country the response included greater government involvement in economic life. Reviglio (2002) provides an excellent description of the spread of government economic activism in western Europe from the 1930s onward. In some countries, this involved outright nationalization of business enterprises, but more often governments attempted to tax, spend, and regulate their way to prosperity—always without success. In Germany and Japan, aggressively expansionist governments centralized economic and political power and launched huge arms-production programs. Even though most of the companies involved remained privately owned, state power in these two countries became both absolute and malignant.

The locust years of the 1930s gave way to the even more cataclysmic years of World War II. State power reached a height (or depth, depending upon one's perspective) never seen before or since, and the war ended with Europe's colonial powers in ruins and the Soviet Union controlling all of central Europe and one-third of Germany. Even in the victorious Western democracies, the total economic and industrial mobilization that occurred during WWII dramatically increased the power (and prestige) of national governments as economic managers, and set the stage for the postwar surge in ideologically motivated state ownership. Finally, the defeat of Japanese imperialism in China opened the way for a death struggle between Nationalist and Communist forces, which Mao Tse-tung's Communists won in 1949. This victory, coupled with the Soviet occupation of eastern Europe, and the spread of Marxist revolutionary movements in Southeast Asia, put much of the Eurasian landmass under communist rule.

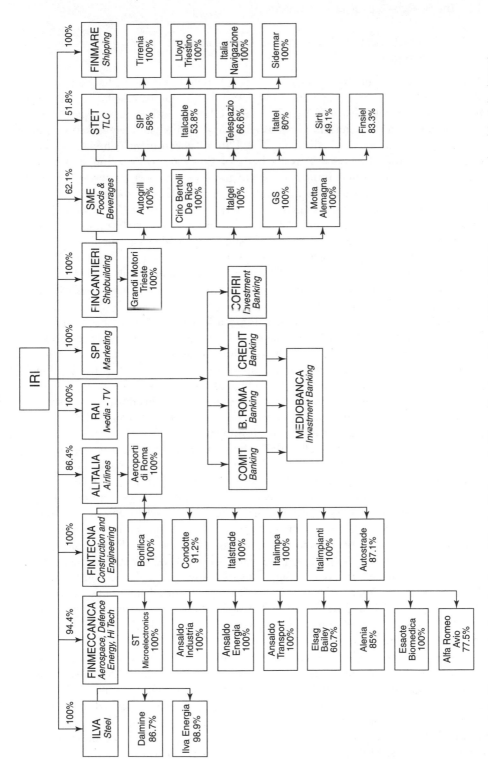

FIGURE 1.1. The organization structure of the Instituto per la Riconstruzione Italiana (RI) in 1992. Source: Bemporad and Reviglio (2002).

The Post–World War II Rise of State Ownership as an Ideology

Though one can argue that democracy emerged victorious from the Second World War, at least in western Europe, this most certainly was not the case for capitalism. Immediately after the defeat of Nazi Germany, Clement Attlee's Labour party won a sweeping electoral victory in Great Britain, and immediately embarked on an ambitious program of nationalization. The Labour government nationalized the coal and steel industries, as well as the Bank of England, civil aviation, and most public transport and utility businesses. Within a few years, over 20 percent of the economy was monopolized in state hands [Reviglio (2002)]. Labour also set out to create the "welfare state," as envisioned by the wartime Beveridge Report. The most important and visible manifestation of this philosophy was the establishment of the National Health Service as a purely state-run, single-payer medical system [Reviglio (2002)]. Even though the Conservative government of Winston Churchill that took power in the early 1950s reversed the nationalization of the steel companies, the basic course of state ownership in the British economy was set and remained so for three decades.

Most of the countries of western Europe adopted the "mixed economy" or "social market economy" model to one degree or another in the postwar period. France, Italy, Spain, and Portugal embraced state ownership enthusiastically, while Germany, the Netherlands, and Sweden opted for less direct state ownership but greater regulation and direction. The ideological impetus toward ever closer economic and political union in western Europe that grew steadily during the postwar era also contributed to the growth of state power, not least because of France's position as the leading player in European integration.

During the three decades after 1945, state ownership extended remorselessly in western Europe and other developed economies (such as Canada). Much of this growth was by deliberate design, as governments sought to control the commanding heights (key sectors) of their economies. Almost without exception, water, oil and gas, electricity, and telecom utilities were state owned, and in many countries (France, Spain, Italy, and Portugal after 1974), state-owned banks were also given either monopoly or protected positions, as discussed in La Porta, Lopez-de-Silanes, and Shleifer (2002). Many politicians also believed the state should control certain "strategic" manufacturing industries, such as steel and defense production. Nationalizations of failing industries also occurred frequently. This, in fact, is how the British government ended up owning most of the country's automotive industry, as well as the aero engine manufacturer Rolls-Royce.

Taking the ideologically motivated and the failing-firm nationalizations together, by the mid-1970s, the state directly owned companies producing more than 10 percent of national output in many Western democracies. Typically, these SOEs accounted for an even higher share of total investment, so they held tremendous sway over most economies. Even as state ownership reached its zenith, however, serious doubts about the efficiency and beneficence of SOEs began to be widely expressed. A seeming aberration occurred at the end of this long period, when the socialist Mitterand government was elected to power in France in 1981.

This government enacted a sweeping nationalization program, but was forced into a major policy reversal within two years.

State-Directed Development Policies Take Root in Developing Countries

Rondinelli and Iacono (1996) argue that government ownership grew in the developing world for slightly different reasons than in developed countries, primarily because government ownership was perceived as necessary to promote growth. In the postcolonial countries of Asia, Africa, and Latin America, governments sought rapid growth through heavy investment in physical facilities. Another reason for government ownership, often through nationalization, was a historical resentment of the foreigners who had owned many of the largest firms in these countries [see also Noll (2000)]. Extreme political factionalism, mentioned above as an explanation for state ownership, was a distressingly frequent motive in developing countries for nationalizing existing private businesses or starting new SOEs from scratch.

Many developing countries also had specific, intriguing reasons for pursuing state ownership as a core political objective. Mahatma Gandhi's philosophy of simplicity and self-sufficiency (a spinning wheel in every village) had an enduring influence on India's economic development—though it is likely that Nehru's love of state-directed industrial development and import substitution contributed far more to India's embrace of state socialism. Unfortunately, the result was much slower economic growth than other Asian countries achieved for the first four decades after India's independence. The "permit Raj" that developed under Nehru's administration stifled entrepreneurship and made the national and state governments the economic masters of India. Since India quickly emerged as a political and intellectual leader of the Third World, its embrace of statist economic policies helped legitimize state ownership and heavy-handed intervention in many developing countries.

China's adoption of a particularly virulent form of Marxism after 1949 precluded any private ownership for almost three decades. Coupled with the policy absurdities enacted during various "great leap forward" plans and the Cultural Revolution, China suffered several severe famines during the 1950s and 1960s. By the time of Chairman Mao's death in 1976, China had become one of the poorest, least educated, and most backward countries on earth. The contrast between China's economic performance during the period after 1949 and that of other ethnic-Chinese states such as Taiwan, Singapore, and Hong Kong could hardly be more striking. It was almost in desperation that the Chinese Communist Party began to experiment with limited private ownership in 1978.

Statist policies triumphed in many other developing countries during the 1950s, 1960s, and 1970s. Latin American countries were particularly keen adherents, primarily because the state-directed development model seemingly offered a way to create enduring economic growth without surrendering control of their economies to the United States. This was especially important for Mexico, which changed its constitution in 1936 to reserve the nation's oil and gas sector exclusively for state ownership. Juan Perón in Argentina was an enthusiastic fan of state ownership, as were the generals who controlled Brazil (and far too many other countries in the region) off and on for much of the postwar era. Vast sums of petrodollars were borrowed by Latin American governments during the 1970s and early 1980s in order to fund large state-sponsored projects and programs. The result was generally default, followed by depression and the resulting "lost decade" of the 1980s. While the origins of state ownership in sub-Saharan Africa were somewhat different from those in Latin America, statist policies were adopted with equal fervor and had the same dismal impact throughout the region.

In sum, by the late 1970s, many countries had embraced state ownership as an economic policy, but many were also becoming disenchanted with the actual performance of state-owned enterprises. In hindsight, the movement toward privatization seems inevitable — but it hardly appeared so at the time.[3] Instead, this was adopted warily, even fearfully, and always in the teeth of fierce opposition. In fact, the story of privatization's rise and eventual triumph is nothing short of epic.

The Rise of Privatization, 1979–2002

Early Attempts at "Denationalization"

Most people associate modern privatization programs with Margaret Thatcher's Conservative government, which came to power in Great Britain in 1979. However, the government of Konrad Adenauer, in the Federal Republic of Germany, launched the first large-scale, ideologically motivated "denationalization" program of the postwar era. In 1961, the German government sold a majority stake in Volkswagen in a public share offering heavily weighted in favor of small investors.[4] Four years later, the government launched an even larger offering for shares in the chemical firm VEBA. These two issues increased the number of shareholders in Germany from 500,000 to almost 3 million, but public enthusiasm for further issues cooled after VEBA's stock price declined, and the government was forced to bail out many small shareholders. Many years were to pass before another major Western nation chose to pursue privatization as a core economic or political policy.

Revealingly, the objectives set for Germany's privatization program by the Adenauer government were virtually the same as those listed 20 years later by the Conservative British government of Margaret Thatcher, and by almost every government in the years since. These goals, as described in Price Waterhouse (1989a, b), are to (1) raise revenue for the state, (2) promote economic efficiency, (3) reduce government interference in the economy, (4) promote wider share ownership, (5) provide the opportunity to introduce competition, and (6) subject SOEs to market discipline.[5] The other major objective mentioned by the Thatcher and subsequent governments was to develop the national capital market and promote wider share ownership among the citizenry.[6]

The only country to pursue a significant privatization program during the 1970s was Chile, and this program is described and assessed by Yotopoulos (1989). The Pinochet government of Chile, which gained power after the ouster of Salvador Allende in 1973, attempted to privatize companies that the Allende government had nationalized. However, the process was poorly executed and required very little equity investment from purchasers of assets being divested. Thus, many of these same firms were re-nationalized once Chile entered its debt and payments crisis in the early 1980s. Chile's second privatization program, which was launched in the mid-1980s and relied less on direct sales to corporate and more on public share offerings to individual investors (including SOE employees), was much more successful.

The Early Thatcher Years, 1979–1984

Although the Thatcher government may not have been the first to launch a large privatization program, it is without question the most important historically. Privatization was not a major campaign theme for the Tories in 1979, but the new Conservative government embraced the policy. Margaret Thatcher adopted the label "privatization," which was originally coined by Peter Drucker and which replaced the name "denationalization" [Yergin and Stanislaw (1998), page 114].[7] Early sales were strenuously attacked by the Labour opposition, which promised that if it were reelected it would to renationalize firms such as British Aerospace and Cable and Wireless. Table 1.2 provides details on the influential early share issue privatizations.

In spite of political opposition, however, the Thatcher government prevailed. The early privatization share offerings were enthusiastically received, and the recently privatized firms were widely perceived as being run more efficiently after divestiture. Further, it soon became clear that the spur of "readying a company for privatization" served to overcome organizational inertia and focus the targeted SOE's employees on the task of improving efficiency and profitability. Finally, the government was able to dramatically lower its public-sector borrowing requirement (PSBR) through the ongoing privatization share sales. When Margaret Thatcher won a second term in 1983, largely on the back of her government's successful prosecution of the Falklands War, the future of privatization in Great Britain was secure.

It was the British Telecom (BT) initial public offering in November 1984 that launched privatization programs on the world stage. This enormous share issue — by far the largest equity offering in history to that time — was met with strong demand by investors (including employees) both in Britain and abroad. The £3.9 billion ($4.8 billion) issue created 2.25 million new shareholders in Britain, and the response of Japanese and American investors to the tranches offered in Tokyo and New York showed that a global market for privatization share offerings existed. Furthermore, the regulatory regime adopted for BT, while necessarily a compromise, appeared workable and fair to consumers, BT's competitors, and its investors. Most critically, the successful sale of BT showed that size alone was not an impediment to successful privatization. A series of increasingly massive SIPs during the last half of the 1980s and early 1990s reduced the role of SOEs in the British economy to essentially nothing after the Tories left office in 1997, from more than 10 percent of GDP 18 years earlier.

TABLE 1.2. Historically Significant Share Issue Privatizations, 1961–2003

Company	Country	Date	Amount US$ Millions	Fraction Sold (%)	Times Offer Subscribed	First Day Return (%)	# Shareholders Created, mln
Volkswagen	Germany	Mar 1961	$315	60%	2	109.3%	—
British Petroleum	United Kingdom	Jun 1977	$972	17	4.7	22.7	—
British Aerospace	United Kingdom	Feb 1981	$339	51.6	3.5	14.0	—
British Telecommunications	United Kingdom	Nov 1984	$4,763	50.2	9.7	86.0	2.25
British Gas	United Kingdom	Dec 1986	$8,012	100	4.0	23.0	—
Banque Paribas	France	Jan 1987	$2,740	100	40.0	18.5	3.81
Nippon Telegraph and Telephone	Japan	Feb 1987	$15,097	12.5	6	55.0	—
British Petroleum	United Kingdom	Oct 1987	$12,430	31.4	<1.0	−21.5	—
Nippon Telegraph and Telephone	Japan	Nov 1987	$40,260[a]	12.5	—	3.1	—
Conrail	United States	Mar 1989	$1,650	85	>1	10.3	—
Telefonos de Chile (ADR)	Chile	Sep 1990	$89	—[b]	>1	7.4	—
Telefonos de Mexico	Mexico	May 1991	$2,170	14.8	>1	0	—
Deutsche Telekom	Germany	Nov 1996	$13,300	26	5	19	2+
France Telecom	France	Oct 1997	$7,080	23	3	15.0	3.91
ENEL	Italy	Nov 1999	$18,900	34.5	heavily	0	3.8
PetroChina	China	Apr 2000	$2,890	10[b]	—	−4.7	—
Statoil	Norway	June 2001	$2,900	20[b]	—	0	—
Bank of China	China	Jul 2002	$2,800	—[b]	—	−4.7	—
Saudi Telecom	Saudi Arabia	Jan 2003	$3,700	30	—	—	—

Source: Financial Times, various issues, as reported in appendix 1.

Note: This table presents financial details about 20 of the most historically significant share issue privatizations since the first postwar "denationalization" of Volkswagen in 1961. More detailed descriptions of each offering are presented in the text.

[a]Seasoned equity offering. All others are IPOs.

[b]Primary, capital-raising share issue, in whole or in part. All others are pure secondary offerings where proceeds accrue to selling government.

Privatization Spreads to Western Europe and Asia, 1984–1988

The perceived success of the British privatization program helped persuade many other industrialized countries to begin divesting SOEs through public share offerings. The next major country to adopt a large-scale privatization, France, was also one of the most important, since it marked such a sharp break with the country's dirigiste tradition of state intervention. The conservative Chirac government came to power in March 1986, committed not only to selling off the industrial and financial groups nationalized by the socialists in 1981 and 1982 [see Dumontier and Laurin (2002)] but also to privatizing the large banks that Charles de Gaulle nationalized in 1945. True to its word, the Chirac government sold 22 major companies worth $12 billion in a 15-month period beginning in September 1986. When the socialists returned to power in 1988, they stopped the sales of further companies, but they did not attempt to renationalize those firms already sold.

In addition to France, Austria, Belgium, Canada, Chile, Denmark, Holland, Italy, Jamaica, Japan, Malaysia, Singapore, Spain, Sweden, and the United States all executed significant privatizations through public share offerings during the mid-1980s. The Japanese sequential privatization of Nippon Telegraph and Telephone (NTT) is significant for several reasons. First, NTT's initial public offering (IPO) of ¥2.34 trillion ($15.1 billion) set a new record for IPO issue size, which was to last until 1999, and this offering yielded an implied market capitalization for NTT of $188 billion.[8] The second and third NTT tranches, in late 1987 and early 1988, raised even larger amounts. As noted earlier, the $40.6 billion NTT tranche in 1988 remains the largest security offering ever, and the three issues collectively raised over $80 billion. Furthermore, the Japanese government deliberately chose not to break up NTT before (or after) its sale, but instead adopted the British RPI-X regulatory regime for a partially privatized telephone monopoly. Finally, the first two NTT offerings were several times oversubscribed and were restricted to Japanese investors only.

Somewhat surprisingly, the only major privatization through public share offering implemented by the United States during the 1980s was also one of the most highly politicized SIPs during this period, as described in Baldwin and Bhattacharya (1991). Even so, the $1.65 billion Conrail issue was successfully executed and was also the largest share offering in U.S. history to that time. In total, roughly $40 billion was being raised worldwide through privatization sales most years during the late 1980s, with the bulk of that coming from European and Japanese SIPs.

Privatization Goes Global, 1989–March 2000

After 1987, privatization programs spread rapidly around the world, particularly to the developing countries of Latin America, Africa, and South Asia. Most of these involved selling an SOE directly to a private corporation or individual in a process called an "asset sale," but several were sold to individual investors through public share offerings. After 1990, the pace of privatization steadily increased, and became positively frenetic after 1995. By that time, several dozen countries were selling SOEs every year, and total annual proceeds topped $100 billion for the first time in 1996. Beginning in 1993, the Balladur government launched a new and even larger French privatization program, which continued under the Jospin administration. The socialists, in fact, launched the two largest French privatizations ever, the $7.1 billion France Telecom IPO in October 1997 and the subsequent $10.5 billion seasoned France Telecom issue in November 1998.

Several other European governments, including Germany, Spain, Portugal, and most spectacularly, Italy, also launched large privatization programs during the 1990s. Italy announced in 1992 that it would begin dismantling its principal state holding company, the IRI, through privatization sales, and the actual divestment program commenced in 1994. Astonishingly, this goal was completed in only eight years, and raised almost $90 billion for the Italian Treasury. IRI shut its doors in October 2002, after transferring the remaining unsold assets to the Treasury for full and timely disposal as market conditions allowed. The 1999 IPO of the electricity company ENEL, which raised $18.9 billion for the Italian government, remains the largest initial public offering in financial history.

European programs typically relied on public share offerings, and were often launched by avowedly socialist governments. Privatization also blossomed in the Pacific Rim, beginning in the late 1980s. Japan sold only a relative handful of SOEs during the 1990s (usually relying on SIPs), but as noted many of these were truly enormous. Elsewhere in Asia, governments took an opportunistic approach to SOE divestment, selling pieces of large companies when market conditions were attractive, or when money was needed to plug budget deficits.

Two Asian countries deserve special attention for their privatization programs (or lack thereof) during the 1990s. These two countries were already the world's second and fifth largest economies on a purchasing-power-parity basis, and promised to become even more important over time. The People's Republic of China launched a major economic reform and liberalization program in the late 1970s that transformed the productivity of the Chinese economy. While there were numerous small privatizations, there were relatively few outright sales of SOEs, so the overall impact of privatization has thus far been quite limited. The other special Asian case was India, which adopted a major economic reform and liberalization program in 1991, after being wedded to state-directed economic development for the first 44 years of its independence. India's reform program shared two key features with China's: it was adopted in response to highly disappointing SOE performance [see Majumdar (1996, 1998)], and privatization did not figure prominently in the reform agenda.

On the other hand, Latin America truly embraced privatization during the 1990s. Chile's program was particularly important, for two reasons. As noted, it was Latin America's first. Additionally, the 1990 Telefonos de Chile privatization, which used a large American depository receipt (ADR) share tranche that was targeted at U.S. investors, opened the first important pathway that developing countries could use to directly tap Western capital markets. Mexico's program was both vast in scope and remarkably successful at reducing the state's role in what had been a highly interventionist economy. La Porta and López-de-Silanes (1999) report that in 1982 Mexican SOEs produced 14 percent of GDP, received net transfers and subsidies equal to 12.7 percent of GDP, and accounted for 38 percent of fixed capital investment. By June 1992, the government had privatized 361 of its roughly 1,200 SOEs and the need for subsidies had been virtually eliminated.

Several other countries in Latin America also executed large divestment programs, as described in McKenzie and Mookherjee (2003), Macedo (2000), Pombo and Ramirez (2001), and others. For example, Bolivia's innovative "capitalization" scheme was widely acclaimed. However, the most important program in the region was Brazil's. Given the size of Brazil's economy and its privatization program, and the fact that the Cardoso government was able to sell several very large SOEs (CVRD in 1997 and Telebras in 1998), in spite of significant political opposition, this country's program was particularly influential.

Privatization in sub-Saharan Africa was something of a stealth economic policy during the 1990s. Few governments openly adopted an explicit SOE divestment strategy, though Bennell (1997, 2003) and Nellis (2003) show that there was substantially more privatization in the region than is commonly believed. For example, Jones, Megginson, Nash, and Netter (1999) show that Nigeria was one of the most frequent sellers of SOEs using public share offerings, although most of these were very small. The experience of the African National Congress (ANC) after it came to power in South Africa also shows the policy realities that governments with interventionist instincts faced in the 1990s—and still face today. Though nationalization and redistribution of wealth were central planks of ANC ideology for decades, the Mandela and Mbeki governments almost totally refrained from nationalizations, and even executed several partial sales of SOEs, though use of the word *privatization* remains taboo.

The Transition Economies Embrace Privatization After 1989

The last major region to adopt privatization programs comprised the former Soviet-bloc countries of central and eastern Europe. These countries began privatizing SOEs as part of a broader effort to transform themselves from command into market economies. Therefore, they faced the most difficult challenges and had the most restricted set of policy choices. After the collapse of communism in 1989–1991, all of the newly elected governments of the region were under pressure to create something resembling a market economy as quickly as possible.

However, political considerations essentially required these governments to significantly limit foreign purchases of divested assets. Since the region's citizens had few financial savings, most of the newly democratic governments of central and eastern Europe launched "mass privatization" programs. These programs generally involved distributing vouchers to the population, which citizens could then use to bid for shares in companies being privatized. These programs resulted in a massive reduction of state ownership and were initially popular politically. However, public disenchantment soon set in, as it became clear that the best divested firms always ended up being controlled by insiders, and that the performance of most "privatized" firms was not improving much—if at all. The net effects of voucher privatizations have been disappointing in most cases but have varied widely. We discuss the workings of voucher schemes in chapter 3 and survey the empirical evidence on mass privatization in chapter 5.

Privatization Since March 2000

By early 2000, the privatization bandwagon seemed set to roll on forever. Governments raised over $140 billion every year from 1997 to 2000—when governments collectively raised a record $180 billion. However, the sharp decline in stock market valuations that commenced on America's NASDAQ in March 2000 soon took the exuberance out of further SIPs. This decline (more like a meltdown) in valuations was especially dramatic for telecom companies, which hit the prospects for additional privatization issues particularly hard since these had been by far the largest and most important share issues. With so many SIPs in the "pipeline" as the market began to tank, 2000 still went on to be a record year for global privatization proceeds, but by year-end a serious contraction was underway.

Total privatization proceeds dropped to a mere $51 billion in 2001, and even further during 2002. Nonetheless, there were several important privatization deals during this two-year period, particularly in Asia. China began selling parts of its three national oil companies in early 2000, beginning with a $2.89 billion offering of a 10 percent stake in PetroChina in April and the public offering of a stake in Sinopec, which raised $3.47 billion, in October 2000. The year 2001 witnessed the sale of an initial stake in China National Offshore Oil Company (CNOOC) in February, raising $1.4 billion, plus the floatation of a second tranche of Sinopec (in August), which also raised $1.40 billion. China executed two large SIPs of its principal telecommunications providers, China Telecom and Unicom, in 2002 and also began selling off its holdings in the "Big Four" state-owned banks with a $2.8 billion partial floatation of the Bank of China in July 2002. All told, the Chinese government raised almost $21 billion through SIPS between April 2000 and the end of 2002.[9]

Elsewhere in Asia, the Korean government began to aggressively divest itself of holdings in commercial businesses after the global stock markets began falling in March 2000. Between September 2000 and October 2002, Korea executed six major public share offerings, raising almost $8 billion in total. Though this sum doesn't appear especially large for so prominent a country, this two-year total is equal to 44 percent of all the proceeds the Korean government has ever raised through public offerings of shares in state enterprises. By contrast, the Japanese government executed only two significant privatization offerings after 2000—of shares in NTT and its cellular phone subsidiary, NTTDoCoMo—but these raised $19.5 billion!

Not all of the post–March 2000 privatization "action" was in Asia. France executed several SIPs of stakes in key companies during this period, including ST Microelectronics, the European Aeronautic Defense and Space Agency (EADS, the parent of Airbus), Thomson Multimedia, Credit Agricole, and Renault. In all, the French government raised almost $23 billion through public offerings alone after March 2000.[10] The Italian, Norwegian, Brazilian, and Austrian governments also executed one or more significant SIPs after March 2000.

At this writing (May 2004), it appears that a slight turnaround may be underway. Although 2003's total volume of $46.6 billion was below 2002's level of $69.2 billion, it exceeded 2001's volume, and the year closed out with several large sales. Perhaps the most intriguing privatizations of 2003 were the $500 million SIP of a 25 percent stake in South Africa's Telkom in March, a series of three tobacco company sales during the spring and summer, and several large Chinese SIPs toward year's end. Beginning in May 2003, the Moroccan, Italian, and Turkish governments auctioned off their ownership in national tobacco companies to multinational bidders, raising almost $5 billion in the process. All three auctions raised significantly more than expected, though it is not clear whether this merely represents increasing scarcity value in a rapidly consolidating industry or a more general increase in overall privatization activity. While only time will tell whether, and how vigorously, privatization sales will resume over the 2004–2006 period, the sharp recent rise in stock market valuations around the world clearly suggests that another secular rise in SIPs and asset sales looks increasingly likely. However, it is unlikely that we will again reach the $140 billion annual sales level any time soon.

Details of Individual National Privatization Programs

This chapter's cursory historical overview of privatization's evolution as a policy, and its dissemination around the world, hardly does justice to the subject. Further, our overview barely hints at the diverse details of the program's design in different countries. Table 1.3 presents a summary of 55 empirical studies that discuss the historical background of state ownership and the subsequent adoption of privatization programs in 40 countries. The interested reader can obtain any of these papers either from the journal cited or by downloading the manuscript from the Social Sciences Research Network (www.ssrn.com) or another Web site. In addition to these country studies, very good regional overviews are presented in Bennell (2003), Cook and Kirkpatrick (2003), Filatotchev (2003), Nellis (2003), Parker (2003), Roland (2002), and Svejnar (2001).

How Much Privatization Has Actually Occurred?

Aggregate Privatization Proceeds

As briefly noted above, different regions have embraced privatization at varying speeds, and for different reasons. However, all governments have found the lure of revenue from sales of SOEs to be attractive, which is clearly a key reason the policy has spread so rapidly. According to Privatisation International (Gibbon, 1998, 2000), the cumulative value of proceeds raised by privatizing governments exceeded $1 trillion sometime during the second half of 1999, and by now has probably surpassed $1.5 trillion. As an added benefit, this revenue has generally

TABLE 1.3. Listing of Country Studies Describing National Privatization Programs

Country	Author(s), Article Name, and Publication Outlet
Argentina, Bolivia, Mexico, Nicaragua	McKenzie, David, and Dilip Mookherjee. 2003. "The Distributive Impact of Privatization in Latin America: Evidence from Four Countries." Working paper, Stanford University, Palo Alto.
Australia	Hodge, Graeme A. 2003. "Privatization: The Australian Experience." In David Parker and David Saal, eds., *International Handbook on Privatization*. Cheltenham, UK: Edward Elgar, pp. 161–186
Bangladesh	Akram, Tanweer. 1999. "Bangladesh's Privatization Policy." *Journal of Emerging Markets* 4, pp. 65–76.
Bolivia	Ruiz-Mier, Fernando, Mauricio Garron, Carlos Gustavo Machicado, and Katherina Capra. 2002. "Privatization in Bolivia: The Impact on Firm Performance." Working paper, Unidad de Analisis de Políticas Sociales y Económicas (UDAPE), Bolivia.
Bolivia	Barja, Gover, and Miguel Urquiola. 2003. "Capitalization and Privatization in Bolivia." Working paper, Cornell University, Ithaca, NY.
Brazil	Macedo, Roberto. 2000. "Privatization and the Distribution of Assets and Income in Brazil." Working paper, Carnegie Endowment for International Peace, Washington, DC.
Canada	Boardman, Anthony E., Claude Laurin, and Aidan R. Vining. 2003. "Privatization in North America." In David Parker and David Saal, eds, *International Handbook on Privatization*. Cheltenham, UK: Edward Elgar pp. 129–160
Chile	Yotopoulos, Pan A. 1989. "The (Rip)tide of Privatization: Lessons From Chile." *World Development* 17, pp. 683–702.
Chile	Ramirez, Miguel D. 2003. "Privatization in Mexico and Chile." In David Parker and David Saal, eds., *International Handbook on Privatization*. Cheltenham, UK: Edward Elgar pp. 262–290.
China	Lin, Cyril. 2000. "Corporate Governance of State-Owned Enterprises in China." Working paper, Asian Development Bank.
China	Sun, Qian, and Wilson H. S. Tong. 2003. "China's Share Issue Privatization: The Extent of its Success." *Journal of Financial Economics* 70, pp. 183–222.
China	Chai, Joseph C. H. 2003. "Privatization in China." In David Parker and David Saal, eds., *International Handbook on Privatization*. Cheltenham, UK: Edward Elgar pp. 235–261.
Colombia	Pombo, Carlos, and Manuel Ramirez. 2001. "Privatization in Colombia: A Plant Performance Analysis." Working paper, Universidad del Rosario: Bogota, Colombia.
Côte d'Ivoire	Jones, Leroy P., Yahya Jammal, and Nilgun Gokgur. 1998. *Impact of Privatization in Côte d'Ivoire: Draft Final Report*. Boston Institute for Developing Economies, Boston University.
Czech Republic, Hungary, Poland	Bornstein, Morris. 1999. "Framework Issues in the Privatization Strategies of the Czech Republic, Hungary and Poland." *Post-Communist Economies* 11:1, pp. 47–77.
Czech Republic	Claessens, Stijn, Simeon Djankov, and Gerhard Pohl. 1997. *Ownership and Corporate Governance: Evidence from the Czech Republic*. Washington, DC: World Bank Policy Research Paper No. 1737.
Czech Republic	Mejstrik, Michal. 2003. "Privatization and Corporate Governance in the Czech Republic." In David Parker and David Saal, eds., *International Handbook on Privatization*. Cheltenham, UK: Edward Elgar pp. 375–401.
Denmark	Christoffersen, Henrk, and Martin Paldam. 2003. "Privatization in Denmark, 1980–2002." CESifo working paper, Aarhus University, Aarhus, Denmark.

Country	Author(s), Article Name, and Publication Outlet
Egypt	Omran, Mohammed. 2001. "The Performance of State-Owned Enterprises and Newly Privatized Firms: Empirical Evidence from Egypt." Working paper, Arab Academy for Science and Technology, Alexandria, Egypt.
Eritrea	Hailemariam, Stifanos, Henk von Eije, and Jos van der Werf. 2001. "Is There a 'Privatization Trap'? The Case of Manufacturing Industries in Eritrea." Working paper, University of Groningen, Groningen, the Netherlands.
Estonia	Nellis, John. 1996. "Finding Real Owners: Lessons from Estonia's Privatization Program." *World Bank Public Policy for the Private Sector Note 66*, Washington DC, World Bank.
Estonia	Jones, Derek, and Niels Mygind. 2001. "Ownership and Productive Efficiency: Evidence from Estonia." Working paper, Hamilton College, Clinton, New York.
Finland	Willner, Johann. 2002. "Public Ownership and Privatisation in Finland." CESifo working paper, °Abo Akademi University, Finland.
France (early), United Kingdom	Jenkinson, Timothy, and Colin Mayer. 1988. "The Privatisation Process in France and the U.K." *European Economic Review* 32, pp. 482–490.
France	Dumontier, Pascal, and Claude Laurin. 2002. "The Financial Impacts of the French Government Nationalization-Privatization Strategy." Working paper, University of Geneva, Switzerland.
Germany (East)	Dyck, I. J. Alexander. 1997. "Privatization in Eastern Germany: Management Selection and Economic Transition." *American Economic Review* 87, pp. 565–597.
Ghana	Appiah-Kubi, K. 2001. "State-Owned Enterprises and Privatization in Ghana." *Journal of Modern African Studies* 39.
Hungary	Jelic, Ranko, and Richard Briston. 1999. "Hungarian Privatisation Strategy and Financial Performance of Privatised Companies." *Journal of Business Finance and Accounting* 26, pp. 1319–1357.
Hungary	Major, Iván. 2003. "Privatization in Hungary and its Aftermath." in David Parker and David Saal, eds., *International Handbook on Privatization*. Cheltenham, UK: Edward Elgar. pp. 427–453.
Ireland	Barrett, Sean. 2003. "Privatisation in Ireland." CESifo working paper, Trinity College, Dublin, Ireland.
Italy	Bemporad, Simone, and Edoardo Reviglio. 2002. "Privatization in Italy and the Role of IRI." Working paper, Italian Ministry of Economics and Finance, Rome.
Italy	Goldstein, Andrea, and Giuseppe Nicoletti. 2003. "Privatization in Italy 1993–2002: Goals, Institutions, Outcomes, and Outstanding Issues." CESifo working paper, OECD, Paris.
Lithuania	Grigorian, David. 2000. "Ownership and Performance of Lithuanian Enterprises." Policy Research working paper 2343, World Bank, Washington, DC.
Macedonia (FYRM)	Glennerster, Rachel. 2000. "Evaluating Privatization in the Former Yugoslav Republic of Macedonia." Working paper, Kennedy School, Harvard University, Cambridge, MA.
Malawi	Chirwa, Ephraim W. 2001. "Industry and Firm Effects of Privatization in Malawian Oligopolistic Manufacturing." Working paper, University of Malawi, Zomba, Malawi.
Malaysia	Sun, Qian, Jin Jia, and Wilson H. S. Tong. 2002. "Malaysian Privatization: A Comprehensive Study." *Financial Management*, pp. 5–31.
Mexico	La Porta, Rafael, and Florencio López-de-Silanes. 1999. "Benefits of Privatization—Evidence From Mexico." *Quarterly Journal of Economics* 114:4, pp. 1193–1242.

(continued)

23

TABLE 1.3. (*continued*)

Country	Author(s), Article Name, and Publication Outlet
Mongolia	Anderson, James H., Georges Korsun, and Peter Murrell. 1999. "Ownership, Exit, and Voice After Mass Privatization: Evidence From Mongolia." *Economics of Transition* 7, pp. 215–243.
Poland	Mickiewicz, Tomasz, and Maciej Baltowski. 2003. "All Roads Lead to Outside Ownership: Polish Piecemael Privatization." In David Parker and David Saal, eds, *International Handbook on Privatization*. Cheltenham, UK: Edward Elgar. pp. 402–426.
Romania	Earle, John, and Almos Telgedy. 2001. "Productivity and Ownership Structure in Romania: Does Privatization Matter?" Working paper, Central European University, Budapest, Hungary.
Russia	Black, Bernard, Reinier Kraakman, and Anna Tarassova. 2000. "Russian Privatization and Corporate Governance: What Went Wrong?" *Stanford Law Review* 56, pp. 1731–1808.
Russia	Earle, John S. 1998. "Privatization, Competition and Budget Constraints: Disciplining Enterprises in Russia." SITE working paper no. 128, Stockholm School of Economics Stockholm.
Russia	Hare, Paul, and Alexander Murayev. 2003. "Privatization in Russia." In David Parker and David Saal, eds., *International Handbook on Privatization*. Cheltenham, UK: Edward Elgar. pp. 347–374.
Slovenia	Smith, Stephen C., Beon-Cheol Cin, and Milan Vodopivec. 1997. "Privatization Incidence, Ownership Forms, and Firm Performance: Evidence From Slovenia." *Journal of Comparative Economics* 25, pp. 158–179.
South Africa	Schwella, Erwin. 2003. "Privatization in South Africa." In David Parker and David Saal, eds., *International Handbook on Privatization*. Cheltenham, UK: Edward Elgar pp. 291–309.
Spain	Arocena, Pablo. 2003. "The Privatisation Programme of the Public Enterprise Sector in Spain." CESifo working paper, Universidad Pública de Navarra, Pamplona, Spain.
Taiwan	Parker, David. 1999. "Policy Transfer and Policy Inertia: Privatization in Taiwan." *Asia Pacific Business Review* 6, pp. 1–20.
Tanzania	Temu, Andrew, and Jean M. Due. 1998. "The Success of Newly Privatized Companies: New Evidence from Tanzania." *Canadian Journal of Development Studies* 19, pp. 315–341.
Turkey	Okten, Cagla, and K. Peren Arin. 2001. "How Does Privatization Affect the Firm's Efficiency and Technology Choice?: Evidence from Turkey." Working paper, Louisiana State University, Baton Rouge.
Ukraine	Pivovarsky, Alexander. 2001. "How Does Privatization Work? Ownership Concentration and Enterprise Performance in Ukraine." Working paper WP/01/42, International Monetary Fund, Washington, DC.
Ukraine	Estrin, Saul, and Adam Rosevear. 2003. "Privatization in Ukraine." In David Parker and David Saal, eds., *International Handbook on Privatization*. Cheltenham, UK: Edward Elgar. pp. 454–474.
United Kingdom	Menyah, Kojo, and Krishna Paudyal. 1996. "Share Issue Privatisations: The UK Experience." In Mario Levis, ed., *Empirical Issues in Raising Equity Capital*. Amsterdam: Elsevier Science, pp. 17–48.
United Kingdom	Florio, Massimo. 2002. "A State Without Ownership: The Welfare Impact of British Privatisations, 1979–1997." Working paper, University of Milan, Italy.
United States	López-de-Silanes, Florencio, Andrei Shleifer, and Robert W. Vishny. 1997. "Privatization in the United States." *Rand Journal of Economics* 28, pp. 447–471.

gone to the divesting governments rather to the SOEs themselves. In finance terminology, asset sales and SIPs have been primarily secondary share offerings — sales of existing shares, with sale proceeds going to the selling shareholder — rather than capital-raising or primary share offerings of newly created shares, where proceeds flow to the firm. In this, SIPs are unique; the vast majority of private-sector share offerings are either wholly or partially capital-raising primary offers. The use of secondary SIP offerings allows governments to raise revenues without raising taxes or cutting other government services.

As noted briefly above, annual privatization proceeds grew steadily before surpassing $160 billion in 1997. Over the next two years, proceeds leveled off at an annual rate of about $140 billion before surging to a record $180 billion in 2000, then falling sharply to $52 billion in 2001. Figure 1.2 shows the annual revenues governments received from privatizations between 1988 and 2002. From early 2002 through the summer of 2003, global privatization revenues remained near 2001's depressed level, though there were signs of increasing activity at the end of 2003. Mahboobi (2002) presents similar figures for privatizations in Organization for Economic Cooperation and Development (OECD) and non-OECD countries. He reports that from 1990 to 1999, privatization in OECD countries raised over $600 billion, which equaled approximately two-thirds of global privatization activity. Western Europe accounted for over half of global proceeds. Finally, Davis, Ossowski, Richardson, and Barnett (2000) report for a sample of transition and

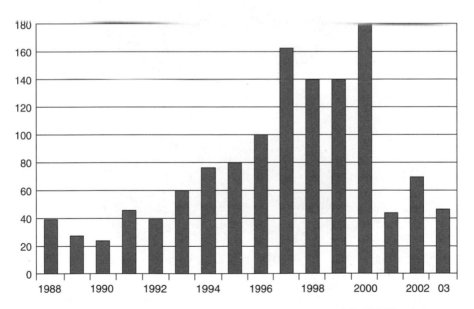

FIGURE 1.2. Worldwide revenues from privatizations, 1988–2003 (US$ billions). Source: *Privatisation International*, as reported in Megginson and Netter (2001), and IFR Thomson database.

nontransition developing countries that privatization proceeds were an average of 1.75 percent of GDP during the peak privatization years of the 1990s.

Not surprisingly, this enormous inflow of cash did wonders for government budgets, especially during the late 1990s, and had a truly transforming impact on the capitalization and efficiency of the world's stock markets—especially those outside the United States. We discuss the fiscal impact of privatization in the next chapter, and analyze more fully the impact of privatization of capital market development in chapter 7.

Geographic and Sectoral Breakdown of Privatization Proceeds

What industrial sectors and geographic regions have accounted for the largest share of privatization proceeds? Figure 1.3 details the answers to these two questions. Telecom offerings accounted for 36 percent of all proceeds raised between 1990 and 2000, with power (16 percent), financial institutions (15 percent), and oil and

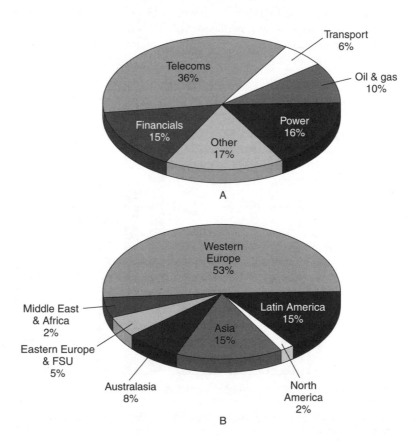

FIGURE 1.3. Privatization proceeds, by sector (A) and region (B), 1990–2000. Source: Gibbon (2000).

gas (10 percent) claiming the next largest shares. Taken together, utilities (telecom, power, oil and gas) account for 62 percent of all proceeds, while regulated industries (telecoms, power, financial institutions) account for 67 percent of the proceeds. A broader definition of "infrastructure" sales that includes national oil and gas companies accounts for 68 percent of total proceeds. Clearly, governments are mostly selling basic industrial and financial infrastructure assets in their privatization programs. The second panel of figure 1.3 shows that the bulk of proceeds have come from western Europe (53 percent), with Asia (15 percent) and Latin America (15 percent) distant seconds.

Table 1.4 provides a much more detailed, and longer term picture of how much individual countries have raised through privatizations from 1977 to 1999. For each country this table shows the number of deals, total privatization revenues, cumulative revenues (between 1977 and 1999) as a percent of 1999 GDP, the market capitalization of privatized firms as a percent of 1999 GDP, and the fraction of total revenues accounted for by public offering versus private sale. Several patterns are evident from this table. First, there is a very wide dispersion in all of these variables across both developed and developing countries, as well as between the two groups. Developed countries raised far larger average amounts ($49.2 billion each) than did developing countries ($5.4 billion each), and total proceeds accounted for an average 7.67 percent of developed country GDP versus only 3.5 percent for developing countries. On the other hand, the market values of privatized companies represented about the same fraction of GDP for developed (47.1 percent) and developing (46.06 percent) countries. Public offerings accounted for a similar fraction of total proceeds in developed (58.9 percent) and developing (51.7 percent) economies.

Privatization's Impact on the State-Owned Enterprise Share of Global Output

The historical discussion presented above suggests that state ownership has been substantially reduced since 1979, and in most countries this has in fact occurred. Using data from Sheshinski and Lopez-Calva (1999), figure 1.4 demonstrates that the role of state-owned enterprises in the economies of high-income (industrialized) countries has declined significantly, from about 8.5 percent of GDP in 1984 to less than 6 percent in 1991. Data presented in Schmitz (1996), Mahboobi (2002), and Bortolotti, Fantini, and Siniscalco (1999), as well as my own empirical work on share issue privatizations, suggest that the SOE share of industrialized-country GDP has continued to decline since 1991, and is now probably below 5 percent.

The low-income countries show an even more dramatic reduction in state ownership, though the bulk of this change has occurred only since 1990. From a high point of almost 16 percent of GDP in 1981, the average SOE share of national output dropped to barely 7 percent in 1995, and has probably dropped to about 5 percent since then. The middle-income countries also experienced significant reductions in state ownership during the 1990s. Since the upper- and lower-middle-income groups include the transition economies of central and east-

TABLE 1.4. Details of Privatization Sales and Proceeds for 34 Countries, 1977–1999

Country	Deals	Revenues	Rev/GDP	Stock	Po/Deals
Switzerland	2	5,734.052	0.02268	74.95000	0.50000
Norway	12	3,106.571	0.02199	56.06943	0.79167
Japan	14	189,400.139	0.04437	34.32778	1
Sweden	21	14,898.401	0.06775	48.01722	0.64444
Germany	75	71,576.558	0.03541	53.80227	0.35014
Finland	26	10,387.738	0.08479	22.49022	0.83333
France	67	81,524.477	0.05952	26.58321	0.84109
Canada	57	21,079.210	0.03546	60.13323	0.47397
Austria	40	10,081.478	0.04967	33.19907	0.68333
The Netherlands	28	15,482.922	0.04143	36.99554	0.37500
Belgium	11	5,963.538	0.02499	42.78714	0.08333
Australia	108	70,596.051	0.18651	70.79184	0.37500
United Kingdom	169	153,394.000	0.11497	71.39784	0.48815
Italy	80	105,936.681	0.09484	33.79306	0.64462
Singapore	22	6,507.614	0.07887	23.22259	1
New Zealand	34	12,077.033	0.23188	78.10296	0.24861
Spain	55	59,421.927	0.10881	34.52101	0.68773
Developed countries avg.	48.29	49,245.200	0.07670	47.12849	0.58944
Israel	52	7,421.008	0.07712	31.18976	0.59303
South Korea	17	14,690.547	0.03717	22.43911	0.89881
Uruguay	2	19.908	0.00101	75.50000	0
Mexico	41	29,487.942	0.06392	56.91530	0.13788
South Africa	13	3,496.831	0.02746	64.12599	0.36667
Chile	16	2,622.630	0.03798	37.18750	0.25000
Malaysia	24	7,821.708	0.10790	49.12484	0.43290
Turkey	60	3,228.023	0.01764	65.61105	0.16429
Colombia	10	5,850.749	0.06799	69.46000	0.20000
Thailand	12	2,061.313	0.01713	32.20139	0.91667
Zimbabwe	5	190.056	0.03423	56.66667	1
Philippines	14	2,166.028	0.02960	38.28922	0.50000
Indonesia	14	5,223.897	0.03815	26.93213	0.71429
Nigeria	19	37.974	0.00090	47.83698	1
Sri Lanka	0	0	0.00000	0	.
Pakistan	12	1,453.027	0.02498	41.58111	0.33333
India	24	5,536.303	0.01240	21.92303	0.76786
Less developed countries avg.	19.71	5,371.055	0.03503	46.0615	0.51723
Test of means (*t*-statistic)	2.58**	3.18***	2.63**	0.17	0.69

Source: Bortolotli, Fantini, and Siniscalco (Forthcoming).

Note: This table reports the aggregate figures on privatization in 34 countries for the period 1977–1999. Countries are ranked by the average GDP per capita in 1997–1999. Deals are the total number of privatizations. Revenues are total revenues (US$ ml 1996) from total privatizations. Rev/GDP is the ratio of total revenues cumulated in the period to 1999 GDP (in US$ ml 1996). Stock is the average of the positive values of the yearly weighed average of privatized stock. PO/Deals is the ratio of the number of privatizations by Public Offer to the total number of privatizations.

***, **, * denote statistical significance at the 1, 5, and 10 percent, respectively.

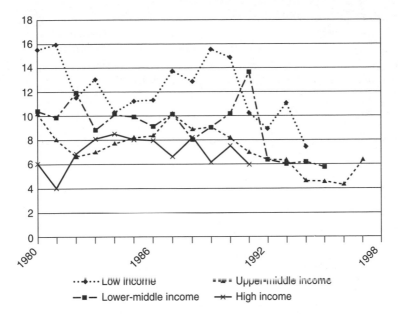

FIGURE 1.4. The percentage share of state-owned enterprises by state of economic development, 1980–1996. Source: World Bank, as reported in Sheshinski and Lopez-Calva (2003).

ern Europe, this decline was expected given the extremely high beginning levels of state ownership. For example, Shafik (1995) reports that the Czechoslovakian government owned 98 percent of all property in 1989. It is not hyperbole to assert that privatization's effect on transition economies has been "transforming."

Summary

Privatization has been a major force in world politics and economics for the past 25 years, and has dramatically reduced the role of state-owned enterprises in both developed and developing countries. This chapter briefly surveys the rise of state ownership as an economic model from antiquity to the late 1970s, and then charts the phenomenal growth in privatization programs since these were first popularized by Margaret Thatcher's Conservative British government in the early 1980s.

The cumulative value raised through privatization programs now probably exceeds $1.25 trillion, and the vast bulk of this money has flowed directly to governments, rather than to the SOEs themselves. This is clearly one important reason governments have so enthusiastically embraced privatization, since these programs raise large sums without having to increase taxes or cut spending on existing government programs. Privatization of utilities, oil and gas companies, and financial institutions have accounted for over two-thirds of total proceeds, and by far the largest fraction of total proceeds have come from western European share issue privatizations. While the absolute importance of privatization varies considerably among countries and regions, developed and developing countries have both embraced privatization and the cumulative proceeds from 1977 to 1999 represent over 7.6 percent of developed countries' GDP in 1999, on average, and 3.5 percent of the average developing country's 1999 GDP.

Why Do Countries Privatize?

One of the truly timeless debates in Western political and economic discourse revolves around the optimality of state versus private ownership of commercial enterprises. Scholars, including economists, have debated the economic role of government throughout history, but these debates reached a crescendo during the twentieth century. Chapter 1 examined the forces that motivated governments to launch state-owned enterprises — or to nationalize existing private businesses — and adopt state ownership as an economic development model during the middle years of the twentieth century. Chapter 1 also described how, over the past quarter-century, many of these same countries reversed course and launched often massive privatization programs designed to reduce the state's role in running these enterprises. This chapter analyzes why governments have so enthusiastically embraced privatization.

Governments typically list multiple reasons for launching privatization programs. Chapter 1 details six rationales presented by the Thatcher government for launching Britain's influential program, while Vickers and Yarrow (1991) present a somewhat different list of what they considered the "real" motivations of the Thatcher government.[1] Raising money is, quite naturally, a very attractive objective, and most governments also hope that privatization will help develop national capital markets. However, the most important rationale given for selling SOEs to private investors is almost always dissatisfaction with the actual performance of state enterprises, coupled with the belief that selling these firms to private investors will significantly improve their performance. In fact, this dissatisfaction with SOE performance and belief in private-sector redemption can be considered a prerequisite for launching a privatization program, since democratic societies that earlier chose state ownership as a deliberate policy do not simply change their minds and choose diametrically opposite economic policies without clear evidence these policies have failed.

By the early 1990s, the state-owned enterprises that were the source of such displeasure for policy makers accounted for a significant fraction of economic activity. Figure 2.1 shows that state enterprises accounted for between 10 and 20 percent of GDP in most high- and middle-income countries during the 1991–1995 period, and for significantly higher percentages of national output in low-income countries. Figure 2.2 shows that SOEs accounted for an even larger fraction of overall investment in many countries. Furthermore, the fact that the SOE share of economic activity and investment declined with per capita GDP meant that poorer countries were more likely to be burdened if, in fact, state enterprises are inherently inefficient.

In launching privatization programs, most governments simply assert as common knowledge that privately owned companies are inherently better managed and more efficient than are state-owned firms. These governments seem not to realize just how controversial these assumptions are within the economics profession, especially among theoretical economists. Theorists generally acknowledge that private ownership causes firms to be more profitable and to operate with greater technical efficiency under most industrial structures, particularly in competitive industries. However, there is far less theoretical consensus about the optimality of private ownership in the presence of significant market failures, and about the ability of private companies to pursue socially desirable goals, such as maximizing employment or providing necessary goods and services at a fair price to all citizens. There is also much controversy about whether commercial enterprises should be asked to pursue social objectives or simply to maximize profits, subject to legal constraints. By far the most controversial issue for theorists is whether natural monopolies—defined as industries with continuously increasing economies of scale, such that only a single producer is economically efficient—should be owned by the state or by private owners subject to state regulation. The

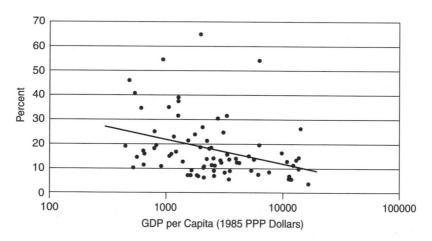

FIGURE 2.1. The average share of state-owned enterprises in GDP across countries, 1991–1995. Source: World Bank, *International Development Indicators* CD-ROM (2000), as reported in Figure 1 of Esfahani and Arkadani (2002).

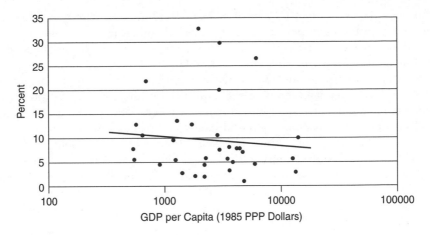

FIGURE 2.2. The average share of state-owned enterprises in total investment across countries, 1986–1990. Source: World Bank, *International Development Indicators* CD-ROM (2000), as reported in Figure 2 of Esfahani and Arkadani (2002).

relative merits of state versus private ownership have enlivened economic debate since the dawn of the profession, and this debate is just as impassioned, and important, today as it was during Adam Smith's era.

The theoretical arguments for the advantages of private ownership of the means of production are based on a fundamental theorem of welfare economics: under strong assumptions, a competitive equilibrium is Pareto optimal, meaning that no other allocation of resources can make someone better off without making someone else worse off. However, the assumptions underlying this competitive equilibrium include requirements that there are no externalities in production or consumption, that the product is not a public good, that the market is not monopolistic in structure, and that information costs are low. Thus, a theoretical argument for government intervention based on efficiency grounds must rest on an argument that markets have failed in some way, or that one or more of these assumptions do not hold—and that the government can resolve the market failure.

Intellectual arguments for government intervention based on efficiency considerations have been made in many areas. Governments perceive the need to regulate (or own) natural monopolies or other monopolies, and to intervene in the case of externalities such as regulating pollution. Governments are also expected to help provide public goods such as national defense and education, or to assist in areas where there is a public good aspect to providing information. The arguments for government intervention become more complicated when they extend to distributional concerns. For example, some argue that the role of government is to act as a "welfare state" [Briggs (1961)], using state intervention in the market economy to modify the actions of the market.[2] Thus, the arguments for state ownership or control rest on some market failure or perceived market failure, and countries have often responded to market failure with state ownership. Privatization, in turn, is a response to the perceived failings of state ownership.

It is important to realize that state ownership must always be a deliberate act that preempts or replaces private ownership. Historically, the act of imposing state ownership is usually accompanied by great controversy, and often by violence and class conflict. Nationalizations of economically healthy companies typically become feasible only after the private owners have been demonized as exploiters or collaborators, while nationalizations of failing companies inevitably occur within the context of economic crises. Nationalizations within developing countries, which occurred frequently during the decades after World War II, were invariably justified as being necessary to overcome decades of colonial exploitation. In other words, state ownership typically occurs either because of the perceived failings of private ownership or out of a desire to use state power to alter market allocations of economic costs and benefits.

Infusing (and inevitably confusing) the debate about the legitimacy and efficiency of state ownership is the fact that each person approaches this question with his or her own worldview about the benevolence of government and the proper limits to state power. Indeed, no question in economics could be more basic. Those who believe that democratic governments act "benevolently," in the best interests of society as a whole, also tend to believe that governments should intervene proactively to address perceived economic injustices. Those who are skeptical of the motives of political actors, and particularly those who ascribe to the "grabbing hand" theory of government activism, tend to favor a much more limited state role in a nation's economic life. Interventionists believe that privately owned corporations will be motivated solely by the profit motive, whereas state-owned companies can be given multiple, socially desirable objectives to pursue. Skeptics decry state enterprises as inherently inefficient for exactly the same reason. This chapter attempts to first frame this theoretical debate and then examine the empirical evidence that has been marshaled for and against state ownership.

The next two sections, which draw heavily on the excellent survey article by Shirley and Walsh (2000), lay out, first, the intellectual case for state ownership of commercial enterprise and, then, the intellectual case against public ownership.[3] The third section then examines whether the empirical evidence supports or refutes the effectiveness and efficiency of public ownership. Since the evidence overwhelmingly indicates that state ownership is inherently less efficient than private ownership in most real industrial settings, we also assesses whether SOEs can be reformed by measures short of privatization, such as exposing state enterprises to competition or imposing hard budget constraints. While the empirical evidence suggests that some economic reforms can be effective in their own right, it leaves unanswered the question of whether these reforms would be even more effective if also coupled with a shift to private ownership. Thus, many countries have decided to launch large-scale privatization programs, and the fifth section examines the fiscal and macroeconomic impact of these programs on the public finances of divesting countries.

The Theoretical Case for State Ownership of Business Enterprises

During the modern era, proponents of state ownership have justified government control of business in three principal ways. First, public ownership has been justified as a way to ensure that business enterprises balance social and economic objectives, rather than focusing exclusively on profit maximization. Second, state ownership has been motivated as a response to significant market failures—particularly the challenges posed to economic efficiency by natural monopolies—and as a method to internalize production externalities such as pollution. Third, proponents assert that public ownership can be justified under certain conditions involving informational asymmetries between principal (the public) and agent (the producer), where complete contracts cannot be written and enforced. Underlying all three cases is the assumption that governments can and do act benevolently, and thus that state ownership is economically efficient. Certainly, state ownership has also been imposed many times in history by ascendant political parties specifically in order to redistribute wealth and income from less to more "deserving" members of society, but this exercise in raw political power is usually justified by dogma rather than by serious economic theory. We evaluate each of the three benevolent motivations for state ownership below.

State Ownership Allows Pursuit of Social Objectives, Not Just Profit Maximization

A classic justification for public ownership of business is that this is the only effective way to ensure that commercial enterprises will pursue socially desirable but noneconomic objectives, in addition to producing outputs at minimum input cost. These objectives may include serving as a "model employer" by hiring members of underrepresented groups and paying above-equilibrium wages, or constructing factories in underdeveloped regions of the country that would be unable to attract industry on arms-length terms, or producing more goods and services than would a private supplier and pricing these outputs at a lower than market clearing price. Since state-owned enterprises will be subject to democratic political control in ways that private enterprises can never be, public ownership should theoretically be able to produce a package of goods and services that comports with the political demands of citizens rather than the dollar demands of consumers.

Perhaps the best theoretical justification for public ownership in a democratic society is presented in Yarrow (1986) and Vickers and Yarrow (1988). Both works offer finely balanced assessments of the costs and benefits of state ownership, assuming that a benevolent government is acting subject to effective democratic political control. Yarrow (1986) suggests that government monitoring of managers has two potential advantages over market alternatives: it reduces the public-good problem associated with dispersed shareholdings, and it can take immediate account of deviations between the social and private returns in goods and factor markets. Yarrow believes that the dissatisfaction with the actual workings of SOEs lies in political market imperfections rather than reflecting inherent weaknesses in state ownership. He also echoes the views of many other observers—such as Kay and Thompson (1986), Cook and Kirkpatick (1988), and Shapiro and Willig (1990)—in asserting that competition is more important than ownership in assuring that firms, state or private, achieve operational and allocative efficiency.

Vickers and Yarrow (1988) expand on the benefits that a benevolent government can achieve by owning commercial enterprises. If political markets work efficiently, competition between politicians will ensure that the correct set of policies will be implemented, and politicians will seek to maximize social welfare—defined as the sum of producer and consumer surplus. Public ownership, without private-sector competition, can adjust output prices to reflect true social cost when there are significant production externalities. In a similar theoretical vein, Shapiro and Willig (1990) model a public manager's utility function as a mix of social and private welfare, where the latter reflects either personal interests or the gap between short-run political benefits and long-run public good. When political markets work effectively, state managers will be forced to maximize social rather than private welfare.

State Ownership as a Response to Market Failures

Most economists accept the idea that natural monopolies are a challenge for pure market economics. Many people go a step further and assert that the only effective response to natural monopoly is public ownership; otherwise, private interests will inevitably restrict output to a level that maximizes profits at a socially excessive price. If the government owns the natural monopolists, however, it can increase production and reduce output cost to optimal levels, since the state is not constrained to maximize profits. Proponents of state ownership suggest that regulated private ownership of natural monopolies will be ineffective, either because informational asymmetries will always give private managers a negotiating advantage over regulators or because of the dangers of regulatory capture.

Many economists have developed theoretical models describing the virtues of state ownership in the presence of market failures. One of the most sophisticated is presented in Sappington and Stiglitz (1987), who argue that state ownership reduces the transactions cost of government intervention in economic affairs, and that this intervention is required in the presence of significant market failures. Their Fundamental Privatization Theorem identifies the conditions that must be met in order to make a transfer from state- to private-ownership efficiency enhancing: when the market will do at least as well as a benevolent government. Sappington and Stiglitz note that both public and private ownership involve significant delegation of production activities between principals and agents; their model simply describes the circumstances under which it will be optimal to entrust oversight duties to public rather than to private owners (principals).

Where Sappington and Stiglitz describe how state ownership can be optimal in theory, other economists make the case for public enterprises by pointing to seemingly massive failures in real markets. In his assessment of state enterprise performance in Britain, Caves (1990) sees monopolies—natural and otherwise—as pervasive, and is thus highly skeptical of the economic utility of privatization. Yarrow (1986), Kay and Thompson (1986), and Florio (2002) also dispute the perception that British SOE performance was uniformly poor. Cook and Kirkpatrick (1988) argue that market failures are especially pervasive and damaging in developing countries. The institutional weaknesses of governments in developing countries, coupled with weak capital markets and national reliance on single commodity exports, means that privatizing SOEs will be extremely hazardous. Cook and Kirkpatrick assert that regulatory capacity in these countries is very weak, and that the best response to market failures will be state ownership with competition.[4]

State Ownership as a Response to Asymmetric Information and Incomplete Contracts

The final rationale for state ownership revolves around informational asymmetries between principals and agents, specifically owners and managers of business enterprises. Because managers have superior knowledge of costs and production possibilities, they will inevitably have a negotiating advantage in setting output levels and pricing. At the extreme, this asymmetry can render regulation of private enterprises ineffective, and the only solution in this case will be public ownership by a benevolent government.

A similar result obtains when it is not feasible to write and enforce complete contracts specifying the rights and responsibilities of each party in all possible economic states. According to Shapiro and Willig (1990), incomplete contracts may make public ownership superior to private ownership if it is optimal for government to intervene in the economy (1) owing to market failures, (2) when managers have private information about costs and profitability, and/or (3) when SOE managers' agendas can be kept in check by an efficient political market. Similarly, Laffont and Tirole (1991) recast the ancient public versus private ownership debate in a modern agency theoretic framework and demonstrate when public ownership will be superior to private ownership. The cost of regulated private ownership is that managers must serve two masters: shareholders and regulators. Under public ownership, this is less of a problem, since there is a single master (the government) to satisfy. The cost of state ownership in the Laffont and Tirole model is a suboptimal investment in those assets that can be redeployed to serve social goals pursued by public owners. This expropriation of assets away from profit-enhancing uses is less likely under private ownership. Finally, Schmidt (2000) uses an incomplete contract model to show that mixed public and private ownership may be the theoretically optimal ownership structure in some cases, since joint ownership mitigates the disadvantages both of public ownership (no incentives to improve quality) and of privatization (too strong incentives for the manager to reduce costs).

On balance, proponents of state ownership make a theoretically credible case. Nonetheless, opponents of public ownership have attacked this case on multiple grounds; by disputing the basic assumptions underlying models of optimal public ownership, by offering differing behavioral models of (nonbenevolent) government motivations, and by spotlighting the actual performance of real state enterprises. We now examine the theoretical case presented by opponents of public ownership.

The Theoretical Case Against State Ownership of Business Enterprises

Economists have offered three principal reasons that state ownership will be inherently less efficient than private ownership, even under the assumption of a benevolent government owner. First, SOE managers will have weaker and/or more adverse incentives than will managers of privately owned firms, and thus will be less diligent in maximizing revenues and (especially) minimizing costs. Second, state enterprises will be subject to less intense monitoring by owners, both because of collective action problems—potential monitors have less incentive to carefully observe managerial performance because they bear all the costs of doing so but reap only a fraction of the rewards—and because there are few effective methods of effectively disciplining SOE managers in the event that subpar performance is detected. Third, the politicians who oversee SOE operations cannot credibly commit to bankrupting poorly performing SOEs, or even to withholding additional subsidized funding, so state enterprises inevitably face soft budget constraints. It bears repeating that these criticisms of state ownership are valid even if one grants that the politicians who create and supervise public enterprises have benevolent intentions. The final, and in many ways most compelling, critique of state ownership is that SOEs will be inefficient by design, since they are created specifically so that politicians can use them to benefit their own supporters at the expense of another group in society. We examine each rationale in turn below.

State-Owned Enterprises Are Inefficient Due to Weak or Adverse Incentives

It is easy to understand the incentives of entrepreneurs or hired executive employees to manage a private firm in a way that maximizes owner wealth. The benefits of any steps taken to increase firm revenues or reduce costs accrue to the company's private owners, and capitalist firms thus have very strong incentives to maximize profits and to invest in efficiency improvements and new product innovation. Shleifer (1998) states that these incentives to minimize costs, improve quality, and innovate new products are the true explanation for the "dynamic vitality" of free enterprise, and thus of capitalism's inherent economic superiority over socialism. These incentives are made even sharper in the typical case where private firms are not protected from competition, as first noted by Hayek (1944) and then by many subsequent observers—including Jensen and Meckling (1979) in their excellent but little-cited theoretical analysis of the weaknesses of labor-managed firms. Hayek asserts that competition promotes operational efficiency both through the incentive effect described above and by revealing information about production costs and market clearing prices to all industry observers.

The managers of state enterprises face much weaker incentives than do private managers. As public employees, they cannot personally reap the benefits of increasing revenues yet they will bear many of the costs (i.e., angry workers, disgruntled suppliers) of reducing the firm's production costs. Thus, they will rationally choose not to aggressively pursue efficiency improvements or to develop innovative new products. The already weak incentives for SOE managers are made even more tenuous in the all too common case where state enterprises are granted a monopoly position as producer of a vital good or service. In this case, the inefficiency of SOEs will not be easy to observe, and since consumers have no alternative, there will be very little market pressure to improve state enterprise efficiency. The economic perils of monopoly state ownership are described in Peltzman (1971), Niskanen (1975), Caves (1990), Hart, Shleifer, and Vishny (1997), and Shleifer (1998).

Schmidt (1996) presents an additional explanation of why state enterprises might be inherently less efficient than private firms. His model is based on incomplete contracting theory, and maintains the benevolent government assumption. If the political overseers of a SOE are unable to perfectly observe the firm's production costs, but still wish to ensure that the firm produces at the allocatively efficient level, they will be willing to subsidize the SOE to entice enterprise managers to produce more than they would otherwise choose to. The state-enterprise managers, who alone know the firm's true production costs, and who understand the government's incentives to subsidize production, will thus have very little incentive to control costs internally. Schmidt therefore predicts that governments will adopt privatization primarily as a means of committing not to subsidize SOE production. Lülfesmann (in press) also presents an incomplete contracting model showing that privatization can be beneficial even if the government is assumed to be rational and benevolent. His model is driven by the conflicting objective functions of a profit-maximizing private manager and a government owner intent on pursuing noneconomic objectives as well as profit.

Finally, Dixit (1997) shows that state-enterprises managers have very weak incentives to pursue efficiency because they are required to serve multiple masters. As political creations, SOEs are accountable to several different constituencies with differing objectives. In the American political context, the constituencies might include Congress, multiple Executive-branch federal agencies, and perhaps state and local government bodies. In comparison with private firm managers, who must satisfy only shareholders, SOE managers must strive to satisfy many competing interests. As a corollary, state managers will thus also face weak and diffuse oversight, which is another problem commonly ascribed to state enterprises.

State-Owned Enterprises Are Inefficient Due to Inadequate Monitoring

Since SOEs are owned by "the state" in general, and thus by all citizens collectively, no single observer has the appropriate incentives to monitor SOE managers. Alchian (1965) was the first to predict that state enterprises are inherently inefficient because the dispersed owners (citizens) have poor incentives to monitor SOE managers. He also asserted that specialization of ownership is one of the key advantages of private firms. Even a politician with society's interest at heart has a very weak incentive to invest the time and effort required to discipline SOE managers, since the cost of doing so will surely be very large whereas the electoral payoff to modestly improving enterprise performance will likely be quite low. Furthermore, since SOE shares cannot be sold by citizens, and since state enterprises are rarely allowed to go bankrupt, Vickers and Yarrow (1988) show that state managers have little reason to fear punishment for inefficiency; short of full privatization, they are very unlikely to be forcibly removed.

Asymmetric information also protects SOE managers from effective monitoring, as noted by Vickers and Yarrow (1988, 1991). Since managers have superior information about firm operations and costs, they will inevitably enjoy a negotiating advantage when dealing with their political overseers. Monitoring of public enterprises is also extremely difficult owing to the aforementioned collective-action problem, since any individual monitor must bear all the search and information costs of supervising public managers, but the benefits of effective monitoring must be shared with the entire (thankless) citizenry. While both publicly owned and privately owned firms suffer from collective action problems, Vickers and Yarrow (1991) assert that the ability of markets to generate information about costs and managerial effort gives private ownership a crucial monitoring advantage.

State-Owned Enterprises Are Inefficient Due to Soft Budget Constraints

If the managers of a private firm are not operating efficiently, they will be replaced either by the current shareholders or as the result of a hostile takeover. If a private firm cannot compete effectively, suppliers of capital will cease funding the company's operations—and in the extreme, the firm will be forced into bankruptcy and liquidated. What are the equivalent public-sector disciplinary tools? We have already noted that SOE managers are rarely punished individually for poor performance, but what about withholding of capital resources? In real life, the state is unlikely to allow a large SOE to face bankruptcy, thus the discipline enforced on private firms by the capital markets and the threat of financial distress is lacking for state-owned firms. Since managers of less-prosperous state firms know they can rely on the government for funding, these firms are said to face "soft" budget constraints.

Kornai (1988, 1993, 1998), Berglof and Roland (1998), Lin, Cai, and Li (1998), Frydman, Gray, Hessel, and Rapaczynski (2000), and several other authors all suggest that soft budget constraints (SBCs) were a major source of inefficiency in communist firms, and that these SBCs have continued through much of the postcommunist transition period. Soft budget constraints are not limited to transition economies, however. Sheshinski and Lopez-Calva (1999) assert that public ownership inevitably leads to SBCs. They present a simple model showing that governments will choose to extend subsidies to failing state enterprises whenever the political costs of allowing a SOE to go bankrupt outweigh the political costs of subsidization.[5] In addition to inhibiting efforts by politicians to impose hard budget constraints, this fear of financial distress can preclude initiatives to force state enterprises to restructure or to open monopolized industries to private-sector competition. Since large SOEs are too big and too politically important to fail, their very weakness protects them from the type of effective discipline to which private firms are continuously subjected.

State-Owned Enterprises Are Inefficient Because Governments Use Them to Pursue Noneconomic Objectives

So far, we have examined theoretical objections to state ownership that nonetheless assume that the government owner is acting benevolently. Once this assumption is weakened, the theoretical case against public ownership becomes especially persuasive. Numerous researchers—including Jones (1985), Vickers and Yarrow (1988, 1991), Stiglitz (1993), Nellis (1994), Shleifer and Vishny (1994), Boyko, Shleifer, and Vishny (1996a,b), Shleifer (1998), Sappington and Sidak (1999), and Shirley and Walsh (2000)—note that state enterprises can be remarkably effective tools of redistributive politics. Since state firms answer to political masters rather than the market, wide divergences from profit-maximizing behavior are not only possible, they are in fact desired. Even in fully competitive markets, Shleifer and Vishny (1994) show that SOEs will be inefficient because politicians force them to pursue noneconomic objectives, such as maintaining excess employment, building factories in politically (but not economically) desirable locations, and pricing outputs at below market clearing prices.

In one of the best analyses of the political motivations underlying state ownership, Jones (1985) asserts that politicians deliberately structure implicit and explicit SOE subsidies to transfer benefits from unknowing groups in society to the politicians' supporters. In a twist on the definition of Pareto efficiency, Jones defines a politically efficient reallocation of resources as one that makes someone better off without making anyone else aware that he or she is worse off. Jones also shows that most transfers generally are structured to run from low-income groups to well-connected groups in the upper or middle classes.

Several authors—including Jones (1985), Nellis (1994), Shirley and Walsh (2000), and particularly Shleifer and Vishny (1994) and Boyko, Shleifer and Vishny (1996b)—note that SOEs are especially attractive vehicles for transferring wealth between groups precisely because their operations are nontransparent. Shleifer and Vishny demonstrate that it would be much harder for politicians to favor one group over another if governmental transfers had to be financed with tax revenues and if subsidies had to be channeled through standard budgetary processes, since doing so would clearly reveal the opportunity costs of the subsidies. Instead, politicians will "bribe" state enterprise managers to pursue favored noneconomic objectives, and in return the politicians will reward SOE managers with higher budgets or other favors of power such as protection from competition. Shleifer and Vishny (1994) and Boycko, Shleifer, and Vishny (1996b) maintain that full privatization is the only sure way to solve state-enterprise inefficiency, since privatization raises the cost of intervention to politicians.

Empirical Evidence on State versus Private Ownership

So which group of theorists worships the True Faith: those who favor state ownership of commercial enterprises or those who oppose public ownership?[6] Ultimately, this question can be resolved only by using the tools of empirical research. Given the importance of this issue, it is not surprising that economists have long attempted to examine whether state ownership is inherently more or less efficient than private ownership. What is surprising is that, until quite recently, empirical research was unable to provide an unambiguous answer to this deceptively simple question. Early empirical studies tended to produce ambiguous or finely balanced results. Whereas several early papers found that private ownership was superior, a roughly equal number found that state ownership was not inherently less value-maximizing than private ownership, and a few even documented that state ownership was superior. In support of private ownership, Davies (1971) compared the performance of Australia's two airlines and found a massive advantage for the privately owned carrier. In a similar vein, Boardman, Freedman, and Eckel (1986) demonstrated that the stock price of Domtar, a Canadian paper company, declined sharply when it was revealed that two Crown corporations had accumulated a controlling interest in the firm—since investors believed the company would be forced to pursue noneconomic objectives once it fell under state control. On the other hand, Caves and Christensen (1980) compared the performance of two competing Canadian railroad companies and found no significant efficiency difference between the state owned and the privately owned companies. Atkinson and Halvorsen (1986) compared the efficiency levels of publicly owned and privately owned electric utilities operating in the United States in 1970 and likewise concluded that there were no significant differences in performance—both were equally cost inefficient. Färe, Groskopf, and Logan (1985) apply a different estimation methodology to this same sample of U.S. electric utility companies and find that the publicly owned utilities are slightly (but insignificantly) more efficient than their private-sector counterparts. Boardman and Vining (1989) and Shirley and Walsh (2000) both present more detailed summaries and analyses of the early empirical research examining the efficiency of state ownership.

Why has it proved so difficult to isolate the impact of ownership on firm performance? Obviously, comparing the performance of government-owned to privately owned firms is one method through which the impact of government ownership on firm performance can be analyzed.[7] However, there are two methodological difficulties that are especially pronounced in attempts to isolate the impact of ownership on performance. First, in comparing SOEs to privately owned firms, it is difficult, if not impossible, to determine the appropriate set of comparison firms or benchmarks, especially in developing economies with limited private sectors. Second, there are generally fundamental reasons that certain firms are government owned and others are privately owned, including the impact of ideology and the degree of perceived market failure within a particular industry. The factors that determine whether the firm is publicly or privately owned likely also have significant effects on performance. As the survey article by Denis and McConnell (2003) makes clear, researchers have found it very difficult to specifically isolate the effect of concentrated versus dispersed ownership on performance even in private companies, so we should expect even greater difficulty in evaluating the effects of government ownership in cases where the ownership structure is itself endogenous to the system that includes both political and economic performance goals.

Despite these problems, researchers have compared SOEs and privately owned company performance in several cases with some success. Given the large volume of research, we break our discussion into two parts, based on the type of sample employed by researchers. We first examine studies that compare the performance of public versus private ownership by employing national or international samples of state-owned and privately owned companies. These studies are summarized in table 2.1. Next, we survey those studies that compare the performance of state and private firms within a given industry, either within a country or internationally. As will be our policy in discussing empirical evidence throughout this book, we first present basic details about each of the key empirical studies and then summarize (and evaluate) the primary results of all the studies at the section's end. Furthermore, we present the studies in the chronological order in which they were written, both because this is how the literature itself developed and because it allows the reader to trace the evolution of intellectual thought over time and to see how practical experience helped guide the work of researchers.

International and Country Studies of State Versus Private Ownership

An important approach to studying the effects of government ownership on efficiency relies on a multi-industry, multinational, time-series, or cross-sectional regression methodology. While cross-sectional studies suffer from well-known methodological problems, they are able to capture differences that are not apparent in single-country or single-industry studies. An extremely influential paper taking this approach is that by Boardman and Vining (1989), who examine the economic performance of the 500 largest non-U.S. industrial firms in 1983. Using four profitability ratios and two measures of X-efficiency, they show that state-owned and mixed (state and private) ownership enterprises are significantly less profitable and productive than are privately owned firms. They also find that mixed enterprises are no more profitable than SOEs, suggesting that full private control, not just partial ownership, is essential to achieving performance improvement. In a later study, Vining and Boardman (1992) use a sample of Canadian firms to reexamine the state versus private ownership question. Their results are qualitatively similar to the earlier findings. In addition, the Canadian study finds that mixed enterprises are more profitable than SOEs, though they fall far short of private-firm levels.

Majumdar (1996) examines differences in efficiency among government-owned, mixed, and private-sector firms in India. He finds support for the superior efficiency of private and mixed ownership firms over SOEs. Using aggregate, industry-level survey data, Majumdar finds that SOEs owned by the central and state governments have average efficiency scores of 0.658 and 0.638, respectively, over the period 1973–1989. Mixed enterprises have scores of 0.92 and private

TABLE 2.1. Summary of Recent Empirical Studies Comparing Public Versus Private Ownership: General and Country Studies

Study	Sample Description, Study Period, and Methodology	Summary of Empirical Findings and Conclusions
Boardman and Vining (1989)	Examine the economic performance of the 500 largest non-U.S. firms in 1983, classified by ownership structure as state-owned, privately owned, or mixed ownership enterprises (ME). Employ four profitability ratios and two measures of X-efficiency.	Find that state-owned and mixed ownership firms are significantly less profitable and productive than privately owned companies. Also find mixed ownership firms are no more profitable than pure state-owned companies—so full private ownership required to gain efficiency. Private ownership superior.
Vining and Boardman (1992)	Ask whether ownership "matters" in determining the efficiency of SOEs, or if only the degree of competition is important. Estimate performance model using 1986 data from 500 largest nonfinancial Canadian companies—including 12 SOEs and 93 mixed enterprises.	After controlling for size, market share, and other factors, find private firms are significantly more profitable and efficient than are MEs and SOEs, though now find that MEs outperform Crown corporations (SOEs). Thus, ownership has an effect separable from competition alone. Private ownership superior.
Majumdar (1996)	Using industry-level survey data, evaluates the performance differences between SOEs, MEs, and privately owned Indian companies for the period 1973–1989. SOEs and MEs account for 37% of employment and 66% of capital investment in India in 1989.	Document efficiency scores averaging 0.975 for privately owned firms, which are significantly higher than the average 0.912 for MEs and 0.638 for SOEs. State-sector efficiency improves during concerted "efficiency drives" but declines afterwards. Private ownership superior.
Kole and Mulherin (1997)	Test whether postwar performance of 17 firms partly owned by U.S. government due to seizure of "enemy" property during WWII differs significantly from performance of private U.S. firms.	Though these firms experience abnormally high turnover among boards of directors, tenure of managers is stable and SOE performance is not significantly different from privately owned firms. No difference based on ownership.
Dewenter and Malatesta (2000)	Test whether profitability, labor intensity, and debt levels of SOEs in the lists of the 500 largest non-U.S. firms during 1975, 1985, and 1995 differs from privately owned firms in the same lists.	After controlling for business cycles, find private firms are significantly (often dramatically) more profitable than SOEs. Private firms also have significantly less debt and less labor-intensive production processes. Private ownership superior.
Frydman, Hessel, and Rapaczynski (2000)	Examine whether privatized central European firms controlled by outside investors are more entrepreneurial—in terms of ability to increase revenues—than firms controlled by insiders or the state. Study employs survey data from a sample of 506 manufacturing firms in the Czech Republic, Hungary, and Poland.	Document that all state and privatized firms engage in similar types of restructuring, but that product restructuring by firms owned by outside investors is significantly more effective, in terms of revenue generation, than by firms with other types of ownership. Concludes the more entrepreneurial behavior of outsider-owned firms is due to incentive effects, rather than human capital effects, of privatization—specifically greater readiness to take risks. Private ownership superior.

Study	Description	Findings
Karpoff (2001)	Examines 35 government financed and 57 privately funded expeditions to the Arctic during 1819–1909 to see if there are systematic differences in productivity of voyages based on the type of backing.	Finds the private expeditions performed better using several measures of performance, despite the higher funding levels enjoyed by publicly backed voyages. More major discoveries were made by private expeditions, while most tragedies (lost ships and lives) occurred on the government-sponsored expeditions. The results are robust in regressions explaining expedition outcomes and the poor performance of public expeditions is not due to different objectives, available technologies, or country of origin. Private ownership superior.
Bartel and Harrison (2002)	Using a 1981–1995 panel of all public and private manufacturing establishments in Indonesia, analyze whether public-sector inefficiency is primarily due to agency-type (ownership/incentive) problems or to the industrial structure and operating environment in which SOEs operated.	Find support for both ownership and environmental causes of public firm inefficiency. Ownership matters because, for a given operating environment, SOEs perform worse than private firms. Environment matters because only SOEs that received government financing or those shielded from import competition performed worse than private firms. Private ownership superior.
Bottasso and Sembenelli (2002)	Using firm-level panel data for 12 Italian manufacturing industries over the 1978–1993 period, examine the relationship between the identity of ultimate owners and the technical efficiency of firms by estimating stochastic production frontiers. Privately owned independent firms are used as control group, and their performance is tested against three alternative ownership forms.	Subsidiaries of foreign multinational firms are found to be more efficient than any other group, while subsidiaries of national (Italian) business groups were insignificantly different. State-owned companies were significantly less efficient than any other group. Private ownership superior.
Tian (2003)	Examines the ownership and control structure of 826 partially privatized companies listed on Chinese stock exchanges from 1994–1998 and tests the relationship between ownership structure and firm value—as measured by Tobin's Q.	Finds that government shareholdings remain very large in partially privatized companies and that the relationship between state holdings and firm value is U-shaped. Going from state ownership levels of 0 to 30%, increasing ownership cause firm value to decline, but after that Tobin's Q increases with increasing state ownership. Private ownership (generally) superior.

enterprises have scores of 0.975. A concern with Majumdar's study is that the aggregated nature of the data, along with problems arising from the reliance on survey data, limits his ability to identify any specific areas where private versus state ownership works best, and whether there are simultaneity and selection-bias problems in trying to estimate the effects of ownership and productivity. In later studies, Majumdar (1998, 1999) and Ahuja and Majumdar (1998) remedy this by documenting that Indian SOEs are inefficient by design. Not only are the companies saddled by their political overseers with noneconomic objectives, they are also forced to operate on an uneconomically large scale. In return, SOE managers are favored with access to credit from state banks at subsidized borrowing rates, so they face soft budget constraints as well. Akram (1999, 2001) shows that Bangladeshi SOEs face similar—but even worse—problems owing to operating inefficiencies, political interference, and soft budget constraints.[8]

Kole and Mulherin (1997) set out to answer the basic question in the public versus private debate as posed by Peltzman (1971), "If a privately owned firm is socialized, and nothing else happens, how will the ownership alone affect the firm's behavior?" Kole and Mulherin study 17 firms with significant German or Japanese ownership when the United States entered World War II. The federal government assumed ownership of the foreign stock in these firms and ended up holding between 35 and 100 percent of the common stock for up to 23 years during and after World War II. Kole and Mulherin find industry controls for five firms, comprising 61 percent of the book value of the 17 firms, and compare the performance of these to the government-owned firms. They find no significant performance differences between their sample and the private-sector firms, and thus conclude "the preceding results stand in contrast to the typical results regarding the inefficiency of government enterprise" (page 15). The authors argue that the fact that these firms were operating in competitive industries forced them to operate efficiently.

The Kole and Mulherin (1997) results are evidence that in a competitive environment, where the government has no agenda other than that of a passive investor, factors other than ownership determine firm performance. Many of the firms were involved in the war effort so the government had an incentive to run them efficiently. In addition, all the firms were eventually reprivatized so the government was also concerned with running the firms efficiently to maximize the later sale value. Kole and Mulherin admit that their sample and the period they study is novel, limiting its generality. Further, their key results are based on only five firms. Still, their findings do illustrate the importance of factors other than ownership in determining firm performance.

Dewenter and Malatesta (2000) follow the general approach of Boardman and Vining (1989), but use multiyear and more recent data. They test whether the profitability, labor intensity, and debt levels of SOEs in the 500 largest international companies, as reported in *Fortune* for 1975, 1985, and 1995, differ from privately owned firms in the same samples. Their data have 1,369 total firm years, of which 147 represent government-owned firms. Since *Fortune* excluded U.S. firms until 1995, the data are mainly international. After controlling for firm size, location, industry, and business-cycle effects, Dewenter and Malatesta find robust evidence that private companies are significantly (often dramatically) more profitable than SOEs, and also have lower levels of indebtedness and fewer labor-intensive production processes than do their state-owned counterparts.

Frydman, Hessel, and Rapaczynski (2000) examine whether privatized central European firms controlled by outside investors are more entrepreneurial, in terms of their ability to increase revenues, than firms controlled by insiders or the state. Their study employs survey data for a sample of 506 manufacturing firms in the Czech Republic, Hungary, and Poland. They document that all state and privatized firms engage in similar types of restructuring, but that product restructuring by firms owned by outside investors is significantly more effective, in terms of revenue generation, than by firms with other types of ownership. They conclude that the more entrepreneurial behavior of outsider-owned private firms is due to incentive effects, rather than human capital effects, of privatization — specifically, the greater readiness of outside shareholders to take risks.

Another paper exploits a very interesting natural experiment to compare the performance of government-organized versus privately organized production. Karpoff (2001) studies a comprehensive sample of 35 government-funded expeditions and 57 privately funded expeditions to the Arctic from 1818 to 1909 seeking to locate and navigate a Northwest Passage, discover the North Pole, and make other discoveries in arctic regions. He finds that the private expeditions performed better using several measure of performance. Karpoff shows that most major arctic discoveries were made by private expeditions, while most tragedies (lost ships and lives) were on publicly funded expeditions. Karpoff notes that the public expeditions might have had greater losses because they took greater risks, but then the public expeditions would have had a greater share of discoveries, which did not occur. Karpoff also estimates regressions explaining outcomes in several ways (crew deaths, ships lost, tonnage of ships lost, incidence of scurvy, level of expedition accomplishment), controlling for exploratory objectives sought, country of origin, the leader's previous arctic experience, or the decade in which the expedition occurred. In essentially every regression, the dummy variable for private expedition is significant, with a sign indicating that the private expedition performed better. Karpoff concludes that the incentives were better aligned in the private expeditions, leading to systematic differences in the ways public and private expeditions were organized. While the uniqueness of the sample limits its generality, Karpoff provides an interesting illustration of the impact of ownership on the performance of an organization.[9]

Bartel and Harrison (2002) use a 1981–1995 panel of all public and private manufacturing establishments in Indonesia to analyze whether public-sector inefficiency is primarily due to agency type (ownership/incentive) problems or to the industrial structure and regulatory environment in which SOEs operate. They find support for both ownership and environmental causes of public-firm inefficiency. Ownership matters because, for a given operating environment, SOEs perform worse than private firms. However, environment also matters because only SOEs that received government financing or those that were shielded from import competition performed worse than private firms. Bartel and Harrison find that if a SOE that is receiving 100 percent government financing is 60 percent privatized, its productivity will rise by four percentage points. That same four percentage-point productivity increase can be achieved by manipulating the operating environment—either by reducing government financing to 30 percent or by raising import penetration by 8.8 percentage points.

Bottasso and Sembenelli (2002) use firm-level panel data for 12 Italian manufacturing industries over the 1978–1993 period to examine the relationship between the identity of ultimate owners and the technical efficiency of firms by estimating stochastic production frontiers. They use privately owned independent firms as a control group, and test their performance against three alternative ownership forms. They find that subsidiaries of foreign multinational firms are more efficient than the reference group, while subsidiaries of national (Italian) business groups are insignificantly different. State-owned companies are significantly less efficient than any other group.

Finally, Tian (2003) examines whether, and how, residual state ownership impacts the valuation of exchange-listed firms. His sample includes 825 companies listed on the Shanghai Stock Exchange from 1994 to 1998, with 513 mixed-ownership firms and 312 private firms. He finds that private firms perform better than mixed ownership firms. In addition, he documents that government share-holdings remain very large in partially privatized companies, and that the relationship between state holdings and firm value is U-shaped. In a range of state ownership levels of from 0 to 30 percent, Tian found that increasing ownership causes firm value to decline, but after that, the Tobin's Q value increases with increasing state ownership.

Industry Studies of State Versus Private Ownership

Studies that employ broad national or international samples typically have the benefit of employing large samples, but they also suffer from the inability to control for factors that are industry-specific. We now briefly survey empirical studies that compare state and private firms within the same industry and thus at least implicitly neutralize differences in the investment opportunity sets facing companies in different industrial sectors. Five of these industries—telecoms, banking, oil and gas, electricity production and distribution, and airlines—are examined in much greater detail in chapters 8–10. The empirical studies we survey here are detailed in table 2.2. One of the very best such studies is by Ehrlich, Gallais-Hamonno, Liu, and Lutter (1994), who provide strong evidence of productivity differences between state-owned and privately owned firms. They use a sample of 23 comparable international airlines of different (and in some cases changing) ownership categories over the period 1973–1983, for which they are able to obtain good and comparable cost, output, and ownership data. They develop a model of endogenous, firm-specific productivity growth as a function of firm-specific capital and use the model as a basis for their fixed-effects regressions estimating a cost function in a simultaneous framework with input-demand equations. They argue that they are able to separate the impact of ownership changes on short-term levels of productivity changes from the long-term effects on the rate of productivity growth, improving on earlier studies that have concentrated on the static rather than dy-

TABLE 2.2. Summary of Recent Empirical Studies Comparing Public Versus Private Ownership: Industry Studies

Study	Sample Description, Study Period, and Methodology	Summary of Empirical Findings and Conclusions
Ehrlich, Gallais-Hamonno, Liu, and Lutter (1994)	Examine impact of state ownership on the long-run rate of productivity growth and/or cost decline for 23 international airlines over the period 1973–1983.	Find that state ownership can lower the long-run annual rate of productivity growth by 1.6–2.0% and the rate of unit cost decline by 1.7–1.9%. Ownership effects are not affected by degree of competition. Private ownership superior.
Ros (1999)	Uses International Telecommunications Union data and panel data regression methodology to examine the effects of competition and privatization on network expansion and efficiency in 110 countries over the period 1986–1995.	Finds that countries with at least 50% private ownership of main telecom firm have significantly higher teledensity levels and growth rates. Both privatization and competition increase efficiency, but only privatization is positively associated with network expansion. Private ownership superior.
Laurin and Bozec (2000)	Compare productivity and profitability of two large Canadian rail carriers, before and after the 1995 privatization of Canadian National (CN). Compares accounting ratios for entire 17-year period 1981–1997 and for three subperiods: the fully state-owned era (1981–91), the pre-privatization period (1992–1995), and the post-privatization era.	Total factor productivity of CN much lower than that of privately owned Canadian Pacific (CP) during 1981–1991 period, but became just as efficient during p e-privatization (1992–1995) period, then exceeded it after 1995. Both firms shed workers after 1992, but CN's employment declined by more (34% versus 18%) as average productivity almost doubled (97% increase). CN's capital spending increased significantly, though CP increased more. Private ownership superior.
LaPorta, López-de-Silanes, and Shleifer (2002)	Using data from 92 countries, examine whether government ownership of banks impacts level of financial system development, rate of economic growth, and growth rate of productivity. Tests whether government ownership of banks is motivated by benevolent, "development" objective or a redistributive "political" objective.	Find government ownership is extensive, especially in poorest countries, that these holdings retard financial system development, and restrict economic growth rates, mostly due to impact on productivity. Higher government ownership in 1970 is associated with slower subsequent financial development and lower growth in per capita income and productivity. Evidence supports the political view of state ownership of banks. Private ownership superior.

(continued)

TABLE 2.2. (*continued*)

Study	Sample Description, Study Period, and Methodology	Summary of Empirical Findings and Conclusions
Kwoka (2002)	Compares the performance of 147 investor-owned electric utilities (IOUs) with that of 396 utilities owned by municipalities operating in the U.S. in 1989. Attempts to determine if there are systematic differences in efficiency between these two groups.	Finds that public and privately owned utilities are largely specialized in different activities, with IOUs dominating electricity generation—where they have cost advantages related to economies of scale. Municipally owned utilities are more competitive. No difference based on ownership.
Wallsten (2002)	Uses an original data set compiled from early 20th century sources to test the effects of government monopoly service, competition and regulation on the development of the telecommunications industry in Europe during the early 1990s. Also examines the effect of very stringent licensing arrangements that allow private firms to operate, but with highly insecure property rights.	Controlling for income and other factors, finds that countries with competition between telephone providers and whose governments did not threaten to expropriate firms' assets saw higher telephone penetration and lower prices, even in rural areas. Telephone penetration was much lower in countries where service was provided by state-owned monopolies than in countries that allowed private service. However, countries that licensed firms under stringent concessions saw even worse penetration. Private ownership superior.

namic effects of state ownership and changes in state ownership. Further, the authors suggest that they are able to isolate the effects of ownership from other factors impacting the rate of productivity growth, including market conditions and exogenous technical changes.

Ehrlich, Gallais-Hamonno, Liu, and Lutter (1994) find a significant link between ownership and firm-specific rates of productivity growth. Their results suggest that private ownership leads to higher rates of productivity growth and declining costs in the long run and that these differences are not affected by the degree of market competition or regulation. Their estimates suggest that the short-run effects of changes from state to private ownership on productivity and costs are ambiguous, providing a possible explanation for some of the anomalous results in studies examining short-run effects of ownership changes. However, their point estimates indicate that the change from complete state ownership to private ownership in the long run would increase productivity growth by 1.6 to 2 percent a year and costs would decline by 1.7 to 1.9 percent. Their empirical results also suggest that a partial change from state ownership to private ownership has little effect on long-run productivity growth—the benefits are based on complete privatization of the firm.[10]

No fewer than 16 studies examine whether state or private ownership is superior in the international telecommunications industry. These studies are described in detail in chapters 4 and 8, so we mention only two here. Ros (1999) and Wallsten (2002) study the state versus private ownership question using data from quite different eras. Ros uses International Telecommunications Union data and panel data regression methodology to examine the effects of competition and privatization on network expansion and efficiency in 110 countries over the period 1986–1995. He finds that countries with at least 50 percent private ownership of the main telecom firm have significantly higher teledensity levels and growth rates. Both privatization and competition increase efficiency, but only privatization is positively associated with network expansion. Most of the studies employing recent ITU data arrive at similar conclusions, though many find that competition is more important than ownership, per se, in improving telecom performance.

Wallsten (2002) examines the impact of state ownership, control, and regulation on telephone penetration rates by going back in time and examining how ownership influenced the speed with which telephone service was provided to citizens of different countries during the industry's infancy. He uses an original data set compiled from early twentieth-century sources to test the effects of government monopoly service, competition, and regulation on the development of the telecommunications industry in Europe during the early 1990s. He also examines the effect of very stringent licensing arrangements that allowed private firms to operate, but with highly insecure property rights. Controlling for income and other factors, Wallsten finds that countries with competition between telephone providers and whose governments did not threaten to expropriate firms' assets saw higher telephone penetration and lower prices, even in rural areas. Telephone penetration was much lower in countries where service was provided by state-owned monopolies than in countries that allowed private service. However, countries that licensed firms under stringent concessions saw even worse penetration rates than countries with state-owned monopolies.

Commercial banking is a key industry in any economy. Banks not only are the principal providers of credit to industry in most countries (other than Britain, the United States, and a few other OECD nations), they also play an indispensable role in every nation's payment system. La Porta, Lopez-de-Silanes, and Shleifer (2002) examine the importance and impact of state ownership in this key industry. Using data from 92 countries, they examine whether government ownership of banks impacts the level of financial system development, rate of economic growth, and growth rate of productivity. They test whether government ownership of banks is motivated by benevolent, "development" objectives or by redistributive "political" objectives. They find that government ownership is extensive, especially in the poorest countries. They also find that these holdings retard financial-system development and restrict economic growth rates, mostly owing to the impact of state ownership—and the monopoly power frequently attendant thereto—on productivity. Higher government ownership in 1970 is associated with significantly slower subsequent financial development and lower growth in per capita income and productivity. This evidence supports the political view of state ownership of banks.

Finally, as noted at the start of this section, a number of early state versus private ownership studies examined the U.S. electric utility industry, with mixed results. Kwoka (2002) revisits this industry using much more recent data. He compares the performance of 147 investor-owned electric utilities (IOUs) with that of 396 utilities owned by municipalities operating in the United States in 1989, and he attempts to determine if there are systematic differences in efficiency between these two groups. He finds that public and privately owned utilities are largely specialized in different activities, with IOUs dominating electricity generation—where they have cost advantages related to economies of scale—but municipally owned utilities are more competitive in electricity distribution. He concludes that any advantages of state ownership are size-dependent and disappear entirely for the largest publicly owned companies.

Summary of Empirical Evidence on State Versus Private Ownership

Given the large number of empirical studies produced during the last 15 years, has empirical research generated a conclusive answer regarding the relative efficiency of state versus private ownership? Fairly clearly, it has, and the answer is that private ownership must be considered superior to state ownership in all but the most narrowly defined fields or under very special circumstances. The only major recent studies surveyed here that do not unequivocally support private over state ownership are Kole and Mulherin (1997) and Kwoka (2002), and their results do not favor state ownership but rather demonstrate only that private ownership is not always superior.

The weight of evidence shows that private ownership is generally better than state ownership, but it does not necessarily follow that all state-owned enterprises can or should be privatized. After all, SOEs originally became state-owned for a reason, and that reason may still be operant. We will examine the empirical evidence on whether privatization "works" to improve firm performance in chapters 4 and 5. In the remainder of this chapter, however, we first ask whether there are effective policy alternatives to privatization and then conclude by examining the fiscal and macroeconomic impact of the privatization programs that have been launched to date.

Are There Effective Policy Alternatives to Privatization?

As discussed earlier, some argue that competition and deregulation are more important than privatization or governance changes in improving performance of firms [Yarrow (1986), Kay and Thompson (1986), Bishop and Kay (1989), Vickers and Yarrow (1991) and Allen and Gale (1999)]. Others maintain that privatization is necessary for significant performance improvements [Vining and Boardman (1992), Boycko, Shleifer, and Vishny (1994, 1996a, 1996b), Nellis (1994), Brada (1996), Shleifer (1998), and Shirley and Walsh (2000)]. A sizable body of empirical research has recently examined this question, and the key studies we will examine are detailed in tables 2.3, 2.4, and 2.5.

The "Ownership Versus Competition" Debate:
Theory and Evidence

Many studies examine whether competition or ownership is more important in explaining actual firm performance—or they examine the corollary question of whether changes in ownership or environment (competition) have greater impact on changes in corporate performance. These studies are summarized in table 2.3. In one of the first such studies, Pinto, Belka, and Krajewski (1993) evaluate the way in which the Polish state sector responded in the three years following Poland's "Big Bang" reforms of January 1990. These reforms deregulated prices, introduced foreign competition to many industries, and signaled that tight monetary and fiscal policies would be pursued. However, the Polish government did not immediately launch a large-scale privatization program. These authors document significant performance improvements on the part of most manufacturing firms, and they conclude that these improvements were due to the imposition of hard budget constraints reinforced by tighter bank lending behavior, consistency in the government's "no bailout signal," import competition, and reputational concerns by SOE managers. During the early transition period, no major Polish SOEs were privatized, and there was no certainty that any would be privatized soon, so the improvements documented cannot be ascribed to an "anticipation effect" by managers preparing for private ownership.

Although Nickell (1996) does not examine the ownership versus competition question directly, he does present one of the first and best studies showing that competition is indeed an important influence on firm behavior. Using an unbalanced panel of data for 147 British manufacturing firms over the period 1972–1986, he examines empirically whether competition—as measured by number of

TABLE 2.3. Summary of Recent Empirical Studies Examining the Impact of Competition on Corporate Performance or Comparing the Efficacy of Ownership Change versus Competition

Study	Sample Description, Study Period, and Methodology	Summary of Empirical Findings and Conclusions
Pinto, Belka, and Krajewski (1993)	Test whether privatization is required to improve performance of SOEs by examining how Polish state sector responded in the three years following the "Big Bang" reforms of January 1990. These liberalized prices, tightened fiscal and monetary policy and introduced competition—but did not include privatization.	Document significant performance improvement due to macroeconomic stabilization package, even without privatization. Improvements mostly due to imposition of hard budget constraints, tight bank lending policies, and enhanced credibility about government's "no bailout" pledge. Competition improves performance without ownership changes.
Nickell (1996)	Using an unbalanced panel of data for 147 U.K. manufacturing firms over the period 1972–1986, examines empirically whether competition—as measured by number of industry competitors—does promote efficiency as predicted by theory. Also employs a much larger, but less informative, data set of 670 companies to verify key results.	Documents that competition, measured either by increased number of competitors or lower level of rents, is associated with higher rates of total factor productivity growth. Also find that market power, as captured by market share, generates reduced levels of productivity. Competition improves performance (doesn't examine ownership's effect).
Li (1997)	Using a panel data set of 272 Chinese SOEs with data from 1980 to 1989, examines the effectiveness of China's incremental reform process. This process emphasized giving SOE managers greater operating discretion and additional incentives, but did not involve (or anticipate) privatization.	Finds marked improvements in the marginal productivity of input factors and total factor productivity. Also finds that over 87% of TFP growth was attributable to improved incentives, intensified product market competition, and improved factor allocation. Competition improves performance without ownership changes.
Wallsten (2001)	Performs an econometric analysis of the effects of telecommunications reforms in developing countries. Using a panel data set of 30 African and Latin American countries from 1984 to 1997, explores the effects of privatization, competition, and regulation on telecommunications performance.	Competition is significantly associated with increases in per capita access and decreases in cost. Privatization alone is not helpful, unless coupled with effective, independent regulation. Increasing competition the single best reform, competition with privatization is the best combination, but privatizing a monopoly without regulatory reforms should be avoided. Performance improves most when competition and privatization are combined.

54

Study	Description	Findings
Zhang, Parker, and Kirkpatrick (2002)	Examine effects of competition, privatization, and regulation on the performance of the electricity industry using a panel data set for 51 developing countries. Econometric technique designed to disentangle separate effects of competition, regulatory change, and ownership change.	Find that competition has the strongest effect in promoting performance improvement. By itself, competition promotes service penetration, capacity expansion, greater labor efficiency, and lower prices for industrial users. Separate effects of privatization and having an independent regulator are insignificant, except that privatization seems to promote higher capacity utilization. Coexistence of these two reforms is correlated with greater electricity availability, more generation capacity and higher labor productivity. Basic conclusion: privatization and regulation, on their own, do not lead to obvious gains in economic performance, while promoting competition does stimulate performance improvements, irrespective of changes in ownership or regulation. Competition more important than ownership change.
Carlin, Fries, Schaffer, and Seabright (2001)	Use data from a 1999 survey of 3,305 firms in 25 transition countries to examine the factors that promote restructuring by firms and enhance subsequent performance—as measured by growth in sales and in sales per employee over a 3-year period. Survey includes about 125 companies from each of the 25 countries, with larger samples from Poland and Ukraine (200+ firms) and Russia (500+ firms). Just over one-half were newly established firms, 8% were privatized to insiders, 22% privatized to outsiders, and 16% remained state owned.	Find that competition has an important and nonmonotonic effect on the growth of sales and labor productivity, with performance improving more for firms facing 1–3 competitors than for monopolists (one-fourth of SOEs faced no competition for their main products in their domestic markets) or firms facing many competitors. Controlling for other factors, find no significant relationship between privatization and performance. Newly created firms generally outperformed all other categories. Old firms (privatized and SOEs) were much more likely to cut employment than new entrants, but some evidence that private firms (new entrants and privatized) more likely to engage in new product development. Overall, find competition to be a more powerful influence on performance than ownership, per se. Competition more important than ownership change.
Angelucci, Estrin, Konings, and Zolkiewski (2001)	Analyze the effect of ownership and competition or firm performance, measured by total factor productivity (TFP), in three transition economies for years 1994–1998. Use reported company accounts data for 1994 and 1998 for 17,570 Polish, and for 1997–1998 for 1,500 Bulgarian and 2,047 Romanian companies. Test whether private foreign-owned firms outperformed private domestic companies, and whether these both outperform SOEs.	Find that (1) competitive pressure (measured by market structure) is associated with higher productivity in all three countries; (2) increased import penetration is positively associated with performance in Poland, but negatively in Bulgaria and Romania; (3) competitive pressure has stronger effects in private firms and privatization is associated with higher performance in more competitive sectors; (4) privatization is associated with better firm performance and privatized firms outperform SOEs in all three countries. Overall, find there are complementarities between competitive pressure and ownership. Performance improves most when competition and privatization are combined.

industry competitors—does promote efficiency as predicted by theory. He documents that competition, measured either by increased number of competitors or lower level of rents, is associated with higher rates of total-factor productivity growth. He also finds that market power, as captured by market share, generates reduced levels of productivity. Nickell verifies these key results using a much larger, but less detailed, data set of 670 companies that lacks details about the number of competitors but does have information about each firm's industrial market share (as proxied by two-digit Standard Industrial Classification).

Li (1997) studies the effectiveness of China's incremental reform process using a panel data set of 272 Chinese SOEs with data from 1980 to 1989. This reform process emphasized giving SOE managers greater operating discretion and additional incentives, but did not involve (or anticipate) privatization. Li documents marked improvements in the marginal productivity of input factors and total factor productivity, and also finds that over 87 percent of total factor productivity (TFP) growth is attributable to improved incentives, intensified product market competition, and improved factor allocation.

Wallsten (2001) performs an econometric analysis of the effects of telecommunications reforms in developing countries. Using a panel data set of 30 African and Latin American countries from 1984 to 1997, he explores the effects of privatization, competition, and regulation on telecommunications performance. Competition is significantly associated with increases in per capita access and decreases in cost. He concludes that privatization alone is not helpful unless coupled with effective, independent regulation. Increasing competition is the single best reform, competition with privatization is the best overall package of reforms, but privatizing a monopoly without regulatory reforms should be avoided.

Zhang, Parker, and Kirkpatrick (2002) examine the effects of competition, privatization, and regulation on the performance of the electricity industry using a panel data set for 51 developing countries. The econometric technique they employ is designed to disentangle separate effects of competition, regulatory change, and ownership change. They find that competition has the strongest effect in promoting performance improvement. By itself, competition promotes service penetration, capacity expansion, greater labor efficiency, and lower prices for industrial users. The separate effects of privatization and having an independent regulator are insignificant, except that privatization seems to promote higher capacity utilization. Coexistence of these two reforms is correlated with greater electricity availability, more generation capacity, and higher labor productivity. Their basic conclusion is that privatization and regulation, on their own, do not lead to obvious gains in economic performance, whereas promoting competition does stimulate performance improvements, irrespective of changes in ownership or regulation.

Carlin, Fries, Schaffer, and Seabright (2001) use data from a 1999 survey of 3,305 firms in 25 transition countries to examine the factors that promote restructuring by firms and enhance subsequent performance—as measured by growth in sales and in sales per employee over a three-year period. The survey includes about 125 companies from each of the 25 countries, with larger samples from Poland and Ukraine (200+ firms) and Russia (500+ firms). Just over one-half were newly established firms, 8 percent were privatized to insiders, 22 percent were privatized to outsiders, and 16 percent remained state owned. The authors find that competition has an important and nonmonotonic effect on the growth of sales and labor productivity, with performance improving more for firms facing one to three competitors than for monopolists (one-fourth of SOEs faced no competition for their main products in their domestic markets) or firms facing many competitors. Controlling for other factors, they find no significant relationship between privatization and performance. Newly created firms generally outperformed all other categories. Old firms (privatized and SOEs) were much more likely to cut employment than new entrants, but there is some evidence that private firms (new entrants and privatized) are more likely to engage in new product development. Overall, these authors find competition to be a more powerful influence on performance than ownership, per se.

Finally, Angelucci, Estrin, Konings, and Zolkiewski (2001) analyze the effect of ownership and competition on firm performance, measured by TFP, in three transition economies for the years 1994–1998. They use reported company accounts data for 1994 and 1998 for 17,570 Polish, and for 1997–1998 for 1,500 Bulgarian and 2,047 Romanian companies to test whether private foreign-owned firms outperformed private domestic companies, and whether these both outperform SOEs. They find that (1) competitive pressure (measured by market structure) is associated with higher productivity in all three countries; (2) increased import penetration is positively associated with performance in Poland, but negatively associated in Bulgaria and Romania; (3) competitive pressure has stronger effects in private firms and privatization is associated with higher performance in more competitive sectors; and (4) privatization is associated with better firm performance and privatized firms outperform SOEs in all three countries. Overall, the authors find there are complementarities between competitive pressure and ownership in promoting superior firm performance.

Imposition of Hard Budget Constraints and Improved Incentives for Managers

Another strand of research examines whether it is, in fact, possible to impose hard budgets constraints on loss-making SOEs and, if so, whether this improves corporate performance. Numerous articles examine whether soft budget constraints are a problem in transition countries. However, in this chapter we discuss only those studies that employ multinational samples and are thus most generalizable. These studies are summarized in table 2.4. A complete listing and analysis of all studies of SBCs in transition economies is presented in chapter 5.

A very important study of the effects of SBCs in transition economies is Frydman, Gray, Hessel, and Rapaczynski (2000), who examine whether the imposition of hard budget constraints is alone sufficient to improve corporate performance in the Czech Republic, Hungary, and Poland. They employ a sample of 216 firms, split among state-owned (31%), privatized (43%), and private (26%) firms, and find that privatization alone adds nearly 10 percentage points to the revenue growth of a firm sold to outside owners. Most important, they find that the threat of hard

TABLE 2.4. Summary of Recent Empirical Studies Examining Whether the Imposition of Hard Budget Constraints (HBC) and Improved Incentives for Managers Improves Corporate Performance

Study	Sample Description, Study Period, and Methodology	Summary of Empirical Findings and Conclusions
Groves, Hong, McMillan, and Naughton (1994)	Using a sample of data for 769 Chinese state-owned enterprises over the years 1980–1989, examine the impact of developing a competitive managerial labor market on firm performance and management productivity.	Find that new positive and negative incentives were effective in promoting improved performance, and that management contracts were widely adopted as part of reform process. Poorly performing managers were more likely to be replaced, and managerial pay was linked to firm sales and profits. Output per worker rose 67 percent in real terms between 1980 and 1989 for sample firms. Competition improves performance without ownership changes.
Frydman, Gray, Hessel, and Rapaczynski (2000)	Examine whether the imposition of hard budget constraints is alone sufficient to improve corporate performance in the Czech Republic, Hungary, and Poland. Employs a sample of 216 firms, split among state-owned (31%), privatized (43%), and private (26%) firms.	Find privatization alone added nearly 10 percentage points to the revenue growth of a firm sold to outside owners. Most important, finds that the threat of hard budget constraints for poorly performing SOEs falters, since governments are unwilling to allow these firms to fail. The brunt of SOEs' lower creditworthiness falls on state creditors. Privatization required to improve performance; threat of HBC not credible.
Bertero and Rondi (2000)	Employing a sample of 150 Italian manufacturing SOEs, with 1,278 firm-year observations, examine whether imposition of a hard budget constraint can improve SOE performance. Exploits the fact that fiscal environment became much tighter for Italian state enterprises during the late 1980s.	Find that the SOE firms' response to increased debt during the hard budget constraint period, 1988–1993, was consistent with financial pressure, but was not during the soft budget constraint period of 1977–87. Only during the later period do firms respond to financial pressure by increasing TFP and reducing employment. Imposition of HBC improves performance without ownership change.

budget constraints for poorly performing SOEs falters, since governments are un-willing to allow these firms to fail. The brunt of SOEs' lower creditworthiness falls on state creditors.

Bertero and Rondi (2000) employ a sample of 150 Italian manufacturing SOEs, with 1,278 firm-year observations, to examine whether imposition of a hard budget constraint can improve SOE performance. They exploit the fact that the fiscal environment became much tighter for Italian state enterprises during the late 1980s, as budget deficits became larger and the public debt reached unsus-tainable levels. They find that the SOE firms' responses to increased debt during the hard budget constraint period, 1988–1993, is consistent with financial pressure, but is not during the soft budget constraint period of 1977–1987. Only during the later period do firms respond to financial pressure by increasing total factor pro-ductivity and reducing employment. In other words, when hard budget constraints can be credibly imposed on SOEs, they do promote greater efficiency even in the absence of ownership changes.

Performance Contracts and Corporatization

The final reforms short of privatization that researchers have examined are cor-poratization and the use of performance contracts for SOE mangers. Studies ex-amining use of management contracts and corporatization in lieu of privatization are summarized in table 2.5. Shirley and Xu (1998) use a sample of 12 manage-ment contracts extended to SOE managers in six developing countries to examine whether these contracts can yield performance improvements without privatiza-tion. The evidence suggests they cannot. Indeed, once the counterfactual is prop-erly accounted for, contracts are negatively correlated with TFP growth.

In a similar vein, but focused on a single country, Shirley and Xu (2001) use a sample with data for 769 Chinese SOEs in 21 cities during the period 1980–1989 to examine whether use of management contracts (MCs) is associated with improved firm performance. The share of sample SOEs under management con-tracts increases from 8 percent in 1986 to 88 percent in 1989. They find that MCs on average are not significantly correlated with productivity improvements, and actually are associated with worse performance once endogeneity is accounted for. However, MCs are associated with improved performance in 38 percent of cases. With respect to improving incentives for SOE mangers, Groves, Hong, McMillan, and Naughton (1994) use a sample of data for 769 Chinese state-owned enterprises over the years 1980–1989 to examine the impact of developing a competitive managerial labor market on firm performance and management productivity. They find that new positive and negative incentives were effective in promoting im-proved performance, and that management contracts were widely adopted as part of the overall reform process. Poorly performing managers were more likely to be replaced, and managerial pay was linked to firm sales and profits. Finally, output per worker rises by 67 percent in real terms between 1980 and 1989 for the sample firms.

Finally, Shirley (1999) uses a sample of 12 developing countries to examine what combination of SOE reforms—including corporatization, use of manage-

TABLE 2.5. Summary of Recent Empirical Studies Examining Whether the Imposition of Performance Contracts and Corporatization Improves Corporate Performance

Study	Sample Description, Study Period, and Methodology	Summary of Empirical Findings and Conclusions
Shirley and Xu (1998)	Use a sample of 12 management contracts extended to SOE managers in six developing countries to examine whether these contracts can yield performance improvements without privatization.	Evidence does not indicate that performance contracts helped improve SOE performance. In fact, once the counterfactual is properly accounted for, contracts are negatively correlated with TFP growth. Management contracts do not improve performance.
Shirley (1999)	Using a sample of 12 developing countries, examine what combination of SOE reforms—including corporatization, use of management contracts, imposition of hard budget constraints, and privatization—yield performance improvements.	Find that only those countries that employ the full spectrum of reforms—including privatization—are able to significantly improve SOE performance. Corporatization or management contracts, used alone or in combination, do not yield performance improvements.
Shirly and Xu (2001)	Using a sample with data for 769 Chinese SOEs in 21 cities during the period 1980–1989, examine whether use of management contracts (MCs) is associated with improved firm performance. The share of sample SOEs under management contracts increases from 8% in 1986 to 88% in 1989.	Find that MCs on average are not significantly correlated with productivity improvements, and actually are associated with worse performance once endogeneity accounted for. However, MCs are associated with improved performance in 38% of cases. Management contracts do not (on average) improve performance.

ment contracts, imposition of hard budget constraints, and privatization—yields the most performance improvement for SOEs. She finds that only those countries that employ the full spectrum of reforms, including privatization, are able to significantly improve SOE performance. Corporatization or management contracts, used alone or in combination, do not yield performance improvements.

Summary: Are There Effective Policy Alternatives to Privatization?

The evidence clearly suggests that injecting competition and imposing hard budget constraints on SOEs can improve the performance of state firms, even without privatization. Other reforms, however, do not seem to have a measurable impact. Can we then conclude that competition and hard budget constraints are an alternative to privatization? Almost certainly we cannot, for two reasons. First, every study that examined both competition and privatization finds either that the combination of the two policies improved performance more than either adopted in isolation or that privatization had an additional measurable effect on performance over and above that of competition alone. Regarding the imposition of hard budget constraints, Nellis (1994), Shirley and Walsh (2000), and others note that this reform is extremely difficult to maintain over time without the threat of ultimate privatization.

At a more basic level, the proposition that competition and hard budgets alone determine corporate performance, and that ownership is unimportant, seems almost surreal to a financial economist in the early twenty-first century. As summarized in Denis and McConnell (2003), one of the primary lessons of financial research over the past quarter-century is that ownership is an extremely important influence on firm performance—and that the system of corporate governance decisively impacts how efficiently corporations will be run, and in whose interests. As we will see in chapters 4 and 5, the empirical research on privatization also clearly documents that changing from state to private ownership improves the economic performance of former SOEs. This discussion, however, is running far ahead of where we need to be, so we will conclude our evaluation of the reasons that governments adopt privatization programs by examining the impact these programs have had on public finances.

The Fiscal and Macroeconomic Impact of Privatization

Governments have two strictly fiscal reasons for adopting privatization programs. First, and most obviously, governments can raise a great deal of revenue by selling their stakes in public firms through either public share offerings or private asset sales. For many countries, an even more important reason to begin privatizing is to stop the outflow of public funds as subsidies for state enterprise losses. Figure 2.3 shows that SOE subsidies—proxied by savings minus investment—accounted for an average of approximately 2 percent of GDP for 38 developing countries during the period 1978–1983, and for roughly 1 percent of GDP during the rest of the 1980s.

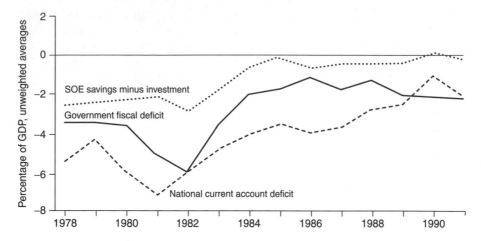

FIGURE 2.3. The fiscal impact of state-owned enterprise subsidies on national income accounts. This figure describes the fiscal drag that subsidizing SOE operating losses has on the national income accounts of 38 developing countries over the period 1978–1991. Source: World Bank, as reported in Figure 1 of Shirley (1999).

However, SOE subsidies were much more burdensome than this for many individual countries. As examples, López-de-Silanes (1997) documents that subsidies accounted for an astonishing 12 percent of Mexico's GDP immediately before that country launched a sweeping privatization program in 1988, and Davis, Ossowski, Richardson, and Barnett (2000) detail subsidies exceeding 3 percent of GDP for the Czech Republic, Uganda, and the Philippines. This section evaluates the fiscal and macroeconomic impact of privatization, and it focuses primarily on those studies that examine whether the proceeds of these programs were saved (used to reduce state borrowing) or spent on launching new programs or maintaining existing programs at unsustainable levels. The recent empirical studies examining the fiscal and macroeconomic impact of privatization are summarized in table 2.6.

Fiscal Motivations for Privatizing State-Owned Enterprises

One of the first published studies examining the fiscal impact of privatization is Jeronimo, Pagán and Soydemir (2000). They use country-level panel data on privatization receipts and budget deficits for OECD countries from 1990 to 1997 to analyze whether the concern with deficits in the 1990s in Spain, Portugal, Italy, and Greece is related to a shift from privatization as a tool of economic restructuring to a tool of European monetary convergence. They document a significantly negative relationship between privatization receipts and deficits in these four countries, but not for other EU members. For the southern European countries, pri-

TABLE 2.6. Summary of Recent Empirical Studies Examining the Fiscal and Macroeconomic Impact of Privatization

Study	Sample Description, Study Period, and Methodology	Summary of Empirical Findings and Conclusions
Jeronimo, Pagán, and Soydemir (2000)	Using country-level panel data on privatization receipts and budget deficits for OECD countries from 1990 to 1997, analyze whether the concern with deficits in the 1990s in Italy, Greece, Spain, and Portugal is related to a shift from privatization as a tool of economic restructuring to a tool of European monetary convergence.	Document a significantly negative relationship between privatization receipts and deficits in these four countries, but not for other EU members. For the southern European countries, privatization seemed to be motivated more as a means to meet the Maastricht convergence criterion than as a tool for economic restructuring.
Macedo (2000)	Examines the fiscal impact of the Brazilian privatization program, which raised over US$71 billion through the sale of 115 companies between 1991 and 1998. Asks whether the proceeds were used responsibly: to improve fiscal situation of Brazilian government, to partially finance very large unfunded pension liabilities, to reduce net government debt or to reduce income inequality within Brazil's population.	Concludes that the proceeds from the Brazilian privatization program were essentially squandered. The revenues contributed to the softening of both the fiscal and external constraints and contributed to delaying (but not preventing) devaluation of the real. Rather than using the proceeds to pay off debt, the proceeds allowed the public debt to expand significantly and the government ended up with *increased* liabilities at the program's end. Income inequality increased as a result of the program, since only middle- and high-income citizens purchased shares of divested companies.
Davis, Ossowski, Richardson, and Barnett (2000)	Discuss the fiscal and macroeconomic implications of privatizing SOEs in developing countries, define how sales should be accounted for in national income accounts, and evaluate how privatization revenues were in fact used by eight transition countries and ten nontransition countries that launched sizable privatization programs between 1987 and 1998. In particular, ask whether proceeds were "saved" (used to pay off debt or reduce new borrowings) or "spent" on launching new programs or maintaining existing programs at otherwise unsustainable levels.	Begin by documenting that sale proceeds were on average equal to 1.75% of GDP (2% for the transition countries) for all 18 countries during the active privatization period. Also demonstrate that net proceeds were on average less than half the value of gross sale proceeds. The econometric evidence indicates that privatization revenues were saved rather than spent, and that the fiscal situation of the case study countries improved as a result of these programs. Emphasizes the need for transparency in the privatization process and recommends accounting for proceeds as a financing item in the fiscal accounts.
Katsoulakos and Likoyanni (2002)	Examine the impact of privatization on public deficits, public debt, employment, and growth by performing an econometric analysis using country-level data of 23 OECD countries for the period 1990–2000. Also re-examine evidence for Spain, Portugal, Italy, and Greece to verify or reject evidence in Jeronimo, Pagán, and Soydemir (2000).	Document a significantly negative relation between privatization receipts and public debt for the OECD as a whole, but not for three most heavily indebted countries (Belgium, Greece, and Italy). Receipts are not significantly correlated with budget deficits for the OECD as a whole or for the four southern European countries. Also find that current privatization receipts have a significantly negative effect on the current unemployment rate but a positive effect on the previous period's rate.

63

vatization seemed to be motivated more as a means to meet the Maastricht convergence criterion than as a tool for economic restructuring.

Katsoulakos and Likoyanni (2002) examine the impact of privatization on public deficits, public debt, employment, and growth by performing an econometric analysis using country-level data for 23 OECD countries for the period 1990–2000. They also reexamine evidence for Spain, Portugal, Italy, and Greece to verify or reject evidence in Jeronimo, Pagán, and Soydemir (2000). They document a significantly negative relation between privatization receipts and public debt for the OECD as a whole, but not for the three most heavily indebted countries (Belgium, Greece, and Italy). Receipts are not significantly correlated with budget deficits for the OECD as a whole or for the four southern European countries. They also find that current privatization receipts have a significantly negative relationship with the current unemployment rate but a positive association with the previous period's rate.

Are Privatization Proceeds Saved or Spent?

In what has become by far the most influential empirical study of the fiscal and macroeconomic impact of privatization, Davis, Ossowski, Richardson, and Barnett (2000) examine the implications of privatizing SOEs in developing countries. They also define how privatization sales should be accounted for in national income accounts, and evaluate how privatization revenues were in fact used by eight transition countries and ten nontransition countries that launched sizable privatization programs between 1987 and 1998. In particular, the authors ask whether proceeds were "saved" (used to pay off debt or reduce new borrowings) or "spent" on launching new programs or maintaining existing programs at otherwise unsustainable levels. They begin by documenting that sale proceeds were on average equal to 1.75 percent of GDP (2 percent for the transition countries) for all 18 countries during the active privatization period. They also demonstrate that net proceeds were on average less than half the value of gross sale proceeds. These key results are detailed in table 2.7. The econometric evidence indicates that privatization revenues were saved rather than spent, and that the fiscal situation of the case study countries improved as a result of these programs. Davis, Ossowski, Richardson, and Barnett conclude by emphasizing the need for transparency in the privatization process and recommend accounting for proceeds as a financing item in the fiscal accounts, rather than as general revenue.

On the other hand, Macedo (2000) clearly shows that at least one country did not husband privatization revenues responsibly. He studies the fiscal impact of the Brazilian privatization program, which raised over U.S.$71 billion through the sale of 115 companies between 1991 and 1998. He specifically asks whether the proceeds were used responsibly to improve the fiscal situation of the Brazilian government, to partially finance very large unfunded pension liabilities, to reduce net government debt, or to reduce income inequality within Brazil's population. Macedo concludes that the proceeds from the Brazilian privatization program were essentially squandered. The revenues contributed to the softening of both the fiscal and external budget constraints and contributed to delaying (but not preventing)

TABLE 2.7. Gross and Net Budgetary Proceeds from Privatization in Eighteen Countries, 1987–1998

	Years of Active Privatization	Gross Privatization Proceeds During Period of Active Privatization[1]		Net Privatization Proceeds Accruing to Budget During Active Privatization Period[2]		Ratio of Net Proceeds Accruing to Budget to Gross Proceeds[3]
		US$ Millions	Percent of GDP[4]	US$ Millions[5]	Percent of GDP[4]	Percent
Argentina	1990–1995	22,885	2.0	11,452	0.9	50
Bolivia	1995–1998	863	4.2	160	0.5	12
Côte d'Ivore	1994–1997	459	1.1	448	1.1	98
Czech Republic	1991–1997	2,369	0.9	1,736	0.8	73
Egypt	1993–1998	2,778	0.8	2,194	0.5	79
Estonia	1992–1998	467	2.9	—	—	—
Hungary	1991–1998	11,841	4.0	6,672	2.2	56
Kazakhstan	1993–1998	5,798	5.5	2,425	2.2	25
Mexico	1989–1994	25,249	1.3	6,310	0.3	25
Mongolia	1994–1998	—	—	45	0.9	—
Morocco	1993–1997	1,489	1.0	1,307	0.9	88
Mozambique	1992–1998	101	1.1	—	—	—
Peru	1994–1997	7,136	3.2	5,821	2.6	82
Philippines	1987–1997	3,810	0.7	3,407	0.5	88
Russia	1992–1998	6,569	0.3	8,632	0.4	—
Uganda	1991–1998	152	0.4	—	—	—
Ukraine	1993–1998	24	—	518	0.2	—
Vietnam	1993–1998	3	—	—	—	—
Avg. of all countries with data		n.a.	1.7	n.a.	0.8	45
Avg. of transition countries with data[6]		n.a.	1.9	n.a.	0.8	31
Avg. of nontransition countries with data[7]		n.a.	1.6	n.a.	0.7	52

Source: World Bank and IMF, as presented in Table 1 of Davis, Ossowski, Richardson, and Barnett (2000).

[1]World Bank Privatization database. Dates are available for 1988–1997.

[2]Executive Board documents and staff estimates. Data through latest available observation.

[3]Ratio calculated for the period of active privatization for which information is available in both sets of data. Differences in coverage in the two series may account for the higher proceeds recorded in IMF data for Russia and Ukraine.

[4]Average of annual ratios of privatization proceeds to GDP during the period of active privatization. For the Philippines, ratios to GNP.

[5]Annual data in national currency converted to U.S. dollars using annual average exchange rates.

[6]Transition case study countries are the Czech Republic, Estonia, Hungary, Kazakhstan, Mongolia, Russia, Ukraine, and Vietnam.

[7]Nontransition case study countries are Argentina, Bolivia, Côte d'Ivore, Egypt, Mexico, Morocco, Mozambique, Peru, the Philippines, and Uganda.

devaluation of the *real*. Rather than using the proceeds to pay off debt, the proceeds allowed the public debt to expand significantly, and the government ended up with increased liabilities at the program's end. Income inequality increased as a result of the program, since only middle- and high-income citizens purchased shares of divested companies.

Have Privatization Programs Strengthened or Weakened Governments Financially?

Fairly clearly, privatization programs have, in fact, financially strengthened most governments, notwithstanding the results for Brazil and a few other, rather profligate national governments. Governments have raised some $1.25 trillion through divestments since 1977, and the net impact of these revenues has surely been to reduce government taxes and net borrowings below what they would have been without privatization.

Summary

The question of whether private ownership of business enterprise is inherently superior to public ownership has enlivened political and economic debate for many centuries, and remains unresolved today. A strong theoretical case can be made for government ownership under certain conditions, especially for natural monopolies producing a vital good or service such as electricity production and distribution or water and sewerage companies. However, the weight of empirical evidence on the state versus private ownership question, which is surveyed in this chapter, now strongly supports those who believe that private ownership is inherently more efficient than state ownership. This is true even for natural monopolies, and the empirical evidence now overwhelmingly indicates that private ownership is decidedly superior for companies operating in industries that are — or can be made to be — competitive.

   The resolution of the private versus public debate in favor of private ownership has had a powerful economic and political impact, since this has provided one key argument in the intellectual justification for privatization programs around the world. The second major justification for divesting state ownership in businesses is a fiscal one. Privatization not only eliminates a government's obligation to subsidize loss-making state enterprises, but the sales of state-owned enterprises have raised about $1.25 trillion for governments over the past quarter-century. Most governments have used these financial windfalls judiciously — to cut net borrowing or reduce existing debt — but there are several examples of countries that effectively squandered their privatization receipts.

   Finally, experience suggests that there is no realistic alternative to privatization as a means to improve the performance of SOEs. While empirical studies clearly show that introducing competition into a monopolized state-owned industrial sector increases efficiency, even without ownership change, those same studies usually also document that privatization has a separate positive impact on performance. Almost without exception, the empirical evidence suggests that the most value-enhancing package of reforms for monopolized state-owned industries is to inject competition, install an effective (but not overbearing) regulatory regime, and sell off some or all of the state's holding in the SOE. The evidence also suggests that the benefits of reforms short of ownership change are very hard to "lock in" without the threat of ultimate privatization. Other measures designed to improve SOE performance without ownership change, such as corporatization or use of employment contracts for managers, have either been found to be ineffective or are less effective than these same reforms coupled with privatization.

How Do Countries Privatize?

This chapter assesses the practical aspects of privatizing state-owned enterprises. We have seen that, beginning in the late 1970s, increasing numbers of people around the world reached the conclusion that state ownership wasn't working, and that private ownership was much more productive. This realization inevitably raised the difficult question of how to shift a society from an economic model stressing government ownership and state direction to one based primarily on private ownership and decision making. That question remains as valid today as it ever was: Exactly how do you privatize the state-owned sectors of an economy? It is easy enough (at least in principle) to allow private ownership to emerge in new business areas. The government must simply allow new private companies to be started, forgo the temptation to overregulate or compete with these new private enterprises, and provide adequate legal protections for the entrepreneurs who start these businesses and for the investors who contribute debt and equity capital. Natural entrepreneurship will take care of the rest.

Over any reasonably finite period of time, however, the bulk of economic activity in an economy will be generated by existing enterprises. Therefore, policy makers intent on shifting from state to private ownership must decide how to convert existing state-owned enterprises into privately owned companies, as well as encouraging "privatization from below" in the form of de novo new business creation. In this chapter, we take as a given that the decision has already been made to privatize state enterprises, rather than attempt to implement nonsale reforms such as management contracts or leasing state assets to private operators. In other words, policy makers have decided that only the hard stuff—full privatization—will do, and are searching for practical guidance regarding how to divest.

Organizing all of the issues that policy makers must confront in the privatization process is a daunting task, which serves to emphasize how difficult privatization is for policy makers to achieve in practice. The first step is to realize that privatization is, in fact, a process and not a single act or event. Furthermore, it is a process that must be repeated for each individual state enterprise being sold.

Additionally, to be done well, privatization does not end with the sale of an SOE to private buyers, but must also be concerned with establishing legal and regulatory systems that protect the property rights of the stakeholders (including consumers) created by privatization. We thus begin by examining the key issues that governments must confront in determining which SOEs to divest, and then describe the steps involved in commercializing and preparing a state-owned enterprise for privatization. Second, we assess the strategic issues a privatizing government must address after completing the commercialization and basic pre-sale preparations of SOEs, but before actually beginning the sales process. It is during this period that a government must (1) decide whether to restructure an SOE before sale, (2) find an acceptable and transparent method to value the company and to set an asking price, and (3) decide whether or not to regulate a newly privatized company after it is divested. Third, the government must decide whether to sell an SOE to private investors for cash or to essentially give the SOE away in a mass privatization program. Phrased this way, the choice seems far-fetched, but of course most of the countries of central and eastern Europe opted, in whole or in part, for mass privatization using vouchers during their initial transition from communism to free-market economics during the early to mid-1990s. Finally, if a government decides to sell an SOE for cash, it must decide on the specific method of sale. This generally boils down to a choice between selling the SOE to a single corporate buyer or group of investors in a trade sale (also called an asset sale) or selling the SOE to investors in a public share offering.

Commercializing and Restructuring SOEs Prior to Sale

The very first step a privatizing government must take is to decide which state-owned enterprises and sectors should be slated for privatization. Though this sounds obvious, the actual choice can be extremely difficult and contentious. This is especially true if privatization is a highly controversial policy adopted by a deeply divided government—which, as Boycko, Shleifer, and Vishny (1996a) make clear, is all too often the case. A privatizing government facing sharp opposition typically feels that it must act quickly and maneuver around opposition from the party out of power, from bureaucrats within the government ministries, and from workers and managers in the state enterprises themselves. Such a government faces the real prospect of both losing power and seeing the entire privatization and economic reform process halted if a major fiasco results from even one botched privatization.

In theory, the choice of which sectors to privatize should be straightforward. Some sectors, such as retail trade and light industry operating in (at least potentially) competitive industries, will be relatively easy to sell off, while other sectors—particularly heavy industry and infrastructure assets—will be far more difficult and require much greater preparation prior to sale. Bornstein (1999) presents one of the best categorizations of how difficult various industrial branches (sectors) will be to privatize, based on observable characteristics of the sector. Bornstein's specific exemplars are the transition economies of Poland, Hungary, and the Czech Republic, but his categorization methods apply to almost any country contemplating how and in what sequence to privatize state assets. The basics of his categorization procedure are reproduced here as table 3.1. The retail trade, consumer services, and housing industries will, at the start of the privatization process in most countries, operate in sectors that are already partly private, and relatively little supplemental capital investment will be required to make the state assets competitive. Therefore, SOEs in these sectors should be attractive to private buyers and thus relatively easy (and noncontroversial) to sell. The agriculture sector in transition economies will be somewhat more difficult to privatize, since it will also need substantial restructuring to become economically viable.

As one moves down table 3.1, the sectors become increasingly difficult for a government to sell off either quickly or easily. In transition economies, the light-industry sector at the start of a privatization process typically is fully state-owned, is badly in need of remedial capital spending, and requires substantial restructuring—and perhaps a large dose of foreign direct investment (FDI)—to become economically viable. In nontransition economies, light industry may not be in such a parlous state, but basic restructuring and supplemental investment will still be required in many cases. Heavy industry has all the investment and restructuring needs of light industry, with the added complication of being considered a "strategic" sector that might be placed off-limits to (often badly needed) foreign investment.

The banking, electricity, and telecommunications sectors face all the challenges of heavy industry, with the additional massively challenging requirement of needing to design, staff, and implement a regulatory regime for the industry in question before a state enterprise can be privatized. These industries are regulated everywhere in the world, and even advanced economies struggle with adequately

TABLE 3.1. Sector/Branch Characteristics Affecting the Scope and Sequence of Divestiture of State Assets

Branch	Characteristic					
	Already Partly Private	Small Capital Investment Required	Substantial Restructuring Needed	Foreign Direct Investment Crucial	Possibly Deemed Strategic	Special Regulatory Framework Essential
Retail trade	?	?				
Consumer services	?	?				
Housing	?	?				
Agriculture	?	?	?			
Light industry			?	?		
Heavy industry			?	?	?	
Banking			?	?	?	?
Electricity			?	?	?	?
Telecommunications			?	?	?	?

Source: Table 1 in Bornstein (1999).

Note: A "?" in a cell denotes that the characteristic significantly influences the divestiture of state enterprises in the branch.

balancing the need to protect consumers from monopoly pricing of vital services, while also protecting the property rights of investors and giving the companies incentives to invest in improving service levels. In transition and developing countries, implementing effective and fair regulation—from scratch—is often a nearly insurmountable challenge. Not only do these countries typically suffer from poorly functioning legal systems, but they also face an extremely high opportunity cost of employing scarce, highly trained professionals in regulatory bodies rather than directly in productive enterprises. All in all, the need to regulate privatized infrastructure industries is the single greatest challenge facing every privatizing government, though this is especially burdensome for transition and developing countries.

Basic Legal Issues to Address at the Start of the Privatization Process

It is axiomatic that a government intent on launching a significant privatization program must take several important, and often extremely difficult, steps at the very start of the process. Furthermore, the government must satisfactorily complete all these prerequisites before any sales revenue can be received from private investors. Immediately after deciding which assets or sectors to sell, a divesting government must pass the basic enabling legislation for privatizations. It may be possible to do this simply by passing one or more national laws, though frequently, reforming governments must actually change the country's constitution to allow privatization in specific industrial sectors such as oil and gas production, surface transportation, and other types of infrastructure services that have been constitutionally reserved for state ownership. For example, the Mexican constitution has (since 1936) reserved much of the nation's oil and gas industry exclusively for state ownership and development, and has prohibited foreign investment in directly related sectors.

All governments also face the choice of whether to enact specific legislation for each privatization or to pass an overall privatization law setting up a framework that can then be employed for most or all subsequent divestitures. Perhaps surprisingly, most countries seem to begin their privatization programs with a case-by-case legislative scheme, either because they wish to "learn by doing" on early sales before enshrining a specific policy framework into law or because political opposition prevents them from enacting a more comprehensive strategy initially. As the program unfolds, most governments enact a comprehensive legal framework that can then be used on all subsequent sales without the need for specific enabling legislation. Seven (2001) presents a detailed analysis of the legal issues involved in designing western European privatization programs, while Gibbon (1997) provides one of the most helpful delineations of the decisions facing a government that wants to privatize through cash sales. Gibbon discusses the steps such a government must take in developing a divestment program. These include (1) setting up a structure for privatization, including legislation, if necessary; (2) providing adequate performance records for SOEs being sold (generating believable accounting data); (3) developing any necessary new regulatory structures; and

(4) determining the appropriate post-sale relationship between the firm and the government. Other authors who examine nonpricing issues relating to the actual divestment contracts involved in privatization include Baldwin and Bhattacharya (1991), Rondinelli and Iacono (1996), Schmidt (1996), Shafik (1996), and Cornelli and Li (1997).

Establishing a Privatization Agency and a Framework for Divestment

So far, we have discussed how "the government" addresses key issues in the privatization process, without specifying how something as amorphous as a government can handle such a complex and detailed process. In fact, national governments almost always create dedicated administrative bodies to oversee various aspects of the privatization process—from initially selecting and commercializing SOEs for divestiture, through actually selling the asset to private investors, to regulating the privatized company, and finally to acting as fiduciary for the state's residual ownership stakes after partial privatizations. As Bornstein (1999) notes, there is wide variation in the specifics of how governments in transition countries have organized their privatization ministries, agents, or bureaus, but all governments (including those in developed and nontransition developing countries) face the same key decisions. Will there be a single agency in charge of all aspects of the privatization process, or will multiple agencies be established to oversee different aspects? Will the privatization agency be controlled by the executive branch of government, or will it be set up as an independent administrative agency? If it is set up under the executive branch, will the agency head have ministerial rank or be a deputy minister under the Ministry of Finance or another governmental department? How will the agency be funded? Will the actions taken by the agency be subject to legislative or judicial review? Will the agency have virtual plenipotentiary powers to override the wishes of sector ministries (Finance, Telecommunications, Energy) or will the ministries retain veto powers over key decisions? Who will initiate the privatization process for a specific company: the agency or the SOE's own managers? Who will develop the specific privatization plan for each company? Who will actually conduct the sale? Will a standing oversight committee be established, or will review be conducted on an ad hoc basis?

All privatizing governments must confront these administrative and organizational issues early in the privatization process, and the optimal course of action will depend on each country's traditions and political environment. The default choice in transition countries seems to be to establish a new Privatization Ministry with great—perhaps extraordinary—powers and with a head who has ministerial rank. This is especially true during the critical early stages of privatization in most transition economies, when the need for centralized decision making and executive power are greatest. Most developed and nontransition developing countries forgo setting up an entirely new governmental department, opting instead for establishing a fairly small privatization office or agency, but still endowing the director with significant authority. The head of this agency may well be given the title of Privatization Minister, but in most cases this agency is expected to have a limited life span, after which the ongoing tasks of administration (acting as fiduciary, regulating the privatized companies, etc.) will be parceled out to standing ministries.

Corporatization of State Ministries and Creation of Joint Stock Companies

Though state-owned enterprises come in many different forms, there are essentially two basic organizational models. First, an SOE can simply be part of a government ministry, or even be a ministry in its own right. Second, an SOE can be organized as a joint stock company that is legally and operationally separate from government ministries, but where the government owns all the stock. This often occurs when a formerly privately owned company becomes an SOE through nationalization or through a failing-firm rescue. Obviously, the challenges facing a privatizing government will be much different depending upon whether a specific SOE is already a joint stock company or is instead an arm of a government ministry.

The ministry form of SOE is how the telecommunications monopoly is organized in many countries, usually as part of the Ministry of Posts, Telegraphs, and Telephones (PTT). As such, these enterprises are legally and operationally indistinct from divisions of the Finance Ministry or the armed forces. They are not organized as commercial enterprises, they do not have separate financial statements from those of the parent ministry, and they have no means of raising external finance. In many cases, SOEs that are state ministries are not even able to hold and manage their own working capital. The employees of such an enterprise are public-sector workers, with government ranks, pay scales, and rights. Needless to say, a great deal of basic preparatory work must be done to convert these ministries into viable business concerns that can be sold to investors, beginning with legally converting these SOEs into wholly government owned joint-stock companies. This process is called *corporatization*, and is not required for an SOE that is already organized as a joint stock company.

Setting Up Accounting, Financial, and Human Resource Systems in SOEs Slated for Sale

The next step in preparing an SOE for ultimate sale is known as *commercialization*, which means converting the mission of the enterprise from maximizing social welfare to maximizing economic profits, as well as developing new private-sector operating procedures and policies. This is frequently a Herculean task. Business commentators often cite the importance of a firm's "corporate culture" and bemoan the difficulty of changing it. This culture is acknowledged to be instrumental in determining how well private business enterprises meet their corporate objectives, and many researchers have documented how difficult it has been for privately owned firms in regulated industries to make the transition to a deregulated business environment. It is even more difficult for managers of firms slated for privatization to inculcate profit-oriented values into a workforce of public-sector employees and to incorporate private-sector accounting, information processing, supply-chain management, and human resource management policies into an SOE's daily operating rhythms.

New accounting systems pose an especially vexing challenge in all transition economies. As Bornstein (1999) notes, communist accounting systems differed in basic ways from capitalist systems, such as in recognizing the production costs of generating goods as "revenue" whether the goods were actually sold or simply transferred to inventory. Additionally, assets such as land were booked at nonscarcity prices because no markets existed to generate realistic valuations. On the other hand, fixed assets were booked at near cost for many years owing to very long (and unrealistically slow) depreciation schedules. All in all, book values have yielded extremely poor estimates of the true market values of SOEs in transition economies. And, since book values have typically been much higher than market values, divesting governments intent on rapid privatization have been open to the charge of "selling off the national silver for a pittance," even when the silver was really almost worthless. Even in nontransition economies, SOEs that were parts of state ministries invariably used government accounting standards rather than generally accepted accounting principles (GAAP) or international accounting standards. Among other critical practical and theoretical differences between public-sector and private-sector accounting standards, there is no such thing as "shareholders equity" in government accounting systems, while this is the core feature of capitalist accounting systems.

Several countries—Poland and India are important examples—have attempted to commercialize state enterprises without planning to subsequently privatize the companies. These attempts have met with limited success, at best. It seems the reforms needed to achieve true commercialization are so all-encompassing that the only way to force the changes through is with the imminent prospect of becoming a private company. Left with state ownership and incentives intact, "commercialized" SOEs have demonstrated a great propensity for backsliding into old ways.

Sequencing and Staging of Sales

Although there is ample prescriptive literature on the art of assessing which companies to privatize, and evaluating which should be divested first, there has been relatively little formal research in this area. However, several authors have studied the closely related questions of whether to privatize rapidly or slowly, what order to follow in privatizing firms (sequencing), and whether to sell an SOE all at once or in stages. Husain and Sahay (1992), Katz and Owen (1993, 1995), Boycko, Shleifer, and Vishny (1996a), Glaeser and Scheinkman (1996), Cornelli and Li (1997), Perotti (1995), and Biais and Perotti (2002) have all theoretically modeled the question of sequencing and staging of SOE sales. Their models illustrate the importance of sequencing and staging in order for the privatizing government to build reputational capital with investors and to build domestic support for the privatization program. This also helps identify bidders who will maximize the efficiency of the firm. However, the complexities of these interrelationships have limited the ability of empiricists to identify specific factors in sequencing and staging.

Several articles that do empirically examine sequencing or staging are Perotti and Guney (1993), Dyck (1997), Dewenter and Malatesta (1997), Jones, Megginson, Nash, and Netter (1999), Gupta, Ham, and Svejnar (2001), and Megginson, Nash, Netter, and Poulsen (forthcoming). Perotti and Guney show that state holdings in firms are typically sold gradually, even when control is transferred rapidly, which they interpret as a confidence-building strategy rather than being caused by limited market capacity. Dyck examines the unique privatization experience of eastern Germany, where a new agency, the Treuhand, was set up with ample funding by the German government and charged with the mission of privatizing the former East German economy as quickly and completely as possible. Unlike most governments, the Treuhand sold off East German companies subject to few political constraints—such as satisfying a desire to ensure that East Germans were able to own some of the divested assets—and instead sold companies for cash to the highest bidders, who tended to be West German businesses and investors. Finally, Gupta, Ham, and Svejnar find strong evidence that the Czech government sold off its most profitable SOEs first, since these were the easiest to sell, which suggests that the government was intent on maximizing revenue and public goodwill rather than maximizing economic efficiency. They also find that the Czech government followed a distinct pecking order in deciding which companies to privatize first. Companies in downstream industries, firms in industries subject to greater demand uncertainty, and firms with greater industrial market shares were the first to be divested.

Before proceeding, it is worth surveying the relative order in which OECD governments privatized companies in different industries. Figure 3.1 describes the total value of privatizations of companies in financial intermediation, telecommunications, public utilities, manufacturing, and other sectors. The pattern that emerges is broadly consistent with Bornstein's (1999) stylized predictions, in that firms in manufacturing and "other" industries—those that are presumably relatively easy to divest—are overrepresented in the early 1990s, while the much larger and more complex privatizations of the public utilities, telecommunications, and transportation sectors are concentrated in the period after 1995.

Should the SOE Be Restructured and, If So, by Whom?

An extremely important and difficult decision that most governments confront early in any privatization process is whether an SOE should be restructured to create a viable commercial enterprise before divestment. If a firm does need restructuring, a related question is who should execute the restructuring—the government prior to sale or the private buyer afterward. There are broadly two types of restructuring. The first, and easiest, is financial restructuring. This usually involves reducing an SOE's total indebtedness, possibly by forgiving claims owed to the government itself, and/or transferring important financial obligations such as

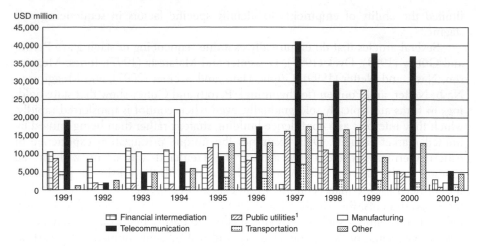

FIGURE 3.1. Privatization in OECD countries by main industrial sectors. 1 = includes electricity, gas, and water; p = provisional. Source: *OECD Privatisation Database* info as depicted in Figure 2 of Mahboobi (2002).

unfunded pension liabilities from the SOE to the government. By far the more difficult process is operational restructuring, which involves selling off or closing down unproductive divisions of an SOE, reconfiguring the company's manufacturing process, changing suppliers and customers, and most painful of all, laying off redundant workers. Since we saw in chapter 2 that one of the distinguishing features of government ownership is massive (and deliberate) overstaffing of state enterprises, there is frequently a need to make significant staff reductions in firms that are slated for privatization.

But who should do the restructuring—the divesting government or the new private buyer? Early advice from the World Bank [Nellis and Kikeri (1989)] was that governments should restructure SOEs prior to divestment, since governments are better able than private owners to cushion the financial blow to any displaced workers by using unemployment or pension payments. Government-led restructuring can thus provide a private buyer of the SOE with a relatively "clean slate." Preparing companies for privatization was standard practice in the United Kingdom during the 1980s, in part to smooth the transition with the trade unions. However, by 1992, the same World Bank authors [Kikeri, Nellis, and Shirley (1992)] had become more nuanced in their interpretation of the optimal strategy. They said (page 54) that small and medium-sized SOEs "should be sold 'as is' at the best price possible, as quickly as possible." However, they also noted that in all cases (page 60) new investments "should be left to private owners once a decision has been made to privatize the enterprise."

The empirical evidence now clearly suggests that the private buyer should be allowed to implement any restructuring necessary. Three empirical papers that examine SOE reform prior to privatization are especially persuasive. First, López-de-Silanes (1997) examines whether prior government restructuring of SOEs improves the net price received by the Mexican government for the SOEs it sold between 1988 and 1992. He finds that restructuring does not pay off. In fact, he shows that prices received by the government would have increased by 71 cents per dollar of assets if the only restructuring step taken by the government had been to fire the CEO and if the assets had been divested an average of one year earlier. He argues that other restructuring steps slow down the process and consume too many resources to be worthwhile. The 71 cents per dollar improvement would be a significant improvement on the average 54 cents per dollar of assets actually received by the Mexican government.

Second, Chong and Lopez-de-Silanes (2002) use data from a random sample of 308 trade sale and share-issue privatizations executed between 1982 and 2000 to test competing hypotheses about the wisdom of government restructuring prior to sale, and the effect of this restructuring on prices paid by buyers and the rehiring policies of new private owners. Summary statistics for their sample are reproduced as table 3.2. On average, the net privatization price—defined as net price received after all costs, adjusted by the number of shares sold, then divided by the average sales over the three years prior to divestiture—is 0.587, and the median is 0.609. A sizable fraction, 43.2 percent, of the firms had net total liabilities (liabilities greater than assets) at the time of sale, and 44.9 percent of the companies experienced management changes prior to sale. An average (median) 50.9 percent (50.6 percent) of the company was sold in the first privatization transaction, and foreign investors participated in 68.2 percent of all sales. Roughly two-thirds (65.3 percent) of the sales were executed via a public share offering exclusively, 19.8 percent were divested only through trade sale, and the remaining firms were sold in a combined trade sale/share offering. The sample companies were heavily (84.4 percent) unionized, and 47.4 percent of the firms had experienced a strike in the three years before the sale. Over three-quarters (78.2 percent) of all firms were restructured by the government in some way prior to sale by the divesting government, with the most common restructuring techniques being voluntary downsizing (32.5 percent) and age-biased downsizing (49.7 percent), which includes both voluntary and involuntary reductions. Employees were given job guarantees in 28.2 percent of the cases, whereas pay was cut by the government prior to sale in 7.5 percent of the transactions. One of the authors' most intriguing findings was the frequency with which the new private owners rehired some of the downsized workers after privatization. This occurred in over one-third (34.7 percent) of all cases.

After controlling for endogeneity, Chong and Lopez-de-Silanes (2002) find that almost all labor retrenchment policies negatively impact the net privatization price (NPP) received, and several types of programs lead to significant rehiring by new owners. The mean and median NPP levels for companies where restructuring was implemented prior to sale versus those that were not restructured are presented in table 3.3. The fifth column of this table details mean and median differences between the "restructuring" and "no restructuring" groups, while the sixth column presents tests of the significance of this difference. Downsizing in general reduces NPP by a highly significant 8 percent, while voluntary downsizing reduces NPP by even more (12 percent). The voluntary downsizing result is probably due to

TABLE 3.2. Characteristics of the Sample Used By Chong and López-de-Silanes (2002) in Their Restructuring and Rehiring Study

Variable	Obs	Mean	Median	St. Dev.	Min	Max
Firm characteristics:						
Net privatization prices/sales	308	0.587	0.609	3.228	0.000	1.367
Sales	308	1.415	0.140	3.167	0.001	21.991
Net total liabilities	308	0.432	0.000	0.496	0.000	1.000
Preprivatization profits	308	0.455	0.000	0.499	0.000	1.000
Mining	308	0.143	0.000	0.350	0.000	1.000
Industry	308	0.231	0.000	0.422	0.000	1.000
Services	308	0.558	1.000	0.497	0.000	1.000
Management change	308	0.449	0.000	0.498	0.000	1.000
Privatization characteristics:						
Foreign participation	308	0.682	1.000	0.467	0.000	1.000
Share sold	308	0.509	0.506	0.282	0.010	1.000
Public offering	308	0.653	1.000	0.477	0.000	1.000
Direct Sale	308	0.198	0.000	0.399	0.000	1.000
Labor characteristics:						
Unions	308	0.844	1.000	0.363	0.000	1.000
Strikes	308	0.474	0.000	0.500	0.000	1.000
Labor policies:						
Downsizing	308	0.782	1.000	0.413	0.000	1.000
Voluntary downsizing	308	0.325	0.000	0.469	0.000	1.000
Age-biased downsizing	308	0.497	0.000	0.501	0.000	1.000
Skill-biased downsizing	308	0.130	0.000	0.337	0.000	1.000
Female-biased downsizing	308	0.058	0.000	0.235	0.000	1.000
Employment guarantee	308	0.282	0.000	0.451	0.000	1.000
Pay cut	308	0.075	0.000	0.263	0.000	1.000
Rehiring	292	0.047	0.000	0.321	0.000	1.000
Rehiring same	292	0.047	0.000	0.321	0.000	1.000
Country-specific variables:						
English common law	308	0.253	0.000	0.436	0.000	1.000
French commercial code	308	0.500	0.5000	0.501	0.000	1.000
German commercial code	308	0.117	0.000	0.322	0.000	1.000
Scandinavian commercial code	308	0.019	0.000	0.138	0.000	1.000
Socialist/communist laws	308	0.110	0.000	0.314	0.000	1.000
Gross domestic product	308	25.398	25.452	1.851	19.448	28.856
Inflation	308	109.876	11.485	292.683	0.618	1667.207
Openess	308	31.137	28.158	31.953	0.000	314.588
Economic growth	308	3.028	2.726	3.811	−11.144	21.320
Fiscal deficits	308	−2.580	−2.279	3.475	−14.003	13.629
ILO conventions	221	54.164	52.000	28.883	1.000	123.000
Labor firing cost	151	2.526	2.718	1.216	0.443	4.756

Source: Table 3 in Chong and López-de-Silanes (2002).

adverse selection, since the best workers are the most mobile and thus the most likely to accept the downsizing offer, yet these are also the workers the SOE most needs to retain after privatization. Age-biased downsizing, female-biased (gender-based) downsizing, and extending employment guarantees also significantly reduce NPP. Not surprisingly, the presence of net total liabilities reduces NPP by an average 31 percent, and increasing the fraction of the company being sold also significantly reduces NPP. Evidence of strong union activism, especially strikes, also significantly reduces NPP. On the other hand, regression results (not shown in table 3.3) document that skill-biased downsizing, implemented after objectively determining (through testing) which workers have the best skills, significantly increases NPP—though the authors point out that this is an extremely difficult policy to implement by a democratic government bent on privatization. Allowing foreign participation in the sale increases NPP by a whopping 32 percent, and public share offerings are associated with a 19 percent average increase in NPP. Any type of downsizing significantly increases the likelihood of some post-sale rehiring of workers, and voluntary downsizing is especially likely to lead to significant rehiring.

TABLE 3.3. Labor Restructuring and Privatization Prices

Type of Restructuring	SOEs Where Measure Was Taken (a)	SOEs Where Measure Was Not Taken (b)	Difference (a)−(b)	T-Statistic for Change in Mean / Z-Statistic for Change in Median
Downsizing				
mean	0.5532	0.7085	−0.1552	3.547[a]
median	0.5711	0.7070	−0.1360	3.576[a]
Voluntary downsizing				
mean	0.4818	0.6376	−0.1557	4.064[a]
median	0.4716	0.6259	−0.1543	3.909[a]
Age-biased downsizing				
mean	0.5265	0.6467	−0.1202	3.320[a]
median	0.5136	0.6320	−0.1184	3.184[a]
Skill-biased downsizing				
mean	0.5616	0.5908	−0.0292	0.534
median	0.6074	0.6157	−0.0083	0.371
Female-biased downsizing				
mean	0.3533	0.6015	−0.2482	3.213[a]
median	0.3765	0.6150	−0.2385	2.977[a]
Employment guarantee				
mean	0.4200	0.6496	−0.2296	5.853[a]
median	0.3664	0.6508	−0.2844	−6.936[a]
Pay cut				
mean	0.6893	0.5787	0.1106	−1.585[c]
median	0.7424	0.6006	0.1417	−1.725[c]

Source: Table 7 in Chong and López-de-Silanes H (2002).

[a] Indicates significance at 1 percent level.
[b] Indicates significance at 5 percent level.
[c] Indicates significance at 10 percent level.

All in all, Chong and Lopez-de-Silanes offer a qualified "do not intervene" recommendation to divesting governments with respect to whether or not they should restructure SOEs prior to sale. The third study, by Chong and Galdo (2002), reaches a similar conclusion. These authors perform much the same analysis as do Chong and Lopez-de-Silanes, but instead use a sample of 84 telecommunications privatizations executed from 1984 to 2000. After controlling for endogeneity, they find that labor force downsizing (insignificantly) reduces NPP, while voluntary downsizing, employment guarantees, the presence of net total liabilities, and evidence of strong union activity all reduce NPP by statistically and economically significant amounts. Pay cuts and allowing foreign participation in a sale significantly increase NPP, while using public offers as a divestment method rather than trade sales effectively doubles the net price received. Chong and Galdo offer as their best policy prescription the advice that governments should not attempt to restructure telecom companies before privatization, but instead should concentrate on transparency and cleanliness (lack of corruption) in the sales, since sales methods significantly impact the net price received.

Taken together, the three studies cited above clearly suggest that governments should concentrate on providing a social safety net for displaced workers in general rather than attempting to make investment and employment decisions in a highly charged political atmosphere. Delay also opens the door for more, and more effective, opposition from the party out of power and others opposed to the privatization and reform process.

Strategic Issues in Planning for the Sale of Specific SOEs

Once the basic preparatory work of selecting and then commercializing the state-owned companies slated for divestment has been completed, any government bent on launching a significant privatization program must confront a series of strategic decisions regarding how to actually sell off these assets. The decision-making process begins with identifying the basic objectives the government wishes to accomplish. This may seem obvious, as governments clearly know they would like to (1) privatize as many companies as possible, (2) as rapidly as possible, while (3) raising as much revenue as possible, (4) without firing any employees of the SOEs being divested, (5) in an open and transparent sale process free of corruption, while (6) also ensuring that ordinary citizens benefit financially from the sale process. Phrased this way, of course, the inherent contradictions in a "wish list" approach to divestment become obvious, and the need to rank-order objectives and make trade-offs becomes clear.

It is often said that governments (and universities) are multi-objective organizations, but since they are able to sell specific state assets only once, they must carefully choose which economic and political objectives are most important and which can be compromised to achieve the greater goal. In the language of economics, governments must maximize a multidimensional objective function, subject to binding political and economic constraints.

Identifying Key Objectives and Trade-offs in the Privatization Process

Essentially, the key trade-offs in designing a privatization program involve choosing between the following objectives: (1) speed of sale versus revenue maximization and transparency, (2) revenue maximization versus favoring citizens and ensuring domestic ownership, (3) promoting economic efficiency versus preserving SOE employment levels and maximizing political benefits for the government, and (4) promoting development of the national stock market versus divesting state assets rapidly and completely. To demonstrate how these trade-offs actually play out, consider the actions that a government wishing to execute a large privatization quickly would take. In a transition economy, the government might choose to divest state assets through a mass privatization program, involving the free distribution of vouchers that can be exchanged for shares in state enterprises to all citizens. This strategy certainly would reduce state holdings quickly (and has done so in many transition countries), but of course it raises no revenue for the government and does nothing to bring new human or financial capital into the firms being divested. In nontransition countries, selling assets quickly usually means selling large numbers of companies either through auctions or through direct negotiations with a limited number of potential buyers, rather than using share issue privatizations—which are very costly and time-consuming to engineer but which also maximize sales revenue and are the most transparent of all divestment methods.

The other trade-offs are also easy to describe, if not to solve. A government wishing to maximize its sale proceeds from divestment would welcome as many potential bidders as possible and would adopt a selling strategy that maximized the competition between bidders for the state assets on offer. This immediately rules out voucher privatization, and also implies that foreign investors should be invited to participate in auctions and public share offerings, and that the SOE or its shares should be sold to the highest bidders. But this might open the way for virtually complete foreign ownership of privatized companies. Which group is more likely to be willing and able to pay top prices for assets: foreign investors and multinational corporations or domestic investors and SOE employees?

The worthy goal of promoting economic efficiency in the privatization process also tends to clash with maximizing revenue and achieving politically important objectives, such as preserving employment in the SOEs being divested. To see this, consider the choice a government faces regarding the sale of the national telecommunications network or the electricity production and distribution grid. These industries have traditionally been structured as state-owned monopolies, but they are competitive industries in a few market economies, particularly the United States. Obviously, a government wishing to promote economic efficiency would either break up its monopoly prior to sale or strongly promote new competitive entry into the market after divestiture, or both. However, selling off an unbroken and unchallenged monopoly would maximize the price that private bidders are willing to pay. Breaking up a monopoly or promoting serious post-sale competition would also increase the likelihood of the new private operator making large staff cuts after the sale. This knowledge increases the temptation for the government either to refrain from breaking up the monopoly—thus forfeiting efficiency gains for the broader economy—or to extend job guarantees to the company's workers after the sale, thus reducing the price private investors will pay for the company.

The final choice, between selling a possibly large number of companies quickly through a trade sale versus selling fewer companies at a much slower pace through multiple share offerings, is arguably the most important for the long-term economic potential of an economy. This surprising assertion is based on two factors. First, as we will see in chapter 7, there is now convincing empirical evidence that well-functioning financial markets are strongly correlated with faster economic growth, so governments wishing to increase their nation's growth potential should promote financial-sector development. And nothing helps promote a nation's financial markets (especially the stock market) more effectively than multiple large SIPs. However, the second counter-balancing factor is that a well-structured program of privatizing trade sales offers the unique possibility of attracting a large amount of foreign direct investment, and of plugging the nation's most important companies into the global trading system.

Valuing SOEs Prior to Sale

Regardless of a government's overall objectives for its privatization program, there is one very practical and inescapable step it must take: determining the value of the assets it plans to sell. Naturally, valuation is essential even for private (non-traded) companies in market economies—especially for taxation and inheritance purposes. Given the size and importance of many state-owned enterprises, the need to establish defensible valuation methods is even greater, yet also more difficult, for several reasons. Most critically, SOEs are often in extremely bad financial and operational shape at the time of privatization, but their prospects under private ownership may be very bright indeed. Should valuation be based on the current state of the company or on its potential? If the latter, how can the selling government commit itself to allow the new private owner to achieve the full profit potential, when the state will have a natural temptation to tax or regulate away these economic gains?

There are four basic methods of valuing a nontraded company for sale: (1) the earnings capitalization approach, which is also known as the P/E ratio method; (2) the discounted cash flow method; (3) the market entry method (or determining the Tobin's Q value for the company); and (4) the comparable-firm approach. The first three of these are described in detail in Bornstein (1999), since these are the most commonly used in transition economies, while the fourth is probably the most commonly used method for valuing private company sales in market economies. The comparable firm method is also the most frequently used valuation method for privatizing trade sales and, especially, SIPs in developed and developing countries. The capitalization approach involves determining the equilibrium level of total profits that a privatized company will likely generate and then applying a multiple (i.e., ten times profits) to determine total firm value.

Naturally, price-earnings ratios are computed for all types of private companies, but this method works only for companies with positive earnings.

The second method, the discounted cash flow (DCF) technique, is the fundamental valuation methodology of modern finance. This involves predicting the future stream of earnings that a company will generate, and then determining the present value of each cash flow by discounting it back to today using an appropriate discount rate. This rate is determined based on the industry the firm is operating in, plus perhaps an adjustment for country and political risk. The individual DCFs are then summed to determine an overall firm value. Third, the market-entry approach involves determining how much it would cost to establish a new company with a market share equal to that of the existing firm. This is quite similar to determining the replacement value, or Tobin's Q, of a company.

Finally, the comparable-firm approach involves determining the value of a publicly traded firm in the same industry as the firm being valued, and making adjustments as necessary for financial and operating differences between the traded and the nontraded companies. In the United States and other developed economies, this is how companies wishing to go public through an initial public offering are typically valued. This technique has also been used with increasing frequency for some trade sales and most large share issue privatizations in recent years—particularly for privatizing telecoms, airlines, electric utilities, and other companies with numerous comparable firms trading in other national markets, many of which were themselves privatized earlier. It was much harder to use this technique in privatization's early years, since almost all of the comparable firms (except American companies) were also SOEs.

In theory, any one of these techniques can yield a defensible firm valuation, but in practice there are often very large differences between the values each technique generates, and the only true "market" value of a company is what an arm's-length buyer is willing to pay. This can be very problematic for privatizing governments, since the natural tendency for commentators is to seize on the highest valuation as the "true" measure. If a government accepts the lower, realistically achievable value, it will often be criticized for selling national treasures on the cheap; if the government instead holds out for too high a price, the privatization will fail. Both outcomes happen with disturbing frequency. Perhaps the best approach for governments to take is to farm out the valuation decision to an objective and respected third party, such as an international investment bank or one of the Big Four accounting firms. When this is done, the firm selected to provide the valuation is then typically prohibited from actually conducting the sale of the company in order to minimize the appearance (or reality) of a conflict of interest. This could arise because a firm charged with both valuing and selling a company would have a clear incentive to set a low valuation, and then profit from the subsequent auction sale at market prices.

Selecting the Method of Sale

As do others [see especially Bornstein (1999)], Brada (1996) presents an excellent taxonomy of privatization methods. Although the context of his paper is central and eastern Europe, his classification of four principal divestment methods is quite general. Of course, there are many variations within each of his four categories, and Brada shows that many privatizations use combinations of the different types of divestment. Brada's first category is privatization through restitution. This method is appropriate when land or other easily identifiable property that was expropriated in years past can be returned either to the original owner or to his or her heirs. This form of privatization is rarely observed outside of eastern Europe, though it has been important there. For example, Brada reports that up to 10 percent of the value of state property in the Czech Republic consisted of restitution claims. A major difficulty with this form of privatization is that the records needed to prove ownership are often inadequate or conflicting.

Governments intent on restitution must decide whether to implement this by physically returning confiscated property or by distributing financial claims exchangeable into shares of other state enterprises being sold. Bornstein (1999) reports that the Czech government concentrated on the actual return of confiscated property to the families of people who were victimized by the communist coup of 1948. Hungary, on the other hand, distributed restitution vouchers to families victimized by confiscations going all the way back to the dawn of the fascist era in 1939.[1]

The second divestment method is privatization through sale of state property, under which a government trades its ownership claim for an explicit cash payment. This category takes two important forms. The first is a trade sale (or asset sale) of a state-owned enterprise, or some parts thereof, to an individual, an existing corporation, or a group of investors. The second form is an SIP, in which a government sells some or all of its holdings in an SOE to investors through a public share offering. These are similar to IPOs in the private sector, but where private IPOs are structured primarily to raise revenue, SIPs are structured to raise money for the divesting government and to achieve political objectives. Figure 3.2 provides a survey of the "market share" of privatizing trade sales and share offerings in OECD economies over the period 1990–2001. The total value of both types of sale increases dramatically from 1990 to 1999, before dropping off sharply in 2000 and especially 2001. However, the share of trade sales also increases fairly consistently over the same time period. In developing economies, trade sales are even more commonly used divestment techniques than in OECD countries.

Brada's (1996) third category is mass or voucher privatization, whereby eligible citizens can use vouchers that are distributed free or at nominal cost. These vouchers give holders the right to bid for stakes in SOEs or other assets being privatized. This method has been used only in the transition economies of central and eastern Europe, where it has brought about fundamental changes in the ownership of business assets in those countries, although not always changes in effective control. Voucher privatization has been the most controversial method of divesting state-owned assets. Boycko, Shleifer, and Vishny (1994) show that the decision to pursue a mass privatization program, and the specific design of the program, is largely dictated by politics. Although asset sales and SIPs account for most of the value of assets that have been moved from state to private employment during the past two decades, it is also true that a much larger number of companies have been

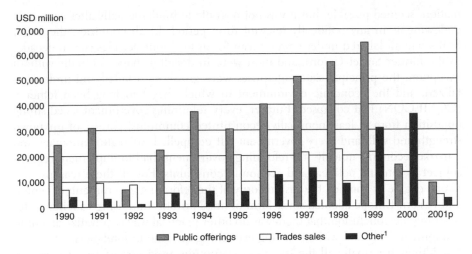

USD million

FIGURE 3.2. Privatization in OECD countries by type of sale transactions. 1 = includes management or employee buyout, asset sales and lease or management contracts; p = provisional. Source: *OECD Privatisation Database* info as depicted in Figure 2 of Mahboobi (2002).

transferred to private ownership through mass privatization programs. It is also likely that more employees have been from firms that were transferred in mass schemes than from firms that were sold in SIPs.

The final method is privatization from below, through the startup of new private businesses in formerly socialist countries.[2] Havrylyshyn and McGettigan (1999) also stress the importance of this type of economic growth in the transition economies. Privatization from below has progressed rapidly in many regions (including China, the transition economies of central and eastern Europe, Latin America, and sub-Saharan Africa). Though not the focus of this book, privatization from below is extremely important to the long-term development of all the transition economies and will be revisited often throughout this book. The most precious resource in any economy is entrepreneurship, and this is nowhere more true than in formerly communist nations. The challenge for all economies is to allow entrepreneurship to flourish while still providing regulatory protection to citizens where needed.

Non-Cash Methods of Privatization: Vouchers and Mass Privatization

The policy makers who took power in central and eastern Europe during the era of "extraordinary politics" after the collapse of communism faced historic opportunities and challenges. For one brief—and no one knew how brief—moment, the Old Regime had been swept away and a new country with a new privatized economy was waiting to be born. Extraordinary political change, even transformation, seemed possible, but it was not possible to fundamentally alter economic endowments in any politically relevant time period. In all countries, the major SOEs had all labored under communism for at least four decades (seven decades in the former Soviet Union), and most were in dreadful shape. Virtually without exception, the principal state enterprises were grossly overstaffed and undercapitalized, and the economic environment to which they had long been tethered (COMECON) had collapsed. Further, every reforming government faced strong opposition from at least nominally reconstituted communist parties, of unknown strength and will, and every government felt compelled to create democracy and a market economy quickly. Yet reforming governments had to implement reforms subject to binding political and economic constraints. For all these reasons, and to one degree or another, the vast majority of the reforming governments of central and eastern Europe adopted some form of mass privatization using vouchers, after reaching the conclusion that there was no other practical way to privatize an entire economy quickly and without selling everything of value to foreigners.

Although virtually all the transition economies used some form of mass privatization (MP), there was in fact immense variation in the specifics of individual national programs and in the time frame during which MP programs were employed. There were also significant differences in how (and by whom) vouchers could be used and in the fraction of the economy that was, in fact, transferred from state to private ownership through these programs. Table 3.4 summarizes the principal and secondary divestment methods used, as well as the scale of divestment achieved, by the 26 transition countries of central and eastern Europe. This table shows that the Czech Republic, Hungary, Slovakia, and Estonia all succeeded in transferring more than 50 percent of state assets to private hands between 1990 and 1999, while an additional 13 countries privatized at least 25 percent of state assets during this time period. The Czech Republic, Russia, Kyrgyzstan, Lithuania, Georgia, Kazakhstan, Moldova, Armenia, and Bosnia used vouchers as their principal divestment technique, while Slovakia, Estonia, Slovenia, Bulgaria, Croatia, Latvia, Romania, Azerbaijan, Albania, Tajikistan, and Belarus used vouchers as their secondary privatization method. The remaining six countries—Hungary, Poland, Macedonia, Uzbekistan, Ukraine, and Turkmenistan—used MP techniques either sparingly or not at all. While much of our discussion in the following paragraphs will focus on the weaknesses and failures of voucher privatization, it bears mentioning that the six countries (particularly the last four mentioned) that did not use MP in a significant way also privatized significantly smaller fractions of state assets than did countries that adopted MP with greater enthusiasm.

Cross-Country Design Differences in Mass Privatization Processes

An observer surveying the academic literature on privatization in transition economies is immediately struck by the massive preponderance of research on the four countries of the Czech Republic, Poland, Hungary, and Russia. Given this focus, and given that these four are indeed the most politically and economically important transition economies, we will limit our discussion to these four countries.

TABLE 3.4. Scope of Privatization and Principal Methods of Divestment Used in 26 Transition Economies (In Descending Order, According to Amount of Privatization Completed)

Country	Large Scale Score*	Primary Method	Secondary Method
Czech Republic	4	Voucher	Direct
Hungary	4	Direct	MEBO
Slovakia	4	Direct	Voucher
Estonia	4	Direct	Voucher
Poland	3.3	Direct	MEBO
Russia	3.3	Voucher	Direct
Kyrgyzstan	3	Voucher	MEBO
Lithuania	3	Voucher	Direct
Georgia	3.3	Voucher	Direct
Slovenia	3.3	MEBO	Voucher
Bulgaria	3	Direct	Voucher
Croatia	3	MEBO	Voucher
Kazakhstan	3	Voucher	Direct
Latvia	3	Direct	Voucher
Macedonia	3	MEBO	Direct
Moldova	3	Voucher	Direct
Armenia	3	Voucher	MEBO
Romania	2.7	MEBO	Voucher
Uzbekistan	2.7	MEBO	Direct
Ukraine	2.3	MEBO	Direct
Azerbaijan	2	MEBO	Voucher
Albania	2	MEBO	Voucher
Tajikistan	2	Direct	Voucher
Turkmenistan	1.7	MEBO	Direct
Belarus	1	MEBO	Voucher
Bosnia	NA	Voucher	Direct

Source: Table 2 in Nellis (2002)

Note: Data for the scores and estimates of methods is from European Bank for Reconstruction and Development, Transition Report 1999, London, p. 32.

*The score is the numerical ranking of the EBRD; its classification system for assessing progress in large-scale privatization is: 1–minimal progress; 2–scheme ready for implementation; some firms divested; 3–more than 25% of assets privatized; 4–more than 50% of assets privatized, and substantial progress on corporate governance; 4+–more than 75% of assets in private hands; standards and performance comparable to advanced industrial countries.

Furthermore, most of this narrative will be based on the reports of Bornstein (1999). Perhaps surprisingly, these countries followed significantly different paths regarding the use of mass privatization techniques, with the Czech Republic and Russia embracing vouchers early and enthusiastically, Poland employing them much later but with some gusto, and Hungary largely shunning them—except to a very limited degree.[3]

Vouchers were a central part of the Czech Republic's first privatization program, which was initiated in 1991. Citizens were offered the chance to purchase, for a nominal fee, vouchers with investment points they could use to bid for shares in companies being privatized. The actual bidding and allocation of ownership resulted from a complex, five-round auction process [see Hingorani, Lehn, and Makhija (1997) for a detailed description of the mechanics of the Czech program]. About 40 percent of the book value of property in the Czech Republic's Large Enterprise Programme was divested, quite rapidly, in this mass privatization scheme [Bornstein (1999)]. A major surprise was that some 450 private investment funds (PIFs) arose spontaneously to collect investment points, with an avowed goal of exercising corporate oversight of the newly privatized companies. Initially, the Czech program was hailed as a major success. By 1996, there were 1,588 companies listed on the Prague Stock Exchange, and by 1997, some 75 percent of the economy was in private hands.

As early as mid-decade, however, it was clear that the Czech MP program was not yielding the hoped-for results, and that insiders had seized firm control of the most valuable privatized enterprises. There was very little trading in the shares of most companies, and the number of publicly traded firms fell to 276 in 1997 and to a mere 154 by March 2000. There were far too many investment funds to be effective, and a disturbing number of the funds turned out to be mere shells that company insiders used to loot their firms. Most critically, the Czech government had never really privatized the largest state-owned banks, which therefore continued a dismal pattern of lending to favored companies—followed by government rescues after these defaulted. By the time the banks were fully sold off to foreign buyers in 2001, the financial sector was in disarray.

Russia also began the 1990s by launching an ambitious voucher privatization program. All citizens were given the opportunity to purchase (for a nominal fee) vouchers with a face value of 10,000 rubles, and some 97 percent of the population purchased vouchers. However, as Frydman, Pistor, and Rapaczynski (1996), Bornstein (1994, 1999), and others make all too clear, the program was hopelessly compromised even before it had a chance to begin by the political necessity of giving enterprise managers and workers disproportionately large share allocations, as well as effective veto rights over major steps in the divestment process. Additionally, Russia was very sharply divided politically throughout the 1990s, with a rebellious and unreconstructed Communist party acting as the government's main opposition. Furthermore, state ministries retained very strong influence, and sometimes control, over entire sectors, including the prized telecommunications and oil and gas industries. At the same time, a huge number of small, weak new commercial banks sprung up—most of which were subsequently wiped out by the government's default on its debt in 1998.

Although most countries' actual experience with vouchers has been poor, none has been quite as dismal as Russia's. While all of the factors described above (and more still) played a role, most observers conclude that insider control of privatized firms has been by far the most important impediment to effective reform. Initially, the Russian government had high hopes that the "voucher privatization funds" (VPFs) formed during the initial voucher distributions might be able to overcome the collective-action problem inherent in mass privatization programs. Such funds might use their concentrated ownership in privatized firms to force managers to restructure. Though most funds attempted to exercise their "voice" in corporate boardrooms, insider dominance completely blocked their efforts. The VPFs turned instead to their "exit" option and sold shares on the secondary market.

Pistor and Spicer (1996) and Bornstein (1994) also examine the early promise and subsequent failure of privatization investment funds in Russia and the Czech Republic. In both countries, citizens have become owners of the worst performing privatized assets, while the "crown jewels" have all come under insider control. In a classic understated phrase, Pistor and Spicer state that "establishing property rights is a longer and more complicated process than allocating title" (page 36).

In contrast to Russia and the Czech Republic, Poland initially concentrated on commercializing its SOEs, without intending to immediately launch a large-scale divestment program. Even as late as 1996, very few companies had actually been sold off and a large-scale MP program had not been implemented. Soon thereafter, a significant voucher privatization program was implemented, and it resulted in over 50 percent of state assets being privatized. Uniquely among the four widely studied transition economies, Hungary consistently stressed trade sales (for real cash) over mass privatization programs. Though initially ridiculed as timid reformers, it is now generally accepted that Hungary's measured pace and emphasis on asset sales, particularly the hard currency sales to Western multinationals, yielded far more impressive results than did the programs that stressed voucher privatization.

Why Have Voucher Privatizations Failed?

The record on mass privatization has indeed been dismal, so why exactly have vouchers largely failed? Anyone looking back today on the academic and policy-oriented literature written about mass privatization programs from 1990 to about 1995 cannot help but notice how confident the vast majority of commentators were about the likelihood that these programs would succeed. Problems were expected and acknowledged when they occurred, but most observers remained optimistic regarding the basic idea that the use of vouchers would ultimately give rise to a group of real owner/investors, with the incentive to restructure and maximize the performance of privatized firms, and with the concentrated shareholdings needed to effectively monitor and discipline the firms' managers. In point of fact, insiders gained uncontestable control of privatized companies virtually everywhere, and in the worst cases they used this power primarily for asset stripping—or tunneling, in the memorable phrasing of Johnson, La Porta, López-de-Silanes, and Shleifer (2000).

Numerous practitioners of "forensic economics" have tried to explain why voucher privatization did not work, and four reasons stand out as especially significant. First, voucher privatizations did not yield any cash inflows, either to the firm or to the government, and thus there were no transfers of technology, capital, and expertise from foreign investors or multinational companies to the privatized companies. Second, voucher privatizations provided the new "owners," who were typically just the existing managers and employees, few incentives to effectively restructure the firm's operations or trim excess staff. Third, governments rarely surrendered full control of important privatized companies to private owners, other than managers, either because the state retained significant shareholdings in the firm or because they deemed the firm too "strategic" to be left unsupervised. The interventions that inevitably resulted were almost always politically rational but economically debilitating, since governments used their influence to ensure that privatized firms did not make serious staffing cuts or implement other, initially disruptive restructuring programs.

The fourth and final reason that mass privatization programs proved ineffective was that the government retained effective control of the banking sector in many countries, even after other sectors were largely privatized. This continued politicization of the credit-extension mechanism ensured that former state firms would continue to face soft budget constraints for indefinite periods. Table 3.5 vividly shows how enduring state influence in the banking sector of several transition economies has been. Even in 1999, the asset share of state-owned banks as a fraction of total banking assets was 23.2 percent in the Czech Republic, 41.9 percent in Lithuania and Russia, 50.3 percent in Romania, 50.7 percent in Slovakia, and an astounding 66 percent in Bulgaria. The state-owned bank share was below 10 percent only in Estonia, Hungary, and Latvia, and these—perhaps not coincidentally—are three of the best performing transition economies.

TABLE 3.5. Indicators of Development and State Ownership in the Banking Sector of 12 Transition Countries in 1999

Country	Concentration[a] (Percentage, 1997)	Number of Banks (1999)	Asset share of State-Owned Banks (Percentage, 1999)	Bad Loans– Total Loans (Percentage, 1999)	Loan-Deposit Rate Spread[b] (1999)
Czech Republic	74.9	42	23.2	31.4	4.2
Estonia	84.5	7	7.9	3.1	4.5
Hungary	67.4	39	9.1	2.8	3.4
Lativia	53.1	23	8.5[d]	6.3[d]	9.2
Lithuania	69.7	13	41.9	11.9	8.2
Poland	42.3	77	25.0	14.5	5.8
Slovenia	71.7	31	41.7	10.2	5.1
Slovakia	84.5	25	50.7	40.0	6.7
Bulgaria	86.7	28[c]	66[c]	12.9[c]	9.6
Romania	85.0	34	50.3	36.6	
Russia	53.7	2,376	41.9[d]	13.1	26.0
Ukraine	64.4	161	12.5	3.3	34.3

Source: Table 4 in Berglof and Bolton (2002).

Note: Data is from IMF International Financial Services, IMF Staff Country report Nr.00/59, WB Database on Financial Development and Structure, EBRD Transition Report 2000.

 [a] Defined as the ratio of three largest banks' assets to total banking sector assets.

 [b] Loan rate is defined as the average rate charged by commercial banks on outstanding short-term credits to enterprises and individuals, weighted by loan amounts. Weighted average of credits of all maturity is used for Czech Republic, Lithuania, and Ukraine. For Poland, only minimum-risk loans are considered. Deposit rate is defined as the average rate offered by commercial banks on short-term deposits, weighted by deposit amounts. Weighted average of deposits of all maturity is used for Czech Republic, Estonia, Lithuania, and Ukraine.

 [c] Data for 1997.

 [d] Data for 1998.

Can Voucher Privatizations Ever Be Successful?

Although the empirical record suggests that voucher privatization is rarely if ever an economically optimal policy, the fact remains that governments typically adopt mass privatization methods only when they feel there is no realistic alternative. Boycko, Shleifer, and Vishny (1994), Nellis (2001), and Bornstein (1999) all conclude that there was no real alternative to mass privatization in transition economies. Therefore, if vouchers must be used, how can mass privatizations be designed to be as successful as possible? The empirical record suggests that four steps should be taken. First, and most important, the government should completely divest its holding in state-owned banks, and then find a way to commit itself not to intervene in credit decisions after divestment. In other words, the government must create a believable hard budget constraint for privatized companies. Second, the state should allow, even encourage, foreign investors to participate in the mass privatization programs as a way of securing badly needed FDI for the company. Third, the government must pass workable bankruptcy legislation and establish effective, independent bankruptcy courts that will protect creditors' rights and make it harder for insiders to loot a company. Finally, the divestment program should allow only a relative handful of investment funds to emerge from the voucher sale process—but it should ensure that the funds that do emerge have the incentive and the power to discipline corporate managers and effect real change in target companies. Needless to say, there are very few countries where the state is strong enough to implement all four of these steps.

Privatizing SOEs Using Trade Sales

Once a government has decided to forgo a mass privatization program, and instead chooses to sell state assets for cash, it must decide on the specific divestment method to use. In effect, this means choosing between a trade sale and a share issue privatization. Generally, this decision is made separately for each individual asset sale, though some countries (i.e., Mexico) have used trade sales almost exclusively for all privatizations. In the next section, we examine empirically the factors that influence the choice between a trade sale and a share issue privatization (SIP) for a large sample of countries, but for now we will simply assert that governments tend to use trade sales for smaller and less profitable state assets and enterprises, while they prefer SIPs for the larger and more profitable companies. Table 3.6 presents a summary of the relative importance of trade sales versus SIPs in the privatization programs of 34 developed and nontransition developing countries over the period 1977–1999, taken from Bortolotti, Fantini, and Siniscalco (forthcoming). The final column presents the number of SIPs as a fraction of the total number of privatization sales, thus indirectly presenting the fraction of divestitures executed by trade sale. On average, 40.0 percent of the privatizations in developed countries and 47.3 percent of those in developing countries were executed by trade sales. However, these market share measures would be much lower if expressed in terms of value rather than number, since trade sales are typically much smaller than public offerings.

TABLE 3.6. Measures of Privatization Activity and Method of Sales in 34 Countries, 1977–1999

Country	Deals	Revenues	Rev/GDP	Stock	PO/Deals
Switzerland	2	5,734.052	0.02268	74.95000	0.50000
Norway	12	3,106.571	0.02199	56.06943	0.79167
Japan	14	189,400.139	0.04437	34.32778	1
Sweden	21	14,898.401	0.06775	48.01722	0.64444
Germany	75	71,576.558	0.03541	53.80227	0.35014
Finland	26	10,387.738	0.08479	22.49022	0.83333
France	67	81,524.477	0.05952	26.58321	0.84109
Canada	57	21,079.210	0.03546	60.13323	0.47397
Austria	40	10,081.478	0.04967	33.19907	0.68333
The Netherlands	28	15,482.922	0.04143	36.99554	0.37500
Belgium	11	5,963.538	0.02499	42.78714	0.08333
Australia	108	70,596.051	0.18651	70.79184	0.37500
United Kingdom	169	153,394.000	0.11497	71.39784	0.48815
Italy	80	105,936.681	0.09484	33.79306	0.64462
Singapore	22	6,507.614	0.07887	23.22259	1
New Zealand	34	12,077.033	0.23188	78.10296	0.24861
Spain	55	59,421.927	0.10881	34.52101	0.68773
Developed countries avg.	48.29	49,245.200	0.07670	47.12849	0.58944
Israel	52	7,421.008	0.07712	31.18976	0.59303
South Korea	17	14,690.547	0.03717	22.43911	0.89881
Uruguay	2	19.908	0.00101	75.50000	0
Mexico	41	29,487.942	0.06392	56.91530	0.13788
South Africa	13	3,496.831	0.02746	64.12599	0.36667
Chile	16	2,622.630	0.03798	37.18750	0.25000
Malaysia	24	7,821.708	0.10790	49.12484	0.43290
Turkey	60	3,228.023	0.01764	65.61105	0.16429
Colombia	10	5,850.749	0.06799	69.46000	0.20000
Thailand	12	2,061.313	0.01713	32.20139	0.91667
Zimbabwe	5	190.056	0.03423	56.66667	1
Philippines	14	2,166.028	0.02960	38.28922	0.50000
Indonesia	14	5,223.897	0.03815	26.93213	0.71429
Nigeria	19	37.974	0.00090	47.83698	1
Sri Lanka	0	0	0.00000	0	.
Pakistan	12	1,453.027	0.02498	41.58111	0.33333
India	24	5,536.303	0.01240	21.92303	0.76786
Less devel. countries avg.	19.71	5,371.055	0.03503	46.0615	0.51723
Test of means (*t*-statistic)	2.58**	3.18***	2.63**	0.17	0.69

Source: Bortolotti, Fantini, and Siniscalco (forthcoming).

Note: Deals are the total number of privatizations. Revenues are total revenues (US$ million 1996) from total privatizations. Rev/GDP is the ratio of total revenues cumulated in the period to 1999 GDP (in US$ million 1996). Stock is the average of the positive values of the yearly weighed average of privatized stock. PO/Deals is the ratio of the number of privatizations by Public Offer to the total number of privatizations.

***, ** Denote statistical significance at the 1 and 5 percent levels, respectively.

Strategic Issues in Designing and Conducting Trade Sales

If a government decides that a trade sale is the optimal method of privatization, it then faces a series of strategic decisions regarding what objectives it most desires to achieve, as well as multiple practical decisions about how to proceed. We have examined many of these issues before. In particular, governments must decide whether to break up the SOE prior to sale — and sell off individual divisions and pieces of the SOE — or retain the enterprise's current structure and sell it off as is. A government must also make choices among the conflicting objectives of speed of sale, revenue maximization, and transparency. But trade sales also yield different strategic options and tactical choices for the seller than do other sales methods, since trade sales offer unique opportunities to tailor the terms of a sale to achieve specific political and economic objectives.

In designing a trade sale privatization program, or even in conducting a single sale, the responsible government agency faces four key decisions. First, the agency must decide whether to conduct all aspects of the sale itself, using agency staff, or to delegate some of the key tasks to third parties such as investment banks or auditing firms. Hiring objective third parties to value and conduct due diligence on the asset being offered for sale has obvious advantages. Involving reputable financial advisers increases the credibility of the sale and helps ensure that it is perceived as being conducted honestly. Globally active banks and accounting firms can also attract international investors to a trade sale that would otherwise be of interest only to local investors, with obvious consequences for net sales proceeds. On the other hand, third party facilitators (especially international banks and auditors) tend to be very expensive and their involvement almost inevitably will slow down the sales process. On balance, most governments use third parties only for large trade sales — which, depending upon the specific country, usually means sales worth $25–50 million or more.

Second, a government must decide whether to allow foreign investors to participate in specific asset sales. Economically, this is a "no-brainer" decision, but in privatization as in many other things, politics often trumps economics. If the asset or enterprise being offered for sale is considered "strategic," most governments will choose to restrict or prohibit foreign participation in its sale. Of course, the danger in granting this practice legitimacy is that governments will be tempted to categorize any politically sensitive privatization as strategic, and promiscuous use of this designation will not only significantly reduce sales revenue for the government but will also prevent the enterprise being sold from receiving an infusion of foreign capital, technology, and expertise. Even more damaging is the effect this strategy will have on a country's international image. Very few countries have been able to attract large amounts of foreign direct investment, and attracting foreign capital will be even harder if a nation is perceived as running a xenophobic privatization program.

The third strategic decision a government privatizing with trade sales must face is whether (and how) to structure the selling terms in order to achieve political and economic objectives other than just maximizing sales price. For example, should the government require bidders for the national telecom company to commit to making specific capital investments and meeting strict service improvement goals if they win the bidding contest? Should the government require the purchaser of the national airline to maintain staffing at current levels and preserve the current route system intact? Should the government require bidders for the local cigarette and cigar monopoly to commit to purchasing only domestically produced tobacco? All of these examples are real, and the single-buyer nature of trade sales uniquely lends itself to the use of such mandates in sales contracts. Of course, these performance mandates are not cost-free, and the more onerous the mandates the lower will be the price received by the government. Additionally, certain mandates (especially those maintaining staffing levels) might scare off potential bidders who might otherwise make attractive offers.

The final and most important strategic decision a divesting government must make is whether to conduct trade sales through auctions or through negotiations with selected potential buyers. This is another case where the economic answer is obvious (auctions), but governments often prefer to conduct "beauty contests" in order to select specific buyers (almost inevitably domestic companies) for high-visibility state assets. Nonetheless, recent academic research clearly shows the superiority of auctions over negotiated sales, and also provides especially clear guidance regarding how to optimally structure auctions to maximize sale proceeds.

Designing Auctions to Maximize Sale Proceeds

Five recent papers study the revenue impact of SOE direct-sale pricing decisions. At a theoretical level, Bulow and Klemperer (1996) ask whether it is more profitable to sell a company through an auction with no reserve price or by using an optimally structured direct negotiation with one less bidder. They show that under most conditions, a simple competitive auction with $N + 1$ bidders will yield more expected revenue than a seller could expect to earn by fully exploiting his or her monopoly selling position against N bidders. López-de-Silanes's (1997) study of Mexican privatizations empirically supports the theoretical proposition that maximizing the number of bidders in an open auction is usually the best way to maximize revenues. He finds that prices received are sensitive to the level of competition in the auction process, but that the Mexican government frequently restricted participation (particularly by foreigners) in spite of this fact. Nonetheless, the amount of revenue generated was the main criterion in selecting the winning bidder for more than 98 percent of the SOEs sold by the Mexican government.

Rondinelli and Iacono (1996) examine auctions in central and eastern Europe, where thousands of small businesses have been auctioned off, as well as in Latin America and Russia, where larger SOEs have been sold. Many types of auctions have been used, including English, Dutch, first price, second price, double, and pro-rata sales. Auctions have been used to sell both lease rights and ownership rights. In other cases, governments have sold SOEs directly to groups of private investors or firms, setting prices and terms by negotiation. These investor groups frequently consist mostly of managers and/or employees. In other cases, the government has liquidated the SOE and sold physical assets to a group of investors.

Hingorani, Lehn, and Makhija (1997) examine an actual voucher privatization program, the first round of the Czech Republic's mass privatization in 1991. Because the mechanics of how companies are divested by this government are actually more similar to an asset sale than to any other method, we discuss their work here. Hingorani, Lehn, and Makhija test whether the level of share demand, as measured by voucher redemptions by Czech citizens, effectively predicts the actual level of stock prices in the secondary market. The authors confirm the predictive power of share demand, and also document that demand is positively related to the level of insider shareholdings and the extent of foreign ownership in a company being sold. They find that share demand is positively related to the level of past profitability, which itself shows that even imperfect accounting statements convey useful information. Additionally, they find that share demand is inversely related to the firm's market risk, which they measure as the post-offering coefficient of variation of stock prices.

Most recently, Klemperer (2002) asks and answers the question, "What really matters in auction design?" His succinct answer is, "discouraging collusive, entry-deterring and predatory behavior" (page 170). By way of illustration, Klemperer points to the contrasting experiences of different western European governments in auctioning off third-generation (3G) cellular phone licenses. Governments such as Britain and Germany conducted well-structured auctions with high minimum-bid or reserve prices—something Klemperer strongly encourages—and received truly staggering payments of $22.5 billion and over $30 billion, respectively. In contrast, the Swiss government set an extremely low reserve price and conducted a poorly structured auction, and received per-capita offers only one-fiftieth as large as those received by the British and German governments.

The importance of properly structuring an auction was demonstrated quite dramatically in the December 2002 auction of the Russian government's 75 percent stake in the oil company Slavneft. As Jack (2002) reports, the Russian government appeared to turn over a new leaf by conducting an open (indeed, televised) and apparently fair auction for this company—but in fact the bidding was a sham. Although many international companies, including the partially privatized Chinese National Oil Corporation, showed interest initially, all but two bidders were discouraged from participating, and after the favored bidder won the auction, it was announced that the two "competitors" were, in fact, controlled by a single corporate parent, and the two bidders would exercise joint control and financing of Slavneft. As this example clearly shows, it is far more important (and difficult) to create real competition in auctions than it is to create the illusion of competition.

Advantages and Disadvantages of Trade Sales

Trade sales have been gaining "privatization market share" for much of the past 15 years, and the reasons are not hard to find. They obviously dominate voucher privatizations in raising real cash and creating real owners, but they also offer many advantages compared to SIPs. Trade sales can be executed much more rapidly than can SIPs, and if properly designed can yield comparable sales proceeds.

Furthermore, trade sales can (and should) be used to attract foreign direct investment into a country or, when absolutely necessary, they can ensure that truly strategic assets remain in domestic hands. Finally, trade sales allow governments to craft sophisticated sale terms to meet political and social objectives.

Though trade sales offer key advantages, they also have several disadvantages relative to SIPs. Three stand out as especially problematic. First, recent empirical research [Gupta, Schiller, Ma, and Thompson (2001); Chong and López-de-Silanes (2002); and Chong and Galdo (2002)] suggests that trade sales typically yield significantly lower sale proceeds than do comparable share issue privatizations. Second, trade sales do nothing to promote development of the national stock market. These sales may, in fact, retard the stock market's growth by reducing liquidity if controlling stakes in key SOEs (especially telecoms) are sold to foreigners and trading in those shares occurs mostly in foreign markets. Finally, trade sales are far less transparent than are SIPs, and the more complex and restrictive the sales process, the greater will be the opportunity for the process to become corrupt. Sometimes corruption enters a sales program inadvertently, but more often the "opportunities" are created deliberately. After all, if governments were always the benevolent, social-welfare-maximizing agents of economic theory, there would be no need for privatization in the first place.

Privatizing SOEs Using Public Share Offerings

Just as it is often said that lawyers live to try major cases, investment bankers live to conduct large share issue privatizations. As we discuss in much greater detail in chapter 6, SIPs are by far the largest share offerings in history, as well as easily the most dramatic. Successful SIPs can also be heroic events for the politicians who engineer SIPs, as well as for the managers of the state enterprise being privatized, since becoming the CEO of a publicly traded company often results in a significant raise in pay and status for the lucky manager. On the other hand, when SIPs go wrong—as more than a few have—the political and economic consequences can be dire. In other words, far more is at stake in large share issue privatizations than just (vast amounts of) money.

Strategic Issues in Designing and Conducting a SIP

Many issues bear on the decision to use a SIP and on how best to design the offering. These are examined in depth in chapter 6, so we will focus here only on how these strategic choices impact the overall design of SIPs. Any government that intends to privatize SOEs using public share offerings faces three sets of interrelated decisions: (1) how to transfer control, (2) how to price the offer, and (3) how to allocate shares. The control transfer decision includes whether to sell the SOE all at once or through a series of partial sales. If the government chooses the latter course, then it must determine how large a fraction of the company's shares to issue in the initial versus subsequent offers. The government must also decide whether to insert any post-privatization restrictions on corporate control.

The pricing decision requires that the government determine whether the offer price should be set by a tender offer, a book-building exercise, or at a fixed price. If the latter, the government must decide whether the offering price should be set immediately prior to the offer or many weeks in advance. The share allocation decision requires the government to choose whether to favor one group of potential investors over another (i.e., domestic investors, SOE employees, or both, over foreign and institutional investors). It also requires deciding whether to use the best available investment banker as lead underwriter (regardless of nationality) or to favor a national champion.

Several papers empirically examine the choices governments actually make in designing SIP programs. First, Bortolotti, Fantini, and Scarpa (2000) empirically examine the choice made by 20 OECD countries regarding whether to sell shares in 233 SIPs internationally and, if so, what fraction of the total offer to sell abroad. The summary statistics from their paper are presented here as table 3.7. This table shows that some shares were sold abroad in 70.8 percent of all offers, and the international portion represented an average 38.5 percent of those share offerings.

Menyah and Paudyal (1996) and Menyah, Paudyal, and Inyangete (1995) investigate the way in which the British government's aims and objectives for privatization influence the procedures and incentives used in the sale of state-owned shares on the London Stock Exchange. Jones, Megginson, Nash, and Netter (1999), Huang and Levich (1998), and Dewenter and Malatesta (1997) all present comprehensive studies of the pricing and share and control allocation decisions made by governments disposing of SOEs through public share offerings. The results are broadly similar, so we concentrate on the paper by Jones, Megginson, Nash, and Netter (JMNN), since it has the largest sample.

JMNN provide evidence of how political factors impact the offer pricing, share allocation, and other terms in SIPs. They analyze a sample of 630 SIPs from 59 countries made over the period June 1977–July 1997. One result JMNN document is the sheer size of SIP offers—the mean (median) size of initial SIPs is $555.7 million ($104.0 million) and the mean size of seasoned issues is $1.069 billion (median $311.0 million), much larger than typical stock offerings. JMNN also find that the selling government significantly underprices SIPs, meaning that the offering price is set below the expected post-offering market price. The mean level of underpricing for initial SIPs is 34.1 percent (median 12.4 percent). Even seasoned SIP offers are underpriced by an average of 9.4 percent (median 3.3 percent).

The evidence of JMNN on the allocation of control in SIPs supports a political interpretation of the divesting government's motives. They find that nearly all SIPs are secondary offerings, in which only the government sells its shares and no money flows to the firm itself. Since the divesting government sells an average (median) of 43.9 percent (35.0 percent) of the SOE's capital in initial offers and 22.7 percent (18.1 percent) in seasoned issues, the offers cited in the JMNN study represent significant reductions in direct government stock ownership. The authors find that although governments typically surrender day-to-day operating control of the SOE to private owners in the initial SIP, they retain effective veto power

TABLE 3.7. Descriptive Statistics for Fraction of Stock Sold Abroad by 20 Countries, 1977–1998

Country	SIPs	ISIPs as a % of SIPs	ABROAD (Means in ISIP Sample)	Company Size (Means in the Domestic SIP Sample, US$ Millions)	Company Size (Means in the ISIP Sample, US$ Millions)
Australia	11	45.45	31.75	1,368.34	2,984.75
Austria	17	88.23	49.06	605.60	777.76
Belgium	1	100.00	33.00	0.00	626.51
Canada	12	50.00	28.75	1,082.69	1,348.26
Denmark	4	50.50	50.50	637.32	3,740.06
Finland	9	66.67	76.15	1,148.06	1,043.98
France	19	100.00	42.70	0.00	8,819.38
Germany	5	60.00	26.67	1,968.99	19,960.98
Greece	3	33.33	48.00	179.47	10,120.18
Ireland	3	66.67	49.50	389.26	1,506.14
Italy	18	94.44	39.58	297.48	12,041.70
Japan	7	14.29	12.85	159,780.94	14,684.29
Netherlands	6	83.33	40.75	198.39	6,829.71
New Zealand	2	50.00	67.00	54.89	3,305.41
Norway	7	85.71	58.50	114.97	810.48
Portugal	27	29.63	42.47	668.42	3,469.53
Spain	17	100.00	33.35	0.00	8,536.44
Sweden	7	100.00	42.00	0.00	2,301.41
Turkey	3	66.67	97.50	57.43	1,043.62
United Kingdom	55	72.73	22.95	4,074.13	6,109.09
TOTAL	233	70.81	38.54	15,563.89	6,034.77

Source: Table 3 in Bortolotti, Fantini, and Scarpa (2000).

Note: This table reports the aggregate data for the 233 privatizations implemented in the 1977–1998Q1 period in 20 OECD countries. SIPs is the number of share issue privatizations in a given country, ISIPs is the number of share issue privatizations with shares listed on a foreign exchange and/or allocated to foreign institutional investors in a given country. ABROAD is the percentage ratio of shares sold abroad to total shares sold, and figures are means computed within the sample of international SIPs. Company size is the implied market value of the company, obtained by dividing total revenues from the SIP in U.S. dollars 1987 by the percentage of capital privatized, multiplied by 100. Means are computed in two sub-samples of domestic and international SIP.

through a variety of techniques. The most common technique is government retention of a "golden share," which gives it the power to veto certain actions, such as foreign takeovers, as we now discuss.

The Controversy Surrounding Golden Shares

In one sense, golden shares seem the answer to a politician's prayer, in that they allow a government to privatize an SOE, withdraw from involvement in day-to-day management, yet still protect the "national interest" by preventing the privatized company to fall into the clutches of an acquirer (especially the evil foreign variety). Of course, there are no free lunches in economics, and employing a golden share involves high opportunity costs that are reflected in the final sales price. These shares are, in fact, rarely worth the cost incurred. Surprisingly, though golden shares have been widely adopted, they are almost never used to affect control contests [McCurry (2000)]. The European Union (EU) is also trying to block new adoptions of golden shares and roll back those already in place, charging they are designed to discourage free cross-border competition for corporate control.[4] An EU court ruling in 2002 upheld the power of governments to use golden shares, but severely restricted the scope and duration of their use.

Advantages and Disadvantages of Using SIPs to Privatize State Assets

Not surprisingly, the advantages and disadvantages of using SIPs are the mirror images of those spelled out above for trade sales. On the plus side, SIPs can raise truly astonishing amounts of revenue. For example, the Japanese government has raised over $111 billion from six rounds of share sales of a single company, NTT, yet the government still owns 46 percent of NTT. For the very largest privatizations, there is simply no realistic alternative to a multi-tranche share offering strategy. After all, just which international company could have purchased NTT in its entirety, even if the Japanese government had wished to sell it in a trade sale? Governments have also discovered that they can design the offer terms in SIPs to achieve important political objectives, such as the aforementioned practice of deliberate underpricing combined with preferential share allocations to domestic investors. If need be, governments can use golden shares to ensure domestic ownership (or to pick the preferred international buyer), yet still have the company's shares publicly traded and thus subject the firm's managers to ongoing market discipline. SIPs are also, by far, the most transparent method of selling off a state enterprise. In fact, there have been very few SIPs with significant evidence of corrupt practices, even in countries where the asset sale process is thoroughly compromised. Finally, SIPs offer governments a powerful, and truly unique, opportunity to develop their national stock markets.

On the other hand, SIPs also have one crucial disadvantage relative to trade sales: they are extremely costly and time-consuming to organize, and most of these costs must be paid whether the offering proceeds or not. Given the high fixed costs of arranging a SIP, this sales method is really only appropriate for very large privatizations—which, depending upon the country, usually means $50–100 million or more. For most privatizations, however, governments have a real choice between using trade sales or divesting via a SIP. We conclude this chapter by assessing the empirical evidence on the determinants of this choice.

Empirical Evidence on the Choice Between Asset Sales and SIPs

Harry Truman once expressed a desire to employ only one-handed economists, since as president he found their (our) habit of saying "on the other hand" so disconcerting and unhelpful. It is much the same for economic theory: since there are two sides to every issue, the only way to resolve theoretical predictions is to insult them with real data. Two recent academic papers have done this for the trade sale versus SIP choice. One explicitly studies the choice between an asset sale and a share issue privatization. Using a sample of 2,477 privatizations that raised $1,189 billion in 108 countries over the period 1977–2000, Megginson, Nash, Netter, and Poulsen (forthcoming) examine why 938 firms are divested using share offerings (in public capital markets), but 1,539 companies are privatized via trade sales (in private markets). They find robust evidence that the choice is influenced by capital market, political, and firm-specific factors. SIPs are more likely to be used when capital markets are less developed, presumably as a way to develop capital markets, and when there is less income inequality. SIPs are also more likely the larger the size of the offering and the more profitable the SOE. On the other hand, governments that have a greater ability to commit to respecting property rights are more likely to privatize via asset sales. Finally, governments choose to privatize the more profitable SOEs through SIPs.

In the second paper, Bortolotti, Fantini, and Siniscalco (1999) estimate the determinants of the fraction of privatization revenues that come from public offerings (SIPs) for privatizations in 49 countries. They find that the greater the selling government's deficit and the more conservative the selling government, the more likely it is that privatization will occur through public offerings. However, SIPs are less likely in French civil law countries.

Summary

A government that has decided to launch a privatization program is somewhat like a person who has decided to go on a diet: the decision, while difficult in itself, marks only the beginning of what promises to be a long and painful process. Governments wishing to privatize one or more state enterprises must follow a fairly standardized process of first preparing the company for sale, then deciding on the optimal method of sale and the offering price, and finally actually selling the firm to private investors. Each step in this process has its own challenges and hazards, and each step is almost always steeped in controversy.

Step one of the privatization process is preparing a company for sale. If the SOE is already a joint stock company operating in a competitive industry, the preparatory phase may be both short and nearly painless. In the much more common case where the SOE is organized as an arm of a government ministry, is staffed by workers with civil service protections, is subject to ministerial working capital and investment spending restrictions, and/or keeps its books according to government accounting principles, a great deal of preparatory work will be required before the firm can be readied for sale. Corporatization, or transforming the state enterprise into a joint stock company legally and operationally separate from a state ministry, is a prerequisite for any further changes. Once the state enterprise is converted into a corporation, the other reforms can be implemented—including adoption of GAAP or international accounting standards and implementing private sector personnel policies. Whether or not a state-owned enterprise should be restructured by government prior to its sale remains a controversial issue; current thinking holds that restructuring should be left to the new private owners in most cases.

There are three basic methods of privatizing state enterprises. First, SOEs can be divested by distributing vouchers to a nation's citizenry that people can then use to "bid" for the companies on offer. Vouchers have been employed in the "mass privatization" programs of the transition economies of central and eastern Europe in the early and mid-1990s. While initially popular, these programs are now generally regarded as failures, since they did not attract new capital or management to the divested firm, and experience showed that these sales did not create effective ownership structures for the newly private firms. Instead, insiders ended up controlling most of the more valuable companies and ordinary investors received claims on the weakest and least promising firms.

The second and third methods of privatizing a company both involve the actual sale of the company to private investors, with cash as payment. In an asset sale (also known as a trade sale or private sale), the government will typically sell all of its holdings—or at least a controlling stake—directly to a single buyer. The buyer can be either an operating company (often a multinational company) or a group of investors. The sales are frequently conducted as auctions, and many governments choose to require buyers to meet numerous mandates after the sale, such as preserving employment at existing levels or achieving high service levels. Though popular, these mandates are costly, in that they reduce the net amount the selling government will receive for its ownership stake. Asset sales are used most frequently for selling off smaller SOEs.

The largest state enterprises can be effectively sold only through a series of public offerings known as share issue privatizations, or SIPs. These are much more costly to arrange than are asset sales, and also require much more time to implement. However, SIPs also have decisive advantages. As noted, the very largest SOEs can only be sold through SIPs—frequently through a series of offerings, or tranches, spread out over several years. SIPs are also the most transparent and least corruptible method of divesting state enterprises, and there is some evidence that these raise more cash for the selling governments than do asset sales. Finally, SIPs are the single most effective tools that governments have to jump-start development of their national stock markets.

Empirical Evidence on Privatization's Effectiveness in Nontransition Economies

Since privatization has been part of government policy toolkits for almost two decades now, academic researchers have had enough time to execute many empirical studies of the effect of divestment on the operating performance of former SOEs. This chapter and the next will survey the rapidly growing body of scientific evidence on privatization's economic effectiveness, but the sheer number of well-executed studies to be examined presents us with a monumental organization challenge. These studies employ many different empirical methodologies, cover many different regions and time periods, and vary greatly with respect to the type and quality of data employed. Over 150 empirical studies performed by academic and professional researchers will be surveyed in this chapter and the next, but only about half of these have been published to date. This also complicates our task, as we must assess which of these unpublished studies are likely to pass the academic market test of peer review to ultimately be published in top academic journals.

Our task, therefore, is to categorize the studies of privatization's effectiveness in a way that allows us to assess the impact of privatization on different countries and on different economic agents. For example, it is likely that privatization has had a much different impact in transition countries than in nontransition economies and, within the much broader latter group, it is likely that the impact has been different in developed versus developing countries. Even within fairly homogeneous groupings such as developed economies, it is very likely that privatization will be viewed differently by consumers, by state-owned enterprise employees, and by the newly created class of shareholders. In other words, we must assess the distributive effect of privatization as well as the effect of privatization on firm performance. Given the vast difference between the experiences, we first categorize papers according to whether they examine privatization in transition or nontransition economies. This dichotomization is necessary, since both direct observation and published research suggest that reforming transition economies invariably requires embracing a great many economic and political changes simultaneously, whereas privatization (and any attendant regulatory changes) is often the sole major component of reform processes in nontransition economies. This chapter thus examines nontransition countries, while chapter 5 evaluates the evidence from transition economies.

This chapter begins with a description of the key objectives in our organizational strategy and a discussion of the methodological problems researchers have been forced to deal with. The second part then surveys the group of studies that gives the broadest assessment of privatization's impact. These are studies that examine how privatization impacts the financial and operating performance of divested firms by comparing the pre versus post-privatization values of several accounting and real output measures. Almost by definition, these studies examine only SIPs, since these are the only companies that are publicly traded and independent after privatization and thus the only firms generating financial statements that are directly comparable to pre-privatization financial values. Later sections survey multinational, multi-industry studies and evaluate the evidence presented in single-country or single-industry studies.

This chapter's latter sections categorize empirical tests by region and industry. The fourth section surveys the large number of studies that examine the effect of privatization on individual countries (country studies), single industries (industry studies), or even single companies (case studies) using a methodology other than simply comparing pre versus post-privatization accounting data from companies divested via public share offerings. This section first surveys studies that examine developed nations, then performs the same task for tests involving developing countries. The fifth section summarizes tests of the economic effectiveness of privatizing infrastructure companies, and emphasizes studies of privatizations of telecommunications companies, electric utilities, and water and sewerage companies. The final section concludes the chapter and summarizes the overall evidence of privatization's effectiveness in nontransition economies.

Strategic Approach to Classifying and Assessing Tests of Privatization's Effectiveness

Besides difficulties in categorization, researchers must grapple with many challenging methodological problems in order to objectively analyze privatization's economic impact.[1] An important problem is that of data availability and consistency. The amount of information that must be disclosed is much less in most countries than in the United States, and these standards vary from country to country as well as over time within individual countries. Furthermore, the possibility of sample selection bias can arise from several sources, including the desire of governments to make privatization "look good" by privatizing the healthiest firms first. Another sample selection problem is that data availability tends to be greater in the more developed countries (and perhaps for the better performing firms within countries), so developed countries (and better performing firms) are overrepresented in empirical analyses.

There are also many problems in measuring performance changes that arise from using accounting or stock data. We discuss the problems with stock return data in chapter 6, but the problems with accounting data are more important since many empirical studies employ primarily accounting information. These problems include determining the correct measure of operating performance, selecting an appropriate benchmark with which to compare performance, and determining the appropriate statistical tests to use. The finance literature has not reached a consensus on the ways to deal with these problems for U.S. companies, much less privatized international firms. Barber and Lyon (1997) argue that test statistics designed to determine whether there is abnormal performance using accounting data are mis-specified when the sample firms have performed unusually well or poorly. They suggest that sample firms must be matched to control firms with similar pre-event performance, which is especially difficult in studies of privatized companies owing to the lack of truly comparable firms.

Given these difficulties, the results of each of the studies we discuss must be kept in perspective. We also note that the studies of post-privatization performance rarely examine the welfare effects on consumers. Most important, few studies control for the possible use of market power by the privatized firms. That is, performance improvements could be due to greater exploitation of monopoly power—which has harmful effects on allocative efficiency—rather than to improved productive efficiency. Many of the studies on performance changes after privatization examine the effects of divestiture on groups such as workers, but few early tests examined the effect of privatization on consumers. This is a serious drawback, since one of the principal reasons for launching privatizations, particularly of monopoly utilities, is consumer dissatisfaction with the service provided by state-owned firms. Fortunately, more recent tests have explicitly measured redistributive and market power effects, though with varying degrees of success. The vast majority of the studies cited below report increases in performance associated with privatization using at least one, and usually several performance measures. This consistency is perhaps the most telling result we report; privatization appears to improve performance measured in many different ways, in many different countries.

With the above caveats in mind, this chapter evaluates the results of 87 studies that employ accounting and/or real output data to examine the impact of privatization on the operating efficiency, ownership structure, and/or financial performance of former SOEs in developed and developing economies. Chapter 5 performs the same task for studies of privatization in transition economies. Though all these studies are detailed in the accompanying tables, and most are discussed at least briefly in the text, we also specify which studies we think are the most important—and why we think this is so. A further organizational step is to present summary information for each of the studies we examine in a series of tables. Presenting this information in tabular form saves us from having to sequentially discuss each paper's sample construction methodology, estimation procedure, and empirical results in the section's text. Instead, we can identify key findings that appear in many different studies, and can discuss methodological pros and cons for entire groups of studies, rather than for each paper in turn.

Empirical Studies Comparing Pre- Versus
Post-Privatization Performance of SIPs

The studies summarized in this section all examine how privatization affects firm performance by comparing pre- versus post-divestment data for companies privatized via public share offering. Since the first study to be published using this methodology is Megginson, Nash, and van Randenborgh (1994), we will refer to this as the MNR methodology. This empirical procedure has several obvious economic and econometric drawbacks. Of these, selection bias probably causes the greatest concern, since by definition a sample of SIPs will be biased toward the very largest companies sold during any nation's privatization program. Furthermore, since governments have a natural tendency to privatize the "easiest" firms first, those SOEs sold via share offerings (particularly those sold early in the process) may well be among the healthiest state-owned firms.[2] Another drawback of the MNR methodology is its need to examine only simple, universally available accounting variables (such as assets, sales, and net income) or physical units such as number of employees. Obviously, researchers must be careful when comparing accounting information generated at different times in many difficult countries. Most of the studies cited here also ignore (or, at best, imperfectly account for) changes in the macroeconomy or industry over the seven-year event window during which they compute pre- versus post-privatization performance changes. Finally, the studies cannot account for the impact on privatized firms of any regulatory or market-opening initiatives that often are launched simultaneously with or immediately after major privatization programs.

In spite of these drawbacks, studies employing the MNR methodology have two key advantages. First, they are the only studies that can examine and directly compare large samples of economically significant firms, from different industries, privatized in different countries, over different time periods. Since each firm's performance is compared to its own results a few years earlier using simple, inflation-adjusted sales and income data (that produce results in simple percentages), this methodology allows one to efficiently aggregate multinational, multi-industry results. Second, while focusing on SIPs yields a selection bias, it also yields samples that encompass the largest and most politically influential privatizations. As discussed in chapter 3, SIPs account for more than two-thirds of the $1.25 trillion of total revenues raised by privatizing governments since 1977. With these methodological caveats in mind, we turn to a summary of the findings of studies using the MNR technique. The multinational, multi-industry studies that employ the MNR methodology are detailed in table 4.1.

Multinational, Multi-Industry Studies

Megginson, Nash, and van Randenborgh (1994) compare three-year average post-privatization financial and operating performance measures with the same three-year average pre-privatization performance measures for 61 companies from 18 countries and 32 industries that were divested during 1961–1989. Using information obtained from prospectuses, annual reports, and secondary sources, they

Study	Sample Description, Study Period, and Methodology	Summary of Empirical Findings and Conclusions
Megginson, Nash, and van Randenborgh (1994)	Compare 3-year average post-privatization financial and operating performance ratios to the 3-year pre-privatization values for 61 firms from 18 countries and 32 industries during 1961–1989. Test significance of median changes in post-versus pre-privatization period. Also employ binomial tests for percent of firms changing as predicted.	Document economically and statistically significant post-privatization increases in output (real sales), operating efficiency, profitability, capital investment spending, and dividend payments, as well as significant decreases in leverage. No evidence of employment declines after privatization, but significant changes in firm directors. Privatization improves firm performance.
Boubakri and Cosset (1998)	Compare 3-year average post-privatization financial and operating performance ratios to the 3-year pre-privatization values for 79 companies from 21 developing countries and 32 industries over the period 1980–1992. Tests for the significance of median changes in ratio values in post-versus pre-privatization period. Also employ binomial tests for percentage of firms changing as predicted.	Document economically and statistically significant post-privatization increases in output (real sales), operating efficiency, profitability, capital investment spending, dividend payments, and employment—as well as significant decreases in leverage. Performance improvements are generally even larger than those documented by Megginson, Nash, and van Randenborgh.
D'Souza and Megginson (1999)	Document offering terms, method of sale, and ownership structure resulting from privatization of 78 companies from 10 developing and 15 developed countries over the period 1990–1994. Then compare 3-year average post-privatization financial and operating performance ratios to the 3-year pre-privatization values for a subsample of 26 firms with sufficient data. Tests for the significance of median changes in ratio values in post-versus pre-privatization period. Also binomial tests for percent of firms changing as predicted.	Document economically and statistically significant post-privatization increases in output (real sales), operating efficiency, and profitability, as well as significant decreases in leverage. Capital investment spending increases—but insignificantly, while employment declines significantly. More of the firms privatized in the 1990s are from telecoms and other regulated industries. Privatization improves firm performance.

Study	Description	Findings
Dewenter and Malatesta (2000)	Compare pre- versus post-privatization performance of 63 large, high-information companies divested during 1981–1994 over both short-term [(+1 to +3) vs. (–3 to –1)] and long-term [(+1 to +5) vs. (–10 to –1)] horizons. Also examine long-run stock return performance of privatized firms and compare the relative performance of a large sample (1,500 firm-years) of state and privately owned firms during 1975, 1985, and 1995.	Document significant increases in profitability (using net income) and significant decreases in leverage and labor intensity (employees ÷ sales) over both short and long-term comparison horizons. Operating profits increase *prior to* privatization, but not after. Document significantly positive long-term (1–5 years) abnormal stock returns, mostly concentrated in Hungary, Poland, and the United Kingdom. Results also strongly indicate that private firms outperform state-owned firms.
Boubakri, Cosset, and Guedhami (2002)	Investigate the role of ownership structure and investor protection in corporate governance using a sample of 170 firms from 26 developing countries that were privatized over 1980–1997. Specifically examine what ownership structure results from privatization, and how it evolves subsequently; how the level of ownership protection impacts post-privatization ownership structure; and how ownership structure and investor protection relate to firm performance.	Document that private ownership tends to concentrate over time after divestment, and that privatization indeed results in a relinquishment of control by the privatizing government over three years after initial sale. Much of the decrease in state ownership is absorbed by foreign and local institutional investors, while the average stake held by individuals is less important. Also find that interaction between legal protection and ownership concentration has a significant negative effect on firm performance, suggesting that ownership concentration matters more in countries with weak legal protection.
Boubakri and Cosset (2003)	Examine pre- versus post-privatization performance of 16 African firms privatized through public share offering during the period 1989–1996. Also summarize findings of three other studies pertaining to privatization in developing countries.	Document significantly increased capital spending by privatized firms, but find only insignificant changes in profitability, efficiency, output, and leverage.

examine whether the performance of these companies improves after they are privatized. They document economically and statistically significant post-privatization increases in output (real sales), operating efficiency, profitability, capital investment spending, and dividend payments, as well as significant decreases in leverage. They find no evidence of employment declines after privatization, and in fact the median level of employment actually increases significantly (at the 10 percent level). They also find significant changes in the number and identity of firm directors around the time of initial privatization.

To more closely examine the sources of any privatization-induced performance changes, MNR also partition their full sample into five matching pairs of subsamples: (1) noncompetitive firms (regulated firms from the telecommunication and utility industries) versus firms from industries open to domestic and international competition; (2) "control privatizations," where the government's divestment lowers its fractional shareholding to less than 50 percent, versus "revenue privatizations," where the government retains majority voting control; (3) firms headquartered in industrialized (OECD) countries versus those headquartered in nonindustrialized (developing) countries; (4) firms where fewer than 50 percent of the pre-privatization board of directors is replaced versus firms with at least 50 percent post-privatization board changes; and (5) firms in which a new CEO is appointed after privatization versus those in which the old CEO is retained. MNR find their basic results are unchanged when they compare firms operating in competitive versus noncompetitive (regulated and/or protected) industries; when they examine privatizations where the government surrenders control, and contrast these with revenue privatizations where the purpose of share sales is primarily to raise cash; and when they compare industrialized (OECD) and developing country privatizations. When MNR partition their data based on the fraction of a firm's board that is replaced, however, they document significantly greater performance improvements for the group of firms that experience 50 percent or greater turnover than for the group of companies experiencing less dramatic change in directors after divestment.

Boubakri and Cosset (BC; 1998) analyze the privatization experience of 79 companies from 21 developing countries and 32 industries divested between 1980 and 1992. They document economically and statistically significant post-privatization increases in output (real sales), operating efficiency, profitability, capital investment spending, and dividend payments—as well as significant decreases in leverage. They also find that employment typically increases, but not significantly. The financial and operating performance improvements they find are generally even larger than those documented by MNR. Several years after the publication of their original study, Boubakri and Cosset (2003) analyze Africa's privatization experience using a sample of 16 African firms divested through public share offering during the period 1989–1996. They document significantly increased capital spending by privatized firms, but find only insignificant changes in profitability, efficiency, output, and leverage.

D'Souza and Megginson (DM; 1999) examine the success of share issue privatization programs in developing and industrialized economies during the period 1990–1996. Their sample includes 85 companies from 28 countries (13 developing and 15 industrialized). They find persuasive evidence that the mean and median levels of profitability, real sales, operating efficiency, and payout of the full-sample firms increase significantly, in both statistical and economic terms, after privatization. In fact, the significance levels of the profitability, output, and efficiency variables in DM are much greater (z values are much higher) than the previous study conducted by Megginson, Nash, and Van Randenborgh (1994), and are similar to those in Boubakri and Cosset (1998). DM also document significantly lower leverage ratios for their firms after divestiture. In contrast to MNR, DM find insignificant changes in employment (as do Boubakri and Cosset) and in capital spending as a fraction of sales after privatization—though the absolute level of capital spending does increase significantly.

DM's subsample analyses also yield important results. Output, operating efficiency, and dividend payments increase significantly for every subsample, while profitability increases and leverage decreases significantly in all but three cases. Employment decreases significantly only for firms that retain their CEO and for firms headquartered in industrialized countries. While capital investment spending as a fraction of sales generally remains statistically unchanged, it decreases significantly for firms with less than 50 percent changes in the board of directors. Additionally, DM test for significant differences between dichotomous subsample pairs using Kruskal-Wallis tests, and these reveal that performance improves significantly more when voting control is relinquished by a divesting government and for firms in noncompetitive industries, but that employment declines significantly more for companies headquartered in developed countries.

Dewenter and Malatesta (2001) estimate the effects of government ownership and privatization using a sample of large firms from three separate time periods (1975, 1985, and 1995) that are listed as the 500 biggest companies in the world by *Fortune* magazine. They estimate regressions explaining profitability after controlling for firm size, location, industry, and the business cycle. They find that net income-based profitability measures increase significantly after privatization, but operating income-based measures do not. Instead, they find that operating profits increase prior to divestiture, supporting the idea that privatization can have a significant anticipation effect.

Boubakri, Cosset, and Guedhami (BCG; 2002) investigate the role of ownership structure and investor protection in corporate governance using a sample of 170 firms from 26 developing countries privatized over the years 1980–1997. After documenting that privatization yields performance improvements for this group of companies comparable to that documented in previous studies, BCG specifically examine what ownership structure results from privatization and measure how it evolves subsequently. They also study how the level of ownership protection impacts post-privatization ownership structure, and how ownership structure and investor protection relate to firm performance. BCG document that private ownership of a privatized firm's stock tends to concentrate over time after the initial offering, and that privatization indeed results in the divesting government's relinquishing control over the three years after initial sale. Foreign and local institutional investors absorb a large fraction of the shares divested by the state, while individual shareholdings remain relatively unimportant. BCG also find that the interaction between legal protection and ownership concentration has a significant negative effect on firm performance, suggesting that ownership concentration matters more in countries with weak legal protection.

Single-Country and Single-Industry Studies

Although the multinational, multi-industry studies using the MNR methodology have proved most influential, numerous studies have also employed this methodology to examine privatization's effectiveness in promoting performance improvements in either a single industry or a single country. Several of these studies initially employ the MNR methodology to estimate the magnitudes of privatization-related performance changes, then use more sophisticated panel data regression methods to identify the specific sources of the performance changes. These studies are summarized in table 4.2.

Macquieira and Zurita (1996) examine Chile's privatization experience using data from 22 companies divested via public share offering between 1984 and 1989. They first test for performance changes without adjusting for overall improvements in the Chilean economy (as in MNR), then with an adjustment for changes experienced by other Chilean firms over the study period. Their unadjusted results are virtually identical to MNR, in that they document significant increases in output, profitability, employment, investment, and dividend payments. After adjusting for market movements, however, the changes in output, employment, and liquidity are no longer significant, and they find that average firm leverage increases significantly.

Boardman, Laurin, and Vining (2003) compare the three-year average post-privatization financial and operating performance ratios to the five-year pre-privatization values of these ratios for nine Canadian firms privatized from 1988 to 1995. They also compute the long-run (up to five years) stock returns for divested firms. They find that profitability, measured as return on sales or assets, more than doubles after privatization, while efficiency and sales also increase significantly (though less dramatically). Leverage and employment decline significantly, while capital spending increases significantly. Privatized firms also significantly outperform the Canadian stock market over all long-term holding periods.

Omran (2001a) studies performance changes for 69 Egyptian companies privatized between 1994 and 1998. Of these, 33 were majority sales (50 percent ownership), 18 were partial sales, 12 were sold to employee shareholding associations (ESAs), and six were sold to anchor investors. Omran finds that profitability, operating efficiency, capital spending, dividends, and liquidity increase significantly after privatization, while leverage, employment, and financial risk (measured as the inverse of times interest earned) decline significantly. He documents pervasive performance improvements across subgroups, but also finds that full privatization works better than partial divestment, and that sales to ESAs work better than others. In a second study, Omran (2002) also compares the performance of privatized companies to a matched set of 54 firms that remain state owned. He finds that SOEs' performance also improves significantly during the post-privatization period, and that privatized firms did not perform any better than

TABLE 4.2. Summary of Single-Country or Single-Industry Empirical Studies Comparing Pre- Versus Post-Privatization Performance Changes for Firms Privatized via Public Share Offerings in Nontransition Economies

Study	Sample Description, Study Period, and Methodology	Summary of Empirical Findings and Conclusions
Macquieira and Zurita (1996)	Compare pre- versus post-privatization performance of 22 Chilean companies privatized from 1984 to 1989. Use Megginson, Nash, and van Randenborgh (MNR) methodology to perform analysis first without adjusting for overall market movements (as in MNR), then with an adjustment for contemporaneous changes.	Unadjusted results virtually identical to MNR: significant increases in output, profitability, employment, investment, and dividend payments. After adjusting for market movements, however, the changes in output, employment, and liquidity are no longer significant, and leverage increases significantly.
Verbrugge, Megginson, and Owens (1999)	Study offering terms and share ownership results for 65 banks fully or partially privatized from 1981 to 1996. Then compare pre- and post-privatization performance changes for 32 banks in OECD countries and 5 in developing countries.	Document moderate performance improvements in OECD countries. Ratios proxying for profitability, fee income (noninterest income as fraction of total), and capital adequacy increase significantly; leverage ratio declines significantly. Document large, ongoing state ownership, and significantly positive initial returns to IPO investors.
Boardman, Laurin, and Vining (2003)	Compare 3-year average post-privatization financial and operating performance ratios to the 5-year pre-privatization values for 9 Canadian firms privatized from 1988 to 1995. Also compute long-run (up to 5 years) stock returns for divested firms.	Find that profitability, measured as return on sales or assets, more than doubles after privatization, while efficiency and sales also increase significantly (though less drastically). Leverage and employment decline significantly, while capital spending increases significantly. Privatized firms also significantly outperform Canadian stock market over all long-term holding periods.
Omran (2001a)	Studies performance changes for 69 Egyptian companies privatized between 1994 and 1998. Of these, 33 were majority sales (>50 percent ownership), 18 were partial sales, 12 were sold to employee shareholding associations (ESAs), and 6 were sold to anchor investors.	Find that profitability, operating efficiency, capital spending, dividends, and liquidity increase significantly after privatization, while leverage, employment, and financial risk (measured as the inverse of times interest earned) decline significantly. Performance changes pervasive across subgroups, but some evidence that full privatization works better than partial, and that sales to ESAs work better than others.

(continued)

111

TABLE 4.2. (continued)

Study	Sample Description, Study Period, and Methodology	Summary of Empirical Findings and Conclusions
Omran (2002)	Perform similar study to Omran (2001a), but also compare performance of privatized companies to a matched set of 54 firms that remained state owned.	Find that SOEs' performance also improves significantly during post-privatization period, and that privatized firms did not perform any better than SOEs.
Okten and Arin (2001)	Test effect of privatization on firm efficiency and technology choice using panel data set of 23 Turkish cement firms privatized between 1989 and 1998. Employ MNR test first, then panel data regression to explore determinants of performance changes.	Document that productivity, capacity utilization, output, and investment significantly increase after privatization, while employment, per unit costs, and prices decline significantly. Capacity increases insignificantly. Panel regression shows output, labor productivity, capital, and capital-to-labor ratio increase significantly, while employment falls. Per unit costs and prices also fall. Privatization clearly induces technology shift.
Sun, Jia, and Tong (2002)	Compare pre- vs. post-privatization financial and operating performance of a sample of 24 Malaysian firms divested via public share offering by the end of 1997. Employ MNR test first, then panel data regression to further examine sources of performance changes.	Find that privatized companies increase their absolute level of profits threefold, more than double real sales, and also significantly increase dividends and reduce leverage. Results are robust across various subsamples. Stocks of privatized firms earn normal returns (insignificantly different from market index). Regression analysis shows that institutional investors and directors have positive impact on privatized firm performance, and that option schemes, rather than direct remuneration, give better incentives to managers.
Feng, Sun and Tong (2002)	Test whether privatization improves financial and operating performance of 31 Singaporean companies divested through public share offering between 1975 and 1998. Employ MNR test first, then panel data regression to further examine sources of performance changes.	Find no significant change after privatization in any variable except output (significant increase) using MNR methods. Then use regression analysis to show that output and leverage improve but efficiency deteriorates after privatization. Conclude that there is little performance improvement after ownership change because Singaporean SOEs were unusually well managed before divestment.

SOEs. It is thus unclear if the performance improvement documented for privatized firms was merely a reflection of an overall improvement in the Egyptian economy during the study period, if the improvement in the performance of state-owned enterprises was itself due to the demonstration (and perhaps anticipation) effect provided by Egypt's privatization program, or if both sets of firms benefited from a general opening of the Egyptian economy during the 1990s. In any case, it is clear that privatization does not harm the divested firms.

Okten and Arin (2001) test the effect of privatization on firm efficiency and technology choice using a panel data set of 23 Turkish cement firms privatized between 1989 and 1998. They examine a single industry in order to specifically measure how privatization impacts the choice of production technology. They develop a simple theoretical model endogenizing the technology choice by elected politicians running SOEs, and predict that SOEs are likely to be undercapitalized and overstaffed in a labor-abundant country (like Turkey). They then use this model to predict how switching to private ownership will impact technology choice. As predicted, they find that privatized companies switch to more capital-intensive production processes. These new processes significantly reduce per unit costs and prices, and substantially raise labor productivity and overall output. They also document that capacity utilization and investment increase significantly after privatization, while employment declines significantly and capacity increases insignificantly. In sum, privatization induces a shift toward more capital-intensive production technology by divested firms.

Sun and Tong (2002) compare the pre- versus post-privatization financial and operating performance of a sample of 24 Malaysian firms divested via public share offering by the end of 1997. As do Okten and Arin, they employ MNR tests first, then use panel data regression to examine the sources of performance changes. Sun and Tong find that privatized companies increase their absolute level of profits threefold, more than double real sales, and also significantly increase dividends and reduce leverage. Results are robust across various subsamples. Stocks of privatized firms earn normal returns (insignificantly different from the market index). Regression analysis shows that institutional investors have a positive impact on privatized firm performance, and that option schemes, rather than direct remuneration, give better incentives to managers.

The final country study surveyed here, by Feng, Sun, and Tong (2002), tests whether privatization improved the financial and operating performance of 31 Singaporean companies divested through public share offering between 1975 and 1998. They find no significant change after privatization in any variable except output (which significantly increases) using MNR methods. They then use regression analysis to show that output and leverage improve after privatization, but that efficiency deteriorates. Finally, they conclude that there is little performance improvement after ownership change because Singaporean SOEs were unusually well managed before divestment.

Verbrugge, Megginson, and Owens (VMO; 1999) investigate bank privatizations that use public security offerings as the divestment mechanism. The problems inherent in a state-owned banking industry have led many countries to at least consider privatizing state-owned banks. Wherever and however banks are privatized, divesting governments all face a common set of concerns and issues. These include (1) the type of privatization process to utilize; (2) whether and how to break up the government-owned banking system, which is especially difficult (but necessary) in the all too common case of a monobank system; (3) transferring ownership claims to the private (domestic or foreign) sector; (4) dealing with an extremely low quality loan portfolio, much of which is in default—albeit likely to be unrecognized on a financial reporting basis; (5) ensuring an enhanced level of managerial talent in the system; and (6) ultimately attracting outside, often foreign, capital and expertise to the banking system. VMO discuss the terms of 58 initial unseasoned and 34 seasoned offerings involving 65 banks from 12 high-information economies and 13 emerging economies. They find that bank IPOs tend to be very large, with a median offering size of nearly $300 million in high-information economies and $140 million in emerging economies. They also document significantly positive average (median) initial returns of 30.5 percent (15.9 percent) for investors, but find that seasoned issues are not significantly underpriced. Privatization leads to only limited improvement in bank profitability, operating efficiency, leverage, and noninterest revenue. Substantial government ownership of banks remains even after privatization, and in only a few cases is the government's stake completely eliminated at the IPO stage, or even in subsequent seasoned offerings. VMO suggest that continued significant government ownership of banks raises serious problems for establishing market-oriented governance and decision-making systems in the banks.[3]

Summary of Pre- Versus Post-Privatization Performance Studies

The 14 studies discussed in this section yield consistently positive results on the effectiveness of privatization in promoting improvements in the financial and operating performance of divested companies. Most of the studies cited here document economically and statistically significant post-privatization increases in real sales (output), profitability, efficiency (sales per employee), and capital spending, coupled with significant declines in leverage. This point is made clear in table 4.3, which summarizes the results of three studies [MNR (1994), BC (1998), and DM (1999)] that use precisely the same empirical proxies and test methodology—and can thus be aggregated and directly compared—yet examine nonoverlapping samples. In total, these three studies examine seven performance criteria for 204 companies from 41 countries. Since the papers examine differing time periods (1961–1989 for MNR, 1980–1992 for BC, and 1990–1996 for DM), and BC study only developing countries, there is very little sample overlap between the studies, which collectively examine 211 companies from 42 countries and no less than 56 different industries. Roughly half (103) of these firms are from 26 developing countries, with the other half (108) coming from 16 industrialized nations. The four countries with the greatest representation in the combined sample are Great Britain (28 firms), France and Portugal (16 each), and Turkey (15 companies), while the following industries were represented by at least ten firms: banking and finance (36 companies), electric utilities (30), telecommunication utilities (22),

TABLE 4.3. Summarized Results from Three Empirical Studies of the Financial and Operating Performance of Newly Privatized Firms (Compared to Their Performance as State-Owned Enterprises)

Variables and Studies Cited	Number of Observations	Mean Value before Privatization	Mean Value after Privatization	Mean Change due to Privatization	z-Statistic for Difference in Performance	% of Firms with Improved Performance	z-Statistic of % Change
Profitability (Net Income ÷ Sales)							
Megginson, Nash, and van Randenborgh (1994)	55	0.0552 (0.0442)	0.0799 (0.0611)	0.0249 (0.0140)	3.15***	69.1	3.06***
Boubakri and Cosset (1998)	78	0.0493 (0.0460)	0.1098 (0.0799)	0.0605 (0.0181)	3.16***	62.8	2.29**
D'Souza and Megginson (1999)	78	0.14 (0.05)	0.17 (0.08)	0.03 (0.03)	3.92***	71	4.17***
Weighted average	218[a]	0.0862	0.1257	0.0396		67.6	
Efficiency (Real Sales per Employee)							
Megginson, Nash, and van Randenborgh (1994)	51	0.956 (0.942)	1.062 (1.055)	0.1064 (0.1157)	3.66***	85.7	6.03***
Boubakri and Cosset (1998)	56	0.9224 (0.9056)	1.1703 (1.1265)	0.2479 (0.2414)	4.79***	80.4	4.60***
D'Souza and Megginson (1999)	63	1.02 (0.87)	1.23 (1.16)	0.21 (0.29)	4.87***	79	5.76***
Weighted average	170	0.9733	1.1599	0.1914		81.5	
Investment (Capital Expenditures ÷ Sales)							
Megginson, Nash, and van Randenborgh (1994)	43	0.1169 (0.0668)	0.1689 (0.1221)	0.0521 (0.0159)	2.35**	67.4	2.44**
Boubakri and Cosset (1998)	48	0.1052 (0.0649)	0.2375 (0.1043)	0.1322 (0.0137)	2.28**	62.5	1.74*

(continued)

115

TABLE 4.3. (continued)

Variables and Studies Cited	Number of Observations	Mean Value before Privatization	Mean Value after Privatization	Mean Change due to Privatization	z-Statistic for Difference in Performance	% of Firms with Improved Performance	z-Statistic of % Change
D'Souza and Megginson (1999)	66	0.18 (0.11)	0.17 (0.10)	−0.01 (−0.01)	0.80	55	0.81
Weighted average	*154*	*0.1405*	*0.1900*	*0.0493*		*60.6*	
Output [Real Sales (adjusted by CPI)]							
Megginson, Nash, and van Randenborgh (1994)	57	0.899 (0.890)	1.140 (1.105)	0.241 (0.190)	4.77**	75.4	4.46***
Boubakri and Cosset (1998)	78	0.9691 (0.9165)	1.220 (1.123)	0.2530 (0.1892)	5.19***	75.6	4.58***
D'Souza and Megginson (1999)	85	0.93 (0.76)	2.70 (1.86)	1.76 (1.11)	7.30***	88	10.94***
Weighted average	*209[a]*	*0.9358*	*1.7211*	*0.8321*		*80.3*	
Employment (Total Employees)							
Megginson, Nash, and van Randenborgh (1994)	39	40,850 (19,360)	43,200 (23,720)	2,346 (276)	0.96	64.1	1.84*
Boubakri and Cosset (1998)	57	10,672 (3,388)	10,811 (3,745)	139 (104)	1.48	57.9	1.19
D'Souza and Megginson (1999)	66	22,941 (9,876)	22,136 (9,106)	−805 (−770)	−1.62	36	−2.14**
Weighted average	*162*	*22,936*	*23,222*	*286*		*49.5*	

	N						
Leverage (Total Debt ÷ Total Assets)							
Megginson, Nash, and van Randenborgh (1994)	53	0.6622	0.6379	−0.0243	−2.41**	71.7	3.51***
		(0.7039)	(0.6618)	(−0.0234)			
Boubakri and Cosset (1998)	65	0.5495	0.4986	−0.0508	−2.48**	63.1	2.11**
		(0.5575)	(0.4789)	(−0.0162)			
D'Souza and Megginson (1999)	72	0.29	0.23	−0.06	−3.08***	67	3.05***
		(0.26)	(0.18)	(−0.08)			
Weighted average	*188*	*0.4826*	*0.4357*	*−0.0469*		*67.0*	
Dividends (Cash Dividends ÷ Sales)							
Megginson, Nash, and van Randenborgh (1994)	39	0.0128	0.0300	0.0172	4.63***	89.7	8.18***
		(0.0054)	(0.0223)	(0.0121)			
Boubakri and Cosset (1998)	67	0.0284	0.0528	0.0244	4.37***	76.1	4.28***
		(0.0089)	(0.0305)	(0.0130)			
D'Souza and Megginson (1999)	51	0.015	0.04	0.025	4.98***	79	5.24***
		(0.00)	(0.02)	(0.02)			
Weighted average	*106*	*0.0202*	*0.0655*	*0.0228*		*80.4*	

Note: This table summarizes the empirical results of three directly comparable academic studies [Megginson, Nash, and van Randenborgh (1994), Boubakri and Cosset (1998), and D'Souza and Megginson (1999)] comparing the three-year average operating and financial performance of a combined sample of 21 [a] newly privatized firms with the average performance of those same firms during their last three years as state-owned enterprises (SOEs). All three studies employ the Wilcoxon rank sum test (with its z-statistic) as the test of significance for the change in median value. All three studies employ multiple proxies for most of the economic variables being measured; this table summarizes only one proxy per topic, and emphasizes the one highlighted in the studies (almost invariably, the variable that uses either physical measures—such as number of employees—or financial ratios using current-dollar measures in the numerator or denominator, or both). Profitability, investment, leverage, and dividend measures are in percent. Efficiency and output measures are index values, with the value during the year of privatization defined as 1.000; inflation-adjusted sales figures are used in the efficiency and output measures.

*** Indicates significance at the 1 percent level.

** Indicates significance at the 5 percent level.

* Indicates significance at the 10 percent level.

[a] Number exceeds 211 because of overlapping firms in different samples.

petroleum (18), steel (14), and airlines (11). The combined sample thus spans a wide variety of industries and stages of national development, and represents the broadest and most comprehensive multinational study of privatization's impact yet produced.

The three studies yield remarkably consistent findings regarding the impact of privatization on firm profitability, efficiency, output, leverage, and dividend payments. All show highly significant performance improvements according to both the Wilcoxon (median) and binomial (proportion) test statistics. Profitability, defined as net income divided by sales, increases from an average value of 8.6 percent before privatization to 12.6 percent afterward, with between 63 and 71 percent of the firms in each sample experiencing increased profitability.[4] Five of the six test statistics in the three studies are significant at the 1 percent level or higher, and the remaining statistic is significant at the 5 percent level.

Efficiency, defined as real (inflation-adjusted) sales per employee, increases from an average level of 96.9 percent of year 0 (the year of privatization) sales during years −3 to −1 to an average level of 116.0 percent during the +1 to +3 post-privatization period. Although the scale of this increase is driven by the DM finding of a 21 percentage point productivity leap, all three studies find efficiency improvements that are significant at the 1 percent level or better, and between 79 and 86 percent of the firms experience output-per-worker increases. The overall increase in output for privatized firms in the three samples is astonishingly large and statistically significant at beyond the 1 percent level according to all the test statistics. On average, real sales revenues rise from 93.6 percent of year 0 levels prior to divestment to 177.1 percent thereafter, a near doubling of real output over a four-year period. Once again, a 176 percentage point increase found by DM drives the magnitude of this result, but the output increase is significant at the 1 percent level in all three studies, and between 75 and 85 percent of all firms increase sales.

The two financial variables (leverage and dividends) studied are of only secondary interest to most governments — though they are naturally of greater concern to firm managers and stockholders. All three studies find that leverage, defined as total debt divided by total assets, declines significantly (at the 5 or 1 percent levels) after privatization, and between 63 and 72 percent of all firms experience reduced debt levels. On average, the debt-to-asset ratio falls from 0.483 prior to divestiture to 0.436 afterward. This is partly due to the fact that a few of the offerings are capital-raising primary share issues, but the vast majority are not, and leverage declines primarily owing to higher retained profitability. Additionally, the three studies also document significant, and fairly dramatic, increases in dividend payments after privatization. On average, cash dividend payments more than triple as a fraction of revenues, from 2.0 percent of sales during the pre-privatization period to 6.6 percent of sales after divestiture, and between 76 and 90 percent of the firms in the three samples increase dividend payments. All of these test statistics are significant at the 1 percent level or higher.

While all three studies document post-privatization increases in capital investment spending as a fraction of sales, only in the MNR and BC papers are the increases significant. On average, capital spending increases from 12.3 percent of sales prior to divestment to 18.7 percent afterward, and between 59 and 67 percent of all firms raise investment outlays. It bears repeating, however, that DM also find a large increase in the level of capital spending, but since sales and assets increase even faster, the increased capital spending as a fraction of sales is insignificant. These capital investment increases help explain the dramatic jumps in output (inflation-adjusted sales revenue) all three papers document.

The most politically charged performance measure is, of course, how privatization impacts employment levels in divested SOEs, and here the three studies diverge somewhat. MNR and BC document employment increases, while DM find that the workforce declines after divestiture. Note that, for ease of presentation, the heading on the fractional change column in table 4.2 is labeled "Percent of Firms with Improved Performance," rather than "Percent of Firms that Change as Expected," so the DM result is entered as 37 percent rather than 63 percent, as in table 4.1. The three studies collectively find that average employment in a SOE being privatized increases from 21,065 pre-divestiture to 21,613 afterward, and 83 of the 164 firms (50.7 percent) examined show an increase in total employment.

One of the most difficult-to-refute challenges leveled at privatization studies showing performance improvements is the assertion that these improvements, particularly profitability increases, may represent nothing other than price increases and/or the exploitation of market power by newly privatized firms. After all, governments face a real financial temptation to sell off SOEs as private monopolies, since this will maximize the price that private investors are willing to pay for shares. None of the three studies summarized here directly examines this question, but all attempt to offer indirect evidence that the performance gains documented are socially beneficial, and are not primarily the result of market power exploitation. MNR examine each firm divested, and find no evidence that product prices increase or that governments increase cash subsidies after divestiture. Quite the reverse; in every case where governments were subsidizing the firm beforehand, these were explicitly terminated after privatization. All three studies also document that governments invariably adopt regulatory schemes for newly privatized utilities, and evidence from supplementary sources indicates that most of these schemes work effectively once fully implemented. Furthermore, all three studies include firms operating in internationally competitive industries, and all three find these firms experience performance improvements comparable to their counterparts in noncompetitive industries.

Additionally, these three studies consistently document that output, efficiency, and capital spending increases dramatically, and significantly, after privatization. Furthermore, leverage declines significantly. Unlike profitability increases, these are all unambiguously socially beneficial outcomes, since they imply that privatized firms use resources more productively and also become financially healthier. That these benefits are achieved without systematically reducing employment also suggests that privatization yields important social benefits. In sum, the weight of evidence in these three studies clearly indicates (1) that privatization improves the operating and financial performance of newly divested firms, (2) that these improvements are the result of socially beneficial improvements in productive efficiency and entrepreneurial effort, and (3) that privatization "works" in a wide variety of countries, industries, and competitive environments.

Case Study, Single-Industry and Single-Country Studies: Developed Nations

The studies surveyed in this section all examine a single industry, a single country, or one or a small number of individual firms in developed economies using a methodology other than the simple pre- versus post-privatization tests developed by MNR. While these studies employ a variety of empirical techniques, most compare actual post-privatization performance changes with either a comparison group of nonprivatized firms or with a "counter-factual" expectation of what would have occurred if the privatized firms themselves had remained state-owned.

Country, Industry, and Case Studies

The studies we examine in this section are summarized in table 4.4. The first study listed merits detailed analysis because it has proved so influential, both owing to the rigor of its methodology and because it was sponsored by the World Bank. Galal, Jones, Tandon, and Vogelsang (1992) compare the actual post-privatization performance of 12 large firms to the predicted performance of these firms had they not been divested. Their sample consists mostly of airlines and regulated utilities in Britain, Chile, Malaysia, and Mexico. Using this counter-factual approach, the authors document net welfare gains in 11 of the 12 cases considered that average 26 percent of the firm's pre-divestiture sales. They find no case where workers are made significantly worse off, and three where workers significantly benefit.

Martin and Parker (1995) examine whether 11 British firms privatized during 1981–1988 improve profitability (measured as return on invested capital) and efficiency (annual growth in value-added per employee-hour) after being divested. They find mixed results. After adjusting for business-cycle effects, fewer than half the firms performed better after being privatized. The authors do, however, find evidence of a "shake-out" effect, where several firms improve performance prior to being privatized (but not afterward). Writing much later, Florio (2001) and Brau and Florio (2002) also examine the overall British privatization experience. Both studies analyze the welfare effect of the massive U.K. divestment program between 1979 and 1997, and compare the actual effects generated against what they feel would have happened if the companies had remained state owned. They acknowledge that the British divestment program yielded major fiscal benefits, lower prices, and increased access in most areas and productivity growth in the divested companies. However, they maintain that these gains would also have been achieved under continued state ownership—and at lower costs in terms of skewed income distribution. They support these assertions by extrapolating productivity trends observed for British SOEs during the 1950s and 1960s, but which were halted for SOEs during the 1970s, as they also were for other areas of British

TABLE 4.4. Summary of Case Study and Country and Industry-Specific Empirical Studies of Privatization: Developed Countries

Study	Sample Description, Study Period, and Methodology	Summary of Empirical Findings and Conclusions
Galal, Jones, Tandon, and Vogelsang (1992)	Compare actual post-privatization performance of 12 large firms (mostly airlines and regulated utilities) in Britain, Chile, Malaysia, and Mexico to predicted performance of these firms had they remained SOEs.	Document net welfare gains in 11 of the 12 cases that equal, on average, 26% of the firms' pre-divestiture sales. Find no case where workers are made worse off, and 3 where workers are made significantly better off.
Green and Vogelsang (1994)	Provide a historical overview of BA's evolution as a state-owned enterprise through its first years as a fully privatized company. Also analyze how operating and financial performance evolves during the time before and after company's sale.	They show that BA suffered severely during the airline depression of the early 1980s, but that the operational changes and restructuring that the management team executes during the mid-1980s paves the way for the successful sale of the government's 100 percent ownership in 1987.
Martin and Parker (1995)	Using two measures (ROR on capital employed and annual growth in value-added per employee-hour), examine whether 11 British firms privatized during 1981–1988 improve performance after divestment. Also attempt to control for business-cycle effects.	Mixed results. Outright performance improvements after privatization found in less than half of firm-measures studied. Several improve prior to divestiture, indicating an initial "shake-out" effect upon privatization announcement.
Price and Weyman-Jones (1996)	Measure the technical efficiency of the U.K. natural gas industry before and after its 1986 privatization and associated regulatory changes using Malmquist indices and nonparametric frontier analysis.	Show that the industry's rate of productivity growth increased significantly after privatization—though not as much as it could have if the industry had been restructured and subjected to direct competition and more appropriate regulation.
Newbery and Pollitt (1997)	Perform a cost-benefit analysis of the 1990 restructuring and privatization of the Central Electricity Generating Board (CEGB). Compare the actual performance of the privatized firms to a counter-factual assuming CEGB had remained state owned.	The restructuring/privatization of CEGB was "worth it," in that there is a permanent cost reduction of 5 percent per year. Producers and shareholders capture all this benefit and more. Consumers and the government lose. Also show that alternative fuel purchases involve unnecessarily high costs and wealth flows out of the country.

(continued)

TABLE 4.4. (continued)

Study	Sample Description, Study Period, and Methodology	Summary of Empirical Findings and Conclusions
Laurin and Bozec (2000)	Compare productivity and profitability of two large Canadian rail carriers, before and after the 1995 privatization of Canadian National (CN). Compare accounting ratios for entire 17-year period 1981–1997 and for three subperiods: the fully state-owned era (1981–1991), the pre-privatization period (1992–1995), and the post-privatization era. Also examine stock returns from 1995–1998. Create a six-firm comparison group of Canadian privatizations, and compute accounting ratios and stock returns for these firms as well.	Total factor productivity of CN much lower than that of privately owned Canadian Pacific (CP) during 1981–1991 period, but becomes just as efficient during pre-privatization (1992–1995) period, then exceeds it after 1995. CN stock price outperforms CP, the transportation industry, and the Canadian market after 1995. Both firms shed workers after 1992, but CN's employment declines by more (34% vs. 18%) as average productivity almost doubles (97% increase). CN's capital spending increases significantly, though CP increases more. Six-firm Canadian privatization comparison group also experience significant increases in investment spending and productivity, and a significant decline in employment.
Villalonga (2000)	Examines the effect of privatization on efficiency for 24 Spanish firms fully divested between 1985 and 1993. Tests for separate effects of ownership change, once other political and organizational factors and time period (state of the business cycle) effects accounted for.	Finds insignificant changes in level and growth rate of efficiency after privatization. Significant positive effect found for business cycle suggests government sold firms during recessions. Capital intensity, foreign ownership, and size also positively related to efficiency improvements. Privatization seems to decrease efficiency for 5 and 6 years after divestiture, but increase efficiency 7 and 8 years after and 4 and 3 years before, suggesting importance of time effects.
Florio (2001)	Presents an analysis of the welfare impact of the U.K. privatization program 1979–1997. Considers the impact on five types of agents: firms, employees, shareholders, consumers, and taxpayers.	Concludes that privatization has modest effects on efficiency of production and consumption, but has important effects on distribution of income and wealth. Acknowledges fiscal benefits, and lower prices in most areas, productivity growth, but asserts these would have been achieved under continued state ownership (due to extrapolation of existing trends). Calculate that, at best, the NPV of the welfare change for each British consumer is less than £1,000, and would be lower if distributional issues accounted for.

| Dumontier and Laurin (2002) | Investigate the value that is created or lost during the state ownership period for each firm nationalized during 1982 and then reprivatized between 1986 and 1995. Then tests whether privatization improves performance over that achieved during post-1982 nationalized period. 46 companies (39 banks and five industrial firms) were nationalized and then reprivatized. | Find that government created value in nationalized firms, but state and taxpayers did not benefit because of premium paid to shareholders upon nationalization (20%) and underpricing of IPO at privatization. Financial and operating performance of companies improved during nationalization phase, then improved even more after privatization. Profits and sales increased after privatization, while efficiency improved over all three periods. Employment fell during nationalized period, but increased (due to higher sales) after privatization. Capital spending highest during nationalized period, due to government subsidies. Leverage declined during nationalized period, but increased after privatization. Dividends decline during nationalized period, but increase after privatization. |
| Saal and Parker (2003) | Examine the productivity and price performance of the privatized water and sewerage companies of England and Wales after the industry is privatized and a new regulatory regime imposed in 1989. Examines joint impact of privatization and new economic regulatory environment on performance. | Find no significant evidence that productivity growth, measured by growth in TFP, is improved by privatization—despite reductions in labor usage. Also find that increases in output prices have outstripped increased input prices, leading to significantly higher economic profits after privatization. |

industry. These two papers calculate that, at best, the U.K. privatization program yielded benefits to British consumers with a net present value of less than £1,000 per capita. If the distributional costs are factored in, they believe the net benefits would be much lower, or even negative.

Price and Weyman-Jones (1996), Newberry and Pollitt (1997), and Saal and Parker (2003) also examine specific aspects of Britain's privatization program. Price and Weyman-Jones measure the technical efficiency of the U.K. natural gas industry before and after its 1986 privatization and associated regulatory changes. They employ Malmquist indices and nonparametric frontier analysis to show that the industry's rate of productivity growth increased significantly after privatization—though not as much as it could have if the industry had been restructured and subjected to direct competition and more appropriate regulation. Newberry and Pollitt perform a counter-factual analysis of the 1990 restructuring and privatization of the United Kingdom's Central Electricity Generating Board (CEGB), and document significant post-privatization performance improvements. However, they find that the producers and their shareholders capture all of the financial rewards of this improvement and more, whereas the government and consumers lose out. The authors conclude that CEGB's restructuring and privatization was in fact "worth it," but could have been implemented more efficiently and with greater concern for the public's welfare.[5] Saal and Parker examine the productivity and price performance of the privatized water and sewerage companies of England and Wales after the industry was privatized and a new regulatory regime imposed in 1989. They study the joint impact of privatization and a new regulatory environment on performance. They document that labor productivity improved significantly after privatization, but find no evidence that total factor productivity grew as a direct result of the ownership change. They do find some evidence of a small increase in the rate of TFP growth after the regulatory regime was tightened significantly in 1995. They also find that increases in output prices have outstripped increased input prices, leading to significantly higher economic profits after privatization.

All in all, British researchers have given their country's privatization program a passing grade, at best. Though most document significant performance improvements along at least some key performance measures, most conclude that the program could and should have been executed with more concern for distributional issues and/or with greater protections built in for consumers. Given that many governments around the world have been inspired by the perceived success of Britain's privatization program, this underwhelming assessment from British academic researchers is disconcerting.

On the other hand, four studies that examine the privatization experience of specific British companies yield much more positive assessments. Two of these studies examine British Airways (BA). First, Green and Vogelsang (1994) provide a historical overview of BA's evolution as a state-owned enterprise through its first years as a fully privatized company. They show that BA suffered severely during the airline depression of the early 1980s, but that the operational changes and restructuring that the management team executed during the mid-1980s paved the way for the successful sale of the government's 100 percent ownership in 1987.

Eckel, Eckel, and Singal (EES; 1997) analyze the effect of British Airways's privatization on the stock prices of its competitors. They also test whether fares on competitive routes decline after privatization. EES find that the stock prices of BA's American competitors declined on average by 7 percent upon BA's privatization, and fares on routes served by BA and competitors fell by 14.3 percent after divestiture. Further, the compensation of BA executives increased and became more performance-contingent. These findings suggest that investors expected a more competitive BA to result from privatization, and the decline in fares indicates that this indeed occurred.[6]

The third study examines a company closely entwined with aviation: British Airports Authority, which was renamed simply BAA after its privatization in 1987. Parker (1997) finds ambiguous results for BAA. Shareholders definitely benefited from an appreciating stock price and rising dividend payments, but Parker documents a decline in the rate of return on net assets after privatization. He also finds no evidence that either productivity or efficiency increased significantly as a consequence of ownership change. Parker does, however, find evidence of economies of scale in airport operations, and cautions against any forced divestiture of BAA assets. Finally, Parker (1994) studies changes in the structure and management, and in the operating and financial performance, of British Telecom during the first decade after its 1984 privatization. He documents significant increases in output, profitability, efficiency, labor productivity, and in the absolute levels of research and development (R&D) and capital spending—though these declined as a percentage of sales. Prices for BT's basket of services fell by 5.1 percent per year from 1984 to 1993, but residential phone service prices increased by 2.7 percent per year. The growth rate in labor productivity accelerated after privatization, and labor costs fell from 42.4 percent of output before to 33.6 percent after divestiture. Parker also describes the history of state ownership of BT, plus its subsequent privatization and the regulatory environment that was developed for a private BT. He notes that the British government promoted competition through new entry, with some success, and describes the retail price index–X percent (RPI-X) pricing scheme imposed on BT.

Two of the remaining studies described in the first section of table 4.3 are country studies, while the third is essentially another case study of an individual privatized company. First, Villalonga (2000) examines the effect of privatization on the operating efficiency of 24 Spanish firms that were fully divested between 1985 and 1993. She tests for separate effects of ownership change, once other political and organizational factors and time period (state of the business cycle) effects are accounted for, and she finds insignificant changes in the level and growth rate of efficiency after privatization. She sees a significant positive effect for the state of the business cycle, suggesting that the Spanish government sold firms during recessions. She also finds that capital intensity, foreign ownership, and size are positively related to efficiency improvements. Privatization seems to decrease efficiency over the intermediate term (five and six years after divestiture), but to increase efficiency over the longer term (seven and eight years) afterwards and in the period leading up to privatization (four and three years before). These findings suggest the importance of time effects.

The second country study, by Dumontier and Laurin (DL; 2002), investigates the value that was created or lost during the state ownership period for each of the 46 French companies (39 banks and five industrial firms) that were nationalized during 1982 and then re-privatized between 1986 and 1995. DL also analyze whether the subsequent privatization of these companies improves performance over that achieved during the post-1982 nationalized period. They find that the French government created value in the nationalized firms, but the state and taxpayers did not benefit because of the premium that was paid to shareholders upon nationalization (20 percent) and because of the underpricing of the IPOs at the time of privatization. The financial and operating performance of companies improved during the nationalization phase, then improved even more after privatization. Profits and sales increased after privatization, while efficiency improved over all three periods. Employment fell during the nationalized period but increased (due to higher sales) after privatization. Capital spending was the highest during the nationalized period, owing to government subsidies. Leverage declined during the nationalized period but increased after privatization. Dividends declined during the nationalized period but increased after privatization. The rather surprising bottom line of this study for our purposes here is that the French government created value in the nationalized firms after 1982, but privatization improved their performance even more!

Laurin and Bozec (2000) compare the productivity and profitability of two large Canadian rail carriers (one state-owned and one private-sector), both before and after the 1995 privatization of Canadian National (CN). They find that CN's relatively poor performance during the "fully state-owned period" (1981–1991) rapidly converges on Canadian Pacific's performance levels during the pre-privatization, but post-announcement period (1992–1995), and then surpasses it thereafter. These findings suggest two separable impacts of privatization on firm performance: an "anticipation" effect prior to divestiture and a "follow-through" effect subsequently. As we have already seen, this phenomenon is observed in other studies as well.

Stock and R&D Performance Studies

In addition to studying accounting measures and technical measures of efficiency, there are two other methods of examining privatization's impact on firm performance. The first is to study how the privatization announcement impacts the stock prices of competitive firms, and the second is to test how privatization impacts research and development intensity and productivity. Studies employing either of these methodologies are summarized in table 4.5. As noted above, EES examine the effect of British Airways's 1987 privatization on competitors' stock prices and find that the stock prices of U.S. competitors fall, suggesting that stock traders expect a much more competitive BA to result from divestiture. Otchere (2002) uses this same methodology to examine the stock-price reaction of 314 industry counterparts to the announcement that 121 firms are to be privatized via share offering in 29 developed and developing countries and 28 industries. He finds that rivals react negatively to privatization announcements, losing 1.72 percent (1.64

TABLE 4.5. Summary of R&D and Stock Price Performance Empirical Studies of Privatization: Developed Countries

Study	Sample Description, Study Period, and Methodology	Summary of Empirical Finding and Conclusions
Eckel, Eckel, and Singal (1997)	Examine the effect of British Airways's privatization on the stock prices of competitors. Also test whether fares on competitive routes decline after privatization. Such findings would suggest a more competitive BA resulting from privatization.	Stock prices of U.S. competitors declined on average by 7 percent upon BA's privatization, and fares on routes served by BA and competitors fell by 14.3 percent after divestiture. Compensation of BA executives increased and became more performance-contingent.
Otchere (2002)	Examine stock price reaction of 314 industry counterparts to the privatization announcement for 121 firms to be divested via share offering to infer the expected impact of privatization on the performance of firms in 29 developed and developing countries and 28 industries.	Found that rivals reacted negatively to privatization announcements, losing 1.72% (1.64%) of their value over the 3-day (5-day) period surrounding the announcement. Also found the reaction of rival firms in developing countries to be stronger than in developed countries, and the reaction of rivals to a full privatization announcement was larger than that of a partial privatization announcement.
Munari and Oriani (2002)	Analyze the impact of privatization on R&D investment, valuation, and performance. Measure ownership-related performance changes using Tobin's Q and a hedonic model. Estimate model on an original data set of 20 Western European companies privatized through public share offerings between 1982 and 1997 and an industry and country-matched set of 20 publicly held private companies.	Showed that newly privatized firms (NPFs) have slightly lower mean values of R&D-to-assets, R&D capital-to-assets, and Tobin's Q, and higher mean debt levels than do matched firms, and that the stock market values the R&D investments of NPFs at less than half the level of private firms. The R&D coefficient on Q is 7.504 for private firms vs. only 1.286 for NPFs. Also found that R&D investments initially decline (relative to assets) after privatization, while Tobin's Q increases, so market valuation of NPFs doesn't respond negatively to decline; in fact, rising Q suggests market is optimistic about ability of NPFs to generate rising profits.
Munari and Oriani (2002)	Compare pre- and post-privatization R&D efforts and patenting behavior of 35 companies that are fully or partially privatized in 9 European countries through public share offering between 1980 and 1997.	Found that, after controlling for inter-industry differences, privatization processes negatively affect different measures of R&D commitment. Shift from public to private ownership also leads to a significant increase in the quantity of patents, and in their quality as measured by citation intensity.

percent) of their value over the three-day (five-day) period surrounding the announcement. He also finds that the reaction of rival firms in developing countries is stronger than in developed countries, and the reaction of rivals to a full privatization announcement is larger than that to a partial privatization announcement.

The final two studies we survey here analyze how privatization affects the R&D investments of divested firms. Munari and Oriani (2002) analyze the impact of privatization on R&D investment, valuation, and performance. They measure ownership-related performance changes using Tobin's Q and a hedonic model, and estimate their model on an original data set of 20 western European companies privatized through public share offerings between 1982 and 1997, as well as an industry- and country-matched control set of 20 publicly held private companies. Munari and Oriani show that newly privatized firms have slightly lower mean values of R&D-to-assets, R&D capital-to-assets and Tobin's Q, and higher mean debt levels than do matched firms, and that the stock market values the R&D investments of privatized companies at less than half the level of private firms. The R&D coefficient on Q is 7.504 for private firms versus only 1.286 for the privatized firms. They also find that R&D investments initially decline (relative to assets) after privatization, while Tobin's Q increases, so the market valuation of divested companies doesn't respond negatively to the decline in R&D spending; in fact, the rising Q suggests that the market is optimistic about the ability of privatized firms to generate increasing profits. Finally, Munari and Oriani (2002) compare the pre- and post-privatization R&D efforts and patenting behavior of 35 companies that were fully or partially privatized in nine European countries through public share offering between 1980 and 1997. They find that, after controlling for interindustry differences, privatization negatively affects different measures of R&D commitment. However, the shift from public to private ownership does lead to a significant increase in the quantity of patents, and in their quality, as measured by citation intensity.

Case Study, Single-Industry, and Single-Country Studies: Developing Nations

For a variety of reasons — in particular, the availability of high-quality data — most of the early academic privatization studies focused on the experience of developed countries. In spite of the fact that the one major exception to this pattern, Boubakri and Cosset (1998), yielded results that were very similar to those documented for industrialized countries, many commentators believed that privatization should yield materially different effects in less developed countries. During the past three years, many excellent studies have been generated that test this proposition, and we summarize those papers in this section.

Survey papers are an author's best friend, and four excellent surveys of privatization's impact in developing countries are now available. All four generally conclude that privatization has been an economically effective policy, but each in its own way cautions about distributional, political, regulatory, and/or market power problems that can result if all of the components of a privatization program are not implemented correctly. First, Kikeri and Nellis (2002) assess the empirical evidence examining privatization in competitive sectors. These authors also provide an appendix summarizing the results of over 100 published and working papers that have examined the effectiveness of privatizing companies that operate in competitive industries. Second, Birdsall and Nellis (2002) assess the distributional impact of privatization in developing countries. As do several other commentators, Birdsall and Nellis try to understand why the public perception of privatization has become so bad in developing countries, when the actual empirical evidence is on balance so favorable, especially regarding improved access to vital utility services in the vast majority of countries. Unfortunately, neither Birdsall and Nellis nor the other commentators can provide a fully satisfactory explanation for privatization's growing unpopularity. The third and fourth survey articles summarize the empirical evidence on privatization's impact in two key regions, Latin America and Africa, and this is why we focus on these surveys in the next two sections. McKenzie and Mookherjee's (2003) survey of the distributive impact of privatization in Latin America provides an excellent summary of the literature dealing with the massive privatization programs executed by this region's governments since 1989, while Nellis (2003) performs a similar survey of African privatization studies. We begin our discussion of individual privatization studies with those examining Latin American countries and companies, and then survey African and South Asian studies. The Latin American studies are summarized in table 4.6.

Studies of Privatization in Latin America

The earliest study in table 4.6, by Ramaurti (1996), is essentially a descriptive analysis of seven privatization programs (four telecom, two airline, and one toll road) in Latin America during the period 1987–1991. He also discusses the economic issues involved in developing these programs, and describes the methods used by privatizing governments to overcome the bureaucratic and ideological opposition to divestiture. Ramamurti concludes that privatization was very positive for the telecom companies, partly due to the scope for making new positive-net present value (NPV) technology and capital investments, but also owing to the attractiveness of the offer terms proffered by the divesting governments. There was much less scope for productivity improvements for the airlines and roads, and little improvement was observed. Ramamurti (1997) also examines the 1990 restructuring and privatization of Ferrocarilla Argentino, the Argentine national freight and passenger railway system. He documents a nearly incredible 370 percent improvement in labor productivity and an equally striking (and not unrelated) 78.7 percent decline in employment, from 92,000 to 18,682 workers.[7] Operating subsidies declined almost to zero, and consumers benefited from expanded and better quality service and lower costs. Ramamurti concludes that these performance improvements could not have been achieved without privatization.

One of the very best empirical privatization studies examining a developing country, by La Porta and López-de-Silanes (1999), performs an in-depth analysis of Mexico's privatization program. Specifically, they test whether the performance of 218 state enterprises privatized through June 1992 improved after divestment.

TABLE 4.6. Summary of Case Study and Country- and Industry-Specific Empirical Studies of Privatization in Latin America

Study	Sample Description, Study Period, and Methodology	Summary of Empirical Findings and Conclusions
Ramamurti (1996)	Surveys studies of four telecom, two airline, and one toll-road privatization programs in Latin America during period 1987–1991. Also discusses political economic issues and methods used to overcome bureaucratic and ideological opposition to divestiture.	Concludes that privatization is very positive for telecoms, partly due to scope for technology, capital investment, and attractiveness of offer terms. Much less scope for productivity improvements for airlines and roads, and little improvement observed.
Ramamurti (1997)	Examines restructuring and privatization of Ferrocarilla Argentinos, the national railroad, in 1990. Tests whether productivity, employment, and need for operating subsidies (equal to 1% of GDP in 1990) change significantly after divestiture.	Documents a 370% improvement in labor productivity and a 78.7% decline in employment (from 92,000 to 19,682). Services were expanded and improved, and delivered at lower cost to consumers. Need for operating subsidies largely eliminated.
La Porta and López-de-Silanes (1999)	Test whether performance of 218 SOEs privatized through June 1992 improves after divestment. Compares performance with industry-matched firms, and splits improvements documented between industry and firm-specific influences.	Output of privatized firms increased 54.3%, while employment declined by half (though wages for remaining workers increased). Firms achieved a 24 percentage point increase in operating profitability, eliminating need for subsidies equal to 12.7% of GDP. Higher product prices explain 5% of improvement; transfers from laid-off workers, 31%, and incentive-related productivity gains account for remaining 64%.
Pombo and Ramirez (2001)	Perform ex post measuring and econometric analysis of 30 large Colombian manufacturing firms and 33 power generation plants privatized during 1993–1998 period. Employ both panel data regression analysis and MNR matched pre vs post-privatization tests.	Panel data analysis finds very positive results for privatized manufacturing firms. Total factor productivity indices increased from 0.27 to 0.50 points, while profit rates increased by 1.2 percentage points. Productive efficiency in power production not systematically related to ownership changes, once other factors accounted for.

| Galiani, Gertler, and Schargrodsky (2001) | Examine the impact of privatizing water services on the mortality of young children in Argentina. Between 1991 and 2000, 30% of Argentina's public water companies covering 60% of the population were privatized. Estimate impact of privatization on child mortality using three different measures. | All three measures showed that child mortality fell 5 to 8 percent in areas that privatized their water services. Increase in access to and quality of water caused the reduction in mortality. Investment increased, service provision became more efficient, and quality improved. The number of people connected to the network increased dramatically, but prices did not. |
| Estache (2002) | Asks whether Argentina's 1990s utilities privatization program was a cure or a disease. Certainly, the privatizations of Argentina's electricity, gas, water and sanitation, and telecommunications utilities are today the object of intense anger within the country, but Estache attempts to determine whether this anger is appropriate. He first notes that privatization occurred just before the country was gripped by a massive political and economic collapse, and he tries to separate the impact of privatization from the overwhelming impact of the collapse. | Privatization, per se, was quite successful: it raised significant revenues for the state and the new private operators increased efficiency and service levels significantly—without significantly raising the rates they charged. The rates charged consumers, however, increased significantly, since the government exploited the new ownership structure to impose indirect taxes that it could not impose through direct levies. Once the economic crisis began, government actions discriminated against the privatized companies and foreign operators were vilified as exploiters when they tried to raise fees in line with inflation and devaluation. |

Using detailed, firm-level data, they compare the performance of the divested companies with industry-matched firms, and find that the former Mexican SOEs rapidly closed a large performance gap with industry-matched private firms that had existed prior to divestment. These firms went from being highly unprofitable before privatization to being very profitable thereafter. Output increased by 54.3 percent, in spite of a reduced level of investment spending, and sales per employee roughly doubled. The privatized firms reduced (blue- and white-collar) employment by half, but those workers who remained were paid significantly more. The authors attribute most of the performance improvement to productivity gains resulting from better incentives, with at most one-third of the improvement being attributable to lower employment costs.

Pombo and Ramirez (2001) study Colombia's privatization program, which was fairly modest by Latin American standards. They perform an ex-post measurement and econometric analysis of 30 large Colombian manufacturing firms and 33 power-generation plants that were privatized during the 1993–1998 period. They employ both panel data regression analysis and the Megginson, Nash, and van Randenborgh [MNR (1994)] matched pre- versus post-privatization tests. The panel data analysis finds very positive results for privatized manufacturing firms, in that total factor productivity indices increased from 0.27 to 0.50 points, while profit rates increased by 1.2 percentage points. On the other hand, they find that productive efficiency in power production is not systematically related to ownership changes, once other factors are accounted for.

In what is likely to prove an extremely influential paper, Galiani, Gertler, and Schargrodsky (GGS; 2001) examine the impact of privatizing water services on the mortality of young children in Argentina. Between 1991 and 2000, 30 percent of Argentina's public water companies covering 60 percent of the population were privatized. GGS estimate the impact of privatization on child mortality using three different measures, and all three measures show that child mortality fell 5 to 8 percent in areas that privatized their water services. The number of people connected to the network increased dramatically, but prices did not, and increased post-privatization access to (and quality of) water caused the reduction in mortality. GGS estimate that approximately 14,300 infants and 55,000 children aged 1–4 years obtained access to water as a result of privatization, which caused a reduction of 414 infant deaths and 110 fewer deaths of young children during the year 2000. The number of employees declined by roughly one-half, but productivity "went through the roof," almost tripling in seven years. Additionally, investment increased, service provision became more efficient, and quality improved.

Estache (2002) asks whether Argentina's 1990s utilities privatization program was a cure or a disease. Certainly, the privatizations of Argentina's electricity, gas, water and sanitation, and telecommunications utilities are today the object of intense anger within the country, but Estache attempts to determine whether this anger is appropriate. He first notes that privatization occurred just before the country was gripped by a massive political and economic collapse, and he tries to separate the impact of privatization from the overwhelming impact of the collapse. He finds that privatization per se was quite successful: it raised significant revenues for the state and the new private operators increased efficiency and service levels significantly—without significantly raising the rates they charged. The rates charged consumers, however, increased significantly, since the government exploited the new ownership structure to impose indirect taxes that it could not impose through direct levies. Once the economic crisis began, government actions discriminated against the privatized companies and foreign operators were vilified as exploiters when they tried to raise fees in line with inflation and devaluation. All in all, Estache concludes that privatization in Argentina was more cure than disease, but the overall experience was a painful one for all involved.

McKenzie and Mookherjee (MM; 2003) present an overview of the results of a project evaluating the distributive impact of privatization in the four Latin American countries of Argentina, Bolivia, Mexico, and Nicaragua. The studies they summarize use existing survey data and try to estimate the effects of privatization on customers, since the lower half of the income distribution level is not likely to become shareholders in the privatization sales. The most significant component of the project focused on privatized utilities and estimates the effect of changes in prices and access on the welfare of families in different expenditure categories. A second component documents the effects on workers, especially the employment changes and possible impact on wage levels and earnings inequality.

MM find strong evidence that privatization leads to significant increases in access to water, telephone, and electricity services in all four countries. Summary results on access changes, presented in table 4.7, show that in general the gains in access are concentrated among lower income groups, since the higher income households typically had access prior to divestiture. Table 4.8 presents similar summary results regarding changes in the price of basic services. Here the interpretation becomes murkier; prices increase in half of the cases examined, but they decrease in the other half. The one clear outlier is the water privatization in Cochabamba, Bolivia, which is generally acknowledged to be a failure—though MM show that even here the actual results are not as disastrous as widely reported. Finally, table 4.9 summarizes the studies' results regarding changes in the quality of service after privatization. As with the access results, the quality of service increases, often dramatically, in every case but one (where quality remains unchanged). Clearly, access to and quality of utility services increased in these four countries after privatization, and in the half of all cases where prices increased the actual burden these increases placed on customers was quite small. These results leave MM in a quandary regarding one of the other tasks they set for themselves—explaining why privatization has become so unpopular in Latin America.

McKenzie and Mookherjee document one potential reason that privatization has acquired a bad name: it unequivocally leads to job losses among SOE employees. In many cases, employment in privatized companies declines by one-half or more, though the available evidence suggests that the majority of displaced workers are reemployed within a year, often in the same industry. Additionally, the aggregate impact of these job cuts is in all cases quite small, since SOEs tend to be among the most capital-intensive firms in most economies. MM find that privatization-related job cuts represent less than 2 percent of the overall workforce in all four countries (much less than this in Bolivia and Colombia), and that the overall employment impact is even more muted once rehiring is accounted for.

TABLE 4.7. Impact of Privatization on Access to Infrastructure in Four Latin American Countries

Country and Sector	Year	Household Expenditure per Capita										Total
		1	2	3	4	5	6	7	8	9	10	
Argentina (urban)												
Water and electricity[a]	1985–86	64.8	81.5	87.8	91.2	93.3	93.9	97.4	96.4	97.8	99.3	90.3
	1996–97	82.5	91.6	94.0	94.5	94.9	94.7	95.9	96.1	96.1	96.9	93.7
Telephone[a]	1985–86	18.4	26.5	33.7	43.6	47.0	49.6	61.4	67.2	75.9	82.3	50.4
	1996–97	22.8	39.6	53.5	57.7	68.5	78.2	82.7	86.7	89.8	92.9	67.2
Bolivia (urban)												
Electricity[b]	1994	89.2	93.3	93.2	94.6	96.6	97.7	98.1	98.0	98.8	99.7	96.0
	1999	98.9	95.0	97.9	96.9	100.0	100.0	100.0	100.0	99.9	100.0	98.8
Telephone[a]	1994	2.9	7.2	8.1	9.4	13.4	22.3	27.4	35.6	48.6	69.7	25.5
	1999	7.9	6.9	13.0	22.9	33.4	35.2	36.7	42.6	58.6	62.0	31.0
Water[c]	1994	64.5	68.1	74.7	73.2	76.4	83.0	85.1	91.1	91.5	95.5	80.6
	1999	89.1	82.5	89.1	89.0	87.8	95.7	98.7	97.7	95.7	97.8	92.1
Mexico (all)												
Telephone[a]	1992	2.0	3.3	5.1	5.7	10.1	14.1	19.9	26.4	39.1	60.8	18.6
	1998	3.9	6.0	9.1	12.6	15.9	21.8	28.4	37.9	54.8	72.8	26.3
Water[c]	1992	22.0	30.5	39.1	44.3	48.8	54.1	63.0	66.0	75.0	87.1	53.0
	1998	27.9	35.8	39.3	44.8	49.4	58.5	64.8	72.1	83.3	89.9	56.6
Nicaragua (all)												
Electricity[d]	1993	11.1	25.2	36.2	53.4	64.4	68.5	78.5	81.7	82.0	78.0	57.9
	1998	11.3	29.5	40.3	58.4	72.0	77.2	88.5	91.4	93.2	84.9	64.7

Source: Table 2 of McKenzie and Mookherjee (2003).

Note: This table shows access to infrastructure in terms of the percent of households with access, by decile. Data from Ennis and Pinto (2002); Barja, McKenzie, and Urquiola (2002); Lopez-Calva and Rosellón (2002); Freije and Rivas (2002)

a Household has access if it reports positive expenditure on the infrastructure item.
b Household has access if the dwelling has electricity.
c Household has access if the water network reaches the building in which the family is living.
d The 1993 figures are obtained from a 1998 survey using a question as to whether the household has installed electricity within the past five years.

TABLE 4.8. Price Changes after Privatization for Utility Services in Four Latin American Countries

Sector	Argentina		Bolivia		Mexico		Nicaragua	
	Before	After	Before	After	Before	After	Before	After
Telephones	100	83.9	100	91.7	100	147.9	n.a.	n.a.
Electricity	100	67.5	100	126.2	n.a.	n.a.	100	124.2
Water	100	84			100	109.2	n.a.	n.a.
La Paz and El Alto			100	89.5				
Cochabamba			100	143				

Source: Table 4 of McKenzie and Mookherjee (2003).

Note: This table shows price changes following privatization. The real price indexes are relative to consumer price index; preprivatization = 100. n.a., not applicable as service was not privatized (or data after privatization is not yet available). Sources for indexes: Argentina: water data from Galiani, Gertler, and Schargrodsky (2002, table 3); electricity prices are residential final prices from FIEL (1999); telephone is based on the communications price index from Instituto Nacional de Estadistica y Censos (INDEC). Bolivia: telephone prices are the minimum fixed tariff from Instituto Nacional de Estadistica (INE); electricity prices are residential tariff rates from Superintendencia de Electricidad de Bolivia; water rates in La Paz and El Alto are the tariff for 10 cubic meters from INE; water rates in Cochabamba are R2 category rates (very poor users) from the Democracy Center. Mexico: water prices are from CONAGUA (Comision Nacional del Agua) and PROFECO (Procuraduria Federal del Consumidor); telephone prices are residential monthly subscription charges from ITU (2001). Nicaragua: electricity prices are from Banco Central de Nicaragua (Central Bank of Nicaragua).

These authors also feel the more basic question is whether privatization promotes job growth in the overall economy, and they find some evidence that this occurs. They also clearly show that privatization leads to higher social spending and lower expenditure on debt service payments by the central government, owing to the positive (and large) fiscal impact of privatization revenues. All in all, MM conclude that privatization must be judged an economic success in Latin America, and it is therefore all the more puzzling why it is popularly perceived as having been a failure.

Studies of Privatization in Africa

John Nellis (2003) presents a survey of studies examining privatization in Africa. He notes that in many (probably most) African countries, the political elites have been opposed to privatization, and have implemented ownership changes only in response to pressure from international financial institutions, particularly the International Monetary Fund (IMF). Additionally, the bulk of the privatizations that have been implemented are concentrated in a handful of countries, with South Africa alone accounting for one-third of the continent's $9 billion in total proceeds since 1990. Nellis concludes that less than 40 percent of Africa's SOEs have been even partially privatized, and very few of the large, economically significant enterprises have been divested at all.

The typical way that "privatization" unfolds is that poor service provision by loss-making SOEs leads first to reforms short of private-sector involvement. These reforms produce no gains, only modest gains, or just unsustainable improvements,

TABLE 4.9. Quality Changes after Privatization for Utility Services in Four Latin American Countries

Country and Sector	Quality Measure	Baseline Value		Post-Privatization Value
		Legal limit of goal		Actual value[a]
Bolivia				
Electricity	Average response time (hours) to users technical complaints	3		2.26
	Average interruption frequency per user	25		4.7
	Index of commercial complaints	12		1.14
Telephone				
Long-distance	Percentage of rural towns connected	25		32.66
	Percentage of national long-distance calls completed	55		69
	Percentage of faults corrected within three days	85		88
Fixed-line	Cotas digitalization (%)	80		96
	Cotel digitalization (%)	5		5
	Cotas incidence of faults (%)	40		8
	Cotel incidence of faults (%)	60		27
		1993		1999
	Waiting list for main lines	50,000		8,000
Mexico		1990	1995	1997
Telephone	Waiting time for new connection (days)	890	72	30
	Faults per 100 lines per year	6.0[b]	4.6	3.3
	Digitalization (%)	38.6[c]	88	90.1
	Number of pending connections	259,875[b]	70,798	91,367
Argentina		1989–1990	1994	1997–1998
Telephone	Digitalization (%)	13	63	100
	Lines in service	3,139,685	4,886,957	6,852,086
	Faults per 100 lines per year	42.4[c]	37.2	17.2
	Average repair waiting time (days)	11	3	n.a.
Water[d]		1992–1993		1994–1999
	Spilled water (millions of m^3/day)	1.49		1.27
	Average delay in attending claims (days)	180		32

Source: Table 5 of D. McKenzie and Mookherjee (2003).

Note: Data from Ennis and Pinto (2002); Barja, Mckenzie, and Urquiola (2002); López-Calva and Rosellón (2002) Data from; ITU (2001).
[a] Electricity results are an average of results reached by five firms: CRE, ELECTROPAZ, ELFEC, and CESSA, in 1999. Telephone results are for 1997.
[b] 1993 data, as 1990 data unavailable.
[c] 1991 data, as 1990 data unavailable.
[d] Argentine water measures are from Galiani, Gertler, and Schargrodsky (2002).

and often lead to a greater financing role for state-owned banks, with all the attendant problems relating to soft budget constraints. As financial losses mount, service quality deteriorates further and fiscal pressures on the government mount to the point that the IMF must be called in. The IMF duly identifies the problem, and insists on reforms that ultimately lead to very grudging privatization. In other words, there have thus far been very few true believers in Africa. In most cases, the divesting governments have insisted on retaining a large stake (typically one-third of the shares) in the firms divested, and have frequently shown hostility toward the multinational companies that are the natural buyers of divested assets. For all these reasons, sales have generally yielded disappointing amounts of revenue to governments, and the results of the studies Nellis surveys are among the least favorable overall toward privatization of any regions'. Five of these studies are discussed below and summarized in table 4.10.

Jones, Jammal, and Gokgur (1998) analyze 81 privatizations in Côte d'Ivoire, covering the electricity sector in infrastructure and other firms operating in competitive or potentially competitive markets in agriculture, agro-industries, and services. They find that (1) firms perform better after privatization; (2) the firms perform better than they would have under continued state ownership; and (3) privatization contributes positively to economic welfare, with annual net welfare benefits equal to about 25 percent of pre-divestiture sales. Andreasson (1998) assesses privatization's impact in Mozambique and Tanzania. In both countries, many SOEs had ceased operations before divestiture, but Andreasson finds that three-fourths of the dormant firms returned to production after privatization. He documents substantial productivity gains after privatization, due partly to workforce reductions, but also due to improved capacity utilization. In most cases, investments, production, sales, and value-added increased sharply post-sale.

Temu and Due (1998) review Tanzania's privatization experience and examine the post-sale performance of 158 SOEs divested through 1999. They begin by documenting the extremely poor physical and financial condition of Tanzanian manufacturing firms before privatization. Temu and Due conclude that, in spite of long and tortuous negotiations required to actually effect most sales (termed "privatization by exhaustion"), privatization increases government revenues, reduces subsidies to SOEs, and forces firms to operate more efficiently. Appiah-Kubi (2001) examines 212 privatizations in Guinea, and reports positive results in terms of reduced pressure on Guinea's balance of payments, increases in both allocative and x-efficiency, stimulation of local capital markets, enhanced inflow of foreign direct investment, widespread quality gains for consumers, and increased employment and remuneration.

Finally, Chirwa (2001) studies the impact of privatization on technical efficiency using data from six privatized Malawian enterprises, three SOEs, and six private companies competing in three oligopolistic industries. Privatization occurs between 1984 and 1991, and Chirwa's panel regression analyses examine data from 1970 to 1997. He finds that privatization increases the technical efficiency of all firms (industry effects) and of privatized firms (firm effects), though he finds that other factors such as capital intensity, multinationality, and structural adjustment programs also promote improved efficiency. These findings suggest that competi-

TABLE 4.10. Summary of Case Study and Country- and Industry-Specific Empirical Studies of Privatization in Africa

Study	Sample Description, Study Period, and Methodology	Summary of Empirical Finding and Conclusions
Jones, Jamma, and Gokgur (1998)	Analyze 81 privatizations in Côte d'Ivoire, covering the electricity sector in infrastructure and other firms operating in competitive or potentially competitive markets in agriculture, agroindustries, and services [described in Nellis (2003)].	Find that (1) firms perform better after privatization; (2) the firms perform better than they would have under continued state ownership; and (3) privatization contributes positively to economic welfare, with annual net welfare benefits equal to about 25% of predivestiture sales.
Andreasson (1998)	Assesses privatization's impact in Mozambique and Tanzania. In both countries many SOEs had ceased operations before divestiture [described in Nellis (2003)].	Find that three-fourths of dormant firms return to production after privatization. Substantial productivity gains also found, due partly to workforce reductions, but also due to improved capacity utilization. In most cases, investments, production, sales, and value-added increase sharply post-sale.
Temu and Due (1998)	Review Tanzania's privatization experience and examine the post-sale performance of 158 SOEs divested through 1999. Begin by documenting the extremely poor physical and financial condition of Tanzanian manufacturing firms before privatization [described in Nellis (2003)].	Conclude that, in spite of long and tortuous negations required to actually effect sale (termed "privatization by exhaustion"), privatization increased government revenues, reduced subsidies to SOEs, and forced firms to operate more efficiently. Second study (2000) found that employment in 16 privatized firms declined by 48%.
Appiah-Kubi (2001)	Examines 212 privatizations in Ghana [reported in Nellis (2003)].	Report positive results in terms of easing pressure on balance of payments, increases in both allocative and X-efficiency, stimulation of local capital markets, enhancing the inflow of FDI, widespread quality gains for consumers, and increased employment and remuneration.
Chirwa (2001)	Studies impact of privatization on technical efficiency using data from six privatized Malawian enterprises, three SOEs, and six private companies competing in three oligopolistic industries. Privatization occurred 1984–1991 and panel regression uses data from 1970 to 1997.	Find that privatization increases technical efficiency of all firms (industry effects) and of privatized firms (firm effects). Find that other factors (capital intensity, multinationality, and structural adjustment programs) also promote efficiency improvement. Suggests competitive environments may be needed to optimize efficiency gains from privatization.

tive environments may be needed to optimize the efficiency gains from privatization.

Studies of Privatization in South Asia and Other Developing Countries

The final region of the developing world we examine is South Asia. Unfortunately, we have no survey paper of the caliber of those discussed above to guide our overview of the empirical literature, so this section will just summarize the results of the relative handful of studies that have focused on this region. These are summarized in table 4.11. It is hoped that an ambitious and competent academic is even now canvassing his or her colleagues for research findings and is busy creating a high quality survey paper. Until then, this summary will have to do.

In one of the earliest published empirical studies on privatization, Bhaskar and Khan (1995) examine the impact of government divestiture on employment in the Bangladeshi jute industry. They exploit a natural experiment involving the privatization of 31 of 62 jute mills after Bangladesh won its independence in 1971. The sale selection process was based solely on ethnicity of ownership at the time the mills were nationalized, not on current financial performance. They find that privatization during the years 1983–1986 had an insignificant effect on output and profitability. Divestment significantly reduced white-collar employment, but had no impact on actual production workers, which suggests that excess employment in public sector is more substantial at the white-collar level than among manual production workers.

Akram (2000) develops a simple model of dysfunctional privatization driven by easy access to state-provided credit and unenforced repayment requirements. He tests this model by examining the debt-default status of 128 Bangladeshi firms privatized through December 1997. He documents that the inability (or unwillingness) of all types of Bangladeshi firms to repay loans is a serious and enduring problem that is not improved by privatization. Of 128 privatized firms, 77 have overdue and outstanding loans to state banks; 33 have outstanding loans that are not yet overdue. Only 18 have neither outstanding nor overdue loans. In a related paper, Akram (1999) describes the practical problems that have bedeviled Bangladesh's privatization program from its earliest days.

Finally, Gupta (forthcoming) examines whether partial privatizations impacted the observed performance of 38 Indian SOEs partially divested between 1990 and 1998. In this excellent study, she employs a panel data set of 2,470 firm years of data for all 341 state-owned Indian enterprises (249 owned by national government, others by states) and the 38 partially privatized firms. She finds that partial privatization has a positive and highly significant impact on firm sales, profits, and labor productivity. Firm effects regressions show that a 10 percentage-point decrease in government ownership increases annual (log) sales and profits by 20 percent and 13 percent, respectively.

Infrastructure Privatization Studies

No privatizations are as controversial or important as those involving basic utility service providers. Telecommunications companies, electric generation and distri-

TABLE 4.11. Summary of Case Study and Country- and Industry-Specific Empirical Studies of Privatization in Asia and Other Developing Countries

Study	Sample Descriptions, Study Period, and Methodology	Summary of Empirical Findings and Conclusions
Bhaskar and Khan (1995)	Examine the impact of privatization on employment in Bangladeshi jute industry by exploiting a natural experiment—privatization of 31 of 62 jute mills, based solely on ethnicity of ownership at the time mills were nationalized, not on current financial performance.	Find that privatization during 1983–1986 has insignificant effect on output and profitability. Significantly reduced white-collar employment, but had no impact on actual production workers. Conclude that excess employment in public sector more substantial at white-collar level than among manual production workers.
Akram (2000)	Develops a simple model of dysfunctional privatization driven by easy access to state-provided credit and unenforced repayment requirements. Tests model by examining debt-default status of 128 Bangladeshi firms privatized through December 1997.	Documents that inability (or unwillingness) of all types of Bangladeshi firms to repay loans is a serious and enduring problem that is not improved by privatization. Of 128 privatized firms, 77 have overdue and outstanding loans to state banks; 33 have outstanding loans that are not yet overdue. Only 18 have neither outstanding nor overdue loans.
Gupta (forthcoming)	Examines whether partial privatizations impact performance for 38 Indian SOEs partially divested between 1990 and 1998. Employs panel data set of 2,470 firm years of data for all 341 state-owned Indian enterprises (249 owned by national government, others by states) and the 38 partially privatized firms.	Finds partial privatization has positive and highly significant impact on firm sales, profits, and labor productivity. Fixed effects regressions show that a 10 percentage point decrease in government ownership increases annual (log) sales and profits by 20% and 13%, respectively. Privatization and competition are not substitutes in their impact on firm performance.
Zhang, Parker, and Kirkpatrick (2002)	Examine effects of privatization, competition, and regulation on the performance of the electricity industry using a panel data set for 51 developing countries. Econometric technique designed to disentangle separate effects of competition, regulatory change, and ownership change.	Finds that competition has the strongest effect in promoting performance improvement. By itself, competition promotes service penetration, capacity expansion, greater labor efficiency, and lower prices for industrial users. Separate effects of privatization and having an independent regulator are insignificant, except that privatization seems to promote higher capacity utilization. Coexistence of these two reforms is correlated with greater electricity availability, more generation capacity, and higher labor productivity. Basic conclusion: privatization and regulation, on their own, do not lead to obvious gains in economic performance, while promoting competition does stimulate performance improvements, irrespective of changes in ownership or regulation

bution companies, oil and gas distribution companies, and water and sewerage utilities have traditionally been state-owned monopolies almost everywhere in the world except the United States. These companies provide basic services that every citizen uses and feels strongly about. Furthermore, these companies tend to be very large and industrially important, and most would have significant market power to set prices in the absence of state ownership or effective regulation. For all these reasons, infrastructure privatizations have been widely studied, and we discuss those studies in the following three sections. We begin by examining studies of telecommunications privatizations, and then evaluate in turn tests of electric utility and water and sewerage company privatizations. These industries are also examined individually, and in greater depth, in chapters 8 (telecoms) and 10 (oil and gas; electric utilities).

Telecommunications Company Privatizations

National telecommunications companies, or "telecoms," have been in state hands since the dawn of the electronics era in most rich countries, with the important exception of the United States, as well as in virtually all the developing nations Therefore, as discussed in Wallsten (2001a) and Noll (2000), telecom privatization represents a truly epochal shift in the balance of state power within every economy where it is attempted. Additionally, citizens have a direct economic stake in the cost and quality of telecom services being provided, so their privatization is always controversial. The financial impact of telecom sales is also immense, since telecom SIPs are almost always the largest share offerings in a nation's history. Furthermore, telecoms usually become the "bellweather" stocks on national exchanges, often accounting for 30 percent or more of total capitalization and an even greater share of total trading volume [Boutchkova and Megginson (2000)]. Additionally, telecom SIPs often involve sizable fractions of the population becoming shareholders for the first time. As examples, almost 4 million French citizens (6 percent of the population) purchased shares in the initial public offering of France Telecom, and by the time Telefonica was fully divested, its shares were owned by more than one in eight Spanish households [Jones, Megginson, Nash, and Netter (1999)]. Finally, it has become painfully obvious to policy makers that an efficient communications sector is vital to a well-functioning modern economy, and that constructing such a system requires capital investment spending on a scale that few governments can either achieve or effectively manage [Röller and Waverman (2001)]. For all these reasons, telecom privatizations are always perceived as high-stakes gambles, and selling governments typically approach divestment with great anxiety.

No less than 16 empirical studies examine the telecommunications industry, which has been transformed by the twin forces of technological change and deregulation (including privatization) since 1984. This was the year that the AT&T monopoly was broken up in the United States and the Thatcher government began privatizing British Telecom. Nine of these studies employ samples created by the individual researchers, usually based on data provided by the International Telecommunications Union (ITU), and most of these studies were begun before 2000. These "early" studies are summarized in table 4.12. The other seven studies em-

TABLE 4.12. Summary of Early Empirical Studies of Telecommunications Company Privatizations

Study	Sample Description, Study Period, and Methodology	Summary of Empirical Findings and Conclusions
Parker (1994)	Examines changes in structure and management, as well as performance changes, of British Telecom during first decade after 1984 privatization. Also describes history of state ownership of BT, plus its subsequent privatization and the regulatory environment developed for private BT. Notes that government promotes competition through new entry, with some success, and describes RPI-X pricing scheme imposed on BT.	Documents significantly increased output, profitability, efficiency, labor productivity, and in the absolute levels of R&D and capital spending—though these decline as a percentage of sales. Prices for BT's basket of services fall by 5.1% per year from 1984 to 1993, but residential phone service prices increase by 2.7% per year. Growth rate in labor productivity accelerates after privatization, and labor costs fall from 42.4% of output before to 33.6% after divestiture.
Boles de Boer and Evans (1996)	Estimate the impact of the 1987 deregulation, and 1990 privatization, of Telecom New Zealand on the price and quality of telephone services. Also examine whether investors benefit.	Document significant declines in price of phone services, due mostly to productivity growth that cut costs at a 5.6% annual rate, and significant improvement in service levels. Shareholders also benefit significantly.
Petrazzini and Clark (1996)	Using International Telecommunications Union (ITU) data through 1994, test whether deregulation and privatization impact the level and growth in teledensity (main lines per 100 people), prices, service quality, and employment by telecoms in 26 developing countries.	Deregulation and privatization both are associated with significant improvements in level and growth in teledensity, but have no consistent impact on service quality. Deregulation associated with lower prices and increased employment; privatization has the opposite effect.
Ros (1999)	Uses ITU data and panel data regression methodology to examine the effects of privatization and competition on network expansion and efficiency in 110 countries over the period 1986–1995.	Finds that countries with at least 50% private ownership of main telecom firm have significantly higher teledensity levels and growth rates. Both privatization and competition increase efficiency, but only privatization is positively associated with network expansion.
Wallsten (2001a)	Performs an econometric analysis of the effects of telecommunications reforms in developing countries. Using a panel data set of 30 African and Latin American countries from 1984 to 1997, explores the effects of privatization, competition, and regulation on telecommunications performance.	Competition is significantly associated with increases in per capita access and decreases in cost. Privatization alone is not helpful, unless coupled with effective, independent regulation. Increasing competitions the single best reform, competition with privatization is best combination of policies, but privatizing a monopoly without regulatory reforms should be avoided.

Boylaud and Nicoletti (2000)	Use factor analysis and a database on market structure and regulation to investigate the effects of liberalization and privatization on productivity, prices, and quality of long-distance and cellular telephony services in 23 OECD countries over the period 1991–1997.	Prospective and actual competition both bring about productivity and quality improvements—and lower prices—in telecom services, but no clear effect found for privatization.
Gutierrez and Berg (2000)	Examine determinants of the number of lines per capita in 19 Latin American countries over the period 1985–1995 using economic, institutional, and regulatory variables—including measures of democracy, economic freedom, and openness to trade. During this period, eight sample countries established regulatory commissions, and 14 out of 24 Latin and Caribbean countries privatized their telecoms between 1984 and 1997 (before Brazil in 1998), raising an estimated $27 billion.	Find that the regulatory framework (the presence and effectiveness of regulation) and freedom variables have a significant positive impact or the penetration rate. The number of cellular phones per capita also significantly positively related to fixed-line penetration, though not certain whether this means cellular and fixed lines are complements or that a competition effect explains the interrelationship.
Cabanda and Ariff (2002)	Examine efficiency growth around privatization for four Asia Pacific countries—Japan, Philippines, Malaysia, and Australia—over an extended time period (up to 12 years) after privatization. Use data envelope analysis (DEA) to measure performance changes.	Document that firms achieve productivity gains ranging from 3% to over 50%, and three of the four countries' telcos see significant increases in total factor productivity. Profitability increases in two of four countries, as does capital spending.
Bortolotti, D'Souza, Fantini, and Megginson (2002)	Examine the financial and operating performance of 31 national telecommunications companies fully or partially divested via public share offering over the period November 1981 to November 1998. Also perform univariate comparisons of the pre-versus postprivatization performance levels of these firms using the MNR univariate testing procedure. They then run panel data estimations to explain performance over time in terms of ownership changes and structural changes due to regulatory reforms occurring during the study period.	Find that profitability, output, operating efficiency, and capital investment spending increase significantly after privatization, while employment and leverage decline significantly. Panel data show that competition significantly reduces profitability, employment, and, surprisingly, efficiency after privatization while creation of an independent regulatory agency significantly increases output. Mandating third-party access to an incumbent's network is associated with a significant decrease in the incumbent's investment and an increase in employment. Retained government ownership is associated with a significant increase in leverage and a significant decrease in employment, while price regulation significantly increases profitability.

Note: This table summarizes the sample selection criteria, methodologies, and empirical findings of several academic studies of privatizations of telecommunications companies that do not use the Stanford University/World Bank database.

ploy the newly completed Stanford University/World Bank Telecommunications Database [described in McNary (2001) and Fink, Matto, and Rathindran (2002)] that couples telecommunications data provided by the ITU with economic, regulatory, and institutional data collected by Stanford and the Bank. These studies are presented in table 4.13.

Perhaps surprisingly, the early empirical studies tell somewhat conflicting stories, probably due in part to differences in the nations covered and methodology employed. Petrazini and Clark (1996), Ros (1999), and Wallsten (2001a) examine developing countries, either exclusively or as separate subsamples, while Ros (1999) and Boylaud and Nicoletti (2000) provide similar coverage of OECD countries. Parker (1994) and Boles de Boer and Evans (1996) study the deregulation and privatization experiences of British Telecom and Telecom New Zealand, respectively.

Though Ros, Wallsten, and Boylaud and Nicoletti all use some variant of panel data methodology, they arrive at slightly different conclusions regarding the relative importance of deregulation/liberalization and privatization in promoting expanded teledensity (number of main lines per 100 population) and operating efficiency of national telecom companies, and the quality and pricing of telecom services. On balance, these studies generally indicate that deregulation and liberalization of telecom services are associated with significant growth in teledensity and operating efficiency, and significant improvements in the quality and price of telecom services. The impact of privatization, per se, is somewhat less clear-cut, but most studies agree that the combination of privatization and deregulation/liberalization is associated with significant telecommunications improvements. This is certainly the result predicted by Noll (2000) in his analysis of the political economy of telecom reform in developing countries.[8]

Gutierrez and Berg (2000) examine the determinants of the number of lines per capita in 19 Latin American countries over the 1985–1995 period using economic, institutional, and regulatory variables — including measures of democracy, economic freedom, and openness to trade. In order to characterize regulatory developments, the authors construct a dichotomous index describing both the enforcement powers of the new regulatory body and its neutrality and independence from political control. They document that eight sample countries established regulatory commissions between 1985 and 1995. Additionally, 14 of the 24 Latin American and Caribbean countries privatized their telecoms between 1984 and 1997 (before Brazil's divestment of Telebras in 1998), raising an estimated $27 billion. Gutierrez and Berg find that the regulatory framework, measured by the presence and effectiveness of regulation, and freedom variables have a significant positive impact on the penetration rate. The number of cellular phones per capita is also significantly positively related to fixed-line penetration, though the authors cannot determine whether this means cellular and fixed lines are complements or that a competition effect explains the interrelationship.

The study by Cabanda and Ariff (2002) is somewhat outside the stream of research described above, but it does examine efficiency growth around privatization for four Asia Pacific countries — Japan, Philippines, Malaysia, and Australia — over an extended time period (up to 12 years) after privatization. The authors

TABLE 4.13. Summary of Empirical Studies of Telecommunications Company Privatizations that Use the Stanford University/World Bank Database

Study	Sample Description, Study Period, and Methodology	Summary of Empirical Finding and Conclusions
Kubota (2000)	Examines the impact of market conditions and policies on telecom-sector performance for 135 countries in 1998 (cross-sectional analysis).	Finds that privatization tends to improve the performance of the incumbent operator, but that an independent regulator and the degree of market competition have mixed or weak effects.
Wallsten (2001b)	Examines the effect of including exclusivity periods (EPs) in 32 telecom privatization sales executed by 28 developing countries between 1987 and 1998. Looks first at the impact of EPs on the sale price received by the government and then on the post-privatization investment levels of the telecom companies.	Other things equal, finds that granting an EP more than doubles the price a buyer will pay for a telco, and that extending the EP for additional years also significantly raises the sale price. The offsetting effect is that EPs are significantly negatively correlated with telecom investment after the sale. EPs also reduce the number of cellular phone subscribers, dampen the growth in the number of payphones provided, and are negatively correlated with international phone traffic after the sale.
McNary (2001)	Compares the relative success of privatization and competition in improving the telecom penetration rates in over 200 countries between 1987 and 1998. Uses pooled time series regression methods, and controls for both sector characteristics and macroeconomic influences. Also adjusts for endogeneity between historic firm performance and the decision to reform.	Finds that local fixed-line and cellular phone competition have significantly positive effects on performance, but that privatization has a significant negative relationship with penetration rates. Concludes the reason for this negative effect is that governments are using privatization primarily as a means to raise revenue rather than to promote economic efficiency.
Li and Xu (2002)	Examine the political economy of privatization and liberalization in the telecoms sector using data for 45 countries from 1990 to 1998. Specifically evaluate whether the degree of democracy and the political power of different interest groups influences the timing, scale, and method of liberalization chosen.	Find that countries with stronger pro-reform interest groups—especially urban consumers and the financial services sector—are more likely to reform in more democratic countries. Less democratic countries are more likely to maintain the public-sector monopoly when the government benefits from ownership, as when the fiscal deficit is high. Democracy affects the pace of reform by magnifying the voices of interest groups in open societies and by moderating politicians' discretion in less democratic countries.

(continued)

TABLE 4.13. (continued)

Study	Sample Description, Study Period, and Methodology	Summary of Empirical Finding and Conclusions
Wallsten (2002)	Using a panel data set with 2,533 observations from 197 countries over the period 1985–1999, examines whether the sequencing of regulation and privatization impacts the effectiveness of reforms and/or the price that investors are willing to pay for the company.	Finds that, as separate reforms, privatization and establishing an independent regulator both have ambiguous effects on telecom performance, but that combining privatization and regulation yields robust, significantly positive results. Establishing an independent regulator before privatization is best policy combination, since this enhances most measures of sector performance and post-sale investment levels. Having a guaranteed monopoly is valuable to investors, and increases the price they will pay, but so does having a regulator in place prior to sale. Investors appear willing to pay a higher price for a firm privatized into an environment with less institutional uncertainty.
Fink, Matto, and Rathindran (2002)	Assess the effectiveness of telecom reforms in developing countries using data for 86 such countries over the 1985–1999 period. Ask three specific questions: (1) What impact do specific policy changes have on sectoral performance? (2) How is the effectiveness of one policy change impacted by the implementation of the others? (3) Does the sequencing of reforms affect performance?	Find that both privatization and competition significantly improve sector performance, but that a comprehensive reform program involving both of these policies and an independent regulator produces the largest gains—an 8% higher level of mainline penetration and a 21% higher level of productivity compared to years of partial or no reform. The sequencing of reforms also matters, with the best performance resulting if competition is introduced before or simultaneously with privatization, rather than after. Also find that autonomous factors, especially the evolution of technology, strongly and positively impact performance.
Li and Xu (2003)	Examine the impact of privatization and competition on telecom-sector performance using a panel data set of privatizations from 166 countries between 1981 and 1998 and information on competition from 43 countries between 1990 and 1998. Evaluates the impact of these reforms on output growth, propensity to shed labor, network expansion, TFP, and improvements in labor productivity. Also examine impact of the method of privatization (SIP versus asset sale) and of granting exclusivity periods.	Find that privatization significantly positively impacts output growth, network expansion, TFP, and labor productivity and is associated with higher labor shedding. Privatizing via a SIP promotes the development of the mobile phone market. Competition leads to higher employment, higher output, faster network expansion, and higher productivity. Granting EPs reduces, but does not negate, gains from other reforms. Also find that competition and privatization are complements, in that competition increases the gains from privatization, and vice versa. Estimate that half of the output growth between 1990 and 1998 is attributable to these two reforms, after controlling for input growth.

Note: This table summarizes the sample selection criteria, methodologies, and empirical findings of several academic studies of privatizations of telecommunications companies that employ the Stanford University/World Bank database.

146

use data envelope analysis (DEA) to measure performance changes, and document that firms achieved productivity gains ranging from 3 percent to over 50 percent, and three of the four countries' telecommunications companies saw significant increases in total factor productivity. Profitability increased significantly in two of four countries (Australia and Malaysia), as did capital spending (in Malaysia and the Philippines).

Bortolotti, D'Souza, Fantini, and Megginson (BDFM; 2002) examine the financial and operating performance of 31 national telecommunications companies fully or partially divested via public share offering over the period November 1981 to November 1998. They first build a data set using balance sheet data for a seven-year period around the privatization dates including various measures for profitability, output, efficiency, employment, capital expenditure, and leverage. This data set also incorporates national measures of telecom service levels, such as number of lines in service. BDFM perform univariate comparisons of the pre- versus post-privatization performance levels of these firms using the Megginson, Nash, and van Randenborgh (1994) univariate testing procedure. They then run panel data estimations to explain performance over time in terms of ownership changes and structural changes due to regulatory reforms occurring during the study period. The authors employ controls such as GDP per capita in their regression estimations to make cross-country comparisons possible.

Using conventional pre- versus post-privatization comparisons, BDFM find that profitability, output, operating efficiency, and capital investment spending increase significantly after privatization, while employment and leverage decline significantly. These comparisons, however, do not account for separate regulatory and ownership effects, and almost all telecoms are subjected to material new regulatory regimes around the time they are privatized. BDFM examine these separate regulatory and ownership effects using both random and fixed-effect panel data estimation techniques for a seven-year period around privatization. They verify that privatization is significantly positively related to higher profitability, output, and efficiency, but significantly negatively related to leverage. However, they also find numerous separable effects for regulatory, competition, retained government, and foreign listing variables. Competition significantly reduces profitability, employment, and, surprisingly, efficiency after privatization while creation of an independent regulatory agency significantly increases output. Mandating third-party access to an incumbent's network is associated with a significant decrease in the incumbent's investment and an increase in employment. Retained government ownership is associated with a significant increase in leverage and a significant decrease in employment, while price regulation significantly increases profitability. Major efficiency gains result from better incentives and productivity, rather than from wholesale firing of employees, and profitability increases are caused by significant reductions in costs, rather than price increases.

On balance, BDFM conclude that the financial and operating performance of telecommunications companies improves significantly after privatization, but that a significant fraction of the observed improvement results from regulatory changes — alone or in combination with ownership changes — rather than from privatization alone.

All of the studies detailed above employ databases created by the researchers themselves, and thus suffer both from relatively small samples sizes and lack of comparability. Recently, however, several studies have employed the new Stanford University/World Bank Telecommunications Database [described in McNary (2001) and Fink, Matto and Rathindran (2002)] that couples telecommunications data provided by the ITU with economic, regulatory, and institutional data collected by Stanford and the Bank. The studies described in this section all employ the Stanford/World Bank database and use advanced econometric estimation techniques, and thus should be considered the state of the art in research into telecom privatization and regulation.

The first such study, by Kubota (2000), examines the impact of market conditions and policies on telecom-sector performance for 135 countries during the single year 1998. It is thus unusual in being a cross-sectional rather than time-series analysis. Kubota shows that privatization tends to improve the performance of the incumbent operator, but that an independent regulator and the degree of market competition have mixed or weak effects. Wallsten (2001b) examines the effect of including exclusivity periods (EPs) in 32 telecom privatization sales executed by 28 developing countries between 1987 and 1998. He examines the impact of EPs first on the sale price received by the government and then on the post-privatization investment levels of the telecom companies. Other things equal, he finds that granting an EP more than doubles the price a buyer will pay for a telco, and that extending the EP for additional years also significantly raises the sale price. The offsetting effect is that EPs are significantly negatively correlated with telecom investment after the sale. EPs also reduce the number of cellular phone subscribers, dampen the growth in the number of payphones provided, and are negatively correlated with international phone traffic after the sale.

McNary (2001) compares the relative success of privatization and competition in improving the telecom penetration rates in over 200 countries between 1987 and 1998. He uses pooled time-series regression methods, and controls for both sector characteristics and macroeconomic influences. He also adjusts for endogeneity between historic firm performance and the decision to reform. McNary's results are unique among this group of studies in that he finds that local fixed-line and cellular phone competition have significantly positive effects on performance, but that privatization has a significant negative relationship with penetration rates. He concludes that the reason for this negative effect is that governments are using privatization primarily as a means to raise revenue rather than to promote economic efficiency.

Li and Xu (2002) examine the political economy of privatization and liberalization in the telecoms sector using data for 45 countries from 1990 to 1998. They specifically evaluate whether the degree of democracy and the political power of different interest groups influences the timing, scale, and method of liberalization chosen. They find that countries with stronger pro-reform interest groups—especially urban consumers and the financial services sector—are more likely to reform in more democratic countries. Less democratic countries are more likely to maintain the public-sector monopoly when the government benefits from ownership, such as when the fiscal deficit is high. Li and Xu conclude that democracy affects the pace of reform by magnifying the voices of interest groups in open societies and by moderating politicians' discretion in less democratic countries.

Wallsten (2002) uses a panel data set with 2,533 observations from 197 countries over the period 1985–1999 to examine whether the sequencing of regulation and privatization impacts the effectiveness of reforms and/or the price that investors are willing to pay for the company. He finds that, as separate reforms, privatization and establishing an independent regulator both have ambiguous effects on telecom performance, but that combining privatization and regulation yields robust, significantly positive results. Establishing an independent regulator before privatization is the best policy combination, since this enhances most measures of sector performance and post-sale investment levels. Having a guaranteed monopoly is valuable to investors and increases the price they will pay, but so does having a regulator in place prior to sale. Wallsten concludes that investors appear willing to pay a higher price for a firm privatized into an environment with less institutional uncertainty.

Fink, Matto and Rathindran (2002) assess the effectiveness of telecom reforms in developing countries using data for 86 such countries over the period 1985–1999. They ask three specific questions: (1) What impact do specific policy changes have on sectoral performance? (2) How is the effectiveness of one policy change impacted by implementation of the others? (3) Does the sequencing of reforms affect performance? The authors find that both privatization and competition significantly improve sector performance, but that a comprehensive reform program involving both of these policies and an independent regulator produces the largest gains—an 8 percent higher level of mainline penetration and a 21 percent higher level of productivity compared to years of partial or no reform. The sequencing of reforms also matters, with the best performance resulting if competition is introduced before or simultaneously with privatization, rather than after. Fink, Matto, and Rathindran also find that autonomous factors, especially the evolution of technology, strongly and positively impact performance.

Li and Xu (2003) examine the impact of privatization and competition on telecom sector performance using a panel data set of privatizations from 166 countries between 1981 and 1998 and information on competition from 43 countries between 1990 and 1998. They evaluate the impact of these reforms on output growth, propensity to shed labor, network expansion, total factor productivity, and improvements in labor productivity. They also examine the impact of the method of privatization (SIP versus asset sale) and of granting exclusivity periods. Li and Xu find that privatization has a significantly positive impact on output growth, network expansion, TFP, and labor productivity and is also associated with more labor shedding. Privatizing via a SIP promotes the development of the mobile phone market. Competition leads to higher employment, higher output, faster network expansion, and higher productivity. Granting EPs reduces, but does not negate, the gains from other reforms. The authors also find that competition and privatization are complements, in that competition increases the gains from privatization, and vice versa. They estimate that half of the output growth between 1990 and 1998 is attributable to these two reforms, after controlling for input growth.

Taken as a whole, the results of these studies offer clear lessons for academics and policy makers alike. Privatization, competition, and establishing an independent regulator all seem to improve telecom performance if adopted in isolation, though there are often painful trade-offs from single reforms (i.e., privatization may promote efficiency, but reduce employment). On the other hand, all of these studies clearly show that adopting a package of reforms—including competition, independent regulation, and privatization—yields economically and statistically significant improvements in telecom performance. Furthermore, those studies that examine the influence of democracy and transparency on the political economy of telecom privatization find that openness improves the process of privatization and increases the amount of improvement achieved by the reform program.

Electric Utility Privatizations

We have already examined several of the electricity privatization studies in earlier sections, and will only recount the key results of these analyses here, before turning to the one important study we have not yet discussed. Table 4.14 summarizes the studies discussed here and in the next section. Newberry and Pollitt (1997) perform a counter-factual analysis of the 1990 restructuring and privatization of the United Kingdom's CEGB, and document significant post-privatization performance improvements. However, they find that the producers and their shareholders capture all of the financial rewards of this improvement and more, whereas the government and consumers lose out. Pombo and Ramirez (2001) study 33 Colombian power generation plants privatized during the period 1993–1998. They find that productive efficiency in power production is not systematically related to ownership changes, once other factors are accounted for.

The one new electric utility study we discuss is by Zhang, Parker and Kirkpatrick (2002). These authors examine the effects of privatization, competition, and regulation on the performance of the electricity service industry using a panel data set for 51 developing countries. Their econometric techniques are designed to disentangle the separate effects of competition, regulatory change, and ownership change. They find that competition has the strongest effect in promoting performance improvement. By itself, competition promotes service penetration, capacity expansion, greater labor efficiency, and lower prices for industrial users. The separate effects of privatization and having an independent regulator are insignificant, except that privatization seems to promote higher capacity utilization. The coexistence of these two reforms (privatization and an independent regulator) is correlated with greater electricity availability, more generation capacity, and higher labor productivity. Their basic conclusion is that privatization and regulation, on their own, do not lead to obvious gains in economic performance, while promoting competition does stimulate performance improvements, irrespective of changes in ownership or regulation.

TABLE 4.14. Summary of Empirical Studies of Privatizations in Infrastructure Industries Other Than Telecommunications

Study	Sample Description, Study Period, and Methodology	Summary of Empirical Findings and Conclusions
Newbery and Pollitt (1997)	Perform a cost-benefit analysis of the 1990 restructuring and privatization of the Central Electricity Generating Board (CEGB). Compare the actual performance of the privatized firms to a counter-factual assuming CEGB remains state owned.	The restructuring/privatization of CEGB is "worth it," in that there is a permanent cost reduction of 5 percent per year. Producers and shareholders capture all this benefit and more. Consumers and the government lose. Also show that alternative fuel purchases involve unnecessarily high costs and wealth flows out of the country.
Zhang, Parker, and Kirkpatrick (2002)	Examine effects of privatization, competition, and regulation on the performance of the electricity industry using a panel data set for 51 developing countries. Econometric technique designed to disentangle separate effects of competition, regulatory change, and ownership change.	Find that competition has the strongest effect in promoting performance improvement. By itself, competition promotes service penetration, capacity expansion, greater labor efficiency, and lower prices for industrial users. Separate effects of privatization and having an independent regulator are insignificant, except that privatization seems to promote higher capacity utilization. Coexistence of these two reforms is correlated with greater electricity availability, more generation capacity, and higher labor productivity. Basic conclusion: privatization and regulation, on their own, do not lead to obvious gains in economic performance, while promoting competition does stimulate performance improvements, irrespective of changes in ownership or regulation.
Saal and Parker (2001)	Examine the productivity and price performance of the privatized water and sewerage companies of England and Wales after the industry is privatized and a new regulatory regime imposed in 1989. Examine joint impact of privatization and new economic regulatory environment on performance.	Find no significant evidence that productivity growth, measured by growth in TFP, is improved by privatization—despite reductions in labor usage. Also find that increased output prices have outstripped increased input prices, leading to significantly higher economic profits after privatization.
Galiani, Gertler, and Schargrodsky (2001)	Examine the impact of privatizing water services on the mortality of young children in Argentina. Between 1991 and 2000, 30% of Argentina's public water companies covering 60% of the population were privatized. Estimate impact of privatization on child morality using three different measures.	All three measures show that child mortality falls 5 to 8 percent in areas that privatize their water services. Increased access to and quality of water cause the reduction in mortality. Investment increases, service provision becomes more efficient, and quality improves. The number of people connected to the network increases dramatically, but prices do not.

151

Water and Sewerage Privatizations

All of the studies of water and sewerage privatizations have been discussed earlier in this chapter, so we provide only a brief recap here. Saal and Parker (2003) examine the productivity and price performance of the privatized water and sewerage companies of England and Wales after the industry was privatized and a new regulatory regime imposed in 1989. They document that labor productivity improved significantly after privatization, but find no evidence that total factor productivity grew as a direct result of the ownership change. They also find that increases in output prices have outstripped increased input prices, leading to significantly higher economic profits after privatization. Nellis (2003) also cites studies of African water privatizations that were generally perceived as unsuccessful.

On the other hand, the evidence on water privatizations in Latin America has been much more positive. With the exception of a failed water privatization in Cochabamba, Bolivia, all of the other national experiences described in McKenzie and Mookherjee (2003) showed striking increases in access to water services (usually achieved without large price increases) and Galiani, Gertler, and Schargrodsky (2002) show that Argentina's water privatizations not only increased efficiency and output but also significantly reduced child mortality by increasing access to clean water. Perhaps the best conclusion that can be drawn from all the studies examining the privatization of infrastructure companies is that ownership change tends to promote performance improvements, but that other reforms—especially promoting competition where possible and adopting an effective regulatory regime—are necessary to ensure that efficiency gains are achieved and that these gains are shared with consumers.

Summary

The 87 studies from nontransition economies discussed in this chapter offer at least limited support for the proposition that privatization is associated with improvements in the operating and financial performance of divested firms. Most of these studies offer strong support for this proposition, and only a handful document outright performance declines after privatization. Almost all studies that examine post-privatization changes in output, efficiency, profitability, capital investment spending, and leverage document significant increases in the first four measures and significant declines in leverage.

The studies examined here are far less unanimous regarding the impact of privatization on employment levels in privatized firms. All governments fear that privatization will cause former SOEs to shed workers, and the key question in virtually every case is whether the divested firm's sales will increase enough after privatization to offset the dramatically higher levels of per-worker productivity. Three studies document significant increases in employment [Galal, Jones, Tandon, and Vogelsang (1992); Megginson, Nash, and van Randenborgh (1994); and Boubakri and Cosset (1998)], but most of the remaining studies document significant—sometimes massive—employment declines. These conflicting results could be due to differences in methodology, sample size and make-up, or omitted factors.

However, it is more likely that the studies reflect real differences in post-privatization employment changes between countries and between industries. In other words, there is no "standard" outcome regarding employment changes.

Perhaps the safest conclusion we can assert is that privatization does not automatically mean employment reductions in divested firms, though this will likely occur unless sales can increase fast enough after divestiture to offset very large productivity gains. Since the empirical studies discussed in this chapter generally document performance improvements after privatization, a natural follow-up question is to ask why performance improves. For utilities, the need to introduce competition and an effective regulatory regime emerges as key, but there is no "silver bullet" answer for what makes privatization successful for firms in competitive industries. As we will discuss in the next chapter, a key determinant of performance improvement in transition economies is bringing in new managers after privatization. No study explicitly documents systematic evidence of this occurring in nontransition economies, but Wolfram (1998) and Cragg and Dyck (1999a,b) show that the compensation and pay-performance sensitivity of managers of privatized U.K. firms increases significantly after divestment. Studies that explicitly address the sources of post-privatization performance improvement using data from multiple nontransition economies tend to find stronger efficiency gains for firms in developing countries, in regulated industries, in firms that restructure operations after privatization, and in countries providing greater amounts of shareholder protection.

In the next chapter, we turn to an examination of research findings about privatization's impact in transition economies. Privatization is both more difficult and more all encompassing in these countries than it is in either industrialized or nontransition developing countries. This is because privatization is only part of the massive changes in transition economies as these countries move from communism to more market-oriented methods of allocating resources and organizing production.

Empirical Evidence on Privatization in Transition Economies

In the middle years of the twenty-first century's first decade, it is hard to remember how fundamentally different the world was prior to the collapse of communism in Europe and North Asia a mere 15 years ago. As noted by Fischer (2001), at its peak, nearly half the world lived in economies describing themselves as centrally planned, and the economic and political system of communism was implacably hostile to private ownership and to allowing market forces to allocate economic resources and rewards. The production-oriented communist system was based on strict orders from a central authority, executed through state-owned firms operating in monopolist industries, and funded by credits from state-controlled banks. Outside of a few, narrowly proscribed areas, private ownership was illegal and consumer demand was ignored. Furthermore, the entire system was militarized, in the sense that the production and resource allocation decisions of an integrated economic union (COMECON) were made principally to support a military alliance (the Warsaw Pact) covering one-sixth of the world's land mass.

The economic system that emerged under communism was so wealth destroying and wasteful that it could be maintained only by pervasive repression. Since rational economic incentives were suppressed whenever these conflicted with Marxist ideology, or the political dominance of the Communist party, people could be induced to comply with the system's demands only through coercion. By the late 1980s, it was obvious that the economic system of communism had failed abjectly, and that only increasingly repressive measures would suffice to maintain the communist political and military system. At critical moments in one country after another, the breaking point was reached when civilized European leaders — even communist ones — simply stopped being willing to kill their own citizens to support a failed ideology. Though communism had been economically bankrupt for many years before the Berlin Wall fell in November 1989, the political collapse this event represented signaled that the people of central and eastern Europe were at last free to rejoin the West, and that the heterogeneous peoples of the former Soviet Union were free to begin a new history. Then what?

   This chapter examines how the 26 countries that emerged from the former Soviet bloc adapted to the new era of political freedom and market economics that emerged after 1989. Given the profound and all-encompassing nature of the changes required to move from a totalitarian political system and a command economy to a democratic society with a market economy, the countries involved in this process have generally been called "transition economies" to reflect that they are involved in a massive evolutionary process. China is typically, if awkwardly, included among transition economies, since it is clearly moving away from a command toward a market economy, and we cover its transition experience at the end of this chapter.

   The first section of this chapter provides an overview of the basic political and economic steps that the various transition countries have taken during the past dozen years, and provides an assessment of their overall effectiveness. The second section looks more specifically at those empirical studies that use multinational samples to examine the effectiveness of privatization in promoting firm-level restructuring and national economic growth. The next two sections survey country-specific privatization studies for, respectively, the nations of central and eastern Europe (CEE) and for the 13 Republics, countries that emerged as sovereign countries after the 1991 break-up of the Soviet Union. Finally, we examine the privatization experience of the "outlier" transition economy: China. This is the one country that has made a truly successful economic evolution away from communism as an economic organizing principle, even though it has retained a communist political system—albeit one far less repressive than in the past.

Overview: The Economic Performance of Transition Economies Since 1989

The collapse of communism in the former Soviet bloc was certainly a liberating event for the people of the countries involved, and one that offered great long-term benefits, but it also promised to be extremely traumatic in the short term. As expected, adopting democratic political institutions and principles proved relatively easy (and popular), but everyone involved understood that dismantling a highly integrated economic system that had been organized along ideological, rather than economic, lines would be extremely disruptive. Every aspect of economic life would have to change, beginning with such basics as the adoption of new currencies, the elimination of guaranteed employment, and the elimination of price controls on virtually all products and services. National central and commercial banking systems needed to be created from the existing mono-bank command and control systems that historically had allocated credit based on a central plan and without regard to project risk and return. Production, sourcing, and distribution arrangements created within the COMECON framework would have to be abrogated and replaced by new relationships resulting from arms-length contracting between consenting parties. Consumers would gain the freedom to purchase goods and services produced anywhere in the world, but would in turn have to earn the wherewithal to pay for these goods and services by competing with workers both in their own countries and those in societies that had been capitalist for many years. Finally, all of these changes would have to be implemented within democratic systems and without using the coercive tools of the former regime.

The challenge of designing effective transition policies was made all the more difficult by the lack of a theory to guide the practical process of transition. Havrylyshyn (2001) points out that in the early 1990s there were theories of capitalism and theories of socialism, but no theories explaining how to move from socialism to capitalism. Kornai (1993) highlights two changes that are needed during transition: forcing a move from a sellers' market to a buyers' market through price liberalization, and enforcing a hard budget constraint through privatization and the elimination of various support mechanisms. These changes provide the two principal incentives for profit maximizing market behavior by all economic agents. Blanchard (1997) defines the core processes of actual transition similarly as comprising two elements: reallocating resources from old to new activities and restructuring within surviving companies. It now seems clear that policy makers had a good understanding of what needed to be done during the initial phases of transition, but they were far less certain about how best to proceed.

It is not that policy makers lacked for advice or ideology. Many of the early leaders of transition states were committed to as rapid a transition as possible, almost regardless of social and economic cost, and the governing ideology of the day supported this objective. This was the set of policies that quickly became known as the "Washington Consensus" because it was strongly supported both by the American government (and most U.S. academics) and by the multilateral institutions headquartered in Washington, especially the World Bank and IMF. As described in Svejnar (2002), the Washington Consensus stressed (1) the need for complete price liberalization, (2) opening the economy up to both free trade and free capital flows, (3) macroeconomic stabilization, (4) the rapid dismantling of communist economic institutions, and (5) complete privatization as rapidly as possible. Though virtually all observers believed these reforms were desirable, there was far less consensus regarding whether the reforms should be implemented in stages or all at once. These two competing approaches quickly became known as the "Big Bang" and "gradualist" strategies, with the former being promoted by those who favored rapid and complete changes and the latter by those who favored a slower pace of change out of concern for the social costs involved. This debate has flared repeatedly over the past 15 years, and we now turn to a more complete discussion of the costs and benefits of each strategy.

The Choice Between Big Bang and Incremental Reforms

Perhaps the key decision all governments faced at the start of the transition process was how rapidly to pursue the goals of economic and political transformation. While there was near universal agreement regarding the ultimate goals of reform — to create democratic, capitalist societies on the western European model — there was little consensus as to the best method and pace of adopting the reforms needed to achieve these goals. Most supporters of the Washington Consensus believed that delaying reforms, or adopting partial reforms, simply provided an opening for reactionary elements to exploit in order to stall or reverse the transition process. These observers felt that the only way to make political and economic changes irreversible was to implement them completely and all at once. Though the transition would obviously be costly, it was best to take this "shock therapy" approach and allow the economy and society to adapt and recover as rapidly as possible.

The followers of the Big Bang approach were clearly in the ascendancy early in the transition process, and there is both anecdotal and empirical support for their position. In particular, Berg, Borensztein, Sahay, and Zettelmeyer (1999) find that the countries that adopted shock therapy did in fact begin to recover lost economic output much sooner than did countries which opted for a delayed and drawn-out reform agenda. Additionally, many reformers felt that the period of "extraordinary politics" that followed the collapse of communist power in most countries offered a window for making major changes that might well close very quickly. The fear of a reaction from conservative or nationalist parties was especially prevalent in Russia, and this fear largely explains why reformers adopted rather dubious methods of implementing reforms, especially privatization. Nellis (1999) and others also conclude that rapid transition was necessary, based on an analysis of the political weakness of many transition governments—again, especially Russia and the former Soviet republics. All too often, reform delayed became reform denied.

On the other hand, the supporters of the gradualist approach also make a strong case that their approach could have yielded better long-run results, and at far lower social cost than shock therapy. The foremost proponent of the gradualist, or "evolutionary institutionalist," approach is Gerard Roland, and this section draws heavily on his writings. Roland (2002) points out that reformers seeking to engineer major societal changes face two types of political constraints. First, *ex ante constraints* are feasibility constraints that can block decision making and prevent reforms from being adopted. The second set of *ex post constraints* are related to backlash and policy reversal after policies have been implemented and outcomes observed. The political economy of reform can be viewed as an issue of how to get reforms enacted in the first place, which involves relaxing the ex ante political constraints, and then how to have the reforms stay in place, which means relaxing the ex post political constraints. Roland feels the best way to create irreversibility of reforms is usually to design reform packages that are properly sequenced and that employ compensating transfers so as to create broad public support.

One of the principal fears expressed almost universally at the beginning of transition was that adopting a gradual restructuring process—and in particular, delaying full privatization would prompt incumbent SOE managers to begin systematically stripping assets from the companies they controlled. This was assumed to be rational behavior for managers, since they held extremely uncertain property rights and had no guarantee that pursuing value-maximizing strategies would redound to their personal benefit after a change in company ownership. Events in many countries justified these fears. Inadequate legal protections in the Czech Republic led to widespread "tunneling" by managers, where corporate wealth was dishonestly, though quite legally, transferred from state-owned and privatized enterprises to newly created private companies through non-arms-length selling strategies and other extractive techniques. These strategies are described in Johnson, La Porta, López-de-Silanes, and Shleifer (2000). Insider privatization also led to massive asset stripping in Russia and many of the republics, as described by Black, Kraakman, and Tarassova (2000).

On the other hand, experience showed that asset stripping is not an inevitable result of a gradualist approach, assuming that other steps—particularly macroeconomic stabilization and some legal reforms—are adopted quickly. Roland and Sekkat (2000) present a theoretical model explaining how career concerns may induce managers of SOEs to restructure their firms once the transition process is launched and a managerial labor market begins to emerge. Under socialism, SOE managers cannot be induced to pursue value-maximizing restructuring policies because of the "ratchet effect" that inevitably results from government's monopsony position as an employer of managers. If a manager does in fact improve his or her firm's performance, the government overseer will simply ratchet up the manager's quota for the next period. Once an open market for managerial talent emerges during the transition process, however, reputational considerations do impart to SOE managers the proper incentive to restructure their firms—and to refrain from asset stripping. Even partial privatization gives the best SOE managers an outside employment opportunity, and thus an inducement to restructure.

Roland (2001) buttresses his case for gradualism by noting that several of the results of Big Bang reform policies were unpleasant surprises. In particular, he notes that the following outcomes were not predicted by the proponents of shock therapy who designed and implemented most of the early reform packages: (1) the huge output fall that typically accompanied price liberalization; (2) the continuous economic decline in Russia and other countries of the former Soviet Union (FSU), and the divergence between the performance of CEE and FSU countries; (3) the extent of insider privatization; (4) the fact that restructuring occurred in many SOEs despite fears of widespread asset stripping before privatization; (5) the extent of the development of the Mafia in many transition economies, especially Russia; (6) the breakup of several countries [the U.S.S.R., Yugoslavia, Czechoslovakia] and the rise of secessionist tendencies in many others; and (7) the huge success of Chinese economic reforms. A disinterested reader may well conclude that many of these surprises were unavoidable, and it is far from certain that a gradualist approach would not have yielded a different, but equally unpleasant set of surprises. However, no one can argue with Roland's assertion that output and employment took an enormous hit in all transition economies (except China) in the years immediately after the Berlin Wall fell, as we now document.

The Collapse and Subsequent Recovery of Output and Employment

Svejnar (2002) presents the best overall assessment of how (and why) output declined so precipitously in transition economies after 1989, and we draw heavily on his work in this section. Figure 5.1, which we reproduce directly from his

Real GDP Percentage Change Index (1989 = Base)

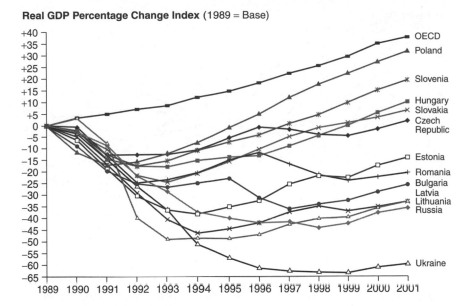

FIGURE 5.1. The evolution of aggregate output in twelve central and eastern European transition economies after 1989. Source: William Davidson Institute data as depicted in Figure 1 of Svejnar (2002).

study, shows the evolution in output for 12 CEE transition economies between 1989 and 2001. Figure 5.2 similarly describes the course of employment in these countries over the same period. As can be seen, all these transition economies experienced very large output declines, ranging from 13 to 25 percent in most CEE countries to over 40 percent for the Baltic states to approximately 45 percent for Russia and even more for the former Soviet republics. Within three years, recovery began in the CEE countries, and this accelerated as the 1990s wore on. By 2000, the CEE countries were growing at 4 to 5 percent per year—not Asian Tiger speed, but certainly faster than most developed and developing economies.

While the collapse in output immediately after transition began proved temporary in many CEE countries, the downturn was much deeper and longer lasting in many other countries, particularly Russia and most of the republics. Although the reason for this divergence in output growth between CEE and FSU has not been fully explained empirically, several studies conclude that the countries that were unwilling or unable to make necessary structural reforms fared the worst [Berg, Borensztein, Sahay, and Zettelmeyer (1999); Havrylyshyn (2001); Zinnes, Eilat, and Sachs (2001); Svejnar (2002)]. This certainly corresponds to the stylized facts that the FSU countries were strikingly unsuccessful at implementing any significant reforms, other than "privatizing" some state assets through nontransparent auctions. Furthermore, Roland (2001), Fischer (2001), and Svejnar (2002) all emphasize that countries that launched mass (voucher) privatization programs without adequate legal protections for investors experienced the most negative results.

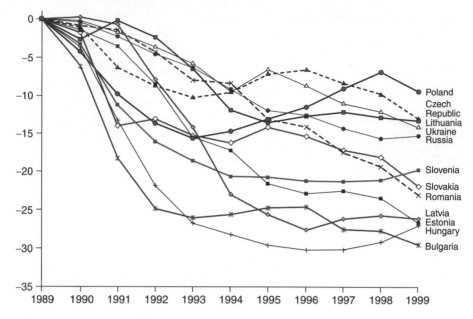

FIGURE 5.2. The evolution of employment in twelve central and eastern European transition economies after 1989. Source: William Davidson Institute data as depicted in Figure 3 of Svejnar (2002).

Accompanying the steep decline in output in all transition economies (except China) was an even sharper drop in employment. Under communism, the joke for workers had always been that "we pretend to work and the state pretends to pay us." Nonetheless, formal unemployment was essentially unheard of. This changed immediately after reforms were adopted and the drop in employment was sharpest in those countries that embraced Big Bang reforms most ardently—though these were also the countries where employment rebounded the soonest and most vigorously. Svejnar (2002) concludes that SOEs rapidly cut employment and real wages and that restructuring led inevitably to an initial decline in labor productivity, as output fell faster than employment. By the mid-1990s, unemployment had reached double digits in all the transition economies of the former Soviet bloc except the Czech Republic, where an efficient labor market reallocated workers to rapidly growing new enterprises relatively quickly. These new enterprises, in fact, have been the source of virtually all of the new jobs created in transition economies since reforms began [Havrylyshyn and McGettigan (1999)].

By the late 1990s, unemployment had stabilized in all but a few countries, though the cumulative loss of jobs had reached 20 percent or more in Slovakia, Romania, Latvia, Estonia, Hungary, and Bulgaria. Employment fell less dramatically in Russia and the republics only because enterprises there were slower to lay off workers. By any standard, a 15 to 30 percent decline in employment within a short period of time would be considered catastrophic, and this was even harder to bear in societies that had not experienced the employment vicissitudes of a market economy for several decades. Furthermore, Svejnar (2002) documents that inequality, as measured by the Gini Coefficient, also increased dramatically during transition (albeit from a low initial level), and reached its highest point in Russia and Ukraine.

The Paramount Importance of Structural Reform in Promoting Economic Growth

As noted above, all of the former Soviet bloc countries faced a pressing need to make major structural reforms in many areas of economic and political life in order to transition to market economies. Several observers have categorized the types of reforms that needed to be adopted; we rely in this section primarily on the classifications offered by Svejnar (2002) and Zinnes, Eilat, and Sachs (2001). Svejnar discusses Type I and Type II reforms.

Type I reforms involve macroeconomic stabilization, price liberalization, the dismantling of communist economic institutions, and the adoption of restrictive monetary and fiscal policies and initial devaluation of a currency, followed by adoption of a fixed exchange rate. Additional steps included eliminating subsidies and promoting restructuring of state ministries and SOEs. Most countries adopted at least some of the Type I reforms, and these proved relatively successful and sustainable in the CEE countries—but much less so in the FSU.

Type II reforms involve the development of laws, regulations, and institutions critical to a market economy, the privatization of large SOEs, establishing a commercial legal system and institutions, banking reform (breaking up and restructuring the mono-bank system), labor market deregulation, and other microeconomic issues. Zinnes, Eilat, and Sachs (2001) present a similar list of structural reforms that they call OBCA, after the firm's objective function (O), its budget constraint (BC), and the principal-agent problems (A) the firm faces. These focus on the need to promote effective corporate governance and prudential regulation, hardening of the budget constraints of SOEs, and promoting effective managerial oversight.

The transition economies faced a pressing need to restructure both at the societal and firm levels. At the national level, this generally implied the need to pass new laws and, more critically, to develop effective institutions and enforcement mechanisms to enforce these laws. It also required governments to reform the nation's financial sector so that SOEs truly faced hard budget constraints. Imposing a hard budget constraint proved to be the single most difficult reform for almost all the transition economies, and it was one that few countries met in the early years. The reason is simple: imposing a hard budget constraint required demanding repayment of credits extended to delinquent firms, and cutting off additional credit to companies that could not compete in the new environment. Since every incentive under socialism had been toward inefficient and excessive use of labor in production processes, the shift to product and capital market competition left almost all SOEs woefully overstaffed, undercapitalized, and utterly bereft of the skills (product design, consumer research, marketing, and distribution) needed to compete with either Western firms or newly created domestic companies. Therefore, imposing a hard budget constraint meant that large swathes of the state-owned sector would be cut off from ongoing financing and would have to cease operations.

For this reason, "restructuring" came to be seen as a code word for massive labor-force reductions and company closures, and many transition economies tried to soften the blow by retaining state influence (or control) over banks. This enabled the new governments to ensure an ongoing flow of credit to the weakest state-owned and privatized companies. The net result of this ongoing state interference in bank credit policies was, however, invariably disastrous. Despite repeated "one-time" recapitalizations of state-controlled banks, by the end of the 1990s, many of the largest banks in the CEE countries had failed—and then were sold to Western banks. Furthermore, since state-owned operating companies had never been forced to effectively restructure, many ended the decade even weaker than at the start of the transition process. Restructuring was also severely hampered by the lack of established bankruptcy courts and procedures for forcing debtor firms to repay their debts or be liquidated.

Numerous empirical studies have employed multinational samples to examine the determinants of national economic performance during the first decade of transition. These studies are discussed in detail below, but we make one key point here. Though these studies differ significantly in many ways, all reach the same conclusion regarding the key driver of success: those countries that most success-fully implement major structural reforms achieve the highest economic growth rates, whereas countries that fail to implement structural reforms continue to fall further and further behind the leading transition economies. The survey articles of Djankov and Murrell (2002), Roland (2001), and Fischer (2001) reach the same conclusion. Unfortunately, the major reforms that yield the largest long-term payoff are also the ones that are the most difficult to achieve and that involve the highest short-term social cost.

An Overall Assessment: Was Reform Worthwhile?

Fifteen years have now passed since the Berlin Wall fell, and even the most de-linquent governments began the transition process over a dozen years ago. So what is the overall assessment of transition in the CEE and FSU countries? Given the pain and dislocation that have resulted from the massive reform processes of the past dozen years, it is logical to ask: What has been achieved and was it worth it? Several commentators have offered their assessments. Fischer (2001) concludes that reform is most advanced in the privatization of small-scale enterprises, the elimination of price controls, and the liberalization of foreign trade and exchange. Less has been achieved in the regulation and supervision of financial sectors, enterprise restructuring, and reform of governance in the public and private sec-tors. Havrylyshyn (2001) notes that the least resolved debate, about the timing and sequencing of institutional reforms, is arguably the most important. His survey of empirical studies concludes that (1) stabilization is a necessary condition for recovery; (2) there is a strong and positive relationship between economic performance and liberalization and adopting structural reforms; (3) initial conditions do seem to matter, but the specific impact is unclear; (4) institutions matter, and their importance grows over time; and (5) traditional factor inputs (investment) do not seem to matter.

Svejnar (2002) provides both an economic and a quality-of-life assessment of the transition experience. At the economic level, he concludes that the performance of former Soviet bloc economies has been disappointing, and the farther east one looks, the worse the performance. The CEE countries performed better for a variety of reasons, including the physical proximity and historical ties to western Europe and because these countries were in a transition "tournament" with each other to attract Western investment and trading relationships. He also concludes that large-scale privatization can be handled in various ways, or even delayed, as long as SOEs face the discipline of needing to earn their own way—and as long as new firms can appear through new creation, the breakup of existing firms, and foreign investment.

Svejnar's noneconomic assessments of the transition experience are perhaps even more interesting than his economic assessments. He examines life expectancy, fertility rates, marriage and divorce rates, and other measures of standard of living and he concludes that quality of life improved moderately in the CEE countries and slightly in the Baltic states. Quality of life remained the same in the (nonwar) Balkans and declined in the FSU. Fertility rates plummeted throughout the region—falling to barely 1.1 births per woman in the Baltic states—while divorce and marriage rates moved closer to western European standards (fewer marriages and more frequent divorces). Surveys of the attitudes of citizens in transition economies suggest that a majority think the political changes were worthwhile, but most also think that the economic and social losses during transition outweighed the gains.

Rather than ask whether transition was "worth the pain," it might be wiser to ask a corollary question instead: Could the beneficial reforms have been adopted and executed more effectively and less painfully? Roland (1994, 2001, 2002) would certainly answer affirmatively, by asserting that a gradualist approach would have yielded superior results at lower cost. Commentators such as Black, Kraakman, and Tarassova (2000) and Stiglitz (1999) would now agree with Roland. Others, such as Nellis (1999) and Shleifer (1997, 1998), would argue that there was no real alternative to shock therapy coupled with a rapid move toward privatization, given the fractured nature of the political process in post-communist states and the inevitability of a painful transition no matter how it was sequenced. Though sympathetic to both camps, I personally am not convinced that there was any real alternative to a rapid and painful transition. Given the awful state of most SOEs after the collapse of communism, and the massive social, political, and economic changes required for these countries to become viable capitalist democracies, it is very hard to honestly envision a transition process that could have been equally successful but less painful.

Privatization's Impact on Economic Performance in Transition Economies

Anyone surveying the privatization literature is immediately struck by the huge number of empirical and survey articles that examine in some way the impact of privatization on economic performance in transition economies. As examples, Djankov and Murrell (2002) cite over 100 academic studies in their survey paper on transition economics, and we cite over 70 articles even in this, much more narrowly focused chapter. In one sense, this is quite strange. After all, the 26 countries of the former Soviet bloc represent a fairly small, and shrinking, share of global GDP—perhaps 10 percent at most—and the experience of the transition economies is seemingly so unique as to offer little in the way of general economic insight. On the other hand, the academic fascination with transition economies is less surprising once one accounts for the massive experiment that transition represents, and the fact that policy makers in many nations are seeking guidance to develop workable policies that yield transformational results at an acceptable short-term cost.

In any case, we are faced with the challenge of efficiently synthesizing several dozen directly relevant empirical studies that in some way examine privatization in the transition countries. Djankov and Murrell (2002) cite 37 studies examining privatization's impact in transition economies, and several new studies have been generated since their survey was published. The task of synthesizing privatization studies is complicated by the fact that while all the studies we survey examine privatization in some way, many do so only as one aspect of the reform agenda, while others make privatization the principal empirical focus of analysis.

Furthermore, the transition countries employed varying methods of privatizing SOEs, including asset sales (Hungary and East Germany), voucher privatizations (the Czech Republic and early Polish divestitures), "spontaneous privatizations" (Slovenia), share offerings (later Polish sales), or a combination of techniques. Studies also cover differing event periods during the 1990s, employ differing empirical methodologies, and ask somewhat different questions—though all directly or indirectly ask how privatization impacts firm-level operating performance. Additionally, all of these studies must contend with the fact that output typically fell dramatically in every central and eastern European country during the period immediately after the collapse of socialism in 1989–1991 though, as noted earlier, output generally snapped back smartly in the CEE.

Many very good empirical studies use samples drawn from multiple countries, while other studies focus more specifically on a single country. Since there is no obviously superior organizing principle, we adopt the following strategy. In the first section below, we survey nine studies that employ multinational samples of privatized, state-owned, and newly created enterprises to determine the overall effectiveness of private ownership in promoting superior economic performance. Subsequent sections examine a broader group of studies to determine the specific impacts of ownership structure and competition on the performance of firms in transition economies. The fourth section then surveys a large group of country-specific empirical studies, beginning with the countries of central and eastern Europe and the former Soviet Union.

As has been our policy in discussing empirical evidence throughout this book, we first present basic details about each of the key empirical studies, and then summarize (and evaluate) the primary results of all the studies at the section's end. Furthermore, we present the studies in the chronological order they were written, both because this is how the literature itself developed and because it allows the reader to trace the evolution of intellectual thought over time and to see how practical experience helped guide the work of researchers. Transition economics is very much a work in progress, and the questions that researchers ask — and the tools they have available to address these questions — will be much different in 2004 than in 1994. Though this methodical approach is defensible, general (non-academic) readers may find it excessively tedious, and so are invited to skip directly to the summaries at the end of each section.

Multinational Empirical Studies of Privatization

We begin by presenting the key details of nine multinational empirical studies. These are summarized in table 5.1. As can be seen, the coverage ranges from three studies that focus exclusively on the transition experience in the Czech Republic, Hungary, and Poland to three studies employing data from 24 or more transition economies. We begin with the three Czech-Hungarian-Polish studies and then progress to the studies encompassing all the transition economies.

THE CZECH REPUBLIC, HUNGARY, AND POLAND

Frydman, Gray, Hessel, and Rapaczynski (1999) compare the performance of privatized and state-owned firms in the "Big Three" transition economies of central Europe, and ask the question, "When does privatization work?" They examine the influence of ownership structure on performance using a sample of 90 state-owned and 128 privatized Czech, Hungarian, and Polish companies and employ panel data regression methods to isolate ownership effects. They find that privatization "works," but only when the firm is controlled by outside owners (other than managers or employees). Privatization adds over 18 percentage points to the annual growth rate of a firm sold to a domestic financial company, and 12 percentage points when sold to a foreign buyer. Privatization to an outside owner also adds about nine percentage points to productivity growth. Further, the gains from privatization do not come at the expense of higher unemployment, since insider-controlled firms are much less likely to restructure, but outsider-controlled firms grow faster. Their study shows the importance of entrepreneurship in reviving sales growth.

Frydman, Gray, Hessel, and Rapaczynski (2000) examine whether the imposition of hard budget constraints is alone sufficient to improve corporate performance. Employing a sample of 216 Czech, Hungarian, and Polish firms, split among state-owned (31 percent), privatized (43 percent), and private (26 percent)

TABLE 5.1. Summary of Multinational Empirical Studies of Privatization in the Transition Economies of Central and Eastern Europe

Study	Sample Description, Study Period, and Methodology	Summary of Empirical Findings and Conclusions
Pohl, Anderson, Claessens, and Djankov (1997)	Compare the extent of restructuring achieved by over 6,300 private and state-owned firms in seven eastern European countries during 1992–1995. Use 6 measures to examine which restructuring strategies improve performance the most.	Privatization dramatically increases restructuring likelihood and success. Firm privatized for 4 years will increase productivity 3–5 times more than a similar SOE. Little difference in performance based on method of privatization, but ownership and financing effects impact restructuring.
Frydman, Gray, Hessel, and Rapaczynski (1999)	Compare the performance of privatized and state-owned firms in the transition economies of central Europe, and asks the question "When does privatization work?" Examine influence of ownership structure on performance using a sample of 90 state-owned and 128 privatized companies in the Czech Republic, Hungary, and Poland. Employ panel data regression methods to isolate ownership effects.	Privatization "works," but only when firm is controlled by outside owners (other than managers or employees). Privatization adds over 18 percentage points to the annual growth rate of a firm sold to a domestic financial company, and 12 percentage points when sold to a foreign buyer. Privatization to an outside owner also adds about 9 percentage points to productivity growth. Further, gain does not come at the expense of higher unemployment; insider-controlled firms are much less likely to restructure, but outsider-controlled firms grow faster. Show the importance of entrepreneurship in reviving sales growth.
Berg, Borensztein, Sahay, and Zettelmeyer (1999)	Using macroeconomic data from 26 transition countries for 1990–1996, examine relative roles of macroeconomic variables, structural policies, and initial conditions in explaining the large observed differences in output performance after transition began.	Results point to the preeminence of structural reforms over both initial conditions and macroeconomic variables in explaining cross-country differences in performance and the timing of recovery from the sharp recession that hit every transition economy in the early 1990s.
Frydman, Gray, Hessel, and Rapaczynski (2000)	Examine whether the imposition of hard budget constraints alone are sufficient to improve corporate performance in the Czech Republic, Hungary, and Poland. Employ a sample of 216 firms, split between state-owned (31%), privatized (43%), and private (26%) firms.	Find privatization alone adds nearly 10 percentage points to the revenue growth of a firm sold to outside owners. Most important, find that the threat of hard budget constraints for poorly performing SOEs falters, since governments are unwilling to allow these firms to fail. The brunt of SOEs' lower creditworthiness falls on state creditors.

166

Frydman, Hessel, and Rapaczynski (2000)	Examine whether privatized central European firms controlled by outside investors are more entrepreneurial—in terms of ability to increase revenues—than firms controlled by insiders or the state. Study employs survey data from a sample of 506 manufacturing firms in the Czech Republic, Hungary, and Poland.	Document that all state and privatized firms engage in similar types of restructuring, but that product restructuring by firms owned by outside investors is significantly more effective, in terms of revenue generation, than by firms with other types of ownership. Conclude that the more entrepreneurial behavior of outsider-owned firms is due to incentive effects, rather than human capital effects, of privatization—specifically greater readiness to take risks.
Zinnes, Eilat, and Sachs (2001)	Employ a unique panel data set of macroeconomic, ownership structure, and indicator variables measuring the depth and breadth of reform and privatization for 24 transition countries to determine whether "change of ownership" (privatization) alone is enough to promote improved economic performance over the period 1990–1998, or whether "deep privatization" involving improved corporate governance, enhanced prudential regulation, and hardening of budget constraints is also required. Develop an OBCA indicator variable for each country measuring the breadth and depth of reforms, and include this variable in regressions. Use four measures of economy-wide macroeconomic performance as dependent variables.	Regardless of performance measure employed, find that economic performance gains come only from deep privatization—meaning that change-of-title reforms yield economic gains only after key institutional and agency-related reforms have exceeded certain threshold levels. By themselves, change-of-title reforms never have a significant impact on performance, but the higher the OBCA level a country has, the more positive is the impact of an increase in change of title on economic performance. While ownership matters, institutions matter just as much.
Carlin, Fries, Schaffer, and Seabright (2001)	Use data from a 1999 survey of 3,305 firms in 25 transition countries to examine the factors that promote restructuring by firms and enhance subsequent performance—as measured by growth in sales and in sales per employee over a 3-year period. Survey includes about 125 companies from each of the 25 countries, with larger samples from Poland and Ukraine (200+ firms) and Russia (500+ firms). Just over one-half were newly established firms, 8% were privatized to insiders, 22% privatized to outsiders, and 16% remained state owned.	Find that competition has an important and nonmonotonic effect on the growth of sales and labor productivity, with performance improving more for firms facing 1–3 competitors than for monopolists (one-fourth of SOEs face no competition for their main products in their domestic markets) or firms facing many competitors. Controlling for other factors, find no significant relationship between privatization and performance. Newly created firms generally outperform all other categories. Old firms (privatized and SOEs) are much more likely to cut employment than new entrants, but authors find some evidence that private firms (new entrants and privatized) are more likely to engage in new product development. Overall, find competition to be a more powerful influence on performance than ownership, per se.

(continued) |

TABLE 5.1. (continued)

Study	Sample Description, Study Period, and Methodology	Summary of Empirical Findings and Conclusions
Angelucci, Estrin, Konings, and Zolkiewski (2001)	Analyze the effect of ownership and competition on firm performance, measured by total factor productivity (TFP), in three transition economies for years 1994–1998. Use reported company accounts data for 1994 and 1998 for 17,570 Polish, and for 1997–1998 for 1,500 Bulgarian and 2,047 Romanian companies. Test whether private foreign-owned firms outperform private domestic companies, and whether these both outperform SOEs.	Find that (1) competitive pressure (measured by market structure) is associated with higher productivity in all three countries; (2) increased import penetration is positively associated with performance in Poland, but negatively in Bulgaria and Romania; (3) competitive pressure has stronger effects in private firms and privatization is associated with higher performance in more competitive sectors; (4) privatization is associated with better firm performance and privatized firms outperform SOEs in all three countries. Overall, find there are complementarities between competitive pressure and ownership.
Claessens and Djankov (2002)	Examine changes in the performance of 6,354 privatized and state-owned firms in seven transition economies over the 1991–1995 period, and test whether privatization improves performance (as measured by increased sales and labor productivity). Sample includes all manufacturing firms that are registered as state owned in 1991 and have more than 25 employees. Have full balance sheet and income statements for 1992–1995, and construct panel data showing evolution of ownership over period.	Find that privatization is associated with significantly increased sales and productivity growth and, to a lesser extent, with fewer job losses. In six of seven countries, privatized firms show higher sales growth or smaller declines in sales than SOEs, and privatized firms reduce their sales forces by an average 6.11% versus 7.42% for SOEs (significant difference). Positive effect of privatization is stronger in economic magnitude and statistical significance as the time elapsed since privatization increases.

firms, they find privatization alone adds nearly 10 percentage points to the revenue growth of a firm sold to outside owners. Most important, they find that the threat of hard budget constraints for poorly performing SOEs falters, since governments are unwilling to allow these firms to fail and thus channel additional credit to the SOEs from state-controlled banks. The brunt of SOEs' lower creditworthiness thus falls on state creditors—and ultimately the country's taxpayers.

Frydman, Hessel, and Rapaczynski (2000) examine whether privatized Czech, Hungarian, and Polish firms controlled by outside investors are more entrepreneurial, in terms of their ability to increase revenues, than firms controlled by insiders or the state. Their study employs survey data from a sample of 506 manufacturing firms, and they document that all state-owned and privatized firms engage in similar types of restructuring, but that product restructuring by firms owned by outside investors is significantly more effective, in terms of revenue generation, than by firms with other types of ownership. They conclude that the more entrepreneurial behavior of outsider-owned firms is due to incentive effects, rather than human capital effects, of privatization—specifically, the greater readiness of outsiders to take risks.

OTHER CEE COUNTRIES

Pohl, Anderson, Claessens, and Djankov (1997) compare the extent of restructuring achieved by over 6,300 private and state-owned firms in seven eastern European countries during the period 1992–1995. They use six measures to examine which restructuring strategies improve performance the most. They find that privatization dramatically increases the likelihood and success of firm-level restructuring. On average, a firm privatized for four years will increase productivity 3–5 times more than a similar SOE. The authors find little difference in performance based on the method of privatization, but ownership and financing effects do significantly impact restructuring.

Angelucci, Estrin, Konings, and Zolkiewski (2001) analyze the effect of ownership and competition on firm performance, measured by TFP, in three transition economies for the years 1994–1998. They use reported company accounts data for 1994 and 1998 for 17,570 Polish firms, and for 1997–1998 data for 1,500 Bulgarian and 2,047 Romanian enterprises to test whether private foreign-owned firms outperform private domestic companies, and whether these both outperform SOEs. They find that (1) competitive pressure (measured by market structure) is associated with higher productivity in all three countries; (2) increased import penetration is positively associated with performance in Poland, but negatively so in Bulgaria and Romania; (3) competitive pressure has stronger effects in private firms and privatization is associated with higher performance in more competitive sectors; (4) privatization is associated with better firm performance and privatized firms outperform SOEs in all three countries. Overall, they find there are complementarities between competitive pressure and ownership.

Claessens and Djankov (2002) examine changes in the performance of 6,354 privatized and state-owned firms in seven transition economies over the period 1991–1995, and test whether privatization improves performance (as measured by increased sales and labor productivity). Their sample includes all manufacturing firms that are registered as state-owned in 1991 and have more than 25 employees. They obtain full balance sheet and income statements for 1992–1995, and construct a panel data set showing the evolution of ownership over this period. They find that privatization is associated with significantly increased sales and productivity growth and, to a lesser extent, with fewer job losses. In six of seven countries, privatized firms show higher sales growth or smaller declines in sales than SOEs, and privatized firms reduce their sales forces by an average 6.11 percent, which is significantly lower than the 7.42 percent decline in employment for SOEs. The positive effect of privatization is stronger in economic magnitude and statistical significance as elapsed time since privatization increases.

ALL TRANSITION COUNTRIES

Berg, Borensztein, Sahay, and Zettelmeyer (1999) use macroeconomic data from 26 transition countries for 1990–1996 to examine the relative roles of macroeconomic variables, structural policies, and initial conditions in explaining the large observed differences in output after transition began. They specifically test whether countries that adopt Big Bang reforms early experience both sharper initial output declines and much quicker recoveries than do countries that delay radical reforms. Their results point to the preeminence of structural reforms over both initial conditions and macroeconomic variables in explaining cross-country differences in performance and the timing of recovery from the sharp recession that hit every transition economy in the early 1990s.

Zinnes, Eilat, and Sachs (2001) seek to determine whether "change of ownership" (privatization) alone is enough to promote improved economic performance in transition economies or whether "deep privatization" involving improved corporate governance, enhanced prudential regulation, and hardening of budget constraints are also required. They employ a unique panel data set of macroeconomic, ownership structure, and indicator variables measuring the depth and breadth of reform and privatization for 24 transition countries over the period 1990–1998, and develop an OBCA indicator variable for each country measuring the breadth and depth of reforms. They include this indictor variable in their regressions, and also use four measures of economy-wide macroeconomic performance as dependent variables. Regardless of the performance measure employed, they find that economic performance gains come only from deep privatization— meaning that change-of-title reforms yield economic gains only after key institutional and agency-related reforms have exceeded certain threshold levels. In isolation, change-of-title reforms never have a significant impact on performance, but the higher the OBCA level a country has, the more positive is the impact of an increase in degree of title change (privatization) on economic performance. While ownership matters, institutions matter at least as much.

Carlin, Fries, Schaffer, and Seabright (2001) use data from a 1999 survey of 3,305 firms in 25 transition countries to examine the factors that promote restructuring by firms and enhance subsequent performance, as measured by growth in sales and in sales per employee over a three-year period. Their survey includes about 125 companies from each of the 25 countries, with larger samples from Poland and Ukraine (200+ firms) and Russia (500+ firms). Just over one-half were newly established firms, 8 percent were privatized to insiders, 22 percent were privatized to outsiders, and 16 percent remained state-owned. They find that competition has an important and nonmonotonic effect on the growth of sales and labor productivity, with performance improving more for firms facing one to three competitors than for monopolists (one-fourth of SOEs faced no competition for their main products in their domestic markets) or firms facing many competitors. Controlling for other factors, they find no significant relationship between privatization and performance. Furthermore, newly created firms generally outperform all other categories. Old firms (privatized and SOEs) are much more likely to cut employment than new entrants, but private firms (new entrants and privatized) seem more likely to engage in new product development. Overall, they find competition to be a more powerful influence on performance than ownership, per se.

Privatization and Ownership Structure: Are All Owners Equally Beneficial?

In nontransition economies, the empirical evidence with respect to the identity of a privatized firm's new owners is unambiguous. Private ownership is better than continued state ownership, concentrated private ownership is better than diffuse ownership, and foreign ownership is generally better than domestic ownership. Further, there are relatively few cases in OECD or developing countries where employees ended up owning a sizable stake in privatized firms, so the importance of insider privatization hasn't been great. However, in transition economies, the identity of a firm's new owners is far more important and the impact of different post-privatization ownership structures on subsequent firm performance is much greater than in nontransition economies. Many studies examine the importance of ownership structure in explaining firm performance in transition economies. Rather than work through each study, we rely on Djankov and Murrell's (2002; hereafter DM) excellent survey of this literature and present their summary results below as our table 5.2.

The results in table 5.2 allow us to draw several conclusions. First, private ownership is unambiguously positively related to a firm's growth in sales (or output) growth in CEE countries, but is negatively associated with output growth in Russia. Second, private ownership is associated with significant (often dramatic) growth in productivity in both CEE and FSU countries, though the studies summarized show widely diverging point estimates of productivity growth. Third, there does not appear to be a uniform relationship between private ownership the overall level of productivity in the transition economies—or even between different studies of the same country. DM themselves (page 748) draw two conclusions from the data summarized in our table 5.2. The first is that privatization has economically significant positive effects, but second, that these effects are far from uniform.

TABLE 5.2. Gains or Losses Due to Ownership Change: A Sampling of Estimates

Output or Sales Growth		Productivity Growth		Levels of Productivity	
% Private Minus % State	Country	%Private Minus % State	Country	Private Minus State as % of State	Country
8.7	Poland[a]	4.3	Central Europe[b]	−43	Russia[k]
7.3	Central Europe[b]	3.5	Russia[c]	62	Russia[l]
−9.7	Russia[c]	10.6	Kyrgyz[f]	14	Estonia[m]
10.9	Bulgaria[d]	3.6	Georgia/Moldova[g] (MBOs)	−30	Lithuania[n] (diffuse owners)
2.5	Czech Republic[d]	0.9	Georgia/Moldova[g] (voucher privatized)	49	Latvia[n] (individual owners)
2.1	Hungary[d]	16.0	Romania[h]	−65	Mongolia[o]
−4.5	Russia[e]	1.0	25 countries[i]	36	Romania[h]
18.0	Kyrgyz[f]	3.1	Eastern Europe[j]	140	Slovenia[p]

Source: Table 1 of Djankov and Murrell (2002).

Note: Estimates of the performance of a 100 percent private firm relative to a 100 percent state firm. Positive signs indicate superior private performance. For the growth measures, relative performance is private-firm yearly growth rate minus state-firm yearly growth rate. For the levels measures, relative performance is private-firm productivity minus state-firm productivity expressed as a percent of state productivity. These estimates are based on the authors' calculations, derived from information presented in the following papers: [a]Grosfeld and Nivet (1999); [b]Frydman et al. (1999); [c]Jones (1998); [d]Pohl et al. (1997); [e]Perevalov, Gimadi, and Dobrodey (2000); [f]Roberts, Gorkov, and Madigan (1999); [g]Djankov (1999a); [h]Earle and Telgedy (2001); [i]Carlin et al. (2001), [j]Claessens and Djankov (2000); [k]Brown and Earle (2000); [l]Earle (1998a); [m]Jones and Mygind (2002); [n]Jones and Mygind (2000); [o]Anderson, Lee, and Murrell (2000); [p]Smith, Cin, and Vodopivec (1997).

Done the right way, and under the right conditions, privatization can yield dramatic improvements in firm performance, but executed improperly, privatization can also be hugely detrimental.

In addition to synthesizing the research making a straightforward comparison of state versus private ownership in transition economies, DM provide a very useful survey of the literature examining different categories of private owners. They offer three main conclusions. The first is that the type of new owner matters almost as much as does the shift from state to private control of a firm. Second, they find that the effects of ownership type are much different in CEE countries than in the FSU.[1] Third, DM reach the intriguing conclusion that retaining some state ownership — rather than fully divesting all state holdings — can be value-enhancing for a partially privatized firm, particularly in countries with very weak systems of corporate governance. The results of DM's survey are reproduced here as figure 5.3, which shows the estimated effects of switching from traditional (100 percent) state ownership to some type of private or mixed state and private control in the CEE region and in the Commonwealth of Independent States (CIS).

Several findings are the same in both regions. In all the transition economies except China, the most value is created when control of state-owned companies is transferred to concentrated private bloc-holders, investment funds, and foreign investors. Ownership by workers is never value-enhancing, and actually reduces

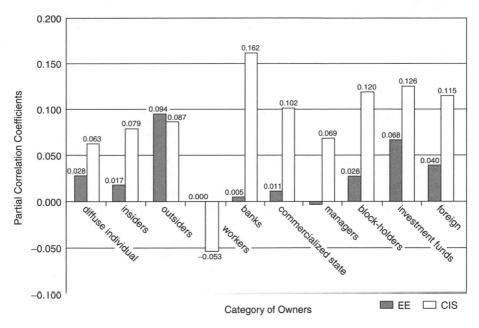

FIGURE 5.3. Regional variation in the effects of different types of owners: comparing ownership effects in eastern Europe to those in the former Soviet Union. Source: Figure 2 of Djankov and Murrell (2002).

value significantly in the CIS, while managers seem to make poor owners in CEE countries but are more effective in the CIS. The real difference between the effects of ownership type in CEE versus CIS countries lies in the valuation impact of banks and retained state ownership. In the CEE region, ownership by banks and retained state ownership have at most a modest positive impact on firm value. However, both types of owners are associated with very strong value creation in the CIS; in fact, banks are associated with the highest value creation of any ownership type. DM speculate that in the weaker institutional environment of the CIS, concentrated ownership is more necessary to ensure effective oversight of firm managers than is the case in the more developed CEE countries. Furthermore, they contend that the state has both the incentive and the ability to be an especially effective monitor and disciplinarian in those countries with the weakest corporate governance regimes.

The empirical results examined above show that privatization is generally associated with improved performance in transition economies, but that the identity of the new private owners is also extremely important. We now turn to a second key question related to the relationship between privatization and firm performance: What is the impact of injecting competition into a formerly monopolistic industry that is also being privatized? This occurs quite frequently in developed, developing, and transition economies, and the result is almost always a significant improvement in firm performance and social welfare. However, the facts that the ownership is changed and the industry is opened to competition simultaneously blur the separable impact of each reform. This has led many researchers to examine whether the policies of privatization and competition are complements or substitutes.

Privatization and Competition: Complements or Substitutes?

Almost by definition, socialist economies were characterized by monopolistic state production in every major industry. After the collapse of communism, there was extremely wide variation in the degree to which different countries dismantled monopolies in key industries, and thus — as noted above — one of the central questions of transition research has been whether the benefits that typically resulted from reform were caused by ownership change, competition, or a combination of the two policies. We again rely primarily on the results presented in Djankov and Murrell (DM; 2002) regarding the impact of competition on the performance of firms in different transition countries. Figure 5.4 presents DM's results, broken down based on CEE versus CIS samples.

As has been found by researchers addressing the competition versus ownership question in nontransition countries, DM's survey leads them to conclude that privatization (to outsiders) and competition have independent, but complementary effects in the CEE countries. However, competition from imported goods leads to significantly poorer firm performance in the CIS countries, whereas domestic

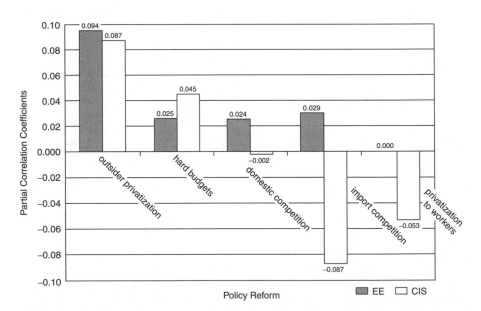

FIGURE 5.4. How policy reform affects enterprise performance: comparing economic effects in eastern Europe to those in the former Soviet Union. Source: Figure 3 of Djankov and Murrell (2002).

competition is associated with insignificantly different performance. This negative relationship between import competition and performance is exactly the reverse of the relationship documented between outsider privatization and firm performance in CIS countries, but is the same as that found between insider privatization and performance. DM conclude that state-owned firms are in such bad shape in CIS countries that they have no real hope of competing effectively with imported goods, and this leads to the observed negative relationship between performance and competition.

Empirical Evidence on Privatization in Central and Eastern Europe

This section presents and evaluates empirical studies that examine privatization's impact in specific central and eastern European transition economies. The country that has attracted the most intense empirical interest is easily the Czech Republic. No fewer than ten papers have analyzed this country's experience, and these studies are summarized in table 5.3. The other countries have attracted less empirical study and will be summarized in the next section.

Empirical Evidence on Privatization's Impact in the Czech Republic

The "Velvet Revolution" of 1989, which did so much to hasten the downfall of communism in central and eastern Europe, occurred in an undivided Czechoslovakia. One of the first major (and certainly the least violent) breakups of any transition economies occurred in 1992, when Czechoslovakia split amicably into the Czech Republic and Slovakia. Since that time, far more academic research has focused on the Czech half of this former union than the Slovak half.

Claessens, Djankov, and Pohl (1997) examine the determinants of performance improvements for a sample of 706 Czech firms privatized during 1992–1995. They test whether a concentrated ownership structure or the presence of an outside monitor (bank or investment fund) improves the level of a firm's Tobin's Q more than does having dispersed ownership. They document that privatized firms do prosper and that the more concentrated the post-privatization ownership structure, the higher is the firm's profitability and market valuation. They also find that large stakes owned by bank-sponsored funds and strategic investors are particularly value-enhancing.

Weiss and Nikitin (1998) analyze the effects of ownership by investment funds on the performance of 125 privatized Czech firms during the period 1993–1995. They assess these effects by measuring the relationship between changes in performance and changes in the composition of ownership at the start of the privatization period. They use robust estimation techniques, in addition to ordinary least squares (since the data strongly reject normality), and find that ownership concentration and composition jointly affect the performance of privatized firms. Concentration of ownership in the hands of a large shareholder, other than an investment fund or company, is associated with significant performance improve-

TABLE 5.3. Summary of Empirical Studies of Privatization in the Czech Republic

Study	Sample Description, Study Period, and Methodology	Summary of Empirical Findings and Conclusions
Claessens, Djankov, and Pohl (1997)	Examine determinants of performance improvements for sample of 706 Czech firms privatized during 1992–1995. Using Tobins Q, tests whether concentrated ownership structure or presence of outside monitor (bank or investment fund) improves Q more than dispersed ownership.	Document that privatized firms do prosper, primarily because of the concentrated ownership structure that results. Find the more concentrated the post-privatization ownership structure, the higher is the firm's profitability and market valuation. Large stakes owned by bank-sponsored funds and strategic investors are particularly value-enhancing.
Weiss and Nikitin (1998)	Analyze the effects of ownership by investment funds on the performance of 125 privatized Czech firms during the period 1993–1995. Assess these effects by measuring the relationship between *changes* in performance and *changes* in the composition of ownership at the start of privatization. Use robust estimation techniques, in addition to OLS, since data strongly reject normality.	Find that ownership concentration and composition jointly affect performance of privatized firms. Concentration of ownership in the hands of a large shareholder, other than an investment fund or company, is associated with significant performance improvements (for all measures of performance). Concentrated ownership by funds does not improve firm performance. Preliminary post-1996 data suggest that changes in investment fund legislation may improve their performance.
Claessens and Djankov (1999a)	Study the effect of management turnover on changes in financial and operating performance of 706 privatized Czech firms over the period 1993–1997. Examine changes in profitability and labor productivity.	Find that the appointment of new managers is associated with significant improvements in profit margins and labor productivity, particularly if the managers are selected by private owners. New managers appointed by the National Property Fund also improve performance, though not by as much.
Claessens and Djankov (1999b)	Examine the relationship between ownership concentration and corporate performance for 706 privatized Czech firms during the period 1992–1997. Use profitability and labor productivity as indicators of corporate performance.	Find that concentrated ownership is associated with higher profitability and labor productivity. Also find that foreign strategic owners and non-bank-sponsored investment funds improve performance more than bank-sponsored funds.
Lizal, Singer, and Svejnar (2000)	Examine the performance effects of the wave of break-ups of Czechslovak SOEs on the subsequent performance of the master firm and the spin-offs. The regressions use data for 373 firms in 1991 and 262 firms in 1992.	There was an immediate (in 1991) positive effect on the efficiency and profitability of small- and medium-size firms (both master and spin-offs) and negative for the larger firms. The results for 1992 are similar but not statistically significant.
Harper (2001)	Examines the effects of privatization on the financial and operating performance of 174 firms privatized in the first—and 380 firms divested in the second—wave of the Czech Republic's voucher privatizations of 1992 and 1994. Compares results for privatized firms to those which remain state owned. Employs Megginson, Nash, and van Randenborgh methodology and variables to measure changes.	Finds that the first wave of privatization yielded disappointing results. Real sales, profitability, efficiency, and employment all declined dramatically (and significantly). However, second-wave firms experience significant increases in efficiency and profitability and the decline in employment—though still significant—is much less drastic than after first wave (–17% vs. 41%).

176

Study	Description	Findings
Lizal and Svejnar (2001)	Examine strategic restructuring and new investment performance of 4,000 Czech companies during 1992–1998. Data set includes over 83,000 quarterly observations. Develop and test a dynamic model of restructuring and investment, allowing them to examine separable impact of private versus public and domestic versus foreign ownership on restructuring, as well as the importance of access to credit and a soft budget constraint on firm investment.	Find that (1) foreign-owned companies invest the most and (domestically owned) cooperatives the least; (2) private firms do not invest more than state-owned firms; (3) cooperatives and small firms are credit rationed; and (4) SOEs operate under a soft budget constraint.
Fidrmuc and Fidrmuc (2001)	Use a sample of 178 Czech firms privatized during first wave of voucher privatization (1992–1994) to test whether ownership change promoted increased efficiency and profitability. Use MNR pre-versus post-privatization comparison techniques to test for performance changes.	Find that efficiency and profitability declined after privatization, and that changes in firms' operations do not vary significantly by size or ownership—but do vary by industry type, with nonmanufacturing firms experiencing more positive (or less negative) changes.
Lizal and Svejnar (2002)	Use panel of over 83,500 quarterly observations from 4,000 medium and large Czech companies over the 1992–1998 period to assess the effects of mass privatization on firm performance.	Find that foreign owners unambiguously improve long-term performance (measured several ways, including profits and investment) of privatized companies, but domestic owners do not.
Kocenda and Svejnar (2002)	Analyze the effect of ownership on post-privatization performance using a data set of 2,529–2,949 observations on an unbalanced panel of 1,371–1,540 medium and large Czech firms. Define six categories of owners and examine impact of each.	Find that concentrated foreign ownership improves economic performance, but domestic private ownership does not, relative to state firms. Foreign-owned firms engage in strategic restructuring by increasing sales and profits, while domestic firms reduce sales and labor costs without increasing profits. Ownership concentration is generally associated with improved performance. Overall, conclude that state ownership plays a much more economically and socially beneficial role in this transition economy than theory would predict.
Cull, Matesova, and Shirley (2002)	Examine the incentive of managers of voucher-privatized Czech companies to "tunnel" (strip assets out of companies at the expense of outside shareholders) and "loot" their companies. Looting occurs when firms face a soft budget constraint and managers are able to borrow heavily, extract funds from the firm, and then default on the debt without penalty. Employ a data set with 1,017 observations from 392 companies spread nearly evenly between 1994–1996. Half of the firms are voucher-privatized joint stock companies (JSCs) while half are limited liability companies (LLCs).	Controlling for size, industry, capital intensity, and initial leverage, find that voucher-privatized JSCs perform significantly worse than firms with concentrated ownership that are purchased for cash. Investment fund-controlled JSCs underperform all other firms, including other JSCs. Fund-controlled JSCs also take on liabilities at a much faster rate than other firms, indicating they are operating under a soft budget constraint. Though not able to measure directly, evidence indirectly shows that looting is a widespread occurrence for many JSCs.

ments for all measures of performance. Concentrated ownership by investment funds does not improve firm performance, though preliminary post-1996 data suggest that changes in investment fund legislation may improve company performance.

Claessens and Djankov (1999a) study the effects of management turnover on the financial and operating performance of 706 privatized Czech firms over the period 1993–1997. They examine changes in profitability and labor productivity, and find that the appointment of new managers is associated with significant improvements in profit margins and labor productivity, particularly if the managers are selected by private owners. New managers appointed by the National Property Fund also improve performance, though not by as much.

Claessens and Djankov (1999b) use this same sample to examine the relationship between ownership concentration and corporate performance. They employ profitability and labor productivity as indicators of corporate performance, and find that concentrated ownership is associated with higher profitability and labor productivity. They also find that foreign strategic owners and non-bank-sponsored investment funds improve performance more than bank-sponsored funds.

Lizal, Singer, and Svejnar (2001) examine the performance effects of the wave of breakups of Czechslovak SOEs on the subsequent performance of the master firm and the spin-offs. Their regressions use data for 373 firms in 1991 and 262 firms in 1992. They document an immediate (in 1991) positive effect of the break-ups on the efficiency and profitability of small and medium-size firms (both master and spin-offs), but find a negative relationship for the larger firms. Their results for 1992 are similar but are not statistically significant. Harper (2001) also examines the effects of privatization on firms privatized in the first (174 firms) and second (380 firms) waves of the Czech Republic's voucher privatizations of 1992 and 1994. He employs the Megginson, Nash, and van Randenborgh (MNR; 1994) methodology and variables to measure changes resulting from privatization, and then compares the results for privatized firms to those for firms that remain state-owned. He finds that the first wave of privatization yields disappointing results. Real sales, profitability, efficiency, and employment all decline dramatically (and significantly). However, the second-wave firms experience significant increases in efficiency and profitability, and the decline in employment, though still significant, is much less drastic than after the first wave (–17 percent versus –41 percent). Fidrmuc and Fidrmuc (2001) similarly use a sample of 178 Czech firms privatized during the first wave of voucher privatization to test whether ownership change promotes increased efficiency and profitability. They also use the MNR pre- versus post-privatization comparison technique to test for performance changes, and find that efficiency and profitability decline after privatization and changes in firms' operations do not vary significantly by size or ownership. However, they find that performance changes do vary by industry type, with nonmanufacturing firms experiencing more positive (or less negative) changes.

Lizal and Svejnar (2001) examine the strategic restructuring and new investment performance of 4,000 Czech companies during the years 1992–1998 using a data set including over 83,000 quarterly observations. They develop and test a dynamic model of restructuring and investment, allowing them to examine the separable impact of private versus public and domestic versus foreign ownership on restructuring, as well as the importance of access to credit and a soft budget constraint on firm investment. They find that (1) foreign-owned companies invest the most and (domestically owned) cooperatives the least; (2) private firms do not invest more than state-owned firms; (3) cooperatives and small firms are credit rationed; and (4) SOEs operate under a soft budget constraint. Lizal and Svejnar (2002) use this same panel to assess the effects of mass privatization on firm performance. They find that foreign owners unambiguously improve long-term performance (measured several ways, including profits and investment) of privatized companies, but domestic owners do not.

Kocenda and Svejnar (2002) analyze the effect of ownership on post-privatization performance using a data set of 2,529 to 2,949 observations from an unbalanced panel of 1,371 to 1,540 medium and large Czech firms. They define six categories of owners and examine the impact of each. They find that concentrated foreign ownership improves the economic performance of privatized companies relative to state firms, but that domestic private ownership does not. Foreign-owned firms engage in strategic restructuring by increasing sales and profits, while domestic firms reduce sales and labor costs without increasing profits. Ownership concentration is generally associated with improved performance. Overall, they conclude that noncontrolling (retained) state ownership plays a much more economically and socially beneficial role in this transition economy than theory would predict.

Cull, Matesova, and Shirley (2002) examine the incentives that managers of voucher-privatized Czech companies have to "tunnel" (strip assets out of companies at the expense of outside shareholders) and "loot" their companies. Looting occurs when firms face a soft budget constraint and managers are able to borrow heavily, extract funds from the firm, and then default on the debt without penalty. They employ a data set with 1,017 observations from 392 companies spread nearly evenly between 1994 and 1996. Half of the firms are voucher-privatized joint stock companies (JSCs) while half are limited liability companies (LLCs). Controlling for size, industry, capital intensity, and initial leverage, they find that voucher-privatized JSCs perform significantly worse than firms with concentrated ownership that had to be purchased for cash. Investment fund-controlled JSCs underperform all other firms, including other JSCs, while fund-controlled JSCs also took on liabilities at a much faster rate than other firms, indicating they were operating under a soft budget constraint. Though not able to measure the activity directly, they conclude that the evidence indirectly shows that looting was a widespread occurrence for many JSCs.

Empirical Evidence on Privatization's Impact in Other CEE Countries

Although the Czech Republic's privatization program has garnered by far the most research attention, the programs of several other CEE countries have also been evaluated empirically. Six studies examining the experience of five countries are surveyed below and are summarized in table 5.4.

TABLE 5.4. Summary of Single-Country Empirical Studies of Privatization in Central and Eastern Europe (Besides the Czech Republic)

Study	Sample Description, Study Period, and Methodology	Summary of Empirical Findings and Conclusions
Eastern Germany Dyck (1997)	Develops and tests an adverse-selection model to explain the Treuhand's role in restructuring and privatizing East Germany's state-owned firms. In less than five years, the Treuhand privatized more than 13,800 firms and parts of firms and, uniquely, had the resources to pay for restructuring itself—but almost never chose to do so. Instead, it emphasized speed and sales to existing Western firms over giveaways and sales to capital funds. Paper rationalizes Treuhand's approach.	Documents that privatized East German firms are much more likely to transfer Western (usually German) managers into key positions than are companies that remain state owned. Also finds that Treuhand emphasizes sales open to all buyers rather than favoring East Germans. Principal message: privatization programs must carefully consider when and how to affect managerial replacement in privatized companies. Plans open to Western buyers, and which allow management change, are most likely to improve firm performance.
Macedonia (FYRM) Glennerster (2003)	Using a panel data set on 470 formerly state-owned firms in the former Yugoslav Republic of Macedonia (FSRM) for 1996–1999, examines whether privatization increases profitability of divested companies. Uses a fixed-effects panel data regression to address selection bias in both the timing and method of privatization.	Finds weak but significant evidence that privatization can yield benefits even with predominantly insider sales and in an environment of weak corporate governance. On average, privatization leads to a 30% increase in revenues and costs, a 16% increase in the number of workers employed, and a $1,200 increase in profits per worker. Firms sold to outsiders and those with more concentrated ownership expand more than other, similar firms after privatization. Employee buyouts perform relatively poorly. Also finds that lack of access to capital is an important reason insider privatizations perform poorly, since those firms where new owners bring in new capital see particularly high growth rates after privatization.

180

Poland

Grosfeld and Tressel (2001)

Examine whether competition and corporate governance are substitutes or complements with respect to promoting performance improvements in Poland's transition. Use the available data for all 200 nonfinancial firms listed on the Warsaw Stock Exchange from 1991–1998. First study the separate effects of competition and ownership concentration on productivity growth at the firm level, then examine their interaction.

Find that product market competition has a positive and significant impact on performance. The effect of ownership concentration, which is quite high in Poland, turns out to be U-shaped. Firms with dispersed ownership and those where one shareholder owns more than 50% of voting shares have higher productivity growth than those with intermediate levels of ownership concentration. Competitive pressure does not affect newly created firms, but does significantly improve performance of privatized companies. Presence of a large foreign owner increases productivity growth significantly. Conclude that good corporate governance and competitive pressures are complements.

Romania

Coricelli and Djankov (2001)

Identify the presence of soft budget constraints and analyze their impact on enterprise restructuring in Romania during the initial transition period. Employ a simple analytical model and a sample of 4,429 enterprises with data from 1992–1995 to test whether hardening budget constraints promotes beneficial restructuring and new investment or whether access to external financing is required to promote new investment.

Find that hard budget constraints (HBCs) do promote passive restructuring, in the form of labor shedding, but not new investment. Active restructuring requires access to external financing. Tightened bank credit can induce HBCs and raise enterprise efficiency in the short run, but at the cost of curtailing investment.

Earle and Telegdy (2001)

Examine impact of privatization—and method of privatization—on firm performance in Romania over the period 1992–1999. Employ a data set of 2,354 firms owned by the State Ownership Fund (SOF) in 1992, and trace evolution of ownership over next six years; most of these (77%) still have some state ownership (50.9% median) in 1998.

Show consistently positive, highly significant effects of private ownership on labor productivity growth, with the point estimate implying an incremental 1.0 to 1.7 percentage point growth in productivity for a 10% rise in private shareholding. Insider transfers and mass privatizations have smaller, but still significantly positive effects.

Slovenia

Smith, Cin, and Vodopivec (1997)

Using a sample with 22,735 firm-years of data drawn from period of "spontaneous privatization" in Slovenia (1989–1992), examine the impact of foreign and employee ownership on firm performance.

Find that a percentage point increase in foreign ownership is associated with a 3.9% increase in value added, and for employee ownership with a 1.4% increase. Also find that firms with higher revenues, profits, and exports are more likely to exhibit foreign and employee ownership.

EAST GERMANY

Dyck (1997) develops and tests an adverse selection model to explain the Treuhand's role in restructuring and privatizing East Germany's state-owned firms. The Treuhand was the agency established and capitalized by the German government to privatize and sell off the state-owned enterprises of East Germany. In less than five years, this agency privatized more than 13,800 firms and parts of firms. The Treuhand, uniquely, had the resources to pay for restructuring itself—but almost never chose to do so. Instead, it emphasized speed and sales to existing Western firms over giveaways and sales to capital funds. This paper rationalizes the Treuhand's approach and documents that privatized East German firms were much more likely to have Western (usually West German) managers transferred into key positions than were companies that remained state-owned. He also finds that the Treuhand emphasized sales open to all buyers rather than favoring East Germans. The principal message of this study is that privatization programs must carefully consider when and how to affect managerial replacement in privatized companies. Plans open to Western buyers and which allow management changes are most likely to improve firm performance.

POLAND

Grosfeld and Tressel (2001) examine whether competition and corporate governance are substitutes or complements with respect to promoting performance improvements in Poland's transition. These authors use the available data for all 200 nonfinancial firms listed on the Warsaw Stock Exchange from 1991 to 1998 to first study the separate effects of competition and ownership concentration on productivity growth at the firm level, and then to examine their interaction. They find that product market competition has a positive and significant impact on performance. The effect of ownership concentration, which is quite high in Poland, turns out to be U-shaped; firms with dispersed ownership and those where one shareholder owns more than 50 percent of voting shares have higher productivity growth than those with intermediate levels of ownership concentration. Competitive pressure does not affect newly created firms, but does significantly improve performance of privatized companies, and the presence of a large foreign owner increases productivity growth significantly. They conclude that good corporate governance and competitive pressures are complements.

ROMANIA

Two studies examine Romania's transition experience. Coricelli and Djankov (2001) identify the presence of soft budget constraints and analyze their impact on enterprise restructuring in Romania during the initial transition period. They employ a simple analytical model and a sample of 4,429 enterprises with data from 1992–1995 to test whether hardening budget constraints promotes beneficial restructuring and new investment, or whether access to external financing is required to promote new investment. They find that hard budget constraints (HBCs) do promote passive restructuring, in the form of labor shedding, but not new investment. Active restructuring requires access to external financing. Tightened bank credit can induce HBCs and raise enterprise efficiency in the short run, but at the cost of curtailing investment. Earle and Telegdy (2001) examine the impact of privatization—and the method of privatization—on firm performance in Romania over the period 1992–1999. They employ a data set of 2,354 firms owned by the State Ownership Fund (SOF) in 1992, and trace the evolution of ownership over the next six years. Most of these firms (77 percent) still have some state ownership (50.9 percent median) in 1998. They find consistently positive and highly significant effects of private ownership on labor productivity growth, with the point estimate implying a 1.0 to 1.7 percentage-point increase in the growth rate of productivity resulting from a 10 percent rise in private shareholding. Insider transfers and mass privatizations have smaller, but still significantly positive effects.

SLOVENIA

Smith, Cin, and Vodopivec (1997) use a sample with 22,735 firm-years of data drawn from the period of "spontaneous privatization" in Slovenia (1989–1992) to examine the impact of foreign and employee ownership on firm performance. They find that a 1 percentage point increase in foreign ownership is associated with a 3.9 percent increase in value added, and a 1 percentage point increase in employee ownership is associated with a 1.4 percent increase. They also find that firms with higher revenues, profits, and exports are more likely to exhibit foreign and employee ownership.

MACEDONIA

Glennerster (2003) employs a panel data set of 470 privatized firms in the former Yugoslav Republic of Macedonia (FYRM) for the period 1996–1999 to examine whether privatization increases the profitability of divested companies. She uses a fixed-effects panel data regression to address selection bias in both the timing and the method of privatization, and finds weak but significant evidence that privatization can yield benefits even with predominantly insider sales and in an environment of weak corporate governance. On average, privatization leads to a 30 percent increase in revenues and costs, a 16 percent increase in the number of workers employed, and a $1,200 increase in profits per worker. Firms sold to outsiders and those with more concentrated ownership expand more than other, similar firms after privatization. Employee buy-out firms perform relatively poorly. She also finds that lack of access to capital is an important reason insider privatizations perform poorly, since those firms where new owners brought in new capital see particularly high growth rates after privatization.

Summary of the Empirical Evidence on Privatization's Impact in the CEE Region

The studies discussed above yield surprisingly consistent results regarding the impact of privatization on the performance of divested central and eastern European firms. Many of these studies explicitly test whether the type of ownership structure that emerges from the privatization process is related to post-privatization performance. Several also test whether soft budget constraints are observed—and whether these help or hinder firm performance. Other things equal, the empirical evidence suggests that:

- Private ownership is associated with better firm-level performance than is continued state ownership. In addition, concentrated private ownership is associated with greater performance improvement than is diffuse ownership.
- Foreign ownership, where allowed, is associated with greater post-privatization performance improvement than is purely domestic ownership.[2] Majority ownership by outside (nonemployee) investors is associated with significantly greater performance improvements than is any form of insider control.
- Firm-level restructuring is associated with significant (sometimes dramatic) post-privatization performance improvements, and this is one key advantage of outsider control. Firms controlled by nonemployee investors are much more likely to restructure than are employee-owned firms.
- Most studies document that performance improves more when new managers are brought in to run a firm after it is privatized than when the original managers are retained. The precise reason for the superior performance of new management is unclear, though there is evidence that the more entrepreneurial behavior of outsider-owned firms is due to incentive rather than human capital effects.
- The role of investment funds in promoting efficiency improvements in privatized CEE firms is ambiguous, though most studies document greater performance improvements for companies controlled by non-bank-sponsored investment funds than by bank-sponsored funds. As we will see in the next section, bank-sponsored funds have the most positive impact on firm performance in FSU countries.
- The impact of privatization on employment is ambiguous, primarily because employment falls for virtually all firms in transition economies after reforms are initiated. While selling firms to outsiders undoubtedly promotes more firm-level restructuring than does insider privatization or continued state ownership, several studies find that sales grow fast enough in outsider-controlled firms to offset the significant increase in labor productivity—causing employment to remain stable or increase.
- There is little evidence that governments have been able to impose hard budget constraints on firms that remain state-owned after reforms begin, since governments are unwilling to allow these firms to fail. Furthermore, the weight of empirical evidence strongly suggests that soft budget constraints retard much needed restructuring and thus hamper (sometimes cripple) economic performance. However, these studies also find that the burden of lower SOE creditworthiness falls on the state (as deferred taxes) or on state creditors, rather than on private creditors or suppliers.

- Arms-length access to external finance is a key prerequisite for value creation by newly created and privatized firms. Whereas many categories of firms are able to cut costs through restructuring, only companies that are able to secure funding for new investment, either domestically or through a foreign parent company, are able to achieve lasting growth in sales and employment.

Given these observed patterns for central and eastern Europe, we next examine how privatization has impacted firm performance in the republics of the former Soviet Union.

Empirical Evidence on Privatization in Russia and the Former Soviet Republics

It is very difficult to reach a simple conclusion regarding privatization's impact in the former Soviet Union in general, and Russia in particular, for four principal reasons. First, as noted earlier, the transition from socialism to capitalism was much more difficult and painful in the former Soviet republics than elsewhere, both because Russia and the other republics were under communist rule the longest and because the transition to capitalism also coincided with dissolution of the Soviet Union. Breaking up any continental-scale nation was likely to prove traumatic; breaking up a country that was also an economic system proved doubly so. Second, the contraction in output that occurred in the former Soviet Union after 1991 was far greater than in central and eastern Europe, making it very difficult to document any kind of relative performance improvement, or to assign causality to any improvement that is found. Third, it seems clear that most of the former Soviet republics took a decided turn for the worse economically after 1997, so competently executed studies examining privatization's impact in the same country, but at different times, might well reach radically different conclusions. Finally, most studies that examine the FSU countries' experiences rely either on survey data or anecdotal evidence, so the "raw material" for empirical analysis is of much poorer quality here than in other regions. For these reasons, we believe that no truly persuasive empirical study of privatization in the former Soviet Union has yet been performed, nor is one likely to be performed until these economies stabilize and several years of reliable accounting (not survey) data become available.

We begin our survey of the empirical evidence of privatization's impact in the FSU by examining two multinational empirical studies, which are summarized in table 5.5. We then examine single-country studies, beginning with the transition experience of Russia, and then proceeding through the experiences of the other former Soviet republics. The single country studies are summarized in table 5.6.

Djankov (1999a) investigates the relation between ownership structure and enterprise restructuring for 960 firms privatized in six newly independent states between 1995 and 1997. He employs survey data collected by the World Bank in late 1997 from Georgia, Kazakhstan, the Kyrgyz Republic, Moldova, Russia, and Ukraine, and shows that foreign ownership is positively associated with enterprise

TABLE 5.5. Summary of Multinational Empirical Studies of Privatization in Russia and Former Soviet Republics

Study	Sample Description, Study Period, and Methodology	Summary of Empirical Findings and Conclusions
Djankov (1999a)	Investigates the relation between ownership structure and enterprise restructuring for 960 firms privatized in six newly independent states between 1995–1997. Employ survey data collected by the World Bank in late 1997 from Georgia, Kazakhstan, Kyrgyz Republic, Moldova, Russia, and Ukraine.	Show that foreign ownership is positively associated with enterprise restructuring at high ownership levels (>30 percent), while managerial ownership is positively related to restructuring at low (<10%) or high levels, but negative at intermediate levels. Employee ownership is beneficial to labor productivity at low ownership levels, but is otherwise insignificant.
Djankov (1999b)	Using same survey data as in Djankov (1999a) above, studies effects of different privatization modalities on restructuring process in Georgia (92 firms) and Moldova (149 firms). Georgia employs voucher privatization, while the majority of Moldovan firms are acquired by investment funds—and numerous others are sold to managers for cash.	Privatization through management buyouts is positively associated with enterprise restructuring, while voucher privatized firms do not restructure more rapidly than firms that remain state owned. Implies that managers who gain ownership for free may have less incentive to restructure, as their income is not solely based on the success of the enterprise.

TABLE 5.6. Summary of Single-Country Empirical Studies of Privatization in Russia and Former Soviet Republics

Study	Sample Description, Study, Period, and Methodology	Summary of Empirical Findings and Conclusions
Russia		
Earle (1998a)	Investigates the impact of ownership structure on the (labor) productivity of Russian industrial firms. Using 1994 survey data, examines differential impact of insider, outsider, and state ownership on the performance of 430 firms—of which 86 remain 100% state-owned, 299 are partially privatized, and 45 are newly created. Adjusts empirical methods to account for tendency of insiders to claim dominant ownership in the best firms being divested.	OLS regressions show a positive impact of private (relative to state) share ownership on labor productivity, with this result primarily due to managerial ownership. After adjusting for selection bias, however, finds that only outsider ownership is significantly associated with productivity improvements. Stresses that leaving insiders in control of firms—while politically expedient—has very negative long-term implications for the restructuring of Russian industry.
Earle and Estrin (1998)	Using a sample very similar to that used by Earle (1998) above, examine whether privatization, competition, and the hardening of budget constraints play efficiency-enhancing roles in Russia.	Find a 10 percentage point increase in private share ownership raises real sales per employee by 3–5%. Subsidies (soft budget constraints) reduce the pace of restructing in state-owned firms, but the effect is small and often insignificant.
Black, Kraakman, and Tarassova (2000)	Surveys the history of privatization in Russia. While mostly descriptive, several case studies are analyzed.	Authors conclude that Russian privatization has created a "kleptocracy" and has essentially failed. Stresses the importance of minimizing incentives for self-dealing in the design of privatization programs.
Estonia		
Jones and Mygind (2002)	Uses fixed-effects production function models estimated on a random sample of 660 Estonian firms with data from 1993 to 1997. Privatization in Estonia created a widely varied ownership structure, and study attempts to estimate relationship between ownership and productive efficiency.	Find that, relative to state ownership, (1) private ownership is 13–22% more efficient, (2) all types of private ownership are more productive, though concentrated managerial ownership has the biggest effect (21–32% improvement), and ownership by domestic outsiders the smallest (0–15%), with ownership by foreigners (21–32%) and employees (24–25%) yielding intermediate levels of improvement.

(continued)

187

TABLE 5.6. (continued)

Study	Sample Description, Study, Period, and Methodology	Summary of Empirical Findings and Conclusions
Kazakhstan		
Djankov and Nenova (2000)	Use data for over 6,600 Kazakh enterprises during 1996–1999 to examine "why privatization failed in Kazakhstan." Trying to explain rapid declines in output for all sectors except oil and gas.	Find that newly created (de novo) private enterprises, established after 1992, perform markedly better than privatized firms or those that remain SOEs. Privatized firms perform as badly as, or worse than, SOEs. Privatization fails to improve performance because divested firms are used as short-term vehicles for extracting private benefits.
Lithuania		
Gregorian (2000)	Examines relationship between ownership and operating performance using a data set of 5,300 small, medium, and large Lithuanian companies with data over period 1995–1997. Performance defined as increased revenues and improved export performance. Also uses regression analysis to study subsample of 618 companies that are fully state owned in 1995; roughly half of these are partially privatized over next two years.	Concludes that privatization has brought significant performance improvements overall. Also finds a negative bias in selecting firms for privatization; once this is accounted for, performance improvement is even more dramatic (there is a ninefold increase in the coefficient on private ownership). Expected subsidies contribute negatively to performance, but study finds no significant impact regarding market competition.
Mongolia		
Anderson, Lee, and Murrell (2000)	Examines effects of competition and ownership on the efficiency of newly privatized firms using a sample of 211 Mongolian companies with (survey-derived) ownership data in 1995. Mongolia's privatization program is implemented in a country lacking the basic institutions of capitalism.	Finds that competition has qualitatively large effects; perfectly competitive firms have nearly double the efficiency of monopolies. Enterprises with residual state ownership appear to be more efficient than other enterprises, reflecting an environment where the government is pressured to focus on efficiency and institutions gave little voice to outside owners.

Ukraine

Estrin and Rosevear (1999)

Use a random sample of 150 Ukrainian firms with data from 1996 to test the relationship between enterprise performance and ownership. Explore whether privatization yields improved company performance and whether specific ownership forms lead to differentiated performance at the enterprise level.

Find that privatization, per se, is not significantly associated with improved performance, and find no benefit to outside (versus insider) ownership. Do find clear positive effects associated with insider ownership. Outside owners are never able to deliver performance superior to SOEs, and insider ownership does not yield a better profit performance than in nonprivatized companies.

Andreyeva (2001)

Examines empirically the responsiveness of firm performance to ownership and market structures, sector and regional specificity, and varying degrees of soft budget constraints. Uses a panel of 524 medium and large firms with performance data for 1996–1998.

Finds that firm efficiency improves significantly with privatization. Also documents a significant influence of industry affiliation and regional location in shaping firm performance; more concentrated markets perform better. Concludes that a policy of attracting strategic investors capable of pushing restructuring and bringing new investment to privatized firms should become a priority for policy makers.

Pivovarsky (2001)

Using data on 376 medium and large Ukrainian firms, investigates relationship between ownership concentration and enterprise performance.

Finds that ownership concentration is positively associated with enterprise performance, and t nat concentrated ownership by foreign companies and banks is associated with better performance than concentrated domestic ownership. Concludes that privatization method has lasting impact on ownership structure; privatization methods that grant significant ownership stakes to single parties have greater efficiency gains than methods that create dispersed ownership.

restructuring at high ownership levels (>30 percent), while managerial ownership is positively related to restructuring at low (<10 percent) or high levels, but negative at intermediate levels. Employee ownership is beneficial to labor productivity at low ownership levels, but is otherwise insignificant. Djankov (1999b) uses this same survey data to study the effects of different privatization modalities on restructuring processes in Georgia (92 firms) and Moldova (149 firms). Georgia employed voucher privatization, while the majority of Moldovan firms were acquired by investment funds—and numerous others were sold to managers for cash. Privatization through management buyouts is positively associated with enterprise restructuring, while voucher privatized firms do not restructure more rapidly than do firms that remain state-owned. This implies that managers who gain ownership for free may have less incentive to restructure than do managers who must actually purchase ownership interests.

Empirical Evidence on Privatization's Impact in Russia

For the people of Russia, transition initially yielded little but pain. In addition to losing an empire, and the world influence that went with it, the only country that these people had known for 70 years disappeared and the historic nation of Russia emerged in its place. Earle (1998a) investigates the impact of ownership structure on the (labor) productivity of Russian industrial firms. Using 1994 survey data, he examines the differential impact of insider, outsider, or state ownership on the performance of 430 firms—of which 86 remained 100 percent state-owned, 299 were partially privatized, and 45 were newly created. Earle adjusts his empirical methods to account for the tendency of insiders to claim dominant ownership in the best firms being divested. OLS regressions show a positive impact of private (relative to state) share ownership on labor productivity, primarily owing to managerial ownership. After adjusting for selection bias, however, Earle finds that only outsider ownership is significantly associated with productivity improvements. He stresses that leaving insiders in control of firms, while politically expedient, has very negative long-term implications for the restructuring of Russian industry.

Earle and Estrin (1998) use a sample very similar to that used by Earle (1998b) to examine whether privatization, competition, and the hardening of budget constraints enhance efficiency in Russia. They find that a 10 percentage point increase in private share ownership raises real sales per employee by 3 to 5 percent. Subsidies (soft budget constraints) reduce the pace of restructuring in state-owned firms, but the effect is small and often insignificant. Finally, Black, Kraakman, and Tarassova (2000) present a damning survey of the history of privatization in Russia. They contend that "privatizing" the assets of the Soviet state, without putting into place the basic legal and institutional supports for private ownership and deregulating economic procedures, simply led to an explosion in criminality and corruption. The authors conclude that Russian privatization has created a "kleptocracy" and has essentially failed. They also stress the importance of minimizing incentives for self-dealing in the design of privatization programs.

Empirical Evidence on Privatization's Impact in the
Former Soviet Republics

BALTIC STATES

Jones and Mygind (2002) use fixed-effects production function models, estimated on a random sample of 660 Estonian firms with data from 1993 to 1997, to examine the effect of ownership change on firm performance. Privatization in Estonia created widely varied ownership structures, and this study attempts to estimate the relationship between ownership and productive efficiency. They find that, relative to state ownership, private ownership is 13 to 22 percent more efficient. While all types of private ownership are more productive, concentrated managerial ownership has the biggest effect (21–32 percent improvement), and ownership by domestic outsiders yields the smallest effect (0–15 percent). Ownership by foreigners (21–32 percent) and employees (24–25 percent) yields intermediate levels of improvement.

Grigorian (2000) examines the relationship between ownership and operating performance using a data set of 5,300 small, medium, and large Lithuanian companies with data available over the period 1995–1997. Performance is defined as increased revenues and improved export performance. He also uses regression analysis to study a subsample of 618 companies that were fully state owned in 1995; roughly half of these were partially privatized over the next two years. He concludes that privatization has brought significant performance improvements overall, but he also find a negative bias in selecting firms for privatization. Once this bias is accounted for, the measured performance improvement is even more dramatic (there is a nine-fold increase in the coefficient on private ownership). Expected subsidies contribute negatively to performance, but this study finds no significant impact regarding market competition.

UKRAINE

Estrin and Rosevear (1999) use a random sample of 150 Ukrainian firms with data from 1996 to test the relationship between enterprise performance and ownership. They explore whether privatization has yielded improved company performance and whether specific ownership forms have led to differentiated performance at the enterprise level. They find that privatization, per se, is not significantly associated with improved performance, and find no benefit to outsider (versus insider) ownership—though insider ownership does seem to have clear positive effects. Outside owners are never able to deliver performance superior to SOEs, and insider ownership does not yield a better profit performance than in nonprivatized companies.

Andreyeva (2001) examines empirically the responsiveness of firm performance to ownership and market structures, sector and regional specificity, and varying degrees of soft budget constraints. Using a panel of 524 medium and large firms with performance data for 1996–1998, she finds that firm efficiency improves significantly with privatization. She also documents a significant influence of industry affiliation and regional location in shaping firm performance, with more concentrated markets performing better, and concludes that a policy of attracting strategic investors capable of pushing restructuring and bringing new investment to privatized firms should become a priority for policy makers.

Pivovarsky (2001) uses data on 376 medium and large Ukrainian firms to investigate the relationship between ownership concentration and enterprise performance. He finds that ownership concentration is positively associated with enterprise performance, and that concentrated ownership by foreign companies and banks is associated with better performance than concentrated domestic ownership. He concludes that the method of privatization has a lasting impact on ownership structure, with privatization that grants significant ownership stakes to single parties having greater efficiency gains than methods that create dispersed ownership.

KAZAKHSTAN

Djankov and Nenova (2000) use data for over 6,600 Kazakh enterprises during 1996–1999 to examine "why privatization failed in Kazakhstan." They try to explain the rapid declines in output that occurred for all sectors except oil and gas. They find that newly created (de novo) private enterprises, established after 1992, perform markedly better than privatized firms or those that remain SOEs, and that privatized firms perform as badly as, or worse than, SOEs. Privatization failed to improve performance because divested firms were used as short-term vehicles for extracting private benefits.

MONGOLIA

Anderson, Lee, and Murrell (2000) examine the effects of competition and ownership on the efficiency of newly privatized firms using a sample of 211 Mongolian companies with (survey-derived) ownership data in 1995. Mongolia's privatization program was implemented in a country lacking the basic institutions of capitalism. They find that competition has qualitatively large effects, with perfectly competitive firms having nearly double the efficiency of monopolies. Enterprises with residual state ownership appear to be more efficient than other enterprises, reflecting an environment where the government was pressured to focus on efficiency and institutions gave little voice to outside owners.

Summary of the Empirical Evidence on Privatization's Impact in the Former Soviet Union

The studies summarized above yield several overall conclusions. Certainly the most important is that insider privatization has been a failure throughout the former Soviet Union, especially in Russia, and that the concentrated managerial ownership structure that characterizes almost all privatized firms will likely hamper these economies for many years. Russian reformers considered rapid privatization to be an imperative, and for this reason they opted for the politically expedient technique of favoring incumbent managers and employees with allocations of controlling shareholdings during the initial mass privatization waves of 1992–1993. The investment funds created during this program proved ineffective, owing primarily to insider control and poor legal protection of (outside) shareholder voting rights. In spite of this, several studies document that privatization was associated with performance improvements in firms that were divested during the mass privatization program of the early 1990s. Many studies also find that post-privatization performance improves the most (or only) for firms that are outsider controlled, and all the studies stress the importance of bringing in new management whenever possible. Additionally, foreign share ownership is associated with significantly greater performance improvement than is purely domestic ownership, and managers who actually pay for divested firms (through management buyouts) improve performance more than do managers who are effectively given control (through voucher schemes).

Russia provides an example of what can go wrong with privatizations in the 1995 "loans for shares" scheme, which transferred control of 12 natural resource firms to a small group of "oligarchs" at very low prices. Black, Kraakman, and Tarassova (2000) argue this was this was a corrupt and nontransparent transfer of assets that precipitated widespread insider expropriation. Further, it contributed to the political unpopularity of privatization in Russia. It provides a cautionary note that privatization is not an economic panacea.[3] Black, Kraakman, and Tarassova also argue that a poorly designed privatization program is worse than none at all. However, Nellis (1999) and other commentators point out that many of Russia's problems resulted from a collapse of central governmental authority, and would thus not likely be solved by renationalization. Perhaps the best long-term hope for economic revitalization in the former Soviet republics is the type of de novo private development described in Havrylyshyn and McGettigan (1999). Certainly, all of the FSU countries seek to emulate the economic success of the transition economy that was arguably the most backwards in 1978, but has now become a byword for economic success and dynamism: China.

The Transition Outlier: Privatization's Impact on China's Economic Performance

No major country has turned in a record of uninterrupted growth comparable to China's since 1978. Even granting that China's remarkable economic transformation occurred after decades of maniacally dysfunctional governance, and thus from a very low developmental base, the country's record of investment, output, and employment growth is extraordinary. While many studies have examined China's economic performance, our focus in this section will be specifically on the role that privatization has played in China's transition to an economy that is capitalist in all but name. We first briefly describe the effect of the policy initiatives adopted by China over the last quarter-century, and then discuss the role and effectiveness of privatization within this reform process.

The Evolution of Economic Reform Policies in the People's Republic of China

China adopted economic reform policies two years after the death of Chairman Mao Tse-tung in 1976, not out of a sudden conviction that capitalism was superior, but rather out of desperation at the wretched state of the Chinese economy—and the attendant political and economic weakness thus engendered. Chinese economic reforms have dramatically increased the total factor productivity [Li (1997)] of Chinese state-owned enterprises, largely by improving incentives [Groves, Hong, McMillan, and Naughton (1994, 1995)] and decentralizing economic decision making [Cao, Qian, and Weingast (1999); Lau, Qian, and Roland (2000)].[4] The progress China has made toward creating a market economy in recent years is nothing short of incredible, as tables 5.7 and 5.8 make clear. The first table describes the relative output shares of state-owned and privately owned manufacturing enterprises in China for the years 1993–1999, while table 5.8 presents similar information about relative employment shares.

These tables clearly suggest that state-owned enterprises represent a rapidly declining share of total Chinese manufacturing output, and an even more rapidly declining share of manufacturing employment. Whereas SOEs accounted for almost half (47 percent) of industrial output in 1993, this had dropped to 28 percent by 1999, and today SOEs probably account for less than 20 percent of output. The pattern of employment in Chinese manufacturing changed even more dramatically between 1993 and 1999 than did output shares. Total employment fell by one-third, from 66.3 million workers in 1993 to 44.2 million in 1999, but the entire drop in employment occurred in the state sector. SOEs employed 45.0 million manufacturing workers in 1993, or 68 percent of the total, but over the next six years the number of workers employed in manufacturing SOEs fell by 24.9 million, and the SOE share of manufacturing employment dropped to 55 percent. The total number of manufacturing workers outside of the state sector remained essentially constant between 1993 and 1999, but the number and share of manufacturing workers employed by privately owned companies increased from

TABLE 5.7. Relative Shares of Chinese State-Owned, Mixed Ownership, and Privately Owned Enterprises in Output, 1993–1999

	Share of Gross Output Value of Chinese Industrial Enterprises (%)						
	1993	1994	1995	1996	1997	1998	1999
SOEs	47	37	34	36	32	28	28
Collectives	34	38	37	39	38	38	35
Individually owned	8	10	13	15	18	17	18
"Other"*	11	15	17	17	18	23	26
TOTAL	100	100	100	100	100	100	100

Source: Table 3 in Broadman (2001).

Note: The shares data do not sum to 100% exactly, owing to rounding and statistical changes in the authorities' reporting tables.

TABLE 5.8. Relative Shares of Chinese State-Owned, Mixed Ownership, and Privately Owned Enterprises in Employment, 1993–1999

	Employment in Chinese Industrial Enterprises (Staff and Workers)				
	1993	1995	1997	1998	1999
SOEs	45.0m	44.0m	40.4m	27.2	24.1
Share	*68%*	*67%*	*65%*	*57%*	*55%*
Collectives	17.0m	15.0m	13.3m	8.0	6.7
Share	*26%*	*23%*	*21%*	*17%*	*15%*
"Others"[a]	4.3m	7.1m	8.5m	12.3	13.4
Share	*6%*	*10%*	*14%*	*26%*	*30%*
TOTAL	66.3m	66.1m	62.2m	47.5	44.2
Share	*100%*	*100%*	*100%*	*100%*	*100%*

Source: Table 4 in Broadman (2001).

[a]"Others" here refers to *all* private sector firms, including "individually owned" enterprises, private firms with more than seven employees, Sino-foreign joint ventures, and fully foreign-funded firms.

4.3 million to 13.4 million, and the private-sector's share of manufacturing employment shot from 6 percent to 30 percent.

Obviously, the share of total Chinese output of goods and services represented by privately owned businesses has increased steadily and dramatically during the past decade. However, most of the growth in the private sector's share has not come from privatized state enterprises. Instead, virtually all of China's economic growth has come either from newly created, domestically owned companies or from ventures funded and controlled by foreign investors. Most of the key reforms have served to promote the formation and development of these new businesses. To date, the privatization of SOEs has not played a central role in the Chinese economic reform agenda; indeed, the Chinese government even denies that it has adopted a privatization program. Instead, the government refers to "opening up the capital of the state sector" and "subjecting state enterprises to market discipline." High-ranking Chinese officials almost never use the word *privatization* when discussing (or defending) the country's divestment program, since the People's Republic of China officially remains a communist nation.

Although shares of several thousand state-owned companies have been sold to private investors, these remain firmly under state control. The reason for this is simple — because the ownership structure of Chinese stock companies is unlike anything seen elsewhere in the world. As described by Xu and Wang (1999), Tian (2003), and Lin (2000), only one-third of the stock in publicly listed former Chinese SOEs can be owned by individuals; the remaining two-thirds of a company's shares must be owned by the state and by domestic (usually financial) institutions. Thus far, these have been exclusively state-owned, though several of the state banks have been partially privatized since 2000.

So-called A-shares may be owned and traded only by Chinese citizens, while B-shares are stocks listed in Shanghai or Shenzhen and may be owned and traded only by foreigners. Other shares are listed in Hong Kong (H-shares) or New York

(N-shares), and these are also reserved for foreign investors. Even though these restrictions were loosened in 2002, the net effect of this fractionalization of ownership has been that, even in publicly listed former SOEs, control is never really contestable. Furthermore, the long-term investment performance of "privatized" Chinese companies has thus far been quite poor, as will be discussed in chapter 6. This is particularly true for the "Red Chip" companies (PRC-controlled enterprises incorporated and listed in Hong Kong) and H-shares sold in Hong Kong.[5]

On the other hand, the sheer number of companies partially privatized by the Chinese government, coupled with the massive potential economic impact of a full-scale privatization program, has prompted a growing number of academic researchers to examine the effectiveness of the partial sales executed thus far. Very few of these manuscripts have thus far been published in academic journals, though this will likely soon change. We now examine these studies.

The Empirical Evidence on Privatization's Impact in China

Table 5.9 summarizes four empirical studies of privatization in China that have either been accepted for publication in top academic journals or are far along in the journal review process. All four studies employ samples of firms that were partially privatized via public share offerings, since only these generate comparable pre- versus post-privatization performance data that are publicly available within the Chinese financial reporting system. Additionally, all four studies employ the MNR (1994) methodology for assessing privatization-related performance changes for individual firms, though most studies also employ panel data estimation techniques to examine specific determinants of performance changes. Almost all Chinese share issue privatizations are executed using primary, capital-raising share offerings rather than the pure secondary offerings favored by most other privatizing countries (except Malaysia). This complicates the analysis of performance changes because primary offerings result in a very large increase in the assets and equity accounts of privatized companies, which artificially depresses measurements such as return on assets and, especially, return on equity in the years immediately after privatization. For this reason, the studies below all measure profitability changes by examining the change in the return on sales ratio or by examining changes in a firm's level of real net profits.

Jia, Sun, and Tong (2002) use a sample of 41 Chinese H-share offerings from 1993 to 1998 to examine whether privatization through listing of Chinese companies in Hong Kong causes performance to improve. They employ both MNR and pooled regression panel data methodology, and find that real net profits are unchanged after privatization, while return on sales declines significantly. Output increases and leverage declines significantly. Regression analysis shows that state ownership is negatively related to performance, but H-share ownership has a significant, positive effect on performance. Wei, Varella, D'Souza, and Hassan (2003) also use MNR methods to test whether performance improves for 208 Chinese companies partially privatized through public share offering between 1990 and 1997. They document significant improvements in real output, assets, and sales,

TABLE 5.9. Summary of Empirical Studies of Privatization in China

Study	Sample Description, Study Period, and Methodology	Summary of Empirical Findings and Conclusions
Sun and Tong (2003)	Evaluate the performance of 634 Chinese SOEs listed on stock exchanges during the period 1994–1998. Use both MNR pre- and post-privatization comparisons and panel data regression methods to examine whether partial divestment improves firm's earnings, output, and efficiency (real output per employee). Also examine differential effect of state and "legal person" shareholdings.	Using MNR methods, find significant improvements in return on sales and the level of real earnings, real sales, and employee productivity after partial privatization. Also find that more recently privatized companies are of higher quality—and perform better after divestment—than do those divested earlier. Panel data regressions verify basic findings that privatization improves performance, and find that different ownership structures have opposite effects on firm's performance. State shareholdings hinder performance, while "legal person" shareholdings promote improvements.
Wei, Varella, D'Souza, and Hassan (2003)	Use MNR methods to test whether performance improves for 208 Chinese companies partially privatized through public share offering between 1990 and 1997.	Document significant improvements in real output, assets and sales, sales efficiency, the level of real profits, and leverage. Firms in which more than 50% voting control is conveyed to private investors improve performance more than do those that remain state controlled.
Tian (2002)	Examines the ownership and control structure of 826 partially privatized companies listed on Chinese stock exchanges in 1994–1998 and tests the relationship between ownership structure and firm value—as measured by Tobin's Q.	Finds that government shareholdings remain very large in partially privatized companies, and that the relationship between state holdings and firm value is U-shaped. Going from state ownership levels of 0 to 30%, increasing ownership causes firm value to decline, but after that Tobin's Q increases with increasing state ownership.
Jia, Sun, and Tong (2002)	Examine whether privatization through listing of Chinese companies in Hong Kong causes performance to improve. Use a sample of 41 Chinese H-share SIPs in 1993–1998. Use MNR and pooled regression panel data methodology.	Find that real net profits are unchanged after privatization, and that return on sales declines significantly. Output increases and leverage declines significantly. Regressions show that state ownership is negatively related to performance. H-share ownership has significant, positive effect on performance.

197

as well as improvement in sales efficiency, the level of real profits, and leverage. Firms in which more than 50 percent voting control is conveyed to private investors improve performance more than do those that remain state controlled.

Tian (2003) examines the ownership and control structures of 826 partially privatized companies listed on Chinese stock exchanges from 1994 to 1998 and tests the relationship between ownership structure and firm value, as measured by Tobin's Q. He finds that government shareholdings remain very large in partially privatized companies, and that the relationship between state holdings and firm value is U-shaped. Going from state ownership levels of 0 to 30 percent, increasing ownership causes firm value to decline, but after that Tobin's Q increases with increasing state ownership. A representation of this relationship is presented in figure 5.5.

Sun and Tong (2003) perform the best and most comprehensive analysis to date of China's privatization program. They evaluate the performance of 634 Chinese SOEs listed on stock exchanges during the period 1994–1998. They use both the MNR and panel data regression methods to examine whether partial divestment improves firms' earnings, output, and efficiency (real output per employee). They also examine the differential effect of state and "legal person" shareholdings. Using MNR methods, they document significant improvements in profitability, as measured by return on sales, and in the level of real earnings, real sales, and employee productivity after partial privatization. They also find that more recently privatized companies are of higher quality—and perform better after divestment—than do those divested earlier. Panel data regressions verify these basic findings that privatization improves performance, though they also find that different ownership structures have opposite effects on firm performance. State shareholdings hinder performance, while "legal person" shareholdings promote improvements. Table 5.10 reproduces the key result of their study.

Taken together, these empirical studies show that privatization in China is associated with dramatic increases in real sales and efficiency (measured as real

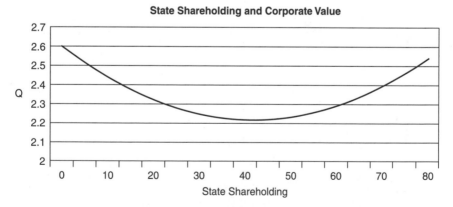

FIGURE 5.5. The relationship between state ownership and corporate value (Tobin's Q) for partially privatized Chinese companies. Source: Tian (2003).

TABLE 5.10. Summary of the Impact of Privatization on the Performance of Partially Divested Chinese Enterprises

Measure	Variable	Number of Obs	Median (Mean) Before	Median (Mean) After	Median (Mean) Change	Wilcoxon Test	Pos (+)/Neg (−) Ratio (Proportion Z)
Profitability	Real net profits (RNP)	634	0.7727 (0.8967)	1.0325 (1.0379)	0.3648 (0.1412)	9.8020**	433/201 (13.5128)**
	Real EBIT (REBIT)	606	0.8149 (0.9000)	1.1386 (1.2722)	0.3237 (0.3723)	9.1090**	413/193 (13.0624)**
	Return on sales (ROS)	634	0.1234 (0.1647)	0.1142 (0.1136)	−0.0092 (−0.0511)	3.0547**	279/355 (−2.6737)**
	Gross profit margin (EBIT/Sales)	614	0.1728 (0.2119)	0.1550 (0.1636)	−0.0178 (−0.0482)	3.9729**	245/369 (−4.0743)**
Output	Real sales (RS)	633	0.8827 (0.9168)	1.2489 (1.4516)	0.3662 (0.5348)	15.7160**	475/158 (21.8289)**
Leverage	Operating cash flow/total debt	288	0.2360 (0.3521)	0.1800 (0.2328)	−0.0560 (−0.1193)	5.3551**	94/194 (−5.892)**
	Times interest earned (TIE)	612	6.2485 (−7.4965)	4.7340 (6.0356)	−1.5145 (13.5321)	4.0230**	278/334 (−2.263)**
Employment	Total employment	113	1,481 (10,818)	1,858 (3,157)	387 (−7,651)	1.0661	63/50 (1.222)
Efficiency	Real sales/employee	113	103.2 (226.1)	126.2 (311.9)	23.04 (65.8)	1.8394*	71/42 (2.728)*

Source: Tables 1–5 of Sun and Tong (2003)

*Denotes significance at the 10 percent level.
**Denotes significance at the 5 percent level.

199

output per worker), as well as with significant declines in leverage. Employment typically does not change significantly following privatization, though this value is not reported frequently enough to allow a firm conclusion. The impact of privatization on profitability is generally misunderstood to be negative, since most empirical studies document a sharp decline in return on assets—and an even larger decline in return on equity—due to the aforementioned fact that Chinese SIPs are almost exclusively primary share offerings. Properly measured, however, profits increase significantly after partial divestiture, since output increases dramatically and the return on sales is essentially unchanged. Thus, the empirical record clearly suggests that privatization "works" quite well in China, even if the government still cannot bring itself to utter the policy's name in polite society.

The Future of Privatization in China

In 1998, the Chinese Communist Party committed the country to what was effectively a massive privatization program [Lin (2000)] under the slogan "seize the large, release the small." This roughly translates as privatizing all but the largest 300 or so SOEs. Over the next five years, such massive changes (and dislocations) occurred within the state sector that the 2003 Party Congress retreated somewhat from planning as rapid a pace of transformation going forward. Nonetheless, even this more modest reform will likely result in a privatization program of unprecedented scale over the next decade. Furthermore, since China joined the World Trade Organization in 2001, broad swathes of heretofore protected Chinese industry—including telecommunications, automobile production, and financial services—will soon be fully opened to international competition for the first time. This process will almost certainly increase the pressure on China to fully privatize its industry.

On the other hand, there are reasons to believe that China's "privatization" program will do little to lessen the state's role in economic decision making, either at the macro- or micro-economic levels. For one thing, the country's convoluted stock ownership restrictions severely hinder effective corporate governance. These ownership restrictions could, however, be rescinded by government fiat at any time. Perhaps the key constraint on privatization in China is the fact that SOEs, rather than the government itself, still serve as the country's social safety net. As described in Bai, Li, and Wang (1997) and Lin, Cai, and Li (1998), Chinese SOEs are burdened with many social welfare responsibilities. Although recent reforms have lessened this burden somewhat, and promise to do so even more in the future, the easy SOE sales and closures have already been made. The enterprises that remain in state hands are generally unprofitable, and often beyond salvage. Thus, it is difficult to imagine the government adopting a privatization program that would either grant these firms discretion over staffing levels or subject them to truly enterprise threatening competition. In sum, the long-term prognosis for privatization in China is unclear; there is great scope for such a program to have a dramatically positive impact, coupled with great danger of social turmoil if handled (or sequenced) incorrectly.

Summary

The countries of central and eastern Europe that were part of the Soviet bloc until the collapse of the Berlin Wall in 1989 have lived through a period of peaceful transition that is unique in modern history. In fact, the changes required to move from police states with centrally planned economies to democracies with market economies have been so vast and all-encompassing that these nations have been labeled "transition states." All 26 countries that emerged from the Soviet bloc have at least begun the political and economic process of transition, and many have made dramatic progress—but the process has invariably been painful and incomplete.

This chapter surveys the economic changes and dislocations involved in the transition of CEE countries, and specifically examines the role that privatization of state enterprises has played in transition. Not surprisingly, given that the state owned as much as 95 percent of productive assets in some countries in 1989, privatization has been far more massive and disruptive in the transition countries than in nontransition developed and developing nations. Not only did the state need to divest its ownership of most of the business assets in these countries, it also had to do so in an environment where few citizens could afford to pay cash for shares divested and where there were literally no domestic companies that could purchase the state enterprises. Rather than sell SOEs to the only parties willing and able to pay cash—foreign companies and investors—most CEE governments opted for mass privatization schemes, wherein citizens received vouchers (free or at very low cost) that could then be converted into shares of SOEs being divested by the state.

Though initially popular, voucher privatizations ultimately proved disappointing. Unlike asset sales, these programs failed to attract any new capital or expertise to the enterprises being divested, which thus languished unreformed and undercapitalized. Unlike share issue privatizations, the voucher schemes also failed to raise any money for the selling governments, which inevitably faced severe fiscal and monetary pressures during transition. More generally, all aspects of the transition process proved to be far more difficult than expected, and many companies—both those that had been privatized and those that remained state owned—encountered severe financial problems. These problems, in turn, made it extremely difficult for governments to impose hard budget constraints on firms, and so easy credit continued to flow to companies from state-controlled banks. Banking crises were the unsurprising and all too common results of these soft budget constraints, and by the end of the 1990s the banking systems of several CEE nations were almost entirely foreign owned.

Another severe problem of transition was the common failure to adopt needed microeconomic and legal reforms to strengthen corporate governance, protect creditors and investors, and prevent managers from looting their companies through a variety of legal and extra-legal means. Researchers have documented a significant, direct relationship between these "deep reforms" and superior economic performance, indicating that the countries able to implement needed legal and regulatory changes were also able to recover most rapidly from the severe decline in output that all transition economies experienced after the collapse of communism. Research also documents that the ownership structures that emerged from various privatization processes were instrumental determinants of the economic performance of divested companies. In general, companies where insiders gained control performed very poorly, whereas firms that gained real owners in the form of financial institutions, foreign corporations, or local entrepreneurs fared much better. This research also documents a surprisingly positive impact of residual state ownership on firm performance.

In contrast with the former Soviet bloc countries, China's transition experience has been immensely successful. Over the past quarter-century, China has enjoyed rapid and almost uninterrupted economic growth, and has attracted more foreign direct investment than any country in the world except the United States. To date, relatively few state-owned enterprises have been even partially privatized, though the empirical evidence suggests that privatization has on average improved firm performance when attempted. Instead, enterprises have been given greater operating freedom and have been subjected to hard (or at least harder) budget constraints. Additionally, new private and mixed ownership companies have emerged as the dominant engines of Chinese economic growth. Finally, a much larger wave of true privatizations seems likely to be executed by the Chinese government over the coming decade.

The Structure and Investment Performance of Privatization Share Offerings

Only 20 years ago, the largest share offering in world history had raised less than $1.5 billion, and very few share offerings ever raised more than $250 million. However, since the first British Telecom offering in November 1984, which raised an unheard of $4.9 billion, no fewer than 183 share issue privatizations have raised at least $1 billion, and 16 have raised over $10 billion! Twenty years ago, a very small fraction of the adult population owned shares in any developed country except the United States, and share ownership was even more highly concentrated in developing countries. Today, between one-sixth and one-third of the adult population owns shares in most developed (and in a few developing) countries, and share ownership exceeds 40 percent in at least three — Sweden, Australia, and the United States.

Twenty years ago, the total value of all of the world's listed companies was a little over $3 trillion, a figure that was less than 40 percent of world GDP. By early 2000, global market capitalization reached $35 trillion, a figure equal to global GDP. Even after world market capitalization declined to its low point of about $20 trillion during the summer of 2002, this still equaled roughly two-thirds of global output, and the global rebound in stock value over the next two years has brought worldwide valuations back near $30 trillion by the summer of 2004. In other words, the past 20 years have witnessed a revolution in global finance and, outside of the United States, the most important factor in this transformation has been the spread of SIP programs around the world.

This chapter examines the structure and investment performance of SIPs. As we will see, these often massive share issues differ fundamentally from private-sector share issues in almost all respects, except that both use the same financial instrument. The insignificantly positive long-term investment performance of SIPs also differs dramatically from the significantly negative long-run returns observed for private share offerings. Additionally, SIPs were the first truly large share offerings of any type in most countries, so privatizations effectively inaugurated those nations' investment banking industries. Even in the handful of countries (Britain,

Japan, Canada, the United States, and a few continental European countries) where significant share offerings were already established, SIPs transformed the size and efficiency of both that country's investment banking industry and its stock market.

Characteristics of Share Issue Privatization Offerings

In all likelihood, you do not now consider common stock offerings to be important instruments of public policy. This section will try to convince you otherwise. In fact, we will see that governments around the world have learned to use share issue privatizations both as a mechanism for raising money and as a tool of political expression. To understand this point, ask yourself what choices the private owner of a company seeking to raise capital by selling stock to public investors for the first time would make regarding the size, structure, and pricing of this IPO of shares. The typical entrepreneur's principal objective in an IPO is to raise as much new capital as possible, at the maximum attainable price per share, while selling a small enough fraction of the company that personal voting control of the firm is not immediately threatened. Expressed in practical terms, this implies that most private-sector share offerings will be primary, capital-raising issues and that entrepreneurs should sell relatively small stakes in their companies through some type of auction mechanism that yields the highest attainable per share price. In the United States—and increasingly in other developed countries as well—this means selling shares through an underwritten initial share offering, where the investment bank handling the offer uses book-building techniques to assess what institutional investors are willing to pay and then sets the offering price at a level that just clears the market. In general terms, this is in fact how most private-sector IPOs are actually priced and marketed in the United States and other developed economies.

When a government sells an SOE via a public share offering, it confronts the same pricing and marketing decisions as faced by corporate issuers, but the empirical evidence shows that governments make significantly different choices from those entrepreneurs make. Unlike entrepreneurs, who seek to maximize the proceeds received from share offerings, a privatizing government pursues multiple objectives and has both political and economic goals. Where entrepreneurs typically sell small stakes in their firms in primary share offerings, governments prefer to sell much larger fractions (averaging about 34 percent) of SOE stock in enormous, purely secondary share offerings that raise revenue for the government but yield no new capital for the firm. Whereas the investment bankers handling private-sector IPOs generally employ book-building techniques and sell shares to the highest bidders, privatizing governments typically use fixed-price offerings, with the (deliberately low) offering price set weeks in advance, and then allocate these shares as widely as possible to citizens—often at discounted prices. Finally, whereas virtually all entrepreneurs are intent on retaining tight control of their firms after the IPO, governments generally commit to not exercising any day-to-day operating control over the privatized firms, though governments often retain ultimate veto power over strategic decisions, especially regarding mergers or restructurings.

SIP Offering Size

The first thing most financially literate observers notice about share issue privatizations is that many of these offerings are truly gargantuan. This is especially true in a relative sense, as compared to other share offerings from a given country or as a fraction of that country's GDP. However, as table 6.1 clearly demonstrates, SIPs are also the largest share offerings in an absolute sense. In fact, the 11 largest share offerings in financial history are all share sales by state-owned firms, and 10 of these are true SIPs that reduce state ownership.[1] Additionally, 30 of history's 34 largest share offerings are SIPs. Apart from the disastrous (for investors) $10.6 billion AT&T Wireless tracking stock IPO in April 2000, no truly private-sector share offering has ever raised more than $7.5 billion, but this has been achieved by 22 SIPs from eight countries.

Several of the issues detailed in table 6.1 bear explicit mention, beginning with the five offerings listed for NTT. Not only is the $40.26 billion seasoned offering in November 1987 the largest share offering in financial history, but when the $15.1 billion IPO in October 1988 and the $22.4 billion seasoned equity offering (SEO) in February 1988 are also added in, the Japanese government raised an astonishing $80 billion from the sale of less than 25 percent of the stock in a single company—in less than one year! The two sales of NTTDoCoMo stock by NTT are really equity carve-outs where a parent company sells off a fraction of the stock it owns in a subsidiary, but since these reduce overall government ownership of a company's equity, they qualify as share issue privatizations. Combining these with the six NTT offerings since 1987 (one was too "small" to make table 6.1's listing) yields total proceeds of almost $135 billion, yet the Japanese government still owns almost half of NTT's shares! It is conceivable that by the time the government fully divests all of its holdings in this one company, the total proceeds may reach $250 billion.

Several other patterns are evident in table 6.1's listing. Note, for example, the disproportionate number of offerings of shares in telecommunications companies. Fifteen of the 20 largest (and 18 of the 29 largest) share offerings in history have been telecom privatization issues—including three from the relatively small countries of Australia (Telstra, ranks 14 and 15) and Sweden (Telia, rank 19). With the exception of five offerings of oil and gas companies (British Petroleum, British Gas, Elf Acquitaine, and two ENI issues) and one bank (Credit Lyonnais), all of the other SIPs in table 6.1 are from regulated industries such as electricity generation and distribution, water and sewage, and rail transport. These are invariably large, well-known companies providing basic services, and the shares are generally marketed very heavily to ordinary citizens. Finally, note that 14 of the 30 SIPs in table 6.1 are initial public offerings, including the largest IPO in history, Italy's November 1999 offering of a one-third stake in the electric utility company ENEL. This issue raised $18.9 billion for the Italian treasury and attracted over 4 million individual investors.

Not surprisingly, table 6.1's listing of the world's largest share offerings is dominated by sales by developed country governments. A similar listing of the largest offerings from emerging markets, presented in table 6.2, shows an even greater dominance by SIPs—in fact, all of the very largest share offerings in emerging

TABLE 6.1. Details of the World's Largest Share Offerings

Date	Company	Country	Amount ($ Millions)	IPO/SEO
Nov 87	Nippon Telegraph & Telephone	Japan	$40,260	SEO
Oct 88	Nippon Telegraph & Telephone	Japan	22,400	SEO
Nov 99	ENEL	Italy	18,900	IPO
Oct 98	NTT DoCoMo	Japan	18,000	IPO
Mar 03	France Telecom	France	15,800	SEO[a]
Oct 97	Telecom Italia	Italy	15,500	SEO
Feb 87	Nippon Telegraph & Telephone	Japan	15,097	IPO
Nov 99	Nippon Telegraph & Telephone	Japan	15,000	SEO
Jun 00	Deutsche Telekom	Germany	14,760	SEO
Nov 96	Deutsche Telekom	Germany	13,300	IPO
Oct 87	British Petroleum	United Kingdom	12,430	SEO
Apr 00	*ATT Wireless (tracking stock)*	*United States*	*10,600*	*IPO*
Nov 98	France Telecom	France	10,500	SEO
Nov 97	Telstra	Australia	10,530	IPO
Oct 99	Telstra	Australia	10,400	SEO
Jun 99	Deutsche Telekom	Germany	10,200	SEO
Dec 90	Regional Electricity Companies[b]	United Kingdom	9,995	IPO
Dec 91	British Telecom	United Kingdom	9,927	SEO
Jun 00	Telia	Sweden	8,800	IPO
Dec 89	U.K. Water Authorities[b]	United Kingdom	8,679	IPO
Feb 01	NTT DoCoMo	Japan	8,200	SEO
Dec 86	British Gas	United Kingdom	8,012	IPO
Jun 98	Endesa	Spain	8,000	SEO
Jul 97	ENI	Italy	7,800	SEO
Apr 00	*Oracle Japan*	*Japan*	*7,500*	*IPO*
Jul 93	British Telecom	United Kingdom	7,360	SEO
Oct 93	Japan Railroad East	Japan	7,312	IPO
Dec 98	Nippon Telegraph & Telephone	Japan	7,300	SEO
Oct 97	France Telecom	France	7,080	IPO
Jul 99	Credit Lyonnais	France	6,960	IPO
Feb 94	Elf Acquitaine	France	6,823	SEO
Jun 97	*Halifax Building Society*	*United Kingdom*	*6,813*	*IPO*
Jun 98	ENI	Italy	6,740	SEO
Feb 01	Orange	France	6,687	SEO

Source: Table 12 of Megginson and Netter (2001). Updated by author.

Note: Offers are reported in nominal amounts (not inflation-adjusted), and are translated into millions of US dollars (US$ millions) using the contemporaneous exchange rate. *Private-sector offerings* are presented in italicized type, while share issue privatizations (SIPs) are presented in normal typeface. Amounts reported for SIP offers are as described in the *Financial Times* at the time of the issue. Private-sector offering amounts are from the *Securities Data Corporation* file or *Financial Times*.

[a] Rights offering, in which the French government participated proportionately, so not a SIP in the traditional sense. Though a share offering by a state-owned firm, government ownership did not decline.

[b] Indicates a group offering of multiple companies that trade separately after the IPO.

markets have been privatizations. Table 6.2 also demonstrates greater industry variation than was true for developed countries, though here as well the 19 telecom offers dominate. Nine of the remaining SIPs are offerings of oil and gas company shares, reflecting the greater resource emphasis of developing country economies.

One pattern that is strikingly obvious in table 6.2 is the financial importance of greater China. Ten of the 35 largest share offerings are from mainland China or Hong Kong, and these span an unusually broad number of industries (telecoms, oil and gas, banking, and mass transit railways). This is particularly impressive since the first publicly traded common stock in modern Chinese history was issued only in 1984, and the two major stock exchanges were not established until 1991. Furthermore, there were no truly "private" share offerings until 2000, and these remain very rare, so all of the phenomenal growth in the capitalization and trading volume of the Shanghai and Shenzhen stock exchanges has come from privatized companies. Yet the state sector remains virtually untouched. The central government has not even begun selling stock in many of its largest SOEs, and retains large majority holdings in those it has partially privatized, so the potential "supply" of Chinese SIPs appears nearly inexhaustible.[2] Since China is already the world's second largest economy on a purchasing power parity adjusted basis, and is enjoying economic growth rates several times higher than those of Western economies, this country seems certain to increase even more in financial importance over coming decades.

In addition to the prominence of Chinese SIPs, table 6.2 reveals that six of the largest emerging market SIPs have been offers by the Korean government for shares in several very different state enterprises. Two of the largest have been offerings of Pohang Iron and Steel (POSCO), historically one of the best managed state-owned enterprises anywhere, and now one of the world's largest steel companies. Four of the large Korean SIPs have been executed very recently, since Korea first began to emerge from the depression brought about by the 1998 East Asian financial crisis. The Korean government remains committed to a very aggressive privatization program emphasizing public share offerings and, unlike most governments that assert their intention to implement such a program, actually seems likely to follow through on its promise successfully.

Tables 6.1 and 6.2 show that the largest SIPs are very large, indeed. But how do SIPs compare, on average, to private sector IPOs and seasoned equity offerings (SEOs)? The most detailed study of SIPs yet published is Jones, Megginson, Nash, and Netter (1999; hereafter JMNN), who examine a sample of 630 initial and seasoned SIPs from 65 countries executed over the period 1977–1997. Many of the results presented in this section are from that paper. JMNN also show that SIPs are large by the standards of private firm offerings. The overall mean (median) size for the full sample of issues is $708 million ($143 million), which is more than 17 (six) times larger than the mean (median) equity offering size reported for U.S. companies in Mikkelson and Partch (1986) and Masulis and Korwar (1986). The initial SIPs are also large.

The total value of the issues in JMNN's sample is $446 billion; of this, initial SIPs constitute $232 billion or 52 percent of the value of the full sample and 66 percent of the number of issues. The overall mean (median) dollar value (hereafter

TABLE 6.2. Details of the Largest Share Offerings (All Share Issue Privatizations) in Emerging Markets

Date	Company	Country	Amount ($ Millions)	IPO/SEO
Jun 00	China Unicom	China	$4,900	IPO
Aug 00	Petrobras	Brazil	$4,030	SEO
Oct 97	China Telecom	China	$4,000	SEO
Jun 02	Korea Telecom	Korea	$4,000	SEO
Jan 03	Saudi Telecom	Saudi Arabia	$3,700	IPO
Oct 01	Sinopec	China	$3,470	IPO
Jun 88	Pohang Iron and Steel	Korea	$3,400	IPO
Apr 00	PetroChina	China	$2,890	IPO
Jul 02	Bank of China	China	$2,800	IPO
Jun 93	Yacimientos Petroliferos Fiscales	Argentina	$2,660	IPO
May 99	Korea Telecom	Korea	$2,490	SEO
Jun 01	Korea Telecom	Korea	$2,490	SEO
May 91	Telefonos de Mexico	Mexico	$2,170	IPO
Jun 89	Korea Electric Power	Korea	$2,100	IPO
Oct 99	China Telecom	China	$2,000	SEO
Oct 93	Singapore Telecom	Singapore	$1,950	IPO
Nov 02	China Telecom	China	$1,650	SEO
Nov 95	PT Telkom	Indonesia	$1,590	IPO
Sep 95	Petronas Gas	Malaysia	$1,443	IPO
May 92	Telefonos de Mexico	Mexico	$1,400	SEO
Feb 01	China National Offshore Oil Company	China	$1,400	IPO
Aug 01	Sinopec	China	$1,400	SEO
Oct 02	Unicom	China	$1,400	IPO
Oct 00	Mass Transit Railway Corp	China (HKSAR)	$1,380	IPO
Oct 89	ISCOR	South Africa	$1,300	IPO
Mar 94	Telecom Argentina	Argentina	$1,227	SEO
Nov 97	Matav	Hungary	$1,200	IPO
Mar 95	Tupras	Turkey	$1,200	IPO
Oct 91	Usinimas	Brazil	$1,170	IPO
Mar 92	Tenaga National	Malaysia	$1,163	IPO
Jul 96	Telefonica del Peru	Peru	$1,100	IPO
Oct 94	Indosat	Indonesia	$1,060	—
Mar 92	Telecom Argentina	Argentina	$1,050	IPO
Nov 98	Telekomunikacja Polska (TPSA)	Poland	$1,020	IPO
Nov 96	CANTV	Venezuela	$1,010	IPO
May 99	Pohang Iron and Steel	Korea	$1,010	SEO
Sep 94	Pakistan Telecommunications	Pakistan	$997	IPO

Note: Amounts reported for SIP offers are as described in the *Financial Times* at the time of the issue. Private-sector offering amounts are from the *Securities Data Corporation* file or *Financial Times*.

referred to as the size of the offer) of the initial SIPs is $556 million ($104 million). The average initial offer is large relative to the mean value of $13.2 million for IPOs floated on U.S. markets between 1960 and 1992 (Ibbotson, Sindelar, and Ritter, 1994) or the median value of $24.4 million for U.S. IPOs from 1990 to 1994 (Lee, Lochhead, Ritter, and Zhao, 1996). The average sizes of non-U.S. IPOs reported in the survey article by Loughran, Ritter, and Rydqvist (1994) vary significantly between markets and over different time periods, but most are less that $15 million.[3]

In addition to being very large by the standards of private sector equity offerings, SIPs are the largest type of privatizations. Megginson, Nash, Netter, and Poulsen (MNNP; forthcoming) report that the average size of 1,526 asset sales of SOEs executed over the 1977–2000 period is $290 million (median $30.3 million) versus the $799 million mean ($105 million median) value for the 931 SIPs reported by MNNP. The value of the firms sold in SIP offerings actually exceeds the value of the firms sold in asset sales by an even greater amount than is suggested by these numbers because usually only about one-third of the SOE is sold in a typical SIP, while almost 75 percent of the typical SOE is sold in an asset sale. As discussed in chapter 3, it clearly seems necessary to use organized stock exchanges and the capital markets to sell the largest SOEs.

Geographic Distribution and Average Age of SIPs

In the early years of privatization, only a handful of mostly developed countries used SIPs to privatize state companies. Since 1990, however, privatizing share offers have become a truly global phenomenon. As an illustration, appendix 1 of this book provides details of SIPs from no fewer than 57 countries, and there have been many other offerings, from several dozen countries, that were too small to be reported by the *Financial Times* and thus are not detailed in the appendix. JMNN's data include share offerings from 59 countries. These issues raise a total of $446 billion ($232 billion in initial SIPs) for selling governments. Two countries, the United Kingdom and China, account for 133 of the offers (21 percent of all offers). There are 238 issues from western Europe, including the United Kingdom (38 percent of all offers, 54 percent of the value of all offers); 160 issues are from Asia, including Australia (25 percent of all offers, 35 percent of the value of all offers); 88 issues are from the Middle East and North Africa (14 percent of all offers, 3 percent of the value of all offers); 64 issues are from eastern Europe (11 percent of all offers, 1 percent of the value of all offers); 31 issues are from the remainder of Africa (5 percent of all offers, 1 percent of the value of all offers); 31 issues are from North America (5 percent of all offers, 2 percent of the value of all offers); and 18 issues are from South America (3 percent of all offers, 2 percent of the value of all offers). Also, the average age of the 54 firms for which they can identify the founding dates is over 50 years (median age 39 years), and one firm (Instituto Bancario San Paolo, an Italian bank) was 429 years old at the time of its privatization. Details of the time pattern of SIPs in the JMNN sample are presented in table 6.3.

We now turn to an examination of the structure and pricing of SIPs, and

TABLE 6.3. Size and Number of Share Issue Privatization Offerings, June 1977–July 1997

Year	Initial SIPs Mean ($ Millions)	Median ($ Millions)	Number	Seasoned Mean ($ Millions)	Median ($ Millions)	Number	All Issues Mean ($ Millions)	Median ($ Millions)	Number
1977				919	919	1	919	919	1
1979				473	473	1	473	473	1
1981	305	305	2				305	305	2
1982	506	506	2				415	415	3
1983	36	36	1	686	686	2	469	448	3
1984	2,500	639	3	85	85	1	1,897	559	4
1985	231	184	3	1,050	898	3	550	424	8
1986	1,536	569	7	989	989	1	1,188	342	10
1987	2,712	207	19	5,586	11,800	6	3,407	658	28
1988	512	116	13	22,800	22,800	1	1,862	152	16
1989	500	240	33	335	285	9	457	240	43
1990	430	319	30	364	157	5	389	157	39
1991	530	103	32	187	193	10	712	131	44
1992	200	67	40	519	478	13	275	85	54
1993	491	52	51	852	252	20	580	80	74
1994	450	132	65	747	215	25	528	170	92
1995	404	92	49	656	127	27	600	105	79
1996	426	56	45	764	393	33	593	180	84
1997	240	58	22	1175	205	14	503	90	45
Overall	556	104	417	1069	311	172	708	143	630

Source: Data from Privatisation International database, as reported in Table 1 of Jones, Megginson, Nash, and Netter (1999).

again rely heavily on the JMNN study. They document several important patterns, which we briefly mention here and then discuss in the paragraphs below. First, they find that governments usually do not sell an entire SOE, or even a controlling stake, in the initial SIP. In many cases, the initial offer is followed by one or more seasoned offers. A government may require four or more of these offerings to fully divest its holdings in the largest state enterprises, particularly telecoms. Second, most SIPs are offered using the fixed-price method, whereby the government sets the share price several weeks in advance of the offering date. Governments typically use tender offers or book building only for the institutional or foreign portions (tranches) of the offering. Third, most initial SIPs are significantly and deliberately underpriced, meaning the offer price is set below the expected post-offer market price, and there is significant variation in the level of underpricing. Fourth, over 90 percent of the SIPs are oversubscribed, meaning that investors demand more shares than the seller is offering. This oversubscription occurs largely because the shares are so conspicuously underpriced, and governments usually allocate the lion's share of the stock on offer to domestic and retail investors, rather than to foreign and institutional investors. Also, employees are virtually always favored with preferential allocations of stock, often at discounted prices. Finally, JMNN find that governments frequently insert control restrictions in the charters of privatized firms, or retain golden shares, which are designed to ensure that the privatized firm will not be fully controlled by foreigners or successfully targeted for hostile takeover.

Fraction of the Company Sold in Initial and Seasoned SIPs

For a variety of reasons, governments rarely sell all of their holdings in an SOE in a single offering. One key reason for this is practical: they are simply too large for markets to absorb in one gulp. Recall that the Japanese government has executed six massive public offerings of NTT shares, yet still owns almost half of the company. Two other reasons for selling SOE shares in multiple tranches have more to do with political imperatives and the need to signal than to the poor absorptive capacity of national stock markets. First, governments find it necessary to retain a large stake in partially privatized companies (particularly regulated utilities) in order to convince investors that the government will not attempt to expropriate shareholder wealth in the divested firm through taxation or discriminatory regulatory policies. By retaining a large residual stake, the government itself would be the biggest loser if its post-offering policies caused stock prices to decline sharply; if the government sold all of its stake in an SOE in the first offering it would not bear the cost of such post-offering strategic behavior. By bonding itself not to expropriate wealth, the government is thus able to sell shares in a partial SIP at a higher price than it could obtain in a complete sale. Finally, governments often feel compelled to retain a stake in high-profile companies or SOEs in strategic industries for nationalistic reasons, especially in order to ensure that the privatized firm will not be acquired by a foreign company. Citizens also demand that the state retain the ability to force privatized company's managers to consider "the public interest" in their operating and investment decisions for the firm.

The empirical evidence on the fraction of an SOE that is typically sold clearly suggests that both practical and political considerations guide SOE divestment policies. This section again relies heavily on the evidence in JMNN, and the key parts of that evidence are reproduced in table 6.4. This indicates that partial offerings are common. Of the 384 initial SIPs, only 11.5 percent involved the sale of an entire SOE. Only the British issues after 1984 and most of the French issues during 1986–1987 involve sales of 100 percent of the company's capital in the initial offer. In addition, only 28.9 percent of initial SIPs involve the sale of more than 50 percent of an SOE, and if we exclude the offers from the United Kingdom, this declines to 20.2 percent. In fact, very few countries routinely sell 100 percent of a company in one offer. The mean (median) percent of capital offered in the 384 initial SIPs is 43.9 percent (35 percent). These numbers are only slightly lower if the United Kingdom is excluded. Not surprisingly, the amount of capital sold in seasoned offers tends to be much smaller.

Pricing and Offer Methods in SIPs

As we will see in chapter 7, the past dozen years has witnessed an unprecedented surge in the number and value of corporate security offerings around the world.

TABLE 6.4. Pricing, Share Allocation, and Control Allocation Patterns in Share Issue Privatizations

Measure	Initial SIPS			Seasoned Offers		
	Mean	Median	Number	Mean	Median	Number
Pricing variables						
Issue size (US$ millions)	$555.7	$104.0	417	$1,068.9	$311.0	172
Initial return	34.1%	12.4%	242	9.4%	3.3%	55
Percent of offer at fixed price	85.0%	100.0%	273	61.0%	100.0%	77
Cost of sales, percent of issue	4.4%	3.3%	178	2.5%	2.6%	61
Share allocation variables						
Percent of offer allocated to employees	8.5%	7.0%	255	4.8%	2.6%	76
Fraction of offers with some allocation to employees	91.0%		255	65.8%		76
Percent of offer allocated to foreigners	28.4%	11.5%	348	35.9%	32.5%	142
Percent of offers with some allocation to foreigners	57.1%		348	67.6%		142
Control allocation variables						
Percent of capital sold in offer	43.9%	35.0%	384	22.7%	18.1%	154
Percent of offers where 100% of capital sold	11.5%		384	0		154
Percent of capital where 50% or more of capital sold	28.9%		384	8.4%		154

Source: Data from Privatization International database, as reported in Tables 3, 4, and 5 of Jones, Megginson, Nash, and Netter (1999).

For example, the total value of all security offerings was a little over $500 billion in 1990, but in 2003, the value was $5.3 trillion! Offerings by U.S.-based issuers always account for over two-thirds of this total, while European and Japanese issues account for most of the rest. Ljungqvist, Jenkinson, and Wilhelm (2003) document that U.S. investment banks—and especially U.S. banking procedures—have been steadily gaining market share since 1990, and the most visible aspect of this growth has been the spread of book building techniques. This means that an investment bank underwriting a share offering will carefully assess investor demand, at each of a rising schedule of per-share offering prices, by institutional investors for shares in a company going public. The bankers will then set the final offering price at a level slightly below that required to clear the market, then they will execute the offer by allocating shares to the institutional investors, after which trading begins. Book building, though expensive in terms of direct costs (such as underwriting fees), allows the issuing firm to sell shares at a sufficiently higher price that the net proceeds from the offering are higher than would otherwise be possible.

The alternative to book building is a fixed-price offering. These have traditionally been the dominant approach to pricing and marketing IPOs outside the United States. In this method, the issuer states the number of shares and the offer price several weeks in advance of taking orders from potential investors. In contrast, book building has been the method of choice in the United States. In this process, the investment banker builds a book as the issue is pre-sold to investors. This pre-selling involves the solicitation of interest but does not legally require investors to buy shares at the price they specify (though reputational concerns generally prompt investors to follow through and place firm orders). Book building has the advantage of aggregating investor demand prior to the offer and thus yields higher expected offer proceeds than the fixed-price method. However, Benveniste and Wilhelm (1997) show that fixed-price offers have an advantage over book building in that they are less likely to fail at the offer price. In fact, the fixed price is set lower than a book-building offer price so as to generate cascading demand that guarantees the issuers' proceeds. This makes fixed-price offers popular with risk-averse issuers, and it follows that these offers are appropriate for SIPs, since a failed offer could endanger the whole privatization program. In addition, cascading demand is useful for eliciting the interest of the politically important median-class voters. However, for less politically sensitive investors, such as institutional investors or foreigners, or for less politically sensitive seasoned offers, governments should be more willing to use book building or auctions to maximize issue proceeds.

The results presented in table 6.4 illustrate the popularity of fixed-price offers. For the 273 initial SIPs for which JMNN can determine the method of offer, 85 percent are at least partially fixed price and 79.9 percent are entirely fixed price. There are offers that are only partially fixed price, in that they use auction pricing for institutional investors. In seasoned offers, shares are sold exclusively at a fixed price 59.7 percent of the time, and 61.0 percent of the average seasoned issue is fixed price. Table 6.4 also presents mean and median values for the cost of selling the share offering as a percent of the issue amount. It is interesting to note that the average level of fees is only 3.9 percent across the full sample of SIPs, and the

4.4 percent average fee for initial offers is only slightly larger than the 2.5 percent value for seasoned issues.

These fees are much lower than the 7.0 percent and 7.9 percent spreads documented for recent American IPOs by Beatty and Welch (1996) and Lee, Lochhead, Ritter, and Xhao (LLRX; 1996), respectively. The fees on seasoned offerings are also much less than the 5.44 percent gross spreads documented by LLRX. Even when JMNN focus exclusively on the very largest ($500 million and up) initial offers in LLRX, they find that the 5.21 percent spread for the largest American IPOs is 18 percent larger than the spread for all initial SIP offers, even though the average size of SIPs is smaller than the top decile of U.S. offers. Evidence also suggests that the fees for larger SIPs are actually falling over time. The low costs of underwriting are consistent with governments deliberately underpricing to such an extent that the underwriters willingly accept low spreads because they perceive there to be very little risk of insufficient demand for shares. In addition, underwriters often view participation in a SIP as reputation enhancing.

Table 6.4 also reports the initial returns (i.e., the underpricing) calculated from the closing secondary market price on the first day of trading, less the offer price, as a percent of the offer price. The mean (median) level of returns is 34.1 percent (12.4 percent) for the initial SIPs and 9.4 percent (3.3 percent) for seasoned SIPs. JMNN find that underpricing has not decreased with time, and also document that the mean and median levels of underpricing are similar across industries with the exception of financials and utilities. We will discuss the theory and empirical evidence on underpricing in much greater detail in the next section. For now, we simply wish to document that underpricing of SIPs is pervasive, and assert that it is politically motivated. By deliberately underpricing SIPs, governments turn these share offerings into political instruments, since they can then allocate the underpriced shares (and implied capital gain) to politically favored groups of citizen/investors. As we now see, governments do in fact allocate shares based on a political calculus, and do so with great effectiveness.

Preferential Share Allocations and the Selection of an Underwriter

The final part of table 6.4 describes how shares are allocated in initial and seasoned SIPs. Governments clearly allocate shares in the politically inspired manner predicted by Biais and Perotti (2002). Officials achieve political goals in part by dividing the issue into tranches, with each tranche targeting a certain number of shares to different clienteles (i.e., employees, domestic, retail, institutional, and foreign). In 91.0 percent of the initial offers, some fraction of the total offering is sold to employees, and these shares are often sold with favorable terms such as discounted prices and lenient payment schedules. The mean (median) fraction allocated to employees is 7.6 percent (5.7 percent). In 9 percent of the initial offerings, domestic retail investors are allowed to purchase shares at a discount. The mean (median) discount is 10.4 percent (7.3 percent). In 16.2 percent of the seasoned offerings, there is an explicit mean (median) discount for domestic retail investors of 5.1 percent (4.3 percent). These discounted offerings are fixed-price transactions in which governments designate a specific block of discounted shares for domestic retail investors.

There are usually additional preferential allocations in the initial offerings to individual versus institutional investors and to domestic rather than foreign investors. Foreigners are explicitly allocated shares in 57.1 percent of the initial offers, but the mean (median) allocation fraction is only 28.4 percent (11.5 percent). An extreme case of preferential allocations occurs in some of the Malaysian offerings, with reserved shares for Malaysian citizens, of which a large fraction must be individual or institutional members of the Bumiputra ethnic group. In addition, domestic investors and employees are effectively always guaranteed their allocation if the offer is oversubscribed. In fact, oversubscribed shares are allocated from institutional and foreign investors to employees and/or domestic retail investors in all but two of the over 150 initial issues for which JMNN can identify the over-subscription allocation mechanism. The other two offers are undersubscribed. JMNN also find that over 90 percent of the initial issues are oversubscribed or fully subscribed, with the major exceptions being the Chinese offers.

Over 20 percent of the offers are more than ten times oversubscribed. Thus, the evidence that employees and domestic investors are preferentially allocated shares in offers that are usually underpriced and oversubscribed suggests that governments are building political support by targeting median-class voters, rather than maximizing issue proceeds. Since López-de-Silanes (1997) documents that opening a bid up to foreign buyers significantly increases proceeds from the sale of Mexican SOEs, the strategy of favoring domestic investors is a costly one for governments, since sale proceeds could be increased by allowing foreign investors to participate in privatization sales.

The share allocations in seasoned offerings are less clear-cut, though they are also generally consistent with political objectives. Fully 65.8 percent of all seasoned issues have specific allocations to employees, with a mean (median) fraction of 4.8 percent (2.6 percent) of the offer being so allocated. However, the median fraction governments allocate to foreigners is significantly larger in seasoned than in initial offerings (32.5 percent versus 11.5 percent), and a larger fraction of seasoned offers have a foreign tranche (67.6 percent versus 57.1 percent).

Perhaps the single most distinctive pattern of share allocation observed for SIPs is the near universal tendency of governments to favor SOE employees with share allocations and to allow these workers to buy shares at a discounted price. One of the most dramatic examples of this was the scheme adopted by the French government for the IPO of France Telecom in 1997. Degeorge, Jenter, Moel, and Tufano (2004) show that the government offered FT employees and retirees not one, but four different share purchase plans, designed to meet four distinct timing and consumption-versus-saving preferences. These four share-purchase plans are described in table 6.5. Degeorge, Jenter, Moel, and Tufano show that over 97 percent of eligible current and former FT workers purchased shares under one or more of these plans.

Although a handful of European (especially British) and American investment banking houses have the most experience in privatization, local investment banks are often included in the underwriting syndicate if they are able to access local

TABLE 6.5. Description of the Four Share Purchase Programs Offered to Employees in France Telecom's 1997 Privatization

Program	Discount[b]	Matching Bonus[c]	Free Shares[d]	Payment Options[e]	Guarantees
Abondix[a] 5 years required holding period	20% off of offer price	100% for first FF3000 50% fro next FF6000 25% for next FF66000	One for each share purchased up to FF 3000 One for each four shares purchased for the next FF3860	In cash In three payments over two years In 36 monthly payments Through transfer from company pension plan	None
Multiplix[a] 5 years required holding period	20% off of offer price	50% for first FF2000 Plus 9 × (personal contribution and bonus) as a guaranteed bank loan The investor forgoes dividends and tax credit	None	In cash In three payments over two years In 36 monthly payments	25% return on personal over five years contribution Guaranteed repayment of the bank loan
Simplix 2 years required holding period (3 years for free shares)	20% off of offer price	None	One for each bought share up to FF3000 One for each four shares purchased for the next FF3860	In cash In three payments over two years In 36 monthly payments	None
Disponix No required holding period (1 year for free shares)	None	None	One for each three shares bought up to FF6860	In cash only	None

Source: Table 1 from Degeorge, Jenter, Moel, and Tufano (2004).

[a] Abondix and Multiplix are held in tax-free retirement accounts. The bonus, capital gains, and paid dividends are therefore tax-free. Social security contributions (CSG/CRDS) are applicable.

[b] The discount is taken off the retail IPO price of FF 182, so that employees only paid FF145.60 for each one of the discounted assets.

[c] The matching bonus is added to the employee's personal investment into the asset. The total bonus added to personal investments into Abondix and Multiplix combined cannot exceed FF22,500, whereby the Abondix bonus is allocated before the Multiplix bonus.

[d] The free shares only vest if the employee holds the assets through the required holding period. The free shares have a global limit of FF6,860 for all share programs combined. Free share payments will be made to Disponix first, then Simplix, and last, Abondix.

[e] The payment plans are interest free.

investor clienteles especially well. In addition, political considerations often require governments to select a local bank as the lead underwriter of the domestic tranche. JMNN find that governments almost always select domestic investment banks as national champions to lead or co-lead the underwriting of the domestic SIP tranche, which is typically the largest portion of the total offer. Governments then select one or more of the top-rated European or American investment banks to be either lead or co-lead (along with the national champion) underwriter for the international tranche. Most governments also retain, either formally or informally, one of the top British or American investment banks to serve in an advisory role during the planning phase of the SIP. In marked contrast to standard U.S. investment banking practice, the advisory and underwriting mandates are usually not awarded to the same bank, suggesting that the advisor plays an important certification role in assuring a fair and transparent SIP pricing process.

Most large SIPs, whether from developed or developing countries, have allocated shares to U.S. investors since this practice was pioneered by the British government with its first British Telecom offering in November 1984. Governments have also favored American investment banks, as described above, at least partly in order to gain access to U.S. markets and investors. This further contributed to the aforementioned spread of U.S.-style investment banking techniques and market share gains by U.S. banks—though, as noted, SIPs represent a distinct exception to the spread of book-building techniques. Ljungqvist, Jenkinson, and Wilhelm (2003) find that the underwriting spreads (fees) charged by banks handling privatization IPOs (PIPOs) are a statistically and economically significant 37 basis points lower than on otherwise comparable private sector IPOs. This in turn seems largely due to the fact that PIPOs are deliberately underpriced (by 13.7 percentage points, on average), so there is very little risk that the underwriter will be forced to retain unwanted shares or intervene to support the IPO's after-market price.

Analysis of the Allocation of Control

One method of maintaining ultimate governmental control over an SOE being privatized is to adopt a multiple-class share structure, with the government retaining a large proportion of the high-vote shares. The main example of this is the golden share, which is especially popular in the United Kingdom (90 percent of the U.K. firms have golden shares). A *golden share* is a special share retained by the government that enables it to veto mergers, liquidations, asset sales, and other major corporate events. The government can also directly insert similar control restrictions into the corporate charter. JMNN find that in 82 percent of their sample firms with sufficient data to make a determination, the government maintains some control by one or both of these methods. Although this retention of control affects offering proceeds, it appears that governments find it necessary to employ control restrictions to reduce nationalistic fears that control of newly privatized firms might be purchased by foreigners or broken up by corporate raiders.

In spite of the pervasiveness of golden shares, JMNN discuss only two cases where a government has threatened to trigger the share. In 1987, the British government used the threat of its golden share to favor Ford over General Motors in the acquisition of Jaguar, and in 1996 a subsequent Conservative government threatened to trigger the golden shares of PowerGen and National Power to discourage bidders who might increase concentration in the U.K. electricity generation market [Holbertson (1996)]. These shares have become extremely controversial over the past five years. The EU attempted to ban their use outright, as a blatant attempt to restrict the intra-European market for corporate control. A recent EU court ruling upheld the basic legality of golden shares, but severely restricted their application and scope.

Initial Returns Earned by Investors in Share Issue Privatizations

As noted earlier, governments generally rely on share offerings as the best method of privatizing large state-owned enterprises, and they routinely adopt highly politicized offer terms in order to achieve political objectives. Offering terms that differ fundamentally from those observed in private-sector offerings, plus the very large average size of privatization issues, have motivated many researchers to examine the initial and long-term returns earned by SIP investors.

Empirical Evidence on Underpricing of SIPs

Table 6.6 summarizes the results of 13 studies examining initial returns. Most of these studies evaluate whether investors who purchase privatization initial public offerings at the offering price, and then sell these shares on the first day of open market trading, earn returns that are significantly different from zero. Thus, these studies test whether PIPOs are underpriced. A few also test whether PIPOs yield initial returns that are materially different from the significantly positive first-day returns earned by investors in private-sector IPOs, as documented in a vast number of articles using both U.S. and international data. The U.S. market experience is summarized in Ibbotson, Sindelar, and Ritter (1994) and international IPO underpricing studies are surveyed in Loughran, Ritter, and Rydqvist (1994).

Seven of the studies in table 6.6 examine PIPO returns from individual countries. All seven studies document significant, often massive, average levels of underpricing, ranging from 8.4 percent for the 53 Egyptian SIPs studied by Omran (2002) to 940 percent for the 308 Chinese PIPOs Class A issues (domestic issuance) examined by Su and Fleisher (1999). Menyah and Paudyal (1996) and Paudyal, Saadouni, and Briston (1998) find, respectively, that British and Malaysian PIPOs are significantly more underpriced than their private-sector counterparts, and Ausenegg (2000) finds the same result for Polish PIPOs. Hungarian PIPOs are also more underpriced than private IPOs, but the difference is not significant [Jelic and Briston (1999)].

Since there are as yet few truly comparable private-sector IPOs in China, Su and Fleisher cannot test whether private offerings also have the incredible underpricing they document for PIPOs. They do find that Class B shares, issued inter-

TABLE 6.6. Summary of Empirical Studies Examining Initial Returns to Investors in Share Issue Privatizations

Study	Sample Description, Study, Period, and Methodology	Summary of Empirical Findings and Conclusions
Menyah and Paudyal (1996)	Examine initial and long-term returns for 40 British privatization IPOs (PIPOs) and 75 private-sector IPOs on the London Stock Exchange between 1981 and 1991.	PIPOs offer a market-adjusted initial return of 39.6%, compared to private-sector IPO initial return of 3.5%. Regression analysis explains up to 64% of variation in PIPO initial returns.
Dewenter and Malatesta (1997)	Test whether privatization IPOs (PIPOs) are more or less underpriced than private-sector IPOs in 8 countries. Compare actual initial returns for 109 companies from Canada, France, Hungary, Japan, Malaysia, Poland, Thailand, and the United Kingdom with national average initial returns reported in Loughran, Ritter, and Rydqvist (1994).	Find mixed results. Initial returns to privatization issues are higher than private-sector IPOs in unregulated industries and in the United Kingdom. Privatization IPOs are lower than private offers in Canada and Malaysia, and they conclude there is not a systematic tendency to underprice PIPOs on the part of all governments.
Huang and Levich (1998)	Study offering terms and initial returns to investors in 507 privatization share offerings from 39 countries during 1979–1996, and test alternative explanations for the observed underpricing.	Document average initial returns of 32.2% for PIPOs and 7.17% for seasoned privatization offerings. Also find that SIPs from non-OECD countries are more underpriced than OECD offers, but conclude there is no evidence PIPOs are underpriced more than private IPOs.
Paudyal, Saadouni, and Briston (1998)	Examine initial and long-term returns offered to investors in 18 PIPOs and 77 private-sector IPOs in Malaysia in 1984–1995. Also provide details of offering terms and share allocation patterns.	Malaysia PIPOs offer market-adjusted initial returns of 103.5% (median 79.9%), which is significantly greater than the private-sector IPO initial returns of 52.5% (29.4%).
Jones, Megginson, Nash, and Netter (1999)	Examine how political and economic factors influence initial returns, as well as share and control allocation patterns, for a sample of 630 SIPs from 59 countries during 1977–1997.	Document that governments deliberately underprice both PIPOs (mean 34.1%, median 12.4%) and seasoned SIPs (9.4% and 3.3%). Also find that share and control allocation patterns are best explained by political factors. Support predictions of Biais and Perotti (2002) theoretical model.
Su and Fleisher (1999)	Study the cross-sectional pattern of underpricing of 308 Chinese PIPOs in 1987–1995. Tests whether observed underpricing for domestic shares can be explained using a signaling model.	Document massive underpricing, with an average initial return of 940% on A shares (issued domestically). Interpret findings as consistent with a signaling model, since 91% of all firms subsequently execute seasoned equity offerings. They find less underpricing for B shares (international).

(continued)

TABLE 6.6. (continued)

Study	Sample Description, Study, Period, and Methodology	Summary of Empirical Findings and Conclusions
Jelic and Briston (1999)	Examine initial and long-term returns for 25 PIPOs and 24 other IPOs in Hungary during 1990–1998.	Find PIPOs are much larger and have higher market-adjusted initial returns than other IPOs (44% mean and 9% median vs 40% and 5%, respectively), but the return differences are not significant.
Jelic, Briston, and Ausenegg (2003)	Examine initial and long-term returns for 55 PIPOs and 110 other IPOs in Poland during 1990–1998.	Using first-day opening prices (not offer prices), find small, though significantly positive, mean abnormal initial returns (1.16%) for PIPOs and insignificant mean abnormal initial returns (0.22%) for other IPOs. The difference is insignificant.
Choi and Nam (1998)	Compare initial returns of 185 PIPOs from 30 countries during 1981–1997 to those of private-sector IPOs from the same countries using mean national initial returns reported in Loughran, Ritter, and Rydqvist (1994).	Finds there is a general tendency for PIPOs to be more underpriced than private-sector IPOs (mean of 31% versus 24.6%), and that the degree of underpricing for PIPOs is positively related to the stake sold and to the degree of ex-ante uncertainty about the value of newly privatized firms.
Florio and Manzoni (2002)	Studies initial return and long-run performance of 55 British SIPs in 1977–1996, and examine sources of any superior performance documented.	Find significant underpricing averaging 13%, and show this to be significantly and negatively correlated with size, profitability, leverage, liquidity, and number of directors. Underpricing also negatively correlated with net proceeds—which they interpret as a measure of ex ante uncertainty.
Omran (2002)	Examines initial underpricing and long-run returns to 53 Egyptian SIPs between 1994 and 1998, and analyzes cross-sectional determinants of excess returns.	Documents significant underpricing averaging 8.4% (median 5%). These are positively correlated with ex ante uncertainty (standard deviation of after-market returns) and excess demand for shares in initial offering.
Ljungqvist, Jenkinson, and Wilhelm (2003)	Analyze both direct and indirect costs (associated with underpricing) of 2,143 IPOs, including 231 PIPOs, in 65 non-U.S. markets during the period 1992–1999. Primarily a private-sector, security underwriting study.	Document that PIPOs are significantly more underpriced (by 13.7 percentage points) than are private-sector IPOs, and the underwriter spreads are a significant 37 basis points lower.

220

nationally, are much less underpriced (37 percent mean initial return). Unlike almost any other comparable group of IPOs, over 90 percent of Chinese PIPOs do in fact execute seasoned equity offerings within a short time after the PIPO. Further, the probability of a seasoned offer occurring is positively related to the level of the initial offer underpricing, which is consistent with various signaling models including Welch (1989).

The other five studies in table 6.6 examine multinational samples of PIPOs, generally using offering data from *Privatisation International* and stock returns from Datastream. The number of countries studied ranges from eight in Dewenter and Malatesta (1997) to 65 in Ljungqvist, Jenkinson, and Wilhelm (2003), though the studies' main results are similar. All these studies document economically and statistically significant underpricing of PIPOs, averaging about 30 percent in the large-sample studies. The two that examine seasoned SIPs [Huang and Levich (1998), and Jones, Megginson, Nash, and Netter (1999)] find these are significantly underpriced as well, though much less so than are PIPOs. Four of these studies — Dewenter and Malatesta (1997), Huang and Levich (1998), Choi and Nam (1998), and Ljungqvist, Jenkinson, and Wilhelm (2003) — also test whether PIPOs are significantly more underpriced than private-sector IPOs. The first three studies find no systematic evidence that PIPOs are significantly more or less underpriced than private IPOs; instead, all three suggest that results vary by country. However, the Ljungqvist, Jenkinson, and Wilhelm study performs the most convincing analysis of the relative underpricing of IPOs and PIPOs, since they use regression methodology and a privatization dummy variable to examine underpricing for a sample of 2,143 IPOs (including 231 PIPOs) from 65 non-U.S. markets. They document that PIPOs are significantly more underpriced (by 13.7 percentage points) than are private-sector IPOs. They also find that the underwriting spreads on PIPOs are significantly lower (by a mean 37 basis points) than on IPOs.

Political and Economic Objectives in Issue Pricing

The principal objective of the Jones, Megginson, Nash, and Netter (1999) study differs from the others in that it tests whether government issuers are attempting to maximize SIP offering proceeds or are instead trying to achieve multiple political and economic objectives, even at the cost of revenue maximization. JMNN test the underpricing models of Perotti (1995) and Biais and Perotti (2002).[4] Both models predict that governments ideologically committed to privatization and economic reform will deliberately underprice SIPs and will privatize in stages, to signal their commitment to protecting investor property rights. "Populist" governments that are pursuing privatization strictly as a means of raising revenue will be unwilling to underprice as much as will "committed" governments. Populist governments will also try to sell larger stakes in SOEs, since they will be unable to commit to not expropriating shareholder wealth; thus retaining a larger stake would cause them to suffer more from the inevitable post-issue stock price decline that would occur once the government's true intentions becomes apparent. JMNN find that initial returns are significantly positively related to the fraction of the firm's capital sold and to the degree of income inequality (Gini coefficient) in a country. They also find that initial returns are negatively related to the level of government spending as a fraction of GDP (a proxy for how socialist a society is) and to a dummy variable indicating that more than 50 percent of a company's stock is being sold. Collectively, these findings strongly support the predictions of Perotti and Biais and Perotti.

JMNN's results support the view that privatizing share offerings are designed by governments primarily to achieve economic and political objectives. Their cross-sectional analyses reveal a mixture of the pricing and marketing strategies of committed and populist governments, as well as of governments that cannot commit but wish to reduce the possibility of a policy reversal. In general, the greater the fraction of an SOE's stock that is offered in the initial SIP, the more under-pricing investors require. This appears to be due to investors' concerns about ex-post interference (policy reversal) rather than capital market constraints. On the other hand, underpricing declines when the government sells more than 50 percent of the SOE's stock.

There is a significant negative relation in the supply equation between initial returns and JMNN's proxy for populist tendencies, suggesting that some privatizations are designed more to raise revenue than to generate economic reform. The political nature of underpricing is further supported by the significance of the coefficient on the Gini income inequality variable, which indicates that under-pricing is being used by governments to attract the support of median-class voters. The U.K. government's extreme market-oriented policies appear to require additional underpricing to garner the necessary political support, and the results presented in Florio and Manzoni (2002) support this hypothesis.

These results indicate that much of the underpricing of initial SIPs is a concession by governments designed to overcome the political obstacles that stand in the way of successful privatization and the economic benefits that might flow from it. This conclusion is based on JMNN's estimate of the determinants of initial returns in a simultaneous-equations model. Specifically, they find that the returns of initial SIPs are (1) positively related to the percent of an SOE sold in an offer, (2) negatively related to their measure of how populist a privatizing government is, (3) positively related to the income inequality within a country, and (4) not inversely related to the offering size as measured by the firm's post-offering market value. Governments certainly wish to raise significant revenues from SIPs, but they are also willing to trade off revenue maximization in order to achieve other political or economic objectives.

Long-Run Returns Earned by Investors in Share Issue Privatizations

Since the seminal article by Jay Ritter (1991), financial economists have paid close attention to estimating the long-run returns earned by investors who purchase unseasoned and seasoned equity issues. Most of these papers find significantly negative long-term returns, whether they examine U.S. offerings or international stock issues, though a few studies document insignificantly positive long-term performance.[5] If true, these findings represent a serious problem for financial econ-omists, since it asks the question: Why don't investors learn that long-term returns to purchasing IPOs or SEOs will be negative and thus shy away from buying new stock issues? This issue is obviously also of concern to governments wishing to privatize state enterprises through SIPs. In this section, we assess whether the long-run, market-adjusted return to SIP investors is significantly positive or negative, and also whether it differs significantly from the returns earned on otherwise com-parable private-sector offerings.

There is a major debate in the empirical finance literature on methodological issues in estimating long-run returns. This is not surprising since findings of sig-nificant negative (or positive) long-run returns can be interpreted as evidence con-tradicting the efficient market hypothesis, a fundamental concept in finance. The debate centers on how to calculate long-run returns and how to construct test statistics.[6] Since the methodological problems identified with estimating long-run returns have not been resolved for studies employing data for U.S. firms, they have not been resolved for privatization studies that are subject to the additional prob-lems of scarce data and the lack of liquid markets. Nevertheless, the fact that most of the studies of long-run returns following privatizations find similar results, using different methodologies and focusing on different countries, lessens some of the methodological concerns.

Empirical Evidence on Long-Run Returns to SIP Investors

This section discusses 19 studies that examine the returns earned by investors who buy and hold privatization share issues for one or more years. These papers are summarized in table 6.7. Eleven of these studies focus on either a single country or a single market for issues, while the other eight examine multinational samples. Levis (1993), Menyah, Paudyal, and Inganyete (1995), and Florio and Manzoni (2002) all examine the British experience and all three document significantly positive long-run abnormal returns for SIP investors. The magnitudes of the long-run returns differ because of varying sample periods and companies covered, though only Florio and Manzoni find excess returns exceeding 50 percent over a five-year holding period. They find these very large returns are concentrated among the water, electricity, and transport utilities, and conclude the excess re-turns resulted from lax regulation. Kerr and Rose (2002) document insignificantly negative one-year excess returns for nine New Zealand SIPs over the 1990–2001 period, but these excess returns are significantly positive and much larger in mag-nitude over three-year and five-year holding periods. Paudyal, Saadouni, and Bris-ton (1998) find that investors earn insignificant long-run returns on 18 Malaysian PIPOs, as well as on 77 private-sector IPOs.

Two studies document significantly negative long-run excess returns for SIPs. First, Aggarwal, Leal, and Hernandez (1993) find their sample of nine Chilean SIPs yields significantly negative one-year market-adjusted returns of approximately −20 percent. Second, Omran (2002) finds that his sample of 53 Egyptian PIPOs yields significantly negative market-adjusted returns over three-year and five-year

TABLE 6.7. Summary of Empirical Studies Examining Long-Run Returns to Investors in Share Issue Privatizations

Study	Sample Description, Study Period, and Methodology	Summary of Empirical Findings and Conclusions
Levis (1993)	Examines long-run return to 806 British IPOs during 1980–1988. Sample includes 12 PIPOs, accounting for 76% of total IPO value.	While private-sector IPOs underperformed the market by over 10% over 3 years, PIPOs outperformed the market by over 15%.
Aggarwal, Leal, and Hernandez (1993)	Examine long-run (one-year) returns for Latin American IPOs, including 9 Chilean PIPOs in 1982–1990.	Using returns from offer price, find significantly negative one-year market-adjusted returns for PIPOs averaging −29.9% (median −32.4%) versus −9.8% (−23.0%) for private-sector IPOs.
Menyah, Paudyal, and Inganyete (1995)	Examine initial and long-term returns for 40 British PIPOs and 75 private-sector IPOs executed on the London Stock Exchange between 1981 and 1991.	Document significantly positive 33% market-adjusted 400-day (80 week) return for PIPO versus an insignificant 3.5% return for private-sector IPOs.
Davidson (1998)	Studies 1-, 3-, 5-, and 10-year market-adjusted returns for SIPs from 5 European countries (Austria, France, Italy, Spain, and the United Kingdom) through March 1997.	After long period of underperformance, averaging 1–1.5% per year, finds SIPs outperformed European market averages during previous 12 months.
Foerster and Karolyi (2000)	Examine long-run return for 333 non-U.S. companies that list stock on U.S. markets in the form of ADRs in 1982–1996. Compare returns for 77 SIPs (38 IPOs, 39 seasoned offers) with private offers.	Document insignificantly positive 4.1% 3-year abnormal returns for SIPs compared to (insignificantly) negative returns of −1.7% for full sample.
Paudyal, Saadouni, and Briston (1998)	Examine initial and long-term returns offered to investors in 18 PIPOs and 77 private-sector IPOs in Malaysia in 1984–1995. Also provide details of offering terms and share allocation patterns.	Find that both PIPOs and private-sector IPOs yield normal returns (insignificantly different from overall market) over 1-, 3-, and 5-year holding periods.
Boubakri and Cosset (2000)	Evaluate the long-term returns to investors in 120 SIPs from 26 developing countries during 1982–1995.	Find significant 3-year raw returns (112% mean, 30% median), but insignificant mean (37% to 46%) and median (−7% to 13%) market-adjusted returns—due to weighting of SIPs in stock market indices. Significant positive long-run returns after adjusting for impact of SIP size on index.
Jelic and Briston (1999)	Examine initial and long-term returns for 25 PIPOs and 24 other IPOs in Hungary during 1990–1998.	Find PIPOs yield insignificantly positive market-adjusted returns over 1-, 2-, and 3-year holding periods, reaching a peak of 21.3% in month 15, while private-sector IPOs yield significantly negative returns.

Jelic and Briston (2000)	Examine initial and long-term returns for 55 PIPOs and 110 other IPOs in Poland during 1990–1998.	PIPO investors earn significantly positive 1-, 3-, and 5-year market-adjusted returns, while other IPO investors earn negative returns. The difference is significant for most holding periods.
Ausenegg (2000)	Examines initial and long-term returns for 52 PIPOs and 107 other IPOs in Poland during 1990–1999.	Finds both PIPO and private-sector IPO investors earn negative—often significant—abnormal returns over 1-, 3-, and 5-year holding periods.
Perotti and Oijen (2001)	Develop a theoretical model suggesting that long-run returns to investors in developing-country SIPs will earn excess returns if and when political risk is resolved. Test the model using data from 22 countries with active privatization programs during 1988–1995.	First document that their proxy for political risk declines by an annual average of 3.6% during the course of a privatization program, and that stock markets develop very rapidly. The decline in risk leads to positive excess returns for SIPs of about 6% per year.
Choi, Nam, and Ryu (2000)	Compute buy-and-hold returns of 204 PIPOs from 37 countries during 1977–1997.	Find significantly positive market-adjusted returns to SIPs over 1-, 3-, and 5-year holding periods.
Megginson, Nash, Netter, and Schwartz (2000)	Examine long-run (1-, 3-, and 5-year) returns for 158 PIPOs from 33 countries in 1981–1997. Compute local-currency and $ returns, versus national and international indices, and versus matching firms.	Document economically and statistically significantly positive holding-period returns in both local currency and U.S. dollars, and versus all market indices. 5-year excess returns exceeding 80% are found for most comparisons.
Dewenter and Malatesta (2000)	Examine long-run returns to investors in 102 SIPs from developed and developing countries in 1981–1994. Also examine long-run stock return performance of privatized firms and compare the relative performance of a large sample (1,500 firm-years) of state and privately owned firms during 1975, 1985, and 1995.	Document significantly positive long-term (1–5 years) abnormal stock returns, mostly concentrated in Hungary, Poland, and the United Kingdom.
Boardman and Laurin (2000)	Examine the factors that influence the long-run returns of 99 SIPs in 1980–1995. Test the effect of relative size, fraction retained (by government), the presence of a golden share, initial return, and timing on 3-year buy-and-hold returns. Also examines whether U.K. utility SIPs earned "excessive" returns.	Find significant positive abnormal returns to all SIPs over 1- (9.2%), 2- (13.5%) and 3-year (37.4%) holding periods. British SIP returns are higher than for non-U.K. issues, and U.K. utilities have highest returns (60.6% 3-year excess returns), but 3-year non-U.K. SIP returns also significant. Excess returns are (significantly) positively related to fraction retained and initial period return, and are negatively related to relative size and presence of a golden share.

(continued)

TABLE 6.7. (continued)

Study	Sample Description, Study Period, and Methodology	Summary of Empirical Findings and Conclusions
Omran (2002)	Examines initial underpricing and long-run returns to 53 Egyptian SIPs between 1994 and 1998, and analyzes cross-sectional determinants of excess returns.	Finds significant positive long-run returns for 1-year holding periods (between 18% and 42%, depending upon calculation method and reference portfolio), but these become significantly negative over 3-year and 5-year holding periods.
Florio and Manzoni (2002)	Study initial return and long-run performance of 55 British SIPs from 1977 to 1996, and examine sources of any superior performance documented.	Document significant positive long-term excess returns reaching 21% after 1 year, 42% after 3 years, and 57.3% after 5 years. SIPs in the water, electricity, and transport industries outperform others, which authors find to be caused by lax regulation.
Kerr and Rose (2002)	Examine long-run (1-, 3-, and 5-year) returns for 9 New Zealand SIPs over 1999 to 2001 period. Compares to return earned on reference portfolio of private-sector companies.	Finds insignificant negative excess returns over a 1-year (−2.4%) holding period, becoming significantly positive over longer holding periods. The 3-year and 5-year excess returns are 36.1% and 82.4%, respectively.
Aybar (2002)	Studies long-term return performance of 143 privatization-related American depositary receipts (ADRs) from 29 industries across 31 developed and developing countries over the period 1984–1999. Returns are compared to local, world, and U.S. market indices.	ADRs generally outperform their respective country indices and the FT World Index, but underperform the S&P 500 Index. Also finds that developed-country ADRs outperform developing country issues.
Jelic, Briston, and Aussenegg (2003)	Examine long-run returns over 3-year holding period for a sample of 143 SIPs—47 Polish, 31 Hungarian, and 65 Czech (in two waves)—from 1990 to 1998 and compare returns to local and U.S. dollar-based indices.	Find that the average buy-and-hold abnormal returns (BHARs) for domestic investors are 41.5% for Poland, −18.2% for Hungary, 15.3% for the first wave of Czech privatizations, and 11.2% for the second. All of these are statistically insignificant. Dollar-based BHARs are positive for all three countries, but are significantly positive only for Poland. Overall, smaller companies with lower percentages of state-retained ownership outperform large state-dominated enterprises.

226

holding periods, though the one-year returns are significantly positive. Several other studies find either insignificant negative long-run returns or mixed returns for different holding periods. Foerster and Karolyi (2000) find insignificantly long-run returns for privatization stocks listing in the United States in the form of American Depository Receipts (ADRs) compared to local benchmarks, though the returns are significantly negative compared to U.S. benchmarks. A similar study of ADRs, conducted later by Aybar (2002), finds that 143 ADRs generally outperform their respective country indices and the FT World Index, but significantly underperform the dollar-denominated S&P 500 Index. Jelic and Briston (1999) find that 25 Hungarian PIPOs yield large but insignificantly positive long-run returns (peaking at 21.3 percent in month 15), though they do find that these cumulative returns are significantly higher than the highly negative returns (reaching–70 percent by month 30) earned on 24 private sector IPOs. A later study by Jelic, Briston, and Ausenegg (2003) of Polish, Hungarian, and Czech privatizations finds significantly positive long-run returns for Polish SIPs compared to a U.S. dollar-denominated stock index, but insignificantly positive excess returns for Hungarian and Czech SIPs versus the same benchmark. All three countries' SIPs yield insignificant, though generally positive, long-run excess returns compared to local currency return indices.

Two of the multinational studies described in table 6.7 focus on long-run returns earned by investors in SIPs from developing countries. A third examines only western European offerings. Boubakri and Cosset (2000) study returns from 120 SIPs from 26 developing countries, while Perotti and van Oijen (2001) develop and test a model of long-term returns using data from 20 developing nations. Both studies document large, highly significant long-run returns, though the mean 112 percent three-year return found by Boubakri and Cosset is not significant once the returns from national markets over the corresponding time periods are subtracted (the absolute returns are converted into market-adjusted, or excess returns). This is primarily due to the extremely large weightings that SIPs themselves have in most developing-country national stock market indices. Once these size biases are accounted for, SIPs significantly outperform most national market indices. Perotti and van Oijen document significantly positive market-adjusted returns, and argue that this excess performance results from a progressive resolution of political risk as governments refrain from expropriating investors' wealth in privatized firms—as had been feared. Their proxy for political risk declines by an average of 3.6 percent annually during the course of a privatization program, and this leads to positive excess returns for SIPs of about 6 percent per year. Davidson (1998) documents that large European SIPs began to outperform market indices in five countries during the mid-1990s. However, these SIPs did so only after an extended period of subpar performance.

Multinational Long-Run Return Studies

The remaining four long-run return studies presented in table 6.8 employ multinational samples that cover a large number of countries and regions. For this reason, and because all the studies are recent enough to employ state-of-the-art techniques for computing net-of-market returns, we consider these the most persuasive evidence on long-term excess returns earned by SIP investors. Boardman and Laurin (2000) examine the factors that influence the long-run returns of 99 SIPs from 1980–1995. They test the effect of relative size, fraction retained by the government, the presence of a golden share, initial return, and market timing on three-year buy-and-hold returns. They find significantly positive abnormal returns to all SIPs over one- (9.2 percent), two- (13.5 percent), and three-year (37.4 percent) holding periods. British SIPs are higher than non-U.K. issues, and British utilities have the highest returns (60.6 percent three-year excess returns), but three-year non-U.K. SIP returns are also significant. Excess returns are significantly positively related to fraction retained and initial period return, and are negatively related to relative size and the presence of a golden share.

Choi, Nam, and Ryu (2000) compute buy-and-hold returns for 204 PIPOs from 37 countries during 1977–1997, and find significantly positive market-adjusted returns to SIPs over one-, three-, and five-year holding periods. Dewenter and Malatesta (2000) find similar results. They examine long-run returns to investors in 102 SIPs from developed and developing countries over 1981–1994. They also examine the long-run stock return performance of privatized firms and compare the relative performance of a large sample (1,500 firm-years) of state and privately owned firms during 1975, 1985, and 1995. They document significantly positive long-term (1–5 years) abnormal stock returns, mostly concentrated in Hungary, Poland, and the United Kingdom.

The most detailed multinational study yet published that examines the long-run stock price performance for privatized firms is Megginson, Nash, Netter, and Schwartz (2000, hereafter MNNS). They improve on earlier studies by using a large sample of 158 SIPs from 33 countries during the period 1981–1997 and by using multiple estimation techniques. They also note the special problems that arise in calculating long-run returns in this setting. MNNS compute one-, three-, and five-year local currency net returns with respect to domestic, international, and U.S. market indices and an industry-matched firm. They do not include the generally large positive initial return documented by Jones, Megginson, Nash, and Netter (1999) and others. MNNS use holding-period and cumulative abnormal returns in the calculations.[7] Empirically, they find systematic evidence of large average positive abnormal performance for the SIPs.

The holding period return (HPR) measures provide evidence that local, international, and U.S. investors receive significantly higher one-year returns from purchasing unseasoned SIP offerings than they could by investing in the national market index (in local currency) over the same time period, or in either the world or U.S. market index or in a U.S. firm in the same industry. A summary of MNNS's key results is presented in table 6.8. The mean (median) one-year HPR for the 158 initial SIPs is 25.1 percent (18.0 percent), while the mean (median) local currency returns on the national market index is 13.2 percent (11.9 percent). The returns on the FT World Index and the S&P 500 Index over the same one-year holding period are 13.1 percent (11.9 percent) and 17.6 percent (19.6 percent), respectively. The HPRs for the industry-matching firm are 15.0 percent (4.9 percent median). These values yield mean (median) net returns for SIPs versus

TABLE 6.8. SIP Holding Period Returns Over One-, Three-, and Five-Year Periods Against Four Different Matching Criteria

| | Matching Samples | | | | | | | | | | | | |
| | (1) SIP | (2) Country | | | (3) World | | | (4) S&P 500 | | | (5) Industry | | |
	HPR	HPR	Diff.	Test Stat.	HPR	Diff.	Test Stat.	HPR	Diff.	Test Stat.	HPR	Diff.	Test Stat.
One-year													
Mean	0.251	0.132	0.118	3.298[a]	0.131	0.120	3.038[a]	0.176	0.074	1.834[c]	0.150	0.100	2.087[b]
Median	0.180	0.118	0.037	2.616[a]	0.119	0.037	2.354[b]	0.196	0.029	1.196	0.049	0.082	2.467[b]
Three-year													
Mean	0.811	0.492	0.319	2.989[a]	0.527	0.284	2.644[a]	0.721	0.090	0.818	0.655	0.156	1.083
Median	0.458	0.460	0.073	1.738[c]	0.415	0.136	1.746[c]	0.565	0.000	0.068	0.342	0.091	1.353
Five-year													
Mean	1.765	0.854	0.911	4.780[a]	0.868	0.897	4.291[a]	1.199	0.566	2.223[b]	2.166	−0.400	−0.310
Median	1.267	0.829	0.469	4.156[a]	0.619	0.501	4.026[a]	0.942	0.200	2.725[a]	0.629	0.628	3.248[a]

Source: Table 4 in Megginson, Nash, J. Netter, and Schwartz (2000).

Note: The share issue privatization (SIP) holding period return (HPR) represents a buy-and-hold return with dividends reinvested in the respective security and is calculated using the *Datastream* return index (RI) datatype. The SIP return uses the first available (base date) post-issue closing price from *Datastream*, so the initial returns are not reflected. For the country (local currency) tests, SIPs are matched to a national stock market return index. The world index test compares the local currency return on the SIP issues with the local currency return on an investment in the *Financial Times* World Index (currency adjustment not shown). The S&P Index test compares the HPR on the SIP issues with the currency-adjusted return of the S&P 500 Index. The Wilcoxon (Z) statistic identifies the differences in median values between the groups. The mean t-statistic tests whether the HPR for the SIP minus the HPR for the firm or index (the net return) is significantly greater than zero. The one-year results are for 158 firms. The three-year results are for 117 firms. The five-year results are for 65 firms.

[a] significant at the 1% level.
[b] significant at the 5% level.
[c] significant at the 10% level.

the four comparison groups of 11.8 percent (3.7 percent), 12.0 percent (3.7 percent), 7.4 percent (2.9 percent), and 10.0 percent (8.2 percent), respectively.[8] In each case, the privatization offers' HPRs are greater than the comparison, and all but one of the differences are significantly positive.

The three-year HPRs are similar. The mean (median) three-year holding period return for the 117 initial SIPs with three years of data is 81.1 percent (45.8 percent), while the mean (median) local currency returns on the national market index is 49.2 percent (46.1 percent). The mean (median) returns on the FT World Index and the S&P 500 Index over the same three-year holding period are 52.7 percent (41.5 percent) and 72.1 percent (56.5 percent), respectively. The three-year HPRs for the industry-matched firms are 65.5 percent (34.2 percent). These values yield mean (median) net returns for SIPs versus the four comparison groups of 31.9 percent (7.3 percent), 28.0 percent (13.6 percent), 9.0 percent (0 percent), and 15.6 percent (9.1 percent), respectively. Again, the privatization offers' HPRs are greater than the comparison groups in all cases, and the differences are statistically significant for the country and world comparisons. The five-year HPRs tell a similar story. The mean (median) five-year holding period return for the 65 initial SIPs with five years of data is 177.7 percent (126.7 percent), while the mean (median) local currency returns on the national market index is 85.5 percent (82.9 percent).

Table 6.9 reports cumulative abnormal returns (CARs) for the SIPs versus the alternative indices and matching firm samples for one, three, and five years. In every case, the CARs are positive, and 10 of the 12 cumulative returns are significantly positive. The one-year CARs for the SIP versus the country index, World Index, S&P 500, and matching firm are 11.8 percent, 12.8 percent, 8.7 percent, and 10.9 percent, respectively. The analogous results for the three-year CARs are 18.0 percent, 20.5 percent, 7.4 percent, and 9.6 percent, respectively. Finally, the results for the analogous five-year CARs are 45.5 percent, 54.6 percent, 36.7 percent, and 35.3 percent.

We should note that the MNNS study ends with data from 1999, and thus does not examine SIP returns after the global bear market in stocks began in earnest in March 2000. The prices of telecom stocks were hammered especially hard from 2000 to early 2003, so it appears certain that SIP investors did not outperform (i.e., they did not lose any less than) other investors over the 2000–2003 period. Indirect evidence suggests they did not do much worse, however. As we will see next chapter, the total market value of privatized firms accounted for a substantially higher fraction (38.6 percent) of the total non-U.S. stock market capitalization in July 2003 than it did one year earlier, and this in turn was a higher fraction than the roughly 20 percent level of 2000 or 1999. Thus it seems that privatization investors did not have to "give back" the excess stock returns they enjoyed over the previous decade. Since early 2003, telecoms and oil companies have performed extremely well, so SIP investors have significantly outperformed private-sector investors, even though all shareholders have benefited from rebounding stock markets.

All four studies surveyed in this section document significantly positive market-adjusted returns over holding periods of up to five years. In general, British

TABLE 6.9. Cumulative Abnormal Returns for Share Issue Privatizations Versus Alternative Indices and Matching Firm Samples

Model	1-Year CAR	3-Year CAR	5-Year CAR
SIP vs. Country Index			
Number	158	117	65
Mean Return	0.1181	0.1804	0.4545
Median Return	0.0659	0.1165	0.5497
t-statistic	3.825[a]	2.871[a]	5.4461[a]
Percent Positive	0.6013	0.6068	0.7846
z-statistic	2.547[b]	2.31[b]	4.589[a]
SIP vs. FT World Index			
Number	158	117	65
Mean Return	0.1279	0.2047	0.5458
Median Return	0.109	0.182	0.5731
t-statistic	3.75[a]	3.363[a]	7.643[a]
Percent Positive	0.6139	0.6325	0.8308
z-statistic	2.8634[a]	2.866[a]	5.334[a]
SIP vs. S&P 500			
Number	158	117	65
Mean Return	0.0871	0.0739	0.3668
Median Return	0.0689	0.131	0.3885
t-statistic	2.4874[b]	1.1829	4.877[a]
Percent Positive	0.5696	0.5727	0.6769
z-statistic	1.7502[c]	1.5717	2.852[a]
SIP vs. industry match			
Number	158	117	65
Mean Return	0.1092	0.0962	0.3531
Median Return	0.0606	0.0971	0.2885
t-statistic	2.7785[a]	1.3296	3.1269[a]
Percent Positive	0.6266	0.5641	0.6923
z-statistic	3.1827[a]	1.3867	3.101[a]

Source: Table 4 in Megginson, Nash, Netter, and Schwartz (2000)

Note: This table presents the cumulative abnormal returns (CARs) for the SIPs net of the local country index return, the *Financial Times* World Index return, the S&P 500 Index return, and the industry-matched firm return, respectively. The returns are all expressed in the currency of the country executing the SIP. The cumulative abnormal returns are calculated by summing the monthly abnormal returns over 1-year, 3-year, and 5-year investment horizons. The mean t-statistic tests whether the CAR is greater than 0. The percent positive measure examines whether the percent of positive CARs is greater than 50 percent.

[a] significant at the 1% level.
[b] significant at the 5% level.
[c] significant at the 10% level.

privatizations yield higher long-run returns than do non-U.K. initial and seasoned SIPs, and British utilities yield the highest returns among the U.K. offerings. However, the net return is significantly positive for most non-U.K. subsamples as well. These studies, and those cited earlier, support the conclusion that the average long-term, market-adjusted return earned by international investors in share issue privatizations is economically and significantly positive. Apart from Perotti and van Oijen, however, few of these studies can offer any convincing explanation of precisely why SIP issues outperform over time, and isolating one or more specific cause-and-effect relationships is likely to prove extremely difficult. Most likely, these excess returns result from a gradual resolution of uncertainty on the part of investors regarding both the microeconomic success of privatization programs and the ability of governments to resist the temptation to expropriate shareholder wealth in privatized firms through direct intervention, or through targeted regulation or taxation. If so, an important implication is that returns on SIPs are likely to be much lower in the future than they have been historically, since investors will no longer require a political risk premium to purchase shares. The determinants of the long-run returns will be an interesting avenue for future research.

Summary

Share issue privatizations have transformed the size and efficiency of non-U.S. financial markets during the past 20 years. Not only have these issues been by far the largest share offerings in financial history, they have also massively increased stock market capitalization and trading volume in many developing (and more than a few developed) countries. SIPs have also massively increased the number of people who own common stock in most countries besides the United States.

This chapter describes how the structure and pricing of SIPs differs fundamentally from private-sector share offerings. Most private-sector share issues are primary, capital-raising offerings involving relatively small fractions of the company, and appear to be designed to maximize per share offering proceeds. Privatization share offerings share none of these characteristics. SIPs are generally pure secondary offerings, where the sale proceeds flow to the government rather than the firm, and governments sell fully one-third of their share holdings in the average initial SIP—and comparable fractions in subsequent seasoned offerings. SIPs are deliberately underpriced, with an average initial return of over 30 percent, and the shares on offer are then preferentially allocated to domestic, retail investors (particularly to employees of the SOE being divested) rather than to foreign or institutional investors. Shares intended for domestic investors are almost never priced using an auction or tender process, but are instead sold through fixed-price offerings where the price is set (deliberately low) weeks before the offering date in order to ensure that the new citizen/investors who buy these shares have the opportunity to capture a short-term capital gain. Although governments seek to raise large amounts from SIPs, empirical studies have verified that governments are willing to sacrifice revenue maximization to achieve other political and economic objectives.

Investors have generally benefited from purchasing SIPs. Several studies verify that the average short-term return to investors who purchase shares at the offer price, and then sell their shares on the first day of trading, earn economically and statistically significant excess returns. Investors who purchase shares at the offer price and then hold the shares for one-, three-, or five-year holding periods also appear to earn significantly higher returns than they could obtain by investing in matching firms or local market stock portfolios. This contrasts sharply with the highly negative long-run returns documented for investors in private-sector share offerings in almost all countries. All in all, SIPs have been positive financial experiences for the first-time citizen/investors who are targeted by most governments as buyers of the stock in state-owned enterprises being privatized through public share offerings.

Privatization's Impact on Financial Market Development

Although governments usually adopt privatization programs primarily to raise revenue, and in order to improve the economic efficiency of former state-owned enterprises, most also hope that privatizations implemented through public share offerings will develop their national stock markets. Successful promotion of national stock market development can yield significant political and economic benefits. The political benefits include the creation of a (presumably grateful) class of citizen/shareholders, plus the reflected glory resulting from the growth of an internationally recognized capital market. Countries and governments that are able to attract international investors to their stock markets tend to attract other types of international investment as well, especially foreign direct investment. All governments, therefore, wish to develop a reputation as being "investor friendly," since this has a halo effect on how a government is perceived in many other political arenas.

As it happens, good politics can also be good policy in this case, since recent economic research shows that large, efficient capital markets promote rapid economic growth. Studies by Levine (1997), Demirgüç-Kunt and Maksimovic (1998), Levine and Zervos (1998), Rajan and Zingales (1998), Subrahmanyam and Titman (1998), Beck, Levine, and Loayza (2000), Henry (2000), Wurgler (2000), and Bekaert and Harvey (2000) and others have now conclusively documented such a direct link between capital market development and economic growth. A looming demographic crisis in the pay-as-you-go pension systems of many European and Asian countries has also lead to a dawning realization that efficient and liquid capital markets are a prerequisite for developing a funded pension system. Therefore, governments have adopted share issue privatization programs at least partly as a means to jumpstart the growth of these markets.

In spite of the obvious importance of capital market development, and of privatization's potential role therein, we are aware of only two academic studies that (indirectly) attempt to document or empirically examine this process. Domowitz, Glen, and Madhavan (2000) examine the dynamics of external corporate financing choices and find that privatization activity is initially followed by foreign equity issuance, but eventually leads to a higher level of domestic bond issuance. Bortolotti, Fantini, and Scarpa (2000) examine governments' choices of selling privatization share offerings domestically versus externally. While both of these studies examine the impact of privatization issues on subsequent external financing, and the Bortolotti, Fantini, and Scarpa paper indirectly measures privatization's impact on stock market development, this chapter focuses much more directly on privatization's role in market development and patterns of stock ownership.

This chapter is organized as follows. The first section documents that capital market-based finance has in fact been increasing in importance, both absolutely and relative to financial intermediary-based finance, in both developed and developing countries over the past two decades. The next section examines the impact of privatization programs, particularly SIP programs, on capital market development since the early 1980s, while the third section evaluates the impact of SIPs on individual and institutional share ownership in non-U.S. stock markets. Here, we also compare the ownership structure of privatized companies to those of private-sector companies of similar size. The fourth section surveys the rapidly growing academic literature documenting the importance of effective corporate governance in promoting financial market development and economic growth, and then describes the positive impact that privatization programs can have on a nation's governance system.

The Rise of Capital Market-Based Finance

It has become something of a truism to assert that capital markets are "winning" the contest with financial intermediaries, especially commercial banks, to become the dominant sources of external financing for companies throughout the developed world. Like most truisms, there is a large grain of truth in this assertion. Unlike most truisms, there is very little reason to also say, "on the other hand," since, as we will document below, capital markets are in fact winning the present and seem likely to dominate the future of corporate finance in developed and developing countries alike. We first document the growth of capital market finance, and then discuss the role privatization programs have played in promoting global capital market development.

The Stable Role of Commercial Banking in Modern Economies

In a very influential article, Kaufman and Mote (1994) asked "Is banking [in the United States] a declining industry?" They provide a highly nuanced answer. As a direct provider of capital to American business, the market share of all financial intermediaries has been declining monotonically for many decades, and this seems certain to continue. Measures such as the fraction of total assets held by intermediaries show similar declines, with the market share of commercial banks showing special vulnerability. Other measures, however, tell a much rosier story about the enduring competitiveness of commercial banks in American corporate life. Their share of total employment and of GDP has been either stable or rising for a quarter-century, and the economic importance of financial intermediation has been rising steadily as incomes have grown. Kaufman and Mote conclude that "banking," broadly defined, is not a declining industry, but that banking defined as the financing of American business most certainly is. Other studies—such as Boyd and Gertler (1994), James and Houston (1996), and James and Smith (2000)—also offer positive, but nuanced, assessments of the enduring role of banking in American business life.

What about banking's role in other OECD countries, and in the developing world? To examine whether banking is gaining or losing "financial market share," table 7.1 documents the fraction of total domestic credit provided by the banking sector, as a percent of GDP, for various countries and groups of countries for the years 1990 and 2000. For the world as a whole, this fraction rose from 120.7 percent of "global GDP" in 1990 to 152.2 percent in 2000. While the importance of bank credit increased significantly over this period for high-income countries, rising from 132.3 to 173.8 percent of GDP, it increased only moderately for middle-income countries (from 65.1 to 72.9 percent of GDP) and remained virtually unchanged for low-income nations (at around 45 percent of GDP). In other words, banking is playing an increasingly important role in the global economy, though the incremental rate of growth is fairly low.

Although the global importance of banking changed only modestly between 1990 and 2000, specific countries experienced much more dramatic changes in the importance of bank lending as a percent of GDP. As examples, this ratio rose from 110.9 to 161.7 percent of America's GDP during this decade, while it leaped from an already remarkable 259.7 percent of Japan's robust GDP in 1990 to an unprecedented 310.5 percent of that country's economy in 2000. Banking's role

TABLE 7.1. Domestic Credit Provided by the Banking Sector as a Percent of GDP, 1990 Versus 2000

Region or Country	1990	2000
Low income	44.6	45.9
China	90.0	132.7
Middle income	65.1	72.9
High income	132.3	173.8
Europe EMU	96.8	118.1
Germany	103.4	147.5
Japan	259.7	310.5
Switzerland	179.0	179.2
United Kingdom	121.4	136.1
United States	110.9	161.7
World	120.7	152.0

Source: World Bank Group (2002).

also increased significantly in China (from 90.0 to 132.7 percent of GDP) and in Germany (from 103.4 to 147.5 percent) between 1990 and 2000, but was virtually unchanged (at 179 percent) in Switzerland.

As is often the case, these aggregate measures of banking's significance in the world economy hide almost as much as they reveal, since they obscure which areas of banking have been growing and which have been shrinking. As it happens, the "plain vanilla" loan products provided by individual banks to individual borrowers have been declining steadily in importance, while provision of both risk management services and syndicated lending have been growing rapidly. Table 7.2 details the dramatic increase in the total value of syndicated lending (and number of loans) over the period 1980–1999.[1] This panel also documents that the syndicated loan market has come to play a vital "capital market" role of providing large-scale, rapid financing for many different types of corporate investments, including acquisition financing. In 1980, barely 1,000 syndicated loans were arranged, and these raised just $83.0 billion. Only three of these loans were used to finance takeovers, and these raised a mere $700 million. By the late 1990s, between 7,000 and 10,000 loans were being arranged each year, and borrowers were routinely raising over $1.5 trillion annually—with between one-fourth and one-third of that amount being raised to finance corporate acquisitions.[2] In fact, the $1.73 trillion raised in 1999 was more than 20 times 1980's total, and was equal to roughly 5 percent of global GDP. Syndicated lending fell along with merger and acquisition activity during the period 2001–03, but remains a trillion-dollar-plus annual business.

To summarize, ordinary "relationship banking" appears to be (at best) holding its own as a source of corporate financing around the world, and is more likely in decline. The bits of banking that are growing rapidly are those parts that provide high value-added products, particularly risk-management tools, and/or provide large-scale syndicated credits to corporate borrowers. These findings are very important because, for many years, a debate has raged within academic finance regarding whether a capital market-based system of corporate finance is inherently better or worse than a bank-based system. During the late 1980s and early 1990s, when Japan and Germany appeared to be outperforming major capital market-oriented countries such as Britain and the United States, the academic literature often favored bank-based systems. Examples of this literature include Prowse (1992), Kester (1992), and Porter (1992), while the supporting arguments are summarized in Maher and Andersson (1999). More recently, however, the weight of opinion has swung strongly in favor of the idea that capital markets have decisive comparative advantages over banks and other financial intermediaries as optimal monitors and financiers of a nation's corporate life. This reassessment has been driven in part by the observation, discussed above, that capital markets have been prospering relative to banks for many years now. Additionally, the repetitive nature and massive costs of banking crises in developing and developed countries alike has convinced many observers that banks are inherently fragile institutions, whose role in corporate finance should be minimized as much and as quickly as possible [*Economist* (1997, 1999)].

While experience and observation have driven much of the reassessment of the optimal role of capital markets in corporate finance, academic research has also been important since it now strongly favors capital markets over banks. The single most important paper in the stream of research documenting that capital markets are essential for good corporate governance is the influential survey article by Levine (1997). Additional papers by Levine and Zervos (1998), Rajan and Zingales (1998), Demirgüç-Kunt and Maksimovic (1998), Henry (2000), and Bekaert and Harvey (2000) all provide direct or indirect support for the capital market optimality hypothesis. The "law and finance" literature developed by La Porta, López-de-Silanes, Shleifer, and Vishny (1997, 1998, 2002) also emphasizes the importance of legal protection for investors in developing national stock and bond markets. Other empirical studies of the impact of financial development on economic growth have documented that the size of the financial system (banks and capital markets) is not as important for growth as is the system's efficiency. Therefore, we examine not only the magnitude of stock markets but also the dynamics in liquidity, measured by the turnover ratio. We now turn to documenting the astonishing rise of capital market-based financing since the early 1980s.

TABLE 7.2. Total Volume of Syndicated Lending Worldwide, 1980–1999

Year	Total Number of Syndicated Loans	Total Value of Loans, $US Billions	Number of Loans for M&A	Value of M&A Loans, $US Billions	Value of M&A Loans as % of Total
1980	1,068	$83.0	3	$0.7	0.8%
1981	1,508	$171.2	5	$2.3	1.3%
1982	1,625	$149.5	13	$2.6	1.7%
1983	1,175	$92.2	7	$1.5	1.6%
1984	1,676	$180.0	38	$51.2	28.4%
1985	1,358	$189.0	29	$21.6	11.4%
1986	1,316	$169.3	122	$48.5	28.7%
1987	1,753	$249.3	151	$43.0	17.3%
1988	2,453	$383.5	414	$121.8	31.8%
1989	3,470	$399.4	685	$125.6	31.5%
1990	4,250	$420.1	539	$59.6	14.2%
1991	4,509	$400.2	401	$35.6	8.9%
1992	5,603	$427.8	447	$27.5	6.4%
1993	5,289	$535.9	460	$39.3	7.3%
1994	6,306	$796.5	780	$92.3	11.6%
1995	6,896	$1,129.7	856	$170.6	15.1%
1996	8,540	$1,360.8	1,039	$194.6	14.3%
1997	9,598	$1,704.9	1,143	$273.7	16.1%
1998	8,778	$1,453.6	1,821	$359.4	24.7%
1999	7,995	$1,733.9	2,053	$528.6	30.5%
TOTAL	87,837	$12,169.0	11,533	$2,213.0	18.2%

Source: Loanware database, Capital DATA Corporation, London, as presented in Table 1 of Boutchkova and Megginson (2000).

The Rapid Growth in Stock Market Capitalization and Trading Volume Since 1983

Table 7.3 describes the growth in the total market capitalization, and in the value of shares traded, on the world's stock exchanges over the 19-year period 1983–2002. Figure 7.1 expresses graphically the growth in market capitalization over this same period, but also updated through September 2003. These years encompassed a period of very rapid growth in the capitalization of markets in every country except Japan, and global stock market capitalization reached an astonishing $37 trillion in early 2000. After March 2000, however, the total market capitalization of the world's stock exchanges declined by a third, to about $22 trillion at the end of 2002. As this book is being written (summer 2004), stock market valuations around the world have risen again, but it is unclear whether market valuations will regain their peak levels in the near future. Even at June 2004 valuation levels, however, stock markets have experienced phenomenal growth over the past two decades.

Total world market capitalization increased over tenfold (to $35.0 trillion) between 1983 and year-end 1999, and the total capitalization of the U.S. market increased almost ninefold (from $1.9 trillion to $16.6 trillion) over the same period. The growth in markets outside the United States was even greater. Perhaps not coincidentally, it is also in these markets where privatization's impact has been greatest, since only two significant share issue privatization (SIPs) have been executed in the United States in the modern era, Conrail in 1987 and U.S. Enrichment Corporation in 1999. The total capitalization of non-U.S. stock markets increased twelvefold between 1983 and 1999, rising from $1.49 trillion to $18.36 trillion. The total market capitalization of developing country stock exchanges increased by 26 times between 1983 and 1999, rising from a mere $83 billion to $2.18 trillion over that 16-year period. Between early 2000 and year-end 2002, all markets fell in value, but the decline was proportionately much smaller for developing countries (14 percent) than for the United States (34 percent), the developed economies of western Europe (38 percent), or Japan (55 percent).

As impressive as the rise in market capitalization between 1983 and 1999 was, trading volumes increased even more. The total value of shares traded worldwide increased over thirtyfold between 1983 and 1999, rising from $1.2 trillion to $37.5 trillion. Volume then increased an additional 50 percent during 2000, reaching an incredible $56 trillion, or roughly 160 percent of global GDP. As before, non-U.S. markets experienced the greatest increases (except during 2000), with the value of shares traded on markets in developing countries rising from a mere $25 billion in 1983 to almost $2.84 trillion in 2000. This 112-fold increase in market liquidity was probably due to two factors: the increasing popularity of "emerging market" investing among Western investors, particularly institutional investors such as pension and mutual funds, and the impact of large scale SIP programs. Since 2000, trading volumes have declined worldwide, but the drop-off has been much milder (except in the United States) than that observed for market capitalization.

TABLE 7.3. The Growth of World Stock Market Capitalization and Trading Volume, 1983–2003

Market Capitalization	1983	1989	1995	1998	1999	2000	2001	2002	2003
Developed countries	3,310,117	10,957,463	15,842,152	24,530,692	32,820,474	28,817,156	24,213,367	20,311,986	27,392,929
United States	1,898,063	3,505,686	6,857,622	12,926,177	16,645,387	15,214,600	13,983,666	11,054,430	14,266,266
Japan	565,164	4,392,597	3,667,292	2,495,757	4,554,886	3,157,222	2,264,528	2,069,299	2,953,098
United Kingdom	225,800	826,598	1,407,737	2,372,738	2,855,351	2,612,230	2,149,501	1,785,199	2,425,822
Developing countries	83,222	755,210	1,939,919	1,908,258	2,184,899	2,146,187	2,013,027	1,884,390	3,936,573
Total World	3,384,339	11,712,673	17,782,071	26,519,773	35,005,373	30,963,343	26,226,394	22,196,376	31,329,502
World, ex. U.S.	1,486,276	8,206,987	10,924,449	13,593,596	18,362,911	15,748,743	12,242,728	11,141,046	17,063,236
U.S. as % of world	56.1%	29.9%	38.6%	48.7%	47.5%	49.1%	53.3%	49.8%	45.5%
Trading Volume									
Developed countries	1,202,546	6,297,069	9,169,761	20,917,462	35,187,632	53,485,364	37,442,525	30,893,445	30,303,833
United States	797,123	2,015,544	5,108,591	13,148,480	19,993,439	32,994,323	22,964,835	18,739,972	17,323,988
Japan	230,906	2,800,695	1,231,552	948,522	1,891,654	2,641,058	1,835,315	1,689,936	2,243,586
United Kingdom	42,544	320,268	510,131	1,167,382	3,399,381	4,558,663	4,550,504	3,998,462	3,624,009
Developing Countries	25,215	1,170,928	1,046,546	1,956,858	2,320,891	2,836,818	2,062,750	2,213,316	3,013,043
Total World	1,227,761	7,467,997	10,216,307	22,874,320	37,508,523	56,322,182	39,505,275	33,106,761	33,316,876
World, ex. U.S.	430,638	5,452,453	5,107,716	9,725,840	17,508,523	23,327,859	16,540,440	14,366,789	15,992,888
U.S. as % of world	64.9%	27.0%	50.0%	57.5%	53.3%	58.6%	58.1%	56.6%	52.0%

Sources: 1983–1998, the World Bank's Emerging Markets Fact Book (various issues), Washington, D.C., 1999–2003 data from the Statistics section of the World Federation of Exchange's Web site (www.world-exchanges.org.)

Note: This table details the growth in the aggregate market capitalization and trading volume, in $US millions, over the 20-year period 1983–2003. Market capitalization figures are year-end values, translated from local currencies into US$ at the contemporaneous exchange rate, while trading volumes represent the total value of all trades executed during the year.

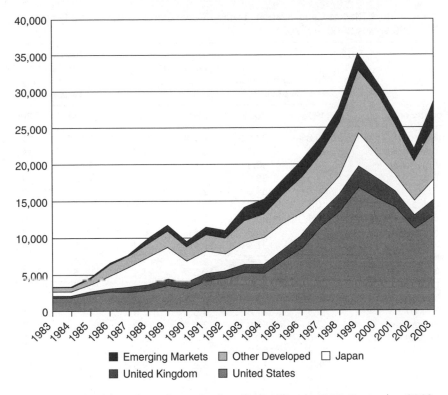

FIGURE 7.1. World stock market valuation ($US millions), 1983–September 2003.
1993–1998 data source: World Bank's *Emerging Markets Fact Book* (various issues).
1999–2002 data source: The statistics section of the World Federation of Exchange's
Web site (www.world-exchanges.org).

Table 7.4 measures the rise of stock market capitalization and trading volumes
somewhat differently, by expressing these as a percentage of national and world
GDP. The aggregate market capitalization of the world's stock markets increased
from 48.0 percent of global GDP in 1990 to 105.1 percent in December 2000.
Even taking account of the subsequent decline in value to perhaps three-fourths
of world GDP in mid-2004, the past fourteen years have witnessed dramatic growth
in stock market valuation relative to global output. These overall figures hide even
more dramatic individual stories, regarding both absolute valuation levels and
rapid increases in relative valuation. As examples of strikingly high ratios of stock
market capitalization to GDP in 2000, consider those of the United States (154
percent), South Africa (163 percent), Singapore (166 percent), the Netherlands
(176 percent), the United Kingdom (182 percent), Switzerland (331 percent), and
Hong Kong (383 percent). Equally revealing are countries with relatively low valuation ratios, including Japan (65 percent), Germany (68 percent), Italy (72 percent), and most developing countries. Examples of countries that experienced
dramatic increases in market capitalization relative to GDP between 1990 and

TABLE 7.4.Stock Market Capitalization, Trading Volume and Turnover as a Percent of GDP, 1990 Versus 2000 and 2001

Country or Region	Market Capitalization as % of GDP		Volume of Shares Traded as % of GDP		Turnover Ratio (Value Shares Traded as % of Capitalization)	
	1990	2000	1990	2000	1990	2001
Low income	19.8%	23.6%	4.7%	32.8%	53.8%	121.3%
Middle income	21.2	41.2	8.0	37.7	78.3	84.9
Argentina	2.3	58.3	0.6	2.1	33.6	0.2
Brazil	3.5	38.0	1.2	17.0	23.6	3.1
Chile	45.0	85.6	2.6	8.6	6.3	0.5
China	0.5	53.8	0.2	66.8	158.9	4.7
Egypt	4.1	29.1	0.3	11.3	—	0.7
Hungary	1.5	26.3	0.3	26.6	6.3	3.8
India	12.2	32.4	6.9	48.4	65.9	15.8
Indonesia	7.1	17.5	3.5	9.3	75.8	2.8
Israel	6.3	58.1	10.5	21.2	95.8	2.7
Korea	43.8	32.5	30.1	121.3	61.3	33.3
Malaysia	110.4	130.4	24.7	65.2	24.6	2.1
Mexico	12.5	21.8	4.6	7.9	44.0	1.7
Philippines	13.4	69.0	2.7	11.0	13.6	0.5
Russian Federation	0.0	15.5	—	8.1	—	3.1
South Africa	122.8	162.8	7.3	61.6	—	3.6
Thailand	28.0	24.1	26.8	19.0	92.6	11.5
Turkey	12.6	34.8	3.9	89.6	42.5	15.3
Venezuela	17.2	6.7	4.6	0.6	43.0	0.5
High income	51.7	120.6	31.4	181.1	59.5	129.9
Australia	35.2	95.6	13.0	58.0	31.6	56.5
Hong Kong, SAR	111.5	383.3	46.3	232.3	43.1	61.3
France	25.9	111.8	9.6	83.7	—	74.1
Germany	21.0	67.8	29.7	57.1	139.3	79.1
Italy	13.5	71.5	3.9	72.5	26.8	104.0
Japan	95.6	65.2	52.5	55.6	43.8	69.9
Netherlands	40.6	175.6	13.6	185.7	29.0	101.4
New Zealand	20.5	37.3	4.5	21.6	17.3	45.9
Singapore	93.6	165.7	55.3	99.2	—	52.1
Spain	21.7	90.3	8.0	176.5	—	210.7
Sweden	41.1	144.4	7.4	171.6	14.9	111.2
Switzerland	70.1	330.5	29.6	254.1	—	82.0
United Kingdom	85.9	182.2	28.2	129.7	33.4	66.6
United States	53.2	153.5	30.5	323.9	53.4	200.8
Europe EMU	21.6	89.9	14.2	83.1	—	90.6
World	48.0	105.1	28.5	153.8	57.2	122.3

Source: World Bank Group (2002).

2000 include China (0.5 to 54 percent), Brazil (3.5 to 38 percent), Israel (6.3 to 58 percent), Australia (35 to 96 percent), Italy (14 to 72 percent), Spain (22 to 90 percent), France (26 to 112 percent), Sweden (41 to 120 percent), and Switzerland (70 to 331 percent). These stock market valuation increases far exceeded any comparable growth in corporate profits or national output, and instead reflect a fundamental reassessment of the value of a nation's common equity. The fact that all of these countries, except Switzerland, executed very large share issue privatization programs suggests that these programs have played a significant role in promoting market development.

Table 7.4 also presents two measures of stock market volume for these same countries and regions. The first, volume of trading as a percent of GDP, simply measures the total value of shares traded as a fraction of GDP, while the turnover ratio is defined as the total value of shares traded during a year divided by prior year-end market capitalization. Both ratios show that market liquidity exploded between 1990 and 2000 (measured by trading volume) and between 1990 and 2001 (turnover). The volume of trading increased almost sixfold between 1990 and 2000 for the world as a whole (from 29 to 154 percent of "global GDP") and for high-income countries (from 31 to 181 percent), while volume of trading increased almost eightfold (from 4.7 to 33 percent of GDP) for low-income countries. Several middle-income countries witnessed truly spectacular increases in trading volumes, including China (0.2 to 67 percent of GDP), South Africa (7.3 to 62 percent), Turkey (3.9 to 90 percent), and Korea (30 to 121 percent). As impressive as these gains are, however, they are dwarfed by the rise in trading volumes in developed economies such as the Netherlands (14 to 186 percent of GDP), Spain (8 to 177 percent), Sweden (7.4 to 172 percent), Hong Kong (46 to 232 percent), Switzerland (30 to 254 percent), and the United States (31 to 324 percent).

The trading volume measure is obviously inflated by the dramatic increase in average stock values between 1990 and 2000, so the turnover ratio is perhaps a better measure of the true increase in the frequency of trading and thus the true liquidity of a nation's stock market. This measure, not surprisingly, shows a much smaller increase than does the value of shares trading, though the ratio more than doubles between 1990 and 2001 for the world and for both low-income and high-income countries. Additionally, several individual countries experienced dramatic increases in turnover, although other countries see a net decline. In these cases, share valuations increase sharply—thus increasing the value of shares traded—but the frequency of trading either remains constant or falls. However, most large countries experience significant increases in the turnover ratio, with the most notable increase being that of the United States, where the value of shares traded as a percent of prior year's capitalization increases from 53 to 201 percent. In summary, the Great Bull Market of the 1990s dramatically increased the overall capitalization and volume of trading of the world's stock markets, and much of the growth that occurred between 1990 and 2000 remains intact today.

*The Dramatic Growth in Securities Issuance Volume
Since 1990*

Another way of measuring the rise of capital markets is to examine whether their share of annual corporate financing activity has grown relative to that of other sources of funding. We have already detailed the stable market share of commercial banking in most countries, but table 7.5 details the phenomenal growth in the total value of securities issuance over the period 1990–2003. This table clearly

TABLE 7.5. Worldwide Securities Issues, 1990–2003

Type of Security Issue	1990	1993	1997	1999	2000	2001	2002	2003
Worldwide offerings	$504	$1,503	$1,816	$3,288	$3,268	$4,112	$4,257	$5,327
(debt & equity)	(7,574)	(9,969)	(15,669)	(21,724)	(14,659)	(16,450)	(18,006)	(19,729)
Global debt (2000–	184	479	635	1,114	2,624	3,610	3,938	4,939
2001) International	(1,376)	(2,701)	(4,066)	(4,122)	(10,827)	(14,033)	(15,811)	(17,309)
debt (1990–1999								
High-grade corp debt	172	388	475	1,069	946	1,367	1,337	1,743
(2001–2002) Euro-	(1,213)	(2,162)	(2,804)	(3,893)	(3,858)	(3,589)	(5,506)	(6,139)
bonds (1990–2000)								
Yankee bonds (2000–	13	59	150	302	47	36	59	94
2002) Foreign	(81)	(270)	(1,177)	(2,706)	(112)	(84)	(212)	(441)
bonds (1990–1999)								
Global equity [exclud-	7	19	34	139	335	141	135	145
ing U.S.]	(132)	(309)	(302)	(817)	(2,662)	(1,534)	(1,481)	(1,412)
U.S. issues worldwide[a]	313	1,049	1,196	2,103	1,958	2,916	2,859	3,397
(debt and equity)	(6,141)	(7,378)	(11,644)	(17,115)	(15,686)	(11,791)	(10,646)	(12,341)
All debt	—	—	—	—	1,726	2,678	2,695	3,210
					(7,824)	(11,009)	(9,964)	(11,470)
Long-term straight	109	386	726	713	744	1,239	1,017	1,248
debt[b]	(1,016)	(3,637)	(9,098)	(7,601)	(2,986)	(4,388)	(3,867)	(4,231)
High-yield corporate	1	55	114	95	43	78	59	134
debt	(7)	(345)	(769)	(434)	(196)	(303)	(261)	(491)
Collateralized securi-	175	475	378	579	488	939	1,261	1,481
ties (asset and	(4,542)	(1,285)	(1,557)	(3,027)	(1,201)	(1,818)	(2,029)	(2,378)
mortgage-backed)								
Convertible debt and	5	15	15	40	56	112	60	96
preferred stock	(43)	(162)	(83)	(143)	(161)	(223)	(137)	(282)
Common stock[c]	14	86	119	175	223	126	104	90
	(362)	(1,374)	(1,341)	(1,069)	(955)	(559)	(545)	(589)
Initial public offerings[c]	5	41	44	64	73	40	27	16
	(174)	(707)	(625)	(531)	(429)	(107)	(97)	(88)

Source: The data are taken from early January issues of the *Investment Dealers' Digest*.

Note: This table details the total value, in billions of U.S. dollars, and number (in parentheses) of securities issues worldwide (including the United States) for selected years in the period 1990–2003.
 [a] From 1998, all figures include Rule 144A offers on U.S. markets.
 [b] Years 1999–2002 are long-term straight debt only, excluding asset-backed debt. Before 1999, figures are for investment grade debt.
 [c] Excludes closed-end funds. Data for 1990–2000 are not comparable to 2001 due to definition change.

shows that the annual volume of global security issues has surged over the past thirteen years, both worldwide and in the United States. Worldwide offerings of debt and equity securities totaled $504 billion in 1990 (and barely $300 billion in 1988); by 2001 this figure had increased tenfold to $5.33 trillion. And these figures do not include privatizations, since these are almost always secondary issues that do not raise capital for the firm itself. Even though security offerings by U.S. issuers accounted for two-thirds or more of the global total throughout this period, that still implies that non-U.S. securities issues increased from $191 billion in 1990 to $1.84 trillion in 2003. Such a massive increase in global security issuance is unprecedented in modern financial history, though domestic bond issues often surge during major wars. The rise in non-U.S offerings also completely dwarfs the increase in bank financing since 1990. As mentioned above, only syndicated lending witnessed comparable growth, and this is the type of bank lending most similar to capital market financing.

The Surge in Mergers and Acquisitions Worldwide

We conclude this examination of the growing importance of capital markets by briefly documenting the almost incredible increase in the total volume of merger and acquisition activity that occurred between 1990 and 2000. The evolution in the aggregate value of announced merger and acquisition (M&A) activity in the United States and the rest of the world is graphically displayed in figure 7.2. The total value of announced mergers and acquisitions on U.S. stock markets rose from less than $200 billion in 1990 (and less than $160 billion in 1991) to over $3.45 trillion in 2000. Even though the 1980s were considered a very active period for M&A, the 1990s dwarfed this decade's total as well as any other in American history. The total value of M&A for the decade topped $5 trillion, with two-thirds of that occurring in 1998 and 1999 alone.

While takeovers have always played an important role in the United States, the rise in M&A activity in Europe during the 1990s was even more dramatic. From less than $50 billion annually in the late 1980s, the total value of M&A involving a European target reached $592 billion in 1998, before more than doubling to $1.22 trillion in 1999—rivaling the U.S total. As noted, the global value of M&A activity in 2000 reached $3.45 trillion, or about 10 percent of world GDP. As with market capitalization, the total value of M&A activity in the United States and other developed economies has contracted sharply since 2000, though 2003's global total of $1.33 trillion was still the fifth most active year in history. If and when stock valuations recover to early 2000 levels, it seems likely that M&A activity will once more take off.

Having documented the growth of capital market– based financing, we now attempt to determine how great a role privatization programs have played in promoting these markets. As we will see, these programs have significantly, often dramatically, impacted the development of most non-U.S. stock markets. We later document that share issue privatizations have also truly transformed share ownership patterns of investors in many different countries.

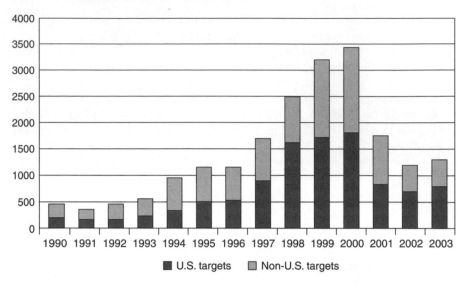

FIGURE 7.2. Value of global mergers and acquisitions, 1991–2003 (US$ billions). Source: *Investment Dealers Digest* (various mid-January issues, 2000–2003).

Privatization's Impact on Stock and Bond Market Development

This section examines the impact of privatization programs on the development of stock and bond markets outside of the United States. Obviously, we should be careful in inferring causation regarding privatization's impact on market growth, since a shift in ideology or some other exogenous political or economic change might have caused both the privatization and the overall boom. On the other hand, a careful examination of the historical evolution of non-U.S. stock markets since 1980 suggests that large SIPs have indeed played a key expansive role almost everywhere, especially because they are generally among the largest and most valuable firms in national markets. This section first documents the size of privatization programs, then examines their impact on stock market capitalization and trading, and describes the importance of SIPs as security offerings and as catalysts for the growth of today's global investment banking industry. We also provide a discussion and interpretation of the econometric evidence regarding privatization's impact on market development.

It is clear that national governments have been among the biggest winners from privatization programs, since these have dramatically increased government revenues, which is clearly one reason the policy has spread so rapidly. *Privatisation International* [Gibbon (1998, 2000)] reports that the cumulative amount raised by privatizing governments since 1977 exceeded $1 trillion sometime during the second half of 1999. This figure probably surpassed $1.25 trillion during 2003. As an added benefit, these revenues have come to governments without their having to raise taxes or cut other public services. Figure 1.2 shows the annual revenues received from privatizations since 1988. Annual proceeds grew steadily before reaching $160 billion in 1997. For the next two years, proceeds continued to flow to governments at an annual rate of $140 billion or more, and hit a record $180 billion in 2000. However, this fell sharply to a mere $43.8 billion in 2001 and to $46.6 billion in 2003, as depressed stock markets discouraged governments from making further sales.

Privatization's Impact on Stock Market Capitalization and Trading Volumes

While it is very difficult to establish a direct, cause-and-effect relationship between SIP programs and stock market development, indirect evidence suggests that the impact has been very significant. At the end of 1983, the total market capitalization of the handful of British, Chilean, and Singaporean firms that had been privatized by then was far less than $50 billion. By the end of May 2000, the 152 privatized firms listed in either the *Business Week* "Global 1000" ranking of the most valuable companies in developed-nation stock markets or in the *Business Week* "Top 200 Emerging Market Companies" ranking had a total market capitalization of $3.31 trillion. This was equal to approximately 13 percent of the combined market capitalization of the firms on the two lists, but was equal to over 27 percent of the non-U.S. total. This is because American firms accounted for 484 of the Global 1000 firms—and $13.1 trillion of the $23.9 trillion Global 1000 total capitalization in May 2000.

The total valuation of privatized companies fell sharply during 2001 and 2002, declining to $2.83 trillion in May 2002. However, the valuations of nonprivatized companies declined even more, to $17.74 trillion. By May 2003, the total valuation of the195 privatized firms on the two *Business Week* lists had rebounded to $3.24 trillion, but the value of the 1,005 nonprivatized companies on the combined 2003 lists continued to decline, falling to $14.58 trillion. Therefore, the privatized companies significantly increased their proportional share of year 2003 global stock market value from 14.5 to 18.2 percent, and raised their share of the non-U.S. total valuation increased even more, from 30.4 percent to 38.6 percent. This implies that investors who purchased privatization share offerings have fared much better since March 2000 than have investors in other type of companies, for whom this has been a financially painful period indeed.

It is almost certainly the case that privatized firms have had an even greater impact on the development of non-U.S. stock markets than these aggregate numbers suggest because they are generally among the largest firms in these markets. Table 7.6 details the total market value and relative size of the 35 most valuable privatized firms on the 2003 Business Week Global 1000 and Top 200 Emerging Market lists. Columns 1 and 2 detail the company names and domicile countries, while column 3 shows the firm's ranking in the Global 1000 list. Firms from the Emerging Market list are given the ranking they would have if included in the Global 1000 ranking, and subsequent rankings are adjusted for the inclusion of firms from the Emerging Market list. Column 4 gives the firm's ranking within its home market, while column 5 lists the firm's total market capitalization. The

TABLE 7.6. Market Values of the Largest Publicly Traded Privatized Firms

Company	Country	Global 1000 Rank	Country Rank	Market Value US$ Millions	Market Value as % National Market
BP	Great Britain	9	1	$153,240	7.76%
NTT DoCoMo	Japan	23	1	$105,306	5.07%
Total	France	24	1	$103,779	6.19%
ENI	Italy	50	1	$64,576	11.47%
Deutsche Telekom	Germany	51	1	$62,850	7.90%
Telecom Italia	Italy	52	2	$60,123	10.68%
France Telecom	France	57	2	$57,448	3.43%
Telefonica	Spain	58	1	$56,802	10.47%
Nippon Telegraph & Telephone	Japan	60	3	$55,578	2.68%
Orange	France	70	5	$45,584	2.72%
China Mobile (Hong Kong)	*China (HK)*	*73*	*1*	*$44,899*	8.37%
TIM (Telecom Italia Mobiliare)	Italy	74	3	$44,761	7.95%
BNP Paribas	France	75	6	$44,325	2.64%
PetroChina	*China*	*77*	*2*	*$43,512*	8.11%
Gazprom	*Russia*	*80*	*1*	*$42,731*	na
ENEL	Italy	81	4	$42,216	7.50%
Aventis	France	84	7	$41,652	2.49%
Telstra	Australia	92	1	$37,814	8.57%
Sinopec	*China*	97	3	$35,696	6.66%
E.ON	Germany	98	4	$35,640	4.48%
Telefonica Moviles	Spain	102	3	$35,450	6.54%
National Australia Bank	Australia	111	3	$33,003	7.48%
ING Groep	Netherlands	113	3	$32,407	9.67%
Banco Bilbao Vizcaya Argentaria	Spain	121	4	$31,574	5.82%
Assicurazioni Generali	Italy	127	5	$30,368	5.40%
Unicredito Italiano	Italy	131	6	$28,803	5.12%
Yukos	*Russia*	*135*	*2*	*$28,186*	na
Credit Agricole	France	136	9	$27,860	1.66%
BT Group	Great Britain	137	12	$27,346	1.38%
AXA	France	144	10	$26,404	1.58%
Societe Generale	France	145	11	$26,387	1.57%
Commonwealth Bank Australia	Australia	164	4	$23,069	5.23%
Banca Intesa	Italy	179	7	$20,910	3.72%
Petrobras	*Brazil*	*180*	*1*	*$20,435*	13.03%
STMicroelectronics	France	186	13	$20,387	1.22%

Source: Data are from Morgan Stanley Capital International (2003) and the Top 200 Emerging Market Companies (*italics*). National stock market valuations are from the June 2003 total market values on the World Federation of Exchanges Web site (www.world-exchanges.org).

Note: Stock market value of the 35 most valuable (largest market capitalization) publicly traded privatized firms as of May 31, 2003.

[a] These firms are from the "Top 200 Emerging-Market Companies," and they are given the rankings they would have if this list was included in the Global 1000 List. From TIM onwards, Global 1000 ranks are also adjusted to include Top 200 Emerging Market Companies.

final column expresses the single firm's market capitalization as a percentage of the entire national market's May 2003 capitalization as detailed in the "Capitalization" section of the World Federation of Exchanges' (www.world-exchanges .org) Web site. This reveals that the largest privatized firms by themselves often account for sizable fractions of the total capitalization of national stock markets, even in advanced economies such as Italy (11.47 percent and 10.68 percent for the two largest firms), Spain (10.47 percent), the Netherlands (9.67 percent), and Australia (8.57 percent). In emerging markets such as Mexico (18.55 percent), China (8.37 percent and 8.11 percent), and Brazil (13.03 percent), individual privatized firms often account for very large fractions of the total national market capitalization.

Tables 7.7 and 7.8 present similar rankings for all 721 non-U.S. firms in the two *Business Week* lists, but details which of the ten most valuable companies in a nation's stock market are privatized firms. These tables clearly reveal the relative importance of SIPs in most non-U.S. stock markets. Privatized firms are the most valuable companies in 13 of the 23 developed markets on the Global 1000 list and in 13 of 20 Top 200 Emerging Markets. Privatized companies have the highest market values in the five largest non-U.S markets—Japan, Britain, France, Germany, and Italy—as well as in the four largest emerging markets—China, India, Mexico, and Brazil. They are the second most valuable firms in Finland, Sweden, Korea, Taiwan, South Africa, Malaysia, and Israel. Privatized companies are the first and second most valuable companies in two countries, France and Indonesia, and they occupy the three (or more) top slots in Italy, Norway, Portugal, China, Russia, Brazil, Hungary, and the Czech Republic.

The Impact of Privatization on Stock Market Liquidity

In an attempt to measure what part of the increased liquidity of world stock markets is driven by privatization, Boutchkova and Megginson (2000; henceforth BM) generate the turnover ratios for individual markets and regress these on the number of privatization deals for each country in a particular year. BM specifically pick the turnover ratio, defined as the total value of trading divided by prior year-end total market capitalization, as their measure of stock market liquidity because it reflects increases in both the value of shares traded and the stock market capitalization measures—rather than just measuring absolute growth in trading volume. In other words, it is a conservative measure of the growth in liquidity. Furthermore, as Levine and Zervos (1998) point out, turnover is one of the few robust stock market-based predictors of long-run economic growth. The *Privatization International* Electronic Database is used to obtain the number of privatization deals (share offerings plus asset sales) each year for each country, and the results of BM's regression estimations are reported in table 7.9. They use pooled cross-section and time series estimation; the first two specifications do not include country dummies, whereas the last three control for country fixed effects. These country intercepts account for omitted variables representing cross country differences and measures of investor protection and rule of law [La Porta, López-de-Silanes, Shleifer, and Vishny (1997, 1998, 2000)].

TABLE 7.7. How Many of the Most Valuable (Largest Market Capitalization) Firms in Developed Countries Are Privatized Companies?

Country	Largest Firm	Second Largest	Third Largest	Fourth Largest	Fifth Largest	Sixth Largest	Seventh Largest	Eighth Largest	Ninth Largest	Tenth Largest
Australia	X		X	X						
Austria	X									
Belgium			X							
Britain	X									
Denmark					X					
Finland	X	X	X	X					X	
France	X	X	X	X	X		X			X
Germany	X		X	X						
Greece	X		X	X		X				X
Hong Kong										
Italy	X	X	X	X	X	X	X			
Japan	X	X	X							
Netherlands			X							
New Zealand	X									
Norway	X	X	X	X						
Portugal	X	X	X	X						
Singapore	X			X	X					
Spain	X		X	X	X	X			X	X
Sweden		X					X			
Switzerland										

Note: Information is from Morgan Stanley Capital International (2003).

TABLE 7.8. How Many of the Most Valuable Firms in Emerging Market Countries Are Privatized Companies?

Country	Largest Firm	Second Largest	Third Largest	Fourth Largest	Fifth Largest	Sixth Largest	Seventh Largest	Eight Largest	Ninth Largest	Tenth Largest
China	X	X	X	X	X	X	X	X		X
Korea		X	X	X	X			X	X	
Russia	X	X	X	X	X	X	X	X	X	X
Taiwan		X							X	
South Africa		X								
Brazil	X	X	X	X	X	X	X	X		X
Mexico	X		X							
India	X			X						
Malaysia		X	X		X					
Chile				X	X	X				
Poland	X	X	X	X						
Israel		X	X	X						
Hungary	X	X	X							
Czech Republic	X	X	X							
Thailand	X				X					
Indonesia	X	X								
Argentina	X									
Turkey	X			X						
Pakistan	X									

Note: Information is from Morgan Stanley Capital International (2003).

TABLE 7.9. Privatization and Stock Market Liquidity

	PCSE		DUM		
	(1)	(2)	(3)	(4)	(5)
TR_{t-1}				0.328	0.344
				(0.000)	(0.000)
PR	0.0177	0.0178	0.023	0.025	0.023
	(0.022)	(0.023)	(0.007)	(0.001)	(0.003)
PR_{t-1}				0.016	0.017
				(0.044)	(0.025)
t		0.006			−0.015
		(0.805)			(0.112)
α	0.493	0.459	**	**	**
	(0.000)	(0.003)			
R^2	0.012	0.013	0.341	0.493	0.497

Source: Table 8 of Boutchkova and Megginson (2000).

Note: Regression results for the impact of the number of privatization deals on stock market liquidity. The measure of liquidity is the turnover ratio (TR_{it}), which is calculated by dividing a county's market capitalization into the value of traded shares over a particular year. PR_{it} is the number of privatization deals in country i in year t.
  PCSE = panel cross-section estimations: (1) and (2)
  $TR_{it} = \alpha + \beta_2 PR_{it} + \beta_4 t + \varepsilon_{it}$
  DUM = pooled estimation with country fixed effects: (3), (4), and (5)
  $TR_{it} = \Sigma \alpha_i + \beta_1 TR_{it-1} + \beta_2 PR_{it} + \beta_3 PR_{it-1} + \beta_4 t + \varepsilon_{it}$
  Regressions (4) and (5) are estimated with the Cochrane-Orcutt AR (1) correction; p-values are given in parentheses.
  ** Multiple country coefficients α_i not reported.

After correcting for first-order autocorrelation, BM arrive at a specification with improved fit ($R^2 = 0.50$). The coefficient (0.023) on the privatization variable is significant at the 1 percent level and the lagged coefficient 0.017 is significant at the 5 percent level. These results indicate that each privatization deal leads to a 2.3 percent increase in a national market's turnover ratio in the first post-divestment year, and a 1.7 percent increase the following year. For example, Portugal's successful sale of the final tranche of Elecrticidade de Portugal (EdP) in June 1998, which was valued at U.S.$2.72 billion, is predicted to have increased the turnover ratio of the Lisbon Stock Exchange from 0.77 then to 0.793 in the 12 months following the deal and to 0.81 in the second year. In terms of value of shares traded, this would represent an increase of $1.774 billion [($57.468 billion current market capitalization + $2.6 billion value of the SIP)*0.023 = $1.774 billion] the first year and $1.311 billion more the second year. An example of the impact for a larger stock market is the sixth offering of NTT in Japan, which was completed in November 2000. It was valued at $11.3 billion and should have increased the value of trading on the Tokyo Stock Exchange over the first year by $83 billion and over the second year by $61 billion more. Though it is impossible to measure the net effect of any single offering on real market trading, the turnover ratio certainly increased in Portugal in 1999 and 2000. However, the Japanese market declined so dramatically in 2001 and 2002 that any incremental increase resulting from NTT6 was swamped by the tidal wave of losses engulfing Tokyo and most other markets after March 2000.

BM cannot show econometrically that privatization programs have been the primary cause of the growth, documented above, in the liquidity of stock and bond markets outside the United States. Conventional causality tests require a system of equations specifying the precise relationship between market liquidity and the scale and format (asset sale versus share offering) of privatization programs. Absent such a fully developed model of the privatization/market development relationship, they implicitly assume that privatization is exogenous to the level of stock market development, yet this seems unlikely to be completely true. In fact, Megginson, Nash, Netter, and Poulsen (forthcoming) show that a government's decision to privatize using a share offering, rather than an asset sale, is significantly negative related to the level of stock market development. This implies that governments choose share offerings as a means of developing their stock markets. On the other hand, BM's sample consists only of countries with sufficiently liquid markets to allow governments to employ share offerings as their privatization method, so by construction they examine the effect of privatization on stock market liquidity only after some critical level of liquidity has been reached. Thus the decision to privatize, conditional on that critical level of market development, can be assumed to be independent of liquidity. Given that privatization is exogenous in their setting, and the significance of the privatization coefficients in the liquidity regression estimates presented in table 7.9, BM conclude that privatization improves stock market development. A more general framework, where all countries are in the sample regardless of their level of financial development, and where both market liquidity and the privatization decision are modeled endogenously, would provide more rigorous conclusions but must await future researchers.

The Impact of Privatization on Individual and Institutional Share Ownership

One aspect of privatization programs that has to date attracted surprisingly little academic interest is its observed ability to massively increase the total number of shareholders in a country. In many cases, a single privatizing share issue will yield over 1 million shareholders, usually in countries with little tradition of share ownership by individual investors. In fact, governments explicitly design SIP offers to attract individual citizen/investors, and they favor certain groups (especially the employees of companies being privatized) with preferential share allocations and pricing. Many governments have also voiced a desire to promote an "equity culture" among their citizenry—meaning a greater willingness to support entrepreneurship through share ownership—as one of the chief rationales for adopting privatization programs. BM therefore examine the pattern of share ownership in privatized firms, and also study how this ownership structure evolves over time.

The Ownership Structure Created by
Share Issue Privatizations

Boutchkova and Megginson (2000) examine stock ownership patterns in privatized firms by comparing the numbers of stockholders in the privatized firms in the

1999 *Business Week* Global 1000 list (discussed above) to capitalization-matched private sector firms from the same national markets. They also compare the number and fractional ownership of institutional investors in these two lists. Next, BM perform a similar comparison of privatized and private-sector companies in the 1999 Top 200 Emerging Market list, but do not examine institutional shareholdings owing to lack of data. For each privatized firm, BM select as a match that private-sector company with the closest total market value in the *Business Week* lists, and they then collect the most recent data on the total number of shareholders for both sets of firms from the June 1999 Worldscope Disclosure CD-ROM database. While this data item is far from universally available, BM are able to collect values for 97 of the 153 privatized companies, and for 99 of the matching privately owned firms. In the majority of those cases where data are available for both the privatized and the matching firm, the privatized companies have a much larger number of shareholders, in spite of the fact that governments usually retain sizable stakes in these firms. This reduces the effective float of privatized firms, since these stakes remain unsold to private investors.

BM use the Wilcoxon signed-rank test to show that the mean number of shareholders of the privatized firms is significantly higher than that of the non-privatized matching firms. The frequency distribution of the number of shareholders in the Global Company Database on WorldScope is strongly skewed to the left. Roughly 91 percent of the 6,410 companies with data on the number of shareholders have fewer than 50,000 individual shareholders, 7.2 percent have between 50,000 and 250,000, and 1.8 percent have more than 250,000. The frequency distribution of the capitalization of their sample of privatized and matching nonprivatized firms is also markedly skewed to the left. However, BM focus on the companies with the highest market capitalizations, which also tend to have the largest number of shareholders, implying a higher proportion of companies with more than 250,000 shareholders. Owing to the limited availability of information on the number of shareholders—especially for the large, traditionally widely held companies—BM are able to construct a sample with complete information on both privatized and nonprivatized companies for only 86 pairs. Using these pairs, they conclude that the number of shareholders of the privatized companies is significantly higher, at the 0.01 level, than the number of shareholders in the matching private-sector (nonprivatized) sample companies.

There are three peculiar cases among the nonprivatized companies that have very large numbers of shareholders: Britain's Abbey National and Woolwich, with 2,028,141 and 1,216,932 stockholders, respectively, and Brazil's Banco Bradesco, with 2,414,603 stockholders. All three of these companies are financial institutions, and the two British firms were very large "de-mutualizations" that by their very nature created a great many new shareholders out of existing depositors. BM do not exclude these companies, and their testing procedure takes into account the magnitude of the differences between the number of shareholders of every pair. Even including these three firms, however, they still find that SIPs have (highly) significantly more shareholders than do the matching firms. The subsample of firms with complete data constructed from table 7.10 shows that the matching private companies have a total market capitalization of $1.2 trillion and 14 million

TABLE 7.10. Law and Finance—English Common Law Systems Promote Capital Market Growth

Country (1)	External Cap/GDP (2)	Debt/GDP (3)	GDP Growth Rate (4)	Domestic Firms/Pop (5)	Rule of Law (6)	Antidirector Rights (7)	Creditor Rights (8)
Australia	0.49	0.76	3.06%	63.55	10.00	4	1
Canada	0.39	0.72	3.36%	40.86	10.00	4	1
Israel	0.25	0.66	4.39%	127.60	4.82	3	1
United Kingdom	1.00	1.13	2.27%	35.68	8.57	4	4
United States	0.58	0.81	2.74%	30.11	10.00	5	1
English origin average	0.60	0.68	4.30%	35.45	6.46	3.39	3.11
Belgium	0.17	0.38	2.46%	15.59	10.00	0	2
France	0.23	0.96	2.54%	8.05	8.98	2	0
Greece	0.07	0.23	2.46%	21.60	6.18	1	1
Italy	0.06	0.55	2.82%	3.91	8.33	0	2
Spain	0.17	0.75	3.27%	9.71	7.80	2	2
French origin average	0.21	0.45	3.18%	10.00	6.05	1.76	1.58
Austria	0.06	0.79	2.74%	13.87	10.00	2	3
Germany	0.13	1.12	2.60%	5.14	9.23	1	3
Japan	0.62	1.22	4.13%	17.78	8.98	3	2
Korea	0.44	0.74	9.52%	15.88	5.35	2	3
Switzerland	0.62	—	1.18%	33.85	10.00	1	1
German origin average	0.46	0.97	5.29%	16.79	8.68	2.00	2.33
Denmark	0.21	0.34	2.09%	50.40	10.00	3	3
Finland	0.25	0.75	2.40%	13.00	10.00	2	1
Norway	0.22	0.64	3.43%	33.00	10.00	3	2
Sweden	0.51	0.55	1.79%	12.66	10.00	2	2
Scandinavian origin average	0.30	0.57	2.42%	27.26	10.00	2.50	2.00
Sample average (44 countries)	0.44	0.59	3.79%	21.59	6.85	2.44	2.30

Source: LaPorta, Lopez-de-Silanes, Shleifer, and Vishny (1997).

Note: This table details the relationship between the type of legal system upon which a country's commercial code is based and the size of that nation's capital markets for selected countries in 1994. Column 2 is the ratio of the Stock market capitalization held by minority (noncontrolling) shareholders to GDP, and column 3 provides a similar measure for private-sector debt (bank loans and bonds). Column 4 presents the country's average annual GDP growth rate during 1970–1993 and column 5 is the ratio of the number of domestic firms in a country to its population, in millions. Columns 6–8 present summary measures of the law and order traditions in a country (column 6) and of how well its legal code protects the rights of shareholders (column 7) and creditors (column 8).

shareholders, whereas the total market capitalization of the privatized firms ($1.6 trillion) is held by more than twice as many shareholders (37.6 million).

BM also compare institutional shareholdings in developed-country privatized firms to those of the matching private-sector companies. The mean (293 versus 281) and median (242 versus 231) number of institutional investors in the privatized and matching firms is surprisingly close. The same is true for mean (15.46 versus 15.78 percent) and median (12.81 versus 12.79 percent) percent shareholdings by these institutional investors. Using the Wilcoxon test of paired differences,

BM cannot reject the null hypothesis that the mean and median values are equal at conventional significance levels. The fact that governments retain sizable stakes in privatized firms—making the fraction of shares available for trading substantially smaller than for matched firms—suggests that institutional investors are at least as interested in investing in privatized companies as they are in private-sector firms of similar size. Additionally, while individual investors are offered the opportunity to profit by initial underpricing by government issuers, institutions are generally not offered similar discounts in the initial offering. Therefore, institutions must reap superior returns by providing monitoring and/or other valuable services.[3]

How Ownership Structure Evolves over Time After Privatization

BM also examine how the total number of shareholders in a company evolves during the years subsequent to a SIP. They collect shareholding data for up to seven years after each privatization, using as a sample those SIPs provided by *Privatization International*, or in the appendix to the Megginson and Netter (2001) survey paper.[4] The pattern thus observed represents one of the most important, and surprising, results of this study—since BM demonstrate that the extremely large numbers of shareholders created by many SIPs are not a stable pattern of corporate ownership! BM test whether the number of shareholders declines significantly in SIPs in the first year after an issue. For the group of SIPs with less than 100,000 initial stockholders, BM are unable to reject the null that the number of shareholders does not change from Year 0 to Year 1. It thus appears that those offerings that yield a reasonable number of shareholders (between 10,000 and 75,000, depending upon the country) do not demonstrate strong tendencies to change in subsequent years. Some of these firms experience increases in the number of shareholdings, while others experience slight declines.

BM normalize the number of shareholders in Year 0 to 1.00, and then measure the number of shareholders in subsequent years as a ratio of Year 0's value. This yields a value less than, greater than, or equal to 1.00 depending upon whether the number of shareholders has increased, decreased, or remained constant. Then they plot the mean coefficients for all SIPs. Figure 7.3 shows the dynamics of share ownership in the full sample of privatized firms, and in various subsamples. BM observe slight increases in all years subsequent to Year 0, and an increase of 23 percent in Year +6, for the subgroup of SIPs with less than 100,000 shareholders. This result is not testable, however, because BM have very few data items for Year +6, owing to the short periods between offerings of the same company or because most privatized companies have short operating histories (as private firms) through 1999. All they can conclude for the SIPs with less than 100,000 initial holders is that there is no statistically significant decrease from Year 0 to Year +1, and there appears to be a tendency for the number of shareholders to increase over time.

However, this is far from true for the 39 SIPs that yield over 100,000 shareholders. In these cases the total number of shareholders declines dramatically and steadily. BM estimate that the total number of shareholders in these highly polit-

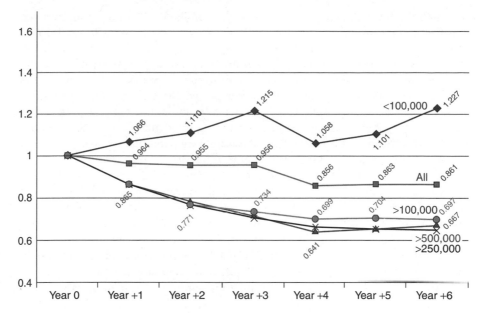

FIGURE 7.3. The evolution of share ownership in privatized firms after initial offering. This figure represents the dynamics of share ownership of privatized firms, where the number of shareholders in Year 0 is normalized to 1 and in subsequent years shows the change with respect to Year 0. The lines are for companies with less than 100,000 initial shareholders, companies with more than 100,000, more than 250,000 and more than 500,000 initial shareholders. Source: Figure 3 of Boutchkova and Megginson (2000).

icized privatizations declines by 33 percent within five years of the share offering. While they again have sufficient data only to test whether the number of shareholders changes significantly during the first post-issue year, BM document a significant (at the 0.01 level) decline in the number of shareholders for those SIPs with more than 100,000 initial stockholders.

The implications of this finding for government efforts to develop an equity culture are unclear. It is certainly true that many new stockholders do not retain the shares they purchase. Further, other evidence suggests that retail investors in privatizations generally own only that one stock, hardly indicative of a rising class of well-diversified shareholders. On the other hand, since the studies detailed in chapter 6 document that the long-run returns to investors in SIPs are strongly positive, this implies that retail investors' first experience in stock market trading is a very positive one—earning a capital gain. Furthermore, the fact that governments are able to entice large numbers of investors to return for subsequent share offerings suggests that these programs are indeed creating stock markets capable of absorbing large new stock issues, just as the governments had hoped.

BM next compare the dynamics of share ownership of privatized and nonprivatized firms. It is not possible to replicate the format of the SIP's shareholder-change table for the nonprivatized (private-sector) companies because of the need to match the IPO of the privatized firms with a similar event for the nonprivatized firms. Although the private companies have had a few new issues or stock splits, indicative of increases in the shareholder base, it is impossible to find sufficient matches with respect to market capitalization, timing of the new issue, and occurrence of a share offering. BM thus examine the dynamics of share ownership for the nonprivatized firms over the ten-year period 1989–1998. The private firms have enough data to examine the dynamics over the entire ten-year period, and these are presented in figure 7.4. In constructing the dynamics table for the non-privatized companies, they move the data series for a particular company that does not have an entry for 1989 so that it begins at Year 0.

As can be seen in figure 7.4, the number of shareholders in nonprivatized firms does not change over the first year, but it does seem to increase in subsequent periods. Yet BM cannot reject the null that the number of shareholders in Year 0 and in Years 1 to 5 is the same. The first significant increase (at the 0.05 level) is recorded for Year 6, and in Years 7 and 8 they find significant increases at the 0.01 level. These results suggest an initially stable number of stockholders in non-privatized companies during the early 1990s, that eventually increases.

Breaking up the nonprivatized companies' sample into subsamples with less

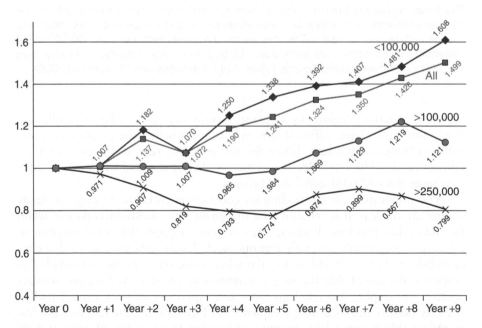

FIGURE 7.4. The evolution of share ownership in private sector (non-privatized) firms, 1989–1998. This figure represents the dynamics of share ownership of matching non-privatized companies over the 10-year period 1989–1998. The lines are for companies with less than 100,000 initial shareholders, companies with more than 100,000, and more than 250,000 initial shareholders. Source: Figure 4 of Boutchkova and Megginson (2000).

than 100,000 and more than 250,000 stockholders in Year 0 reveals two different patterns. The former sample shows an increase in the number of shareholders, with a cumulative increase of more than 60 percent by the final year, while the latter sample shows a cumulative decrease of more than 20 percent. The decline in shareholder numbers is consistent with increasing institutionalization of ownership for large capitalization firms. Unfortunately, BM have too few private companies with a large number of shareholders, and thus cannot use any meaningful testing procedure to determine whether the decline in shareholder numbers is significant. However, the reported patterns suggest that the number of shareholders in private firms is generally increasing with time, though the shareholder base of the largest companies decreases. To summarize, BM document a significant decrease in the number of shareholders of the SIPs in their sample, especially those with 100,000+ initial stockholders, contrasting with an increasing shareholder base for the nonprivatized matching companies.

Privatization's Impact on International Corporate Governance

Every sovereign nation has a system of corporate governance, though very few countries are content with their system as it currently functions. A nation's corporate governance system can be defined as the set of laws, institutions, practices, and regulations that determine how limited-liability companies will be run—and in whose interest. Not surprisingly, given the economic primacy of publicly traded firms in most national economies, the current (heated) debate about corporate governance centers on these large companies. Specifically, the debate focuses on how to create a legal and regulatory system that will give the managers of publicly listed companies the incentive to operate their firms in a way that maximizes economic value and financial performance, and yet still protect the legitimate interests of noncontrolling corporate stakeholders.

While developing an effective, value-maximizing system of corporate governance is an increasing concern for most nations, doing so becomes a political and economic imperative for countries wishing to launch privatization schemes, particularly share issue privatization programs. Both the financial success of the program and the electoral survival of the sponsoring government typically hinge on the post-privatization operating performance of the former state-owned enterprises being divested, and on the financial return earned by the newly created class of citizen/shareholders on the stocks they purchase. However, almost by definition, countries that are contemplating a significant privatization program will lack many or most of the necessary ingredients of an effective corporate governance system, and will instead have to create such a system on the fly. This is typically a much more difficult task than simply selling off large numbers of state-owned firms (itself no mean feat), since it involves the necessity of reforming so many laws and institutions simultaneously. Creating a satisfactory corporate governance system generally involves at least the following: (1) changing a nation's corporate and securities laws, (2) strengthening (or creating) the listing and disclosure requirements for its stock exchanges, (3) enhancing the independence and competence of the national judiciary, and (4) establishing a regulatory regime capable of balancing the competing claims of managers, outside shareholders, and creditors. The economic pay-off from success in this endeavor can be extremely large, but so can the penalties for failure.

Components of a Nation's Corporate Governance System

Much of the "central plumbing" of an effective national corporate governance system is apparent to all observers. Obvious components include a nation's system of corporate and securities law, its court system (and the independence and activism of its judges), the regulatory bodies established to enforce governance regulations, and the rules of the nation's capital markets. A nation's corporate and securities laws should clearly establish the rights and responsibilities of managers, investors, creditors, and other corporate stakeholders, and these laws should provide mechanisms for stakeholders to protect their rights and to resolve disputes. Of particular importance are those laws defining the voting and cash flow rights of noncontrolling shareholders and the rights of creditors to force nonpaying corporate borrowers into bankruptcy in the event of nonpayment. The legal system should also establish clear information disclosure requirements on firms, since outside shareholders and creditors must have timely, ongoing access to corporate information in order to enforce their claims, and managers are generally unwilling to disclose this data absent a legal mandate to do so. A nation's courts are at least as important to effective governance as is the body of law itself. These must be capable of enforcing commercial laws, adjudicating claims, and enforcing private property rights in a timely and effective manner. Finally, the legal system's disclosure rules in most countries are also buttressed by the listing requirements that the nation's stock and bond markets impose on firms wishing to list securities for public trading.

Less obviously relevant to effective corporate governance are such cosmic issues as the degree of product market competition and the level of macroeconomic and political stability, as well as seemingly mundane topics such as the national commitment to transparent and internationally accepted accounting standards. Historical experience suggests that it is very difficult for businesses to operate effectively in a nation wracked by political or macroeconomic instability. These are especially damaging for capital spending, since entrepreneurs are typically unwilling to make long-term, potentially expropriable investments in a country where legal rules are prone to sudden change or where taxes, inflation, or high interest rates can quickly eviscerate an investment's value. An equally damaging aspect of instability is the set of incentives this gives to corporate managers. Even in the best of circumstances, managers will face a tension between maximizing a firm's long-term market value and looting the firm for their own short-term gain. When managers must operate in an uncertain macroeconomic and legal environment, this balance usually shifts heavily in favor of self-dealing over value-maximization. Perhaps the worst of all possible environments for effective corporate governance is the all-too-frequent case of a country's suffering from political and economic instability, high inflation (itself usually the result of fiscal profligacy), and endemic corruption. This adds the necessity of paying an unending stream of bribes to all the other burdens and temptations of managing a business.

The importance of product market competition in promoting effective corporate governance becomes fairly obvious upon reflection. Firms exposed to intense competition in product and factor markets must be efficient and responsive to customer needs to survive. Phrased differently, highly competitive industries generate relatively few economic rents and thus provide few opportunities for corporate managers to enrich themselves at the expense of outside investors. Additionally, competitive industries tend to be characterized by competitive labor markets. Therefore, managers who develop a reputation for maximizing firm value will be rewarded financially and professionally, whereas those with a reputation for exploiting outside investors will be penalized. On the other hand, protected or monopolistic industries tend to generate significant economic rents, over which managers exercise effective control. The temptation managers have to consume these rents is made all the stronger by their nontransparent nature, and by the reality that noncompetitive industries (or economies) are unlikely to have competitive labor markets capable of punishing managerial self-enrichment.

While few would doubt that economic stability and product market competition are critically important in promoting effective corporate governance, the importance of mandating nationwide adoption of internationally accepted accounting standards is less clear-cut. In fact, however, both academic research and accumulated experience clearly show that investors will shun any capital market that does not require public companies to regularly disclose a great deal of detailed financial information, prepared according to the accounting standards observed in best-practice countries. Domestic investors will be unwilling to commit their savings to informationally opaque markets, and international investors will avoid them in favor of markets characterized by transparent accounting and information disclosure standards. Being thus relegated to the second (or lower) tier of international financial markets can be crippling for a nation's long-term economic prospects. This is because global investment capital flows have often exceeded $500 billion dollars annually in recent years, and the relative importance of capital markets in the world's economies has more than doubled over the past decade.

Academic Research on the Importance of Corporate Governance

At its best, the relationship between academic research and public policy-making can be symbiotic, with academics bringing their objectivity and analytical skills to bear in addressing issues of abiding interest to elected officials. This happy confluence has in fact occurred regarding academic research into corporate governance during the past ten years, it has flourished just as governments have begun reaching for policy guidance. One of the first, and most influential, papers was Shleifer and Vishny (1997), since it synthesized the existing strands of research to that time, and was in fact named "a survey of corporate governance." Since then, two specific lines of research have emerged, and these will be discussed in turn below. The first line examines how a country's legal system—especially whether the system is based on English common law—influences the size, efficiency, and productivity of that nation's capital markets. This stream is complemented by the second line of inquiry, discussed in the first section of this chapter, which studies whether the size and efficiency of a nation's capital markets influences the rate of economic growth the country can achieve.

Since we are focusing on international systems of corporate governance, we will not survey the vast theoretical and empirical literature on U.S. mergers and acquisitions or the management compensation policies adopted by American corporations, unless a study's results are truly generalizable to a global context. Additionally, we will not devote much attention to any one of the several survey articles on corporate governance that have been written over the past decade, though five highly readable and informative surveys deserve specific mention.

Maher and Andersson (1999) present a comparative analysis of the "shareholder" versus the "stakeholder" models of corporate governance, and conclude that neither has decisive competitive advantages. Though we disagree with this conclusion, believing instead that only the shareholder model has real survival value, this paper provides a sophisticated assessment of what other researchers label the "capital-market based" versus "bank-based" (or "Anglo-Saxon" versus "European") models of corporate finance and governance. Black, Kraakman, and Tarassova (2000) focus primarily on the causes of Russia's dismal privatization experience, though they also provide an excellent overview of corporate governance principles. Coffee (1999) emphasizes the importance of legal systems generally, and securities law in particular, in an effective system of corporate governance. Lin (2000) presents the single best discussion we have read of the multifaceted nature of a value-maximizing corporate governance system. Lin's focus is on China, but he also discusses topics that are globally relevant, such as the need to promote product and labor market competition, mandate international accounting standards, and set up effective legal and regulatory bodies as a counter-weight to managerial control. Finally, Denis and McConnell (2003) provide an excellent, up-to-date survey of the international corporate governance literature.

Capital Markets and National Legal Systems

While several authors have commented on the importance of legal systems to effective corporate governance, the works of La Porta, Lopez-de-Silanes, Shleifer, and Vishny (hereafter LLSV) have had unprecedented impact owing to their number and the fact that the papers have been published in very prestigious academic journals. Using a sample of 49 countries, LLSV (1997) show that countries with poorer investor protection—measured both by the character of legal rules and the quality of law enforcement—have smaller and less liquid capital markets. This is true for both debt and equity markets, suggesting that stock and bond markets are complements rather than supplements, and both require the proper legal infrastructure to reach maturity. LLSV (1997) also show that French civil law countries offer much poorer investor protection than do common law countries, and La Porta, Lopez-de-Silanes, and Shleifer (LLSV; 1998) describe why this is so. They examine the investor protection characteristics of the world's four basic legal systems (English common law, French civil law, and German and Scandinavian law), and find that the common law countries offer by far the greatest protection to noncontrolling investors. Further, LLSV (1998) document (and provide a rationale for) the fact that ownership concentration is highest in countries offering poor investor protection, which is consistent with the idea that small, diversified shareholders are unlikely to be important in countries that fail to protect outside investors. In a specific investigation of the ownership structures of the largest publicly traded companies in the world's developed economies, LLSV (1999a) show that dispersed ownership structures are common only in the United States, Japan, and Britain. Effective family control over even the largest companies, often exercised through pyramidal share ownership structures, is the norm everywhere else. LLSV (2000) also find that dividend policies in different nations are related to the agency costs of different ownership structures. Table 7.10 reproduces key results from LLSV (1997) showing the impact of a nation's legal system on economic growth and financial market size and depth.

Empirical studies by LLSV and others support their proposition that a nation's legal system influences the optimal ownership structures of publicly listed companies, and that ownership structure "matters." LLSV (1999b) find that the size of a nation's government is related to its efficiency, honesty (the legal system again), and the demographic makeup of its citizenry. LLSV (2002) document that countries with the greatest legal protection for investors also assign the highest valuation to publicly traded shares. The clear implication of this finding is that individual investors are more willing to entrust their savings to capital market investments when they are confident that their wealth will not be expropriated by insiders. Demirgüç-Kunt and Maksimovic (1998) show that in countries whose legal systems score high on an efficiency index, a greater proportion of firms use long-term external financing. Since their measure of efficiency is different from LLSV's, the results are not a direct test of the LLSV hypothesis that common law countries offer better investor protection than civil law countries (especially since France receives higher efficiency scores than Britain). Nonetheless, Demirgüç-Kunt and Maksimovic document that an active stock market and large banking sector are associated with externally financed firm growth, and that companies in countries with weak financial sectors are unable to fund maximum achievable growth. Finally, though Coffee (1999) takes issue with LLSV's focus on the transcending importance of a nation's system of corporate law—he emphasizes differences in national securities laws and regulations—he agrees that the commercial legal system is a vitally important part of an effective corporate governance system.

The Impact of Privatization Programs on Corporate Governance

In many countries contemplating SIP programs, stock markets are sleepy, rather backward places that play little active role in corporate finance or governance. Few people own shares, and the stock ownership that does exist is highly concentrated in controlling blocks of family-dominated businesses. This is an intolerable situation for a government that wishes to raise very large sums of money by selling blocs of shares in state-owned businesses to a citizenry ignorant of—or, worse, hostile toward—the entire idea of stock ownership. To have any chance of success, a government must create a new and trustworthy corporate governance system literally from scratch. Though this is always a difficult task, it is made easier by the fact that many other countries have successfully executed SIP programs since 1979, and there is now a vast store of accumulated experience available to guide novice privatizers.

As documented in Jones, Megginson, Nash, and Netter (1999) and Menyah and Paudyal (1996), governments adopting large-scale SIP programs are at least as concerned with political and economic objectives in designing the share offerings as they are in raising revenues. In fact, the findings in Jones, Megginson, Nash, and Netter examined in chapter 6 show that governments deliberately structure privatizing share offerings to maximize political and economic benefits at the expense of revenue maximization. Taken as a whole, this pattern of behavior clearly suggests that governments care very deeply whether their citizens have a positive investment experience after purchasing shares of SOEs being privatized. Governments therefore take great care in designing share offerings, and must then be equally concerned that the stock markets on which citizen/shareholders trade their shares are fair and honest markets. To ensure this, governments must take a number of steps more or less simultaneously—including adopting a new regime of corporate and securities law, establishing a regulatory body to oversee privatized utilities, and perhaps setting up an investor protection body comparable to the U.S. Securities and Exchange Commission. But governments are not the only actors who play critical roles in constructing post-privatization systems of corporate governance; in particular, no institution is more dramatically affected by large SIP programs than is the nation's stock exchange.

Having examined why governments have become so concerned with corporate governance, we now change gears from positive economics (what has been observed) to normative prescriptions of what should be done. Specifically, we describe the steps governments and concerned private-sector agents should take to develop an effective corporate governance system in their countries—whether or not a large-scale privatization program is being contemplated.

What Must Be Done to Develop an Effective Corporate Governance System?

The prescriptions presented in this section will be based primarily on the findings of academic research, and will implicitly assume we are advising government policy makers about priorities to be followed in establishing (or reforming) a workable governance system. We will thus emphasize specific, realistic policy actions and will refrain from admonitions such as "encourage honesty and discipline among workers and managers." While there is nothing magical about creating a system of governance that protects legitimate stakeholder interests and provides incentives for managers to make value-increasing investments, the steps required to achieve this can be extraordinarily difficult to implement. To quote an old World Bank saying, "there are no short cuts to development."

Though the needs of every country are different, it is possible to specify what steps most governments should take to improve (or create) an effective corporate governance system. For most non-OECD countries (and a few OECD nations as well), the following reforms should be encouraged:

1. *Legal reforms.* While it is essentially impossible for a nation to change its entire system of corporate law (say, from civil law to common law), it is within the grasp of most governments to reform existing laws to provide better protection for noncontrolling investors. Academic research has clearly shown that in the absence of strong investor protection laws, and courts willing and able to enforce these laws, investors will be unwilling to purchase debt and equity securities and capital markets will remain small and inefficient. In particular, a nation's laws, regulations, and courts must protect outside investors from expropriation by insiders who have an incentive to enrich themselves through a variety of self-dealing schemes. An important part of this reform process is simply to mandate and enforce sufficient information disclosure for outside stockholders and creditors to know they are in danger of being expropriated, and then to provide timely and effective venues for investors to protect their rights. This venue could be the nation's court system, or it could involve a special purpose agency—provided this agency has real power.

2. *Mandate international accounting standards.* The "simple" act of requiring publicly traded domestic companies to use internationally accepted accounting standards can be an important, perhaps vital, adjunct to strengthening investor protection through reform of a nation's corporate and securities laws.[5] This accomplishes three main purposes. First, it transfers much of the burden of reforming a country's corporate governance system from the state to the private sector. Second, it prevents domestic companies from concealing financial and operating problems behind nontransparent accounting conventions, and ensures that all domestic companies can be compared both to each other and to the international competition. Third, mandating international accounting standards will help attract international investors to a nation's stock and bond markets. These investors bring not only vast wealth, but also much needed professionalism and demands for managerial accountability. Unfortunately, simply mandating use of modern reporting systems will help only marginally if a nation does not have a sufficient number of professionally trained accountants, or if domestic accountants are themselves not trustworthy. In this case, the only alternative will be to allow foreign accounting firms unlimited access to the domestic market.

3. *Promote high standards for listing on the national stock market.* Transparency begins at the stock exchange. If a country's stock market does not take transparent information disclosure requirements seriously, then neither will the firms that choose to list on that exchange nor

the country's investors. This is an especially critical problem in countries where stock exchange rules are set by government fiat, rather than by private owners of the exchange. Member or investor-owned exchanges have an inherent incentive to maximize the exchange's "brand value," and are thus far more likely to mandate rigorous listing standards and to police the disclosure and governance policies of companies once they begin trading. To an extent, exchange credibility can be imported by establishing ongoing relationships with major Western exchanges and international organizations such as the World Federation of Exchanges (www.world-exchanges.org). Domestic companies should also be encouraged to cross-list on one or more foreign markets as well as the domestic exchange.

4. *Set clear rules for corporate control contests.* Few societies are comfortable with hostile takeover battles; these are controversial even in the countries where they are witnessed the most, the United States and Great Britain. Nonetheless, it is vitally important to establish mechanisms that allow poorly performing corporate managers to be effectively challenged by outsiders. The best way to do this is to set rules for takeover contests, and to not tilt these rules too much in favor of incumbents. While the most extreme control contests, such as hostile takeover battles, may be socially unacceptable, most countries can take less dramatic but practically more important steps to promote managerial accountability. These can include mundane steps such as allowing the use of signed proxies, rather than requiring personal attendance at shareholder meetings, and mandating that companies hold shareholder meetings in accessible locations and at reasonable times. To paraphrase Lord Acton, "managerial entrenchment corrupts; unchallenged entrenchment corrupts absolutely."

5. *Encourage institutional investors to become major players in the national stock market.* The past three decades have witnessed a nearly incredible increase in the liquidity and efficiency of capital markets in the United States, Great Britain, Switzerland, and the Netherlands. Most other countries have experienced far less dramatic growth in trading volume and securities issuance volume (though capitalization has increased comparably). Not coincidentally, the four countries listed above all have large funded (private) pension systems and the largest number of active institutional investors, especially pension funds. These investors bring a number of significant strengths to the market with them. They are sophisticated financial analysts, they command significant (often vast) resources, and they have the clout to demand that corporate managers perform effectively and attend to shareholders' interests. Countries wishing to develop an effective corporate governance system should both encourage the growth of domestic institutional investors and attract participation by foreign institutions.

6. *Establish workable, efficient bankruptcy systems.* At first blush, it may

seem odd to assert that a country wishing to develop an effective corporate governance system should also develop an efficient bankruptcy system. However, upon reflection, most people understand that protecting investors also means protecting creditors, and this is usually impossible without providing creditors with a mechanism for penalizing borrowers who default and forcing the liquidation of hopeless or fraudulent debtors. This is often a very difficult step to take politically, especially in newly democratic transition economies, since the natural impulse is to favor debtors' rights over those of creditors. But without assurance that they will be able to enforce their legal rights, creditors will be unwilling to make loans in the first place.

7. *Clarify—but limit—government's role in corporate governance.* An efficient corporate governance system does not arise in a vacuum, nor will it spring full-blown strictly from private sector initiatives. Many of the reforms detailed above, especially the legislative and regulatory reforms, cannot be accomplished without the national government playing a leading role. On the other hand, government's role can easily become too dominant. In fact, a core problem with corporate governance in most countries is that state-owned firms play much too large a role in the nation's economy or that the government's claim on available private-sector credit is too high, or both. Perhaps the most straight-forward assertions we can safely make is to say that, to the maximum extent possible, government should be a catalyst for change and it should serve as an unbiased referee and regulator of private-sector economic activity. The two great economic dangers for all political economies are, first, a state that is so powerful that it strangles private initiative; and second, a state that is too weak to ensure political stability and enforce property rights. Reform-minded, democratic leaders must walk a fine line between these extremes.

Perhaps the single most compelling argument in favor of developing an effective national corporate governance system is the fact that such a system must be in place before a truly productive entrepreneurial culture can emerge. All countries dream of creating domestic equivalents of America's Silicon Valley or NASDAQ stock market, but very few have taken the necessary steps to create a vibrant venture capital industry. To achieve this, the corporate governance system must protect investors and reward entrepreneurs, and the national government must establish a legal and regulatory system that promotes competition, protects the property rights of legitimate corporate stakeholders, and encourages the growth of efficient capital markets.

Summary

Recent financial history can be encapsulated in a phrase: the rise of global capital markets. This chapter presents an overview of the rise of capital market-based finance and the relative eclipse of financial intermediary-based financing, and examines the impact of SIPs on the growth of world capital markets, especially stock markets. This chapter also studies privatization's impact on the pattern of share ownership by individuals and institutional investors. We begin by documenting the increasing importance of capital markets, and the declining role of commercial banks, in corporate financial systems around the world. We then show that privatization programs—particularly those involving public share offerings— have had a dramatic impact both on the development of non-U.S. stock markets and on the participation of individual and institutional investors in those markets. We conclude by describing the components of a nation's corporate governance system, and discuss how privatization programs can promote (and have promoted) the development of an effective corporate governance system.

Our research documents the following key points: (1) the fraction of total domestic credit provided by the banking sector, as a percent of GDP, has increased only modestly since 1990 for the world as a whole, as well as for most major country groupings. During the 1990–2000 period, stock market capitalization as a percent of GDP increased from 48 to 105 percent for the world as a whole, though it has declined by perhaps a third since then, and from 52 to 121 percent for high-income countries. (2) SIPs contributed significantly to the nearly elevenfold increase, from $3.4 trillion to $35.0 trillion, in the total capitalization of the world's stock markets that occurred between 1983 and 2000. During that same period, the aggregate valuation of SIPs grew from less than $50 billion to over $3.3 trillion—about 13 percent of the world's total, but over 27 percent of the non-U.S. total. Though the aggregate valuation of the world's stock markets declined to about $18 trillion by year-end 2002, privatized firms have fared much better than other companies and they now account for a significantly higher fraction of total non-U.S. market value (38.6 percent in May 2003) than in 2000. SIPs also played a significant role in the even more dramatic increase in global stock market trading volume, from $1.23 trillion in 1983 to $33.1 trillion in 2002. (3) Privatizations have significantly improved stock market liquidity during the last ten years. On average, each additional privatization deal is associated with a 2.3 percent increase over the first year and a 1.7 percent increase over the second year in the turnover ratio of the respective stock market. (4) Privatized firms are now the most valuable companies in most non-U.S. stock markets, including four of the five largest, as well as in most developing countries. (5) Privatizations have dramatically increased the number of shareholders in many countries. Almost two-thirds of the 54 non-U.S. firms with over 500,000 shareholders are privatized companies, and roughly a dozen SIPs have more than 1 million initial shareholders. SIPs generally have a far larger number of stockholders than do capitalization-matched private firms in the same country. (6) However, we also find that the extremely large numbers of shareholders created by many SIPs are not a stable ownership structure. For the 47 offers that initially yield over 250,000 shareholders, the total number of shareholders declines by one-third within five years.

What policy recommendations can we offer to governments contemplating the launch of a large-scale privatization program, based on the results presented in this chapter? First, we can confidently assert that, if executed properly, a series of share issue privatizations can indeed promote the growth of a liquid stock market, which will yield economic and political dividends for many years to come. Second, we would advise governments not to overreach when setting the price for these share offerings. Those governments that have willingly underpriced SIPs, particularly early in their privatization programs, have been far more successful than have those governments that set very high offering prices. Most governments consider it vital to design SIP offering terms that attract large numbers of domestic investors, and to price share issues so that these first-time investors earn capital gains, in order to maximize political support for privatization and thus for ongoing economic reforms.

Our third recommendation is aimed at government policy makers who have decided to launch a large-scale privatization program, but who are struggling with designing the optimal processes and procedures to be used. Absent a truly compelling reason to do otherwise, privatizing governments should sell SOEs as quickly and completely as possible, for cash, to any investors willing to pay a fair price—including foreigners.

Our final recommendation involves the need to encourage the development of an effective system of corporate governance for publicly traded companies. A large volume of empirical research [see especially Shleifer and Vishny (1997)] has clearly shown that countries that offer investors effective legal protection have large, liquid capital markets, while those countries that have neglected investor protection have smaller and less efficient stock and bond markets. Share issue privatization programs involve immense share offerings targeted at a politically sensitive group of investors (first-time citizen/investors), and governments often must develop an entire regulatory system from scratch to ensure that these investors are protected from expropriation by corporate insiders. The lesson of recent research is that such an effort is well worth making for any government wishing to enter the brave new world of modern finance.

Privatization Industry Studies

Telecommunications

No other industry has become more closely associated with privatization in the popular imagination than has telecommunications. Beginning with the first large, and immensely controversial, sale of British Telecom shares in 1984, governments of over 80 countries have fully or partially divested their holdings in the national telecommunications service provider (hereafter, telecom or telco), which was almost always a monopoly service provider prior to divestiture. More than 150 separate offerings have been made, and these have raised almost $450 billion for the divesting governments.

Few governments approach the telecom privatization decision lightly. Not only do these companies provide a basic service, they are invariably one of the nation's most important industrial companies and are often the largest single employer after the government itself. Privatizing these firms successfully can yield significant political, economic, and financial benefits—not the least of which is the opportunity to massively increase the number of citizens who own shares and to dramatically improve the depth and liquidity of the country's stock market. On the other hand, few governments survive the political fallout from a botched telecom privatization, and any economic and regulatory mistakes made during the initial sale will haunt the economy for many years thereafter. Telecom privatizations are thus the highest of all high-stakes privatization gambles.

This chapter begins by providing an overview of how state ownership of telecommunications evolved during the twentieth century, and discusses why this model has fallen out of favor over the past two decades. The next section details the key issues of regulation that must be faced whenever a government decides to privatize its telecom provider, and also offers policy recommendations based on the experience of those countries that have already privatized their telcos. We then describe the two basic methods used to divest telecom ownership stakes and detail how asset sales and public offerings of share in these companies have transformed global capital markets in the years since stock in British Telecom was first offered to the public in 1984. The fourth and fifth sections discuss the empirical evidence on the effectiveness of privatization and related reforms in improving telecom performance and describe the size and value of the stakes in telecom providers that governments have left to sell.

Overview of the Global Telecommunications (Telecom) Industry

Along with the automobile and the airplane, telecommunications transformed life during the twentieth century. The growth of modern telephone service — and more recently, cellular phone service and Internet access — over the past century has been extremely rapid, but also extremely varied. Each nation's experience has been influenced by many factors, including initial wealth, economic growth rate, and geopolitical stability, but policy has been the single most decisive factor explaining the diffusion of telecoms in the population.

The Historic Industrial Structure of National Telecom Markets

As Wallsten (2002b) shows, many countries allowed private ownership of telecoms during the early years of the twentieth century. However, this pattern started to change around the time of World War I, as governments began to co-opt private ownership, and the trend toward state ownership accelerated sharply during the Great Depression and after World War II. In western Europe, a mixture of ideology and financial necessity prompted the governments of industrialized countries to nationalize the few remaining private telecoms during the postwar era, and to grant sweeping monopolies to state-owned operators. Developing countries typically nationalized the concessions of the departing colonial powers (or started telecom companies from scratch) and made these central components of their overall state-directed development strategy. So thoroughly did modern governments accept the premise that telecoms should be state-owned that by the early 1980s the only major countries with privately owned telecom providers were Canada and the United States.

As discussed at length in chapter 2, the basic rationale for state ownership was that telecommunications were considered a natural monopoly, with ever increasing returns to scale, so that only one supplier was economically rational. Natural monopolies have always been problematic for economists, and the customary response of political leaders to such an industry structure was to mandate state ownership in order to spur development and to protect consumers from exploitation. Many also felt that state ownership was required to ensure that something like universal service would be provided to all citizens at "fair" prices. The alternative of allowing private ownership of telecoms, with regulation, was rejected as either unworkable or unfair (or both) everywhere outside of North America.

This political equilibrium of state ownership of telecoms remained intact for three decades after World War II, but was finally disrupted by four developments. The first was the powerful demonstration effect provided by the technological and economic success of telecom equipment and service providers in North America. Whereas telecom monopolies in most countries acquired reputations for bad service provided at high cost, telecommunications service in the United States and Canada was fast, innovative, and provided at steadily declining real prices. The pace of innovation accelerated even more after the American Telephone and Telegraph Company (AT&T) was broken up by court order in 1984. The second factor was the observed inability of state-owned telecoms to achieve the objectives set for them. Far from delivering universal service at low cost, these firms demonstrated all of the bad habits of monopolies (high prices, poor service, technological backwardness), with none of the compensating benefits (cost efficiency, system-wide interoperability). Third, advances in economic theory began to cast serious doubt on the idea that telecoms actually were natural monopolies, or that state ownership was the best way to handle the problems of market power. Finally, powerful new communications technologies began to emerge that could not be effectively commercialized under the existing state monopoly structure.

The (Changing) Mix of Goods and Services Offered by Telecom Providers

Until about two decades ago, telecommunications was a very simple business, where the provider offered basic fixed-line telephone service to businesses and individuals, and these consumers paid a fixed and regulated monthly fee. Since then, as we all know, the variety of products and services offered by telecom providers has changed beyond recognition. The rapid evolution of digital systems during the 1970s and early 1980s, powered by advances in information technology, rendered the analog systems used in most countries obsolete. Cellular telephone networks moved from the laboratory to widespread consumer use, requiring massive investments in new equipment and service capabilities, and eventually revolutionizing how people communicate. Cable television emerged as a major technological counterpart and competitor to basic telephony in North America, prompting an accelerating technological "arms race" to determine who would provide digital communications/information/entertainment services to the home. Even basic, fixed-line telephone service was transformed by the development of rapid new switching and routing systems, fiber optic networks, and computerized private branch exchanges. By the time the Internet burst on the scene as a major communications and information technology medium in the mid-1990s, it was clear that the old state-owned monopoly structure for telecoms was doomed.

Given the emergence of these new technologies, it is not surprising that the policy of privatizing state-owned telecoms really took off during the 1990s. Table 8.1 details the growth in various telecom services from 1991 to 2003, revealing how completely the global telecommunications industry was transformed over this 13-year period. The total value of telecoms services increased from $403 billion in 1991 to $1.07 trillion in 2003, while the value of equipment sold increased proportionally even more, from $120 billion to $300 billion. Even these figures understate the true increase in telecom usage, since the real price of both services and equipment fell steadily throughout the 1991–2003 period. A better indication

TABLE 8.1. Key Revenue and Service Indicators for the World Telecommunications Sector

	1991	1992	1993	1994	1995	1996	1997	1998	1999	2000	2001	2002[a]	2003[b]
Telecom market revenue (current prices and exchange rates), US$ billions													
Services	403	448	470	517	596	672	712	767	854	920	968	1,020	1,070
Equipment	120	132	135	158	183	213	234	248	269	290	264	275	300
Total	523	580	605	675	779	885	946	1,015	1,123	1,210	1,232	1,295	1,370
Telecom services revenue breakdown (current prices and exchange rates), US$ billions													
Telephone[c]	331	350	359	386	428	444	437	456	476	477	472	465	455
International[d]	37	43	46	47	53	53	54	56	58	60	63	65	68
Mobile	19	26	35	50	78	114	142	172	223	278	317	364	414
Other[e]	53	72	77	81	89	114	133	139	155	165	180	190	200
Telecom services capital expenditure (current prices and exchange rates), US$ billions													
Total[f]	124	130	135	138	161	174	177	177	186	198	201	205	215
Other statistics													
Main telephone lines (millions)	546	572	604	643	689	738	792	846	905	983	1,053	1,129	1,210
Mobile cellular subscribers (millions)	16	23	34	56	91	145	215	318	490	740	955	1,155	1,329
International telephone traffic minutes (billions)[g]	38	43	49	57	63	71	79	89	100	118	127	135	140
Personal computers (millions)	130	155	175	200	235	275	325	375	435	500	555	615	650
Internet users (millions)	4.4	7.0	10	21	40	74	117	183	277	399	502	580	665

Source: International Telecommunications Union Web site (www.itu.org).

Note: All data in millions of current US$ converted by annual average exchange rates. Country fiscal year data aggregated to obtain calendar year estimates.

[a] Estimation.

[b] Forecast.

[c] Revenue from installation, subscription and local, trunk and international call charges for fixed telephone service.

[d] Retail revenue.

[e] Including leased circuits, data communications, telex, telegraph and other telecom-related revenue.

[f] Note that the data of the growing number of new market entrants are not always reflected in national statistics.

[g] From 1994 including traffic between countries of former Soviet Union.

273

of the mushrooming demand for telecommunications services is provided by the statistics measuring physical use. International telephone traffic almost quadrupled between 1991 and 2003 — from 38 billion to 140 billion minutes — while the number of personal computers in use rose more than fourfold, from 130 million to 650 million. Impressive as these compound annual growth rates (of around 11 percent) might be, however, the increased demand for cellular and Internet service was nothing short of exponential. The number of cellular phone subscribers worldwide rose from 16 million in 1991 to 1.33 billion in 2003, while the number of Internet users increased 150-fold over this time period, from 4.4 million to 650 million. Telecommunications has grown so rapidly, in fact, that Li and Xu (2002) report that telecom services alone now represent 2 to 3 percent of GDP in most countries.

Raw statistics can impress, but what ordinary citizens (and voters) care about is the availability and cost of telecom services. It is very hard to come up with a single summary measure of "average" cost of service, since the number and mix of services to choose from has changed substantially over time. Nonetheless, it seems clear that the real cost of a three-minute local call has dropped significantly (sometimes dramatically) in almost all industrialized countries since the early 1990s, and a similar decline has occurred in the majority of developing countries. Additionally, the real prices of long distance and international calls have been more than halved in most countries over this period.

Measuring the availability of telecom services is easier than measuring price changes, since availability can be proxied by the penetration rate, or the number of telephone lines per 100 inhabitants. As Noll (2000) reports, the number of telephone lines per 100 people in the industrialized countries of Europe ranged from 11.3 (Portugal) to 58.5 (Sweden) in 1981, with most countries clustering in the range of 30 to 45 percent coverage. By 1996, telephone service had reached 37.5 percent of Portugal's population and 68.2 percent of Sweden's, and most European Union countries had between 50 and 60 lines per 100 inhabitants. The industrialized "tiger" economies of Asia witnessed even more rapid growth in coverage between 1981 and 1996, with the number of lines per 100 people rising from 8.4 to 43.0 in Korea and from 15.5 to 46.6 in Taiwan. Japan, Canada, and the United States all had high coverage rates (of 34.2, 41.3, and 46.7 percent, respectively) in 1981, which nonetheless increased by about 50 percent over the next 15 years. More recent data from the ITU (www.itu.org) reveals continued growth in the number of telephone lines per 100 inhabitants in all industrialized countries since 1996.

While the average annual growth in the number of telephone lines per 100 people over the past quarter-century can best be described as "significant, but incremental" in developed economies, the growth has been far more rapid in developing countries — albeit from a much lower base. Table 8.2 documents the evolution of telecom service coverage, productivity, and prices in 16 Latin American and 15 African countries over the period 1984–1997. The first column of this table reports the same measure we have been using so far, the number of lines per 100 inhabitants.[1] The second and third columns report the number of pay phones and the connection capacity per hundred people, while the fourth

TABLE 8.2. Telecom Utilization Statistics for Latin America and Africa (Excluding South Africa), 1984–1997

Year	Mainlines per Hundred Population		Pay phones per Hundred Population		Connection Capacity per Hundred Population		Employees per Line		Price of 3-Min Local Call (USD)	
	Latin America	Africa	Latin America	Africa	Latin America	Africa	Latin America	Africa	Latin America	Africa
1984	4.56	0.74	0.06		5.83	1.16	0.03	0.08		
1985	4.95	0.82	0.06	0.01	5.77	1.11	0.03	0.07		
1986	5.22	0.88	0.07	0.01	5.92	1.46	0.02	0.07	0.03	0.16
1987	5.54	0.94	0.08	0.01	6.85	1.48	0.02	0.07	0.05	0.11
1988	5.86	1.00	0.09	0.01	7.61	1.29	0.02	0.07	0.06	0.11
1989	6.16	1.08	0.09	0.01	7.16	1.58	0.02	0.06	0.06	0.09
1990	6.66	1.17	0.09	0.01	8.23	1.55	0.02	0.06	0.05	0.07
1991	7.14	1.30	0.09	0.01	8.54	1.86	0.02	0.05	0.05	0.06
1992	7.77	1.48	0.10	0.01	9.17	1.97	0.02	0.06	0.04	0.09
1993	8.50	1.72	0.11	0.01	10.07	2.26	0.02	0.05	0.05	0.09
1994	9.19	1.95	0.12	0.01	10.78	2.40	0.01	0.04	0.05	0.07
1995	9.91	2.15	0.14	0.02	12.47	2.66	0.01	0.04	0.05	0.08
1996	10.86	2.45	0.15	0.03	13.49	3.36	0.01	0.04	0.07	0.09
1997	11.67	2.94	0.18	0.05	15.34	4.14	0.01	0.03	0.07	0.06
Average annual percent charge	7.51	11.25	9.40	19.57	7.93	11.01	−7.97	−7.31	11.20	−5.58

Source: Table 2 of Wallsten (2001a).

275

line reports the number of workers employed by the telecom service provider per installed phone line. The final column details the evolution in price for an average three-minute local call.

As can be seen, the number of lines per 100 inhabitants in Latin America increased at a 7.5 percent compound annual rate, from 4.56 to 11.67 percent of the population, between 1984 and 1997. The coverage rates for pay phone and connection capacity increased somewhat more rapidly (9.4 and 7.9 percent average annual growth, respectively) over the same period. Productivity per worker in Latin American telecoms increased sharply between 1984 and 1997, with the number of workers per line dropping at an average rate of 7.9 percent per year. However, the benefits from this increased productivity were not passed on to consumers, since the average price of a local call in Latin America increased 11.2 percent per year. Although service quality and penetration rates expanded, and other services (long distance and international) either had more moderate price hikes or outright declines, these increased prices for basic service help explain why telecom reforms have been so controversial throughout Latin America.

The evolution of telecom service levels and prices in Africa over the 1984–1997 period was significantly different from that in Latin America. In 1984, less than one person (0.74) per hundred had access to a telephone line; by 1997, the number of lines per 100 inhabitants had increased to 2.94. The average annual growth rate implied by these figures is 11.25 percent. The number of pay phones per 100 people grew at an even faster rate of almost 20 percent per year, though from an extremely low base of one pay phone per 10,000 people in 1985. The productivity of African telecom workers also increased rapidly between 1984 and 1997, with the number of workers per line falling at a 7.3 percent annual rate. Unlike in Latin America, however, African consumers did benefit from these productivity increases, as the average price of a three-minute local call fell from U.S.$0.16 to U.S.$0.06 between 1985 and 1997. As was true for developed countries, more recent ITU data indicate that these trends in Latin America and Africa have continued in the years since 1997.

So far, we have discussed the rapid changes in the global telecommunications industry in isolation from changes in their ownership structures to focus on the changes in service observed by consumers in various countries and regions. However, these physical and price changes were accompanied by equally dramatic changes in ownership and regulation of telecom providers. Li and Xu (2002) report that less than 2 percent of the telecom providers in 167 countries were privately owned in 1980, but this had increased to 42 percent by 1998. Expressed as a fraction of global industry revenues, the increasing share of private ownership would be even more striking, since almost all of the telcos in developed countries have been at least partially privatized, and these account for the vast majority of worldwide industry revenues.

Although the first major telecom privatization, British Telecom 1, took place in 1984, most telecom privatizations have occurred only during the past dozen years. Figure 8.1 shows the cumulative distribution of the 84 telecom privatizations documented as occurring between 1984 and 2000 by Chong and Galdo (2002).

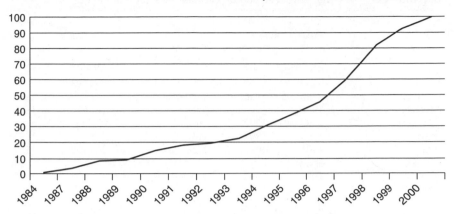

FIGURE 8.1. The evolution of telecommunication privatization over time. This figure details the cumulative distribution of the dates of 84 telecom privatizations executed between November 1984 and December 2000, with the graph reaching 100 percent of the sample in 2001. Source: Figure 1 of Chong and Galdo (2002).

Clearly, governments around the world have enthusiastically adopted telecom privatization programs. On the other hand, Li and Xu also report that 72 percent of all telecom providers remained monopolies in 1998, which indicates that the majority of governments have not been willing to fully expose their telecom markets to competition. Table 8.3 details when the national telecommunications provider was privatized and/or subjected to independent regulation in various countries. As we will see later in this chapter, the primary reason governments have chosen not to inject competition into their "privatized" telecom markets is that selling off a telecom with a protected (if not actually monopoly) position maximizes the sale proceeds governments receive from private investors. We now analyze the regulatory choices governments must face when they decide that the time has come to privatize their national telecom providers.

Regulating Privatized Telecoms

One of the undeniable benefits of a state-owned telecom system is its simplicity. It may be inefficient, technologically backward, overstaffed, and offer consumers little choice and high costs, but at least a state-dominated telecom industry does not require any elaborate regulatory processes to be developed. Instead, the government is the monopoly provider, it owns all of the network assets, and it sets all of the rules regarding access, pricing, distribution, and allowable substitutes. Historically, the telecom service provider might have been structured as a corporatized SOE, but as often as not was simply an arm of the Communications Ministry and was frequently part of a single Postal, Telephone, and Telegraph (PTT) organization. In any case, the telecoms were usually given a monopoly in the provision of telecom services and telecom workers were almost always state employees.

TABLE 8.3. Countries That Privatized and/or Established a Separate Regulator

Country	Year Privatized	Year Regulator Established	Country	Year Privatized	Year Regulator Established
Albania	n.a.	1998	Kenya	n.a.	1999
Angola	n.a.	1999	Kiribati	1983	n.a.
Argentina	1990	1990	Kyrgyzstan	n.a.	1997
Armenia	1998	n.a.	Latvia	1994	1992
Australia	1997	1992	Lithuania	1998	n.a.
Austria	1998	1997	Luxemburg	n.a.	1997
Bahrain	1981	1996	Madagascar	1995	1997
Barbados	always	n.a.	Malawi	/a	1998
Belgium	1996	1993	Malaysia	1990	1998
Belize	1996	1988	Maldives	1988	n.a.
Bhutan	n.a.	1998	Mali	n.a.	2000
Bolivia	1995	1995	Malta	1998	1997
Botswana	n.a.	1996	Mauritania	n.a.	1999
Brazil	1998	1997	Mauritius	n.a.	1988
Bulgaria	n.a.	1998	Mexico	1990	1996
Burkina Faso	n.a.	1999	Mongolia	1995	1995
Burundi	n.a.	1997	Morocco	n.a.	1998
Cameroon	n.a.	1998	Mozambique	n.a.	1992
Canada	always	1976	Namibia	n.a.	1992
Cape Verde	1995	1992	Nepal	n.a.	1998
Central African Republic	1990	1996	Netherlands	1994	1997
Chile	1988	n.a.	New Zealand	1990	n.a.
Colombia	n.a.	1994	Nicaragua	n.a.	1995
Costa Rica	n.a.	1996	Nigeria	n.a.	1992
Croatia	1999	2000	Norway	n.a.	1987
Cuba	1994	n.a.	Pakistan	1996	1996
Czech Republic	1994	1993	Panama	1997	1996
Denmark	1991	1991	Papua New Guinea	n.a.	1997
Ecuador	n.a.	1995	Paraguay	n.a.	1995
Egypt	n.a.	1998	Peru	1994	1993
El Salvador	1997	1996	Philippines	always	1979
Equatorial Guinea	1987	n.a.	Poland	1998	n.a.
Eritrea	n.a.	1998	Portugal	1995	1989
Estonia	1993	1998	Qatar	1998	n.a.
Ethiopia	n.a.	1996	Romania	1998	n.a.
Finland	1998	1988	Russia	1997	n.a.
France	1997	1997	Senegal	1997	n.a.
Gabon	n.a.	2000	Serbia	1997	n.a.
Georgia	1994	n.a.	Seychelles	1954	n.a.
Germany	1996	1998	Singapore	1993	1992
Ghana	1997	1997	Slovakia	2000	1993
Greece	1996	1995	Slovenia	1996	n.a.
Grenada	1989	n.a.	Solomon Islands	1990	n.a.
Guatemala	1998	1996	South Africa	1997	1997
Guinea	1996	1995	South Korea	1993	n.a.
Guinea-Bissau	1990	n.a.	Spain	1992	n.a.
Guyana	1991	1992	Sri Lanka	1997	1991
Haiti		1969	Sudan	1994	1996
Honduras	n.a.	1995	Sweden	2000	1992

Country	Year Privatized	Year Regulator Established	Country	Year Privatized	Year Regulator Established
Hungary	1993	1990	Switzerland	1998	1992
Iceland	n.a.	1997	Tanzania	n.a.	1994
India	n.a.	1997	Togo	n.a.	1999
Indonesia	1995	n.a.	Trinidad and Tobago	1989	n.a.
Ireland	1996	1997	Turkey	n.a.	2000
Israel	1990	n.a.	Uganda	2000	1997
Italy	1998	1998	United Arab Emirates	1976	n.a.
Ivory Cost	1997	1995	United Kingdom	1984	1984
Jamaica	1989	1995	United States	always	1934
Japan	1985	n.a.	Vanuatu	1990	n.a.
Jordan	2000	1995	Venezuela	1991	1991
Kazakhstan	1994	n.a.	Zambia	n.a.	1994

Source: Table 2 of Wallsten (2002).

Note: n.a. = firm not privatized or regulator not established. Data from ITU-BDT Telecommunications Regulatory Database, 1999.

Naturally, the capital investment policies of state-owned telecoms were also set by the government, and the aggregate amounts available for maintenance of existing assets and purchase of new equipment were almost always inadequate, for four reasons. First, as wholly state-owned enterprises the telecoms were by definition excluded from raising capital in public equity markets. Second, the amount the firms were allowed to raise in debt markets was usually constrained by the overall public-sector borrowing requirement (PSBR), and the government's own funding needs were always met first. Third, governments had every incentive to mandate low prices for telecom services, which meant that these services were often provided (to favored groups) below cost, thus reducing the telecom companies' profitability and minimizing the amount of cash flow available for reinvestment in the firm. Finally, state-owned telecoms were almost always starved of cash by their nature as de facto government employment agencies.

Since these companies were often seriously overstaffed, it was natural for their political overseers to substitute labor for capital whenever possible, and to place a higher priority on paying wages and salaries on time than on investing in new equipment or maintaining the existing capital stock. In fact, it can be said that a defining characteristic of state-owned telecoms is that they are financially weak, have too little capital equipment, and are far off the technological frontier in terms of service capability. One of the key objectives of privatization is therefore to structure the business so that it can commence a massive, sustained capital investment program — and to sell the company in a way that provides the new owners with the proper incentives to actually launch such an investment program.

Key Regulatory Issues Facing a
Privatizing Government

Before telecom privatization can even be attempted, however, a government must ask and answer a series of important questions regarding the regulation of the divested company. Simply selling the firm off as an unregulated private monopoly is almost never an option, for both economic and political reasons. Economically, nothing is gained by turning a public monopoly into a private one. Although the private owners might have an incentive to increase the operational efficiency of the company, they have no incentive to reduce prices or to invest in improved service. Furthermore, while the benefits of creating a private monopoly will accrue only to the new owners, the costs will be borne by consumers generally and by laid-off workers in particular. Arguably, this "privatization of monopoly profits and socialization of costs" could be reflected in a higher price paid to the government during the initial sale of the company, but even this "benefit" would be constrained by the fact that investors understand the political impossibility of allowing a private monopoly to be created, and would reduce their offering price accordingly. Quite simply, citizens of democratic societies will not stand for a service as basic as telecommunications to be monopolized by a private company, and will demand that this firm be subjected to effective, politically accountable regulation. For this reason, truly exploitative privatizations are observed only in countries with the murkiest forms of democracy, such as Russia in the mid-1990s and some of the seamier countries of eastern Europe, Latin America, Central Asia, and sub-Saharan Africa.

Since a government cannot simply sell off the national telecom and wash its hands of the service, all governments must pass enabling legislation and create a new regulatory authority either before or immediately after privatization. However, creating an effective regulatory regime is neither simple nor easy. The overarching problem that all governments must face is that a privatized incumbent will inevitably have significant market power over any potential rivals immediately after the initial privatization sale is executed. This argues for promoting competition in any way possible. On the other hand, the incumbent will often be much weaker financially and operationally than many potential rivals—especially Western operators that might enter the market—and could easily be crushed by these players before it could adjust to a fully open and competitive environment. Additionally, all privatizing governments face the temptation of choosing a policy that maximizes sale proceeds, by selling the provider off intact and with light regulation, and subject to little new competition, rather than one that promotes competition and maximizes economic efficiency after the sale. Among the basic issues that all privatizing governments must address are the following.[2]

- Should the monopoly provider be broken up before privatization—either along geographic lines or based on the type of product or service offered—or sold off intact?
- Should the new private owners be granted an exclusivity period, when

they will not be subject to new competition, or should competition be allowed immediately after the initial sale?

- If competition is desired, how can this be encouraged without inflicting severe damage on the incumbent operator, which often bears large "legacy" costs of stranded assets and excess labor?
- Should the company be sold directly to a private operator in an asset sale, or should the company be sold to investors through one or more public share offerings?
- If a trade sale is selected, should foreign telecom companies by allowed (or encouraged) to participate? If so, how can the enduring national interest be protected under foreign ownership?
- What powers should the new regulatory authority be given, how independent should it be from political influence, and how should this new body be financed and staffed?
- How can it be ensured that the new regulatory body will judiciously weigh the interests of consumers versus producers, and not be captured by the incumbent operator?
- How can it be ensured that telecom providers have the wherewithal and incentive to undertake the capital investments needed to expand and improve service?
- Most important of all, how will prices for basic services be set, and who will have the power to change these prices?

Although economists have theoretically "correct" answers to all of these questions, the real world of political economics renders all these choices difficult. The fundamental choices governments face are twofold. First, policy makers must choose between maximizing sales revenue at the time of privatization and maximizing economic efficiency afterward. Second, privatizing governments must choose between protecting the interests of the privatized incumbent and protecting consumers and ensuring that citizens gain access to the full range of telecommunications services at the lowest possible price. Additionally, no government is keen to see its national telecom provider fall under foreign control, so the decision to allow foreigners to bid for a controlling interest is always excruciating—and this decision is rarely taken unless the foreign operator can offer something (capital, technology, management expertise) that cannot be obtained locally.

Regulatory Regimes and Best Practices

Since the empirical evidence on telecom regulation and privatization is discussed at length in a later section, our purpose here is simply to detail what empirical research and practical experience has shown to be "best practices" regarding the regulation of telecommunications providers at the time of their privatization. Although most of the examples cited here come from developed countries, many developing countries have also achieved extremely beneficial results. The key difference is that developing countries usually are forced to sell controlling interests in their telecoms to foreign operators, so the choices these governments face generally revolve around the investment and service extension commitments to extract from these operators before the sale is executed—since this is the only time when the divesting government is likely to have significant bargaining power. Empirical evidence and expert commentary offers six key lessons for governments wishing to privatize their national telecom monopolies.

BREAK UP TELECOMS PRIOR TO SALE

First, if at all possible politically, the telecoms should be broken up before the initial privatization sale since, as a practical matter, it will be impossible to do so at any time after that. This draconian step is always fiercely resisted by the incumbent provider's managers, workers, and suppliers—and in industrialized countries by nationalists who envision creating a "national champion" capable of competing in the global telecommunications market. However, this is the only truly effective method of rapidly engendering competition in the domestic market. The American experience in particular shows that de-monopolization strongly promotes innovation and the development of new products and services. It is axiomatic (though nonetheless true) that to become competitive, a company must compete. Since no rational company will choose to compete if there is a viable option to do otherwise, governments must ensure that privatized telecoms face competition immediately. Alas, very few governments have been willing or able to choose the breakup option, so those concerned with promoting competition have generally been forced to embrace other strategies.

ENCOURAGE AND PROTECT COMPETITION AFTER PRIVATIZATION

If an incumbent operator is not broken up prior to sale, the privatizing government should make it clear that competition from new entrants will not only be allowed but also strongly encouraged, and that the financial and legal interests of the new entrants will be protected. This can be done in three ways. First, the enabling legislation for privatizing the incumbent operator should clearly spell out the legal and regulatory structure that will govern the telecom market after the sale. Actual laws passed by democratic legislatures have greater force than do regulatory rulings or official promises, so potential competitors will be reluctant to enter a national market against a powerful incumbent unless the basic rules of competition are spelled out in statute. Second, promoting competition should be one of the cardinal mandates given to whatever regulatory regime is established to supervise the privatized telecom market, and clear rules for adjudicating conflicts between the incumbent and new competitors should be enacted. Third, foreign investment in the privatized telecom market should be encouraged. This is always a tough sell, since nationalism (perhaps even xenophobia) is a powerful force in every society, and all governments are loathe to surrender domestic control over basic services to foreigners. Nonetheless, only the largest multinational telecommunications companies have the resources to challenge entrenched incumbent telecoms, and these firms also have the incentive to do so—at least in richer national markets.

ESTABLISH AN INDEPENDENT REGULATORY AUTHORITY, AND DO SO BEFORE THE FIRST SALE

The third lesson for governments contemplating privatization of their monopoly telecom provider is that a complete and transparent regulatory system must be established before the initial privatization sale. This includes not only mandating the establishment of an independent regulatory commission but also detailing the commission's powers, staffing requirements, and funding sources. Ideally, this commission should be established before privatization, but in any case its duties and powers must be clearly mandated at least by the time of the sale. Though many governments are tempted to sell the telecom first and regulate later, this rarely works. For one thing, as noted above, potential competitors will be unwilling to enter the market unless the competitive rules of the game are in place. Additionally, empirical research has now conclusively shown that investors are frightened by regulatory uncertainty and are willing to offer a high price for a telecom operator only if an understandable regulatory regime is already in place.[3] Finally, the danger of regulatory capture by the privatized incumbent will always be high, but becomes a virtual certainty unless an independent regulator is established before the initial privatizing sale is made.

NEVER GRANT EXCLUSIVITY PERIODS TO BUYERS

These grants of temporary protection from competition are often demanded by companies that buy the incumbent provider from the selling government, in the event of an asset sale, as well as by the incumbent's managers if the firm is being offered to investors through a public share offering. The reasons why buyers request EPs and why governments are tempted to offer them are obvious, since common sense and empirical research both suggest that investors highly value a monopoly position in a market for a basic necessity, and are willing to pay a high price to obtain it. However, Wallsten (2001b) and others show that granting EPs significantly reduces post-privatization investment and service extension, and thus acts as a severe constraint on economic efficiency.

FIND A WAY TO CREDIBLY COMMIT TO NONINTERFERENCE

The divesting government must allow the privatized firm's managers to run the firm along truly commercial lines, even when the state retains an overwhelming majority of the firm's shares—which is often the case with telecoms, given their massive size. Keeping "hands off" almost inevitably means that the government must allow the partially privatized firm to reduce staff, increase some service prices, expand operations into other national markets (by acquisition or organic growth), and adopt modern corporate governance practices. Even if they feel entitled to exercising continuing strategic control after selling off only minority equity stakes, governments are often shocked by the ferocity and effectiveness of the stock market's response to interventions that would have been routine under state ownership. Where allowed (outside the EU), a possible compromise is for governments to retain a golden share in their partially privatized telecoms. This gives governments the right to veto certain corporate actions, such as a major asset sale or acquisition by a foreign company, yet still precludes the government from intervening in the day-to-day operations of the firm. Naturally, nothing in economics is free, so including a golden share will also reduce the price investors are willing to pay for the company.

ESTABLISH CLEAR AND OBJECTIVE PRICING RULES BEFORE THE INITIAL SALE

Telecom service is considered a necessity in most countries, so the single most important regulatory step to take before the first privatization sale is to specify how prices for services will be established initially and how these prices will be changed over time. There is no perfect method of accomplishing this, since any pricing regimen must balance the interests of consumers and providers, unless competition can be counted on to do this without regulation. Adequately protecting producers is especially problematic, since the pricing system must give the incumbent an incentive to innovate and control costs, while still allowing the firm to earn a return high enough to cover its cost of capital and to finance new investment programs. Furthermore, the pricing rules must cover the rates that incumbents are allowed to charge new entrants for access to the existing network and for other connection charges levied between competing providers. If incumbents are allowed to set these connection charges too high, they will use this mechanism to stifle new entry; if the charges are mandated to be too low, this could encourage economically wasteful entry and inflict serious financial damage on the incumbent. The best principle is probably to mandate a clear and transparent pricing formula for all services, such as the RPI-X pricing regime adopted for British Telecom before its initial privatization in 1984 (discussed in the following section). The second best method—devolving the pricing decision to the independent regulator, but mandating open and contestable rule-making procedures—is often the more practical option.

We will return to the issue of regulating privatized telecoms in a later section, when we survey the empirical evidence on telecom privatization and regulation. Our next step, however, is to examine how the wave of telecom privatizations has evolved since 1984, and to examine the impact this phenomenon has had on global capital markets. We begin by summarizing the methods governments use to sell their telecoms, and then describe how three key early sales set precedents that have influenced all 150 telecom offerings that have been executed since 1990.

The Privatization Wave in Telecoms

As we discussed at length in chapter 3, governments have two basic methods of selling equity in state-owned enterprises to private investors. First, they can sell either the entire company or a controlling interest directly to another company (or group of investors) in an asset sale, which is also known as a trade, private or direct sale. Alternatively, the government can sell some or all of its share holdings to investors through a public share offering. This technique is called a SIP, or public offering. Governments have employed both methods to privatize their telecom operators, with the key choice variable usually being the country's size and state of economic and technical development. As a general rule, larger industrialized countries usually opt for SIPs, whereas smaller and developing countries usually sell their operators directly to one of the relatively small group of international telecommunications companies. Developing countries, in particular, have found asset sales to be the most reliable and effective method of attracting the capital, technology, and expertise needed to modernize their telecom providers. During the period from 1990 to 2000, these countries found that by cleverly structuring their telecom auctions they were often able to extract very aggressive promises of post-sale investment and service extension from foreign bidders. The bargaining power of sellers has been seriously curtailed by the global stock market crash that began in March 2000, which hit Western telecommunications companies especially hard, since the international operators have become much more concerned with their own survival and much less eager to bid on telecom providers in developing nations.

In every country, the national telecom is one of (if not the) largest companies in terms of sales, assets, investment, and employment, so its sale inevitably has a major impact on the economy and the financial system. Telecoms also have the potential to be extremely valuable companies, which means that it is often very difficult to find a single buyer with the financial resources to purchase the entire company directly from a government, or to sell the company in its entirety in a single public offering. Therefore, the governments of industrialized countries that opt to sell their telecom through public offerings generally must do so in multiple tranches (offerings) spread over several years. In any case, both economic theory and practical experience suggest that it is usually wise to sell large, politically sensitive infrastructure companies in pieces rather than all at once. Doing so allows the government to build credibility early in the privatization process, such as by allowing the firm's managers to operate without political interference and by not subjecting the company to punitive regulation or the shareholders to expropriative taxation. By reducing perceived political risk, governments encourage investors to pay higher prices for shares in subsequent rounds.[4] For all these reasons, governments typically adopt a strategy of selling telecoms in separate tranches, spread out over several years. As with so many other features of share issue privatization, the first British Telecommunications offering in November 1984 (hereafter, BT1) pioneered what became the standard method of selling telecoms in OECD countries.

The Pioneers: British Telecom, NTT, Telefonos de Chile

When the Thatcher government decided to partially privatize British Telecom, the decision makers involved understood that they were entering a brave new era politically, industrially, and financially. BT1 was revolutionary in many aspects. First, at £3.9 billion ($4.8 billion), it was by far the largest share offering in history to that time. Second, most of the issue was explicitly targeted at ordinary British citizens, and was supported by a massive advertising campaign, thus raising the political stakes for the government almost beyond measure. Third, international tranches were specifically allocated to continental European, American, and Asian investors, making BT1 the first truly global share offering in history. Fourth, this was the first major privatization of a core infrastructure company by any industrialized country's government, and the regulatory structure proposed for BT was completely untested.[5]

To general amazement, BT1 was met with strong demand by investors, including employees, both at home and abroad. The issue was almost ten times over-subscribed, which means that investors demanded 9.7 times as many shares as were offered. Furthermore, the initial return to investors who bought shares at the offering and sold these by the end of the first day's trading was a stunning 86 percent. This set a pattern of deliberate underpricing that would be followed in almost all subsequent British offerings, as well as in most other national programs. Given the widespread participation by ordinary British citizens, most of whom became stockholders for the first time with this issue, BT1 was also considered a major political success, and helped generate enthusiasm for subsequent, even larger British SIPs. Most important, this issue demonstrated that a global market existed for privatization share offerings, and that size alone need pose no difficulty. Japan became the next major country to take this lesson to heart in a telecom privatization program.

To call the Japanese sequential privatization of NTT a "program" hardly does it justice, since the three SIPs executed between February 1987 and October 1988 dwarfed all security offerings ever executed before—or since! The initial public offering of NTT shares was, at ¥2.34 trillion ($15.1 billion), far and away the largest share offering in history. But this record lasted a mere nine months. In November 1987, the second NTT tranche raised an almost unimaginable ¥4.97 trillion ($40.3 billion), which remains the largest single security offering of any type in the history of financial markets.[6] By the time the third NTT tranche [¥3.30 trillion ($22.4 billion)] was successfully executed in October 1988, the Japanese government had raised no less than $77.8 billion in an 18-month period—and still owned 65 percent of NTT! A very unusual feature of the first two NTT tranches was that they were reserved exclusively for Japanese investors. This turned out to be a dubious favor for the home team, however, since the value of NTT shares fell sharply, and more or less continuously, over the next 15 years.

The third pioneering telecom share issue was Telefonos de Chile. Though not an especially large SIP by privatization standards, it was extremely important because it was sold as an ADR offering primarily to U.S. investors, and was very well received. The success of the Telefonos de Chile offering opened a pathway for many other developing countries to follow, and a stream of privatization ADRs followed over the next dozen years. More generally, 1990 marked the year when all types of privatization offerings, especially telecoms, kicked into high gear.

The Telecom Privatization Deluge (1990–2000) and the Big Chill (after 2000)

Financial history has never seen a decade remotely comparable to the 1990s in terms of security issuance volume or stock market capitalization growth, and telecom privatizations were star performers in this most extravagant of periods. Table 8.4 details 158 separate telecom privatization sales executed by either asset sale or share offering by 74 countries between November 1984 and July 2003. These sales raised a total of $441.9 billion for divesting governments, an equity issuance total unmatched save by the entire U.S. corporate sector over the same period. The vast majority of these sales—all but eight of the offerings and 81 percent of the value—were executed after the September 1990 Telefonos de Chile offering described above.

The "telecom deluge" of the 1990s began quietly enough, with only three sales (Argentina's Telefonica, Telekom Malaysia, and Telecom New Zealand) during the final quarter of 1990 and five in all of 1991, but one of the offers from this period set a pattern that was to be followed by many subsequent telecom sales by developing countries. This was the initial privatization of Telefonos de Mexico (Telmex), which began when the Mexican government sold a controlling fraction of Telmex shares to a consortium of international companies that included America's Southwestern Bell Company. In exchange for gaining operating control of Telmex, and an effective exclusivity period in the Mexican telecoms market, the consortium committed itself to a multibillion dollar capital-spending program and to very ambitious promises of service extension. The consortium also promised to sell a sizable fraction of its holding in a public offering, which it did in May 1991 in a very successful SIP targeted primarily at U.S. investors. The Mexican government also sold roughly half of its residual 30 percent stake in Telmex during the May 1991 offering, and had fully divested its holdings by May 1994.

The Telmex privatization became a blueprint for subsequent developing country telecom privatizations for several reasons. First, by using an asset sale as the initial divestment technique, the Mexican government was able to attract vital capital and expertise—and extract very favorable development promises—from international operators. Second, by also insisting on a subsequent public share offering, the Mexican government was able to promote development of the national stock market, since a sizable fraction of the Mexican population eventually purchased Telmex shares, and the company immediately became the most valuable (and widely held) company on the Bolsa de Mexicanos. Third, by opening its heretofore protected domestic telecoms market to foreign investment, and by undertaking other privatizations that dramatically reduced the state's role in what had been a highly interventionist economy, Mexico signaled an entirely new openness to international trade and investment. Over the next dozen years, Mexico was

TABLE 8.4. Telecommunications Privatizations

Country	Company	Date	Amount of Offer (US$ Millions)	Method of Sale	Fraction Sold
Albania	Albanian Mobile Communications	Aug 00	$128.6	Asset sale[1]	—
Argentina	Telefonica de Argentina	Nov 90	$2,830	Asset sale[2]	60%
Argentina	Telefonica de Argentina	Dec 91	$849	SIP	30%
Argentina	Telecom Argentina	Mar 92	$1,050	SIP	30%
Argentina	Telecom Argentina	Mar 94	$1,277	SIP	—
Armenia	Armentel*	97	$79.9	Asset sale	—
Australia	Telstra	Nov 97	$10,530	SIP	33.3%
Australia	Telstra	Oct 99	$10,400	SIP	16.5%
Austria	Mobilkom	Jun 97	$700	Asset sale	25%[3]
Austria	Telekom Austria	Oct 98	$2,400	Asset sale	25%[4]
Austria	Telekom Austria	Nov 00	$853	SIP	27%
Belgium	Belgacom	95	—	Asset sale	49.9%[5]
Bolivia	Empresa Nacional de Telecomunicaciones*	95	$610	Asset sale	—
Brazil	Companhia Riograndese de Telecomunicaciones*	96	$656	Asset sale	—
Brazil	CRT*	Jun 98	$1,020	Asset sale	50.1%
Brazil	Telebras	Jul 98	$18,920	Asset sale[6]	
Brazil	Eletronet*	Aug 99	$157	Asset sale	51%
Bulgaria	Bulgarian Telecommunications Company	Apr 00	$600	Asset sale	51%[7]
Canada	Manitoba Telecom Services	96	$670	SIP	—
Chile	Telefonos de Chile	Sep 90	$89	SIP	—
China	China Telecom (Hong Kong)	Oct 97	$4,000	SIP	25%
China	China Telecom (Hong Kong)	Oct 99	$2,000	SIP	4%
China	China Unicom	Jun 00	$4,900	SIP	25%
China	China Unicom	Oct 02	$1,400	SIP	—
China	China Telecom (PRC)	Nov 02	$1,650	SIP	10%
Cote D'Ivoire	CI-Telecom*	Jan 97	$193	—	51%
Croatia	Croatian Telecom	Oct 99	$850	Asset sale	35%[8]
Czech Republic	Cesky Telecom	Jul 95	$1,460	Asset sale	27%[9]
Czech Republic	Ceske Radiokomunikace*	Sep 97	$11.5	Asset sale	20.8%
Czech Republic	Ceske Radiokomunikace	Jun 98	$134	SIP	19%
Denmark	Tele Denmark	May 94	$2,894	SIP	38.9%
Denmark	Tele Denmark	97	$3,200	Asset sale	—
Egypt	Egyptian Mobile Telephone Company	Mar 98	$53	SIP	28%
El Salvador	Intel	Jul 98	$41	Asset sale	51%[10]
El Salvador	CTE	Jul 98	$275	Asset sale	51%[11]
Estonia	Estonian Telecom	Feb 99	$221	SIP	23.7%
Europe	Eutelsat	Feb 03	$478	Asset sale	23%[12]
Europe	Eutelsat	Feb 03	$225	Asset sale	10.8%[13]
Finland	Sonera	Jan 99	$1,400	SIP	21.2%
Finland	Sonera	Oct 99	$3,600	SIP	18%

Country	Company	Date	Amount of Offer (US$ Millions)	Method of Sale	Fraction Sold
Finland	Sonera	Mar 00	$1,900	SIP	3.1%
Finland	Sonera	Nov 01	$887	SIP	—
France	France Telecom	Oct 97	$7,080	SIP	23%
France	France Telecom	Nov 98	$10,500	SIP	13%
France	Wanadoo	Jul 00	$1,770	SIP	29.4%
France	Orange	Feb 01	$6,687	SIP	13.1%
Germany	Deutsche Telecom	Nov 96	$13,300	SIP	26%
Germany	Deutsche Telecom	Jun 99	$10,200	SIP	—
Germany	Deutsche Telecom	Jun 00	$14,760	SIP	6.6%
Ghana	Ghana Telecom*	Dec 96	$38	Asset sale	30%[14]
Greece	Hellenic Telecom (OTE)	Mar 96	$398	SIP	6%
Greece	Hellenic Telecom (OTE)	Jun 97	$1,967	SIP	12%
Greece	Hellenic Telecom (OTE)	Nov 98	$1,100	SIP	10%
Guatemala	Telgua	Oct 98	$700	Asset sale	95%[15]
Guinea	Sotelgui*	Mar 96	$45	Asset sale	60%[16]
Hungary	Matav*	93	$875	Asset sale	30%
Hungary	Matav*	95	$852	Asset sale	—
Hungary	Matav	Nov 97	$1,200	SIP	17%
Iceland	Islandssimi	Jun 01	$49	Asset sale	19.7%
India	VSNL	Mar 97	$527	SIP	17%
India	MTNL	Dec 97	$358	SIP	49%
India	VSNL	Feb 02	$307	Asset sale	25%[17]
Indonesia	Indosat	Oct 94	$1,060	SIP	35%
Indonesia	PT Telkom	Nov 95	$1,590	SIP	19%
Indonesia	PT Telkom	Dec 96	$600	SIP	4.5%[18]
Indonesia	PT Telkomsel	Apr 02	$429	Asset sale	12%[19]
Indonesia	Indosat	Dec 02	$631.5	Asset sale	42%[20]
Ireland	Telecom Eirann*	96	$290	Asset sale	—
Ireland	Telecom Eirann	Jul 99	$4,300	SIP	65%
Israel	Bezeq	Jul 97	$274	Asset sale	11.5%
Israel	Bezeq	Mar 98	$223	SIP	9.5%
Italy	Societa Finanziaria Telefonica (STET)	Nov 85	$103	SIP	3.1%
Italy	STET	Jul 91	$232	SIP	3.7%
Italy	STET	Jun 92	$593	SIP	7.6%
Italy	Telecom Italia	Oct 97	$15,500	SIP	41.2%
Italy	Telecom Italia	Dec 02	$1,400	SIP	3.5%
Japan	Nippon Telegraph and Telephone (NNT)	Feb 87	$15,097	SIP	12.5%
Japan	NNT	Nov 87	$40,260	SIP	12.5%
Japan	NNT	Oct 88	$22,400	SIP	9.6%
Japan	NNT DoCoMo	Oct 98	$18,400	SIP	32.9%
Japan	NNT	Dec 98	$7,300	SIP	6.5%
Japan	NNT	Nov 99	$15,000	SIP	6%
Japan	NTT	Nov 00	$11,300	SIP	7%
Japan	NTT DoCoMo	Feb 01	$8,200	SIP	—
Jordan	Jordan Telecom	Oct 02	$150	SIP	15%
Kazakhstan	Kazakhtelecom*	97	$370	Asset sale	—

(continued)

289

TABLE 8.4. (continued)

Country	Company	Date	Amount of Offer (US$ Millions)	Method of Sale	Fraction Sold
Korea	Korea Telecom*	93	$100	Asset sale	10%
Korea	Korea Telecom	May 99	$2,490	SIP	12.2%
Korea	Korea Telecom	Jun 01	$2,200	SIP	18%
Korea	Korea Telecom	Jun 02	$4,000	SIP	28%
Korea	Korea Telecom	Dec 02	$1,200	Public offer[21]	—
Latvia	Lattelecom	Jan 94	$160	Asset sale	49%
Lithuania	Lithuanian Telecom	Jun 00	$160	SIP	25%
Macedonia	Macedonian Telecommunications	Dec 00	$326[22]	Asset sale	51%
Malaysia	Telekom Malaysia	Oct 90	$872	SIP	24%
Malaysia	Telekom Malaysia	Apr 92	—	SIP	—
Mauritania	Mauritanian Telecom (Mauritel)	Feb 01	$48	Asset sale	54%[23]
Mauritius	Mauritius Telecom	Dec 00	$261	Asset sale	40%[24]
Mexico	Telefonos de Mexico (Telmex)	Dec 90	—	Asset sale[25]	—
Mexico	Telmex	May 91	$2,170	SIP	14.8%
Mexico	Telmex	May 92	$1,400	SIP	4.67%
Mexico	Telmex	May 94	$550	SIP	1.53%
Morocco	Mobil Maroc*	May 94	$13	Asset sale	50%
Morocco	Maroc Telecom	Dec 00	$2,200	Asset sale	35%[26]
Netherlands	Koninklijke PTT Nederland (KPN)	Jun 94	$3,868	SIP	30%
Netherlands	KPN	Oct 95	$3,514	SIP	22%
Netherlands	KPN	Nov 00	$4,600[27]	SIP	8%
Netherlands	KPN	Dec 01	$4,500	SIP	—
New Zealand	Telecom New Zealand	90	—	Asset sale	54%[28]
New Zealand	Telecom New Zealand	Jul 91	$819	SIP	27%[28]
Nicaragua	Enitel	Sep 01	$83[29]	Asset sale	40%
Norway	Telenor	Dec 00	$1,600	SIP	21%
Pakistan	Pakistan Telecommunications	Sep 94	$997	SIP	12%
Panama	Instituto Nacional de Telecomuni-caciones*	97	$652	Asset sale	—
Peru	Entel-Peru*	Feb 94	$901	Asset sale	35%
Peru	CPT*	Feb 94	$1,100	Asset sale	35%
Peru	Telefonica del Peru	Jul 96	$1,100	SIP	23.6%
Peru	Telefonica del Peru	Jul 99	$88.4	Asset sale	2.72%
Poland	PZT Telekom; Teletra*	93	$37	Asset sale	80%
Poland	Telekomunikacja Polska (TPSA)	Nov 98	$1,020	SIP	15%
Poland	TPSA	Jul 00	$4,300	Asset sale	35%[30]
Portugal	Portugal Telecom	Jun 95	$988	SIP	27.3%
Portugal	Portugal Telecom	Jun 96	$950	SIP	22%
Portugal	Portugal Telecom	Oct 97	$2,030	SIP	26%
Portugal	Portugal Telecom	Jul 99	$1,630	SIP	13.5%
Portugal	Portugal Telecom	Dec 00	$1,773	SIP	8.2%
Puerto Rico	Puerto Rico Telephone Company	Jul 98	$2,000[31]	Asset sale	51%
Qatar	Qatar Telecom	Dec 98	$740	SIP	45%
Romania	Rom Telecom	Nov 98	$675	Asset sale	35%[32]
Russia	Svyazinvest	97	$1,870	Asset sale	25%[33]
Russia	Mobile Telesystems (MTS)	Jun 00	$384	SIP	—
Saudi Arabia	Saudi Telecom	Jan 03	$3,700	SIP	30%
Senegal	SONATEL*	Jul 97	$90	Asset sale	33%[34]
Senegal	SONATEL*	97	$84	SIP	—

Country	Company	Date	Amount of Offer (US$ Millions)	Method of Sale	Fraction Sold
Serbia	Serbia Telecom	Jun 97	$869	Asset sale	49%[35]
Singapore	Singapore Telecom	Oct 93	$1,950	SIP	7.2%
Singapore	Singapore Telecom	Jul 96	$260	SIP	0.67%
Slovakia	Slovak Telecom	Jul 00	$950	Asset sale	51%[36]
South Africa	Telkom*	Mar 97	$1,261	Asset sale	30%[37]
South Africa	Telkom	Mar 03	$500	SIP	25%
Spain	Telefonica	Jun 87	$375	SIP	—
Spain	Telefonica	Sep 95	$1,300	SIP	12%
Spain	Telefonica	Feb 97	$4,360	SIP	21%
Spain	Telefonica Internacional (Tisa)*	97	$852	Asset sale	—
Sri Lanka	Sri Lanka Telecom*	97	$225	Asset sale	—
Sweden	Telia	Jun 00	$8,800	SIP	30%
Switzerland	Swisscom	Oct 98	$5,600	SIP	34.5%
Taiwan	Chunghwa Telecom	Sep 00	$988	SIP	2.8%
Tunisia	Sotetel	Jun 98	$3	SIP	40.6%
Turkey	Teletas	Mar 88	$13	SIP	22%
Turkey	Teletas*	93	$21	Asset sale	18%
Turkey	Turkcell	Jul 00	$1,900	SIP	11%
Ukraine	Ukrainian Mobile Communication	Nov 02	$194	Asset sale	57.67%[38]
United Kingdom	British Telecommunications	Nov 84	$4,763	SIP	50.2%
United Kingdom	British Telecommunications	Dec 91	$9,927	SIP	26.1%
United Kingdom	British Telecommunications	Jul 93	$7,360	SIP	21.9%
United Kingdom	BR Telecommunications	95	$205	Asset sale	—
Venezuela	CANTV	Nov 96	$1,010	SIP	49%
Total			$441,906.90		

Table Summary

Method of Sale	Number of Transactions	Value (US $ million)
SIP	95	$382,780.00
Asset sale	60	$58,983.90
Unknown	1	$193
Total	156	$441,906.90

Source: Most of the data presented here are from the *Financial Times* and/or the FT.COM Web site, but other sources are employed as well. In particular, sales marked with an asterisk are taken from various issues of *Privatisation International* (1997–2000) and *Privatisation International Yearbooks* (1998–2001).

Note: This table presents key information about telecommunications privatizations executed by governments around the world. The method of sale refers to whether the company was divested via a share issue privatization (SIP) or asset sale.

(continued)

TABLE 8.4. *(continued)*

[1] Payment made in two tranches: $85.6 million initially and then $85.6 million six months later. Stake sold to a Cosmote/Telenor company, a consortium of OTE (Greece) and Telenor (Norway). Buyers also pledged to invest an additional $120 million to expand the network and improve service quality.

[2] Stake sold to a joint venture between Telefonica de Espana and Citicorp Venture Capital, COINTEL.

[3] Stake sold to Telecom Italia Mobile.

[4] Stake sold to Telecom Italia.

[5] Stake sold to consortium of SBC, Tele Denmark and Singapore Telecommunications.

[6] Telebras broken into 13 separate operating companies and stakes in individual units sold to foreign and domestic buyers.

[7] Stake sold to consortium of OTE (Greece) and KPN (Netherlands). Buyers also agreed to invest in additional $350 million over three years and to share $200 million in profits with local government authorities.

[8] Stake sold to Deutsche Telekom.

[9] Stake sold to consortium of Swisscom and KPN.

[10] Stake sold to Spain's Telefonica.

[11] Stake sold to France Telecom.

[12] France Telecom sold its stake to Eurazeo.

[13] Deutsche Telekom sold its stake to a private equity firm owned by De Agostini, an Italian publishing group.

[14] Stake sold to consortium headed by Telekom Malaysia.

[15] Luca, a conglomerate of local businesses, outbid Telmex to win this auction. Within weeks, two senior government officials left Congress to run Telgua, and then Telmex announced it had gained control of Luca—and thus indirectly of Telgua.

[16] Stake sold to Telekom Malaysia.

[17] Stake sold to the Tata conglomerate group.

[18] Sold to institutional investors.

[19] Stake of cellular phone unit sold by PT Telekom to Singapore Telecom.

[20] Stake sold to ST Telemedia.

[21] Public offer of convertible bonds.

[22] The buyer, Hungary's Matav, also promised to make capital investments of $229 million.

[23] Stake sold to Maroc Telecom.

[24] Stake sold to France Telecom.

[25] Controlling stake sold to a consortium headed by Southwestern Bell.

[26] Stake sold to Vivendi Universal.

[27] Combined primary share offering ($3,350 million) and convertible bond offering ($1,250 million).

[28] Approximately 54% of company sold to Bell Atlantic and Ameritech in 1990, and the July 1991 share issue represents 49.9% of the two companies' holdings.

[29] Stake sold to a consortium led by Telia Swedtel, which paid $33.1 million initially, and $10 million annually for the next five years.

[30] Stake sold to France Telecom–led consortium. France Telecom acquired a 25% stake, while its Polish partner, the private conglomerate Kulczyk Holding, purchased the remaining 10% stake.

[31] Amount to be received by Puerto Rican government. America's GTE is to pay $444 million for 51% plus one share, and PTRC will borrow $1,560 million to pay a special dividend to the government. GTE is to sell 5% to Popular, a Puerto Rican bank, holding company, and another 5% to a group of Puerto Rican investors.

[32] Stake sold to Greece's OTE, which will gain management control of Rom Telecom.

[33] 25 percent plus one share sold to the Mustcom consortium, which includes George Soros, and to the Interos financial group headed by "oligarch" Vladimir Potanin.

[34] Stake sold to FCR, a France Telecom subsidiary.

[35] Stake sold to OTE of Greece and Italy's Stet.

[36] Stake sold to Deutsche Telekom.

[37] Stake sold to Thintana consortium, 60% owned by SBC and 40% by Telekom Malaysia.

[38] The Russian company Mobile Tele Systems (MTS) bought this stake, which includes 25% of Ukrtelecom shares, and signed option agreement to buy the remaining 42.33% for $142.6 million in 2003–2005.

able to attract more foreign direct investment than any other developing countries except China and Brazil.

Several countries successfully executed initial telecom sales (either asset sales or SIPs) between 1992 and the middle of 1996, including Argentina, the Czech Republic, Denmark, Greece, Guinea, Hungary, Indonesia, Latvia, Morocco, the Netherlands, Pakistan, Peru, Portugal, and Singapore. The next pivotal sale, however, was the $13.3 billion Deutsche Telekom (DT) offering in November 1996. This SIP was important both for its size and for the fact that one of the German government's prime objectives for this offering was nothing less than to promote an "equity culture" among its citizens. Despite being champion savers, prior to DT1 only four million Germans (five percent of the population) owned any shares, and the German government believed this deadened the entrepreneurial spirit and held the nation back from developing a large pool of venture capital. Emboldened by calls to duty, and prompted by a $133 million advertising campaign, roughly 2 million German citizens purchased shares in DT1 alone. This offering capped both a successful year and a successful half-decade of telecom privatizations.

For telecom sales, however, no period even remotely compared to the two years of 1997 and 1998, during which 39 sales worth $108 billion were executed. This period witnessed the largest asset sale in history: Brazil's auction of 13 operating companies to domestic and foreign buyers, which raised $18.9 billion. These years also witnessed a series of truly colossal SIPs, including Australia's Telstra ($10.5 billion), France Telecom ($7.1 billion in 1997 and $10.5 billion in 1998), Telecom Italia ($15.5 billion), Japan's NTT4 ($7.3 billion), and the $18.4 billion NTT DoCoMo initial public offering. All six of these issues rank among the 30 largest share offerings in financial history. There were also several SIPs and asset sales during 1997–1998 that were smaller in absolute size, but were extremely large relative to the nation's economy and financial system, including Telekom Austria ($2.4 billion), Greece's OTE ($1.97 billion), Hong Kong-based China Telecom ($4.0 billion), Hungary's Matav ($1.2 billion), Kazakhtelecom ($370 million), Panama's INT ($652 million), Portugal Telecom ($2.03 billion), Puerto Rico Telephone Company ($2.0 billion), Russia's Svyazinvest ($1.87 billion), and Swisscom ($5.6 billion).[7]

The initial privatization of France Telecom (FT) in October 1997 was another pivotal event in the history of telecom privatization both for what it represented and for what it created. State-owned infrastructure companies had long been central to the French national identity, so the decision to begin divesting one of the state's crown jewels represented a major break with France's dirigiste past, especially since both FT1 and FT2 were executed by a socialist government.[8] This sale also created an aggressive competitor, determined to go head-to-head with the other privatized European telecoms—such as BT, Spain's Telefonica, Deutsche Telekom, and Holland's KPN—in acquiring telecom operators in developing countries and commercializing major new technologies such second- and third-generation cellular service in continental Europe.

The time from 1999 to early 2001 witnessed continuing large SIPs and asset sales, and by the end of this period over 80 countries had at least partially privatized their telecom operators. This period also saw an unprecedented investment and acquisitions spending boom, which transformed the global telecommunications industry, but which also left all the major players in severe financial distress once the technology bubble burst. The global stock market crash that began in March 2000 wiped nearly $4 trillion off the market values of technology companies world-wide, with telecommunications companies in Europe and America being especially hard hit. Several U.S. companies, including WorldCom and Global Crossing, went bankrupt, and all of the major European telcos were forced to take drastic action to cut the debt loads they had taken on during The Boom. Both British Telecom and Holland's KPN executed large rights offerings during 2001 in order to shore up their balance sheets, and France Telecom followed suit with the largest rights offering in history ($15.8 billion) in March 2003. The CEOs of both France Telecom and Deutsche Telecom were fired in late 2002 and early 2003, respectively, and almost all the large European telecom companies began aggressively divesting assets.

This switch from asset acquirers to asset sellers on the part of the major Western telcos had a particularly devastating impact on developing country governments hoping to auction off their telecom operators. Where before such auctions would have attracted multiple (and aggressive) bidders, the locust years of 2001 and 2002 saw a mere 17 sales executed worldwide, and these raised only $33.1 billion. Excluding the two equity carve-outs of cellular phone subsidiaries (France Telecom's $6.7 billion initial offering of Orange and NTT's $8.2 billion secondary offering of NTT DoCoMo), and the $1.4 billion offering of the pure cellular phone operator China Unicom, there were only 14 sales of fixed-line telecom operators during 2001–02, and these raised less than $17 billion, not even one-sixth of the 1997–1998 total. China's experience with its IPO of China Telecom during late 2002 was symptomatic of the problems many countries faced. After a dismal road show to promote the offering, the government and its underwriters were forced to delay the issue, and ultimately cut the number of shares being offered in half, before finally launching the IPO in November. Likewise, the Korean government had to aggressively price the two tranches of Korea Telecom that it offered public investors during 2002. Most other governments simply foreswore the public markets, and resorted to asset sales during this period.

This dismal picture began to brighten somewhat during 2003. Two asset sales and two SIPs (South Africa's $500 million secondary offering of Telkom and the $3.7 billion IPO of Saudi Telecom), worth a combined $4.9 billion, were executed during the first quarter alone, and during July, the Belgium government announced that it might sell all or part of its 49.9 percent stake in Belgacom in an IPO that could value the company at up to $11 billion. As we will discuss later, the long-term future of telecom privatizations appears to be bright, but the short- and intermediate-term prospects are heavily dependent on continuing improvements in global stock market valuations.

Patterns Observed in Telecom Privatization Structures and Strategies

In addition to those discussed above, a close examination of the history of telecommunications privatizations reveals several intriguing patterns. As noted, it is clear that governments of developing countries have a different preferred method for privatizing their telcos than do their counterparts in OECD countries, with developing country governments relying more on asset sales rather than on SIPs. What the raw data do not show, however, is that this reliance on asset sales makes telecom privatizations more politicized, more prone to corruption, and less likely to succeed than are SIPs. By their nature, public share offerings are politically visible and financially transparent. Very few SIPs fail to sell all the shares on offer, and even fewer are marred by scandal. On the other hand, there are numerous examples of telecom asset sales to "connected" buyers, and many sales stretch inconclusively for years because government sellers and private buyers cannot agree on a price.

An example of a rather dubious asset sale occurred in October 1998, when the Guatemalan government announced a surprise winner for the auction of Telgua, its national telecom provider. Luca, a conglomerate of local businesses, outbid Telmex to win this auction. Within weeks, however, two senior government officials resigned from Congress in order to run Telgua, and shortly thereafter Telmex revealed that it had gained control of Luca (and thus indirectly of Telgua). On the other hand, executing SIPs can also be fraught with difficulty if these are foolishly designed. For example, the Taiwanese government's repeated attempts to sell off stakes in Chunghwa Telecom offer an object lesson in how share offering prices should not be set. Owing to political concerns that it would be accused of selling Chunghwa shares "too cheaply," the government has consistently asked the maximum conceivable price for the telecoms shares—and has just as consistently failed to sell any significant amounts. In a dismal September 2000 offering, the government was able to find buyers for only 18 percent of the shares on offer, and the company itself had to rescue a 2003 issue by purchasing its own shares from the government. A sizable fraction of all Japanese SIPs executed since 1987 have also failed owing to unrealistically high minimum bid prices demanded by the Ministry of Finance, and the same has occurred for planned telecom sales in Paraguay and several other countries.

No region has experienced the highs and lows of telecom privatization quite as spectacularly as has eastern Europe, especially Poland, Hungary, and the Czech Republic. As the three "stars" of transition economics, these countries all attracted significant investment from Western operators when they were put on sale in the mid-1990s, but all three were saddled with antiquated Soviet bloc equipment and severely bloated (and protected) workforces. While Hungary's Matav developed extremely well industrially, and the government was able to complete its stock divestment by 1999, Poland and the Czech Republic had much rougher experiences. Both countries were able to attract strategic investors as partners in their telecom operators, but major disagreements regarding investment policy and control soon developed, and several promised (and much needed) restructuring steps were not taken. The collapse in telecom market values since March 200 has prevented either country from resolving its telecom problems, and both governments retain large and unwanted stakes in their fixed-line providers.

The Empirical Evidence on Telecom Privatization (and Regulation)

Has telecom privatization worked? Has this massive gamble paid off for governments, politically and economically, or would they have been wiser to retain these firms and try to reform them under state ownership? We address these issues here, and pay particular attention to the issue addressed initially in chapter 2: Are competition and privatization supplements or complements? The reader should note that most of the material in this section was presented earlier in chapter 4, where we discussed the empirical evidence on telecom privatization within the broader context of surveying all empirical evidence on privatization in nontransition economies. We reproduce that discussion here, since some readers will select specific chapters to read, rather than working through the entire book sequentially. The reader who has already waded through chapter 4 may thus choose to skip this section and go directly to the next section.

Empirical Evidence on the "Ownership Versus Competition" Debate in Telecoms

The academic literature examining the industrial structure and regulation of telecommunications companies is truly voluminous. This is hardly surprising, given the economic significance of this sector and the theoretical issues that arise naturally in the study of telecommunications operations. For our purposes, we need examine only a small subset of this literature—specifically 16 empirical studies that directly or indirectly evaluate the impact of privatization on telecom performance. Nine of these studies employ samples created by the individual researchers, usually based on data provided by the ITU, and most of these studies were begun before 2000. These "early" studies are summarized in table 8.5. The other seven studies employ the newly completed Stanford University/World Bank Telecommunications Database [described in McNary (2001) and Fink, Matto, and Rathindran (2002)] that couples telecommunications data provided by the ITU with economic, regulatory, and institutional data collected by Stanford and the Bank. These studies are presented in table 8.6.

Researchers studying telecom privatization have often encountered difficulty in separating the effects of ownership transfer from other factors that might be influencing telecom performance at the same time. This is because most countries that choose to reform their telecom sectors do so by adopting an entire set of policies more or less simultaneously. In addition to partially privatizing their telecoms, many governments choose to establish an independent regulator and allow new competitors to enter the market at the same time. Ideally, researchers would like to be able to test whether telecom performance changed significantly after

TABLE 8.5. Summary of Early Empirical Studies of Telecommunications Company Privatizations

Study	Sample Description, Study Period, and Methodology	Summary of Empirical Findings and Conclusions
Parker (1994)	Examines changes in structure and management, as well as performance changes, of British Telecom during first decade after 1984 privatization. Also describes history of state ownership of BT, plus its subsequent privatization and the regulatory environment developed for a private BT. Notes that government promoted competition through new entry, with some success, and describes RPI-X pricing scheme imposed on BT.	Documents significantly increased output, profitability, efficiency, labor productivity, and in the absolute levels of R&D and capital spending—though these declined as a percentage of sales. Prices for BT's basket of services fell by 5.1% per year form 1984 to 1993, but residential phone service prices increased by 2.7% per year. Growth rate in labor productivity accelerated after privatization, and labor costs fell from 42.4% of output before to 33.6% after divestiture.
Boles de Boer and Evans (1996)	Estimate the impact of the 1987 deregulation, and 1990 privatization, of Telecom New Zealand on the price and quality of telephone services. Also examine whether investors benefited.	Document significant declines in price of phone services, due mostly to productivity growth that cut costs at a 5.6% annual rate, and significant improvement in service levels. Shareholders also benefited significantly.
Petrazzini and Clark (1996)	Using International Telecommunications Union (ITU) data through 1994, test whether deregulation and privatization impact the level and growth in teledensity (main lines per 100 people), prices, service quality, and employment by telecoms in 26 developing countries.	Deregulation and privatization both are associated with significant improvements in the level and growth in teledensity, but have no consistent impact on service quality. Deregulation is associated with lower prices and increases employment; privatization has the opposite effect.
Ros (1999)	Uses ITU data and panel data regression methodology to examine the effects of privatization and competition on network expansion and efficiency in 110 countries over the period 1986–1995.	Finds that countries with at least 50% private ownership of main telecom firm have significantly higher teledensity levels and growth rates. Both privatization and competition increase efficiency, but only privatization is positively associated with network expansion.
Wallsten (2001a)	Performs an econometric analysis of the effects of telecommunications reforms in developing countries. Using a panel data set of 30 African and Latin American countries from 1984 to 1997, explores the effects of privatization, competition and regulation on telecommunications performance.	Competition is significantly associated with increases in per capita access and decreases in cost. Privatization alone is not helpful, unless coupled with effective, independent regulation. Increasing competition is the single best reform, competition with privatization is best overall combination, but privatizing a monopoly without regulatory reforms should be avoided.

(continued)

TABLE 8.5. (continued)

Study	Sample Description, Study Period, and Methodology	Summary of Empirical Findings and Conclusions
Boylaud and Nicoletti (2000)	Use factor analysis and a database on market structure and regulation to investigate the effects of liberalization and privatization on productivity, prices, and quality of long-distance and cellular telephony services in 23 OECD countries over the 1991–1997 period.	Prospective and actual competition both bring about productivity and quality improvements—and lower prices—in telecom services, but no clear effect could be found for privatization.
Gutierrez and Berg (2000)	Examine determinants of the number of lines per capita in 19 Latin American countries over the 1985–1995 period using economic, institutional, and regulatory variables—including measures of democracy, economic freedom, and openness to trade. During this period, sample countries established regulatory commissions, and 14 out of 24 Latin and Caribbean countries privatized their telecoms between 1984 and 1997 (before Brazil in 1998), raising and estimated $27 billion.	Find that the regulatory framework (the presence and effectiveness of regulation) and freedom variables have a significant positive impact on the penetration rate. The number of cellular phones per capita is also significantly positively related to fixed-line penetration, though it is not clear whether this means cellular and fixed lines are complements or that a competition effect explains the interrelationship.
Cabanda and Ariff (2002)	Examine efficiency growth around privatization for 4 Asia Pacific countries—Japan, Philippines, Malaysia, and Australia—over an extended time period (up to 12 years) after privatization. Use date envelope analysis (DEA) to measure performance changes.	Document that firms achieved productivity gains ranging from 3% to over-50%, and 3 of the 4 countries' telcos saw significant increases in total factor productivity. Profitability increased in 2 of 4 countries, as did capital spending.
Bortolotti, D'Souza Fantini, and Megginson (2002)	Examines the financial and operating performance of 31 national telecommunications companies fully or partially divested via public share offering over the period November 1981 to November 1998. Also perform univariate comparisons of the pre- versus post-privatization performance levels of these firms using the MNR univariate testing procedure. Then run panel data estimations to explain performance over time in terms of ownership changes and structural changes due to regulatory reforms occurring during the study period.	Find that profitability, output, operating efficiency, and capital investment spending increase significantly after privatization, while employment and leverage decline significantly. Panel data show that competition significantly reduces profitability, employment, and, surprisingly, efficiency after privatization while creation of an independent regulatory agency significantly increases output. Mandating third-party access to an incumbent's network is associated with a significant decrease in the incumbent's investment and an increase in employment. Retained government ownership is associated with a significant increase in leverage and a significant decrease in employment, while price regulation significantly increases profitability.

Note: This table summarizes the sample selection criteria, methodologies, and empirical findings of several academic studies of privatizations of telecommunications companies that do not use the Stanford University/World Bank database.

298

TABLE 8.6. Summary of Empirical Studies of Telecommunications Company Privatizations that use the Stanford University/World Bank Database

Study	Sample Description, Study Period, and Methodology	Summary of Empirical Findings and Conclusions
Kubota (2000)	Examines the impact of market conditions and policies on telecom-sector performance for 135 countries in 1998 (cross-sectional analysis).	Finds that privatization tends to improve the performance of the incumbent operator, but that an independent regulator and the degree of market competition have mixed or weak effects.
Wallsten (2001b)	Examines the effect of including exclusivity periods (EPs) in 32 telecom privatization sales executed by 28 developing countries between 1987 and 1998. Looks first at the impact of EPs on the sale price received by the government and then on the post-privatization investment levels of the telecom companies.	Other things equal, finds that granting an EP more than doubles the price a buyer will pay for a telco, and that extending the EP for additional years also significantly raises the sale price. The offsetting effect is that EPs are significantly negatively correlated with telecom investment after the sale. EPs also reduce the number of cellular phone subscribers, dampen the growth in the number of payphones provided, and are negatively correlated with international phone traffic after the sale.
McNary (2001)	Compares the relative success of privatization and competition in improving the telecom penetration rates in over 200 countries between 1987 and 1998. Uses pooled time series regression methods, and controls for both sector characteristics and macroeconomic influences. Also adjusts for endogeneity between historic firm performance and the decision to reform.	Finds that local fixed-line and cellular phone competition have significantly positive effects on performance, but that privatization has a significant negative relationship with penetration rates. Concludes the reason for this negative effect is that governments are using privatization primarily as a means to raise revenue rather than to promote economic efficiency.
Li and Xu (2002)	Examine the political economy of privatization and liberalization in the telecoms sector using data for 45 countries from 1990 to 1998. Specifically evaluate whether the degree of democracy and the political power of different interest groups influence the timing, scale, and method of liberalization chosen.	Find that countries with stronger pro-reform interest groups—especially urban consumers and the financial services sector—are more likely to reform in more democratic countries. Less democratic countries are more likely to maintain the public sector monopoly when the government benefits from ownership, as when the fiscal deficit is high. Democracy affects the pace of reform by magnifying the voices of interest groups in open societies and by moderating politicians' discretion in less democratic countries.

(continued)

TABLE 8.6. (continued)

Study	Sample Description, Study Period, and Methodology	Summary of Empirical Findings and Conclusions
Wallsten (2002)	Using a panel data set with 2,533 observations from 197 countries over the period 1985–1999, examines whether the sequencing of regulation and privatization impacts the effectiveness of reforms and/or the price that investors are willing to pay for the company.	Finds that, as separate reforms, privatization and establishing an independent regulator both have ambiguous effects on telecom performance, but that combining privatization and regulation yields robust, significantly positive results. Establishing an independent regulator before privatization is the best policy combination, since this enhances most measures of sector performance and post-sale investment levels. Having a guaranteed monopoly is valuable to investors and increases the price they will pay, but so does having a regulator in place prior to sale. Investors appear willing to pay a higher price for a firm privatized into an environment with less institutional uncertainty.
Fink, Matto, and Rathindran (2002)	Assess the effectiveness of telecom reforms in developing countries using data for 86 such countries over the period 1985–1999. Ask three specific questions: (1) What impact do specific policy changes have on sectoral performance? (2) How is the effectiveness of one policy change impacted by the implementation of the others? (3) Does the sequencing of reforms affect performance?	Find that both privatization and competition significantly improve sector performance, but that a comprehensive reform program involving both of these policies and an independent regulator produce the largest gains—an 8% higher level of mainline penetration and a 21% higher level of productivity compared to years of partial or no reform. The sequencing of reforms also matters, with the best performance resulting if competition is introduced before or simultaneously with privatization, rather than after. Also find that autonomous factors, especially the evolution of technology, strongly and positively impacted performance.
Li and Xu (2003)	Examine the impact of privatization and competition on telecom-sector performance using a panel data set of privatizations from 166 countries between 1981 and 1998 and information on competition from 43 countries between 1990 and 1998. Evaluates the impact of these reforms on output growth, propensity to shed labor, network expansion, TFP, and improvements in labor productivity. Also examine the impact of the method of privatization (SIP versus asset sale) and of granting exclusivity periods.	Find that privatization is significantly positively related to output growth, network expansion, TFP, and labor productivity and is associated with higher labor shedding. Privatizing via a SIP promotes the development of the mobile phone market. Competition leads to higher employment, higher output, faster network expansion, and higher productivity. Granting EPs reduces, but does not negate, gains from other reforms. Also find that competition and privatization are complements, in that competition increases the gains from privatization, and vice versa. Estimate that half of the output growth between 1990 and 1998 is attributable to these two reforms, after controlling for input growth.

Note: This table summarizes the sample selection criteria, methodologies, and empirical findings of several academic studies of privatizations of telecommunications companies that employ the Stanford University/World Bank database.

reforms were adopted and be able to determine what fraction of any performance change found should be allocated to (1) the switch to private ownership, (2) the advent of new competition, and/or (3) the structure and objectives of any new regulatory regime established to oversee privatized telcos.

Unfortunately, the early empirical studies of telecom privatization tell somewhat conflicting stories with respect to both how much performance changed after privatization and what caused the changes noted. This was due in part to differences in the nations covered and methodology employed. Petrazini and Clark (1996), Ros (1999), and Wallsten (2001a) examine developing countries, either exclusively or as separate subsamples, while Ros (1999) and Boylaud and Nicoletti (2000) provide similar coverage of OECD countries. Parker (1994) and Boles de Boer and Evans (1996) study the deregulation and privatization experiences of British Telecom and Telecom New Zealand, respectively.

Though Ros, Wallsten, and Boylaud and Nicoletti all use some variant of panel data methodology, they arrive at somewhat different conclusions regarding the relative importance of deregulation/liberalization and privatization in promoting expanded teledensity (number of main lines per 100 population) and operating efficiency of national telecom companies, and the quality and pricing of telecom services. On balance, these studies generally indicate that deregulation and liberalization of telecom services are associated with significant growth in teledensity and operating efficiency, and significant improvements in the quality and price of telecom services. The impact of privatization, per se, is somewhat less clear-cut, but most studies agree that the combination of privatization and deregulation/ liberalization is associated with significant telecommunications improvements. This is certainly the result predicted by Noll (2000) in his analysis of the political economy of telecom reform in developing countries.

Gutierrez and Berg (2000) examine the determinants of the number of lines per capita in 19 Latin American countries over the 1985–1995 period using economic, institutional, and regulatory variables — including measures of democracy, economic freedom, and openness to trade. In order to characterize regulatory developments, the authors construct a dichotomous index describing both the enforcement powers of the new regulatory body and its neutrality and independence from political control. They document that eight sample countries established regulatory commissions between 1985 and 1995. Additionally, 14 of the 24 Latin and Caribbean countries privatized their telecoms between 1984 and 1997 (before Brazil's divestment of Telebras in 1998), raising an estimated $27 billion. Gutierrez and Berg find that the regulatory framework, measured by the presence and effectiveness of regulation, and freedom variables have a significant positive impact on the penetration rate. The number of cellular phones per capita is also significantly positively related to fixed-line penetration, though the authors cannot determine whether this means cellular and fixed lines are complements or that a competition effect explains the interrelationship.

The study by Cabanda and Ariff (2002) is somewhat outside the stream of research described above, but it does examine efficiency growth around privatization for four Asia Pacific countries — Japan, Philippines, Malaysia, and Australia — over an extended time period (up to 12 years) after privatization. The authors use data envelope analysis (DEA) to measure performance changes and document that firms achieve productivity gains ranging from 3 percent to over 50 percent. Three of the four countries' telecommunications companies see significant increases in total factor productivity. Profitability increases significantly in two of four countries (Australia and Malaysia), as did capital spending (in Malaysia and the Philippines).

Bortolotti, D'Souza, Fantini, and Megginson (BDFM; 2002) examine the financial and operating performance of 31 national telecommunications companies fully or partially divested via public share offering over the period November 1981–November 1998. They first build a data set using balance sheet data for a seven-year period around the privatization dates including various measures for profitability, output, efficiency, employment, capital expenditure, and leverage. This data set, reproduced in chapter 4 as table 4.14, also incorporates national measures of telecom service levels, such as number of lines in service. BDFM perform univariate comparisons of the pre- versus post-privatization performance levels of these firms using the Megginson, Nash, and van Randenborgh (1994) univariate testing procedure. They then run panel data estimations to explain performance over time in terms of ownership changes and structural changes owing to regulatory reforms occurring during the study period. The authors employ controls such as GDP per capita in their regression estimations to make cross-country comparisons possible.

Using conventional pre- versus post-privatization comparisons, BDFM find that profitability, output, operating efficiency, and capital investment spending increase significantly after privatization, while employment and leverage decline significantly. These comparisons, however, do not account for separate regulatory and ownership effects, and almost all telecoms are subjected to material new regulatory regimes around the time they are privatized. BDFM examine these separate regulatory and ownership effects using both random and fixed-effect panel data estimation techniques for a seven-year period around privatization. They verify that privatization is significantly positively related to higher profitability, output, and efficiency, but significantly negatively related to leverage. However, they also find numerous separable effects for regulatory, competition, retained government ownership, and foreign listing variables.

Competition significantly reduces profitability, employment, and, surprisingly, efficiency after privatization while creation of an independent regulatory agency significantly increases output. Mandating third-party access to an incumbent's network is associated with a significant decrease in the incumbent's investment and an increase in employment. Retained government ownership is associated with a significant increase in leverage and a significant decrease in employment, while price regulation significantly increases profitability. Major efficiency gains result from better incentives and productivity, rather than from wholesale firing of employees, and profitability increases are caused by significant reductions in costs, rather than price increases. On balance, BDFM conclude that the financial and operating performance of telecommunications companies improves significantly after privatization, but that a significant fraction of the observed improvement results from regulatory changes—by themselves or in combination with ownership changes—rather than from privatization alone.

*Empirical Studies Using the Stanford University/World
Bank Telecom Database*

All of the studies detailed above employ databases created by the researchers themselves, and thus suffer both from relatively small samples sizes and lack of comparability. Recently, however, several studies have employed the new Stanford University/World Bank Telecommunications Database [described in McNary (2001) and Fink, Matto, and Rathindran (2002)] that couples telecommunications data provided by the ITU with economic, regulatory, and institutional data collected by Stanford and the Bank. The studies described in this section all employ the Stanford/World Bank database and use advanced econometric estimation techniques, and thus should be considered the state of the art in research into telecom privatization and regulation.

The first such study, by Kubota (2000), examines the impact of market conditions and policies on telecom sector performance for 135 countries during the single year 1998. It is thus unusual in being a cross-sectional rather than a time-series analysis. Kubota shows that privatization tends to improve the performance of the incumbent operator, but that an independent regulator and the degree of market competition have mixed or weak effects.

Wallsten (2001b) examines the effect of including EPs in 32 telecom privatization sales executed by 28 developing countries between 1987 and 1998. He examines the impact of EPs first on the sale price received by the government and then on the post-privatization investment levels of the telecom companies. Other things equal, he finds that granting an EP more than doubles the price a buyer will pay for a telco, and that extending the EP for additional years also significantly raises the sale price. The offsetting effect is that EPs are significantly negatively correlated with telecom investment after the sale. EPs also reduce the number of cellular phone subscribers, dampen the growth in the number of pay phones provided, and are negatively correlated with international phone traffic after the sale.

McNary (2001) compares the relative success of privatization and competition in improving the telecom penetration rates in over 200 countries between 1987 and 1998. He uses pooled time-series regression methods, and controls for both sector characteristics and macroeconomic influences. He also adjusts for endogeneity between historic firm performance and the decision to reform. McNary's results are unique among this group of studies in that he finds that local fixed-line and cellular phone competition have significantly positive effects on performance, but that privatization has a significant negative relationship with penetration rates. He concludes that the reason for this negative effect is that governments are using privatization primarily as a means to raise revenue rather than to promote economic efficiency.

Li and Xu (2002) examine the political economy of privatization and liberalization in the telecoms sector using data for 45 countries from 1990 to 1998. They specifically evaluate whether the degree of democracy and the political power of different interest groups influence the timing, scale, and method of liberalization chosen. They find that countries with stronger pro-reform interest groups—especially urban consumers and the financial services sector—are more likely to reform in more democratic countries. Less democratic countries are more likely to maintain the public-sector monopoly when the government benefits from ownership, such as when the fiscal deficit is high. Li and Xu conclude that democracy affects the pace of reform by magnifying the voices of interest groups in open societies and by moderating politicians' discretion in less democratic countries.

Wallsten (2002) uses a panel data set with 2,533 observations from 197 countries over the period 1985–1999 to examine whether the sequencing of regulation and privatization impacts the effectiveness of reforms and/or the price that investors are willing to pay for the company. He finds that, as separate reforms, privatization and establishing an independent regulator both have ambiguous effects on telecom performance, but that combining privatization and regulation yields robust, significantly positive results. Establishing an independent regulator before privatization is the best policy combination, since this enhances most measures of sector performance and post-sale investment levels. Having a guaranteed monopoly is valuable to investors and increases the price they will pay, but so does having a regulator in place prior to sale. Wallsten concludes that investors appear willing to pay a higher price for a firm privatized into an environment with less institutional uncertainty.

Fink, Matto, and Rathindran (2002) assess the effectiveness of telecom reforms in developing countries using data for 86 such countries over the period 1985–1999. They ask three specific questions: (1) What impact do specific policy changes have on sectoral performance? (2) How is the effectiveness of one policy change impacted by implementation of the others? (3) Does the sequencing of reforms affect performance? The authors find that both privatization and competition significantly improve sector performance, but that a comprehensive reform program involving both of these policies and an independent regulator produces the largest gains—an 8 percent higher level of mainline penetration and a 21 percent higher level of productivity compared to years of partial or no reform. The sequencing of reforms also matters, with the best performance resulting if competition is introduced before or simultaneously with privatization, rather than after. Fink, Matto, and Rathindran also find that autonomous factors, especially the evolution of technology, strongly and positively impact performance.

Li and Xu (2003) examine the impact of privatization and competition on telecom sector performance using a panel data set of privatizations from 166 countries between 1981 and 1998 and information on competition from 43 countries between 1990 and 1998. They evaluate the impact of these reforms on output growth, propensity to shed labor, network expansion, TFP, and improvements in labor productivity. They also examine the impact of the method of privatization (SIP versus asset sale) and of granting exclusivity periods. Li and Xu find that privatization has a significantly positive impact on output growth, network expansion, TFP, and labor productivity and is also associated with more labor shedding. Privatizing via a SIP promotes the development of the mobile phone market. Competition leads to higher employment, higher output, faster network expansion, and higher productivity. Granting EPs reduces, but does not negate, gains from other reforms. The authors also find that competition and privatization are com-plements, in that competition increases the gains from privatization, and vice versa. They estimate that half of the output growth between 1990 and 1998 is attributable to these two reforms, after controlling for input growth.

Taken as a whole, the results of these studies offer clear lessons for academics and policy makers alike. Privatization, competition, and establishing an indepen-dent regulator all seem to improve telecom performance if adopted in isolation, though there are often painful trade-offs from single reforms (i.e., privatization may promote efficiency but reduce employment). On the other hand, all of these studies clearly show that adopting a package of reforms — including competition, independent regulation, and privatization — yields economically and statistically significant improvements in telecom performance. Furthermore, those studies that examine the influence of democracy and transparency on the political economy of telecom privatization find that openness improves the process of privatization and increases the amount of improvement achieved by the reform program.

The Future of Telecom Privatization

We conclude this chapter by evaluating the probable future course of telecom privatization. Though the early years of the new millennium have not been kind to governments wishing to privatize their telcos, or to the established private and state-owned providers, the most important question to address is whether this funk is likely to endure, or will the market return to something approaching the glory days of the late 1990s?

What Do Governments Have Left to Sell?

While the ultimate path of telecom privatization is unknowable, what we can clearly document is that governments have not run out of telecom assets to sell. Table 8.7 details the size and approximate value of the remaining stakes held by 51 national governments in 64 telecom companies as of July 31, 2003. As can be seen, even at the fairly depressed prices of mid-2003, governments retain over $391 billion worth of telecom shares — a total that is not dramatically less than the $442 billion raised by these governments through telecom divestments over the past two decades. In other words, there is plenty of "inventory" left to sell, and governments can be expected to avail themselves of this opportunity in steadily increasing num-bers if and when market valuations return to something near pre-crash levels.

Several notes of caution in interpreting the market value totals in table 8.7 are, however, called for, since the individual listings almost certainly represent valuations that are not actually realizable. Several factors bias the valuations above what might be truly achievable. First, the valuations that are based on historic prices from previous asset sales are certainly too high — since those sales occurred during the telecoms boom and the prices paid have not been offered in the years since. Second, financial research has now firmly established that the mere an-nouncement of a plan to issue new shares depresses that firm's stock price, so the valuations in table 8.7 would likely drop as soon as any government announced

TABLE 8.7. Residual Stakes of Telecom Firms Remaining in State Hands, July 2003

Country	Company	Retained Stake %	Approximate Value $US Millions
Australia	Telstra	50.1%	$18,945
Austria	Telekom Austria	48%	$2,642
Austria	Mobikom	75%	$2,100*
Brazil	CRT	49.9%	$1,016*
Brazil	Eletronet	49%	$151*
Bulgaria	Bulgarian Telecom	49%	$576*
China	China Mobile (Hong Kong)	72%	$32,327
China	Unicom	77%	$5,732
China	China Telecom	90%	$14,747
Cote D'Ivoire	CI-Telecom	49%	$185*
Croatia	Croatian Telecom	65%	$850
Czech Republic	Cesky Telecom	73%	$3,067
El Salvador	Intel	49%	$39*
El Salvador	CTE	49%	$264*
Finland	TeliaSonera	19.4%	$3,572
France	France Telecom	56%	$32,171
France	Orange	86.3%[a]	$39,339
France	Wanadoo	70.6%[a]	$7,959
Germany	Deutsche Telekom	59%	$37,082
Germany	T-Online	71.90%[b]	$8,228
Ghana	Ghana Telecom	70%	$89*
Greece	Hellenic Telecom (OTE)	65%	$3,437
Greece	CosmOTE	55%	$1,956
Guatemala	Telgua	5%	$37*
Guinea	Sotelgui	40%	$30
Iceland	Islandssimi	90.3%	$225*
Indonesia	PT TelKom	76.5%	$4,338
Indonesia	PT TelKomsel	88%[c]	$3,146*
Israel	Bezeq	54%	$1,556
Japan	Nippon Telegraph and Telephone (NTT)	46%	$25,566
Japan	NTT DoCoMo	67.1%[d]	$37,293
Jordan	Jordan Telecom	85%	—
Latvia	Lattelecom	51%	$167*
Lithuania	Lithuanian Telecom	75%	—
Macedonia	Macedonian Telecommunications	49%	$313*
Malaysia	Telekom Malaysia	76%	$4,909
Mauritania	Mauritanian Telecom (Mauritel)	46%	$41*
Mauritius	Mauritius Telecom	60%	$392*
Morocco	Mobil Maroc	50%	$13*
Morocco	Maroc Telecom	65%	$4,086*
Netherlands	Koninklijke KPN	34.77%	$6,041
New Zealand	Telecom Corp. of New Zealand	46%	$2,645
Nicaragua	Enitel	60%	$125
Norway	Telenor	79%	$6,427
Pakistan	Pakistan Telecommunications	88%	—
Peru	Entel-Peru	65%	$1,673*
Peru	CPT	65%	$2,043*
Poland	Telekomunikacja Polska (TPSA)	50%	$2,536
Puerto Rico	Puerto Rico Telephone Company	49%	$1,922*
Qatar	Qatar Telecom	55%	—

Country	Company	Retained Stake %	Approximate Value $US Millions
Romania	Rom Telecom	65%	$1,254*
Russia	Svyazinvest	75%	$5,610*
Saudi Arabia	Saudi Telecom	70%	$8,633 ᵉ
Serbia	Serbia Telecom	51%	$904*
Singapore	Singapore Telecom	87.5%	$13,308
Slovakia	Slovak Telecom	49%	$913*
South Africa	Telkom	45%	$1,028
Sweden	Telia Sonera	46%	$8,471
Switzerland	Swisscom	65.5%	$13,035
Taiwan	Chunghwa Telecom	95%	$13,154
Tunisia	Sotetel	59.4%	—
Turkey	Teletas	60%	—
Turkey	Turkcell	89%	$2,879
Ukraine	Ukrainian Mobile Communications	42.33%	$142*
TOTAL			$391,329

Table Summary		
Asset Sale Prices (*)	Market Prices	Total
$27,301	$364,284	$391,329

Note: This table details the size and approximate market value of the residual state holdings of telecommunications firms as of July 2003. For publicly listed firms, value is determined based on the fractional retained holdings in appendix 1, times the total market value of these firms in the *Business Week* "Global 1000" or "Top 200 Emerging Market" listing of the world's most valuable companies as of May 31, 2003. For telecoms that were partially divested through an asset sale, value is computed based on the implied valuation from the last asset sale (indicated by an asterisk).

ᵃ Stake held by France Telecom rather than directly by French state.
ᵇ Stake owned by Deutsche Telecom rather than directly by German government.
ᶜ Stake owned by PT TelKom rather than Indonesia government.
ᵈ Stake owned by NTT, rather than Japanese government.
ᵉ Implied value based on January 2003 IPO offer price.

its intention to sell. One possible mitigating factor is that these are not ordinary companies, but are in fact partially privatized firms, so investors already understand the desires of governments to sell additional shares as market conditions allow. Since the issues are already partially anticipated, the announcement effect of a new secondary offering should be less than would be the case for a typical fully private firm.

Third, several of the more valuable stakes detailed in this table actually represent shares held by the parent company in separately listed cellular phone or Internet subsidiaries—as in the relationships between France Telecom and its subsidiaries Orange and Wanadoo, or between NTT and NTT DoCoMo. If additional shares in these companies were to be sold off, the proceeds would flow directly to the parent company, rather than to the national government. Naturally, the proceeds of such a sale could then be paid out to the government as a dividend, or reinvested profitably in the parent's own operations. The key point is that proceeds from sales of listed subsidiaries would not automatically become revenues for the national government, even though such sales count as privatizations since they serve to reduce total state ownership in telecom operators. These subsidiary holdings account for $98.9 billion of the $391.3 billion total valuation presented in table 8.7.

Fourth, since the retained stakes listed in this table are based on the data we have collected and presented in table 8.4 (and in the full-length SIP appendix in the back of this book), it is a near certainty that we missed recording some offers that were actually made, thus imparting an upward bias to the percentage retained values recorded here. On the other hand, we did not include any values for companies for which we could not collect retained ownership data, so these are also missing entirely from table 8.7.

There are also two important political reasons the values in table 8.7 probably represent an unachievable maximum. First, many governments are very reluctant to allow their holdings in telecom providers to drop below a certain level—usually the 20 to 25 percent required to be a "blocking minority" shareholder. Some governments are even constitutionally prohibited from allowing their holdings to drop below this level. Second, the stock prices of almost all of the publicly traded companies in table 8.7 remain below the levels at which domestic investors originally purchased their shares. This makes all governments leery of issuing new shares and thus forcing citizen/shareholders to realize capital losses on the investments these same governments had encouraged them to make years before. On the other hand, if stock markets around the world continue the steady recuperation they have enjoyed of late, stock values will rise above the original offering prices and this constraint will become less binding.

How Will Telecom Privatization Techniques and Practices Change?

Fairly clearly, telecom privatizations will remain the centerpieces of national privatization programs in almost all countries for the foreseeable future. Most telecoms have already been partially divested, so a ready market exists for new share sales—either to stockholders or to strategic corporate investors. On the other hand, many telecoms remain wholly state owned, particularly in the Arab world. The recent and successful privatization of Saudi Telecom may well break the logjam for these offerings, but a true worldwide revival in telecom sales will have to await a rebound in the values of the leading Asian, American, and European operators. Only then will OECD-country governments be willing to divest additional shares, and only when their own balance sheets are repaired will the companies themselves be ready to resume the hunt for telecom operators in emerging markets.

Furthermore, the specific terms and structures of telecom sales are likely to change significantly from those observed during the 1990s, even when the pace of telecom privatization picks back up. The boundless optimism that underpinned that most exuberant period for the global telecommunications industry has now been destroyed; when individual company share prices again reach IPO levels it will be because earnings per share have more than doubled, rather then because investors are again willing to accept price-to-earnings (P/E) ratios of 60 or more. Capital spending by the industry is also likely to remain severely depressed for many years to come, for two main reasons. First, capacity growth has far outpaced growth in final demand in all the major OECD countries throughout the past decade, and what new equipment is needed can be obtained very cheaply either through the acquisition of competitors or through distressed asset sales resulting from the wave of bankruptcies in the United States and the desire of European telcos to divest noncore operations. Second, all the major telecom operators, especially those in Europe, suffered severe financial damage by paying excessive prices in auctions for new spectrum and technology licenses.

The most dramatic examples of telecom overexuberance are the now-infamous 3G cellular licenses that were purchased for fantastic sums during 1999 and 2000, yet remain unused in most countries. The telecom companies all swear they will not again succumb to frenzy and repeat their bidding errors, and at least in the short term they will likely stick to this promise. On the other hand, the onward march of technology is relentless and recent history shows this march has often turned into a stampede for telecom operators. As the lines between telecommunications, entertainment, and information processing continue to blur, the technology winners will see their market values and investment opportunities brighten dramatically.

With respect to telecom privatization in developing countries, the future offers both continuity and significant change. Once the overall market recovers, Western telcos will likely again be willing to bid aggressively for shares in developing country telecom operators, but only in the most promising national markets and only for stakes that allow buyers to exercise effective operational control. The days when almost any country could sell minority stakes in their telcos to Western companies at high prices and encumbered with significant investment commitments are probably gone forever. The balance of negotiating power has swung decisively in favor of the bidders during the past several years, and even the most robust global economic recovery is unlikely to fully redress this situation.

Privatization Industry Studies

Commercial Banking

During the past 15 years, over 250 commercial banks have been fully or partially privatized by governments of 59 countries, either publicly through public offerings of shares or privately through an asset sale. In many cases, this represented a fundamental break with a national past that emphasized the strategic role of commercial banking in funding the nation's economic development, and the national government's key role in planning and directing that development. This chapter examines why governments are choosing to privatize their state-owned banks (SOBs), how they are selling SOBs, and whether these sales have, on average, achieved the goals set by the divesting governments.

As a first step in determining why governments are privatizing banks, we examine why these banks became state-owned in the first place and then ask what caused societies to decide that state-owned banking was not a good idea. Next, we present and discuss the historical record of bank privatizations before surveying the empirical evidence regarding bank privatization in, respectively, developed countries, nontransition developing countries, and transition economies. We then briefly assess the evidence on the merits of foreign ownership of privatized banks, and then discuss the future of banking privatization—and specifically ask how many banking assets governments still have left to sell. The final section summarizes and concludes.

Why Has State Ownership of Commercial Banks Been So Prevalent Historically?

Economists have debated the relative merits of state versus private ownership for centuries. There is an enormous theoretical and empirical literature on government versus private ownership of nonfinancial firms, which we surveyed in chapter 2. We focus here specifically on how this debate relates to state ownership of commercial banking, since this is arguably the most basic industry in a modern economy because of its central role in allocating capital and monitoring corporate borrowers.

Regardless of where they are located, how they are organized, or the structure of their ownership, banks tend to perform three basic functions in any economic system. First, they play a central role in the country's payments system and also serve as a clearinghouse for payments. Second, they transform claims issued by borrowers into other claims that depositors, creditors, or owners are willing to hold. Third, banks provide a mechanism for evaluating, pricing, and monitoring credit extension in an economy. Of course, the efficiency, safety, effectiveness, and transparency of these functions varies widely across countries depending on, among other things, who owns the banks, how the credit-granting process is managed, and to whom credit is granted, and the degree to which bank-issued claims are held with some confidence by the nonbank public. In the context of a country with a long history of state ownership of commercial banks — or even significant state influence over commercial banking — these efficiency, safety, and transparency concerns are often infinitely more complex and intractable than in more laissez-faire economies.

The Theoretical Case for State Ownership of Banks

During the modern era, proponents of state ownership have justified government control of business in three principal ways. First, public ownership has been justified as a way to ensure that business enterprises balance social and economic objectives, rather than focusing exclusively on profit maximization. Second, state ownership has been motivated as a response to significant market failures — particularly the challenges posed to economic efficiency by natural monopolies — and as a way to address production externalities such as pollution. Third, proponents assert that public ownership can be justified under certain conditions involving informational asymmetries between principal (the public) and agent (the producer), where complete contracts cannot be written and enforced. Underlying all three cases is the assumption that governments can and do act benevolently, and thus that state ownership is economically efficient. Certainly, state ownership has also been imposed many times in history by ascendant political parties specifically in order to redistribute wealth and income from less to more "deserving" members of society, but this exercise in raw political power is usually justified by dogma, rather than by serious economic theory.

State ownership of banking grew as a result of the post–World War II trend toward state ownership, but was also driven by industry-specific factors. "Benevolent" reasons include a perceived lack of private capital with sufficient risk tolerance to finance growth; inadequate funding to sectors and groups with low financial but high social returns; a desire to promote industrialization and development at a pace more rapid than private financing would allow; and a desire to maintain domestic control over a nation's financial system. Less attractive, but equally compelling reasons include ideology (punishing capitalists), a desire to disenfranchise politically unpopular groups (postwar France's perception that many banks had collaborated with the Nazi occupiers); a reaction to foreign dominance for newly independent former colonies and a desire to use banks as tools for political patronage and advantage.

The Extent of State Ownership in Practice

There can be little doubt that state ownership of banking has proved popular historically. Table 9.1 shows the extent of government ownership as of the year 1999. This table uses 1999 data, presented in Barth, Caprio, and Levine (2004), but organizes the countries listed by their commercial legal system, as suggested by La Porta, Lopez-de-Silanes, Shleifer, and Vishny (1998, 2002).

Several trends can be observed from this table. First, it is clear that state ownership is widespread, particularly in developing countries. What this cross-sectional listing does not show, however, is that state ownership has been declining steadily over time, and this has accelerated dramatically since the late 1980s. Second, state ownership is higher in countries with a socialist legal tradition than in any other. This is hardly surprising, since banks were central tools of control and credit allocation in the command-and-control communist system that developed in the Soviet Union after 1917, and was then imposed on central and eastern Europe (again, CEE) after World War II. These countries began privatizing after winning their independence in 1989, but have had insufficient time to completely divest their holdings.

Third, countries with French civil law commercial codes have generally higher state ownership than those with German law, Scandinavian law, or English common law codes. This difference was vastly more pronounced before 1990, however, when the core French civil law states in western Europe (France, Italy, Spain, Portugal, Belgium) all had banking sectors that were dominated by state ownership. Beginning with France in 1986–1987, however, all these countries launched massive privatization drives that peaked during the 1990s, and now very few banks remain in state hands in any of these countries.

This observation, that the Western countries most wedded to state ownership historically have almost completely privatized their banking sectors, brings up the natural question: Why did the most enthusiastic supporters of state-owned banking decide to divest their ownership, and why did other countries also launch significant banking privatization programs during the past two decades?

Why Have Governments Launched Bank Privatization Programs?

As discussed briefly above, large segments of the global banking system have been transferred from state to private hands over the past two decades, and much more is poised to be sold in the near future—particularly in the emerging powerhouses of India and China. What has caused this fundamental reassessment of state ownership of banking? Two factors stand out as especially important. First, compelling evidence began to accumulate showing that state ownership was not working as planned. The second factor was a dawning realization that this really mattered—

TABLE 9.1. Banking System Details and State Ownership Levels, 1999

Country	Percent of Total Bank Assets State Owned	Percent of Total Bank Assets Foreign Owned	Percent of Deposits Held by 5 Largest Banks	Total Bank Assets/GDP (Percent)	Explicit Deposit Insurance Scheme
Australia	0	17	73		No
Bahrain	4	28	71	186	Yes
Bangladesh	70	6	65		Yes
Canada	0		76	154	Yes
Cyprus	3	11	80	76	Yes
India	80	0	42	48	Yes
Ireland					Yes
Israel			80	147	No
Kenya			62	56	Yes
Malaysia	0	18	30	166	No
New Zealand	0	99	91	154	No
Nigeria	13	0	51	28	Yes
Saudi Arabia	0		69	93	No
Singapore	0	50			No
South Africa	0	5	85	90	No
Sri Lanka	55				No
Thailand	31	7	75	117	No
Trinidad and Tobago	15	8	75		Yes
United Kingdom	0			311	Yes
United States	0	5	21	66	Yes
English origin average	15.94	19.54	65.37	120.86	
English origin median	0	8	72	105	
Argentina	30	49	48	54	Yes
Belgium			74	315	Yes
Bolivia	0	42	68	52	No
Brazil	52	17	58	55	Yes
Chile	12	32	59	97	Yes
Egypt	67	4	65		No
El Salvador	7	13	75	62	Yes
France	0		70	147	Yes
Greece	13	5	70	100	Yes
Guatemala	8	5	38	28	Yes
Honduras	1	2	52		Yes
Indonesia	44	7	53	101	Yes
Italy	17	5	25	150	Yes
Jordan	0	68	68	214	No
Kuwait	0	0		109	No
Lebanon	0	27	40		Yes
Mexico	25	20	80	30	Yes
Morocco	24	19	75	89	Yes
Netherlands	6		88	358	Yes
Oman	0	11	77	64	Yes
Panama	12	38	30	386	No
Peru	3	40	81	36	Yes
Philippines	12	13	46	91	No
Portugal	21	12	82	238	Yes

(continued)

313

TABLE 9.1. (*continued*)

Country	Percent of Total Bank Assets State Owned	Percent of Total Bank Assets Foreign Owned	Percent of Deposits Held by 5 Largest Banks	Total Bank Assets/GDP (Percent)	Explicit Deposit Insurance Scheme
Qatar	43	15	76		No
Spain	0	11	49	156	Yes
Turkey	35	66	50		Yes
Venezuela	5	34	64	6	Yes
French origin average	16.18	22.2	61.52	127.74	
French origin median	12	15	65	97	
Austria	4	5	38		Yes
Germany	42	4	12	313	Yes
Japan	1	6	31		Yes
Switzerland	15	9	65	539	Yes
Taiwan	43		15		No
German origin average	21	6	32.2	426	
German origin median	15	5.5	31	426	
Denmark	0		79	121	Yes
Finland	22	8	97		Yes
Iceland	64	0			Yes
Sweden	0	2		129	Yes
Scandinavian origin average	21.5	3.33	88	125	
Scandinavian origin median	11	2	88	125	
China			75		No
Croatia	37	7	57		Yes
Czech Republic	19	26	74	125	Yes
Hungary	3	62			Yes
Poland	44	26	57	54	Yes
Romania	70	8	59	25	Yes
Russia	68	9	80	16	No
Slovenia	40	5	64	66	No
Vietnam			65		No
Socialist origin average	40.14	20.43	66.37	57.2	
Socialist origin median	40	9	64.5	54	
Average with socialist	19.67	18.96	61.64	130.83	
Average without socialist	16.96	18.73	60.88	139.80	
Median with socialist	12	11	65	98.5	
Median without socialist	7	11	66.5	101	

Source: Table 1 in Barth, Caprio, and Levine (2001).

that financial system development promoted economic growth. We look at each influence below.

The Theoretical Case Against State Ownership of Banks

Economists have suggested three principal reasons state ownership will be inherently less efficient than private ownership, even under the assumption of a benevolent government owner. First, SOE managers will have weaker and/or more adverse incentives than will managers of privately owned firms, and thus will be less diligent in maximizing revenues and (especially) minimizing costs. Second, state enterprises will be subject to less intense monitoring by owners, both because of collective action problems—potential monitors have less incentive to carefully observe managerial performance because they bear all the costs of doing so but reap only a fraction of the rewards—and because there are few effective methods of disciplining SOE managers in the event that subpar performance is detected. Third, the politicians who oversee SOE operations cannot credibly commit to bankrupting poorly performing SOEs, or even to withholding additional subsidized funding, so state enterprises inevitably face soft budget constraints. It bears repeating that these criticisms of state ownership are valid even if one grants that the politicians who create and supervise public enterprises have benevolent intentions.

The final, and in many ways most compelling, critique of state ownership is that SOEs will be inefficient by design, since they are created specifically so that politicians can use them to benefit their own supporters at the expense of another group in society. Numerous researchers—including Jones (1985), Vickers and Yarrow (1988, 1991), Stiglitz (1993), Nellis (1994), Shleifer and Vishny (1994), Boycko, Shleifer, and Vishny (1996), Shleifer (1998), Sappington and Sidak (1999), and Shirley and Walsh (2000)—note that state enterprises can be remarkably effective tools of redistributive politics. Since state firms answer to political masters, rather than the market, wide divergences from profit-maximizing behavior are not only possible, they are in fact desired. Even in fully competitive markets, Shleifer and Vishny (1994) show that SOEs will be inefficient because politicians force them to pursue noneconomic objectives, such as maintaining excess employment, building factories in politically (but not economically) desirable locations, and pricing outputs at below market clearing prices.

The Empirical Evidence on State Ownership of Commercial Banks

We surveyed the empirical evidence on state versus private ownership of nonfinancial businesses in chapter 2, and concluded that private ownership should now be considered superior in most real instances. Does the evidence regarding state ownership of banking point to a similar conclusion? Table 9.2 details the empirical evidence on state versus private ownership of banking, and the overall picture that emerges is extremely damaging for proponents of government ownership. How-

TABLE 9.2. Summary of Empirical Studies on State Versus Private Ownership of Banking

Study	Sample Description, Study Period, and Methodology	Summary of Empirical Findings and Conclusions
Bhattacharya, Lovell, and Sahay (1997)	Employ data envelope analysis to examine the relative efficiency of 70 state-, foreign- and privately owned banks in India during the early stages (1986–1991) of liberalization.	Find that, during the study period, publicly owned banks are the most efficient and privately owned banks the least efficient at delivering financial services to customers. However, they also find that foreign-owned banks increase market share significantly during this period, primarily at the expense of state banks.
LaPorta, Lopez-de-Silanes, and Shleifer (2002)	Using data from 92 countries, they examine whether government ownership of banks impacts the level of financial system development, rate of economic growth, and growth rate of productivity. They test whether government ownership of banks is motivated by benevolent "development" objectives or by redistributive "political" objectives.	They find that government ownership is extensive, especially in the poorest countries. They also find that these holdings retard financial system development and restrict economic growth rates, mostly due to the impact of state ownership on productivity. Higher government ownership in 1970 is associated with significantly slower subsequent financial development and lower growth in per capita income and productivity. This evidence supports the political view of state ownership of banks.
Bonin, Hasan, and Wachtel (2002)	Examine the impact of ownership structure (state, private, and foreign ownership) on bank performance in the 6 transition economies of Bulgaria, Croatia, the Czech Republic, Hungary, Poland, and Romania. Their sample has 222 observations with financial and ownership data from these countries for the years 1999 and 2000.	The authors find robust evidence that profitability—measured by return on assets and return on equity—is higher for fully private banks than for banks with some state ownership, and is the highest of all for wholly foreign-owned banks. Foreign banks also experience the most rapid increase in customer loans.

Barth, Caprio, and Levine (2003)	Use a new database on bank regulation and supervision in 107 countries to assess the relationship between specific regulatory and supervisory practices and banking-sector development, efficiency, and fragility. They also examine the relationship between state ownership and these measures of banking-sector development.	They find that government ownership of banks is negatively correlated with favorable banking outcomes and positively linked with corruption. However, government ownership does not retain an independent, robust association with bank development, efficiency, or stability when other features of the regulatory and supervisory environment are controlled for.
Sapienza (2004)	Studies the effects of government ownership on bank lending behavior using information on individual loan contracts between Italian banks and customers over the period 1991–1995. She employs a matched set of 110,736 company-bank-year observations of lines of credit extended to 6,968 companies. 55,393 observations refer to borrowers from state-owned banks, and 55,393 refer to borrowers from privately owned banks.	Finds that borrowers from state-owned banks pay an average of 44 basis points less than do borrowers from private banks. She also shows that the voting pattern of the region where the loan is booked and the party of the state bank's CEO significantly influence the price of loans. These results strongly support the political view of state bank ownership over the competing social and agency cost views.
Cornette, Guo, Khaksari, and Tehranian (2003)	Examine performance differences between privately owned and state-owned banks in 16 Far East countries from 1989 through 1998.	They find that state-owned banks are significantly less profitable than privately owned banks due to state banks' lower capital ratios, greater credit risk, lower liquidity, and lower management efficiency. While the performance of all banks deteriorated significantly at the beginning of the Asian economic crisis in 1997 and 1998, state banks' performance deteriorated more than did that of private banks and performance differences are most acute in those countries where government involvement in the banking system is the greatest.

ever, one of the first studies is an outlier. Bhattacharya, Lovell, and Sahay (1997), employ data envelope analysis to examine the relative efficiency of 70 state-, foreign- and privately owned banks in India during the early stages (1986–1991) of liberalization. Prior to 1970, only one bank in India was state-owned, but a wave of nationalizations in that year and in 1980 created a banking system that was dominated by government-owned institutions. They find that, during the study period, publicly owned banks are the most efficient and privately owned banks the least efficient at delivering financial services to customers. However, their most striking finding is that foreign-owned banks increase market share significantly during this period, primarily at the expense of state banks. These results are rather surprising, since studies of the relative efficiency of state-owned, mixed, and privately owned nonfinancial enterprises in India show diametrically opposite results.[1]

La Porta, Lopez-de-Silanes, and Shleifer (2002) examine the importance and impact of state ownership in this key industry. Using data from 92 countries, they examine whether government ownership of banks impacts the level of financial system development, rate of economic growth, and growth rate of productivity. They test whether government ownership of banks is motivated by benevolent, "development" objectives or by redistributive "political" objectives. They find that government ownership is extensive, especially in the poorest countries. They also find that these holdings retard financial system development and restrict economic growth rates, mostly due to the impact of state ownership on productivity. Higher government ownership in 1970 is associated with significantly slower subsequent financial development and lower growth in per capita income and productivity. This evidence supports the political view of state ownership of banks.

Bonin, Hasan, and Wachtel (2002) examine the impact of ownership structure (state, private, and foreign ownership) on bank performance in the six transition economies of Bulgaria, Croatia, the Czech Republic, Hungary, Poland, and Romania. Their sample has 222 observations with financial and ownership data from these six countries for the years 1999 and 2000. About three-quarters of the banks are fully private and about 40 percent of these are completely foreign owned. Not surprisingly, wholly foreign-owned banks tend to be created by greenfield investment, while the majority foreign-owned banks tend to be banks privatized to a foreign strategic investor. Almost 60 percent of the banks in the region are at least majority foreign owned, while less than 15 percent remain majority state owned. These authors find robust evidence that profitability — measured by return on assets and return on equity — is higher for fully private banks than for banks with some state ownership, and is the highest of all for wholly foreign-owned banks. Foreign banks also experience the most rapid increase in customer loans.

Barth, Caprio, and Levine (2004) use a new database on bank regulation and supervision in 107 countries to assess the relationship between specific regulatory and supervisory practices and banking-sector development, efficiency, and fragility. They also examine the relationship between state ownership and these measures of banking-sector development. They find that government ownership of banks is negatively correlated with favorable banking outcomes and positively linked with corruption. However, government ownership does not retain an independent, robust association with bank development, efficiency, or stability when other features of the regulatory and supervisory environment are controlled for. On the other hand, there is certainly no evidence, even in weak institutional settings, that government-owned banks are associated with positive outcomes.

Sapienza (2003) studies the effects of government ownership on bank lending behavior using information on the pricing of individual loan contracts between Italian banks and customers over the period 1991–1995. She exploits the fact that all Italian banks have access to an unusually detailed and informative database on corporate borrowers, which negates the impact of differential credit evaluation skills on the loan pricing decision. She further controls for within-sample differences by examining a matched set of 110,786 company-bank-year observations of lines of credit extended to 6,968 companies. Some 55,393 observations refer to borrowers from state-owned banks and 55,393 refer to borrowers from privately owned banks. Sapienza finds that borrowers from state-owned banks pay an average of 44 basis points less than do borrowers from private banks. She also shows that the voting pattern of the region where the loan is booked and the political party of the state bank's CEO significantly influence the price of loans. These results strongly support the political view of state bank ownership over the competing social and agency cost views.

Cornett, Guo, Khaksari, and Tehranian (2003) examine performance differences between privately owned and state-owned banks in 16 Far East countries from 1989 through 1998. They find that state-owned banks are significantly less profitable than privately owned banks owing to state banks' lower capital ratios, greater credit risk, lower liquidity, and lower management efficiency. While the performance of all banks deteriorates significantly during the early phases of the Asian economic crisis in 1997–1998, state banks' performance deteriorates more than does that of private banks and performance differences are most acute in those countries where government involvement in the banking system is the greatest. Economic growth is also slower in these countries, and there is less financial development.

Finally, Weintraub and Nakane (2003) examine the privatization experience of roughly 250 Brazilian banks over the period 1990–2001. All Brazil's banks were severely impacted by the Real Plan's halting of inflation in 1994–1995, since they had profited from financial intermediation activities during the preceding inflationary and (especially) hyper-inflationary periods. The halting of easy profits from inflation brought on a banking crisis, which resulted in a complete restructuring of industry during the late 1990s. This paper examines the impact of these changes on total factor productivity and uses a sample of 3,958 annual observations. The authors find that bank size and ownership are important determinants of productivity. In particular, they find that state-owned banks are significantly less productive than private banks and that privatization significantly increases productivity.

In sum, the weight of empirical evidence now clearly suggests that state ownership of commercial banks yields few benefits, yet is associated with many negative economic outcomes. Whatever the motivations once were for launching state-owned banks, this experiment in state planning must now be considered a systemic failure, and this conclusion helps explain why so many governments have launched large-scale bank privatization programs. We are thus almost ready to analyze how governments privatize, and to assess which specific institutions are selected for divestment. Before doing so, however, we should briefly examine the evidence showing a positive link between financial development and economic growth. We then assess how governments select banks for privatization.

Financial System Development and Economic Growth: Theory and Evidence

In addition to dissatisfaction with the observed performance of state-owned banks, governments have one powerful reason to discard any flawed financial-sector development model. There is now little doubt that the financial sector in general, and banking in particular, plays an important role in fostering a nation's economic development.[2] Rajan and Zingales (1998) provide evidence supporting the positive influence of financial development on economic growth by means of reducing the cost of external financing to firms. They find that financial development is especially important for the process of creating new firms in an economy.

Levine and Zervos (1998) also provide evidence suggesting that banking efficiency is critically important to the development of an economy and that banking services are different from those provided by stock markets. In fact, an entire stream of research has now emerged documenting the critical importance of an efficient financial system to sustainable economic growth. Important recent papers in this literature are Demirgüç-Kunt and Maksimovic (1998), Levine (1997), Demirgüç-Kunt and Huizinga (1998), Wurgler (2000), Cetorelli and Gambera (2001), and Beck, Demirgüç-Kunt, and Levine (2003). Related papers stress the importance of creating the proper legal and regulatory framework for encouraging the development of efficient, liquid banking and capital markets. This literature is largely encompassed in a series of articles by La Porta and Lopez-de-Silanes (1999) and La Porta, Lopez-de-Silanes, Shleifer, and Vishny (1997, 1998, 2002).

The basic themes that emerge from these research streams are that an efficient financial system is vital, and that it is very difficult to construct such a system from scratch or in place of existing (typically less effective) systems, owing to the determined opposition from entrenched parties. The most important source of opposition to development of a modern, nonpoliticized financial system is usually the state — and those with close ties to the existing power structure. This fact makes banking privatization at least as important as a tool of political economy as it is as a mechanism for banking reform.

How Do Governments Select Banks to Be Privatized?

Two studies examine the determinants of privatization choice — or which banks governments will choose to sell and under what conditions. Clarke and Cull (2002) examine the political economy of sales of 13 banks by Argentine provincial governments after the passage of the April 1991 Convertibility Act. They find that (1) poorly performing banks are more likely to be privatized than those performing well; (2) overstaffing tends to reduce the probability of privatization because the post-sale staff cuts needed will be too politically painful; (3) larger banks are less likely than smaller banks to be privatized; (4) higher levels of provincial unemployment and higher shares of public employees reduces the likelihood of privatization; and (5) the onset of the Tequila Crisis in 1995 increased the likelihood of privatization by raising the financial costs of continued state bank subsidization. In other words, both economic and political factors impact the privatization decision for individual banks, but political buyoffs seemed especially important factors.

Boehmer, Nash, and Netter (2003) use their comprehensive sample of bank privatizations from 51 countries to examine how political, institutional, and economic factors influence a country's decision to privatize its state-owned banks. They specifically examine whether the determinants of bank privatization are the same in OECD and non-OECD countries. They find that, in non-OECD economies, bank privatization is more likely the lower the quality of the nation's banking sector, the more right-wing the government is, and the more accountable the government is to its people. None of these factors is significant in developed economies; instead, poor fiscal conditions are the most important determinants of bank privatization in OECD countries.

The Record on Privatizing State-Owned Banks

Wherever and however banks are privatized, they all face a common set of concerns and issues, beginning with the type of privatization process to utilize: asset sale, public share offering or, in transition economies, vouchers. The empirical record suggests that no one form of sale is the "standard" or default method of divesting state-owned banks. The most comprehensive bank privatization study, that of Boehmer, Nash, and Netter (2003, hereafter BNN), examines 270 transactions from 51 countries over the period 1982–2000, which raised a total of $119 billion for divesting governments. BNN find that 46.7 percent of these sales are executed using share issue privatizations (SIPs), while the remaining 53.3 percent employ asset sales. The average (median) transaction raises $442 million ($15 million) and involves the sale of 47.7 percent (41 percent) of the bank's total capital. This is but the first of many pieces of evidence we will see suggesting that governments are very hesitant to surrender effective control of the banks they are "privatizing," much less divest them completely.

We do not have data on voucher privatizations of banks, but the basic terms of bank asset sales and share issue privatizations from August 1985 through May 2003 are presented in table 9.3. This table documents that governments raised $142.9 billion through 144 public share offerings and 139 private sales over that 18-year period. The SIPs raised $76.2 billion in total, an average of $529.1 million each, while the asset sales raised an average of $479.9 million each, for a total of $66.7 billion.

As with almost all other industries, the first banking privatizations occurred during the 1980s, but the vast bulk of all sales occurred during the 1990s, and then fell off sharply after the NASDAQ stock market began crashing in March 2000. We examine each period in turn below, beginning with the earliest sales in 1986 and 1987.

TABLE 9.3. Details of Banking Privatization

Country	Company	Date	Amount of Offer (US$ Million)	Method of Sale	Fraction Sold
Argentina	Banco de Santa Fe*	May 98	$57.3	Asset sale	90%
Argentina	Banco Hipotecario*	Jan 99	$496.5	SIP	46%
Australia	Commonwealth Bank	Jul 91	$1,017	SIP	29.75%
Australia	Commonwealth Bank	Oct 93	$878	SIP	19.90%
Australia	State Bank of New South Wales*	Sep 94	$426.75	Asset sale[1]	—
Australia	Bank of Western Australia (Bank West)*	Dec 95	$672	Asset sale[2]	—
Australia	Bank of South Australia (Bank SA)	1995	$525	Asset sale	—
Australia	Bank West*	1996	$325	SIP	—
Australia	Commonwealth Bank	Jul 96	$3,100	SIP	50.4%
Australia	Bank of Queensland*	Nov 99	$86.7	SIP	39.6%
Australia	Trust Bank*	Dec 99	$96.2	Asset sale	100%
Austria	Salzburger Sparkasse*	Oct 95	$188	Asset sale	70%
Austria	Hypo Niederoesterreichische*	Jun 96	—	Asset sale	26%
Austria	Oberoesterreiche Hypo	Nov 96	$158.9	Asset sale	49%
Austria	Creditanstalt	Jan 97	$1,586	Asset sale	70%[3]
Austria	Bank Austria	Feb 98	$389	Asset sale	9.6%[1]
Austria	Salzburger Landes-Hypothekenbank	Oct 98	—	Asset sale	50.01%
Belgium	Credit Agricole/Landbouw Krediet*	1995	$55	Asset sale	—
Belgium	Credit Communal de Belgigue	Nov 96	$1,100	SIP	34.5%
Belgium	Credit Agricole/Landbouw Krediet*	1996	$33	Asset sale	—
Belgium	ASLK-CGER*	Dec 98	$1,500	Asset sale	25.1%
Brazil	Banco Meridional	1997	$241.5	Asset sale	—
Brazil	Bemge*	Sep 98	$494	Asset sale	—
Brazil	Bandepe*	Nov 98	$154	Asset sale	99.97%
Brazil	Baneb*	Jun 99	$144.8	Asset sale	94%
Brazil	Banestado	Oct 00	$871	Asset sale	88%[5]
Brazil	Banespa	Nov 00	$3,600	Asset sale	76%[6]
Bulgaria	United Bulgarian Bank	Jul 97	$30	Asset sale	65%[7]
Bulgaria	Post Bank*	Aug 98	$38	Asset sale	78.23%
Bulgaria	Express Bank*	Sep 99	$39.5	Asset sale	67%
Bulgaria	Bulbank	Jul 00	$345	Asset sale	98%[8]
Bulgaria	DSK Bank	Apr 03	$336	Asset sale	100%[9]
China	Bank of Shanghai	2001	$62	Asset sale	8%[10]
China	Bank of China	Jul 02	$2,800	SIP	—
China	Pudong Development Bank	Dec 02	$67	Asset sale	5%[1]
Colombia	Banco Corpavi	1994	$170	SIP	34.2%
Colombia	Banco Ganadero	1996	$328	Asset sale	40%
Colombia	Banco Popular	1996	$271	Asset sale	80%
Cote d'Ivoire	SGBCI	Jun 99	$5.75	SIP	—
Croatia	Zagrebacka Bank	Jun 96	$25	SIP	—
Czech Republic	Komercni Bank	Jul 95	$85	SIP	4%
Czech Republic	Komercni Bank	May 96	$50	SIP	3.2%
Czech Republic	Investicni a Postovni Banka (IPB)*	Jan 98	$81.8	Asset sale	36%
Czech Republic	Ceskoslovenska Obchodni Banka (CSOB)	Jun 99	$1,175	Asset sale	69.99%[12]

322

Country	Company	Date	Amount of Offer (US$ Million)	Method of Sale	Fraction Sold
Czech Republic	Komercni Bank	Jun 01	$1,210	Asset sale	60%[13]
Denmark	Girobank*	1993	$110	SIP	51%
Egypt	Commercial International Bank*	1993	$115	SIP	26.25%
Egypt	Commercial International Bank*	1996	$119	SIP	—
Egypt	Egyptian American Bank*	1996	$35	SIP	—
Egypt	Misra International Bank*	1996	$34	SIP	—
Egypt	Alexandria Commercial & Maritime Bank*	1997	$26.6	SIP	—
Egypt	Cairo Barclays Bank*	Jan 99	$4	Asset sale	11%
Finland	Skopbank Loan Portfolio*	1995	$134	Asset sale	—
France	Banque Paribas	Jan 87	$2,740	SIP	100%
France	Banque de Batements de Travaux Publics	Apr 87	$67	SIP	100%
France	Banque Industrialle & Mobiliere Privee (BIMP)	Apr 87	$60	SIP	100%
France	Credit Commercial de France	Apr 87	$732	SIP	100%
France	Credit Local de France	Nov 91	$340	SIP	22%
France	Credit Local de France	Jun 93	$738	SIP	30.5%
France	Banque Nationale de Paris	Oct 93	$4,920	SIP	60%
France	Banque Francaise du Commerce Exterieur*	1995	$500	Asset sale	—
France	CIC	Apr 98	$2,200	Asset sale	67%[14]
France	Societe Marseillais de Credit*	Oct 98	$1,795	Asset sale	100%
France	Credit Lyonnais	Jul 99	$6,960	SIP	90%
France	Credit Foncier de France (CFF)	Jul 99	$700	Asset sale	90.6%
France	Banque Hervet	Feb 01	$413	Asset sale	90%[15]
France	Credit Agricole	Dec 01	$3,158	SIP	—
France	Credit Lyonnais	Nov 02	$2,200	Asset sale	10.9%[16]
Germany	Deutsche Verkehrs–Kredit–Bank (DVKB)	Mar 88	$34	SIP	24.9%
Germany	Deutsche Siedlungs-Und Landesrentenbank (DSL)	Oct 89	$241	SIP	48%
Germany	Deutsche Kreditbank (DKB)	1995	$3,234	Asset sale	—
Ghana	Ghana Commercial Bank*	1996	$26	Asset sale	—
Ghana	Ghana Commercial Bank*	1996	$35	SIP	—
Ghana	Social Security Bank*	1997	$16.6	Asset sale	—
Greece	Bank of Athens*	1993	$28	Asset sale	66.67%
Greece	General Hellenic Bank	Apr 98	$67	SIP	50%
Greece	National Bank of Greece	May 98	$379	SIP	10%
Greece	Cretabank	Jul 98	$304	Asset sale[17]	—
Greece	Bank of Central Greece	Aug 98	$59	Asset sale	56%
Greece	National Bank of Greece	Apr 99	$553	SIP	4%
Greece	National Bank of Greece	Oct 99	$348	SIP	2.9%
Greece	Ionian Bank	1999	$623	Asset sale	51%
Greece	Commercial Bank of Greece	Jun 00	$283	Asset sale	6.7%[18]
Guyana	National Bank of Industry	Oct 97	$20	Asset sale	47.5%[19]
Hungary	Magyar Kulkereskedelmi Bank	Jul 94	$92	Asset sale	42%
Hungary	Budapest Bank	1995	$87	Asset sale	—

(*continued*)

TABLE 9.3. (*continued*)

Country	Company	Date	Amount of Offer (US$ Million)	Method of Sale	Fraction Sold
Hungary	National Savings & Commercial Bank (OTP)	1995	$89	SIP	30%
Hungary	Magyar Hitel Bank*	1996	$89	Asset sale	—
Hungary	OTP Bank	Oct 97	$213	Asset sale	25%
Hungary	OTP Bank	Oct 97	$140	SIP	16.4%
Hungary	Kereskedelmi es Hitelbank (K&H Bank)	1997	$30	Asset sale	—
Hungary	Mezobank	1997	$25	Asset sale	—
Hungary	Penzintezeti Kozpont Bank (PK Bank)	1997	$18.9	Asset sale	—
Hungary	OTP Bank	Nov 99	$162	SIP	14.1%
Iceland	National Bank of Iceland*	Sep 98	$24.5	SIP	15.75%
Iceland	Iceland Investment Bank (FBA)*	Nov 98	$67	SIP	49%
Iceland	Bunadarbanki*	Dec 98	$10	SIP	8.5%
Iceland	Iceland Investment Bank	Nov 99	$136.5	Asset sale	51%
Iceland	National Bank of Iceland	Oct 02	$138	Asset sale	45.8%[20]
India	State Bank of India	Dec 93	$713	SIP	29.4%
India	Industrial Development Bank of India	1995	$758	SIP	—
India	State Bank of India	Oct 96	$370	SIP	—
India	State Bank of India	Oct 96	$370	SIP	—
India	Bank of Baroda	1997	$235	SIP	—
India	Bank of India	1997	$186	SIP	—
India	Corporation Bank	1997	$84	SIP	—
India	Dena Bank	1997	$50	SIP	—
Indonesia	Bank Negara Indonesia	Nov 96	$400	SIP	25%
Indonesia	Bank Central Asia	Mar 02	$539	Asset sale	51%[21]
Israel	IDB Holding	1992	$350	Asset sale	42.5%
Israel	Israel Union Bank	May 93	$85.5	Asset sale	60%
Israel	Bank Hapoalim	May 93	$120	SIP	6.9%
Israel	Bank Leumi*	Aug 93	$272	SIP	14.8%
Israel	Bank Hapoalim*	Nov 93	$122	SIP	6.4%
Israel	Bank Mizrahi	Nov 94	$110	Asset sale	26%[22]
Israel	Bank Mizrahi*	1995	$110	Asset sale	—
Israel	Israel Discount Bank	Mar 96	$80	SIP	16%
Israel	Israel Discount Bank*	Apr 97	$180	SIP	19.1%
Israel	Bank Leumi*	May 97	$406	SIP	18.4%
Israel	Bank Mizrahi*	Jul 97	$129	SIP	25%
Israel	Bank Hapoalim	Sep 97	$1,370	Asset sale	43%[23]
Israel	Bank Hapoalim*	Feb 98	$168	SIP	7.5%
Israel	Bank Leumi	Apr 98	$52	SIP	2%
Israel	Bank Mizrahi	Jun 98	$200	SIP	31.7%
Israel	Bank Leumi	Sep 98	$160	SIP	7.5%
Israel	Bank Hapoalim*	Apr 99	$59	SIP	2%
Israel	Bank Hapoalim	Jul 99	$160	SIP	4%
Israel	Bank Hapoalim	Jun 00	$582	SIP	17%
Italy	Banca Commerciale Italiana	Aug 85	$118	SIP	12%
Italy	Banco di Napoli	Nov 91	$323	SIP	9.7%
Italy	Credito Italiano	Nov 91	$140	SIP	7%

Country	Company	Date	Amount of Offer (US$ Million)	Method of Sale	Fraction Sold
Italy	Istituto Bancario San Paolo	Mar 92	$709	SIP	20%
Italy	Credito Italiano	Dec 93	$1,079	SIP	58%
Italy	Credito Italiano	Dec 93	$100	SIP	—
Italy	Istituto Mobiliare Italiano	Jan 94	$1,513	SIP	30%
Italy	Banca Commerciale Italiana	Feb 94	$1,700	SIP	54%
Italy	Istituto Mobiliare Italiano	Jul 95	$733	Asset sale	3.5%[24]
Italy	Istituto Mobiliare Italiano	Jul 96	$327	SIP	6.93%
Italy	Istituto San Paolo di Torino	May 97	$730	SIP	46%
Italy	Banca di Roma	Nov 97	$1,740	SIP	36.5%
Italy	Banco di Napoli	1997	$39	Asset sale	—
Italy	Cariplo Bank	1997	$5,000	Asset sale	—
Italy	Banca Nazionale del Lavoro	Nov 98	$4,600	SIP	85%
Italy	Banca Monte dei Paschi di Siena	Jun 99	$2,302	SIP	27%
Italy	Mediocredito Centrale	Nov 99	$2,148	Asset sale	100%
Italy	Banca Regionale Europea	Dec 99	$1,421	Asset sale	56.73%
Jamaica	NCB Group	Nov 86	$16	SIP	100%
Japan	Nippon Credit Bank	Jun 00	$932	Asset sale	80%[25]
Kazakhstan	Turanalem Bank*	Mar 98	$100	Asset sale	72%
Kenya	National Bank of Kenya	Nov 94	$10	SIP	20%
Kenya	Kenya Commercial Bank*	1996	$11	SIP	—
Kenya	Kenya Commercial Bank	May 98	$29.4	SIP	25%
Korea	Citizens National Bank	Aug 94	$264	SIP	10%
Korea	Seoul Bank	Mar 99	$700	Asset sale	70%
Korea	Woori Financial Group	Jun 02	$509	SIP	12%
Korea	Seoul Bank	Sep 02	$965	Asset sale	—
Korea	Chohung Bank	Jun 03	$2,530	Asset sale	80%[26]
Kuwait	Kuwait Real Estate Bank*	1996	$42	Asset sale	—
Kuwait	Burgan Bank*	1997	$158	Asset sale	—
Kuwait	Burgan Bank*	1997	$270.6	SIP	—
Kuwait	Commercial Bank of Kuwait*	1997	$32.7	Asset sale	—
Kuwait	Gulf Bank*	1997	$56	Asset sale	—
Kuwait	Gulf Bank*	1997	$57	Asset sale	—
Latvia	Latvijas Unibanka	May 96	$10	Asset sale	23%[27]
Lithuania	Lithuanian Agricultural Bank	Mar 02	$20	Asset sale	76.10%[28]
Macedonia	Stopanska Banka	Sep 97	$17.6	Asset sale	55%[29]
Malta	Mid-Med Bank*	Apr 99	$250	Asset sale	67.1%
Mexico	Grupo Financiero Bancomer*	Oct 91	$2,798	Asset sale	56%
Mexico	Banco Nacional de Mexico (Banamex)*	Aug 91	$4,430	Asset sale	70.7%
Mexico	Grupo Financiero Bancomer	Mar 92	$837	SIP	—
Mexico	Grupo Financiero Serfin	Dec 93	$420	SIP	—
Mexico	BBVA Bancomer	Jan 02	$865	Asset sale	11.6%[30]
Mongolia	Trade and Development Bank	May 02	$12.23	Asset sale	76%[31]
Morocco	Banque Marocaine du Commerce Exterieur	Jan 95	$169	SIP	50%
Morocco	Credit-Eqdom	Jun 95	$9	SIP	18%
Morocco	Banque Marocaine du Commerce Exterieur	Apr 96	$50	SIP	—

(continued)

325

TABLE 9.3. (*continued*)

Country	Company	Date	Amount of Offer (US$ Million)	Method of Sale	Fraction Sold
Morocco	Banque Marocaine du Commerce Exterieur*	1997	$80	Asset sale	—
Morocco	Banque Marocaine du Commerce Exterieur*	1997	$64	SIP	—
Mozambique	Commercial Bank of Mozambique*	1996	$11	Asset sale	—
Mozambique	Banco Populaire de Desenvolvimento*	1997	$21	Asset sale	—
Norway	Christiania Bank	Dec 93	$259	SIP	22%
Norway	Christiania Bank	Nov 95	$150	SIP	17%
Norway	Fokus Bank	1995	$291	SIP	96%
Norway	Den Norske Bank	1996	$376	SIP	19.8%
Norway	Union Bank of Norway*	1996	$275	SIP	—
Norway	Christiania Bank*	Mar 99	$348	SIP	16%
Norway	Christiania Bank	Oct 00	$2,900	Asset sale	35%[32]
Pakistan	Habib Credit ad Exchange Bank	Jun 97	$39	Asset sale	70%[33]
Pakistan	First Women Bank*	1997	$6.5	Asset sale	—
Pakistan	Schon Bank*	1997	$11.2	Asset sale	—
Pakistan	United Bank Limited	Oct 02	$208	Asset sale	51%[34]
Peru	Banco Popular*	1993	$6	Asset sale	100%
Peru	Interbanc*	Jul 94	$51	Asset sale	100%
Peru	Banco Continental*	Apr 95	$256	Asset sale	60%
Peru	Banco Continental	Jul 98	$68	SIP	20%
Philippines	Philippine National Bank	Mar 92	$89	SIP	10%
Philippines	International Corporate Bank*	1993	$114	Asset sale	93.7%
Philippines	Philippine National Bank	1995	$71	SIP	8%
Philippines	Philippine National Bank*	Dec 99	$230	Asset sale	35%
Philippines	Philippine National Bank	Jul 00	$141	Asset sale	30%[35]
Poland	Bank Slaski	Jan 94	$64	SIP	30%
Poland	Bank Premyslowo Handlowy	Jan 95	$150	SIP	50.1%
Poland	Bank Gdanski	Dec 95	$67	SIP	—
Poland	Polish Development Bank*	1995	$17	SIP	—
Poland	Bank Slaski	Jun 96	$196	Asset sale	7.25%[36]
Poland	Petrobank*	1996	$48	Asset sale	—
Poland	Wielkopolski Bank Kredytowy*	1996	$60	Asset sale	—
Poland	Bank Gdanski	Feb 97	$83.4	Asset sale	32%[37]
Poland	Powszechny Bank Kredytowy	1997	$300.2	SIP	65%
Poland	Polish Investment Bank	Apr 97	$67	Asset sale	100%[38]
Poland	Bank Premyslowo Handlowy	Jun 97	$660	SIP	—
Poland	Export Development Bank	Sep 97	$94.5	Asset sale	15.9%[39]
Poland	Powszechny Bank Kredytowy	Sep 97	$264	SIP	65%
Poland	Polish Development Bank	May 98	$52.8	Asset sale	44.54%
Poland	Bank Pekao*	Jun 98	$260	SIP	15%
Poland	PKBL*	Oct 98	$51.9	Asset sale	99.93%
Poland	BPH*	Nov 98	$600.6	Asset sale	36.7%
Poland	Bank Pekao*	Jun 99	$1,090	Asset sale	52.09%
Poland	Bank Zachodni*	Jun 99	$580	Asset sale	80%
Poland	Powszechny Bank Kredytowy	Jun 00	$76.06	Asset sale	10.3%
Poland	Bank Pekao	Oct 00	$133	SIP	—
Portugal	Banco Totta and Acores	Jul 89	$195	SIP	—

Country	Company	Date	Amount of Offer (US$ Million)	Method of Sale	Fraction Sold
Portugal	Banco Totta and Acores	Jul 90	$153	SIP	31%
Portugal	Banco Portugues do Atlantico	Dec 90	$382	SIP	33%
Portugal	Sociedad Financeria Portuuesa	May 91	$109	SIP	7.5%
Portugal	Banco Espirito Santo e Comercial de Lisbon (BESCL)	Jul 91	$385	SIP	40%
Portugal	Banco Fonsecas & Burnay	Aug 91	$247	SIP	80%
Portugal	BESCL	Feb 92	$590	SIP	60%
Portugal	Banco Portugues do Atlantico	May 92	$346	SIP	17.64%
Portugal	Banco Fonsecas & Burnay	Jul 92	$61	SIP	20%
Portugal	Credito Predial Portugues	Dec 92	$279	SIP	100%
Portugal	União de Bancos Portugues	Dec 92	$167	SIP	61.2%
Portugal	Banco Portugues do Atlantico	Jul 93	$221	SIP	17.5%
Portugal	Banco Portugues do Atlantico	Mar 94	$105	SIP	7.5%
Portugal	Banco Pinto & Sotto Mayor	Nov 94	$255	SIP	80%
Portugal	Banco Fomento Exteroir	Dec 94	$133	SIP	80%
Portugal	Banco Pinto & Sotto Mayor	Mar 95	$46	SIP	20%
Portugal	Banco Fomento Exteroir*	1996	$892	Asset sale	—
Portugal	Banco Totta e Acores	1996	$135	SIP	—
Portugal	Banco Fomento Exteroir*	1997	$35.9	SIP	3.5%
Romania	Banca Romana pentru Dezvoltare	Dec 98	$200	Asset sale	41%
Romania	Banc Post	Apr 99	$42.8	Asset sale	42%
Romania	Banca Agriola	Apr 01	$52	Asset sale	98%[41]
Russia	Vneshtorgbank	Dec 02	$300	Asset sale	20%[42]
Singapore	Keppel Bank	1993	$235	SIP	—
Slovakia	Slovenska Sporitelna	Dec 00	$347	Asset sale	87%[43]
Slovakia	Vseobecna Uverova bank (VUB)	Jun 01	$473	Asset sale	94.5%[44]
Slovenia	Nova Ljubljanska Banka (NLB)	2002	$427.7	Asset sale	34%[45]
Spain	Argentaria	May 93	$1,027	SIP	24.9%
Spain	Argentaria	Nov 93	$1,214	SIP	25%
Spain	Argentaria	Mar 96	$1,200	SIP	25%
Spain	Argentaria	Feb 98	$2,300	SIP	25%
Sri Lanka	National Development Bank of Sri Lanka*	1997	$75	SIP	—
Sweden	Nordbanken	Oct 95	$893	SIP	30%
Sweden	Nordbanken	1997	$907.3	SIP	—
Taiwan	Chiao-Tung Bank*	1996	$219	SIP	—
Taiwan	Chiao-Tung Bank*	Aug 97	$982.7	Asset sale	—
Taiwan	Chang Hwa Commercial bank*	Dec 97	$381.7	SIP	—
Taiwan	Taiwan Business Bank*	Jan 98	$554	SIP	—
Taiwan	First Commercial Bank*	Jan 98	$1,372	SIP	—
Taiwan	HuaNan Commercial Bank*	Jan 98	$798	SIP	—
Taiwan	Farmers' Bank of China*	Sep 99	$143	SIP	—
Taiwan	Chiao-Tung Bank*	Sep 99	$363	SIP	—
Taiwan	Bank of Kaohsiung*	Sep 99	$25	SIP	—
Thailand	Nakomthon Bank	Sep 99	$317	Asset sale	75%
Thailand	Radanasin Bank	Nov 99	$166	Asset sale	75.02%
Thailand	Bank Thai	Oct 02	$130	SIP	36.2%
Turkey	Sekerbank	1993	$4	Asset sale	10%
Turkey	Sumerbank	Sep 95	$103.5	Asset sale	—

(continued)

327

TABLE 9.3. *(continued)*

Country	Company	Date	Amount of Offer (US$ Million)	Method of Sale	Fraction Sold
Turkey	Denizbank	May 97	$66	Asset sale	—
Turkey	Anadolubank*	May 97	$69.5	Asset sale	—
Turkey	Etibank	Jan 98	$155.5	Asset sale	100%
Turkey	Turkiye is Bankasi (Isbank)	May 98	$651	SIP	12.3%
Uganda	Uganda Commercial Bank	1997	$5	Asset sale	—
Uganda	Barclays Bank	Oct 98	$3.8	Asset sale	100%
Venezuela	Banco Popular	1993	$23	Asset sale	—
Venezuela	Banco de Fomento de Coro	1994	$4	Asset sale	—
Venezuela	Banco Guyana	1995	$7	Asset sale	—
Venezuela	Banco Consolidado	1996	$124	Asset sale	—
Venezuela	Banco de Venezuela	Dec 96	$338	Asset sale	90%
Venezuela	Banco Republica	Jun 97	$56.7	Asset sale	56.7%
Venezuela	Banco Populary de los Andes	Dec 97	$47.4	Asset sale	47.25%
Venezuela	La Confederacion del Canada Venezolana	Aug 98	$6.4	Asset sale	—
Zimbabwe	Commercial Bank of Zimbabwe	Sep 97	$43.7	SIP	80%
TOTAL			$142,902.59		

Table Summary

Method of Sale	Number of Transactions	Value (US $ Million)
SIP	144	76,187.85
Asset sale	139	66,174.74
TOTAL	283	142,902.59

Sources: Most of the data presented here is from the *Financial Times* and/or the FT.COM Web site, but other sources are employed as well. In particular, sales marked with an asterisk are taken from various issues of *Privatisation International* (1998–2000) and *Privatisation International Yearbooks* (1998–2001).

Note: This table presents key information about banking privatizations executed by governments around the world. The method of sale refers to whether the company was divested via a share issue privatization (SIP) or asset sale.

[1]Stake sold by New South Wales state government to Colonial Mutual, a Melbourne-based insurance group. Colonial Mutual also promised to inject $259 million in new capital at the end of four years and not to sell the firm to any of Australia's Big Four banks.

[2]Stake sold by Western Australian state government to Bank of Scotland.

[3]In a highly politicized sale, the state's controlling stake was sold to Creditanstalt's main rival, Bank Austria.

[4]The state's remaining stake in Bank Austria was sold to Dresdner Bank of Germany.

[5]Stake sold to Banco Itau.

[6]Stake sold to Spain's Banco Santander Central Hispano.

[7]Purchase paid for through a $30 million rights issue after the sale. Stake sold to Oppenheimer (U.S.) and the European Bank for Reconstruction and Development.

[8]Stake sold to a consortium of Italy's UniCredito and Germany's Allianz.

[9]Stake sold to Hungary's OTP Bank.

[10]Stake sold to HSBC.

[11]Stake sold to Citigroup.

[12]Stake sold to Belgium's KBC.

[13]Stake sold to France's Societe Generale.

[14]Sake sold to France's Credit Mutuel.

[15]Stake sold to CCF, which had recently been acquired by Britain's HSBC.

[16]Stake sold to BNP Paribas.

TABLE 9.3. (*continued*)

[17]Sold to Latsis Oil and shipping group for an unexpectedly high price.

[18]Stake sold to France's Credit Agricole.

[19]Stake sold to Republic Bank of Trinidad and Tobago.

[20]Stake sold to Samson, Iceland's second largest bank, leaving the government with a 2.5% holding—which it plans to retain.

[21]State residual holding sold to Farallon Capital, a U.S.-based investment group.

[22]Stake sold to the Ofer-Wertheim consortium, which also acquired an option to purchase an additional 25% within 18 months.

[23]State's remaining stake sold to a group of investors led by Ted Arison, a well-known U.S. Israeli billionaire.

[24]Private placement of shares to Istituto Bancario San Paolo di Torino.

[25]After being nationalized by the Japanese government in 1998, Nippon Credit bank was sold to a group led by Softbank.

[26]After nationalizing much of the Korean banking system after the Asian financial crisis of 1997, and then injecting $132.5 billion into bailing out these banks, the government's stake in Chohung was sold to Shinhan Financial Group.

[27]Stake sold to the European Bank for Reconstruction and Development.

[28]Stake sold, after five years of trying, to the Germany's Norddeutsche Landesbank Girozentrale.

[29]Stake sold to group including Austria's Giro Bank, the European Bank for Reconstruction and Development and the International Finance Corporation.

[30]The Mexican government sold its remaining stake in the former Bancomer to Spain's Banco Bilbao Vizcaya Argentaria, which already had a 48.5% stake in the bank

[31]Stake sold to Banca Commerciale Lugano/Gerald Metals, a Swiss–U.S. consortium.

[32]The government's residual stake sold to Nordic Bank Holding.

[33]Stake sold to the U.A.E.'s Sheikh Nahayan bin Mubarak Al Nahyan. The state planned to retain its 20% stake indefinitely.

[34]Stake sold to a group of investors from Abu Dhabi and Bestway Holdings, a company that represents expatriate Pakistanis. The state plans to retain the remaining 49% stake.

[35]State's remaining stake sold to Lucio Tan, a Philippine businessman and friend of President Joseph Estrada.

[36]ING, the Dutch financial services group, raised its stake to 33.15%.

[37]Stake sold to the Polish bank IG, giving the bank a 63% holding.

[38]Stake sold to Poland's Kredyt Bank.

[39]Commerzbank, which already owned a 32.8% stake, increased its holding to 48.7% through a $94.5 million share offering reserved for it alone. Italy's BCI also acquired a 5% stake at the same time for an undisclosed price.

[40]Bank of Austria increased its stake in PKB to 57% with this sale.

[41]Stake sold to a consortium including Raiffeisen Zentralbank, an Austrian bank, and the Romanian-American Enterprise Fund.

[42]Stake sold to European Bank for Reconstruction and Development, leaving the Russian government with a 79.9% holding.

[43]Stake sold to Austria's Erste Bank.

[44]Stake sold to Italy's Banca Intesa.

[45]Stake sold to Belgium's KBC.

[46]This offering was only partially successful, with just 77% of the offer subscribed. The government's stake was thus reduced only from 96% to 59.8%, rather than to 49% as planned. Additionally, shares of Bank Thai fell sharply soon after the offer, yielding a 3% loss to investors who bought shares at the purchase price—despite the fact that shares were sold at a 9% discount to the previous market price.

Influential Early Bank Privatizations, 1985–1990

The first bank privatizations we identify are two SIPs in 1986. In August of that year, Italy sold a 10 percent stake in Banca Commerciale Italiana, and the Jamaican government followed three months later with the sale of its entire stake in NCB Group. These were rather small sales, even by mid-1980s standards, but the same cannot be said about the next group of sales—those executed by the newly elected Chirac government in France, which came to power in late 1986.

Over the next two years, the Chirac government divested 12 companies, but the centerpieces of this program were the four complete bank privatizations (by SIP) that occurred between January and April 1987. Two of these were small, raising only $60 million and $67 million, respectively, but the Banque Paribas offering raised $2.74 billion and Credit Comercial de France raised $732 million. The Paribas sale was especially noteworthy because this offer created 3.7 million shareholders, a truly remarkable number for a country with a total population of less than 60 million.

After the Socialists were voted back into power in 1988, the French government ceased all privatizations for several years, but the new government did not move to renationalize any of the companies sold off by the Chirac administration. From early 1988 through the end of 1989, Germany was the only country to divest any banking assets. The Kohl government sold minority stakes, using public offerings, in DVKB and DSL.

Bank Privatizations During the 1990s

As with all industries, the number and cumulative value of banking privatizations surged during the 1990s, and gathered strength as the decade wore on. The sale of banks by the newly independent countries of central and eastern Europe, though relatively small in value, were arguably the most economically significant sales because they were central planks of these governments' transition strategies. Unfortunately, most of the early sales (through about 1995), which involved partial sales using vouchers, ended badly when the volume of nonperforming loans booked by these banks—often to the same state-owned enterprises as before—reached disastrous levels. These banks typically had to be recapitalized, at great expense, by governments, and were then completely divested during the late 1990s, usually to strategic foreign investors. As described in Bonin, Hasan, and Wachtel (2003), over 75 percent of the banking assets in Poland, Hungary, the Czech Republic, Slovakia, and Croatia were controlled by foreigners by 2002.

Many nontransition countries also launched bank privatization programs during the 1990s, which ranged in scale from relatively trivial to truly colossal. One of the earliest and most influential sales was the 1991 SIP of 29.75 percent of Commonwealth Bank of Australia (CBA), which raised $1.017 billion and fundamentally altered the Australian banking industry. CBA had long been Australia's largest bank, and by the time it was fully privatized in 1996 the bank's competitive position had become even more formidable. In addition to CBA, the Australian government sold sakes in six other banks during the 1990s, typically using asset sales. Other OECD countries that launched significant bank privatization programs include Austria, Belgium, France, Greece, Iceland, Italy, Norway, Portugal, Spain, and Sweden. The programs of France, Italy, Portugal, and Spain are especially noteworthy because these were all civil law countries that historically had developed very large state banking sectors—which were sold off almost entirely during the 1990s. Remarkably, the Italian government raised almost $25 billion, the most of any country, through bank sales during the 1990s.

Latin American countries also enthusiastically embraced banking privatizations, usually selling majority stakes to private buyers using asset sales. In the early 1990s, most governments favored domestic over foreign bidders, but this was to change over the course of the decade as several of the early programs either met with limited success or failed outright. By the late-1990s, Spanish banks had become voracious acquirers of privatized banks in Latin America, either purchasing stakes directly from a divesting government or acquiring control of already private banks in the open market. Argentina, Brazil, Colombia, Mexico, Peru, and Venezuela all launched major bank privatization programs during the 1990s, and the national programs of Argentina, Brazil, and Mexico are discussed in studies that we survey in the next section. As described in Unal and Navarro (1999) and Haber and Kantor (2003), Mexico's experience was nothing short of catastrophic.

Many other nontransition developing countries outside of Latin America also launched significant bank privatization programs during the 1990s, often emphasizing asset sales to foreign strategic investors. This group includes Egypt, Ghana, India, Indonesia, Israel, Kenya, Kuwait, Morocco, Mozambique, Pakistan, the Philippines, Taiwan, Thailand, Turkey, and Uganda. Israel's program was especially important because it represented a deliberate attempt to return to private ownership the institutions nationalized in 1984 after the banking system collapsed. The programs of Egypt, India, Israel, Kenya, and Taiwan emphasized SIPs, while the other national programs emphasized asset sales or a mix of public and private offers.

Bank Privatizations Since March 2000

The meltdown in stock market valuations that began on NASDAQ in March 2000 and spread around the world over the next three years had a predictably negative impact on the number of banking privatizations since March 2000, and on the average size of the sales that did occur. We document 27 offerings after March 2000, of which 23 were assets sales and four SIPs; only seven of the 27 sales raised $1 billion or more. The most important recent offerings have been the $2.8 billion SIP of 25 percent of Bank of China in July 2002, the $3.2 billion SIP of France's Credit Agricole in December 2001 and the $2.2 billion SIP of Credit Lyonnais in November 2002, and Korea's direct sales of three banks nationalized after the East Asian Crisis began in 1997. There were very few bank sales during 2003, and it is unclear if and when these sales will resume—though a continued rebound in stock market valuations would certainly promote new sales, especially in India, China, and the Moslem nations.

Empirical Evidence on Banking Privatizations

Unlike privatizations of nonfinancial firms, where a substantial body of theoretical and empirical literature has emerged, relatively few empirical analyses of bank privatizations have been generated, and most of these have appeared only very recently. This is somewhat surprising since banks, or least the banking function, is indispensable in all economies. At the same time, it is not unexpected since data on banks that have been privatized are so difficult to obtain, especially regarding financial performance before and after privatization. Furthermore, banks have always been one of the favorite tools that politicians and governments employ to channel funding to chosen sectors, industries, and firms on favorable terms. As such, they are even more opaque than usual for an industry that under the best of circumstances suffers from lack of transparency in financial reporting.

Nonetheless, over two dozen empirical studies of bank privatizations have been generated since 1997, and we survey these studies in this and the following two sections. This section discusses empirical studies of bank privatizations in developed countries (defined as countries that were OECD members in 1990), while the next two sections survey studies of privatizations in nontransition developing countries and in the transition economies of central and eastern Europe and the former Soviet Union.

Empirical Evidence on Banking Privatizations in Developed Countries

Four studies examine the effectiveness of bank privatization in OECD countries, and these are summarized in table 9.4. Two of these are multinational studies, while the other two examine the experience of individual countries. Verbrugge, Megginson, and Owens (1999; hereafter VMO) study the offering terms and share ownership results for 58 unseasoned IPOs and 34 seasoned offerings of 65 banks that were fully or partially privatized from 1981 to 1996. They then compare pre and post-privatization performance changes for 32 banks in OECD countries and five in developing countries. VMO document moderate performance improvements in OECD countries; ratios proxying for profitability, fee income (noninterest income as fraction of total income), and capital adequacy increase significantly, while leverage ratio declines significantly. They also find significantly positive initial returns to IPO investors. On the other hand, VMO document large, ongoing state ownership, with very few governments selling majority control of their banks—and even fewer selling their entire ownership stake.

Gleason, McNulty, and Pennathur (2003) examine the short- and long-term stock returns to successful bidding firms that participate in the purchase of a financial service firm being privatized. They study bidders that are United States–based or have stock traded in a U.S. market and examine 86 transactions from 1980 through 2002, though most sales occur between 1995 and 1998. They find that the CARs to bidding firm shareholders are positive around the date of the announcement, but that this short-run superior performance is not sustainable over longer periods. While the long-run CARs are (insignificantly) negative, the authors find that bank bidders are able to significantly reduce their systematic risks, relative to the home market, following such acquisitions.

Braz (1999) examines the nationalization of Portugal's private banking system following a military coup in 1974, as well as the "re-privatization" of these same banks after 1990. He describes the (multiple) objectives of the Portuguese government in launching this bank privatization program, and also discusses the primary method of sale (public offer) and offer terms of these divestitures. Drawing on both his own analyses and other published work, Braz shows that (1) the productive

TABLE 9.4. Summary of Empirical Studies on the Effectiveness of Bank Privatization in OECD Countries

Study	Sample Description, Study Period, and Methodology	Summary of Empirical Findings and Conclusions
Verbrugge, Megginson, and Owens (1999	Study the offering terms and share ownership results for 58 un-seasoned (IPOs) and 34 seasoned offerings by 65 banks that were fully or partially privatized from 1981 to 1996. They then compare pre-and post-privatization performance changes for 32 banks in OECD countries and 5 banks in developing countries.	Document moderate performance improvements in OECD coun-tries. Ratios proxying for profitability, fee income (noninterest income as fraction of total), and capital adequacy increase signif-icantly; leverage ratio declines significantly. Document large, on-going state ownership, and significantly positive initial returns to IPO investors.
Gleason, McNulty, and Pennathur (2003)	Examine the short-and long-term stock returns to successful bid-ding firms that participate in the purchase of a financial service firm being privatized. They study bidders that are U.S.-based or have stock traded in a U.S. market and examine 86 transactions from 1980 through 2002, though most sales occur between 1995 and 1998.	Fnd that the cumulative abnormal returns (CARs) to bidding firm shareholders is positive around the date of the announcement, but that this short-run superior performance is not sustainable over longer periods. While the long-run CARs are (insignifi-cantly) negative, the authors find that bank bidders are able to significantly reduce their systematic risks, relative to the home market, following such acquisitions.
Braz (1999)	Examines the nationalization of Portugal's private banking system following a military coup in 1974, as well as the "reprivatiza-tion" of these same banks after 1990. He describes the (multi-ple) objectives of the Portuguese government in launching this bank privatization program, and also discusses the primary method of sale (public offer) and offer terms of these divestitu-res.	Shows that (1) the productive efficiency of privatized banks in-creases significantly after divestiture, with assets per worker showing an especially large differential increase; (2) privatized banks reduce staff at a significantly more rapid rate than do public banks; and (3) privatized banks experience significantly more rapid growth in their branch networks than do state banks.
Otchere and Chan (2003)	Perform a clinical analysis (case study) of the impact that Com-monwealth Bank of Australia's (CBA's) privatization had on the bank itself as well as on its domestic rivals. The initial sale of CBA was executed in 1991, and the bank was fully divested in 1996.	Find that (1) the stock prices of major rival banks reacted nega-tively to CBA's sales, with especially negative reactions to the in-itial and final sales; (2) CBA's long-run stock price performance is significantly positive, and increases steadily as the govern-ment's ownership stake declines; (3) the financial and operating performance of CBA improves significantly after privatization, and surpasses that of its major rivals.

333

efficiency of privatized banks increases significantly after divestiture, with assets per worker showing an especially large differential increase; (2) privatized banks reduce staff at a significantly more rapid rate than do public banks; and (3) privatized banks experience significantly more rapid growth in their branch networks than do state banks. He concludes by offering several "lessons" for government officials weighing the privatization of their nation's banking system.

Finally, Otchere and Chan (2003) perform a clinical analysis (case study) of the impact that CBA's privatization had on the bank itself, as well as on its domestic rivals. The initial sale of CBA was executed in 1991, and the bank was fully divested in 1996. They find that (1) the stock prices of major rival banks react negatively to CBA's sales, with especially negative reactions to the initial and final sales; (2) CBA's long-run stock price performance is significantly positive, and increases steadily as the government's ownership stake declines; (3) the financial and operating performance of CBA improves significantly after privatization, and surpasses that of its major rivals.

In sum, the evidence from developed countries is that bank privatization yields significant performance improvements, though these seem to be smaller and less pervasive than the improvements typically documented in studies of nonfinancial company privatizations in OECD countries. We now assess the privatization experiences of non-OECD countries.

Empirical Evidence on Banking Privatizations in Nontransition Developing Countries

Several papers describe bank privatizations in nontransition developing countries, though only seven of these actually perform empirical analyses of privatization's impact. These are summarized in table 9.5. Two of these are multinational studies, while the other five examine the national experiences of Brazil, China, Egypt, Nigeria, and Pakistan. Boubakri, Cosset, Fischer, and Guedhami (2003) examine the post-privatization performance of 81 banks divested in whole or (much more frequently) in part by governments of 22 developing countries over the period 1986–1998. They find that (1) privatization alone does not seem to significantly impact profitability or operating efficiency; (2) ownership type and industry concentration significantly impacts risk taking behavior by privatized banks, with banks controlled by industrial groups taking the highest risk exposure, followed by locally controlled banks and with foreign owned banks taking the least exposure; (3) foreign owned banks have lower net interest margins than do locally owned banks, suggesting that foreign ownership makes a significantly greater contribution to a divested bank's economic efficiency.

The second multinational study, Otchere (2003), performs a similar pre- versus post-privatization analysis of operating performance changes, as well as an assessment of stock price performance, for 21 banks privatizations (18 unseasoned and three seasoned offerings) in low- and middle-income countries from 1989 to 1997. He also computes the same measures for 28 rival firms for comparison purposes. He finds that privatization announcements elicit significantly negative stock price reactions from rival banks, which are more negative the larger the state

TABLE 9.5. Summary of Empirical Studies on the Effectiveness of Bank Privatization in Non-Transition Developing Countries

Study	Sample Description, Study Period, and Methodology	Summary of Empirical Findings and Conclusions
Boubakri, Cosset, Fischer, and Guedhami (2003)	Examine the post-privatization performance of 81 banks divested in whole or (much more frequently) in part by governments of 22 developing countries over the period 1986–1998.	Find that (1) privatization alone does not seem to significantly impact profitability or operating efficiency; (2) ownership type and industry concentration significantly impacts risk taking behavior by privatized banks, with banks controlled by industrial groups taking the highest risk exposure, followed by locally controlled banks and with foreign owned banks taking the least exposure; and (3) foreign-owned banks have lower net interest margins than do locally owned banks.
Otchere (2003)	Performs a similar pre- versus post-privatization analysis of operating performance changes, as well as an assessment of stock price performance, for 21 bank privatizations (18 unseasoned and 3 seasoned offerings) in low- and middle-income countries from 1989 to 1997. He also computes the same measures for 28 rival firms for comparison purposes.	Finds that privatization announcements elicit significantly negative stock price reactions from rival banks, which are more negative the larger the state ownership fraction that is divested. These findings support the "competitive effects" hypothesis and suggest that investors view privatization announcements as foreshadowing bad news for rival banks. He finds that the privatized bank stocks significantly underperform their respective stock markets, and these returns are also (insignificantly) lower than those achieved by rival bank stocks.
Beck, Cull, and Jerome (2003)	Examine the effect of privatization on performance using an unbalanced panel of 69 Nigerian banks with annual data for the period 1990–2001. The authors focus on the banks that were completely privatized during this period.	Document a significantly positive impact from privatization, even in a macroeconomic and regulatory environment that was inhospitable to financial intermediation. Privatization helped close the very wide gap between the performance of state-owned banks and private banks in Nigeria, though the performance of divested firms never surpassed that of private banks.

ownership fraction that is divested. These findings support the "competitive effects" hypothesis and suggest that investors view privatization announcements as foreshadowing bad news for rival banks. On the other hand, Otchere finds that the privatized bank stocks significantly underperform their respective stock markets, and these returns are also (insignificantly) lower than those achieved by rival bank stocks. He also finds little evidence of significant improvements in the operating performance of privatized banks.

Beck, Crivelli, and Summerhill (2003) examine empirically the transformation of state banks in Brazil after the industry's collapse in 1995. They utilize an unbalanced panel of 207 banks with quarterly data from January 1995 to September 2003, with a total of 4,864 observations. They describe the four options that Brazilian state governments could choose from in repairing the collapsed banks — liquidation, federalization, privatization or restructuring, and retention. As expected, the authors find that political economy variables explained states' choices regarding bank transformation. States that are more dependent on federal transfers, whose banks are already under federal administration, and those that convert state banks into development agencies are more likely to surrender control to the federal government. These banks perform much better than those that remain stateowned, and privatized banks significantly improve their performance after state divestment.

Moshirian, Chan, and Li (2003) test whether the July 2002 partial privatization of Bank of China Hong Kong (BOCHK) was viewed as creating a stronger banking competitor by examining the impact of this announcement on the stock prices of 23 bank and nonbank financial institutions in Hong Kong and mainland China. These authors use competitors' stock returns over the period from March 1999 to July 2003. They find that many rivals' stock prices react negatively both to the announcement of China's entry into WTO and to the announcement of BOCHK's privatization. The stocks of Hong Kong financial institutions (particularly nonbank institutions) generally react significantly negatively to BOCHK privatization announcements, implying that investors believe that the bank will become a stronger competitor. Mainland banks and nonbank financial institutions react positively, probably interpreting the privatization announcement as a signal that the Chinese government will continue to deregulate and reform China's financial system. They also document significant negative cumulative abnormal returns for BOCHK's new shareholders over the first year of trading.

Omran (2003) examines the financial performance of 12 Egyptian banks privatized between 1996 and 1999. He tests whether the banks' performance changes over the −2 to +2 year period surrounding the sale date using measures of profitability, capital risk, asset quality, efficiency, liquidity risk, and growth rate. He finds generally insignificant changes resulting from privatization, though some profitability and liquidity measures decline significantly after 1999 owing to worsening macroeconomic conditions. He also finds that banks with higher private ownership are associated with superior performance.

Beck, Cull, and Jerome (2003) examine the effect of privatization on performance using an unbalanced panel of 69 Nigerian banks with annual data for the period 1990–2001. The authors focus on the nine banks that were completely privatized during this period. They document a significantly positive impact from privatization, even in a macroeconomic and regulatory environment inhospitable to financial intermediation. Privatization helps close the very wide gap between the performance of state-owned banks and private banks in Nigeria, though the performance of divested firms never surpasses that of private banks.

Bonaccorsi di Patti and Hardy (2003) describe the evolution of Pakistan's banking system from the time of its nationalization in 1974 through its transformation and partial privatization during the 1990s. Major reforms and deregulation events occurred in 1991–1992 and 1997. By 1997, Pakistan had fully privatized two banks, but still had four major state banks competing with 21 private domestic and 27 foreign-owned banks. Bonaccorsi di Patti and Hardy examine the impact of the 1991–1992 and 1997 changes on bank performance using annual data for between 33 and 40 banks, with 547 total observations. They find that the principal short-run effect of both sets of reforms was to increase both the revenues and costs of all banks, but not overall profitability. Efficiency increased after the 1991–1992 reforms, but there was no convergence between lagging state-owned banks and private (domestic and foreign) banks, since all improved. Because only two banks were fully privatized (one to the bank's own employee unions), no real differences were observed between these and other banks. After the 1997 reforms, profitability first declined, then increased significantly for the average bank.

In addition to these six empirical papers, several studies provide either descriptive analyses of bank privatization programs in developing countries or analyses of the pricing of bank sales, particularly in Latin America. Clarke and Cull (2003) develop a simple theory that models the inherent trade-offs between (1) sales price offered, (2) layoffs allowed, and (3) loan portfolios guaranteed faced by governments and potential buyers in bank privatization transactions. They then test this model using data drawn from 15 provincial Argentine bank privatizations during the 1990s. They find that provinces with high fiscal deficits were willing to accept layoffs and to guarantee a larger fraction of the privatized bank's portfolio in return for a higher price. The Tequila Crisis also forced politicians to protect fewer jobs and retain a higher share of the public banks' assets in the "bad bank" residual entity.

Baer and Nazmi (2000) describe the origins of Brazil's state and private banks and examine how the decades of inflation produced distortions in how they functioned. They then describe how the Real Plan's success in halting inflation — which was good for the overall economy — severely impacted the profitability (even the viability) of both state and private banks in Brazil and led the state and national governments to take increasingly desperate steps to rescue the banking system from collapse. Ness (2000), Makler (2000), and Weintraub and Nakane (2003) present similar discussions of the Brazilian banking system's evolution and outlook.

Brock (1999) describes and examines Chile's two bank privatization programs. The first program was implemented in 1975, soon after the Allende government was overthrown, and used highly leveraged direct sales — primarily to the banks' previous owners. This program ended in failure after the Debt Crisis broke out in 1982, when the Central Bank was forced to close or renationalize most of the privatized banks. The second, and much more successful, program began in 1985 and employed mostly public share offerings targeted at small investors and offered on very favorable terms. Brock describes the difficulties faced by the Chilean government, and especially the Central Bank, in recapitalizing and then re-privatizing the nation's banks and other financial institutions, though these efforts were ultimately far more successful than those in other Latin American countries.

Four studies — Lopez-de-Silanes and Zamarippa (1995), Unal and Navarro (1999), Gruben and McComb (2003), and Haber and Kantor (2003) — examine Mexico's highly controversial bank privatization program, which began in 1991 and ended five years later in default and collapse. All of the authors show that the Mexican government, which had first seized all private banking assets in a foolish nationalization in 1982, deliberately structured the 1991 privatization sales to max-imize the proceeds received by the national treasury, regardless of buyer compe-tence or the need to promote sound banking practices. The government implicitly promised to allow the new owners to achieve high profits by protecting domestic banks from competition, by allowing the newly private banks to use very forgiving accounting rules, and by practicing an extreme form of regulatory forbearance. The resulting boom in domestic borrowing masked fundamental flaws in the bank-ing system created by this privatization program, and the system collapsed com-pletely after the disastrous December 1994 devaluation of the Mexican peso. The banking system then had to be recapitalized at great cost to Mexico's taxpayers, and by 2001 foreign banks controlled over 60 percent of the country's banking assets.

All in all, the empirical record on bank privatization in nontransition devel-oping countries does not offer overwhelming support for the idea that privatization alone can improve the (usually dreadful) financial and operating performance of state-owned banks. Simply selling off state banks seems to yield only negligible improvement, and poorly designed privatizations (i.e., Mexico's) can backfire badly. On the other hand, empirical evidence also shows that leaving banks under public ownership is an even worse strategy, given the state's dismal fiduciary rec-ord. We now conclude our assessment of bank privatization's empirical record by examining how these sales have worked in the transition economies of central and eastern Europe and the former Soviet Union.

Empirical Evidence on Banking Privatizations in Transition Countries

Bank privatizations in the CEE and FSU economies differ significantly from bank sales elsewhere in two important respects. First, these sales involved a transfor-mation from a socialist command economy, in which banks played a central co-ordinating and credit-rationing role, to a market economy in which banks are expected to have vastly different functions. Second, many banks were sold through voucher privatizations. Ensuring a smooth shift from state-owned banks to private banks is difficult even in mixed capitalistic systems where only a few sectors may have been nationalized. Engineering smooth shifts in the banking sectors of econ-omies that are virtually completely state owned (transition economics) is far more difficult.

A number of theoretical and empirical papers outline the special difficulties encountered by banks in transition economies. Perotti (1993) shows theoretically that banks in these countries have a strong, perverse incentive to fund large former debtors, although these state-owned enterprises are less efficient and more risky than private firms because by doing so they gain the potential repayment of previous debts. This inevitably leads to lower productivity of investment and a greater concentration of risk. Furthermore, since privately owned banks feel this incentive just as strongly as state-owned ones, merely privatizing the banking industry will not solve the problem. The incentive to subsidize former debtors is, however, magnified in the all-too-frequent case where the state retains significant influence over the banks or the debtor companies (or both) after these are nominally privatized. Perotti concludes that liquidation of economically hopeless SOEs will generally be preferable to eternal subsidization, since this will both recognize the true value of the debt and remove the "debt overhang" from banks so they can increase their lending to the more dynamic private sector.

Bonin and Wachtel (2000) provide an excellent analysis of the difficulties of achieving market-based banking systems in transition economies. They emphasize that bank privatization is only one step in the always painful process of disengaging the state from virtually complete control over the banking system. In a later study, Bonin and Wachtel (2002), these same authors examine the structure of the banking sectors of six transition countries in which privatization of state-owned banks is well advanced. Their most striking finding is that foreign banks now dominate banking in Hungary, Poland, the Czech Republic, Croatia, and Bulgaria—and are making substantial inroads in Romania. The rise of foreign bank ownership is at least partly a result of the essential failure of domestic ownership to satisfactorily address the financial problems of borrowers (especially SOEs) in transition countries or to impose hard budget constraints that would force these firms to restructure. Commander, Dutz, and Stern (1999) show that this failure to restructure had an especially woeful impact on the post-privatization performance of firms in all transition economies, but particularly the former Soviet Republics.

Meyendorff and Snyder (1997) study the "transactional structures" of banking privatizations in central and eastern Europe, which they define as having three elements: (1) antecedent actions that determine the characteristics of the unit being privatized; (2) ownership transfer and governance after privatization; and (3) follow-on actions and ongoing government intervention. They note that most of the governments in the region made similar policy choices when they began privatizing their banking systems, which have proved highly influential over time. As examples, most governments chose not to seriously break up the socialist mono-bank system, and most severely restricted new competition—particularly from foreign banks. For these reasons, the former monobanks retain dominant market shares in most of the transition economies almost a decade after reforms were initiated. Further, none of the politically feasible ownership transfer methods (voucher privatization, insider sales) brought in new capital or talent, so all the region's banking systems remain weak and noncompetitive. The pressure exerted by joining the EU in 2004 offers some hope that true restructuring might begin soon.

The same special issue of the *Journal of Comparative Economics* in which Meyendorff and Snyder's paper appears also presents three case studies of specific bank privatizations in transition economies. Abarbanell and Bonin (1997) study the 1993 privatization of Poland's Bank Slaski in a mixed asset sale (to ING) and public offering. They suggest that this experience shows the benefits of attracting a strategic foreign investor, but also highlights the costs of pursuing this strategy too obsessively. Abarbanell and Meyendorff (1997) describe Russia's disbanding of Zhilotsotsbank and the subsequent creation of its private successor, Mosbusinessbank, in a way that left incumbent mangers largely in control of the bank's strategy and operations. They describe how the Russian government's bank privatization and deregulation policies have engendered a system that is 75 percent private and surprisingly innovative—but also highly unstable. Finally, Snyder and Kormendi (1997) describe the 1992 voucher privatization of Komercni Banka, the Czech Republic's largest bank, in a way that left the state in effective control of the company's operating and lending policies. These authors show that this decision to pass up an opportunity to create a strong private bank and to harden budget constraints for borrowers was to have lasting, negative consequences for the bank and the nation.

Bonin and Wachtel (2000) describe the bank privatization experiences of six CEE transition economies—Bulgaria, Croatia, the Czech Republic, Hungary, Poland, and Romania—after 1991. They pay particular attention to the role of foreign strategic investors in bank privatization processes. Outside of Hungary, this was very limited until the late 1990s. They document significant variation in the pace of privatization and in the methods used by different countries, and find that the early experiences were generally quite negative for all countries except Hungary. After a halting start with partial privatizations (often involving voucher sales), and numerous recapitalizations, they show that full privatization improves performance—though this usually involves sales to foreign banks. By 2002, foreigners control over 75 percent of bank assets in five of the six countries studied.

Finally, and perhaps most persuasively, Bonin, Hasan, and Wachtel (2003) test whether privatization improves the financial and operating performance of the 10 largest banks in each of the six CEE transition economies covered by Bonin and Wachtel (2003) over the period 1994–2002. After unsuccessful partial privatizations in the early and mid-1990s, most of the privatized banks were recapitalized and then sold to foreign strategic investors. The data set they employ has 471 total annual observations, and they document significant performance improvement after privatization; they also find that privatized banks begin to compete successfully for fee-for-service businesses. The performance of privatized banks in the late 1990s is significantly better than state-owned banks and becomes comparable to foreign greenfield banks. Privatization to a strategic foreign owner brings a cost advantage in the source of funds for lending, but the authors find no evidence of improved financial intermediation after privatization.

In sum, the evidence from transition economies is somewhat more favorable regarding the impact of privatization on bank performance than was the case for nontransition developing countries. The natural temptation for governments in all the transition economies was to retain effective control of banks after other nonfinancial firms had been divested in order to lessen the shock of transition by propping up borrowers with easy credit. This is exactly what the state overseers did in virtually all cases where they retained control (or even influence), and the results were invariably disastrous for the banks, the government, and the nation's taxpayers. After repeated "one-time" recapitalizations, governments throughout the region finally ceded control entirely to private owners, who more often than not were foreign. By 2002, foreign banks controlled the banking system of the largest CEE economies, though they have not yet had the same impact in FSU countries.

Empirical Evidence on the Impact and Efficiency of Foreign Ownership of Banks

The body of evidence discussed above allows us to draw conclusions, but also leaves several issues unresolved. One key finding is that many bank privatization programs result in virtually complete foreign ownership of banking systems, particularly in developing and transition economies. We conclude our assessment of the empirical literature on banking privatization with a systematic assessment of the evidence regarding the efficacy of foreign ownership of banking assets.

It is not much of an exaggeration to state that the expected final outcome of bank privatizations—especially flawed privatizations—in developing countries is foreign ownership and control of a nation's banking system. Several studies examine the impact of foreign ownership of banks, and these studies are summarized in table 9.6. Claessens, Demirgüç-Kunt, and Huizinga (1998) examine the extent of foreign ownership in 80 national markets over the period 1988–1995, and test whether net interest margins, operating costs, taxes paid, and profitability are different between domestic and foreign-owned banks. They find that foreign banks achieve higher profits than domestic banks in developing countries, but exactly the opposite is observed in developed markets. Regression analyses also suggest that an increase in foreign bank share leads to lower profitability for domestic banks.

Clarke, Cull, and Martinez Peria (2001) use survey data from over 4,000 borrowers in 38 developing and transition countries during 1999 to examine whether foreign bank penetration reduces access to credit in developing countries. Their empirical results strongly support the assertion that foreign bank penetration improves firms' access to credit. Borrowers in countries with high levels of foreign bank penetration tend to rate access to long-term loans and interest rates as lesser constraints on enterprise operations and growth than enterprises in countries with low foreign penetration. The authors also find that the benefits of enhanced credit availability apply to small and medium businesses as well as large ones.

Majnoni, Shankar, and Várheggi (2003) study the dynamics of foreign bank ownership in Hungary using a sample of 26 commercial banks active in the period 1994–2000. By the end of the year 2000, foreign controlled banks account for over two-thirds of total banking assets in Hungary. They find that, after controlling for the nature of investment (greenfield versus acquisition), management style, and duration of ownership, foreign banks are pursuing a lending policy that does not differ significantly from domestic banks. Foreign banks are, however, able to

TABLE 9.6. Summary of Empirical Studies on the Economic Impact of Foreign Bank Ownership in Developing Countries

Study	Sample Description, Study Period, and Methodology	Summary of Empirical Findings and Conclusions
Claessens, Demirgüç-Kunt, and Huizinga (2001)	Examine the extent of foreign ownership in 80 national markets over the period 1988–1995, and test whether net interest margins, costs, taxes paid, and profitability are different between domestic and foreign-owned banks.	Find that foreign banks achieve higher profits than domestic banks in developing countries, but exactly the opposite in developed markets. Regression results also suggest that an increase in foreign bank share leads to lower profitability for domestic banks.
Clarke, Cull, and Martinez Peria (2001)	Use survey data from over 4,000 borrowers in 38 developing and transition countries during 1999 to examine whether foreign-bank penetration reduces access to credit in developing countries.	Their empirical results strongly support the assertion that foreign bank penetration improves firms' access to credit. Borrowers in countries with high levels of foreign bank penetration tend to rate interest rates and access to long-term loans as lesser constraints on enterprise operations and growth than enterprises in countries with foreign penetration. The authors also find that the benefits of enhanced credit availability apply to small- and medium-sized businesses as well as large ones.
Majnoni, Shankar, and Várheggi (2003)	Study the dynamics of foreign bank ownership in Hungary using a sample of 26 commercial banks active in the period 1994–2000. By the end of the year 2000, foreign-controlled banks accounted for over two-thirds of total banking assets in Hungary.	Find that, after controlling for the nature of investment (greenfield versus acquisition), management style, and duration of ownership, foreign banks are pursuing a lending policy that does not differ significantly from domestic banks. Foreign banks are, however, able to achieve consistently higher profitability levels.

achieve consistently higher profitability levels. Bonin, Hasan, and Wachtel (2003) find significantly different results in their study of bank privatizations in six transition economies after 1994. Most of these sales were made to foreign strategic investors, and the authors find clear evidence that privatization improves performance and that foreign ownership is value maximizing for the acquired and greenfield banks.

In addition to the empirical studies discussed above, Clarke, Cull, Martinez Peria, and Sánchez (2003) survey the extant evidence on foreign bank entry in developing countries, while Berger (2003) performs a similar survey that also includes developed economies. Clarke, Cull, Martinez Peria, and Sánchez show that foreign ownership increased substantially in many developing countries between 1994 and 1999, and exceeded 30 percent of all banking assets in Peru, Venezuela, Argentina, the Czech Republic, Poland, Chile, and Hungary in 1999. In sum, the evidence clearly suggests that foreign bank ownership is efficiency enhancing—at least in developing countries—and may well be the default outcome for many national bank privatization programs.

The Future of Banking Privatization

As noted above, there were very few bank privatizations during 2003, and it is not clear if or when these sales will resume. Nonetheless, we believe that once these programs resume, there is reason to believe that the scale of new programs might rival that of the late 1990s.

What Do Governments Have Left to Sell?

Table 9.7 details the stakes in partially privatized banks that governments have left to sell. As we did in assessing the value of residual telecom stakes in chapter 8, we present either the market values of retained stakes, where available, or the last asset sale or SIP valuation in the far more frequent case where stock market prices are unavailable. As this table shows, the total estimated value of retained stakes is $64.3 billion, or a little less than one-half of what states have already raised through bank sales since 1986. Governments hold 19 stakes valued at $1 billion or more, with Italy's retained 73 percent stake in Banca Monte dei Paschi di Siena being the most valuable ($6.6 billion).

Of those countries that have already begun divesting bank assets, China and India probably have the most valuable retained stakes, since state banking has historically played such an important role in these two large countries and neither has really touched the core of the government-owned banking sector. On the other hand, table 9.7 does not include any estimate of the value of retained stakes of countries that have not yet begun privatizing their wholly-owned banks. This includes much of the Moslem world and many transition and nontransition developing countries. Thus, in one sense, the future of banking privatization is quite literally inestimable, but our reading of the historical record and plans expressed by many national governments suggests that the future could be very bright, indeed.

Country	Company	Fraction Retained, %	Approximate Value, US$ millions
Argentina	Banco de Santa Fe	10%	$ 6.4
Argentina	Banco Hipotecario	54	583
Australia	Bank of Queensland	60.4	132
Austria	Salzburger Sparkasse	30	81
Austria	Oberoesterreiche Hypo	51	165
Belgium	Credit Communal de Belgique	65.5	2,088
Belgium	ASLK-CGER	74.9	4,476
Bulgaria	United Bulgarian Bank	35	16
Bulgaria	Post Bank	21.77	11
Bulgaria	Express Bank	33	19
China	Bank of Shanghai	92	713
China	Bank of China	75	8,400
China	Pudong Development Bank	95	1,273
Colombia	Banco Corpavi	65.8	327
Colombia	Banco Ganadero	60	492
Colombia	Banco Popular	20	68
Czech Republic	Investicni a Postovni Banka (IPB)	64	145
Czech Republic	Ceskoslovenska Obchodni Banka (CSOB)	30.01	504
Czech Republic	Komercni Bank	32.8	971
Denmark	Girobank	49	106
Egypt	Cairo Barclays Bank	89	32
France	Credit Local de France	47.5	1,149
France	CIC	33	1,084
Germany	Deutsche Verkehrs—Kredit—Bank (DVKB)	75.1	103
Germany	Deutsche Siedlungs Landesrentenbank	52	261
Greece	Bank of Athens	33.33	14
Greece	General Hellenic Bank	35.5	48
Greece	Bank of Central Greece	44	46
Greece	National Bank of Greece	83.1	3,127
Greece	Ionian Bank	49	599
Greece	Commercial Bank of Greece	93.3	3,941
Guyana	National Bank of Industry	52.5	22
Hungary	Magyar Kulkereskedelmi Bank	58	127
Hungary	National Savings & Commercl Bank (OTP)	70	2,219
Iceland	Bunadarbanki	91.5	108
Indonesia	Bank Negara Indonesia	75	2,428
Israel	IDB Holding	57.5	474
Israel	Israel Union Bank	40	57
Israel	Israel Discount Bank	80.9	762
Israel	Bank Leumi	92.5	2,063
Italy	Istituto Bancario San Paolo	80%	$2,836
Italy	Istituto San Paolo di Torino	54	857
Italy	Banca Monte dei Paschi di Siena	73	6,587
Italy	Banca Regionale Europea	43.27	1,084
Kazakhstan	Turanalem Bank	28	39
Kenya	National Bank of Kenya	80	40
Korea	Citizens National Bank	90	2,376
Korea	Seoul Bank	30	300

Country	Company	Fraction Retained, %	Approximate Value, US$ millions
Korea	Woori Financial Group	88	3,177
Latvia	Latvijas Unibanka	77	33
Lithuania	Lithuanian Agricultural Bank	23.99	6
Macedonia	Stopanska Banka	45	14
Malta	Mid-Med Bank	32.9	123
Mongolia	Trade and Development Bank	24	4
Morocco	Credit-Eqdom	82	41
Norway	Fokus Bank	4	12
Pakistan	Habib Credit ad Exchange Bank	20	17
Pakistan	United Bank Limited	49	200
Poland	Bank Slaski	62.75	1,696
Poland	Export Development Bank	84.1	500
Poland	BPH	63.3	1,036
Poland	Bank Zachodni	20	145
Portugal	União de Bancos Portugues	38.9	106
Portugal	Banco Portugues do Atlantico	24.36	341
Romania	Banca Romana pentru Dezvoltare	59	288
Romania	Banc Post	58	59
Russia	Vneshtorgbank	79.9	1,200
Slovakia	Slovenska Sporitelna	13	52
Slovenia	Nova Ljubljanska Banka (NLB)	66	830
Thailand	Nakomthon Bank	25	106
Thailand	Radanasin Bank	24.98	55
Thailand	Bank Thai	59.8	215
Turkey	Sekerbank	90	36
Venezuela	Banco de Venezuela	10	38
Venezuela	Banco Republica	43.3	43
Venezuela	Banco Popular de los Andes	52.75	53
Zimbabwe	Comercial Bank of Zimbabwe	20	11
TOTAL			$64,326

Source: For publicly listed firms, value is determined based on the fractional retained holdings in appendix 1, times the total market value of these firms in the *Business Week* "Global 1000" or "Top 200 Emerging-Market Companies" listing of the world's most valuable companies as of May 31, 2003, presented in "The Business Week Global 1000," *Business Week* (July 14, 2003). If prices are unavailable from this source, we use the most recent sale price. For telecoms that were partially divested through an asset sale, value is computed based on the implied valuation from the last asset sale.

Note: This table details the size and approximate market value of the residual state holdings of telecommunications firms as of July 2003.

Summary

Bank privatizations are among the biggest challenges facing many governments around the world. The reluctance of states to remove themselves from the banking and credit systems is well documented, and the overall impact of state ownership on banking has been disastrous in almost every country where government ownership of banks has been pervasive. However, if the objective of a country is to establish a more efficient and market-oriented economy, reducing the influence of the state on credit allocation decisions is critically important. Perhaps the key lesson the articles surveyed here teach is that privatizing governments should completely divest their ownership in banks whenever and wherever it is politically feasible to do so.

In addition, the studies cited above show that privatization is associated with significant performance improvements in divested banks, though the extent of improvement varies by region and stage of national development. Privatization has resulted in clear performance improvements in OECD countries, as well as in the transition economies. In the transition economies, however, the beneficial results only emerged after the banks were sold to foreign strategic investors during the middle and late 1990s, usually after partial privatizations using vouchers had failed to improve performance owing to continued government intervention in bank lending policies. The record on bank privatization in nontransition developing countries is much more mixed. In general, privatization improves bank performance, but this usually occurs only after painful trial and error and when a majority (preferably all) of the bank's shares are sold to a strategic (preferably foreign) investor via an asset sale. In general, share issue privatizations of banks do not seem to be successful outside of OECD countries.

The studies surveyed in this paper lead us to conclude that a series of very important issues and questions must be addressed in order for bank privatization to be successful. Some, if not most, of these issues do not come into the equation in nonfinancial privatizations. For bank privatization to be successful in any country, a series of steps should be taken to establish a viable banking system. These steps include the following:

- Full privatization is best, but if the government does retain partial ownership, there must be assurances that it will act only as a passive investor. This is essential to prevent the continuation of past credit-allocation decisions made by the government, usually on some political or central-planning basis.
- Effective methods of dealing with bad loans prior to and/or during the privatization process are essential. This problem is especially severe in situations where uncollectible loans are outstanding to state-owned enterprises (SOEs).
- It is essential to eliminate the culture and propensity of banks to lend to these SOEs after privatization, especially in economies with large remaining concentrations of state enterprises.
- A bank regulatory system must be developed that is sufficiently independent from political influence. This is essential for effective bank examination, supervision, and monitoring. Financial reporting systems must also be developed that allow for transparency, especially with regard to asset quality and true profitability.
- Governments should avoid setting up 100 percent deposit insurance schemes for privatized banks, since the well-documented moral hazard

problems these guarantee problems create are also severe in a privatized banking system.
- Finally, and perhaps most controversially, governments may well need to emphasize sales to foreign banks in order to attract badly needed capital, expertise, technology, and financial legitimacy.

Privatization Industry Studies

Energy and Airlines

Along with telecoms and banking, the two major industries that have accounted for the largest number and highest value of privatizations over the past quarter-century are oil and gas companies and electric utilities. These four industries collectively account for almost $900 billion of the total $1.25 trillion or so that governments have raised through asset sales and public share offerings since 1977. This chapter examines the privatization histories and regulatory regimes adopted for these two energy industries, as well as for a third, national airlines. Although airlines are much less important in terms of aggregate proceeds or number of sales, these are arguably the most internationally visible of all privatizations. While only a nation's citizens or visitors will experience the service provided by most state-owned enterprises, the entire population of international air travelers will likely observe a nation's airline, and a sizable fraction will actually experience that carrier's service.

We also present estimates of the value of retained government stakes in firms in these three businesses. While this exercise is inherently difficult and can generate approximate valuations at best, even these are striking. For example, we find that while governments have raised about $300 billion through sales of oil and gas, electricity, and airline companies since 1977, their retained stakes in partially privatized companies are worth almost the same amount. This means that these governments have roughly as much left to sell as they have already sold. However, the value of fully state-owned electricity, and particularly oil and gas, companies is far higher. Though we do not prepare a detailed estimate of the value of fully state-owned electric utilities, these are certainly worth at least $100 billion, and perhaps far more. We estimate the value governments could raise through an aggressive privatization of the national oil companies of OPEC and non-OPEC countries using three different valuation methods. The lowest estimate obtained is $1.45 trillion, and the highest is $3.21 trillion—more than twice as much as governments have raised through all types of privatizations over the past quarter-century!

This chapter examines the privatization experiences of each of these industries in turn. The first section details the history of oil and gas sales by governments, and presents our estimates of the value of retained government stakes, as well as the value of national oil companies that remain wholly state-owned. The second section provides a similar treatment of electric utility privatizations, though this section also delves much more deeply into the regulatory challenges that arise naturally when governments decide to sell off operating companies in their electric service industries. The final section describes the history of airline privatizations and assesses the (fairly dreadful) current and likely future prospects for further sales of state-owned airlines.

Privatizing Oil and Gas Companies

After telecommunications, the most valuable state-owned enterprises to be privatized during the past quarter-century have been oil and gas companies. Firms such as British Petroleum (now BP Amoco), France's Total and Elf Acquitaine (now Total Elf Fina), Spain's Repsol, Norway's Statoil, and Italy's ENI all are among the 100 most valuable (highest market capitalization) companies in the world. However, by far the largest and most important oil and gas companies remain wholly state owned. These are the national oil companies (NOCs) of the nine members of OPEC, as well as such key non-OPEC producers as Mexico, Oman, and Malaysia. With the one potentially decisive exception of Iraq, none of these countries is currently even contemplating the privatization of its NOC. However, this could well change over time, as the generally dismal economic performance of "petro states" becomes undeniable and the amount of money these countries could raise becomes apparent. Though we do not predict when the OPEC countries will begin selling off their NOCs, we believe that this will eventually occur, and present defensible estimates of the value that governments could raise by divesting their wholly state-owned NOCs.

The History of State Ownership of National Oil Companies

In terms of economic theory, it may seem strange that so many countries have opted for national ownership of oil and gas (O&G) companies. After all, petroleum is the most widely traded and international of all commodities, it is produced on every continent (and ocean), and it is consumed in even the poorest nations. The refining and trading of petroleum products has no natural monopoly aspects, and the global market is so competitive that oil trading does not require regulation. The transport and retail distribution of natural gas is usually considered a natural monopoly, and thus the sale of gas distributors does require development of an appropriate regulatory framework prior to transfer from state to private ownership. However, this is one of the easier utilities to regulate owing to the competitive nature of gas production, the transparent nature of the distribution system, and the fact that the product is regularly traded and priced in competitive international markets.

Of course, the reason so many oil-producing states have in fact chosen state ownership lies not with economic theory but with political ideology and power politics. Several of the governments of oil-producing states that are members of OPEC have always owned their NOCs. Those that allowed Western-owned oil companies to operate within their territories nationalized these operations soon after the Arab oil embargo during the Yom Kippur War of 1973 resulted in a quadrupling of world oil prices. This price increase fundamentally shifted the balance of power in the global oil industry from consumers, represented by oil companies, to producers and gave the members of OPEC an extremely powerful incentive to exercise political control over joint production levels and prices. The second oil shock following the Iranian revolution in 1978–1979 tripled prices again, further strengthening OPEC's bargaining position and increasing the cartel's incentive to control production and prices.

Non-OPEC oil-producing states also exhibited mixed ownership of the primary oil companies operating in their territory prior to the first oil price shock. Most, however, followed the strategy of Mexico, which nationalized Western (principally American) oil interests during the 1930s and thereafter enshrined purely domestic ownership of the country's oil "patrimony" in the nation's constitution and politics. Of all the extractive industries, none has quite so much historical baggage as does petroleum, and many oil-producing countries have painful memories (some real, some imagined) of Western exploitation of petroleum resources. Once these nations achieved independence from colonial rule, almost all opted for state ownership of their oil companies, and most organized these as monopoly NOCs. The shift in the balance of power resulting from Oil Shocks I and II gave non-OPEC governments the same incentives as their OPEC counterparts to exercise political control over oil production and prices in order to guard against a sharp price decline. This game was even more fun for the non-OPEC governments, however, since they were generally able to produce at maximum output levels, since OPEC could usually be counted on to take the necessary actions to restrict output and prop up prices. Non-OPEC governments were thus able to free-ride on OPEC's production limitation actions.[1]

In spite of the manifest benefits to oil-producing countries that resulted from state ownership of NOCs, and the attendant political control of prices, the costs of state control became increasingly burdensome over time. Although the NOCs could not help but operate at a profit, most were grossly inefficient and overstaffed, and the (politically logical) monopoly over production operations was almost always extended as well to domestic refining and distribution. Given the innate profitability of NOCs, governments tended to treat them as national kitty banks that could be raided for the bulk of national tax revenues, as well as for off-balance sheet funding. The financial burdens imposed by these policies meant that NOCs were often unable to fund expensive exploration and development projects with internally generated funds, and their intimate ties to national governments restricted the NOC's access to global capital markets. Additionally, almost all governments with state-owned NOCs maintained domestic prices for petroleum products at artificially low levels, thus encouraging wasteful consumption and dissipating the gains achievable through an export maximization policy. Finally, the NOCs lacked the technological expertise of Western oil companies, and the protectionist investment policies made it difficult to attract Western technology through co-production deals and joint ventures.

Thus far, the (perceived) benefits of state ownership of NOCs in major oil-exporting developing countries have outweighed the costs, and only one of these countries has broken ranks to allow even partial foreign ownership in its oil industry. Russia is the only emerging-market oil exporter to have privatized its oil industry, and even here foreigners were effectively excluded from the divestment process.[2] Nonetheless, the Russian experience has proved instructive, since the privatized companies have thus far pointedly refused to participate in OPEC's production limitation schemes, and instead appear intent on ramping up their production and export sales as rapidly as the nation's oil infrastructure will allow.

In contrast to the general attitude of developing country oil exporters, Western governments have enthusiastically embraced privatization of their national oil companies. As in so many other areas, Britain led the way, first by privatizing British Petroleum and Britoil in stages from 1977 to 1987, and then by fully divesting Enterprise Oil and British Gas during the mid-1980s. Shortly thereafter, Spain began restructuring its hydrocarbon processing industry and sold its first tranche of Repsol in May 1989, and completed this divestment in 1997. According to Arocena (2003), the Spanish government's intent was to create a single large, integrated company able to compete on a global scale. During the 1990s, several other countries followed the British lead, including Canada, France, Italy, and most important of all, the major oil exporting nation of Norway. These sales are described below.

The Record on Privatizing National Oil and Gas Companies

Table 10.1 presents a listing of oil and gas company privatizations from the first British Petroleum share offering in June 1977 through July 2003. As we did previously with telecoms and banking sales, we group the SIPs and asset sales by country and in chronological order. We document 161 sales, which raised $137.26 billion in all. The 79 SIPs raised $101.77 billion, or an average of $1.29 billion each, while the 82 asset sales raised $35.49 billion for divesting governments, averaging $432.8 million apiece.

Several of these sales merit specific comment. As noted above, the sequential sales of British Petroleum—at progressively higher per share prices—not only raised some $14 billion for the U.K. government, but the final $12.43 billion offering in October 1987 was one of the ten largest share offerings in history and was executed even as the U.S. stock market was experiencing its worst crash ever. Though several underwriters lost money on this BP offering, it was completed successfully. Britoil was also sold in separate tranches, but by June 1984 the British government was confident enough, and trusted by investors enough, to sell its entire ownership in Enterprise Oil in a single offering. With the $8.01 billion SIP

TABLE 10.1. Oil and Gas Privatizations

Country	Company	Date	Amount (US$ Millions)	Method of Sale	Fraction Sold
Argentina	Yacimientos Petroli-feros Fiscales (YPF)	Jun 93	$2,660	SIP	45.3%*²
Argentina	Transportadora de Gas del Sur*	May 94	$520	SIP	27%
Argentina	Metrogas*	Nov 94	$130	SIP	20%
Argentina	YPF*	Jan 99	$2,010	Asset sale	14.99%
Argentina	YPF*	Jul 99	$842	Asset sale	5.3%
Australia	GFE Resources*	Aug 95	$42	Asset sale	100%
Australia	Power Net	1997	$1,887	Asset sale	—
Australia	Dampler-Bunbury Gas Pipeline*	Mar 98	$1,619	Asset sale	100%
Australia	Kinetik Energy/Westar*	Feb 99	$1,000	Asset sale	100%
Australia	Energy ZI / Stratus*	Mar 99	$1,300	Asset sale	100%
Australia	Ikon Energy/Multinet*	Mar 99	$1,100	Asset sale	100%
Australia	TPA*	Mar 99	$600	Asset sale	100%
Australia	Alinta Gas	Jul 00	$187.8	Asset sale	45%ᵇ
Australia	Alinta Gas	Oct 00	—	SIP	55%
Austria	OMV	Dec 87	$117	SIP	15%
Austria	OMV*	May 94	$427	Asset sale	20%
Austria	OMV*	May 96	$393	Asset sale	14.9%
Austria	OMV*	1996	$393	SIP	—
Austria	Energie Steiermark (Es-tag)*	1997	$488	Asset sale	—
Belgium	Distrigaz*	1994	—	Asset sale	67%
Belgium	Distrigaz*	Jun 96	$104	SIP	16.62%
Bolivia	YPFB*	1996	$835	Asset sale	—
Bolivia	Gualberto Villarroel/ Guillermo Elder Bell*	Nov 99	$102	Asset sale	100%
Brazil	Petroflex	Apr 92	$222	SIP	89%
Brazil	Petroquimica Uniao*	Jan 94	$272	Asset sale	40.5%
Brazil	CEG (and its Riogas subsidiary)*	1997	$576	Asset sale	—
Brazil	COMGAS*	1997	$70.9	Asset sale	—
Brazil	Petrobras	Aug 97	$534	SIP	—
Brazil	Comgas	Apr 99	$992	Asset sale	52.7%*ᵈ
Brazil	Petrobras	Aug 00	$4,030	SIP	24.2%
Bulgaria	Neftochim	Oct 99	$101	Asset sale	58%ᵉ
Canada	Petro Canada	Jul 91	$478	SIP	19.5%
Canada	Petro Canada	Nov 92	$198	SIP	10.5%
Canada	Petro Canada	Sep 95	$1,170	SIP	50%
Canada	Alberta Energy Com-pany	May 93	$355	SIP	—
China	Petro China	Apr 00	$2,980	SIP	10%
China	Sinopec	Oct 00	$3,470	SIP	—
China	China National Off-shore Oil Comp (CNOOC)	Feb 01	$1,400	SIP	27.5%
China	Sinopec	Aug 01	$1,400	SIP	—
Colombia	Promigas*	1996	$101	Asset sale	—

Country	Company	Date	Amount (US$ Millions)	Method of Sale	Fraction Sold
Colombia	Gas Natural*	1997	$160	Asset sale	39%[f]
Czech Republic	Litvinov and Kralupy*	Jul 95	$173	Asset sale	49%
Czech Republic	Unipetrol	1997	—	SIP	37%
Czech Republic	Transgas	May 02	$3,700	Asset sale	97%[g]
Czech Republic	Unipetrol	May 03	$271	Asset sale	63%[h]
Egypt	Misr Petroleum Processing*	Jul 98	$105	SIP	34.3%
Estonia	Estongaz*	1995	$4	Asset sale	—
Estonia	Esoil*	1996	$10	Asset sale	—
Estonia	Estongaz*	1997	$5.6	Asset sale	—
Finland	Fortum	Dec 98	$573	SIP	22%
Finland	Fortum	Jan 02	$403	SIP	9%
France	Elf Acquitaine	Sep 86	$493	SIP	11%
France	Elf Acquitaine	Jun 91	$440	SIP	2%
France	Elf Acquitaine	Mar 92	$367	SIP	2.3%
France	Total SA	Jul 92	$906	SIP	19%
France	Elf Acquitaine	Feb 94	$6,823	SIP	38%
France	Total SA	Feb 96	$621	SIP	6%
France	Elf Acquitaine	Nov 96	$2,000	SIP	9.1%
Germany	Berliner Gaswerke (Gasag)*	Feb 98	$866	Asset sale	51.2%
Greece	Hellenic Petroleum	Jun 98	$311	SIP	23%
Hungary	Primagaz Hungaria Industrial Comm.*	1993	$19	SIP	—
Hungary	DEGAZ*	1995	$23	Asset sale	—
Hungary	KOGAZ*	1995	$67	Asset sale	—
Hungary	MOL	Nov 95	$153	SIP	28.3%
Hungary	DEGAZ*	1996	$85	Asset sale	—
Hungary	DDGAZ*	1996	$52	Asset sale	—
Hungary	EGAZ*	1996	$84	Asset sale	—
Hungary	FOGAS*	1996	$129	Asset sale	—
Hungary	KOGAZ	1996	$67	Asset sale	—
Hungary	TIGAZ	1996	$172	Asset sale	—
Hungary	MOL	May 97	$304	SIP	19.3%
Hungary	MOL	Mar 98	$300	SIP	11%
India	Indian Oil	Nov 95	—	SIP	10%
Israel	Naphta Petroleum Corporation*	Nov 93	$49	SIP	35.5%
Israel	Naphta Petroleum Corporation*	1993	$70	SIP	57%
Israel	Lapidot Oil Exploration*	Jan 96	$8	Asset sale	58.9%
Israel	Naphta*	Jul 96	$16	Asset sale	44.1%
Israel	Lapidot Oil Exploration*	1996	$8	Asset sale	—
Italy	Liquipibigas and CGL	Mar 94	$160	Asset sale	100% + 35%
Italy	ENI	Nov 95	$3,907	SIP	15%

(continued)

TABLE 10.1. (continued)

Country	Company	Date	Amount (US$ Millions)	Method of Sale	Fraction Sold
Italy	Saipem	Aug 96	$85.6	SIP	—
Italy	ENI	Oct 96	$5,864	SIP	14%
Italy	ENI	Jul 97	$7,800	SIP	18%
Italy	Agip Servizi*	1997	$36	Asset sale	—
Italy	Saipem*	Mar 98	$634	SIP	26%
Italy	ENI	Jun 98	$6,740	SIP	15.4%
Italy	Acegas	Feb 01	$143	SIP	41.8%
Italy	Snam Rete Gas	Dec 01	$1,800[i]	SIP	—
Jamaica	Petrojam*	1996	$68	Asset sale	—
Kazakhstan	Yuzhneftegaz	1996	$120	Asset sale	—
Latvia	Latvian Gas	1997	$48.7	Asset sale	—
Lithuania	Mazheikiu Nafta	Oct 99	$150	Asset sale	33%[j]
Macedonia	OKTA	Sep 99	$190	Asset sale	54%[k]
Malaysia	Petronas Gas	Sep 95	$1,443	SIP	25%
Montenegro	Jugapetrol Kotor	Oct 02	$105.5	Asset sale	54.33%[l]
Morocco	Shell-Maroc*	1993	$47	Asset sale	—
Morocco	Societe Petrole du Maghreb (Petrom)*	1993	$15	Asset sale	—
Morocco	SAMIR (oil refinary)*	Mar 96	—	SIP	31.11%
Morocco	SAMIR/SCP	Oct 98	$39	Asset sale	67.7% + 73.9%
New Zealand	Petrocorp	Jul 87	$75	SIP	18%
Norway	Statoil	Jun 01	$2,900	SIP	20%
Peru	Petroleos del Mar (Petromar)*	1993	$200	Asset sale	100%
Peru	Petrolera Transoceanica*	1993	$25	Asset sale	100%
Peru	Refineria de Ilo*	Apr 94	$69	Asset sale	100%
Peru	La Pampilla (Petroperu)	Jun 96	$181	Asset sale	60%
Peru	Petrolube	Aug 96	$18.9	Asset sale	100%
Philippines	Petron*	1993	$502	Asset sale	40%
Philippines	Petron	Aug 94	$400	SIP	21.5%
Poland	Polgaz*	1993	$40	Asset sale	70%
Poland	Polski Koncern Naftowy (PKN)	Nov 99	$513	SIP	31%
Poland	PKN	Jon 00	$520	SIP	36%
Portugal	Petrogal	Jun 92	$279	SIP	25%
Portugal	Petrogal*	1995	$265	Asset sale	—
Russia	Lukoil-Kogalym	Apr 94	$318	Asset sale	—
Russia	Lukoil Holding	Apr 94	$293	Asset sale	—
Russia	Purneftegaz	Apr 94	$187	Asset sale	—
Russia	Noyabrskneftegaz	May 94	$442	Asset sale	—
Russia	Gazprom	Jun 94	$228	Asset sale	—
Russia	Megionneftegaz	Jun 94	$222	Asset sale	—
Russia	Nizhnevartovskneftegaz	Jun 94	$168	Asset sale	—
Russia	Lukoil*	1995	$320	SIP	—

Country	Company	Date	Amount (US$ Millions)	Method of Sale	Fraction Sold
Russia	East Siberian Oil and Gas (VSNK)*	1996	$8	Asset sale	—
Russia	Yukos*	1996	$23	Asset sale	—
Russia	Gazprom	Oct 96	$430	SIP	—
Russia	VSNK*	1997	$19.8	Asset sale	—
Russia	Eastern Oil Company	1997	$875	Asset sale	—
Russia	Tyumen Oil Company*	1997	$820	Asset sale	—
Russia	Slavneft*	1997	$39.3	SIP	—
Russia	Onako	Sep 00	$1,080	Asset sale	85%[m]
Russia	Slavneft	Dec 02	$1,860	Asset sale	37.5%[n]
Russia	Lukoil	Dec 02	$775	SIP	5.9%
Singapore	Singapore Petroleum Corp.	Oct 90	$58	SIP	—
Slovakia	Slovnaft	Jul 95	$112	SIP	20%
Slovakia	Slovnaft	1997	$11.1	Asset sale	—
Slovakia	SPP	Jul 02	$2,700	Asset sale	49%[o]
Spain	Repsol	May 89	$1,140	SIP	26.6%
Spain	Repsol	Apr 93	$952	SIP	13.3%
Spain	Enagas	Jun 94	$410	Asset sale	91%
Spain	Repsol	Apr 95	$1,600	SIP	19%
Spain	Repsol	Feb 96	$1,100	SIP	11%
Spain	Repsol	Apr 97	$1,170	SIP	10%
Spain	Gas Natural	Dec 96	$284	SIP	3.8%
Sri Lanka	Colombo Gas Company Ltd.*	1995	—	Asset sale	51%
Sri Lanka	Lanka Lubricants Ltd.*	1996	—	SIP	39%
Sweden	OK Petroleum*	Mar 94	$830	Asset sale	100%
Thailand	PTT Exploration and Production	Jun 93	$52	SIP	15%
Thailand	PTTEP*	Jun 98	$112	SIP	10%
Thailand	PTT	Nov 01	$725	SIP	—
Thailand	Bangchak Petroleum	Jun 94	$128	SIP	20%
Turkey	Turpas	Apr 00	$1,200	SIP	31.5%
Turkey	POAS	Aug 00	$1,260	Asset sale	51%[q]
Turkey	POAS	Mar 02	$183	SIP	16.5%
Turkey	Petkim	Jun 03	$605	Asset sale	89%[r]
United Kingdom	British Petroleum	Jun 77	$972	SIP	17%
United Kingdom	Britoil	Nov 82	$911	SIP	51%
United Kingdom	British Petroleum	Sep 83	$849	SIP	7%
United Kingdom	Britoil	Aug 85	$582	SIP	49%
United Kingdom	Enterprise Oil	Jun 84	$524	SIP	100%
United Kingdom	British Gas	Dec 86	$8,012	SIP	100%
United Kingdom	British Petroleum	Oct 87	$12,430	SIP	31.4%
Zambia	Refined Oil Products (ROP)*	1995	$4	Asset sale	—
Total			$137,262.20		

(continued)

TABLE 10.1. *(continued)*

Table Summary

Method of Sale	Number of Transactions	Value (US $Million)
SIP	79	101,771.90
Asset sale	82	35,490.30
Total	161	137,262.20

Source: Most of the data presented here is from the *Financial Times* and/or the FT.Com Web site, but other ources are employed as well. In particular, sales marked with an asterisk are taken from various issues of *Privatisation International* (1998–2000) and *Privatisation International Yearbooks* (1998–2001).

Note: This table presents key information about oil and gas privatizations executed by governments around the world. The "method of sale" refers to whether the company was divested via a share issue privatization (SIP) or asset sale.

[a] All of the state's remaining shares were distributed to state governments, an employee trust fund and pensioners after the sale.

[b] Stake sold by State of Western Australia to consortium of Utilicorp (U.S.) and United Energy (Australia).

[c] Stake sold to Tractebel and Belgian government retained a golden share.

[d] Stake (52.7% of cash flows, 63.8% of voting rights) sold to consortium of British Gas and Royal Dutch/Shell.

[e] Sold to Lukoil (Russia), which also promised to invest $403 million in modernizing facilities.

[f] Stake sold to Enron (U.S.).

[g] Stake sold to RWE Gas (Germany).

[h] Letter of intent for sale of stake to PKN Orlen (Poland) and Agrofert (Czech Republic) in late May 2003.

[i] Proceeds received by parent company, ENI, rather than Snam Rete Gas or the Italian government.

[j] Controlling stake sold to Williams Company (U.S.) in a very controversial deal.

[k] Stake sold to consortium led by Hellenic Petroleum.

[l] Sold to Hellenic Petroleum in exchange for $65 million payment, $5.5 million to cover social security taxes, and a promise to make $35 million of new investments.

[m] Sale to Tyumen Oil Company (Russia).

[n] Asset sale of 50% of government's controlling 75% stake in a controversial, noncompetitive auction.

[o] Stake sold to consortium of Ruhrgas (Germany) and Gas de France.

[p] Stake sold to Shell Investments B.V.

[q] Stake sold to Turkish consortium.

[r] Sold to Standard Kimya (Turkey) in a televised auction.

of 100 percent of British Gas in December 1986 and the October 1987 BP offering, the British government completed the sale of all of its holdings in major oil and gas companies.

France was the next major Western country to begin divesting its state-owned oil companies. The government sold Elf Acquitaine in six tranches, beginning in September 1986 and ending in November 1996. France also fully divested its holdings in Total SA in two offerings, with the second occurring in early 1996. These eight share offerings raised $11.65 billion for the French state, but more important, the privatization of these two companies created a powerful new force in the global petroleum industry. Shortly after their full privatization, Total and Elf Acquitaine merged to form a company called TotalElf, and then a few years later this company acquired Belgium's PetroFina to create TotalElfFina. This is now the world's fourth largest publicly traded oil company in terms of sales, and third largest in terms of market capitalization. The French government actively supported these mergers as a way to create a national champion with the heft to compete toe-to-toe with the international oil giants.

This strategy of growth through mergers was also pursued by the Spanish and Italian national champions. Repsol SA, which was privatized by the Spanish government in a series of five tranches between May 1989 and April 1997, acquired Argetina's YPF and several other smaller companies in quick succession. Repsol YPF quickly established itself as a key player in the second tier of the global petroleum industry, ranking eighth among publicly traded companies in terms of both sales and market value. Given that Repsol had been created by the Spanish government only during the late 1980s out of several disparate companies, and that Spain had no history as a competitor in the world oil industry, this was a remarkable achievement. Italy began selling its much more valuable national oil company ENI in November 1995. The four ENI tranches raised an impressive $24.31 billion for the Italian state in less than four years, and ENI also began acquiring stakes in other petroleum companies. Given its late start, however, ENI today finds itself much more of a potential target than a potential acquirer. Despite the fact that the company's sales of $56.36 billion during 2002 and market value of $64.58 billion in May 2003 place it respectively in seventh and sixth place among publicly traded petroleum companies, the Italian government has refrained from divesting its remaining 36.9 percent stake in ENI, principally out of fear that the company would be acquired by one of the global giants very shortly thereafter.

During the transition period after the fall of the Berlin Wall in 1989, the governments of central and eastern Europe began selling off their state-owned oil and gas companies. A handful of these sales were executed via SIPs, including Hungary's MOL (three tranches) and Poland's PKN (two tranches), but most of the privatizations involved asset sales to Western or Russian operators. Control of Russia's vast oil and gas sector was passed to private ownership through a series of complex, frequently nontransparent asset sales that included the notorious "loans for shares" program in 1994. This scheme gave the insiders who were allowed to participate in the bidding control over companies with immense potential value in exchange for relatively tiny cash sums. For example, a controlling stake in Gazprom, the world's largest producer of natural gas, was sold for a mere $228 million. Later Russian oil and gas privatizations, such as the $1.08 billion sale of Onako to Tyumen Oil Company, were conducted using somewhat more transparent methods, but the December 2002 auction of a controlling stake in Slavneft was widely considered a noncompetitive insider deal—despite being conducted in a televised auction with all the trappings of transparency [Jack (2002)].

The most important oil and gas privatizations of the past five years have involved two countries, Norway and China. Norway's sale of 20 percent of Statoil through a SIP that raised $2.90 billion in June 2001 was significant because of Norway's position as a major producer and exporter of North Sea oil and gas. Further sales of Statoil shares are planned, though it remains unclear whether the Norwegian government is willing to allow its holdings to drop below 50 percent. Finally, after restructuring its hydrocarbon sector into one principal offshore and two main onshore producing companies during the 1990s, China began selling minority stakes in these three companies in 2000. The government raised $9.16 billion through two SIPs of shares in Sinopec and one offering each in PetroChina and CNOOC.

Oil and Gas Privatization's Future: The Value of Residual Stakes in Partially Divested Firms

Despite the impressive list of full and partial privatizations of NOCs described above, the international oil and gas business remains the most state controlled of all global industries, since none of the truly key players has been even partially divested. All of the NOCs of the nine OPEC members remain 100 percent state owned, and this is also the case for the NOCs of most of the other major oil-exporting developing countries. Additionally, only a few of the major non-OPEC oil and gas companies have been fully privatized, so governments still retain sizable (and valuable) stakes in NOCs that they can and probably will continue selling off over the next several years. Table 10.2 presents the actual market value of the retained stakes in these partially privatized companies as of May 2003. We attempt the much more difficult task of estimating the market value of those NOCs that remain wholly state owned in the next section.

Column eight of table 10.2 shows that governments retain stakes in partially privatized NOCs worth more in total, $173.95 billion, than what they have raised through all previous sales ($137.26 billion). In other words, even those governments that have already begun selling NOCs have more to sell than they have sold thus far. Several of the remaining stakes are strikingly large, particularly Italy's retained 36.9 percent holding in ENI, worth $23.83 billion, and the Chinese government's 77.4 percent residual stake in Sinopec, worth $27.64 billion in May 2003. The Indian government has sold only a small fraction of its NOC, Oil and Gas Natural, and so its residual 84.1 percent stake is worth over $12 billion at current market prices. Other noteworthy residual holdings include China's 72.5 percent stake in CNOOC (worth $8.32 billion), Brazil's 32 percent holding in Petrobras (worth $6.54 billion), and Italy's majority stake in Snam Rete Gas, worth $4.52 billion.

Two other features of the data presented in table 10.2 bear explicit mention. First, this estimate of the value of retained state ownership is almost surely biased low, both because we do not include several of the oil companies headquartered in Russia, Kazakhstan, Ukraine, and other former Soviet republics, since we were unable to conclusively determine the fraction of equity retained by the state, and because we present values only for companies partially divested through public share offerings. In other words, we do not include estimated market values of retained stakes in oil and gas firms that were partially divested using an asset sale. The total market value of all fully and partially privatized oil and gas companies, $652.8 billion in May 2003, also clearly shows how important these sales have been both as a source of revenue for divesting governments and in developing global stock markets.

Oil and Gas Privatization's Future: Valuing Wholly State-Owned OPEC and Non-OPEC Companies

As important as the retained stakes in partially divested companies are, the future of oil and gas privatization—and perhaps of privatization itself—will be based on

TABLE 10.2. Total Market Values of Retained Government Stake in Fully and Partially Privatized Oil and Gas Companies

Company Name	Country	Total Market Value, 5/30/03 US$ Millions	P/E Ratio	Proven Petroleum Reserves, YE 2000 Million Barrels	Crude Oil Production Average, Year 2000 mmbpd	Government Retained Ownership %	Market Value of Retained Government Stake, US$ Millions
BP	Great Britain	$153,240	32.7	7,643	1,928	0	0
Total	France	$103,779	13.7	6,950	1,433	0	0
ENI	Italy	$64,576	12.0	3,553	748	36.9%	$23,829
Repsol YPF	Spain	$19,299	8.4	2,378	636	0	0
Statoil	Norway	$19,139	7.6	1,994	733	80%	$15,311
BG Group	Great Britain	$15,657	22.6	—	—	0	0
Petro Canada	Canada	$10,003	9.3	414	95	20%	$2,001
Snam Rete Gas	Italy	$7,565	14.9	—	—	59.77%	$4,522
Fortum	Finland	$6,635	8.5	—	—	61%	$4,047
Petro China	China	$43,512	7.7	11,032	2,091	90%	$39,161
Gazprom	Russia	$42,731	-134.1	7,215	198	40%	$17,092
Sinopec	China	$35,696	9.6	2,552	676	77.42%	$27,636
Yukos	Russia	$28,186	9.2	11,769	986	3.6%	$1,015
Petrobras	Brazil	$20,435	4.5	8,356	1,324	32%	$6,539
Lukoil Holdings	Russia	$15,659	8.5	14,280	1,557	14%	$2,192

(continued)

359

TABLE 10.2. (continued)

Company Name	Country	Total Market Value, 5/30/03 US$ Millions	P/E Ratio	Proven Petroleum Reserves, YE 2000 Million Barrels	Crude Oil Production Average, Year 2000 mmbpd	Government Retained Ownership %	Market Value of Retained Government Stake, US$ Millions
Oil & Gas Natural	India	$14,478	10.2	5,478	534	84.11%	$12,177
Surgutneftegaz	Russia	$11,876	52.5	6,992	813	No data	—
CNOOC	China	$11,481	10.3	—	—	72.5%	$8,323
SASOL	South Africa	$7,814	6.6	—	—	No data	—
Indian Oil	India	$5,905	9.6	—	—	53%	$3,130
Petronas Gas	Malaysia	$3,605	24.2	—	—	75%	$2,704
MOL	Hungary	$2,904	8.6	—	—	28.7%	$833
Tatneft	Russia	$2,451	7.1	—	—	31.31%	$767
PTT Exploration and Production	Thailand	$2,218	7.7	—	—	70%	$1,553
Naftowy Orlen	Poland	$2,065	18.2	—	—	28%	$578
Tupras	Turkey	$1,909	15.7	—	—	68.5%	$1,308
TOTAL		$652,818					$173,951

Note: This table presents the estimated market value (in US$ millions) of retained government holdings in 4 fully and 22 partially privatized national oil companies, as of August 2003. The first two columns present the company name and country of origin, while the third and fourth columns present the total market value of the company as of May 31, 2003 and the price-earnings ratio (P/E ratio) implied by this valuation and current-year net profits, as presented in the *Business Week* "Global 1000" or "Top 200 Emerging Market" listing of the world's most valuable companies (*Business Week*, July 14, 2003). Columns 4 and 5 detail the proven petroleum reserves (in millions of barrels) for each company and the average daily crude oil production (in thousands of barrels per day, mbpd) during the year 2000, as presented in "Le Classement Annuel de PIW met en Evidence L'Emergence d'un Nouveau Groupe 'Major,' " *Le Bulletin de L'Industrie Petroliere* (19 December 2001), pp. 1–3. The government's retained stake is from the SIP appendix to this book or from the company's listing in *Hoover's Handbook of World Business 2003* (Hoover's, Inc., Austin, TX, 2003), and the estimated market value is this fraction times the total market value.

whether and when governments of major oil exporting countries begin privatizing their wholly state-owned NOCs. In this section, we try to determine how much revenue these governments could raise from an aggressive and complete sale of their NOC holdings. Unfortunately, since none of these firms is publicly traded, and (surprisingly) we were unable to locate a formal valuation estimate on any publicly accessible database, we must estimate their values indirectly. We develop three different valuation measures for this task, and the inputs to this process and our results are presented in table 10.3.

Our first valuation method assumes that global oil companies are valued as a multiple of their proven petroleum reserves, while the second and third methods compute market value as a multiple of annual oil production and estimated annual profits, respectively. The third column of table 10.3 presents the proven reserves of wholly state-owned NOCs in the nine OPEC countries and in seven key non-OPEC exporting countries as of year-end 2000. Column 4 presents the average daily production for all of these NOCs during 2000, while column 5 presents the market price of the Reference Crude Oil of each country in August 2003. We use year 2000 values for reserves and production since these better represent "equilibrium levels" than do more recent figures, which were distorted first by global recession and then by the run-up to the Second Iraq War and its aftermath. Note that we use only proven petroleum reserves and production levels in our valuation estimates, since we do not have comparable data on the natural gas reserves and production levels of these NOCs. Clearly, the value of gas reserves and production would be significant in many cases, and this fact alone suggests that our valuation estimates may be biased low.

To compute reserve and production multiples we use the data for the fully and partially privatized, publicly traded petroleum companies presented in table 10.2. Year 2000 oil reserves and production data are available for 14 of the companies listed in table 10.2, and the stock market values each barrel of proven reserves at $9.12, on average. While this might be a defensible multiple to use for valuing the reserves of wholly-owned NOCs, we feel a better multiple is the $4.03 per barrel average value-to-reserve ratio computed using only the eight companies in developing and emerging markets (excluding the Western multinational oil companies). Since an international investor buying into the privatization of an OPEC or non-OPEC national oil company in the Middle East, Latin America, or East Asia would be accepting a significant amount of political risk, including a high risk of expropriation, it seems more reasonable to use a lower average value-to-reserve multiple. The estimated market values computed using proven reserves are detailed in column 6 of table 10.3.

Even using this "conservative" value-to-reserve multiple, however, we end up with an eye-popping $3.21 trillion estimated value for government holdings in the NOCs of the nine OPEC and seven non-OPEC nations detailed in table 10.3. Based on its reserves, Saudi Arabia's Aramco is alone worth over $1 trillion, and the nine OPEC national oil companies are collectively worth $3.04 trillion since they hold the vast bulk of the world's proven reserves. The only non-OPEC company with large proven reserves, Mexico's Pemex, would be valued by this method

TABLE 10.3. Estimated Market Values of Fully State-Owned National Oil Companies (NOCs)

Company Name	Country	Proven Petroleum Reserves, Year 2000 Million Barrels	Average Daily Production Year 2000 mbpd	Reference Price for Barrel ($) August 2003	Estimated Market Value of Government Stake		
					Multiple of Reserve Valuation Method US$ Millions	Multiple of Daily Production Method US$ Millions	Capitalization of Estimated Profits US$ Million
OPEC countries							
Aramco	Saudi Arabia	261,698	8,602	$25,58	$1,054,643	$376,705	$401,571
INOC	Iraq	112,500	2,597	$26.03	$453,375	$113,730	$123,370
KPC	Kuwait	96,500	1,653	$26.66	$388,895	$72,389	$80,426
NIOC	Iran	89,700	3,787	$26.03	$361,491	$165,843	$179,900
PDVSA	Venezuela	77,685	3,295	$27.51	$313,071	$144,297	$165,428
ADNOC	Abu Dhabi	53,790	1,350	$27.92	$216,774	$59,120	$68,788
Libya NOC	Libya	23,600	1,336	$27.49	$95,108	$58,507	$67,026
NNPC	Nigeria	13,500	1,312	$28.40	$54,405	$57,456	$68,001
Qatar Petroleum	Qatar	13,200	858	$26.66	$53,196	$37,574	$41,746
Sonatrach	Algeria	8,740	1,336	$28.02	$35,222	$58,507	$68,318
Pertamina	Indonesia	4,000	970	$26.95	$16,120	$42,479	$26,142

Non-OPEC countries							
Petroecuador	Ecuador	3,402	259	$25.19	$13,710	$11,343	$11,907
PDO	Oman	3,080	538	$26.68	$12,412	$23,560	$26,196
Petronas	Malaysia	2,640	529	$28.67	$10,639	$23,166	$27,679
Syrian Petroleum	Syria	1,500	300	$26.77	$6,045	$13,138	$14,657
Ecopetrol	Colombia	1,464	443	$25.19	$5,900	$19,400	$20,365
EGPC	Egypt	1,450	398	$25.95	$5,844	$17,429	$18,849
Pemex	Mexico	28,260	3,450	$27.40	$113,888	$151,085	$172,517
TOTAL					$3,210,737	$1,445,728	$1,582,885

Note: This table represents the estimated market value (in US$ millions) of government holdings in 17 wholly state-owned national oil companies, as of August 2003. The first two columns present the company name and country of origin, while the third and fourth columns detail the proven petroleum reserves (in millions of barrels) for each company and the average daily crude oil production (in thousands of barrels per day, mbpd) during the year 2000, as detailed in "Le Classement Annuel de PIW met en Evidence L'Emergence d'un Nouveau Groupe 'Majors,'" *Le Bulletin de L'Industrie Petroliere* (19 December 2001), pp. 1–3. Column 5 presents the world market price for the nation's "Reference" crude oil as of August 1, 2003, as listed in Table 13, "World Crude Oil Prices" of the U.S. Department of Energy's *Weekly Petroleum Report*, Energy Information Agency's (Washington, D.C.), as presented on the Web site www.eia.doe.gov/pub/oil_gas/petroleum. The last three columns present estimated market values (in US$ million) computed three ways: (1) as a multiple of reserves, (2) as a multiple of annual production, and (3) as a capitalized stream of earnings [a perpetuity], assuming a 50 percent net profit margin on all production, stable production rates, and a 10 percent required rate of return.

at $113.9 billion, while the remaining six non-OPEC companies have market values of between $5.8 billion and $13.7 billion.

Our second valuation method multiplies the year 2000 annual production levels of each of the wholly owned NOCs in table 10.3 by $119.98. This is the value computed by dividing the market value of each of the 13 publicly traded oil companies in table 10.2 by its respective annual production rate in barrels, and then averaging the results. We delete Gazprom from this calculation, since it is primarily a gas producer and produces only 198 thousand barrels of petroleum per day (72.27 million barrels per year), yet has a market capitalization of almost $43 billion. On the other hand, we use all the remaining petroleum companies to compute our average multiple, since the average ratios for Western companies and for companies headquartered in developing countries are much more similar than was the case for reserve ratios.

The estimated values of each of the wholly-owned NOCs, computed using annual production levels, are detailed in column 7 of table 10.3. These differ from the values computed using reserve measures in two principal ways. First, the total estimated value of government holdings, $1.45 trillion, is less than half that computed using reserves. Phrased differently, valuing these companies using a "flow" measure (annual production) yields a significantly lower figure than does valuing the companies using a "stock" measure (proven reserves). Second, it is perhaps not surprising to observe that companies such as Nigeria's NNPC, Indonesia's Pertamina, and all of the non-OPEC producers, which have relatively high production levels but low levels of proven reserves, are valued more highly using production multiples than they were using reserve multiples. On the other hand, companies that have reserves equal to many years' worth of production, such as Aramco, Kuwait's KPC, and Abu Dhabi's ADNC, have much lower estimated values when production multiples are employed rather than reserve multiples.

Our third valuation method, capitalization of earnings—also known as the discounted cash flow, or DCF valuation method—is probably the most defensible theoretically and is the valuation method any finance professional would prefer to use whenever possible. The DCF method involves generating an estimated stream of future net profits for each NOC, and then determining the present value of that earnings stream by discounting each expected future cash flow using an appropriate risk-adjusted discount rate. Unfortunately, in order to generate overall valuations with any accuracy, one must not only estimate the entire future stream of sales revenues but also predict what the net profit margins will be on those sales. Predicting future sales revenues is notoriously difficult for any particular national oil company, and estimating operating profits is problematic since few NOCs voluntarily disclose profitability data. Therefore, we are once more forced to use fairly crude parameter estimates in our valuation formulas.

Specifically, we must estimate four variables for each company: (1) the expected path of output for the foreseeable future; (2) the expected path of prices for each company's output in the future; (3) the net profit margin earned by the company on each barrel of sales; and (4) the appropriate risk-adjusted discount rate for each NOC. As a first approximation, we assume that sales will remain at their year 2000 levels indefinitely for each NOC, that per-barrel prices received by each company will remain at their August 2003 levels for the foreseeable future, that each NOC has and will maintain a 50 percent net profit margin on all crude oil produced, and that 10 percent is an appropriate risk-adjusted discount rate (RADR) for each company. With these assumptions, we can generate the valuation estimates presented in column 8 of table 10.3.

It should come as no surprise that the valuations developed using the discounted cash flow (DCF) technique are quite similar to those generated previously using the multiple of sales method, since both techniques use current output levels as one of the primary inputs into the valuation formulas. The overall estimated value of wholly state-owned NOCs increases to $1.53 trillion, but the DCF valuations for most companies are comparable to (though higher than) those generated as a multiple of output. However, the principal sources of bias are quite different. Whereas the multiple of sales method yields high valuations for companies with high output levels and low levels of reserves, and the multiple of reserves method does exactly the opposite, the DCF method assigns too low a value to NOCs such as Aramco with lower than average production costs and assigns excessively high valuations to NOCs such as Nigeria's NNPC or Indonesia's Pertamina that have higher than average production costs. Whereas Aramco's net profit margin is almost certainly higher than 50 percent, the margins of NNPC and Pertamina are probably much lower. On balance, however, a 50 percent profit margin seems appropriately conservative, as does a 10 percent RADR, so there does not appear to be a systematic bias in our valuation formula.

So which, if any, of these three valuations is most accurate? Stated differently, how much could the 16 OPEC and non-OPEC governments in our list actually obtain from a comprehensive privatization program involving the complete divestment of government ownership in currently wholly state owned national oil companies? In all likelihood, these governments could probably raise between $1.5 trillion and $2.5 trillion over a period of perhaps a decade through a competently designed and executed privatization program. Of course, today it is inconceivable that any of these governments (except perhaps Iraq) might be willing to consider even partially privatizing its NOCs, much less selling it off entirely. It is also difficult to believe that international investors would initially be willing to pay top dollar for shares in any company as exposed to re-nationalization risk as these NOCs would be, especially if state ownership was to be reduced below 50 percent.

On the other hand, anyone predicting in 1977 that European governments would raise almost $1 trillion, and drastically reduce state holdings in nationalized industries, over the next quarter-century would have seemed mad. The fact remains that almost all of the 16 OPEC and non-OPEC nations discussed above have long underperformed other developing countries economically, and most of these governments are plagued by structural financial problems. By raising economic efficiency and filling the state's coffers, privatization of the national oil company could both remedy the government's financial problems and raise the long-run growth rate of the nation's economy. Even the skepticism of international investors could be overcome through careful sequencing of sale tranches, with small initial share offerings targeted at domestic investors being followed only much later by large global offerings—after governments had established their reputations as protectors of shareholder rights. Though history suggests that "politics trumps economics" in the normal course of political life, we think that the financial opportunity discussed above will prove too tempting for the citizens of oil-exporting countries to ignore. Specifically, we believe that governments will raise at least $1 trillion over the next 15 years through the sale of (first minority, then majority) stakes in what are now wholly state-owned NOCs. By 2019, the global petroleum business will be much larger and much more privately owned than anyone believes possible today!

Privatizing Electricity Utilities

Although both oil and gas companies and electric utility companies are primarily concerned with the processing and distribution of energy, the industrial structures of the two industries could hardly be more different. Whereas oil and gas is a truly global commodity business, many parts of the electric service industry (ESI) are natural monopolies within specific geographic areas, and the generation, transmission, and retail distribution of electric power is regulated (or owned) by the state in every major country. Any government that is considering privatizing some or all of its national ESI must therefore make a series of decisions regarding whether to restructure the industry before divestment, and how to regulate the privatized components. Getting the regulatory regime right is particularly important, since economic and technical regulation must balance the interests of producer and consumer and give the newly privatized companies the incentive to make large new investments to modernize and expand their businesses.

The Industrial Structure of National Electric Supply Industries

The industrial structure of every national electric service industry (ESI) is essentially the same, though key aspects of the industry can differ fundamentally, especially regarding the ownership and regulatory structure of the industry and the mix of generation units employed to produce electric power. Every ESI has three basic components, and the characteristics of each sector are described in table 10.4.

The first component is generation. Electricity can be generated on an industrial scale in several different ways and using several different fuels — including coal, natural gas, heavy and light fuel oil (petroleum products), hydro and wind energy, and most controversially, nuclear power. Even moderate-sized countries will have dozens of individual generating plants, and some larger nations will have several hundred. The plants are typically dispersed throughout the country, and most are located outside of metropolitan areas (especially the newer plants). Since the individual plants were built at different times, using different generations of production technology, a nation's generation "system" is usually much more akin to a collection of individual plants rather than a seamlessly integrated network. Regardless of what generation technology is used, however, electric power is a pure commodity, so no producer can charge a premium for product quality dif-

TABLE 10.4. Functional Structure of the Electric Services Industry

Function	Key Economic Characteristics	Implications
Generation	Limited scale economies at plant level Coordination economies at system level Complementary with transmission	Potentially competitive
Transmission	Network externalities In general not a natural monopoly Large sunk costs	Investment incentives need special attention One grid but possibly several owners
Distribution	Often a natural monopoly Large sunk costs	No competition
System operation	Monopoly (due to technical constraints)	No competition
End user supply	Limited scale economies No special features	Potentially competitive

Related services:
  Power exchanges
  Financial contracts
  Construction and maintenance of assets
	No special features	Potentially competitive

Source: Table 1 of International Energy Administration and Organization of Economic Cooperation and Developments (2001).

ferences. Furthermore, since electricity cannot be efficiently stored, it must be consumed as it is produced, so no producer can charge a premium for reliability of supply.

Because of these technological characteristics, the generating sector of a nation's ESI is not a natural monopoly and so can be structured as a competitive business. In fact, the generation sector is already competitive in many countries, especially OECD members. In countries where generation is currently organized as a monopoly, competition can usually be introduced by restructuring the sector into multiple smaller companies and by designing a market structure that ensures that the new firms must compete. However, while restructuring the generating sector is technically and administratively feasible, it is also hard to get the economics right, since it will be difficult to ensure that the mix of plants in the newly created business units are similar enough in terms of production efficiency to survive competition.

Once electricity is generated, it must be transmitted—often over extended distances—to local substations, where the high-voltage power is reduced to the level required by industrial, commercial, and residential customers. The transmission network is a large, expensive, technically sophisticated network that must be operated as a single integrated grid. Large and ongoing capital investments are also required to maintain, modernize, and expand the network. Since it would be economically wasteful to duplicate such a network, transmission is considered a classic natural monopoly, where only a single provider is rational for any given geographical area. The network's coordinating entity must also balance electricity supply and demand and allocate costs among different producers. For all these reasons, most countries have only a single entity owning and operating the transmission network. An especially large country might have multiple transmission operators, but even in this case each operator will have a monopoly within its own (typically large) geographic region.

The final sector of a nation's ESI is distribution, the delivery of electric power to industrial, commercial, and residential customers. Since distribution involves the use of the physical grid to deliver electricity to final users, this segment has characteristics of a natural monopoly. On the other hand, because many of the tasks involved in obtaining, metering, billing, and servicing electricity customers rely more heavily on information technology and marketing skills than on electrical systems engineering, several parts of transmission can be competitive. It is particularly easy to structure wholesale distribution as a competitive business, since industrial and commercial electricity consumers have the technical expertise and financial incentive to negotiate on equal terms directly with the transmission company (or even with individual producers). The only effective method of injecting competition into the retail distribution business is through regulation mandating that companies not affiliated with the transmission company be given access to the network's "final mile" of wires connecting electrical substations directly to residences on the same terms afforded to transmission company affiliates. Some countries go further and prohibit transmission companies from owning a distribution company.

In sum, the technology of electric power generation, transmission, and distribution does not impose any single structure on a nation's ESI. While generation is, or can be made to be, inherently competitive, transmission is a natural monopoly for all but the geographically largest countries—and is organized as a series of regional monopolies even in these. While distribution is, or can be made to be, innately competitive for large electricity users, it is more difficult to structure retail distribution as a competitive business, though this can be achieved with proper regulation. It is therefore not surprising to observe great heterogeneity in the organizational and ownership structures of electric power industries around the world.

The Organizational and Ownership Structures of Different National ESIs

Great Britain represents one extreme on the industrial and ownership spectrum, having fully privatized all segments of its ESI over the past 14 years, and also having injected a great deal of competition into the generation and distribution sectors. The regulatory authority set up to oversee the U.K. electricity industry has been remarkably innovative, and the "British experiment" has proved highly influential for other countries seeking to restructure their ESI to become more competitive.[3] Britain has led the way in many areas of electricity deregulation and privatization, and as a result consumers have enjoyed falling real prices. Spain has also restructured and fully privatized its ESI, while Germany, Portugal, Italy, and several other continental European countries have restructured and partially privatized key segments of their ESIs. Most western European nations have begun opening their electricity markets to foreign producers, as required by EU regulations. Table 10.5 describes the current industrial and ownership structures of the world's 25 largest electricity markets, based on electricity produced during the year 2001.

Electric power has traditionally been a provincial/state responsibility in Australia and Canada, so both countries have decentralized networks. However, these countries differ significantly with respect to competition and ownership. Two of the largest Australian states privatized key segments of their grids during the late 1990s, and most other states have announced plans to follow suit. Substantial competition is also allowed in generation. On the other hand, Canada's ESI remains state owned (by regional governments), and only limited steps toward deregulation have so far been attempted. There are no announced plans for privatization.

The world's largest electricity market, the United States, demonstrates a surprising mixture of state and private ownership in all segments of its ESI. There are several hundred American electric utilities, and while most of the industry is privately owned, every level of government is involved in generation, transmission, and distribution. The federal government generates power through its network of hydroelectric power plants, and interstate electricity transmission is regulated by the Federal Electricity Regulatory Commission (FERC). Many smaller electric utilities are owned and operated by states and municipalities, while larger companies are owned by large, publicly traded holding companies. States are generally responsible for regulating generation and distribution, but there is considerable regulatory overlap and divided responsibility. Though America's ESI has traditionally been considered one of the world's most efficient, this assumption was shaken by the massive power failure that plunged much of the northeastern United States and eastern Canada into darkness in August 2003. It is unclear what impact this blackout will have on the structure of America's electric power regulatory system, but there is little chance of the blackout prompting a large-scale privatization program. The peculiarities of the industry's financing, particularly the heavy use of tax-favored municipal bond financing, largely precludes municipalities from selling off their government owned facilities.

The national government has traditionally played a leading role in developing electric power industries in developing countries, and this is reflected in the current ESI structures of the larger emerging market ESIs described in table 10.5. China's rapidly growing electric power industry is still dominated by state-owned monopolies in generation, transmission, and distribution, though several state enterprises are allowed to generate power and the country is actively encouraging foreign private investment in the generation sector. Generation and transmission in Brazil are state-owned monopolies, and are not slated for privatization. Distribution is mostly in private hands, though Brazil's recent economic difficulties have caused severe financial difficulties for the private operators. Financial problems have also had a devastating impact on India's attempts to expand and modernize

TABLE 10.5. Current Ownership and Market Structure of Electric Service Industries (ESIs) in the World's Largest Electricity Markets

Rank	Country	Electricity Generation in Terawatt-Hours (2001)	Current Ownership and Market Structure of Electric Utility Companies
1	United States	3,968	Mixture of private (shareholder) and municipal (state and local) ownership of electric power generation, transmission, and distribution.
2	China	1,478	State-owned monopoly in generation, transmission, and distribution, but some SOEs have been partially privatized and sector is being restructured to promote competition.
3	Japan	1,075	Privately owned but heavily regulated, and a large fraction of generation comes from nuclear plants. Japan has by far the highest electricity rates in OECD.
4	Russian Federation	890	Electricity market dominated by partially privatized (52% retained state ownership) United Energy Systems (UES), which controls 70% of Russia's distribution system. Breakup and restructuring of UES planned.
5	Canada	582	Mostly state-owned by provincial governments, which historically have been responsible for providing electricity. Some regional governments have implemented limited deregulation.
6	Germany	571	Almost fully privatized, competitive and open to foreign entry, but generation still dominated by four "super-regional" companies.
7	India	562	Though private ownership allowed in generation, transmission is monopolized by state electricity boards (SEBs), which are in very poor financial condition. Electricity demand far outstripping supply.
8	France	550	Electricite de France (EdF) is the last major state-run electricity monopoly in the EU. Wholesale market liberalized. EdF privatization planned 2004 but labor opposition, nuclear power reliance are problematic.
9	United Kingdom	384	Fully privatized, competitive, and open to foreign entry. RPI-X regulatory model adopted after privatization in early 1990s has been widely emulated around the world.
10	Brazil	326	Generation and transmission remain state owned and not slated for privatization. Distribution is mostly private, but recent economic problems have caused severe financial difficulties for private operators.
11	South Korea	311	Historically one of the fastest growing markets. State-owned KEPCO currently a near monopoly, but firm has been partially privatized and government plans to restructure ESI.
12	Italy	280	ENEL partially privatized (66% remains state owned) and market being progressively opened to domestic and foreign competition according to EU timetable.
13	Spain	237	Former state-owned monopoly has been broken up and almost fully privatized. Market being opened to foreign and domestic competition faster than required by EU.

14	South Africa	210	Parastatal Eskom accounts for 95% of generation, and also dominates transmission and distribution. No plans to privatize Eskom yet announced.
15	Australia	208	Electricity traditionally a state responsibility and states have varied widely in extent to which they have privatized. Victoria and South Australia have already fully privatized and most others are doing so.
16	Mexico	206	State-owned Federal Electricity Commission (CFE) has enjoyed an electricity monopoly for decades, though limited liberalization has occurred since 1992. Reform proposals proposed but not enacted.
17	Taiwan	188	State-owned Taipower dominates all aspects of ESI. Legislation to privatize Taipower proposed but not yet passed. Firm would retain transmission/distribution monopoly, but generation assets would be broken up.
18	Ukraine	172	State-owned ESI burdened by heavy debt and old equipment. Partial privatization of generators begun in 1998, but halted by presidential decree in 2001. Sales to resume soon; heavy reliance on nuclear a problem.
19	Sweden	162	Electricity is generated and traded in a competitive market, but transmission is still a regulated monopoly. No announced privatization plans.
20	Poland	146	Traditionally state-owned monopoly, but limited market opening allowed from 1998. Full privatization and market opening planned as preparation for EU accession.
21	Saudi Arabia	135	State-owned but recently corporatized. Privatization being considered, and government is promoting a restructuring of ESI to separate generation, transmission and distribution. Demand growing 4.5%/year.
22	Iran	127	Apparently state-owned monopoly, with no announced plans for liberalization or privatization. Demand growing 7% per year, so significant capacity increases lately. Nuclear program causing major tensions.
23	Turkey	123	Until recently, one of the fastest growing electricity markets. TESI controls 91% of ESI, but pressure on Turkey to privatize. New law to break-up, privatize TEAS passed 2001 but not yet implemented.
24	Norway	122	State-owned Statkraft dominates ESI and no announced plans to privatize. Norway has one of the world's highest per capita electricity consumption rates, and 99% of electricity comes from hydroelectric plants.
25	Indonesia	112	Independent power producers (IPPs) allowed limited access to market during mid-1990s, but 1997 Crisis halted expansion and left state-owned distributor PLN with massive debts. Liberalization restarted in 2002.
26	Thailand	101	Generation open to competition, but distribution apparently a monopoly of state-owned EGAT. Asian financial crisis forced a slowdown in new construction, but state-owned generators partially privatized.

Source: The primary data source for this table is the "Country Analysis Briefs" Web site operated by the U.S. Department of Energy's Energy Information Administration (http://www.eia.doe.gov/cabs/).

Note: This table describes the current ownership and regulatory structure of the companies generating, transmitting, and distributing electricity in the world's 26 largest electricity markets (those generating at least 100 terawatt-hours in 2001).

its ESI. Competition and foreign investment is allowed—indeed encouraged—in India's generation and distribution sectors, but transmission is a monopoly of the state electricity boards. These boards are virtually bankrupt, and because they control all transmission networks, foreign and domestic investors have been very reluctant to build new generating capacity or to modernize distribution systems. Unfortunately, it is hard to see how this impasse will be broken any time soon, since political and financial difficulties preclude the privatization of the state electricity boards, and investment in other sectors will not increase as long as the boards are unreliable purchasers or suppliers of electric power.

At the other extreme of the ownership and organizational spectrum, France has the most centralized and state-dominated ESI in the developed world. Although wholesale distribution has been liberalized, state-owned Electricite de France (EdF) retains a monopoly on almost all other generation, transmission, and distribution activities. In spite of intense pressure from the EU, France adamantly refused to allow foreign producers to sell power in its home market until very recently. This caused considerable friction with France's neighbors, since EdF has aggressively pursued a strategy of international acquisitions since the mid-1990s. In addition to having the last remaining large state-owned electricity monopoly in the EU, France stands out because of its heavy reliance on nuclear power for over two-thirds of its electricity needs.[4] This, plus opposition from trade unions, has complicated the French government's plans to privatize EdF in the near future. Even though a complete sale of EdF could raise as much as $40 billion, this is unlikely to occur until the issue of who will be liable for decommissioning nuclear reactors is resolved.

The Record on Privatizing National ESIs

Although the discussion above might suggest that very little ESI privatization has occurred, this is far from true, as we discuss in this section. Table 10.6 presents a listing of ESI privatizations between June 1986 and July 2003. We document 136 sales, which raised $129.12 billion. The 49 SIPs raised $75.54 billion, or an average of $1.54 billion each, while the 85 asset sales raised $53.22 billion for divesting governments ($626.1 million apiece).

An interesting feature of ESI privatization is that divestments began much later than in most other industries. The first ESI privatization we find is the sale of 40 percent of Germany's Viag through public share offering in June 1986, which was followed by a second tranche of the remaining 60 percent in May 1988. Spain sold a small stake in its newly reorganized electric utility Endesa in May 1988, but this was considered a one-off sale at the time, rather then the beginning of full-scale divestment. Austria was next, with a share offering of a 49 percent stake in Verbund in November 1988, and a second public offering of EVN the next year. Korea also sold a stake in its ESI during the 1980s, raising $2.1 billion through a SIP of a 21 percent stake in Korea Electric Power in June 1989.

As in many other industries, Britain emerged as a privatization leader when it sold off 12 regional electricity distribution companies in a massive SIP in De-

TABLE 10.6. Electric Utility Privatizations, 1986–2003

Country	Company	Date	Value (US$ Million)	Method of Sale	Stake Sold (%)
Argentina	Edesur*	1995	$390	Asset sale	—
Argentina	Edenor*	1996	$157	Asset sale[1]	—
Argentina	Edemsa*	Jun 98	$237	Asset sale	51%
Australia	Loy Yang B Power Station*	Jan 93	$1,010	Asset sale	40%
Australia	United Energy*	Aug 95	$1,150	Asset sale	100%
Australia	Solaris Energy*	Nov 95	$700	Asset sale	100%
Australia	Eastern Energy*	Nov 95	$1,532	Asset sale	100%
Australia	Powercor Australia*	Nov 95	$1,589	Asset sale	100%
Australia	Citipower*	Nov 95	$1,179	Asset sale	100%
Australia	Yallourn Energy*	Mar 96	$1,876	Asset sale	100%
Australia	Hazelwood*	Aug 96	$1,830	Asset sale	100%
Australia	Loy Yang B*	Apr 97	$782	Asset sale	49%
Australia	Loy Yang A	Apr 97	$3,800	Asset sale	100%
Australia	Powernet Australia*	Oct 97	$2,000	Asset sale	100%
Australia	Southern Hydro*	Nov 97	$273	Asset sale	100%
Australia	Kinetik Energy/Westar*	Feb 99	$1,000	Asset sale	100%
Australia	Ikon Energy/Multinet*	Mar 99	$1,100	Asset sale	100%
Australia	Energy 21/Stratus*	Mar 99	$1,300	Asset sale	100%
Australia	ETSA Utilities/ETSA Power	Jan 00	$1,973	Asset sale	—
Australia	Optima Energy	May 00	$183	100-yr lease	—
Australia	Synergen	May 00	$20	Asset sale	—
Australia	Flinders Power	Aug 00	$180	100-yr lease	—
Austria	Verbund	Nov 88	$153	SIP	49%
Austria	Energie-Versorgung Niederös-terreich (EVN)	Nov 89	$125	SIP	—
Austria	Burgenland Holdings*	Dec 93	$5	Asset sale	30%
Austria	Kelag*	Feb 95	$178	Asset sale	32.15%
Austria	Estag	Dec 97	$450	Asset sale	25.1%[2]
Bolivia	ELFEC*	Aug 95	$50.2	Asset sale[3]	—
Brazil	Light*	May 96	$2,271	Asset sale	55.8%
Brazil	Enersul	Nov 97	$565[4]	Asset sale	—
Brazil	Companhia Paulista de Forca e Luz (CPFL)	Nov 97	$2,700	Asset sale	57.6%[5]
Brazil	Coelba*	May 98	$235	Asset sale	—
Brazil	Eletropaulo Metropolitana*	Apr 98	$1,780	Asset sale	74.88%
Brazil	COELCE*	Apr 98	$867	Asset sale	89.77%
Brazil	Gerasul*	Sep 98	$801	Asset sale	42%
Brazil	Bandeirante*	Sep 98	$859	Asset sale	74.8%
Brazil	Companhia Paranaese de Energia (COPEL)*	Jun 99	$138	SIP	5.96%
Brazil	Cesp Parapanema	Aug 99	$685	Asset sale	—
Brazil	Celb*	Nov 99	$46	Asset sale	83.72%
Brazil	Cesp Tiete*	Nov 99	$469	Asset sale	38.66%
Canada	Nova Scotia Power	Aug 92	$675	SIP	—
Canada	Alberta Energy Corp.	May 93	$355	SIP	—
China	Shandong Huaneng Power	Aug 94	$337	SIP	27%
China	Huaneng Power International	Oct 94	$650	SIP	25%
Colombia	Chivor*	1996	$625	Asset sale	100%[6]

(continued)

TABLE 10.6. (*continued*)

Country	Company	Date	Value (US$ Million)	Method of Sale	Stake Sold (%)
Colombia	Betania*	1996	$489	Asset sale	99%[7]
Colombia	Termotesajero*	1996	$19	Asset sale	57%[8]
Colombia	Termocartagena*	1996	$27	Asset sale	100%[9]
Colombia	Empresa de Energia de Bogota Condesa, Emqesa*	Sep 97	$2,181	Asset sale	48.5%
Colombia	Empresas de Energia del Pacifico*	1997	$550	Asset sale	57%[10]
Colombia	Codensa*	1997	$1,085	Asset sale	49%[11]
Colombia	Emgesa*	1997	$951	Asset sale	49%[12]
Colombia	Transelca*	1998	$142	Asset sale	65%[13]
Colombia	Electrocosta/Electrocaribe*	1998	$1,030	Asset sale	65%
Dominican Republic	Dominican Electricity Company	99	$750	Asset sale	50%[14]
El Salvador	CLESA (formerly part of CEL)*	Jan 98	$109	Asset sale	79.66%
El Salvador	Delsur (formerly part of CEL)*	Jan 98	$180	Asset sale	75.47%
El Salvador	CAESS and EEO (formerly part of CEL)*	Jan 98	$297	Asset sale	82%
France	Societe Nationale d'Electricite et de Thermique (SNET)	Nov 00	$327	Asset sale	30%[15]
Georgia	Telasi	98	$25	Asset sale	75%[16]
Germany	VIAG	Jun 86	$327	SIP	40%
Germany	VIAG	May 88	$877	SIP	60%
Germany	OBK*	May 98	$72	Asset sale	25%
Germany	Stadtwerke Leipzig (SWL)*	May 98	$237	Asset sale	40%
Greece	Public Power Corp	Dec 01	$417	SIP	16%
Greece	Public Power Corp	Dec 02	$360	SIP	13.2%
Guatemala	Guatemalan Electric Company*	Aug 98	$520	Asset sale	80%
Guyana	GEC*	Jul 98	$24	Asset sale	50%
Guyana	Guyana Electricity Corp	Sep 99	$23	Asset sale	50%[17]
India	Orissa Power Generation Corporation*	Jun 98	—	Asset sale	49%
Italy	AEM Milan	Jul 98	$900	SIP	49%
Italy	ACEA*	Jul 99	$970	SIP	49%
Italy	ENEL	Nov 99	$18,900	SIP	34.5%
Italy	AEM Torino	Nov 00	$263	SIP	29.9%
Italy	Elettrogen	Jul 01	$2,297	Asset sale[18]	—
Korea	Korea Electric Power	Jun 89	$2,100	SIP	21%
Korea	Korea Electric Power	Oct 94	$300	SIP	21%
Korea	Korea Electric Power	Mar 99	$750	SIP	5%
New Zealand	Contact Energy	Mar 99	$636	Asset sale	40%[19]
New Zealand	Contact Energy	May 99	$583	SIP	60%
Nicaragua	Dissur and Disnorte	Sep 00	$115	Asset sale	95%[20]
Panama	Chiriqui/Metro Oeste*	Oct 98	$212	Asset sale	51%
Panama	Noreste*	Oct 98	$90	Asset sale	51%
Panama	Bahia las Minas	Nov 98	$92	Asset sale	51%[21]
Panama	Fortuna	Nov 98	$118	Asset sale	49%[22]
Panama	Chiriqui and Bayano	Nov 98	$92	Asset sale	49%[23]
Panama	Distribution companies	Sep 98	$301	Asset sale[24]	—
Peru	Edelnor*	Jul 94	$176	Asset sale	60%
Peru	Edelsur*	Jul 94	$212	Asset sale	60%

Country	Company	Date	Value (US$ Million)	Method of Sale	Stake Sold (%)
Peru	Cahua*	Apr 95	$42	Asset sale	60%
Peru	Edegel*	Oct 95	$524	Asset sale	60%
Peru	Ventanilla*	Dec 95	$120	Asset sale	60%
Peru	Egenor Peru*	96	$228	Asset sale	60%
Peru	Luz del Sur	Nov 96	$200	SIP	30%
Peru	Electro Sur Medio*	Feb 97	$51	Asset sale	90%
Peru	Electro Norte; Electro Noroeste; Electro Centro; Electro Norte Medio	Dec 98	$146	Asset sale	—
Poland	Bedzin Heat and Power*	Dec 98	$3	Asset sale	25%
Poland	Patnow-Adamow-Konin*	Mar 99	$90	Asset sale	20%
Poland	Titasz/Dedasz*	Oct 99	$20	Asset sale	—
Portugal	Electricidade de Portugal	Jun 97	$2,100	SIP	30%
Portugal	Electricidade de Portugal	Jun 98	$2,720	SIP	18%
Portugal	Galp	Jan 00	$976	Asset sale	33%[25]
Senegal	Senelec	99	$65	Asset sale	34%[26]
Slovakia	Three Electricity Distributors	May 02	$450	Asset sale	49%[27]
Spain	Gas y Electricidad de Espana	Nov 86	$61	SIP	38%
Spain	Endesa	May 88	$750	SIP	—
Spain	Endesa	May 94	$1,050	SIP	11%
Spain	Endesa	Oct 97	$4,500	SIP	34%
Spain	Endesa	Jun 98	$8,000	SIP	33%
Spain	Red Electrica Espanola	Jul 99	$349	SIP	35%
Sweden	C 4 Energi*	Apr 98	$7	Asset sale	—
Thailand	Electricity Generating Co (EGCO)	Jan 95	$178	SIP	50%
Thailand	Egcomp*	Jul 98	$241	Asset sale	14.9%
Thailand	Ratchaburi Electricity Generating Holding	Nov 00	$67	SIP	55%
Ukraine	Rivenoblenergo	May 01	$23	Asset sale	75%[28]
Venezuela	Sistema Isla de Margarita Nueva Esparta (SENE)*	Sep 98	$90	Asset sale	70%
United Kingdom	Eastern Electricity Plc	Dec 90	$1,249	SIP	100%
United Kingdom	East Midlands Electricity Plc	Dec 90	$1,010	SIP	100%
United Kingdom	London Electricity Plc	Dec 90	$1,010	SIP	100%
United Kingdom	Manweb Plc	Dec 90	$550	SIP	100%
United Kingdom	Midlands Electricity Plc	Dec 90	$969	SIP	100%
United Kingdom	Northern Electric Plc	Dec 90	$570	SIP	100%
United Kingdom	Norweb Plc	Dec 90	$800	SIP	100%
United Kingdom	SEEBORD Plc	Dec 90	$589	SIP	100%
United Kingdom	Southern Electric Plc	Dec 90	$1,249	SIP	100%
United Kingdom	South Wales Electricity Plc	Dec 90	$470	SIP	100%
United Kingdom	South Western Electricity	Dec 90	$570	SIP	100%
United Kingdom	Yorkshire Electricity Group	Dec 90	$959	SIP	100%
United Kingdom	Scottish Power	May 91	$2,933	SIP	100%
United Kingdom	Scottish Hydro-Electric	May 91	$1,380	SIP	100%
United Kingdom	National Power	Mar 91	$2,278	SIP	60%
United Kingdom	National Power	Mar 95	$3,657	SIP	40%
United Kingdom	Powergen	Mar 91	$1,395	SIP	60%

(*continued*)

TABLE 10.6. (*continued*)

Country	Company	Date	Value (US$ Million)	Method of Sale	Stake Sold (%)
United Kingdom	Powergen	Mar 95	$2,543	SIP	40%
United Kingdom	British Energy	Jul 96	$2,200	SIP	77.75%
UAE	Power and desalination plant	Jun 98	$280	Asset sale	40%[29]
TOTAL			$129,118.20		

Table Summary

Method of Sale	Number of Transactions	Value (US $ Million)
SIP	49	$75,536
Asset sale	85	$53,219.20
100-year lease	2	$363
TOTAL	136	$129,118.20

Source: Most of the data presented here are from the *Financial Times* and/or the FT.COM Web site, but other sources are employed as well. In particular, sales marked with an asterisk are taken from various issues of *Privatisation International* (1998–2000) and *Privatisation International Yearbooks* (1998–2001).

Note: This table presents key information about electric utility privatizations executed by governments around the world between 1986 and 2003, though the data are more complete from 1994 onward. The method of sale refers to whether the company was divested via a share issue privatization (SIP) or asset sale.

[1] Sold to Electricite de France.

[2] Sold by Austrian state of Styria to Electricite de France.

[3] Sold to EMEL S.A.

[4] Purchase price paid by Brazilian utility much higher than expected.

[5] Stake sold to consortium of Brazilian utilities.

[6] Sold to Chilgener (Chile).

[7] Sold to Endesa (Spain).

[8] Sold to company's employees.

[9] Sold to Houston Industries (U.S.) and Electricidad de Caracas (Venezuela).

[10] Sold to Endesa (Spain), Enersis, and Chilectra (Chile).

[11] Sold to Endesa (Spain).

[12] Sold to ISA.

[13] Sold to Houston Industries (U.S.) and Electricidad de Caracas (Venezuela).

[14] Distribution and generation facilities separated prior to sale.

[15] Sale to Endesa (Spain) reduces stake held by French SOEs from 100% to 70%.

[16] Sold to AES Energy (U.S.).

[17] Stake sold to Anglo-Irish consortium.

[18] Sold to Spanish-Italian consortium of Endesa (Spain), BSCH (Spain), and the Brescia municipal services company (Italy).

[19] Stake sold to Edison Mission (U.S.).

[20] Controlling stake sold to Union Fenosa (Spain). Remaining 5% retained by employees.

[21] Generator company stake sold to Enron (U.S.).

[22] Generator company stake sold to consortium of Coastal Power (U.S.) and Hydro-Quebec (Canada).

[23] Stakes in two generators sold to AES Corporation (U.S.).

[24] Stakes in three distribution companies sold to Union Senosa and Constellation Power.

[25] Stake sold to Eni (Italy), with remainder held by SOEs and private investors.

[26] Sale to French-Canadian consortium.

[27] Stakes in ZSE, SSE, and VSE sold to E. On Energie (Germany), Electricite de France, and RWE Plus (Germany).

[28] Stake sold to AES Corporation (U.S.)

[29] Sold to CMS Energy (U.S.).

cember 1990. Collectively, these share offerings raised $10 billion for the British government. A mere six months later, the government raised an additional $8 billion by selling four other electric companies. During the late 1980s, the British government had restructured the Central Electricity Generation Board (CEGB) into separate generation and transmission components, as described and analyzed in Newberry and Pollit (1997) and Littlechild (2001). The transmission company National Grid was floated in 1995. Two of the three generating companies, National Power and Powergen, were sold off in two tranches in 1991 and 1995, raising $9.9 billion in total. The nuclear generating plants were grouped into a separate entity called British Energy. This company was floated in 1996, but had to be effectively renationalized several years later after mounting losses threatened to force the company into liquidation, which would have had untold implications given the firm's nuclear reactors.

After the formerly communist countries of central and eastern Europe gained their independence in the early 1990s, most were eager to privatize and modernize their ESIs as quickly as possible. Unfortunately, most of these transition economies were saddled with antiquated electricity generation, transmission, and distribution systems based on Soviet technology, and many were also totally dependent on Russia for oil and gas fuels—at least initially. Most of these countries tried to attract Western capital and expertise by conducting asset sales of stakes in their ESIs, but success was initially quite limited, and remains so today. We document privatization sales only for Poland, Slovakia, Ukraine, and Georgia, and these four asset sales and one SIP collectively raised a mere $611 million. Russia's electricity privatization was vastly larger, but also much more shrouded in mystery. We are unable to obtain concrete estimates for the amount of money raised by the sale of United Energy Systems to private investors (oligarchs) during the mid-1990s, but most estimates are amazingly low—perhaps only a few hundred million dollars.

The privatization boom of the middle and late 1990s exerted a powerful influence on government owners of ESIs, and many electricity companies were fully or partially privatized during this period. Spain completed its divestment of Endesa with three increasingly large SIPs between May 1994 and June 1998 that collectively raised over $13.5 billion (the 1998 offering alone raised $8 billon). Portugal sold two tranches (totaling 49 percent) of Electricidade de Portugal, raising $4.8 billion, while Brazil raised $11.28 billion through 11 asset sales between May 1996 and November 1999. The Australian state of Victoria also employed asset sales to dispose of most of its holdings in ESI companies between 1993 and 1999. Argentina, Austria, Bolivia, China, Colombia, Germany, Greece, Korea, New Zealand, Panama, Peru, and Thailand also executed significant ESI privatizations during the middle and late 1990s, while Greece sold two tranches of its Public Power Corporation in 2001 and 2002.

Although many countries have privatized some or all of their ESI, none has raised an amount remotely comparable to the $23.33 billion that Italian (national and city) governments received from four SIPs and one asset sale over a three-year period beginning in July 1998. The $18.9 billion initial public offering of a 34.5 percent stake in ENEL was not only the largest IPO in financial history but it also attracted a record 3.8 million individual shareholders [Bates (1999), Lane (1999)]. Unfortunately, most of these new stockholders were destined for disappointment, as ENEL's share price began to fall soon after the IPO, and lost almost half of its value over the next five years, before recovering some ground during 2003.[5] The Italian government has announced its intention to sell more of its holdings in ENEL once the stock price rises back near its IPO offering price, and actually sold a $2.3 billion tranche through an accelerated book-building operation in November 2003. However, it is unclear whether full divestment is under consideration. More generally, this is the stance that other governments have taken with respect to ESI privatization, as we discuss below. Once stock market valuations fully recover from the swoon that commenced in March 2000, a surge of ESI share offerings and asset sales can be expected.

The Future of ESI Privatization

So what electricity company assets do governments have left to sell? As was the case with national oil companies, this is a difficult question to answer definitively because the ESIs of so many countries remain 100 percent state owned. Unlike the case for oil companies, however, we cannot estimate the value of wholly state-owned ESIs, for two reasons. First, there is no comprehensive listing of these companies, much less an accounting of their assets, liabilities, costs, and revenues. Second, there are very few fully or partially privatized electric power companies listed on stock markets that we can use to generate the type of valuation multiples we were able to employ for national oil companies. Instead, table 10.7 presents our estimate of the market values of retained government stakes in those ESI companies that have been partially privatized either by asset sales or SIPs. As we did in chapters 8 and 9 for telecom and banking privatizations, respectively, we value these residual stakes using actual stock prices for listed companies and the original purchase price for those firms partly divested using asset sales.

Italy's ENEL stake stands out as the most valuable retained holding; its 65.5 percent stake is worth an impressive $27.65 billion. The Korean government's stake in Korean Electric Power is worth $6.3 billion, while Russia's 52.5 percent holding in Unified Energy System has a market value of $5.14 billion. Various German municipalities collectively hold a 35 percent stake in RWE, which is currently worth $5.67 billion, while the Greek and Portuguese governments retain stakes in their electric power companies with values in excess of $2 billion each.

Several developing country governments also retain valuable stakes in partially privatized ESI companies. Malaysia's 64.0 percent holding in Tenaga Nasional is worth $4.67 billion, and China's retained stakes in three companies are valued at $10.28 billion; the government's stake in Huaneng Power International alone is worth $7.69 billion. Three Latin American governments also have valuable stakes in ESI firms. Brazil's holdings have a theoretical value (based on asset sale prices) of $9.34 billion, while those of Colombia and Peru are theoretically valued at $5.48 billion and $867 million, respectively.

In total, the retained government stakes detailed in table 10.7 are worth $92.8

TABLE 10.7. Market Values of Retained Government Stakes in Partially Privatized Electric Utility Companies

Country	Company Name	Retained Stake	Approximate Market Value US $ mm
Argentina	Edemsa	49%	$228*
Austria	Kelag	67.85%	$369*
Austria	Estag	74.9%	$1,343*
Belgium	Electrabel	4.6%[a]	$639
Brazil	Light	44.4%	$1,799*
Brazil	Companhia Paulista de Forca Luz (CPFL)	42.4%	$1,988*
Brazil	Electropaulo Metropolitana	25.12%	$597*
Brazil	COELCE	10.23%	$99*
Brazil	Gerasul	58%	$1,106*
Brazil	Bandeirante	25.2%	$289*
Brazil	Companhia Paranese de Energia (COPEL)	55.4%[b]	$232
Brazil	Electrobras	58.1%[c]	$2,470
Brazil	Cesp Tiete	61.34%	$744*
China	Guangdong Electric Power Development	51.79%	$1,678
China	Huaneng Power International	75%	$7,689
China	Shandong Power Internationa	73%	$911*
Colombia	Empresa de Energia de Bogota Condesa, Emgesa	51.5%	$2,316*
Colombia	Empresa de Energia del Pacifico	43%	$415*
Colombia	Condesa	51%	$1,129
Colombia	Emgesa	51%	$990*
Colombia	Transelca	35%	$76*
Colombia	Electrocosta/Electrocaribe	35%	$555*
Czech Republic	Ceske Energeticke Zavody (CEZ)	67.61%[d]	$1,703
Dominican Republic	Dominican Electricity Company	50%	$750*
El Salvador	CLESA	20.34%	$28*
El Salvador	Delsur	24.53%	$59*
El Salvador	CAESS and EEO	18%	$65*
France	SNET	70%	$763*
Germany	RWE	35%[c]	$5,670*
Germany	OBK	75%	$216*
Germany	Stadtwerke Leipzig (SWL)	60%	$356*
Greece	Public Power Corporation	71.3%	$2,642
Guatemala	Guatemalan Electric Company	20%	$130*
Italy	ENEL	65.5%	$27,651
Italy	AEM Milan	51%	$1,188
Italy	ACEA	51%	$506
Italy	AEM Torino	70.1%	$617
Korea	Korea Electric Power	53%	$6,301
Malaysia	Tenaga Nasional	64.02%[f]	$4,666
Panama	Noreste	49%	$86*
Panama	Bahia las Minas	49%	$88*
Panama	Fortuna	51%	$123*
Peru	Edelnor	40%	$117*
Peru	Edelsur	40%	$141*
Peru	Cahua	40%	$28*
Peru	Edegel	40%	$349*
Peru	Ventanilla	40%	$80*
Peru	Egenor Pera	40%	$152*

(continued)

TABLE 10.7. (*continued*)

Country	Company Name	Retained Stake	Approximate Market Value US $ mm
Poland	Patnow-Adamow-Konin	80%	$360*
Portugal	Electricidade de Portugal	32.6%	$2,082
Portugal	Galp	67%	$1,982*
Russia	Unified Energy System	52.5%	$5,136
Senegal	Senelec	66%	$126*
Slovakia	Three Electricity Distributors	51%	$468*
Spain	Red Electricia Espanola	28.5%	$503
Thailand	Electricity Generating Company (EGCO)	25.52%	$184
Thailand	Ratchaburi Electricity Generating	45%	$451
Venezuela	Sistema Isla de Margarita Nueva Esparta	30%	$39*
Total			$92,829

Note: This table details the size and approximate market value of the residual state holdings in partially privatized electric utility companies as of August 2003. For publicly listed firms, value is determined based on the fractional retained holdings, presented in table 10.6 and/or the SIP appendix to this book, times the total market value of these firms in the *Business Week* "Global 1000" or "Top 200 Emerging Market" listing of the world's most valuable companies as of May 31, 2003 (*Business Week*, July 13, 2003). For utilities that were partially divested through an asset sale, value is computed based on the implied valuation from the last asset sale (indicated by an asterisk,) presented in table 10.3.
  [a] Stake held by Belgian municipalities.
  [b] Combined holdings of State of Parana (31.1%) and BNDESRAP (24.3%) of common stock and two preferred stock share classes.
  [c] Fraction of common shares.
  [d] Stake held by National Property Fund.
  [e] Stake held by German municipalities.
  [f] Stake held by Khazanah Nasional Berhad (35.63%), Minister of Finance (17.07%), and Bank Negara (11.32%).

billion. As with oil and gas, however, it is likely that the combined market value of wholly state-owned ESI companies is significantly larger than the total value of retained stakes in partially divested electricity companies. Our earlier discussion of the organizational and ownership structures of the 25 largest electricity markets revealed that key segments of the ESIs in most of these countries remain wholly state owned, and many governments have not even begun privatizing their electricity industries. Depending upon how completely and aggressively governments pursue privatization, we (crudely) estimate the value of wholly-owned stakes as at least $100 billion, and perhaps much more.

Privatizing National Airlines

The final industry whose privatization experience we examine is global air transport. Though this international airline business is dominated by U.S. based carriers, there are over 150 airlines operating today and the vast majority of these are (or recently were) state-owned enterprises. This section details the airline divestments that have been executed by governments since 1985, and then assesses the likely future course of national airline privatizations. Based on the recent experience of this most distressed of all major global industries, the future looks rather bleak.

As we asserted for oil and gas, there is little justification in economic theory for requiring a country's international airline to be state owned. Nonetheless, this pattern has characterized global aviation since its birth in the pre–WII era, and this remains the basic industry structure for most of the airlines operating today. Governments have traditionally launched national airlines for prestige reasons, to show the national flag in world airports, as well as to ensure that the country is serviced by a regularly scheduled air carrier. Few of these national airlines have ever been highly profitable, and many required (and still require) significant operating subsidies from sponsor governments to continue operating. These financial obligations become especially burdensome during recessions, which is when the idea of privatization seems most attractive. Unfortunately, airline recessions occur with disturbing frequency, and this is precisely when the pool of potential investors is also the most limited.

The Record on Privatizing National Airlines

Table 10.8 presents a listing of airline privatizations between October 1985 and July 2003. The first sale was a SIP of 30 percent in Malaysia Airlines, while the most recent involved the floatation of Israel's El Al—after many years of planning and several previous, abortive attempts. We document 50 sales, which collectively raise $21.4 billion. The 27 share offerings raise $16.3 billion, an average of $605.2 million each, while the 23 asset sales raised a mere $5 billion ($217.6 million each, on average) for divesting governments.

Several of the early share offerings detailed in table 10.8 were large by the standards of the day and highly successful for the divesting governments. Numerous Western governments were able to completely divest their national airline holdings between 1987 and 1994, including Australia (Qantas), Canada (Air Canada), Germany (Lufthansa), Japan (Japan Air Lines), New Zealand (Air New Zealand), and the United Kingdom (British Airways). The floatation of Britain's 100 percent stake in British Airways in December 1987 is especially noteworthy, since this sale occurs a mere five years after BA suffered massive operating losses during the recession of 1981–1982. As described by Green and Vogelsang (1994), BA's management restructured the company and laid of several thousand staff members in response to the losses—and in anticipation of being privatized.[6]

During the mid-1990s, several Western airlines began pursuing a global expansion strategy based upon acquiring stakes in smaller national airlines through asset sales. These strategies allowed countries as diverse as Belgium, Fiji, Hungary, Portugal, and South Africa to divest sizable stakes in their respective national carriers on attractive terms. By the late 1990s, however, this strategy had largely been discredited, and countries such as Greece were unable to find buyers for their troubled national carriers under any terms. The last truly successful airline privatization of the 1990s was France's floatation of a 22 percent stake in Air France in

TABLE 10.8. Airline Industry Privatizations

Country	Company	Date	Value (US $ Million)	Method of Sale	Fraction Sold
Argentina	Aerolineas	Nov 90	$1,870	Asset sale	85%[a]
Argentina	Aerolineas	Feb 94	$700	Asset sale	55%[a]
Australia	Qantas	1994	—	Asset sale	25%[b]
Australia	Qantas	Jul 95	$1,070	SIP	75%
Austria	Austrian Airlines	Jun 87	$73	SIP	24.2%
Austria	Austrian Airlines	Jun 88	$73	SIP	20%
Austria	Austrian Airlines	May 89	$65	SIP	14%
Belgium	Sabena	1994	—	Asset sale	49.5%[c]
Belgium	Sabena	2000	—	Asset sale	37%[d]
Bulgaria	Balkan Airlines	1999	$0.175	Asset sale	75%[e]
Canada	Air Canada	Sep 88	$246	SIP	43%
Canada	Air Canada	Jul 89	$452	SIP	57%
Chile	LAN*	May 94	$11	Asset sale	23.8%
China	China Southern	Aug 97	$631	SIP	30%
China	China Eastern Airlines*	1997	$245	Asset sale	—
China	Hainan Airlanes*	1997	$33.4	Asset sale	—
Cyprus	Cyprus Airways	Jul 00	$37.5	SIP[f]	14%
Estonia	Estonian Air	1996	$4	Asset sale	49%[g]
Fiji	Fiji Air	May 98	$8	Asset sale	28.5%[h]
Finland	Finnair	Jan 95	$74	SIP	9.3%
France	Air France	Feb 99	$337	SIP	22%
Germany	Lufthansa	Sep 89	$475	SIP	17%
Germany	Lufthansa	Sep 94	$730	SIP	10.4%
Germany	Lufthansa	1997	$2,650	SIP	37%
Hungary	Malev	1993	—	Asset sale	35%[i]
Italy	Alitalia	May 98	$450	SIP	18.4%
Jamaica	Air Jamaica*	May 94	$27	Asset sale	70%
Japan	Japan Air Lines	Dec 87	$4,645	SIP	34.5%
Kenya	Kenya Airways*	1995	$26	Asset sale	—
Kenya	Kenya Airways	Mar 96	$48	SIP	51%
Malaysia	Malaysian Airline System	Oct 85	$78	SIP	30%
Malaysia	Malaysian Airline System	1994	$702	Asset sale	29.09%*[j]
Mexico	Aerovias de Mexico*	Oct 88	$339	Asset sale	100%
Mexico	Mexicana*	Aug 89	$140	Asset sale	11%
Netherlands	KLM Royal Dutch Airlines	Apr 86	$295	SIP	16%
Netherlands	KLM Royal Dutch Airlines	Dec 96	$570	Asset sale	13.2%[k]
New Zealand	Air New Zealand	Oct 89	$99	SIP	100%
Peru	AeroPeru	1993	$54	Asset sale	72.2%
Poland	Polskie Linie Lotnicze (LOT)*	Nov 99	$33.7	Asset sale	10%
Portugal	TAP—Air Portugal	Feb 00	$150	Share sale[l]	34%
Russia	Aeroflot	May 01	—	Asset sale	26%[m]
Singapore	Singapore International Airlines	Nov 85	$233	SIP	14%
Singapore	Singapore International Airlines	Jun 87	$284	SIP	9.4%
South Africa	Sun Air*	Sep 97	$10.7	Asset sale	80%

Country	Company	Date	Value (US $ Million)	Method of Sale	Fraction Sold
South Africa	South African Airways (SAA)*	Nov 99	$230	Asset sale	20%[n]
Spain	Iberia	Mar 00	$1,054	SIP	46.1%
Spain	Iberia	Apr 01	$518	SIP	53.9%
Thailand	Thai Airways International	Mar 92	$225	SIP	53%
Tunisia	Tunis Air*	1995	$22	SIP	—
United Kingdom	British Airways	Feb 87	$1,327	SIP	100%
TOTAL			$21,345.48		

Table Summary

Method of Sale	Number of Transactions	Value (US$ Million)
SIP	26	16,191.50
Asset sale	23	5,003.98
Share sale	1	150
TOTAL	50	21,345.48

Source: Most of the data presented here from the *Financial Times* and/or the FT.COM Web site, but other sources are employed as well. In particular, sales marked with an asterisk are taken from various issues of *Privatisation International* (1998–2000) and *Privatisation International Yearbooks* (1998–2001).

Note: This table presents key information about airline industry privatizations executed by governments around the world. The "method of sale" refers to whether the company was divested via a share issue privatization (SIP) or asset sale.

[a] Original sale was of an 85% stake sold to Iberia and local partners. When partners defaulted, Argentina government took back 55% of this. In 1994, Iberia converted $700 million of debt into additional 55% stake (to 85%). After Iberia's privatization, the Spanish government was left with an 85% stake in Aerolinas, which it sold in November 2001.

[b] Stake sold to British Airways.

[c] Stake sold to Swissair.

[d] Swissair exercised an option to increase its stake to 86.5%, but by mid-2001 Belgian government was suing Swissair for damages and trying to force the company to make additional capital injections into Sabena. Both Swissair and Sabena collapsed shortly after September 11, 2001.

[e] Controlling stake sold to Zheevi, and Israeli management group, for $175,000. The company collapsed in April 2001, with debts of $113 million.

[f] Rights offering to raise capital for the airline.

[g] Controlling stake sold to Maersk Air. In 2003, Maersk sold its stake to SAS, another bidder in 1996.

[h] With sale, Qantas increased its stake in Fiji Air to 46%. Original purchase details unknown.

[i] Stake sold to Alitalia, but renationalized in 1998 after failure of alliance.

[j] Controlling stake sold to local businessman. In December 2000, the Malaysian government repurchased this stake at the same Malaysian ringgit price (M$1,790 million), roughly double the open market price as a rescue.

[k] Government cut its stake from 38.2 to 25%, by selling stake back to KLM.

[l] Private share sale (capital increase) to Swissair.

[m] Stake purchased by businessman/politician Roman Abramovich. He later sold this stake to NRB bank for $ 140 million in March 2003.

[n] Stake sold to Swissair. South African government renationalized stake after Swissair collapsed in late 2001.

February 1999. This offering, which occurred only after years of opposition from the carrier's unionized workforce, raised a mere $337 million, but helped position Air France as one of the world's most profitable and highly rated airlines.

The global economic slowdown that began in early 2001 had the typical deleterious effect on airline profits, but it was the World Trade Center attack that September that created a "perfect storm" for the industry. Air traffic fell drastically, particularly on international routes, and the airlines found themselves saddled with massive new security expenses at the same time that fuel, insurance, and other operating costs were also rising sharply. The industry's most recent near-death experience occurred in late 2002 and early 2003, first with the lead-up to war between Iraq and the American-led coalition and then the troubled aftermath, which saw international tourist travel briefly fall to multi-year lows.

The Future of Airline Privatization

By late 2003, signs began to appear suggesting that the prospects for the industry were changing from catastrophic to merely dismal. Most of the surviving U.S.–based carriers had used a trip through Chapter 11 bankruptcy, or the threat of doing so, to significantly reduce their operating costs—especially labor. The sharp decline in interest rates after 2000 also helped airlines reduce their capital costs associated with acquiring new airplanes and servicing the debt of previously acquired aircraft. Finally, air traffic began to rebound somewhat, albeit from truly horrific levels. El Al's successful floatation in July 2003 seemed to indicate that the worst for the industry had perhaps passed.

Nonetheless, the future of the national airlines with their current cost and route structures appears grim. The only airlines that are truly prospering are either discount carriers, such as America's Southwest and Jet Blue and Europe's Ryannair and EasyJet, or a handful of long-haul carriers such as Singapore Airlines that are still able to attract full fare business travelers. Few national airlines have either the low-cost structures of the discount carriers or the loyalty-inspiring service levels of the prestige carriers, and thus seemed doomed to operating in an increasingly hostile business environment. This is not primarily related to state ownership, since all the globally active U.S.–based carriers are also in very poor shape and none has ever been state owned, but state ownership certainly does not help the national carriers cut costs or improve service levels.

Table 10.9 presents our estimate of the market values of retained government stakes in the 33 non-U.S. airlines that rank among the 50 largest in the world based on year 2001 revenue passenger miles. Only a few of the companies in which the government retains any shares are publicly traded, and market values are unavailable even for several of these. Therefore, we are once more forced to develop a method for valuing non-traded airline ownership stakes. Since 19 of these 33 airlines have negative net income (net losses) during 2001 and four of the 14 profitable companies earned less than $10 million, we cannot use the theoretically preferable earnings capitalization valuation model. We therefore value the retained government stakes in non-traded airlines using a multiple of sales methodology, with the sales multiplier derived from the sales and market

TABLE 10.9. Market Value of Residual State Holdings in National Airlines

Top 50 Rank	Company Name	Country	Residual State % Ownership	2001 Revenue Passenger Miles (Millions)	Total Revenues (US $ Million)	Net Income (US $ Millions)	Market Value of Residual State (US $ Millions)
5	British Airways	Great Britain	0	64,236	$12,113	$(187.4)	0
6	Air France	France	56%	59,543	$9,316	$137.2	$1,889[a]
8	Lufthansa	Germany	0	56,755	$9,380	$(567.4)	0
9	Japan Airlines	Japan	0	50,767	$9,583	$357.9	$3,829[a]
12	Singapore Airlines	Singapore	56.8%	42,765	$5,353	$357.9	0
13	Qantas	Australia	0	42,144	$5,473	$223.2	0
14	Air Canada	Canada	0	41,495	$6,045	$(788.7)	0
15	KLM Royal Dutch Airlines	Netherlands	14.1%	35,757	$5,070	$(139.9)	$63[a]
18	Thai Airways	Thailand	100%	37,429	$2,961	$43.7	$1,066
19	Iberia Airlines	Spain	0	25,642	$4,024	$44.9	0
20	Korean Airlines	South Korea	100%	23,731	$4,418	$(459.2)	$1,590
21	Alitalia	Italy	53%	22,447	$4,698	$(798.2)	$896
22	Malaysia Airlines	Malaysia	100%	22,289	$2,288	$(219.9)	$824
25	Varig Brazilian Airlines	Br0azil	100%	16,018	$2,578	$(204.3)	$928
26	China Airlines	Taiwan	71%[b]	16,002	$2,071	$52.9	$529
27	Emirates	UAE	100%	14,370	$2,128	$164.2	$766
28	Scandinavian Airlines System	Sweden, Denmark, and Norway	50.0%[c]	14,265	$4,337	$(103.1)	$781
29	Air New Zealand	New Zealand	82%	13,544	$1,900	$(578.6)	$561
30	South African Airways	South Africa	100%	12,697	$1,709	$39.7	$615
31	Saudi Arabian Airlines	Saudi Arabia	100%	12,562	$3,050	N/A	$1,098
32	Air China International	China (PRC)	100%	12,391	$1,769	$4.9	$637

(continued)

TABLE 10.9. (*continued*)

Top 50 Rank	Company Name	Country	Residual State % Ownership	2001 Revenue Passenger Miles (Millions)	Total Revenues (US $ Million)	Net Income (US $ Millions)	Market Value of Residual State (US $ Millions)
35	Turkish Airlines	Turkey	98.2%	9,346	$1,371	$16.4	$485
37	Philippine Airlines	Philippines	4.26%	8,357	$810	$6.0	$12
38	P.T. Guarda Indonesia	Indonesia	100%	8,146	$998	$(26.2)	$359
40	El Al Israel Airlines	Israel	85%[d]	7,889	$1,104	$(85.2)	$623[a]
41	Gulf Air Company	Abu Dhabi, Bahrain, Oman, Qatar	100%[e]	7,646	$906	$(132.4)	$326
42	Pakistan International Airlines	Pakistan	84.0%[f]	7,283	$670	$(39.1)	$203
43	Air India	India	100%	7,098	$990	$3.2	$357
44	TAP Air Portugal	Portugal	100%	6,426	$1,123	$(39.4)	$404
45	Egypt Airways	Egypt	100%	5,526	$1,104	$(85.2)	$397
46	Olympic Airways	Greece	100%	5,241	$885	$(75.0)	$319
47	Austrian Airlines	Austria	39.7%	5,059	$1,135	$(148.8)	$162
48	Finnair OYJ	Finland	58.4%	4,929	$1,506	$6.4	$317
49	Indian Airlines Ltd.	India	100%	4,522	$840	$(51.0)	$302
TOTAL							$20,338

Note: This table presents financial and operating statistics for 34 fully and partially privatized national airlines that are ranked as among the Top 50 largest in the world, in terms of year 2001 revenue passenger miles (RPM), in *Aviation Week and Space Technology* (January 13, 2003), pp. 331–366 [the 4 largest, and most the other 12 Top 50 airlines are U.S.-based carriers]. All of the data presented in columns 1–7 are from the *AW&ST* article, while the market value of residual state ownership (in US$ millions) is either from data obtained from the company's Web site in August 2003 or from the *Business Week* "Global 1000" or "Top 200 Emerging Market" listing of the world's most valuable companies as of May 31, 2003 (*Business Week* July 13, 2003).

[a] Actual market value.

[b] Stake held by state controlled foundation.

[c] The combined holdings of the Swedish (21.4%), Danish (14.3%), and Norwegian (14.3%) governments.

[d] The Israeli government sold shares representing 15% of El Al's total equity plus warrants for the remaining 85% in June 2003, raising $110 million.

[e] Each government owns a 25% stake.

[f] Stake held by Pakistani government (57.7%) and state-owned institutions (26.3%).

values of the (fully and partially) privatized, publicly traded airlines. Specifically, we have both market capitalization (as of May 2003) and year 2001 sales for eight large companies—British Airways, Air France, Lufthansa, Japan Airlines, Singapore Airlines, Qantas, Air Canada, and KLM—and compute a price-to-sales (P/S) ratio for each company by dividing total market value by total sales.[7] The P/S ratio ranges from a high of 1.238 for Singapore Airlines to a low of 0.004 for Air Canada, and the average P/S for these eight airlines is 0.36. This is also quite close to the hypothetical median value of 0.32, computed by averaging the P/S of fourth-ranked Air France (0.39) and fifth-ranked British Airways (0.25).

We use actual market prices to value the retained government stakes in four of the carriers detailed in table 10.9, and use our price to sales multiple of 0.36 to value the stakes of the other 24 national carriers—most of which remain 100 percent state owned. These valuations are presented in column 8 of table 10.9, and only five of the 28 stakes retained by governments are worth more than $1 billion. The Singaporean government's holding in SAL has a value of $3.83 billion, and the French state's holding in Air France is valued at $1.89 billion, but the total value of all retained state holdings is only $20.34 billion. This is an absurdly small value for a major global industry that remains largely government owned, and even this measure may be too high. Recall that we used an average of eight established Western carriers to compute the P/S multiple used to value all the non-traded stakes, and it is likely that most developing-country carriers would be valued at a discount to global players such as British Airways and Air France. Therefore, the $20.34 billion estimate should be considered a maximum value that could be realized from an aggressive and complete program of airline privatization over the next several years. Of all the industries whose futures we have assessed, the global airline industry's prospects are clearly the worst.[8]

The Lessons and Future
of Privatization

Privatization has been a part of economic life for a quarter-century now, and seems likely to remain firmly entrenched in the public policy debate for the foreseeable future. What have we learned from this experience, and what lies ahead? Since these questions have been addressed in depth in earlier chapters, we do not attempt a full summary here, but instead provide only a distillation of the key lessons of privatization in the section below. The section after that describes unresolved issues in privatization research. We then close out this work by assessing the likely future course of privatization in the short, medium, and long term.

Lessons Learned from a Quarter-Century of Privatization Experience

By definition, privatization represents a change in the ownership of business enterprises from state to private hands. It also invariably represents a sharp break with a past where state ownership of business had been deliberately created, so privatization also implies that a society has changed its mind in an important way. After much theoretical and empirical research, it now seems clear that private ownership is superior to public ownership of commercial enterprise in almost all realistic business settings. Thus the first true lesson of privatization is that state ownership of most productive assets must be considered a historical failure, and the policy of privatization has been adopted in order to improve business performance. The other key lessons of privatization are presented and discussed below.

Privatization Works by Itself, but Works Better as Part of a Reform Program

No fewer than 300 empirical analyses of privatization have been produced over the past 15 years, with most of these being performed quite recently. Collectively, these studies examine many thousand companies divested by governments in over 125 countries. Given this wide range of studies, it is possible to find at least one to support almost any interpretation of privatization's effectiveness that someone might wish to put forth. The vast weight of evidence, however, clearly supports two conclusions. First, it seems clear that moving a company from state to private ownership will usually improve that company's financial and operating performance, even if no other changes are made to the company or to the firm's operating environment. In other words, privatization "works," even if adopted in isolation.

On the other hand, the second clear lesson offered by research is that the best results come about when ownership change is combined with deregulation, injecting competition, and other reforms to the firm and to its operating environment. In many cases, an SOE slated for privatization should be broken up into smaller operating companies before being divested, either to better engender competition or to make the newly private firm more responsive to market forces, or both. Changes to management are almost always required, and preferably should be made before privatization, since few of the political appointees who manage most SOEs will have the skills or mindset required to operate an entrepreneurial company. Governments should also review the regulatory environment into which a SOE providing a basic service is being privatized, and in many cases the industry should be deregulated prior to (or simultaneously with) privatization of the incumbent operator.

More painful restructuring steps may also be required to position a newly privatized company for prosperity. The typical state enterprise is overstaffed—often grossly so—and if this is the case, the new owners of a divested firm must be allowed to trim the workforce in an economically rational way. All governments fear lay-offs resulting from privatization, and most seek to cushion the blows of any reductions that do occur. This is both rational and just in democratic societies; the trick is to structure the incentives from severance payments and early retirement packages to ensure that the most valuable workers remain with the newly privatized company and the state's financial support goes to those laid-off workers who need help the most. Chong and Lopez-de-Silanes (2002) document just how difficult it is for governments to properly structure these severance packages in order to retain the most valuable employees and soften the financial blow of redundancy for the most vulnerable.

Privatization Works, but Is No Panacea: Don't Raise Unrealistic Expectations

One of the quandaries facing reform-minded policy makers around the world today is that a disconnect has emerged between the true effectiveness of economic reform policies—such as free trade, deregulation, and privatization—and the popular image of those policies. Hard statistical evidence clearly shows that these economic reforms deliver significant and lasting benefits, yet all have become unpopular in many countries. In some regions, and particularly in Latin America, privatization has become so unpopular that politicians dare not propose extending the program's reach, or even defend past divestments. Given the financial weaknesses of governments, and the intellectual bankruptcy of state ownership as a model of economic development, there is no realistic alternative to continued economic reform and privatization in these regions. Therefore, ongoing privatization can and must be promoted; the question is, "how?"

As is generally true in real life, there are no easy answers to this question. Capitalism is always a hard concept to sell in democratic societies, in spite of its obvious dynamism and productivity. The enduring popularity of an elusive "third way" to organize economic and political life, one that combines the best aspects of capitalism and socialism, shows how conflicted open societies are about allowing economic processes to generate winners and losers. And whatever its other merits may be, privatization of state enterprises invariably creates easily identifiable winners (consumers in general, new managers and shareholders in particular) and losers (displaced workers, uncompetitive former suppliers, competing firms), and will always be subject to criticism for doing so.

Perhaps the best advice we can offer to policy makers seeking to promote privatization programs is not to over-sell the benefits that the programs can deliver. While real, these benefits are never large enough to solve a society's ills, and disappointment at privatization's inability to transform lies at the root of much of today's popular dissatisfaction with the policy. It is understandable why policy makers are tempted to promise much from privatization, since this allows them to overcome powerful vested interests arrayed against reform, but all too often this becomes a Faustian bargain.

Efficiency Maximization Is Better than Revenue Maximization

Policy makers planning the privatization of a state-owned monopoly almost always face the choice between privatizing in a way that maximizes economic efficiency and privatizing in a way that maximizes revenue for the divesting government. Selling off a state-owned monopoly intact, either in an asset sale or in a SIP, will indeed yield much more revenue to a government than will selling off a company that must compete with new entrants in a deregulated industry. Selling the company intact is also generally the more popular approach with politicians and the incumbent firm's managers and workers, especially if the alternative is to dismember the existing firm into smaller, competitive pieces.

Unfortunately, both practical experience and empirical evidence clearly show that monopolies should always be broken up and industries deregulated before incumbent service providers are privatized. There are far too many examples of privatization creating what effectively become private monopolies, which have every incentive to continue restricting output and charging very high prices. This is especially damaging in industrially crucial businesses such as telecommunications and electric power generation and distribution, where high costs and poor service can cripple an entire economy's competitiveness. In other industries, such as water and sewerage, the burden of continuing poor service and high costs will fall most painfully on the poorest members of society.

There is simply no alternative to competition as a spur to lower prices and better service, so policy makers should always make engendering competition the principal objective of privatization. Since this is rarely in the individual interest of any single political actor, professional economists and other commentators must often make this case, frequently and publicly. All involved should also realize that governments have only one chance to engender competition—at the beginning of the privatization process. Experience has clearly shown that it is virtually impossible to revisit a botched privatization to either break up a private monopoly or to impose an aggressive regulatory regime on an already privatized company. Any such restructuring will be strongly opposed by the firm's managers, workers, and suppliers—as well as by the new owners and shareholders who purchased the company under the original offering terms.

Privatizing Well Is Better than Privatizing Fast

A natural corollary to the above two lessons is that, if a choice must be made, it is better to privatize well than to privatize quickly. Economic reformers often believe that they have only a narrow window of opportunity in which to implement changes such as price liberalization or privatization before the forces of reaction return to power. Acting on this belief, reformers often ram through a raft of major policy changes in a very short time, in an approach that has come to be known as "shock therapy." While the proponents of shock therapy can make a case that their approach worked in the transition economies of central and eastern Europe (again, CEE) during the 1990s, many would dispute that the therapy really had to be as shocking as it was. In particular, China's much more measured (and successful) approach to reform suggests that a "slow but steady" approach may work better in many cases. Even in the context of CEE transition, it became clear after the fact that there was far less danger of a return to socialism or a reaction to market-oriented policies than reformers had initially feared.

The guiding philosophy for policy makers should be to sequence reforms in a way that maximizes political support for further reforms, by building on success. With respect to privatization, this means that the easiest and least controversial sales should be executed first, and that policy makers should allow sufficient time to elapse for these sales to be perceived as successful. Once this is achieved, more controversial privatizations of core service providers and companies requiring significant restructuring can be implemented. Not only does a measured approach help defuse political opposition to privatization, it also allows time for capital markets to develop and for practitioners to learn the skills of modern financial capitalism.

Full Privatization, for Cash, Is Always the Best Policy

For a variety of reasons, most initial privatizations involve partial sales of state enterprises. Phrased differently, initial privatizations rarely create companies that are 100 percent privately owned, but instead create mixed ownership enterprises in which governments retain large (often majority) equity stakes. This is especially true for extremely large state enterprises such as telecommunications companies, which must be sold in multiples tranches over several years in order not to overwhelm the absorptive capacity of national stock markets. There are also sound theoretical reasons that governments choose to privatize slowly, primarily in order to demonstrate their commitment to noninterference in the affairs of the privatized company even when they retain the majority voting power to do so.

On the other hand, while we acknowledge that privatization will usually be a multistage, multiyear process for most companies, we need to clearly state that full privatization should be the ultimate goal. As long as a government retains ownership in any important company, there will be both political pressure to intervene in the firm's operations and a convenient mechanism for doing so. In practice, governments around the world have demonstrated an ability to refrain from politicized intervention in the affairs of most industries, but this has never been true for banking. Governments simply cannot constrain themselves to impose hard budget constraints on borrowers as long as they retain any significant ownership in former state-owned banks. These simply must be either privatized completely or not at all.

A natural corollary to the proposition that full privatization should always be preferred to partial privatization is the maxim that state enterprises being divested through an asset sale should be sold, for cash, to the highest bidder, even if that bidder is a foreign company. All too often, governments will choose the politically expedient course of selling SOEs to favored local buyers on concessionary terms, in order to avoid being charged with "selling the family silver to foreigners." This is a mistake on both policy and political grounds, since foreign bidders—particularly multinational companies—will usually make more capable and value-maximizing owners than will local champions, and by favoring the local bidder the government forgoes the opportunity to maximize sale proceeds.

Ownership Matters: Be Careful Who You Sell Your Company To

Not all potential buyers of a divested SOE will make equally capable owners. If a company is to be divested using an auction (asset sale), those responsible for conducting the sale should always try both to attract as many bidders as possible and to attract potential buyers who can manage the divested company most effectively. In general, this means attracting established companies operating in the same industry, since only these companies have the managerial knowledge, industry-specific technology, and financial strength required to restructure the privatized firm in a way that positions it for long-term prosperity. Since state enterprises are almost invariably overstaffed, undercapitalized, and far off the industry's technological frontier, it is imperative that these companies be sold to strategic buyers that have both the incentive and ability to restructure them in a value-maximizing way. In many real cases, this means that SOEs should be sold to Western multinational corporations (MNCs), if it is possible to attract such bidders.

The terms upon which SOEs can be sold through asset sale auctions will depend upon a number of factors. The most important influences are the condition of the company being sold, the attractiveness of the country as a target for foreign direct investment, and the global health and competitiveness of the industry. For example, during the telecoms boom of the late 1990s, many countries were able to auction off their state-owned telcos on very favorable terms because the industry worldwide was growing rapidly and was flush with cash. Both the newly privatized European telecoms and the American operating companies that emerged from the breakup of AT&T were aggressively bidding for stakes in emerging markets, and all these firms competed fiercely for mandates that came up for bid. After the telecom crash of 2001–2002, the European and American telecoms retrenched and were no longer interested in bidding for telcos in emerging markets, no matter how potentially attractive.

As a practical matter, of course, no country can manufacture a perfect timing opportunity to divest its SOEs. Countries can, however, be prepared to exploit opportunities that present themselves by having plans in place to sell companies when market conditions are right, and actively working to attract the desired bidders. At this writing (summer 2004), the world economy seems on the verge of another period of rapid growth, which suggests that a much more positive environment for auctioning off SOEs may be on the horizon for many industries. Those governments that prepare for this market turn will be able to sell companies at the best price to value-maximizing buyers.

Process Matters: Structure a Sale to Maximize Transparency and Legitimacy

Privatization is an acutely political process and, as such, how a government structures any given sale will always be a matter of general interest. The first key choice regarding method of sale is whether a government should choose an asset sale or a public share offering as a divestment technique. Asset sales can generally be arranged more rapidly than can a SIP, and a larger fraction of the company (perhaps even a government's entire stake) can be divested in a private as opposed to a public sale. Asset sales are also the only efficient method of selling relatively small state enterprises.

However, our reading of the empirical evidence suggests that governments should generally favor share issue privatizations over asset sales whenever there is a real choice of divestment methods. In addition to sound financial reasons, discussed in the next section, SIPs are also inherently more transparent and less subject to corruption than are private sales. Every aspect of a privatization share offering is open to public view, from performing an initial appraisal and valuation, to selecting an investment banker to handle the offering, to pricing the share offering, to actually conducting the sale and distributing shares to investors. Governments have also learned how to structure SIP offering terms to achieve political objectives and to maximize public support for the privatization process.

Finance Matters: Use Privatization to Develop Capital Markets

We have dwelled at length in this book on the question of how to choose the best method for selling a state enterprise. As noted above, asset sales offer many benefits, including speed and ease of sale, and the ability to sell a large fraction of a company in one transaction. A private sale should thus be considered the method of choice for selling small companies. In spite of the benefits offered by asset sales, however, we believe that privatization through public share offering should be considered the default choice for selling medium and large companies.

While SIPs are costlier and more difficult to arrange than asset sales, they have three decisive advantages. First, the empirical evidence now clearly indicates that SIPs raise more money for a given fraction of the company sold than do asset sales. Second, SIPs are inherently transparent financial operations, whereas asset sales are prone to real or perceived abuse by insiders. Third, and most important, privatization through public share issuance offers the single best—and perhaps the only—opportunity for governments to massively promote the development of their national capital markets.

There is now a consensus among economists that well-developed financial markets promote economic growth. Unfortunately, it is also painfully obvious that efficient capital markets do not arise spontaneously, but must be nurtured through deliberate public policy actions. This includes adopting legal and institutional reforms to protect private property rights, as well as establishing an effective regulatory regime with a capable supervisory body. Though these reforms are vital, they are rarely sufficient to promote financial market development because markets also require a supply of financial assets to trade. Owners of private companies will be reluctant to issue tradable securities until the markets are informationally efficient and highly liquid, yet investors will be unwilling to trust their savings to securities markets until there is an adequate supply of quality securities available for trade. This chicken-or-egg problem can be solved in a short period of time only by governments' selling large quantities of shares in well-known companies to individual and institutional investors, and repeating this process many times over many years.

Political Support Is a Prerequisite for Successful Privatization

It is no coincidence that privatization has occurred almost exclusively in democratic societies. Privatization emerged from the contest of ideas, and its economic success has solidified its position as a core tool of public policy. Yet privatization also has massive economic, industrial, and social impacts, and because it produces losers as well as winners, the policy has become very controversial in many (perhaps most) countries. This presents a challenge for policy makers, who understand the need for continuing privatization, but who also must confront opposition from those who wish to halt or slow the policy.

There is no silver bullet that can make the process of "selling" privatization easy, though certain actions can help overcome opposition—at least from open-minded people. First, one can marshal the empirical evidence on privatization's effectiveness, and then present this evidence in a systematic and objective manner. This book has been written in part to do just that. Second, care should be given to ensuring that privatizations are conducted in as open, honest, and equitable a manner as possible, and that the benefits are shared by many segments of society. The third suggestion is to be patient and allow companies to be privatized slowly and incrementally. Democratic processes are slow, but they also produce enduring results when there is strong public support for a policy that works.

Unresolved Issues in Privatization Policy and Research

A quarter-century of practical experience and a large and rapidly growing empirical literature have taught us a great deal about privatization's economic and political impact. The impact of ownership change on the operating and financial performance of individual companies is now well understood, and we also have a working understanding of the macroeconomic and fiscal impact of privatization. However, there is much that we still do not understand about this immensely significant policy, particularly how divestment impacts the lives of a privatized firm's workers, or how different privatization's impact is depending upon the overall level of development of a particular country. This section briefly highlights several areas where our level of understanding is particularly low relative to the importance of the issue.

Labor Economics of Privatization: Does Privatization Cost or Create Jobs?

By far the most contentious issue surrounding privatization is whether selling a state-owned enterprise to a private buyer or to stock market investors inevitably costs jobs. The empirical research has not yet answered this question definitively, though we can offer a partial conclusion since these studies generally show that privatization increases both a divested company's sales and the productivity of its workforce. If the productivity of a privatized company's employees increases faster than do its sales, then the firm almost surely will have to shed workers under private ownership. If sales increase as fast as or faster than productivity, then employment levels should remain stable or even rise. Therefore, the overall impact of privatization on any individual company can be predicted using the tools of Economics 101.

It is much more difficult to predict whether a privatization program will create or destroy jobs for an entire economy, and the empirical record offers very little guidance thus far. Here again, the basic question is whether the privatized companies can increase sales fast enough to offset the impact of increasing per-worker productivity, but it is rarely possible to address this question econometrically, since so many factors impact an economy's performance over any given study period. This is particularly true if, as is often the case, privatization is but one of several economic reforms adopted simultaneously by a government, since it will be impossible to assign causation for any economic improvement that is observed to a specific policy change.

Secondary and spillover effects pose an additional challenge to measuring the employment impact of privatization. For example, suppose that privatizing a nation's monopoly telecom provider not only makes the divested company significantly more efficient and profitable but also promotes rapid growth in industries directly related to communications, such as equipment manufacturing, information technology, and business services. The direct effect of privatization, making the telecom company more efficient, will probably cause the firm to reduce its direct employment levels, but the indirect effect of increased industrial dynamism may cause aggregate employment to increase. Although some research has attempted to measure the aggregate employment effects of privatization, much more is needed.

The Income and Wealth Distributional Effects of Privatization: Must There Be a Tradeoff Between Efficiency and Fairness?

Perhaps surprisingly, very little research has directly examined privatization's impact on national wealth and income distribution. This is partly because the first generations of studies have focused on the impact of ownership change on the performance of individual companies and/or on the financial impact of divestiture on capital market development and on government budgets. These are tests of whether net economic benefits are produced by privatization, and of how large these gains are, and thus are relatively simple tests to execute. It is much more difficult to determine how these gains are split among different groups in society.

For example, most studies show that SIPs are highly beneficial for investors who purchase the shares on offer and for the fiscal health of divesting governments, so we can conclude that privatization eases national budget constraints even as it creates and enriches a new class of shareholders. However, we cannot measure the overall fiscal and distributional impact of privatization on different groups of citizens until we know what governments do with these financial windfalls. If the proceeds are saved—used to reduce outstanding debt or to minimize additional debt issuance in the future—then the net financial position of the government is improved. On the other hand, if the proceeds are spent on social programs or redistributed among citizens through fiscal transfers, then the favored groups will naturally benefit more than others. Of course, if the sale proceeds are spent wastefully (for example, to defend an overvalued currency in order to fuel additional domestic consumption), a society's overall economic health will be harmed.

We also know far less than we should about the impact of privatization on income distribution within a country, though Birdsall and Nellis (2003) provide a very useful survey of the existing literature. This is particularly true regarding how divestment impacts a state enterprise's own workers. In general, studies show that most privatizations result in some employment shedding, but that the workers who remain at privatized companies are usually paid significantly more. We know far less about what happens to the workers who are made redundant after privatization. We would particularly like to know whether, and under what terms, workers who are laid off by privatized companies are rehired by other private-sector firms. If displaced workers are able to quickly find work at comparable wages elsewhere, then the income distribution impact of privatization will not be severe. If, on the other hand, laid-off workers cannot find alternative employment quickly, or if the alternative jobs pay significantly less, then national incomes will be severely impacted by privatization.

How to Design an Optimal Sequencing Strategy for a National Privatization Program

Very little research has examined how governments choose to sequence the sales of particular companies—and most of what has been written is normative (what should be done) rather than analytical (what has been done, and why) in nature. Most governments seem to pursue a commonsense strategy of selling off the financially healthiest SOEs first, since this can be done quickly and with relatively little need for pre-sale restructuring. As programs evolve, most governments then move on to selling core service companies, typically beginning with telecommunications providers, then electric utilities, and only later water and sewerage companies. These large enterprises are typically sold in stages, with many months or even years separating sale tranches for specific companies. Unfortunately, there is little in the theoretical or empirical literature to guide policy makers regarding how much of a particular company should be sold in one tranche versus in later sales. Nor can economists yet offer much guidance about sequencing the sales of different industries, or even specific companies within a given industry.

Perhaps the single biggest gap in our knowledge in this area is that we can offer very little research-based guidance regarding how and when to privatize commercial banks. As described in Megginson (2003), these are vital institutions in all economies, and state-owned banks often dominate (or monopolize) the financial sectors in many countries, yet we cannot answer seemingly simple questions such as whether to recapitalize a state bank before selling it off and whether to sell all state banks at once or in sequence. We also can offer far too little guidance to policy makers who are trying to balance banking-sector restructuring with promoting development of stock and bond markets, even though this is an issue that many countries—particularly China and India—are now struggling with.

How Should Severely Underdeveloped Countries Privatize State Enterprises?

The policy of privatization developed in Great Britain and has been most closely associated with sales by governments in developed economies. Of course, many developing and transition economies have also pursued privatization, and the empirical evidence suggests that this policy is effective in these economies as well. However, very little research has examined the record of privatization in the poorest and least developed countries, so the question remains whether these represent a special case requiring special procedures and/or special assistance.

Economic life is certainly unfair to citizens of the poorest countries, and even the all too rare benevolent governments in these countries face excruciating policy trade-offs in promoting development and in privatizing SOEs and para-statal companies. Poverty and illiteracy are endemic, governments are often corrupt and/or incompetent, and native entrepreneurs are all too often stifled by government control, wretched infrastructure, or simply lack of capital. State-owned or controlled companies often dominate all aspects of economic life, and these tend to be technologically backwards and extremely poorly run, so the potential payoff from ownership change should, in theory, be very large. On the other hand, there is precious little margin for error if one of the core SOEs is either privatized badly or simply allowed to fail. Finally, since these economies are so poor and unpromising, Western multinational companies rarely line up to purchase state enterprises being divested, so what little external support that is available to privatizing governments tends to come from international institutions such as the World Bank.

Despite this litany of problems, governments of severely underdeveloped countries should actively pursue privatization as a core policy, but they should also try to line up as much support as possible from development agencies and aid organizations beforehand to help with the transition. In these countries, no policy that forces companies to shed workers without transitional support can be justified — no matter how large the economic payoff may be in the long term. Fortunately, development agencies are usually very willing to support financially any poor-country government that truly commits itself to economic reform and privatization, especially since so few have to date made this commitment except under duress. On the other hand, policy makers and development agency officials must be particularly careful not to "over promise" the benefits that privatization can indeed deliver. Ownership change will usually make a state enterprise more efficient and productive; privatization alone will not convert a dilapidated sugar refinery into a world-beating manufacturer or allow a country to massively raise its citizens' standard of living. As a World Bank consultant once noted, "there are no short cuts to development."

How Important and Effective Has Privatization Been in the United States?

Anyone researching privatization soon notes that this word means different things in different regions of the world. In western Europe, Japan, Canada, and most developing countries, privatization refers to the sale of state-owned business enterprises to private investors, via either a public share offering or a private asset sale. Today this is also what privatization means in the transition economies of central and eastern Europe, but during the early and mid-1990s, the term also referred to the transfer of ownership of enterprises from the state to ordinary citizen using vouchers, restitution, or other free or nearly free methods. In China, there has been little true privatization of large SOEs; instead, newly created shares in these companies have been sold to domestic and foreign investors, and the sale proceeds have flowed to the firm itself rather than to the national or local governments. Thus far, the Chinese government has not surrendered ultimate control of any major SOE.

Since there are very few true SOEs in the United States, privatization means something entirely different here as well. As discussed in López-de-Silanes, Shleifer and Vishny (LSV; 1997) and Boardman, Laurin, and Vining (2003), privatization in America refers to contracting out the provision of services currently provided by the public sector to the private sector. LSV examine empirically why certain activities are contracted out by different governments, and find that the more binding are state fiscal constraints and the less powerful are public-sector unions, the greater the likelihood of contracting out public services.

Are There Industries That Should Not Be Privatized?

While the weight of empirical evidence generated over the past decade indicates that privatization generally improves the financial and operating performance of most companies and in most countries, the evidence also clearly suggests that privatization yields systematically different effects in different industries. Privatization of manufacturing firms (i.e., automobile assembly, oil and gas exploration and production, and steel-making) and of service businesses such as telecommunications and gas distribution that operate in globally competitive industries generally yields immediate, and often dramatic, performance improvements. In fact, privatizations of these businesses have become almost noncontroversial, since the performance improvements observed have been so obvious and the need to change ownership in order to gain access to new sources of capital and technology has been so pressing.

In regulated service businesses besides telecoms and gas distribution, there is compelling evidence that privatization can yield significant performance improvements, but only if appropriate supplemental policy steps are also adopted. For electric utilities, the evidence clearly shows that privatization works best when governments simultaneously adopt an effective regulatory regime and promote competition and new entry into a deregulated industry. The empirical evidence is even more mixed for airlines and commercial banking. While most studies of these industries do find that privatization improves performance, the improvements documented thus far are neither large in economic terms nor especially robust, and are consistently observed only when the state firms are sold to foreign companies.

The discussion above raises a critical question: Are there any industries that simply should not be privatized because the costs of ownership change outweigh the benefits? At one level, the answer to this question is an obvious yes; there are many government services (national defense, administration of courts of justice, basic social welfare services) that should not be contracted out no matter what the cost savings from doing so might be. In other cases—such as administration of parks and monuments, provision of health-care services, higher education, and administration of prisons—privatization may yield both quantifiable economic benefits and less quantifiable noneconomic costs.

But are there any fee-for-service businesses that should not be privatized? Our answer is a cautious no, but there is one industry that has proved very difficult to transfer to private ownership in a way that yields unambiguous welfare improvements. That is water and sewerage provision. As described in various World Bank and United Nations reports, it is extremely difficult to operate water and sewerage businesses at a price that is both profitable for service providers and affordable for consumers—especially in poor countries that require large capital investments to upgrade their networks. Only three (European) water companies are actively involved in water privatizations internationally, and these companies have generally had dismal experiences with developing country privatizations. Therefore, divesting governments wishing to sell their water and sewerage companies cannot count on strong demand from multinational companies. All too often, in fact, these sales fail to attract a single qualified buyer.

Unfortunately, the empirical evidence on water and sewerage privatization is both scant and mixed. Whereas Saal and Parker (2003) finds no performance improvements related to privatization itself in the water and sewerage industry of England and Wales, Galiani, Gertler, and Schargrodsky (2001) document very strong improvements (and service extensions) after Argentina privatized its water companies during the early 1990s. On balance, therefore, we conclude that water and sewerage companies probably should be privatized, but also caution that ownership change alone will yield major service improvements only if prices charged are allowed to rise significantly and consumers are able to pay these higher fees.

The Future of Privatization

We have seen that privatization has spread rapidly around the world during the past quarter-century, but what does the future hold for this policy? We conclude this book with an (always hazardous) attempt to predict how much privatization will occur both in the immediate future—say the next five years—as well as over a longer period out to 20 years. Our near-term predictions will mostly be region-specific, beginning with western Europe and ending with Latin America, while our long-term forecasts will focus much more on which new industries and government services will be transferred to private ownership by the year 2025.

The Immediate Future of Privatization (2005–2010)

WESTERN EUROPE

A strong prima facie case can be made that the next few years will see far less privatization by western European governments than did the period 1995–2000 for the simple reason that these governments are beginning to run out of assets to sell. Indeed, state-owned enterprises have largely been eliminated from the economic lives of Great Britain, Portugal, Spain, and (to a lesser extent) Italy, and their importance has been dramatically reduced almost everywhere else in western Europe. Every major EU country launched a significant privatization program during the 1990s, and very few wholly state-owned telecoms, banks, airlines, water and sewerage companies, or oil and gas production and distribution networks still exist in this region.

On the other hand, while most EU state enterprises have been partially privatized, few governments were able to fully divest their SOE holdings before the stock market collapse of 2000–2002 halted additional large share issue privatizations. In particular, only a handful of the EU telecom providers have been fully privatized, and majority stakes in the national telco are still held by the governments of Germany, France, Iceland, Norway, and Switzerland, while the governments of Austria, the Netherlands, and Sweden still retain 35 to 48 percent stakes in their national telecom providers. Collectively, these telecom stakes alone are worth almost $100 billion.

While the retained telecom holdings of EU governments probably represent their single most valuable residual ownership stakes, other holdings may prove almost as important over time. As we discussed in chapter 10, few European governments have fully divested their holdings in the national electricity production and distribution network, and many have not even begun privatizing their electric service industries. Italy, Norway, and Finland still hold large stakes in state oil and gas companies—worth roughly $50 billion collectively—while France has not even begun to privatize either Gaz de France or Electricité de France, each of which may be worth over $30 billion. National and regional governments in Germany, Italy, and several other countries retain majority ownership (sometimes 100 percent ownership) of large savings banks and nonbank financial institutions, while the governments of France, Italy, Greece, and the Scandinavian countries retain majority ownership of their national airlines, and the Dutch government retains a 14 percent stake in KLM.

All in all, the stakes retained by EU governments in wholly owned or partially privatized state-owned enterprises are probably worth around $250 billion at today's market values. If stock markets continue to rise in value over the next five years, and if EU governments once more begin aggressively selling their retained SOE stakes, this region could see new sales totaling as much as $300 billion through the year 2010.

EASTERN EUROPE AND THE FORMER SOVIET UNION

To say that the past decade has been tumultuous for the countries of CEE and the former Soviet Union (again, FSU) would be a major understatement. After a very painful and fitful start, most of the transition countries have at least partially privatized their core SOEs, though in many cases governments still retain sizable ownership stakes. Perhaps surprisingly, the one industry that has now been privatized most completely by transition governments is commercial banking, though the end result of this process in the CEE economies has been near total foreign ownership—which is hardly what most governments wished to see in the early days of transition.

With respect to network industries, privatization has made much less progress in CEE and FSU countries. Telecoms, oil and gas production and distribution, and electric power generation and distribution all remain largely state owned. The governments of Croatia, the Czech Republic, Latvia, Lithuania, Poland, Romania, Russia, Serbia, and Slovakia still hold at least 49 percent stakes in their principal fixed-line or wireless (or both) telecom providers, and these stakes are collectively worth almost $15 billion at current market prices. Few of the region's electric power companies have even been partially privatized, so the potential payoff from a full-scale divestment program could easily top $20 billion if properly sequenced, and if buyers are allowed to restructure these companies after purchase.

Without doubt, however, the most valuable retained stakes held by CEE and FSU governments are in national oil and gas companies. The Polish and Hungarian governments hold minority stakes in their national oil companies, worth about $2 billion together, but this is dwarfed by the value of Russia's retained stakes in Gazprom and three other companies. The state's holdings in Gazprom alone are worth $17 billion at current market prices, and the other three stakes collectively could be sold today for perhaps $3 billion more. The region's pipelines and other distribution networks also remain state owned. All told, the governments of central and eastern Europe and the former Soviet Union retain complete or partial ownership stakes in SOEs worth perhaps as much as $75 billion, and the next five years are likely to see many of these assets divested.

AFRICA

Privatization has been something of a stealth policy in Africa over the past two decades. While several hundred transactions have been recorded across the continent, the total value of all divestments has been less than $20 billion—and most of that has been generated by sales in Nigeria and South Africa [see Bennell (2003)]. Furthermore, very few of the core SOEs dominating economic life in most sub-Saharan African nations have been majority privatized, and most have not even been partially divested. Therefore, the potential for a significant number and value of African privatizations certainly exists. Given the current political and ideological environment, however, such a surge in privatization seems highly unlikely over the next few years. The best intermediate-term prediction is for a small but steady stream of sales worth perhaps $5 billion per year through the end of this decade. Longer term, the potential for African privatizations looks much brighter.

SOUTH AND EAST ASIA

This vast region is by far the most promising area for privatization over the next five year, for two principal reasons. First, privatization has generally been less widespread in most Asian countries than it has been in Europe or Latin America, so there is much more left to sell. Second, many Asian countries continue to achieve economic growth rates that are two or more times higher than those achieved in other regions, so international investors will continue to have a strong appetite for Asia's privatized assets. Most Asian governments retain full or majority ownership of their national telecommunications companies, and few have even begun to privatize their electric supply industries. State-owned banks have played important roles in many of the countries in this region, and most of these remain majority state owned. This region is also unusual in that many of the state-owned airlines have significant value, which could yield a financial windfall for divesting governments over the next several years if the global airline industry continues its recent slow but steady recovery.

There can be little doubt, however, that the promise of privatization in the two Asian countries of China and India dwarfs all others. On a purchasing-power-parity basis, these countries are already the second- and fifth-largest economies in the world, and both are growing extremely rapidly. Furthermore, privatization thus far has not figured prominently in the economic reform agendas of either country. Although the Chinese government has sold minority stakes in several hundred SOEs, as described in Lin (2000) and Sun and Tong (2003), none of these sales has involved nearly complete ownership transfer and few of the large, core state enterprises has even been partially privatized. A series of announcements in early 2004 that China would be investing almost $100 billion of its exchange reserves to recapitalize three of the four largest state-owned banks suggests the potential scale of a complete privatization of China's financial system. The Chinese state also retains telecom stakes worth over $50 billion at current market prices, and its residual holdings in the major national oil and gas companies are worth around $40 billion.

While China has at least begun a serious privatization program, this really has not been the case in India. Despite repeated promises to raise large sums for the national budget, Gupta (2004) shows that very few of India's large SOEs have even been partially privatized—and all of the sales through early 1999 were of very small minority stakes. Furthermore, India has an unusually extensive state sector, so the potential for large-scale privatization is vast. On the other hand, most of the large SOEs are very poorly run and almost all previous attempts to sell these companies have met with vocal and effective opposition—especially in the banking sector. Thus one should be careful in making excessively bold predictions about the intermediate-term prospects for privatization in India, and to a lesser extent for China and the other continental Asian economies as well. Even so, we believe that governments in the region might be able to raise as much as $400 billion through asset sales and SIPs over the next five years, with roughly half of that coming from China and India.

JAPAN AND OCEANIA

Japan is a puzzle for privatization researchers. This country has raised more from privatization sales since 1985 than any other country, yet the Japanese government has (repeatedly) executed some of the most poorly designed auctions and has suffered the indignity of seeing several SIPs fail outright. Even after divesting almost $150 billion worth of assets over the past two decades, the Japanese governments still retains immensely valuable SOE holdings. Just the state's holdings in NTT and NTT DoCoMo are worth over $70 billion at today's prices, and the Japanese government has not even to begin privatizing the Postal Savings system or other para-statal financial entities. Significant portions of Japan's electricity and transport networks also remain state owned, as are all of the major airports and seaports. In sum, the potential payoff from a determined Japanese privatization program could run to $100 billion or more, but there is little evidence that this is being seriously contemplated.

Paradoxically, the situations in Australia and New Zealand are almost exactly the opposite of Japan's. These two countries have nearly run out of assets to sell. Both Australia and (especially) New Zealand were privatization leaders during the

1980s and 1990s, and most of their core state enterprises have been at least partially privatized. Even so, Australia retains a 50.1 percent stake in the national telecom (Telstra), worth over $20 billion at current market prices, and New Zealand owns 46 percent of Telecom Corporation of New Zealand, which is worth some $3 billion. The Australian electric supply industry, which has traditionally been owned and operated by regional governments rather than the national government, is now partially privatized and will likely be fully private within a few years. All in all, international investors will see few privatization offerings from Down Under over the next few years.

LATIN AMERICA

The region offering the least promising intermediate-term outlook for privatization must be Latin America. This conclusion is based on three principal observations. First, Latin America went further down the path toward complete privatization of state enterprises during the 1990s than any other region (including western Europe), so the regions' governments have relatively few easily marketable assets left to sell. Second, privatization has become such an unpopular policy in Latin America that few governments would dare propose a major new round of asset sales, even if the governments had large numbers of assets left to sell. In fact, it will be surprising if several privatized companies are not re-nationalized over the next few years in Peru, Bolivia, Venezuela, Argentina, Brazil, and other countries. Third, international investors currently seem to be shunning Latin America in favor of other emerging markets, both because the near-term economic growth prospects for many of the region's economies seem so poor and because investors perceive a rising chorus of populist and left-wing rhetoric from many of the region's political leaders. So far, this rhetoric has not been translated into material policy changes, so investor sentiment could well change if global economic expansion lifts Latin America's economic prospects. Over the next few years, however, we doubt that more than $20 billion in total will be raised through new privatization sales in the entire region, and long-term prospects do not appear particularly promising either.

NORTH AMERICA

The three countries of North America have immensely different privatization histories, and offer significantly different near-term divestment prospects. Mexico underwent a sweeping, and highly successful privatization program during the period 1988–1992, but then suffered through an extremely costly failed bank privatization program during the mid-1990s. There have been few additional sales of Mexican state assets since 1995, and few are likely over the next few years.

Even though Mexico's national oil company, Pemex, and the nation's electricity network both remain 100 percent state owned, and could be sold for a combined total of perhaps $150 billion or more, neither sale is politically conceivable any time soon. Other than these two assets, Mexico has few easily marketable state enterprises left to sell.

Canada has blithely wandered on and off the privatization path repeatedly over the past two decades, selling a few state assets one year, then forgoing additional sales the next. Ideology has played little role thus far in Canada's privatization program, which nonetheless has raised over $20 billion since 1985. Recently, most of the action has been at the regional level, with various regional governments partially divesting ownership in electric power grids and other energy assets. The safest prediction for Canadian privatizations over the next five years is for more of the same—rather ad hoc sales totaling perhaps $5 billion in peak years, but less than $100 million in lean ones.

For no other large nation are the intermediate-term privatization prospects as enigmatic as they are for the United States. As noted above, there have been few "classic" American privatizations for the simple reason that state-owned enterprises have traditionally played little role in American economic life. Instead, privatization has meant the contracting out of services previously provided by the public sector, and even under this tamer definition the total proceeds raised by all levels of government in the United States have been quite small. The safest bet for the next five years is that this trend of incremental small "privatizations" will continue. However, the final months of 2003 offered a glimpse of a possible alternative political future in the election of Arnold Schwarzenegger as governor of California in a truly bizarre special election. Given the monumental state budget deficit that Governor Schwarzenegger must somehow close—without raising taxes—and the stated philosophies of many of his economic advisors, there is a fair chance that California will launch a massive program of contracting out and asset sales over the next few years. If such a program is indeed launched and is perceived to be successful, this could well prompt a nationwide trend toward shifting more service provision from the public to the private sector.

In sum, the maximum likelihood estimate for the total value of privatizations worldwide over the next five years is a cumulative total of between $250 billion and $500 billion. The years 2004 and 2005 should see a continued rebound from the severely depressed global levels of around $50 billion annually witnessed during 2001 and 2002, but it is difficult to imagine annual total proceeds again reaching the $160–180 billion levels of 1997–2000 any time in the near future. The most promising regions for privatization during the period 2005–2010 will likely be South and East Asia, especially China and India, followed by western Europe, the transition economies of central and eastern Europe and the former Soviet Union, and Japan.

Long-Term Prospects and Challenges for Privatization

What are the truly long-term prospects for privatization worldwide—say over the next 20 years? Obviously, the further in the future one predicts, the less confident one must be, so readers should treat the predictions we make in this section with a proper skepticism. Nonetheless, we can identify three possible "mega-trends" that, if they emerge as we predict, will have the potential to transform the global economic and political impact of privatization. The first, and potentially most powerful, trend that we believe will emerge is that governments of oil-producing states will decide to privatize their NOCs. Such a step is currently unimaginable for most "petro-state" governments, particularly those that are OPEC members, but the economic logic of divesting NOCs is compelling. Few oil economies have performed even modestly well over the past two decades, and the potential revenues that could be raised from a concerted NOC privatization program are enormous. In chapter 10, we calculated that the complete privatization of the 17 NOCs that are now wholly state owned by OPEC and non-OPEC governments could raise a minimum of $1.45 trillion and a maximum of $3.21 trillion. The critical test of whether this trend is at all realistic will come when the newly elected government of Iraq decides whether, and how, to privatize the Iraqi National Oil Company. If this sale occurs and is perceived to be successful, more will certainly follow.

The second trend that we believe will emerge over the next two decades is the economic awakening of the Moslem world, and particularly the Arab nations in the Middle East. As documented in a recent United Nations (2002) publication entitled *Arab Human Development Report 2002*, the Arab world severely lags almost all other regions in economic growth and in economic and political freedom. For far too long, the Arab world has suffered under oppressive and intrusive regimes, and the SOEs that dominate economic life throughout this region are among the most backward and least productive in the world. In order for these countries to make any significant progress toward greater political freedom, they will also have to massively reform their lumpen state sectors and open their economies to trade and investment. Currently, few Arab SOEs (outside of the oil sector) would be considered especially valuable, but if these were to be reformed as part of a general market opening process, many Arab state enterprises could become very attractive both to foreign strategic buyers and to local stock market investors. To phrase this a bit differently, the "inventory" of Arab SOEs is both massive and potentially very valuable.

Mega-trend number three might be called the privatization of public transport. Despite full or partial divestment of many national airlines, much of the core public transportation network remains wholly state owned in both developed and developing countries. Most of the world's seaports, airports, passenger rail networks, subways, and bus services are state owned, as are key nontransportation networks such as pipelines and roadways, yet there is no overriding economic reason that this must be so. Many of these assets are, or could readily be made to be, extremely valuable and could be sold very easily. Of course, most passenger rail services require heavy government subsidies, but even here there is scope for at least private management—if not outright ownership.

Regardless of what happens regarding outright privatization of existing assets, there seems little doubt that private financing of infrastructure investments will continue to increase in importance over time. The spectacular rise of project finance as a method of developing and funding large infrastructure projects clearly shows that private capital can be mobilized to finance what have traditionally been considered public works. This blurring of the lines between what economic activities are considered inherently "public" and "private" has driven privatization to the forefront of public policy over the past two decades, and seems likely to continue over the next two.

Appendix 1: Sample Firms Privatized Through Public Share Offerings, 1961–August 2003

This table provides descriptive information for our sample of SOEs that were fully or partially privatized through a public offering of shares during the period March 1961 through the end of August 2003. The table documents basic information, such as date and size of the offering, and also documents whether it was an IPO, a seasoned issue, or a rights offering. Information about offering characteristics (primary versus secondary), geographic allocation, investor demand and initial return, and government policies and share ownership is also provided.

Company Name[1]	Issue Date	Initial Share Issue			Government % Share Capital		Fraction of Issue Allocated to			Multi-Class (Y/N)	Other Restrictions (Y/N)	Special Share (Y/N)[6]	Times Issue Over-subscribed[7]	Initial Period Return[8]
		Issue Size ($US million)	Privatization Issue (Y/N)[2]	Fraction Secondary[3]	Before Issue	After Issue	Employees	Foreign Investors[4]	U.S. Investors[5]					
Argentina														
Telefonica de Argentina*	Dec 91	849	Y+	100	40[9]	10	—	75	—	Y	Y	N	2.5	—
Telecom Argentina	Mar 92	1,050	Y+	100	30[10]	0	—	20	—	—	—	—	6	—
	Mar 94	1,227	N	100	100									
Yacimientos Petroliferos Fiscales (YPF)	Jun 93	2,660	Y	100	100	54.7[11]	10[12]	75	46	Y	Y	—	—	—
Australia														
Commonwealth Bank*	Jul 91	1,017	Y	0	100	70.25	3.6[13]	0[14]	0	N	Y[15]	N	3.5	—
	Oct 93	878	N	100	70.25	50.35	—	—	—	—	—	—	—	—
	Jul 96	3,100	N	100	50.4	0	—	—	—	—	—	—	Y	0[16]
Government Insurance Office	Jul 92	1,766	Y	100	100	0	—	—	—	—	—	—	>1	36%

(continued)

Appendix 1 (continued)

Company Name[1]	Issue Date	Initial Share Issue			Government % Share Capital		Fraction of Issue Allocated to			Multi-Class (Y/N)	Other Restrictions (Y/N)	Special Share (Y/N)[6]	Times Issue Over Subscribed[7]	Initial Period Return[8]
		Issue Size ($US million)	Privatization Issue (Y/N)[2]	Fraction Secondary[3]	Before Issue	After Issue	Employees	Foreign Investors[4]	U.S. Investors[5]					
SGIO*	Mar 94	125	Y	100	100	0								
Tabcorp*	Aug 94	504	Y	100	100	0								
Qantas	Jul 95	1,070[17]	Y	100	75[18]	0								
Telstra	Nov 97	10,530	Y	100	100	66.6	3.8[19]	12	—	N	Y[20]	N	4.5[21]	
	Oct 99	10,400	N	100	66.6	50.1	0[22]	13.5	B	N	—	—	—	0[23]
TAB	Jun 98	644	Y	100	90	0		0[24]		N			heavily	7.3%
Austria														
Austrian Airlines	Jun 87	73	Y	100	99.2	75	—	—	—	—			—	—
	Jun 88	73	N	100	75	55								
	May 89	65	N	100	55	41								
ÖMV Aktiengesellschaft*	Dec 87	117	Y	100	100	85	25	—	—	N	N	N	2	—
Vorarlberger Kraftwerke(VKW)*	Oct 88	56	Y	100	100	0		—	—					
Verbund*	Nov 88	153[25]	Y	0	100									
Energie-Versorgung Niederösterreich(EVN)*	Nov 89	125	Y	100	100	51	10.6	13.2	—	Y	Y	N	—	—
Flughafen Wein*	Jun 92	162	Y	100	100	73								
	Jun 95	197	N	100	70.4	52.14								
Voest-Alpine Eisenbahnsysteme*	Dec 92		Y	100	100	51								

Company	Date										
VA Technologie*	Nov 93	49	N	100	51	0					
Austria Mikro Systeme*	Nov 94	43	N	100	26	0	11.5				
	May 94	655	Y	100				60.0			1.6%
	Jul 94	25	N	100				19.2[26]			
Bohler Uddeholm*	Mar 95	165	Y	0	72.7	72.7	—	—	—		—
	Apr 96	393	N	100	72.7	25	—	—	—		
Austria Tabak	Nov 97	340	Y	100	100	56[27]		45		5	4%
Telecom Austria	Nov 00	853	Y	100	75[28]	48[29]				heavily	-7.7%
Belgium											
Credit Communal de Belgique	Nov 96	1,100	Y	100	100	65.5[30]	—	—	—	4	4.7%
Brazil											
Usinimas	Oct 91	1,170	Y[31]	100	100	25		5.9[32]			
Petroflex*	Apr 92	222	Y	100	100	11					
Copesul	May 92	839	Y	100	100	37					
Goiás Fertilizantes*	Oct 92										
National Steel Company	Apr 93	801									
Ultrafertil*	Jun 93	206									
Cosipa	Aug 93	586									
Acominas	Sep 93	599									
COPERBO*	Jun 94										
Acrilinitrila do Nordeste (Acrinor)*	Jul 94										
Petrobras	Aug 97	534	Y	100	79.2	55		60[33]			
	Aug 00	4,030	N	100					100		
Embraer	Jul 01	750	N	100						4	

(continued)

Company Name[1]	Issue Date	Initial Share Issue — Issue Size ($US million)	Initial Share Issue — Privatization Issue (Y/N)[2]	Initial Share Issue — Fraction Secondary[3]	Government % Share Capital — Before Issue	Government % Share Capital — After Issue	Fraction of Issue Allocated to — Employees	Fraction of Issue Allocated to — Foreign Investors[4]	Fraction of Issue Allocated to — U.S. Investors[5]	Multi-Class (Y/N)	Other Restrictions (Y/N)	Special Share (Y/N)[6]	Times Issue Over Subscribed[7]	Initial Period Return[8]
Canada														
Fishery Products International (FPI)*	Apr 87	134	Y	100	92	0	8.5[34]	—	—	N	Y	N	—	—
Air Canada*	Sep 88	246	Y	0	100	57	—	25	—	N	Y[35]	N	—	6.3%
	Jul 89	452	N	100	57	0	—	25	—	N	Y[36]	N	—	6.3%
Potash Corp. of Saskatchewan*	Nov 89	197	Y	100	100	63		60	40					
Saskatchewan Oil & Gas*	Oct 91	745	N											
	Oct 90	129												
Telus	Oct 90	835	Y	100	100	40		0					1.47	
	Nov 91	745	N	100	38	0								
Petro Canada*	Jul 91	478	Y	0	100	80.5	6[37]	14	7.1	N	Y[38]	N	—	
	Nov 92	198	N	0	80.5	70	—	—	—	N	Y	N	—	9.1%
	Sep 95	1,170	N	100	70	20		20	20					
Nova Scotia Power*	Aug 92	675	Y	100	100									
Co-enerco Resources*	Mar 93	86	Y	100	100	68.5								
Alberta Energy Comp.*	May 93	355	Y	100	100			[39]						
Canadian National Railway	Nov 95	1,500	Y	100	100	60							10	—

Company	Date													
Chile														
CAP de Inversione*	Mar 85	82[40]	Y	0	100	53	—	—	—	N	Y	N	—	—
Telefonos de Chile*	Sep 90	89	Y+	0	—	—	—	100	75	Y	Y	N	>1	7.4%
China (P.R.C.)														
Shanghai Vacuum Electronic Devise	Jan 92	78	Y	0	—	—	—	100[41]	—	Y	—	—	4.0	26%
Shanghai Tyre & Rubber	Aug 92	217		0										
Brilliance China Automotive Holdings Ltd.[42]*	Oct 92	80	Y	100	91.5	65.2	—	100[43]	—	Y	N	N	—	26%
Shanghai Chlor-Alkali	Jul 93	217	Y	0	100	70								
Yizheng Chemical Fibre	Mar 94	279												
Dongfang Electronic	Jun 94	62	Y	0										
Shandong Huaneng Power	Aug 94	337	Y	0	100	73			100[44]					
Huaneng Power Intl	Oct 94	650	Y	100	75			50						
	Mar 98	142	N	0										
Jilin Chemical Industrial	Jun 95	200					100							
Guangshen Railway	May 96	442	Y	0[45]	—	—	—	100[46]	—	—	—	—	7	—
Guangdong Tannery	Dec 96	14.6	—	0	—	—	0	100	—	—	—	—	600+	
China Southern	Aug 97	631.1	Y	0	100	70	0	100[47]	93	N	—	—	2.5	3.7%
China Telecom	Oct 97	4,000	Y	100	100	75	0	95.5[48]	10.7	—	—	—	30	-10.6%[49]
	Oct 99	2,000	N	0	76	72		100					2	
	Nov 02	1,650	Y	0	100	90		95	95[50]					
China Unicom	Jun 00	4,900	Y	0	100	75								
	Oct 02	1,400	N	0										
Great Wall Technology	Aug 99	144	Y		90			100					90	

(continued)

411

Appendix 1 (continued)

Company Name[1]	Issue Date	Initial Share Issue: Issue Size ($US million)	Privatization Issue (Y/N)[2]	Fraction Secondary[3]	Government % Share Capital: Before Issue	After Issue	Fraction of Issue Allocated to: Employees	Foreign Investors[4]	U.S. Investors[5]	Multi-Class (Y/N)	Other Restrictions (Y/N)	Special Share (Y/N)[6]	Times Issue Over Subscribed[7]	Initial Period Return[8]
Beijing Capital Intl Airport	Jan 00	462	Y	0										-4.7%
PetroChina	Apr 00	2,890	Y	10	100	90		100						
China Unicom	Jun 00	4,900	Y		100	75	0	100[51]						
Baoshan Iron & Steel	Dec 00	943	Y	0				0[52]					27	46%
China National Off-shore Oil Comp	Feb 01	1,400	Y	0	100	72.5		100[53]					3.2	+
Sinopec	Oct 00	3,470	Y	0				100[54]					4	-3%
Unicom	Aug 01	1,400	N					0					160	3.3%
	Oct 02	1,400	Y	0				0						25%
Bank of China	Jul 02	2,800	Y		100			100[55]						-4.7%
Mass Transit Railway Corp (HKSAR)	Oct 00	1,380	Y	100	100	77		0					30 retail; 15 instit.	24%
Croatia														
Pliva	Mar 96	142	—[56]	100	—	—	—	100[57]	—	—	—	—	20	—
	May 98	238	N	100	14	0[58]	—	86[59]	0	—	—	—		1.2%
Zagrebacka Bank	Jun 96	25	—[60]	100	—	—[61]	—	100[62]	—	—	—	—	15	—
Czech Republic														
Komercni Bank	Jul 95	85	Y	100	100	96[63]			—	—	—	—		—
	May 96	50	N	100	94.7	91.5	0	67	33	—	—	—		—
Ceska Sporitelna	Jun 96	48.5	N	100	—	—[65]	—	—	—	—	Y[64]	—		—

Country / Company	Date													
Ceske Radiomuni-kace	May 98	134	N	0	70	51		100		N			6	11.8%[66]
Denmark														
Copenhagen Airports*	Mar 94	112	Y	100	100	75	3.7[67]	80	—	N	Y	N	3.3	−6.1%
Tele Danmark AS*	May 94	2,894	Y	0	89.9	51	2.1[68]	—	—	Y	Y	N	4	7.3%
Egypt														
Nasr City Housing & Construction	May 96	53.7	Y	100	100	23[69]	6.7	0	—	—	—	—	71.0	—
Medinet Nasr Housing & Development Company	Aug 96	172	Y	100	100	25	—	—	—	—	—	—	—	—
Al-Ahram Beverages	Feb 97	52.2	N	0	75	0	0[70]	95	—	—	—	—	7.5	21%
El-Nasr Clothing & Textile	Jun 97	57	Y	100	100	0	—	—	—	—	—	—	Yes	
Estonia														
Estonian Telecom	Feb 99	221	Y	100	100	76.3		85.8		Y	Y		15	
Finland														
Valmet	Aug 88	188	Y	0	100	80	—	0	—	—	—	—	—	14.5%
Rautaruukki	Jun 89	101	Y	0	99.3	86.8	22.7	0	—	—	Y	—	5	8.9%
Outokumpu	Dec 93	66	N	15.6	86.8	81.1	0	—	—	—	Y	—	—	15.7%
	May 89	78	N	0	60	57	11.1	0	—	—	Y	Y	7	4.7%
	Dec 93	148	N	0	57	50.1	—	—	—	—	—	—	—	2.5%
Finnair	Jan 95	74	N	0	71.5	62.2	—	70	—	—	—	—	2	—
Kemira	Oct 96	285	N	69	72.3	55	—	—	—	—	—	—	—	−1.1%
Fortum	Dec 98	573	Y	100	97.5	75.5	—	—	—	—	—	—	—	−5.13%
	Jan 02	403	N	100	70	61	—	31	—	—	—	—	5	

(continued)

Appendix 1 (continued)

Company Name[1]	Issue Date	Issue Size ($US million)	Privatization Issue (Y/N)[2]	Fraction Secondary[3]	Government % Share Capital — Before Issue	Government % Share Capital — After Issue	Employees	Foreign Investors[4]	U.S. Investors[5]	Multi-Class (Y/N)	Other Restrictions (Y/N)	Special Share (Y/N)[6]	Times Issue Over Subscribed[7]	Initial Period Return[8]
Sonera	Jan 99	1,400	Y	100	100	78.8	1.4	80.9[71]	—					
	Oct 99	3,600	N	100	75.6	57.6								
	Mar 00	1,900	N	100	57.6	54.5								
	Nov 01	887	N	0[72]										
Stora Enso	Sep 00	238	N						100					
	Jun 02		N	100										
France														
Elf Acquitaine	Sep 86	493	Y	100	66.8	55.8	—	—	—	—	Y	Y[73]	4	11.2%
	Jun 91	440	N	100	55.8	53.8	—	66.7	42.1	—	Y	Y	—	0%
	Mar 92	367	N	100	53.8	51.5	—	35	—	—	Y	Y	3.22	0.56%
	Feb 94	6,823	N	100	51	13	7.5	27	—	—	Y	—	3	—[75]
	Nov 96	2,000	N	100	9.85	0.75	0	70+[74]	0	—	Y	—	—	
Saint Gobain	Nov 86	2,091	Y	100	100	0	—	20[76]	—	Y	Y	—	14	36.7%[77]
Banque Paribas	Jan 87	2,740	Y	100	100	0	—	20	—	Y	Y	—	40[78]	18.5%
Sogenal	Mar 87	250	Y	100	100[79]	0	—	—	—	—	Y	—	46	80.0%[80]
Banque de Batement et des Travaux Publics	Apr 87	67	Y	100	100	0	—	—	—	—	Y	—	65	20.8%
Banque Industrielle & Mobiliere Privee (BIMP)	Apr 87	60	Y	100	100	0	10	—	—	—	Y	—	29	27.1%

(continued)

Company	Date													
Credit Commercial de France	Apr 87	Y	732	100	100	0	10	20	—	—	Y	—	10.7	15.9%
Agence Havas	May 87	Y	405	100	40.3	0	—	—	—	Y	Y[81]	Y	20	8.0%
Compagnie Generale D'Electricite	May 87	Y	1,927	100	100	0	10	20	1.8	—	Y	—	—	10.3%
Societe Generale	Jun 87	Y	3,577	100[82]	100	0	10	16	—	—	Y	—	—	B
Television Francaise 1 (TF1)	Jul 87	Y	207	100			10	—	—	—	Y	—	—	
Compagnie Financiere de Suez*	Oct 87	Y	2,929	100	100	0	10	11.8[83]	—	Y	Y	N	5	-17.8%
Credit Local de France	Nov 91	Y	340	100	72.5	50.5[84]	0	20	—	—	Y	—	1.74	-3.81[85]
Total S.A.*	Jun 93	N	738	100	50.5	20.0	0	40.4	—	—	Y	N	13.0	7.38[86]
Total S.A.	Jul 92	N	906	100	34	15	0	65	32	Y	Y[87]	Y	2	—
Total S.A.	Feb 96	N	621	100	15	9[88]	—	—	—	—	—	—	—	—
Rhone-Poulenc*	Jan 93	Y	564	100[89]	77.5	67[90]	10	45	16.7	Y	—	N	>1	34.8%
Rhone-Poulenc	Nov 93	N[91]	2,200	100	43	0	10	27.5	19	—	—	—	3	-0.5%
Rhone-Poulenc	Feb 97	N	449	100	5.1[92]	0.5	0	17	—	—	—	—	—	—
Banque Nationale de Paris	Oct 93	Y	4,920	100	100	40	7.4[93]	—	—	—	—	—	8.5	—
Union Des Assurances De Paris	Apr 94	—	3,250	—	50	0	—	—	—	—	—	—	—	—
Renault	Nov 94	Y	2,340	100	80.1	50.1	10						15[94]	—
Renault	Apr 02	N	1,300	100	37.8	27.14							—	—
SGS-Thomson[95]	Dec 94	Y	470	0	95.5	80	Y[96]						—	—
Seita	Feb 95	Y	1,100	100	100	10	0	100[97]					6.55	0
Seita	May 98	N	124	100	10.3	5	4.6	—					—	—
Usinor Sacilor	Jul 95	Y	3,930	74	100	8							—	0
Usinor Sacilor	Oct 97	N	335	100	7.7	0	0						—	—
Pechiney	Dec 95	Y	1,350	64.2	100	44	—		30[98]				1.25[99]	-6.4%
Pechiney	Apr 98	N	371	100	10.5	1[100]	0						—	-0.8%

Appendix 1 (*continued*)

Company Name[1]	Issue Date	Initial Share Issue			Government % Share Capital		Fraction of Issue Allocated to			Multi-Class (Y/N)	Other Restrictions (Y/N)	Special Share (Y/N)[6]	Times Issue Over Subscribed[7]	Initial Period Return[8]
		Issue Size ($US million)	Privatization Issue (Y/N)[2]	Fraction Secondary[3]	Before Issue	After Issue	Employees	Foreign Investors[4]	U.S. Investors[5]					
Assurances Generales de France [AGF]	May 96	1,670	N	100	—	—	9.1	67[101]	—	—	—[102]	—	6[103]	
Machines Bull	May 97	106	N	100	29[104]	17	10	—	—	—	—	—	—	-4.9%
France Telecom	Oct 97	7,080	Y	100	100	77	10	—	—	—	—	—	3[105]	15.0%
	Nov 98	10,500	N	62	75	62							Comfortably	11%[106]
	Mar 03	15,800	N	0	56	56[107]							1	-1%
Thomson-CSF	Jun 98	1,700	N	0	58.3	42.9[108]		0						
Caisse Nationale de Prévoyance	Oct 98	1,590	Y	83.5	100	78	4						retail 6; instit. 7	6%
Air France	Feb 99	337	Y	100	100	78	50[110]	23.7[109]					12.4	0
Aerospatiale Matra	Jun 99	1,400	Y	100	64.7	47.7	13.5						retail 2.1 7; instit. 36	17%
Credit Lyonnais	Jul 99	6,960	Y	100	100	10		42[111]						
STMicroelectronics	Sep 99	2,000	N	90.1										
	Dec 01	2,300	N	0[112]										
European Aeronautic Defense & Space Agency (EADS)	Jul 00	2,852	Y	0		15[113]	7.3[114]							
Wanadoo	Jul 00	1,770	Y	100	100[115]	89.5							retail 5.6; Instit. 16	10%

Thomson Multimedia	Oct 00	2,331[116]	N	66.7	51.7	35								
Orange	Feb 01	6,687[117]	N	100[118]	100	86.29							16.8 instit.	−6%
Credit Agricole	Dec 01	3,158	Y	0	100								19	5.6%
Autoroutes du sud de la France	Mar 02	2,400	Y	100	100	51								11%
Germany														
Volkswagen AG	Mar 61	315	Y	100	100	40	—[119]	C			Y[120]		2	109.3%
	Mar 88	674	N	100	16	0		C			Y		>1	2.7%
VEBA AG	Apr 65	132	Y	29	100	43.8					Y		>1	13.8%
	Mar 87	1,380	N	100	25.6	0	—[121]							1.4%[122]
VIAG	Jun 86	327	Y	100	100	60								—
	May 88	877	N	100	60	0								0.3%[123]
Industrie Verwaltungs Gesellschaft (IVG)	Oct 86	81	Y	100	100	55		0						—
Deutsche Verkehrs-Kredit-Bank (DVKB)	Mar 88	34	Y	100	100	75.1	49.8	0	0					—
Lufthansa	Sep 89	475	N	0	69	52	00	O	0		Y			—[124]
	Sep 94	730	N	0[125]	51.4	41			0				Heavily	2%
Deutsche Siedlungs- Und Landesrentenbank (DSL)	Oct 89	241	Y	100	100	52								—
Deutsche Telekom	Nov 96	13,300	Y	0	100	74		62[127]	21[128]	N	N	N	5[126]	19%
	Jun 99	10,200	N	0	65.6	59	2	80[129]	10			N	2	−3.3%[130]
	Jun 00	14,760	N	100	46.1	19.2[131]								
Jenoptik	Jun 98	424	Y	100	100[132]								30	39%
T-Online	Apr 00	2,700	Y	100	100								19	2.4%
Deutsche Post	Nov 00	5,600	Y	100	100	71							1+	

(continued)

417

Appendix 1 (continued)

| Company Name[1] | Issue Date | Initial Share Issue | | | Government % Share Capital | | Fraction of Issue Allocated to | | | Multi-Class (Y/N) | Other Restrictions (Y/N) | Special Share (Y/N)[6] | Times Issue Over-Subscribed[7] | Initial Period Return[8] |
		Issue Size ($US million)	Privatization Issue (Y/N)[2]	Fraction Secondary[3]	Before Issue	After Issue	Employees	Foreign Investors[4]	U.S. Investors[5]					
Fraport (Frankfort Airport)	Jun 01	784	Y	0										−4.6%
Ghana														
Ashanti Goldfields	Apr 94	373	Y+	84.7	55	31.3	—[133]	71.8	—	—	—	Y	5	3.0%
Greece														
Hellenic Sugar Industries	Jul 93	33	Y	—	100	70.5	—	—	—	—	—	—	5	—
OTE	Mar 96	398	Y	100	100	94	17	—	—	—	—	—	6	8[134]
	Jun 97	1,967	N	65	92	80	—	48	—	—	—	—	1.8	
	Nov 98	1,100	N	100	75	65	—	—	40[135]	—	—	—	1.8	
Hellenic Petroleum	Jun 98	311	Y	30	100	77		63.4[136]					15	
General Hellenic Bank	Apr 98	67	Y	100[137]	85.5	35.5								
Nation Bank of Greece	May 98	379	Y	100	51	41		100					3.5	
	Apr 99	553	N	0	38	34								
	Oct 99	348	N	43.5									1.3	
Athens Stock Exchange	Dec 98	36	Y	100	88	49		25	16				2.5	
CosmOTE	Oct 00	328	Y	100[138]	70	55							4	neg

(continued)

Company	Date													
Public Power Corp	Dec 01	417	Y	100	100	84	31.8	44[39]	—	—	—	—	6[140]	—
	Dec 02	360	N	100	84.5	71.3	—	—	—	—	—	—	—	46.9%
Hungary														
Ibusz	Jun 90	33	Y	—	100	66.6	—	54.5	—	—	—	—	23	—
Egis	Jun 94	44	Y	—	70	41	—	16	—	—	—	—	2	—
	Jun 94	89[141]	Y	100	100	71	—	16	—	—	—	Y	—	—
Mol	Nov 95	153	N	100	88.3	60	6	18.8	32	—	—	—	—	—
	May 97	304	N	100	59	39.7	0[142]	79	—	—	—	—	5[144]	7.4%[145]
	Mar 98	300	N	100	39.7	28.7	—	70[143]	—	—	—	Y	—	—
Borsodchem	Feb 96	64	Y	45	100	39	Y	86	—	—	—	—	Heavily	—
TVK	Jul 96	180	Y	100	100	15	12	83.5	—	—	—	—	—	—
OTP Bank	Oct 97	213	N	100	25	0	20[146]	66	7	—	—	Y	—	−10%[147]
Matav	Nov 97	1,200	Y	100	22.75	5.75	—	72	22	—	—	—	3	0.7%
	Sum 99[148]													
Iceland														
Islandssimi	Jun 01	49	Y	0	100	80.3	—	—	—	—	—	—	oversub	—
India														
State Bank of India	Dec 93	713	N	100	98.2	68.8	—	100	100	—	—	—	—	—
	Oct 96	370	—	—	—	—	—	—	—	—	—	—	—	—
Indian Oil	Nov 95	—	—	—	63	53	—	100	—	—	—	—	—	—
VSNL	Mar 97	527	N	100	82	65	—	100	100	—	—	—	10	18%
MTNL	Dec 97	358	Y	67	100	51	—	—	—	—	—	—	3	positive
Container Corporation	Nov 98	53		100				3[149]						
Gas Authority of India (GAIL)	Feb 99	42						13[150]						
Indonesia														
Indosat	Oct 94	1,060		0	100	65								20%
Tambang Timah	Oct 95	220	Y	100	65	0		72					3	

Appendix 1 (continued)

Company Name[1]	Issue Date	Initial Share Issue			Government % Share Capital		Fraction of Issue Allocated to			Multi-Class (Y/N)	Other Restrictions (Y/N)	Special Share (Y/N)[6]	Times Issue Over Subscribed[7]	Initial Period Return[8]
		Issue Size ($US million)	Privatization Issue (Y/N)[2]	Fraction Secondary[3]	Before Issue	After Issue	Employees	Foreign Investors[4]	U.S. Investors[5]					
PT Telkom	Nov 95	1,590[151]	Y	100	100	81		33		a			>1	2.4%
	Dec 96	600	N	100	81	76.5[152]								
Bank Negara Indonesia	Nov 96	400	Y	100	100	75		43					4.5	50%[153]
Ireland														
Greencore (formerly Irish Sugar Corporation)*	Apr 91	136	Y	100	100	49	10[154]	—	—	N	Y	Y	2.8	B
Telecom Eireann	Jul 99	4,300	Y	100	65[155]	0	23	45[156]					retail 2; instit. 12	18.5%
Israel														
Israel Chemical	Feb 92	235	Y	100	100	75								
	Q1 95		N	100	75	50								
	Dec 98	287	N	100	31.5	0								
Bank Hapoalim	May 93	288	Y	100[157]	97	80.5	—	—	—	—	—	—	120	B
	Apr 99	59	N	74	24	22								
	Jul 99	160	N	100	22	18		100						
	Jun 00	582	N	100	17	0								
Israel Discount Bank	Mar 96	80	Y	100	87	71	—	—	—	—	—	—	1.7	-2.8%
Bezeq	Mar 98	223	N	100	63.5	54[158]	—	—	—	—	—	yes		—

Company	Date													
Bank Leumi	Apr 98	52	N	100	63.5	61.5			100[159]	—	—	—	4.6	12%
	Sep 98	160[160]	N	100	61	44				—	—	—	4.5	—
United Mizrahi Bank	Jun 98	200	Y[161]	49	22[162]					—	—	—	—	—
Italy														
Banca Commerciale Italiana	Aug 85	118	N	100	73	61	—	50		—	—	—	—	—
Societa Finanziaria Telefonica (STET)	Feb 94	1,700	Y	100	54	0	—[163]	—		—	Y	—	10	—
	Nov 85	103	Y	100	87.9	84.8	—	—		Y	Y	—	—	—
Enimont	Jul 91	232	N	100[164]	63.6	59.9	—	—		Y	Y	—	1.9	[165]
	Jun 92	593	N	100[166]	59.3	51.7	—	—		—	Y	—	7	—
Banco di Napoli*	Sep 89	936	Y	100	100	20	—	49		Y	—	N	—	—
	Nov 91	323	N	0	58.8	49.5	—	25		—	—	—	—	—
Credito Italiano	Nov 91	140	N	100	65	58	—	—		Y	—	—	6	11.8%
	Dec 93	1,079	N	100	58	0	—	25.1	10.8	Y	Y	—	—	—
	Dec 93	100	N	—	—	0	100	—		Y	Y	—	—	—
Istituto Bancario San Paolo	Mar 92	709	Y	100	100	80	—[167]	—		—	—	—	—	—
Istituto Nazionale D. Assicurazioini	Jun 94	3,100	Y	100	100	49	—	—		Y	—	—	>1	—
Instituto Mobiliare It-aliano	Jun 96	2,100[168]	N	100	39	5	—	—		—	—	—	>1.0	10%
	Jan 94	1,513	Y	90	60	30	—	46	16	—	—	—	9	—
Eni	Jul 96	327	N	100	8.03	1.1[169]	—	—		—	—	—	—	—
	Nov 95	3,907	Y	100	100	85	—	€7[170]		—	—	—	3[171]	0.4%
	Oct 96	5,864	N	100	85	71	Y[173]	15		—	—	—	—	0[172]
	Jul 97	7,800	N	100	69.1	51.5	—	12.8		—	—	—	Y	—
	Jun 98	6,740	N	100	51.5	36.9[174]	—	14[175]	8.6	—	—	—	2.5	—
Alitalia	May 98	450	Y	100[176]	85.4	67	—	<0		—	—	—	—	—
Saipen	Aug 96	85.6	N	100	80[177]	20	—	—		—	—	—	—	—
Istituto San Paolo di Torino	May 97	730	N	100	66	20	0.8[178]	—		—	—	—	3	—

(continued)

421

Appendix 1 (continued)

Company Name[1]	Issue Date	Initial Share Issue			Government % Share Capital		Fraction of Issue Allocated to			Multi-Class (Y/N)	Other Restrictions (Y/N)	Special Share (Y/N)[6]	Times Issue Over Sub-scribed[7]	Initial Period Return[8]
		Issue Size ($US million)	Privatization Issue (Y/N)[2]	Fraction Secondary[3]	Before Issue	After Issue	Employees	Foreign Investors[4]	U.S. Investors[5]					
Aeroporti di Roma	Jul 97	315	Y	100	75	34	5	—	—	—	—	—	14	
Telecom Italia	Oct 97	15,500	N	100	44.7	3.5	—	—	—	—	—	—	—	3%
	Dec 02	1,400[179]												
Banca di Roma	Nov 97	1,740[180]	Y	0	36.5	0	—	—	—				3	
Banca Nazionale del Lavoro	Nov 98	4,600	Y	100	85	0							retail 6; instit. 3	
AEM[181]	Jul 98	900	Y	100	100	51							retail 5; instit. 23	
Enel	Nov 99	18,900	Y	100	100	65.5							heavily[182]	0%
Autostrade	Dec 99	4,600	N	100	47.7	0							4	
Finmeccanica	Jun 00	5,360	Y	100	60	14.7		24					2.4	
Acegas	Feb 01	143	Y	100	96.8	55[183]							2.6	
Snam Rete Gas	Dec 01	1,800	Y	100[184]	100								5	
ASM Brescia	Jul 02	323	Y	0	100	75[185]								0%
Jamaica														
N.C.B. Group*	Nov 86	16	Y	100	100	0	13	0	0[186]	N	Y	N	—	—
Caribbean Cement*	Jun 87	90	Y+	100	90	0	3.9	0	0	N	Y	Y	—	—
Japan														
Nippon Telegraph and Telephone	Feb 87	15,097	Y	100	100	87.5	—	0[187]	0	—	Y	—	6	55.0%[188]
	Nov 87	40,260[189]	N	100	87.5	75	—	0	0	—	Y	—	—	3.1%[190]

(continued)

Company	Date	Amount											
Japan Air Lines	Oct 88	22,400	N	100	75	65.4	—	0	0	—	Y	—		3.7%[191]
	Dec 98	7,300	N	100	65.5	59		29	10.5	—			2.9	
	Nov 99	15,000	N	100	59	53	B	13.76	13.76	—		7.4		
	Nov 00	11,300	N	100	53	46				—		1.5		
Japan Railroad East	Dec 87	4,645[192]	N	100	34.5	0							1	3.4%[193]
	Oct 93	7,312	Y	—	100	50							29	57.9%
	Jul 99	5,800	N	100	38	12.5								
Japan Tobacco	Sep 94	3,400	N	100	100	80.6							0.34[194]	
	Jun 96	2,040	Y	100	67	0[195]		12.9						
JR West	Oct 96	4,400	Y	100	100	67.1							<1.0[196]	2.8%
NTT DoCoMo	Oct 98	18,400	Y[197]	100[198]	100			30	12				2	
	Feb 01	8,200	N	0	100								2.6 retail	2
Jordan														
Jordan Telecom	Oct 02	150	Y	100	100	85								
Kenya														
Kenya Airways	Mar 96	48	Y	100	74[199]	23	3[200]	14						
Korea														
Pohang Iron and Steel (POSCO)	Jun 88	3,400	Y	0	100	66		100					>1	186.7%
	Oct 94	300	N	0	26.6	21.6								
	Dec 98	300	N	100	21.6	12.8			100[201]					
	May 99	1,010	N	100	6.84	0	33[203]		100[202]					
	Sep 00	336	N	100			73.2[204]							
Korea Electric Power	Jun 89	2,100	Y	100	100	79								-4.6%
	Oct 94	300	N	0	79	58								
	Mar 99	750	N	100	58	53			100					
Korea Telecom	May 99	2,490	N	mixed	71.2	59			100[205]					
	Jun 01	2,200	N	100	58	40			100				>2	
	Jun 02	4,000	N	100	28	0[206]								

Appendix 1 (continued)

Company Name[1]	Issue Date	Initial Share Issue — Issue Size ($US million)	Privatization Issue (Y/N)[2]	Fraction Secondary[3]	Government % Share Capital — Before Issue	After Issue	Fraction of Issue Allocated to — Employees	Foreign Investors[4]	U.S. Investors[5]	Multi-Class (Y/N)	Other Restrictions (Y/N)	Special Share (Y/N)[6]	Times Issue Over Subscribed[7]	Initial Period Return[8]
Korea Tobacco & Ginseng	Oct 01	550	N	100	53	33			100					
Woori Financial Group	Oct 02	230	N	100	14.5	0[207]								
	Jun 02	509	Y	100	100	88		100						6.3%
Kuwait														
Commercial Facilities Company	Sep 94	225		100	54	37							heavily	
Arab Insurance Group[208]	Nov 97	290	Y	100	100	49.5	—	—		—	—	—	5	
MALAWI Press Corp.	Mar 98	12.8	Y	100	93	71		64.4						
Lithuania														
Lithuanian Telecom	Jun 00	160	Y	100	100	75				—				-12.7%
Malaysia														
Malaysian Airline System*	Oct 85	78	Y	100	100	70	16.7[209]	—	—	N	Y	Y	6	—
Telekom Malaysia*	Oct 90	872	Y	0	100	76	15	25[210]	—	N	Y	Y[211]	2	—
	Apr 92	—	N	100	—	—		—	—	N	N	Y	—	—
Tenaga National*	Mar 92	1,165	Y	100	100	77	12.4	10	—	N	Y	Y	2.3	~100
Petronas Gas	Sep 95	1,443	Y	100	100	75	Y	30					1.0	6.25

424

	Date													
Malaysia Airports	Nov 99	293	Y	44	100	72	10	—	48	Y	N	N	1.9	0
Mexico														
Teléfonos de Mex- ico*	May 91	2,170	Y	100[212]	29.8[213]	15	—	79.5	48	Y	N	N	>1	5.6%
	May 92	1,400			6.2	1.53								
	May 94	550			1.53	0[214]								
Grupo Financiero Bancomer	Mar 92	837	Y+	100[215]	44[216]	44	—	—[217]	36	Y	—	—	>1	5.6%
Grupo Financiero Serfin	Dec 93	420	—	—	—	—	—	—	50	Y	—	—	—	5.6%
Morocco														
Compagnie de Transports au Maroc*	Jun 93	12	Y	100	100	60								
Les Ciments de L'Oriental (CIOR)*	Dec 93	40	Y	100	100	66								
Sofac Credit*	Apr 94	5	Y	100	100	81.63								
Societe Nationale D'Investissement (SNI)*	Oct 94	41	Y	100	100	84.37								
Banque Marocaine du Commerce Ex- térieur*	Jan 95	169	Y	100	100	50		100					5	
Crédit-Eqdom*	Apr 96	50	N	100	—	—		100						—
	Jun 95	9	Y	100	100	82								
Netherlands														
KLM Royal Dutch Airlines*	Apr 86	295	Y	20	55	39		55	45	Y	Y	Y[218]	—	0.9%

(continued)

Appendix 1 (continued)

Company Name[1]	Issue Date	Issue Size ($US million)	Privatization Issue (Y/N)[2]	Fraction Secondary[3]	Government % Share Capital — Before Issue	Government % Share Capital — After Issue	Fraction Allocated — Employees	Fraction Allocated — Foreign Investors[4]	Fraction Allocated — U.S. Investors[5]	Multi-Class (Y/N)	Other Restrictions (Y/N)	Special Share (Y/N)[6]	Times Issue Over Subscribed[7]	Initial Period Return[8]
Naamloze Vennootschap DSM*	Feb 89	619	Y	100	100	65.7	5.5	50	—	N	Y	Y	4.5	5.6%
NMB Postbank	Oct 89	715	N	100	65.7	31.3	5.7	49[219]	—	N	Y	Y	>1	0.2%[220]
														—[221]
	Dec 89	649	Y	100	54	24	—	—	—	—	—	—	2.5	
Koninklijke PTT Nederland (KPN)	Jun 94	3,868	Y	100	100	70	—	—	—	—	—	—	4	7%
	Oct 95	3,514	N	100	70	48		45						
	Nov 00	4,600[223]	N	0	43	35		87[224]					2[222]	
	Dec 01	4,500	N	0[225]	34.77	34.77								−8%
Pink Roccade	Jul 99	120	y	100	100	74								0.2%
	Jun 00	280	N	100	74	74								
	Dec 01	38	N	0		37								
New Zealand														
Petrocorp*	Jul 87	75	Y	—	82	64	6	25	—	N	N	N	—	—
Air New Zealand*	Oct 89	99	Y	100	100	0	20[226]	0	0	Y[227]	N	Y[228]	1.9	—
Telecom New Zealand*	Jul 91	819	Y+	100	46[229]	46	—	66.7	33.3	N	N	Y	>1	15.2%
Contact Energy	May 99	1,420	Y	100	100	85		70						11.2%
Norway														
Christiania Bank	Dec 93	259	Y	100	91	69	6[230]							
Statoil	Jun 01	2,900	Y	51	100	80		78						0

(continued)

	Date												
Telenor	Dec 00	1,600	Y	0	100	79		50					
Den Norske Bank (DnB)	Apr 01	474	N	100	60.6	35		81				2.5	−7%
Pakistan													
Pakistan Telecommunications	Sep 94	997	Y	100	100	88							
Papua New Guinea													
Orogen Minerals	Nov 96	188	Y	0	51		70[231]						
Peru													
Telefonica del Peru	Jul 96	1,100	Y	100	28.6	5		86.4[232]	—	—	—	5	>10%
Luz del Sur	Nov 96	200	N	100	30	0		40	—	—		0.8	
Banco Continental	Jul 98	68	N	100	20	0		50[233]	—			4	
Phillipines													
Phillipine National Bank	Mar 92	89	Y	100	67	57		—	—	—	—	—	
Petron	Aug 94	400	Y	100	60	41.5		63	—				
Poland													
Bank Slaski*	Jan 94	64	Y	100	100	70	33	—	N	N	N	>1	1240.%[234]
Jelfa Pharmaceutical*	Apr 94	20	Y	100	100	30							
Polifarb Wroclaw*	May 94	30	Y	100	100	25							
Kutno Pharmaceutical*	94												
Polifarb Cieszyn*	Jun 94												
Rolimpex*	Jul 94												
Stalexport*	Aug 94	74	Y	100	100	40							
Debica*	Sep 94	56	Y	100	100	51.3							

Appendix 1 (*continued*)

Company Name[1]	Issue Date	Issue Size ($US million)	Privatization Issue (Y/N)[2]	Fraction Secondary[3]	Gov't % Before Issue	Gov't % After Issue	Employees	Foreign Investors[4]	U.S. Investors[5]	Multi-Class (Y/N)	Other Restrictions (Y/N)	Special Share (Y/N)[6]	Times Issue Over Subscribed[7]	Initial Period Return[8]
Zaklady Przemyslu Odziezowego*	Sep 94													
Krosno*	Oct 94													
Bank Premyslowo Handlowy	Jan 95	150	Y	100	100	49.9		30.8[235]						
	Jun 97	660	N	100										
Rafako Boiler Engineering Factory*	Feb 95	20	Y	100	100	75								
Bank Gdanski	Dec 95	67	N	100	—	—[236]		0[237]					1.3	
KGHM Polska Miedz	Jul 97	415	Y	100	100	49	29[238]	41	—	—	—	—	4.3	13%
Telekomunikacja Polska SA (TPSA)	Nov 98	1,020	Y	100	100	85		70						11.2%
Polski Koncern Naftowy (PKN)	Nov 99	513	Y	100	85[239]	54		81					4	
Bank Pekao	Jun 00	520	N	100	58	32		0[240]					3	
	Oct 00	133												
Portugal														
Unicer	May 89	63	Y	100	100	51	30	—	—	—	—	—		
	Jun 90	91	N	100	51	0								
Banco Totta & Acores	Jul 89	195	Y	100	100	51		—	—	—	—	—	3	—
	Jul 90	153	N	100	51	20								

428

Tranquilidade	Dec 89	176	Y	100	100	51								
Centralcer	Oct 90	129	N	100	51	0								
	Nov 90	236	Y	100	100	0								
Banco Portugues do Atlantico	Dec 90	382	Y	100	100	67							1.20	
	May 92	346	N	100	67	49.36								
	Jul 93	221	N	100	49.36	31.86								
	Mar 94	105	N	100	31.86	24.36								
Sociedad Financeira Portuguesa	May 91	109	Y	100	100	0								
Banco Espirito Santo e Comercial de Lisboa*	Jul 91	385	Y	100	100	60	25[241]	5	—	N	Y	N	>2	—
Companhia de Seguros Bonanca	Feb 92	590	N	100	60	0	11.3	10	—	N	Y	N	—	| |
	Jul 91	97	Y	100	100	40	—[242]	0	0	—	—	—	>1	| |
Banco Fonsecas & Burnay	Dec 92	29	N	100	40	25								
	Aug 91	247	Y	100	100	20								
Mundial Confianca	Jul 92	61	N	100	20	0								
	Apr 92	229	Y	100	100	0								
Petrogal	Jun 92	279	Y	100	100	75								
Império	Nov 92	174	Y	100	100	0								
Crédito Predial Português	Dec 92	279	Y	100	100	0								
União de Bancos Português	Dec 92	167	Y	100	100	38.9								
Companhia Maceira Pataias	May 94	217	Y	100	100	20								
SECIL	Jul 95	53	N	100	20	0								
	May 94	217	Y	100	100	49								

(continued)

Appendix 1 (*continued*)

Company Name[1]	Issue Date	Initial Share Issue			Government % Share Capital		Fraction of Issue Allocated to			Multi-Class (Y/N)	Other Restrictions (Y/N)	Special Share (Y/N)[6]	Times Issue Over Subscribed[7]	Initial Period Return[8]
		Issue Size ($US million)	Privatization Issue (Y/N)[2]	Fraction Secondary[3]	Before Issue	After Issue	Employees	Foreign Investors[4]	U.S. Investors[5]					
CIMPOR	Jul 94	241	Y	100	100	80	33[243]	55–60					1.05	3.82%
	Sep 96	799	N	100	80	35	Yes[244]						150	
Banco Pinto & Sotto Mayor	May 98	720	N	100	35	10		30[245]						
	Nov 94	255	Y	100	100	20								
	Mar 95	46	N	100	20	0								
Banco Fomento Exterior	Dec 94	133	Y	100	100	20	10[246]							
Portugal Telecom	Jun 95	988	Y	100	100	72.7		39	13				4	3.82%
	Jun 96	950	N	100	73	51	—	60	—	—	—	—	—	—
	Oct 97	2,030	N	100	51	25[247]	—		—	—	—	—	14	0.67%
	Jul 99	1,630	N	82	23.5	10		54					retail 8.5[248]	
	Dec 00	1,773	N	34	8.2	0								
Electricidade de Portugal	Jun 97	2,100	Y	100	100	70	—	44	—	—	—	—	37[249]	
	Jun 98	2,720[250]	N	100	70	52		35[251]					63	0.9%
	Oct 00	1,340	N	100	50.6	32.6[252]							3 instit.	
Brisa-Auto Estradas	Nov 97	549	Y	100	100	65	—	37	—	—	—	—	130 retail 18[253]	3.56%
	Nov 98	928	N	100	75	34								

Country / Company	Date												
Qatar													
Qatar Telecom	Dec 98	740	Y	100	100	55		0[254]	0			—	—
Russia													
Gazprom	Oct 96	430[255]	Y	100	51[256]	50	50						
Mobile Telesystems (MTS)	Jun 00	384	Y	100		50							
Lukoil	Dec 02	775	N	100	13.5	7.6		100	100				
Saudi Arabia													
Saudi Telecom	Jan 03	3,700	Y	100	100	70							
Singapore													
Neptune Orient Lines*	Apr 81	84	Y	0	100	67.7	—	—	—	N	N	N	—
Singapore International Airlines	Dec 87	88	N	0	62.3	52.8	—	—	—	N	N	N	—
	Nov 85	233	Y	50	77	63	—	37	N	Y	—	3.1	—
Singapore National Printers*	Jun 87	284	N	100	62.9	53.5	—	20[257]	—	N	Y	—	—
	Feb 87	3	Y	29	100	63	14.3	—	—	N	N	N	119
Singapore Aerospace*	Jun 90	87											
Singapore Shipbuilding & Engrg*	Jul 90	32											
Singapore Petroleum Corp*	Oct 90	58											
SAL Industrial Leasing*	Jul 91	17											
Singapore Electronic & Engrg*	Jul 91	15											
Singapore Computer*	Oct 91	35											

(continued)

431

Appendix 1 (continued)

Company Name[1]	Issue Date	Initial Share Issue: Issue Size ($US million)	Privatization Issue (Y/N)[2]	Fraction Secondary[3]	Government % Share Capital: Before Issue	After Issue	Fraction of Issue Allocated to: Employees	Foreign Investors[4]	U.S. Investors[5]	Multi-Class (Y/N)	Other Restrictions (Y/N)	Special Share (Y/N)[6]	Times Issue Over Subscribed[7]	Initial Period Return[8]
Singapore Technologies*	May 93	114	Y	100	100	75								100.7%
Singapore Telecom*	Oct 93	1,950	Y	—	100	92.8	3.7	50	—	N	Y	Y	4	—
	Jul 96	260	N	100	88.17	87.5	—	100[258]	—					
Singapore MRT	Jul 00	172	Y	100	100	67	4.6							5%
Slovakia														
Slovnaft	Jul 95	112	Y	100	86	66		50+[259]						
South Africa														
Iscor	Oct 89	1,300	Y	100	100		6	10						
Telkom	Mar 03	500	Y	100	100	75		37	25				4	0.8%
Spain														
Gas y Electricidad de Espana (GESA)	Nov 86	61	Y	100	94	56	—	—	—	—	—	—	4	—
Telefonica	Jun 87	375	N	0	—	47	—	100[260]	100	—	—	—	—	7.8%
	Sep 95	1,300	N	100	32	20		46	22	—	—	—		
	Feb 97	4,360	N	100	21	0	—	33[261]	—	—	—	—	10	
	May 98	2,840	N	0[262]						—	—	—		4.8%
Endesa	May 88	750	Y	100			—	27		—	—	—	1.47	
	May 94	1,050	N	100	74	65				—	—	—	2.5	
	Oct 97	4,500	N	100	66	31				—	—	—	—	1.3%

	Jun 98	8,000	N	100	33	0		5						
Repsol*	May 89	1,140	Y	100	100	73.4	9	14	14	N	Y	N	3	2.26%
	Apr 93	952	N	100	54.4	41.1[263]	—	89	42.1	N	Y	N	—	0%
	Apr 95	1,600	N	100	40	21	6.3						3[264]	
	Feb 96	1,100	N	100	21	10	Y[265]	Y	Y	—	—	Y[266]	8–15	
	Apr 97	1,170	N	100	10	0	17.7[267]	—	—	—	—	—	44	0.5%
	Jul 99	5,500	N	0[268]	0	0	10[269]							
Argentaria Corp.	May 93	1,027	Y	100	100	75.1	—	37	13	—	—	—	6	13.3%
	Nov 93	1,214	N	100	75.1	50.1							4.5	
	Mar 96	1,200	N	100	50	25	—	Y[270]	Y	—	—	—	2.1-7	
	Feb 98	2,300	N	100	29	0		40[271]					18[272]	
Gas Natural	Dec 96	284	N	100	3.8	0	—	40	—	—	—	—	3.4	
Aceralia	Dec 97	818	Y	100	47.4	0	—	27 7[273]						
Tabaclera	Apr 98	2,230	N	100	52.3	0		30[274]				Y	13.6[275]	−4%[276]
Red Electrica Espan-ola	Jul 99	349	Y	100	100	65		30					retail 8; instit. 3	
Indra	Mar 99	433	Y	100	66	0							retail; 36; instit. 18	
Iberia	Mar 00	1,054	Y	100	100	53.9								
	Apr 01	518	N	100	53.9	0								
Sweden														
Procordia	Jun 87	165	Y	0	100	83.9	19.1	—	—	—	—	—	—	—
Svenskt Stal AB (SSAB)*	Jun 92	364	N	100[277]	47.8[278]	0	9.5	11.8	—	Y	N	N	>1	—[279]
Assi Domän	Mar 94	962	Y	100	100	51	70	—	—	N	N	N	2	
Pharmacia	Jun 94	1,040	Y	—	57.5	10.1	13.9	—	—	Y	—	—	25	−0.13%
	Jun 94	1,300	N	100										
Stadshypotek	Oct 94	463	Y	100									5	
Telia	Jun 00	8,800	Y	83.3	100	70							4[280]	4.1%
Switzerland														
Swisscom	Oct 98	5,600	Y	100	100	65.5		65					3	10%

(continued)

Appendix 1 (continued)

Company Name[1]	Issue Date	Initial Share Issue			Government % Share Capital		Fraction of Issue Allocated to			Multi-Class (Y/N)	Other Restrictions (Y/N)	Special Share (Y/N)[6]	Times Issue Over Subscribed[7]	Initial Period Return[8]
		Issue Size ($US million)	Privatization Issue (Y/N)[2]	Fraction Secondary[3]	Before Issue	After Issue	Employees	Foreign Investors[4]	U.S. Investors[5]					
Zurich Airport	Nov 00	193	N	100	83.2	55[281]	—	—	—	—	Y	—	—	—
Taiwan (R.O.C.)														
China Steel Corporation	Apr 91	—	Y	100	100	91.1	—	—	—	—	Y	—	—	—
	May 92	904	N	100	91.1	76.5	16.3	14.4[282]	14.4	—	Y	—	—	11.8%
	Mar 94	300	N	100										
	Aug 94	170	N	100										
	Mar 95	1,200	N	100	67.8	47.9	30.7							
Chunghwa Telecom	Sep 00	988	Y	100	100	97.2[283]							5	−3.2%[284]
General Environment Conservation	Sep 00	7.2	Y	0	100									2.1%
Thailand														
Thai Airways International	Mar 92	225	Y	0	100	94.7[285]	5	15	—	—	Y	—	—	—
PTT Exploration and Producation	Jun 93	52	Y	100	100	85	—	35	—	—	—	—	6[286]	43.9%
Bangchak Petroleum	Nov 01	725	Y	100	85	70								10%
	Jun 94	128	Y	Y	100	80								83.9%
Electricity Generating Co (EGCO)	Jan 95	178	Y	100	100	50		28					41.6	173.0%

434

Company	Date													
Ratchaburi Electricity Generating Holding	Nov 00	67	Y	100	100	45	27	20	—	N			4	28.0%
Turkey														
Teletas*	Mar 88	13	Y+	100	48[287]	26	20		—			Y[288]		
Tofas	Mar 94	333	N	100	12.3							N		
Turkiye Is Bankasi	May 98	651		100		0[289]		55	22			N	4[290]	
Tupras	Apr 00	1,200	Y	100	100	68.5		25				Y		
United Kingdom														
British Petroleum*	Jun 77	972	Y	100	68	51	—[291]			N	N	N	4.7	22.7%
	Sep 83	849	N	100	38.4	31.4	—			N	Y[292]	N	1.3	−0.23%
	Oct 87	12,430	N	79	31.4	0	0	50	22	N	N	N	<1.0	−21.5%
British Aerospace	Feb 81	339	Y	33.3	100	48.4	3.3[293]			N	N	Y[294]	3.5	14.0%
	May 85	714	N	65.9	48.4	0	2.0			N	Y	Y	12	16.3%
Cable and Wireless*	Oct 81	466	Y	47.5	100	50	10			N	Y	N	5.6	17.3%
	Dec 83	416	N	100	45	23	5			N	Y	N	0.7	4.7%
	Dec 85	1,378	N	64.5	23	0	1			N	N	Y	2	1.4%
Amersham International*	Feb 82	131	Y	92	100	0	5			N	N	Y	24	32.4%
Britoil*	Nov 82	911	Y	100	100	49	1			N	N	Y	0.27	−19.0%
	Aug 85	582	N	100	48	0	6.2	20		N	N	Y	10	17.8%
Associated British Ports*	Feb 83	33	Y	100	100	48.5	10.9			N	N	N	34	23.2%
Enterprise Oil*	Apr 84	70	N	100	48.5	0	—[295]			N	N	N	1.6	1.8%
	Jun 84	524	Y	100	100	0				N	N	Y	0.7	0.0%
Jaguar plc*	Jul 84	384	Y	100	100		15			N	N	Y	8.3	8.5%
British Telecommunications*	Nov 84	4,763	Y	100	100	49.8	10	11.8	6	N	N	Y	9.7	86.0%
	Dec 91	9,927	N	100	48	21.9	—	34.3	3	N	N	Y	2.5	0.4%
	Jul 93	7,360	N	100	21.9	0	—	21.6	8	N	N	Y	3	5.0%

(continued)

Appendix 1 (continued)

Company Name[1]	Issue Date	Issue Size ($US million)	Privatization Issue (Y/N)[2]	Fraction Secondary[3]	Gov % Share Capital Before Issue	Gov % Share Capital After Issue	Employees	Foreign Investors[4]	U.S. Investors[5]	Multi-Class (Y/N)	Other Restrictions (Y/N)	Special Share (Y/N)[6]	Times Issue Over Subscribed[7]	Initial Period Return[8]
British Gas*	Dec 86	8,012	Y	100	100	0	3[296]	20	7.1	N	N	Y	4.0	23.0%
British Airways*	Feb 87	1,327	Y	100	100	0	9.5	25	11	N	Y	N	32	67.7%
BAA plc (British Airports Authority)*	Jul 87	2,028	Y	100	100	0	5	0	0	N	N	Y	9.3	37.0%
	Jan 96	223	N	100	2.9	0	0							
Rolls Royce*	May 87	2,234	Y	79.1	100	0	5	—	—	N	N	Y	9.6	68.2%
British Steel*	Dec 88	4,524	Y	100	100	0	10	38	12	N	N	Y	3.3	3.8%
Anglian Water plc*	Dec 89[297]	1,172	Y	100	100	0	3	18.5	1.7	N	N	Y	5.7	49.0%
Northumbrian Water Group plc	Dec 89	261	Y	100	100	0	3	18.5	1.7	N	N	Y	5.7	57.0%
Severn Trent plc*	Dec 89	1,403	Y	100	100	0	3	18.5	1.7	N	N	Y	5.7	31.0%
Southern Water plc*	Dec 89	651	Y	100	100	0	3	18.5	1.7	N	N	Y	5.7	41.0%
South West Water plc*	Dec 89	486	Y	100	100	0	3	18.5	1.7	N	N	Y	5.7	47.0%
North West Water Group plc*	Dec 89	1,415	Y	100	100	0	3	18.5	1.7	N	N	Y	5.7	35.0%
Thames Water plc*	Dec 89	1,528	Y	100	100	0	3	18.5	1.7	N	N	Y	5.7	36.0%
Welsh Water plc*	Dec 89	573	Y	100	100	0	3	18.5	1.7	N	N	Y	5.7	42.0%
Wessex Water plc*	Dec 89	408	Y	100	100	0	3	18.5	1.7	N	N	Y	5.7	54.0%
Yorkshire Water*	Dec 89	782	Y	100	100	0	3	18.5	1.7	N	N	Y	5.7	49.0%
Eastern Electricity plc*	Dec 90	1,249	Y	100	100	0	4	20	7	N	N	Y	10.7	48.0%

Company	Date													
East Midlands Electricity plc*	Dec 90	1,010	Y	100	100	0	4	20	7	N	N	Y	10.7	50.5%
London Electricity plc*	Dec 90	1,010	Y	100	100	0	4	20	7	N	N	Y	10.7	42.0%
Manweb plc*	Dec 90	550	Y	100	100	0	4	20	7	N	N	Y	10.7	66.0%
Midlands Electricity plc*	Dec 90	969	Y	100	100	0	4	20	7	N	N	Y	10.7	44.0%
Northern Electric plc*	Dec 90	570	Y	100	100	0	4	20	7	N	N	Y	10.7	42.5%
Norweb plc*	Dec 90	800	Y	100	100	0	4	20	7	N	N	Y	10.7	52.0%
SEEBOARD plc*	Dec 90	589	Y	100	100	0	4	20	7	N	N	Y	10.7	42.0%
Southern Electric plc*	Dec 90	1,249	Y	100	100	0	4	20	7	N	N	Y	10.7	50.0%
South Wales Electricity plc*	Dec 90	470	Y	100	100	0	4	20	7	N	N	Y	10.7	64.0%
South Western Electricity plc*	Dec 90	570	Y	100	100	0	4	20	7	N	N	Y	10.7	50.0%
Yorkshire Electricity Group plc*	Dec 90	959	Y	100	100	0	4	20	7	N	N	Y	10.7	59.5%
Scottish Power*	May 91	2,933	Y	100	100	0	—[298]	17.3	—	N	N	Y	3.2	—
Scottish Hydro-Electric*	May 91	1,380	Y	100	100	0	—[299]	17.3	—	N	N	Y	3.2	—
National Power	Mar 91	2,278	Y	100	100	40								
	Mar 95	3,657	N	100	40	0		22.1					8	
Power Gen	Mar 91	1,395	Y	100	100	40								
	Mar 95	2,543	N	100	40	0		22.1					8	
Railtrack	May 96	3,100	Y	100	100	0								
British Energy	Jul 96	2,200	Y	100	100	12.25[300]	—	70[301]	—	—	—	—	2.5	—6.0%[302]
AEA Technology	Sep 96	349	Y	100	100	0	—					—	7	
United States														
Consolidated Rail Corp.	Mar 89	1,650	Y	100	85	0	—[303]	11.5	88.5	—	N	N	>1	10.3%

(continued)

437

Appendix 1 (*continued*)

| Company Name[1] | Issue Date | Initial Share Issue | | | Government % Share Capital | | Fraction of Issue Allocated to | | | Multi-Class (Y/N) | Other Restrictions (Y/N) | Special Share (Y/N)[6] | Times Issue Over Subscribed[7] | Initial Period Return[8] |
		Issue Size ($US million)	Privatization Issue (Y/N)[2]	Fraction Secondary[3]	Before Issue	After Issue	Employees	Foreign Investors[4]	U.S. Investors[5]					
United States Enrichment Corp	Jul 98	1,425	Y	100	100	0								
Venezuela CANTV	Nov 96	1,010	Y	100	49	0	9	40						11.7%

Notes:
1. * Denotes that data was derived from some form of a prospectus.
2. + Denotes that some or all of the state owned firm's stock had been sold previously in a private asset sale.
3. Fraction secondary refers to the percent of the total issue that was strictly secondary in nature (a sale of existing shares by the government) rather than a new equity issue.
4. Denotes the allocation to foreigners and/or the maximum amount of the offer foreigners were allowed to purchase.
5. This often includes Canada as well as the United States.
6. In many privatizations, the government retains a "special share" (or golden share) giving it special powers, such as the right to veto a takeover of a newly privatized company, the right to veto CEO candidates, or the right to appoint a given number of directors.
7. This is a measure of excess demand for the share issue, and measures the number of shares demanded at the offer price as a multiple of the number of shares being offered.
8. This is a measure of how severely an issue is underpriced, and is computed using the ratio of the first available open market share price divided by the offer price.
9. A joint venture between Telefonica de Espana and Citicorp Venture Capital, COINTEL, purchased 60% of this company from the Argentine government in November 1990 for $2.83 billion.
10. A majority stake in this company was purchased by the French and Italian state telephone companies.
11. All of the state's remaining shares were distributed to state governments, an employee trust fund, and pensioners.
12. Pensioners also received 12.7% of the shares.
13. Employees could purchase shares at a 10% discount.
14. Offer limited to Australian citizens only.
15. No shareholder besides the government was allowed to own more than 5% of the stock.
16. Issue had a partly paid structure with 60% required up front. The issue closed unchanged in price on the first day of trading.
17. Individual investors were given a 5% discount for the first 20,000 shares.

18. In 1994, the government sold a 25% stake in Qantas to British Airways.

19. Australian investors are guaranteed up to 70% of the issue.

20. Foreign investors were limited to a minimum 35% shareholding level.

21. Retail investors were given the opportunity to purchase shares on an installment plan and at a 5% discount (10% if held for one year).

22. Domestic institutions were allocated 20% of the issue, Australian private investors 66.5%. The participation of 1.7 million investors pushed the fraction of Australian population owning shares to 43.3%, the world's highest.

23. Installment receipts (the first part of a two-stage payment) closed on the first day of trading at A$4.51, just above the discounted retail price of A$4.50, but well below the institutional price of A$4.75.

24. No special allocation to foreigners. 35% of offer allocated to institutions, who paid A$2.15 per share (and who bid through book-building) versus A$2.05 for retail investors who were allocated 65% of offer.

25. The ASch 365 offer price was actually payable in two installments, with only ASch 165 being payable on subscription. Investors who retained their shares until October 31, 1991 were eligible for one free "loyalty" share for every ten shares purchased.

26. This issue was sold internationally via a private placement, with a Rule 144A issue in the United States.

27. An additional 6.6% of the firm's capital was available for greenshoe option exercise.

28. In 1998, the Austrian government sold a 25.1% stake in Telecom Austria to Telecom Italia.

29. This offering was very disappointing for the Austrian government, which had hoped to raise twice as much. The actual offer price had to be set so low that Telecom Italia was given an extra 4% free as compensation for dilution.

30. These shares were owned by local authorities rather than the central government.

31. Shares were sold through auction to individual and corporate buyers. Government debt could be used (at par) as payment.

32. There was no limit on foreign purchases, yet they only demanded 5.9% of the offering.

33. Forty percent sold to domestic investors, 310,000 of whom participated in a scheme that allowed them to use part of their unemployment insurance funds to buy shares at a 20% discount.

34. Employees were allowed to purchase shares through payroll deductions, with the company contributing 10% of the cost.

35. The shares were not registered for sale in the United States, and foreigners were limited to a maximum ownership of 25% of the company's shares.

36. The enabling legislation mandated that the company's headquarters remain in Montreal and specified that no investor could own more than 15% of the stock.

37. Employees receive a 1-year, no-interest loan to purchase shares. If the loan was repaid after one year, employee receives a matching share free. Employees may purchase additional shares at a 10% discount.

38. No more than 25% of voting shares may be held by nonresidents. Furthermore no single investor may own more than 10% of the voting shares.

39. This was the first Canadian privatization without a ceiling on foreign ownership.

40. Shares are to be purchased in installments within three years.

41. A separate offer of a different class of shares will be sold to Chinese investors. This ADS issue consists solely of "A" shares.

42. This is actually a Bermuda-registered holding company that owns 51% of the principal Chinese assembler of passenger cars and trucks. Chinese agencies retain ownership of the rest of the firm, as well as high vote stock in this firm.

43. All shares sold were initially to be traded only on the NYSE. A subsequent listing in Hong Kong was planned.

44. This became the first Chinese company to obtain a primary listing of ADRs on the NYSE.

45. Proceeds to be used to purchase rolling stock, reduce debt, and for working capital.

46. ADR and H-share (Hong Kong) issues.

47. Approximately 7% of the issue was allocated to Hong Kong.

(continued)

48. 4.5% of shares sold to Hong Kong investors, an additional 69.5% of the issue sold through ADRs to Asian investors, 10.7% sold through ADRs in the U.S., while 14.25% sold to international investors as ADRs.
49. The Hong Kong market itself fell by 10% on the offer date, so market-adjusted returns were essentially zero.
50. 95% of offering sold as N-shares in New York, while 5% are H-shares sold in Hong Kong.
51. Shares sold in New York and Hong Kong.
52. This was an A-share offering, strictly for the Chinese domestic market.
53. This was an offering of H-shares (Hong Kong) and N-shares (New York) only.
54. Three international oil companies—ExxonMobil, BP Amoco and Royal Dutch Shell—subscribed to over half of the offer.
55. H-share (Hong Kong) listing only.
56. Unable to determine if this was an initial or a seasoned offering. A 27.5% stake was sold, but shareholding levels were not given.
57. This was a GDR issue, with a domestic issue to follow.
58. Total offer was a 17% stake, with the Croatian government selling its remaining 14% stake, and EBRD selling 3% of its 11% stake (leaving 8%). Government pension funds still retain part of Pliva though direct holdings cease.
59. The domestic tranche was set at a 10% discount to the institutional and foreign price, which was set at market level. Domestic investors must hold their shares two months to earn the discount.
60. Cannot determine if this was an initial offering.
61. 10% stake sold, but cannot determine initial and after-sale shareholding levels.
62. GDR issue. The lead underwriter, UBS, purchased a 2% equity stake for its own account at a discounted price.
63. This was a GDR offering of non-voting shares.
64. GDR and ADR issues carry no voting rights.
65. 7.9% stake sold, but initial and after-sale shareholding levels not determined. Shares priced at 7% discount to closing price on Prague exchange.
66. Offer price set at 8% discount to pre-issue market price, and structured as a GDR offering.
67. Employee shares were purchased at a discount.
68. Employee shares were purchased at a discount.
69. This was the first sale of a majority stake in an Egyptian state-owned firm.
70. Prior to this issue, employees already owned 10% of firm's capital; two Egyptian firms held 5% each.
71. Shares allocated to Finnish and international institutions, plus underwriter over-allotment.
72. Rights offering designed to provide funding for the company to reduce its net debt. The Finnish government participated proportionately in the offering.
73. No accumulation of 10% or more of the company's stock allowed without government approval.
74. This was a block sale, with roughly half placed with an Elf subsidiary and half placed with French and international institutional investors.
75. Block offered at a 2% discount to market price.

76. Foreign investors limited to a maximum 20% ownership of company's voting securities. This became standard on most subsequent issues.

77. The Chirac government was charged with deliberate underpricing of this, the first large nationalized company to be privatized after the Conservatives came to power in early 1986.

78. This issue resulted in 3.81 million new Paribas shareholders.

79. Only 47% of Sogenal was owned directly by the French government. The remaining shares were owned by Societe Generale (a state-owned enterprise), which was itself privatized three months later.

80. After reaching this very large initial premium over the issue price, the stock price plunged dramatically over the next several months.

81. The government retains the right to veto a takeover it disapproves of.

82. Current holders of non-voting stock were allowed to convert into these shares at no charge.

83. Foreigners could hold no more than 20% of the stock, and French nationals were given preference in allocation of shares. Investors who held their shares for 18 months received a free "loyalty" share for every 10 shares owned.

84. This includes holdings of other SOEs. The state directly held 47.5% before and 27.5% after the issue.

85. Calculated using end-of-month prices (the only ones available to us), which was three weeks after trading began.

86. Initial return calculated using end-of-June prices. The shares were priced 3.1% below the end-of-May price, but there was no mention that this price was used as a reference.

87. The government retains the right to control international agreements, veto CEO candidates, and select two board members.

88. Stake sold through auction directly to institutional investors.

89. Issue also allows for conversion of non-voting equity securities into common stock on a one-for-one basis one month after issue is completed.

90. The government retained 87% of the voting power.

91. Price for new issue set at a 12.2% discount (for individual investors) to market price.

92. Sale of shares owned by state-owned bank Credit Lyonnais executed by RTC-like entity charged with selling failed bank's assets.

93. Allocations were initially higher for employees, foreigners, and bloc-holders, but were cut back to help meet retail demand.

94. This excess demand calculated using oversubscription only of the institutional tranche. The public was offered shares at a 6.25% discount from the institutional price.

95. Company actually owned equally by French and Italian state-owned holding companies.

96. "Some" shares reserved for employees. Core shareholders bought a 25% stake at a 2% premium over institutional price.

97. Stake sold in a private placement to Deutsche Morgan Grenfell at a 0.73% discount to pre-offer market price. Shares were then resold to European and American investors.

98. French institutional investors were also allocated 19% of issue.

99. This excess demand calculated using over-subscription only of the domestic tranche. Demand or the international tranche was much weaker.

100. While state's direct holding reduced to a residual, state-owned Electricité de France upped its holding from 4.75 to 7.75%.

101. 67% of this issue was allocated to French and international institutional investors.

102. Unlike other French privatizations, AGF has no core shareholdings designed in.

103. This excess demand calculated using oversubscription only of the international tranche.

104. This represents the direct holding of the French state. France Telecom, employees, and other public-sector entities own an additional 26.5% of capital.

105. This excess demand calculated using oversubscription only of the retail tranche. The institutional tranche was 17 times oversubscribed. The sale yielded a record 3.9 million individual shareholders.

106. Return calculated over the two-week offering period.

107. Rights offering in which the French state fully participated. Thus this would not be considered a SIP under most definitions.

108. Primary offer sold primarily to new core shareholders: Alcatel (16.4% of company, 41% of offer), Dassault (6% and 24.3%), and Aerospotiale (4% and 16.3%). Government did not participate in capital increase.

441

(continued)

Appendix 1 (continued)

109. Shares allocated to foreign and French institutional investors.
110. This represents the allocation to the 2.4 million French retail investors who applied for shares, rather than just employees.
111. Shares allocated to foreign and domestic institutional investors.
112. Offering of 7% of STM shares raised $1,330 million for France Telecom and $970 million for Italy's Finmeccanica, STM's two controlling shareholders.
113. Ownership retained by the French government.
114. Employees were allowed to purchase EADS shares at a 15% discount.
115. Prior to this offering, Wanadoo was the wholly owned internet subsidiary of France Telecom, and both remain majority-owned by the French state.
116. Offering coupled with a $731 million issue of convertible and exchangeable bonds.
117. Sale accompanied by a $2,500 million bond issue.
118. Proceeds retained by France Telecom, not the company or the French government.
119. Shares were allocated at a 20% discount to low-income investors, including employees, who agreed to hold their shares until March 1963.
120. There was no special share, but all shareholders have only one vote each, regardless of the number of shares owned.
121. Shares were preferentially allocated first to employees, then to low-income investors.
122. Issue was priced at a 1.4% discount to the closing price on March 20, 1987.
123. Issue was priced slightly below closing price the day before the issue was announced.
124. The government issued stock on a one-for-four rights allocation at a price of DM155/share, when the market price was DM 200.5/share.
125. Rights offer that the German government chose not to participate in.
126. Roughly 2 million individual Germans purchased Telekom shares, partly as a result of a $133 million advertising campaign. Prior to this issue, only 4 million Germans owned any stock, and engendering an "equity culture" was an explicit objective of the German government.
127. Shares allocated to German and European institutional investors.
128. Shares allocated to Japanese and U.S. institutional investors.
129. Issue sold primarily to retail investors in 18 countries.
130. Shares closed after first day of trading at Eu65.8, or 3.3% below the Eu66.50 offer price, but above the discounted retail price of Eu63.50.
131. Offer represented 61% of Jenoptik's shares, and government holdings were those of the state of Thuringia.
132. Prior to the offering, T-Online was a wholly-owned internet subsidiary of Deutsche Telekom.
133. Each employee received 5 free shares.
134. Shares quickly hit 8% maximum one day price increase on first trading day.
135. Shares allocated to Canadian and U.S. institutional investors.
136. Domestic investors were offered shares at Dr 1,800 per share; international investors offered shares at Dr 1,900/share.
137. First part of a two-part offer involves a private placement of stock by Greek Army Pension Fund. This will then be followed by a rights offering at one-third of current market price. Approximate offer value computed.

138. Offering proceeds received by Hellenic Telecommunications (OTE), rather than the company or the Greek government.
139. More than 20,000 participating Greek retail investors were offered shares at a 3% discount and bonus shares if those purchased were retained for 6 months.
140. Retail price set at 3% discount to institutional offer and retail investors allocated 43% of shares.
141. $44mm of this is a public issue, while the European Bank for Reconstruction & Development will pay $45mm.
142. Roughly 20% of offer allocated to domestic investors; half to institution, half to individuals. There was no mention of specific employee allocation.
143. International offer price set at Ft 6,330/share while retail domestic price set at Ft 6,100/share.
144. This excess demand calculated using over-subscription only of the domestic retail tranche. International tranche "heavily" oversubscribed. Due to high demand, government transferred 1.5 percent (of the original 9.22%) of the international offer to the domestic tranche and underwriters exercised a 1% green shoe option.
145. Return on international tranche only. The retail domestic offer yielded an 11.5% return.
146. Offering to staff made at a 36% discount to pre-offer closing price.
147. Shares fell 10% during a trading day when share prices were falling dramatically worldwide.
148. These terms were based on indirect evidence of sale only; unable to conclusively document terms of offering.
149. Indian state-owned financial institutions purchased about 60% of the shares on offer, and a total of only 40 investors purchased shares.
150. Indian state-owned financial institutions purchased most of the shares.
151. Offer size cut by 31% due to poor market response.
152. Offering was a private placement to institutional investors.
153. Observers attributed most of this to domestic investor demand.
154. Shares offered to employees and sugar beet growers at a 20% discount from offering price.
155. KPN of the Netherlands and Sweden's Telia own 35% of company's shares. After the IPO, employees will own 14.9% of company's equity.
156. Shares sold to foreign and domestic institutions.
157. This was a bloc purchase of shares from the Israeli government by Goldman Sachs.
158. Offer a mixture of shares, warrants and convertible bonds. The post-issue holdings value assumes full conversion of warrants and convertibles.
159. This was a private placement of shares with Lehman Brothers, a U.S. investment bank.
160. Sale was of shares and warrants. Share proceeds and government holdings after the sale assume full exercise of all warrants.
161. A 51% stake in UMB was sold to private investors in 1997, but this was the first public offering.
162. This will fall to 1% if all warrants issued are exercised.
163. Employees could purchase shares at a 10% discount.
164. Savings shares issued in units of 10 shares plus warrants to purchase 10 additional shares.
165. This was a unit offering of shares and warrants.
166. Unit offering, with warrants to purchase 20 additional shares for every 1000 shares held.
167. 30% of the issue was allocated to customers.
168. Convertible bond issue convertible into shares of INA.
169. These shares were retained for distribution as bonus shares for 1994 offering.
170. 67% of the offer was allocated to international and domestic institutions; 33% to small domestic shareholders.
171. Institutional investor demand only. Retail investor demand described as "heavy." Greenshoe option exercised, raising number of shares offered by 15%.
172. Institutional investors paid the market price for their shares, while retail investors were offered a 3.5% discount.
173. Employees and retail investors were offered shares at a 3% discount and were offered a loyalty bonus (one-for-ten) if shares were held at least one year.

(continued)

Appendix 1 (*continued*)

174. This value assumes the exercise of the over-allotment option.
175. Shares allocated to domestic and international institutional investors. Almost half the original tranche was reallocated to retail domestic offer. Retail investors were not offered a price discount, but were offered one bonus share for every 10 held if retained for 12 months.
176. This will be followed by a capital increase later in 1998. The government will use part of the offer proceeds to pay off a capital contribution made in 1997.
177. Ownership held by partially-privatized Eni, rather than by the state itself.
178. Employees and retail investors were offered shares at a 2.5% (retail investors) and 5% (employees) discount to the offer price.
179. Accelerated book-building operation, targeted exclusively at institutional investors, mostly international.
180. Share issue is part of a $2.84bn recapitalization, which also includes a convertible bond issue and purchase of core shareholdings.
181. Electric utility sold by the Milanese government, not the Italian Treasury.
182. This offering attracted 3.8 million investors.
183. This company is owned by—and offering made by—the City of Trieste.
184. Proceeds received by parent company, ENI, rather than by Snam Rete Gas itself or the Italian government.
185. This company is owned by—and offering made by—the City of Trieste.
186. Only Jamaicans may hold shares, and no investor may hold more than 7.5% of voting shares.
187. Foreigners are not allowed to directly own NTT shares.
188. NTT shares closed up limit (without meaningful trading volume) for two days in a row. A closing price was only established on the third day of trading.
189. Each share of this $40 billion issue was priced at ¥2,550,000, or $20,650.
190. The offer price was set at a 3% discount to the last closing price before issue announcement.
191. Offer price set 3.5% below previous closing price.
192. JAL shares had lost 22% of their value in the two weeks prior to issue. Nonetheless, even at their lowest points, these shares sold at a price/earnings ratio of 350.
193. Offer price set 3.4% below previous closing price.
194. After an excessively high price ($14,100/share) was set in an auction, investors canceled two-thirds of the shares originally demanded.
195. The government was selling 273,000 shares remaining from unsuccessful 667,000 share issue in 1994. This was the first Japanese privatization to use "book building" techniques.
196. The government hoped to sell 1,700,000 shares, but was only able to sell 1,365,000 (80%).
197. This was the largest IPO in financial history at the time.
198. This is technically an equity carve-out (ECO) by NTT, rather than a privatization by the Japanese government, but NTT itself is still majority state-owned (65.5%).
199. KLM purchased 26% of company through direct sale in January 1996.
200. This was the first ESOP in Kenyan history. For tax reasons, structured as a unit trust rather than sale of shares to employees.
201. This was an ADR issue. This was increased in size, and priced at a 26% premium to previous day's closing price in Seoul, due to high demand.
202. These were ADRs priced at a 10% premium to previous day's closing price in Seoul.
203. Shares were purchased by POSCO for their employees' account.

204. The majority of the issue was offered to employees and low-income Koreans at a 30% discount from institutional offer price.
205. ADRs were priced at a 20% premium to previous week's average closing price in Seoul.
206. The Korean government was seriously embarrassed to learn that almost half (11.34% of 28% of issue) of the stake sold acquired by SK Telecom, Korea's dominant mobile phone company.
207. Offering targeted at international investors, but only ⅔ of offer successfully placed. Company itself purchased the unsold shares, allowing the government to dispose entirely its ownership.
208. The company is owned equally (33.3% each) by the governments of Kuwait, Libya, and the United Arab Emirates.
209. In addition to allocating shares for employees, 33.3% of the issue was reserved for Buma Putra (ethnic Malay) investors.
210. Foreigners may hold no more than 25% of issued shares. Additionally, no individual investor (except the government) may own more than 5% of voting securities.
211. The government must consent to acquisitions, major assets sales, or the firm's liquidation and the government may appoint 6 of 12 directors.
212. Control of the company was sold to an international consortium in December 1990. This issue represented a partial divestment of the Mexican government's stake.
213. The government controls a larger fraction (but still a minority) of the voting stock, and retains the right to elect 2 of 19 directors.
214. The remaining stake was sold via a global convertible bond issue.
215. This group was formed to purchase 56% of Bancomer from the Mexican government in 1991 for $2.88 billion. This issue thus was a primary (capital-raising) offer for Grupo Bancomer, but the money raised was simply used to pay the installment on the government's note and is therefore classified as a pure secondary offering.
216. The sale was by a group (not the Mexican government) that had previously purchased 56% of the firm.
217. This was a Rule 144 private placement in the United States.
218. The Dutch government retains the right to appoint a simple majority of the firm's board of directors.
219. The U.S. tranche, which was not itemized, was in the form of a Rule 144 private placement.
220. Offer price set at a 2% discount from the closing stock price.
221. Offer price set at a small (1%) discount to the closing price.
222. 55% of the issue sold to Dutch investors. Retail buyers received a 4.55% discount for up to 100 shares.
223. Combined primary share offering ($3,350 million) and convertible bond issue ($1,250 million).
224. Shares allocated to institutional investors—mostly outside the Netherlands. Individuals offered shares at a 4% discount and a bonus share for each share held one year.
225. Rights offering designed to reduce firm's very high net debt. The Dutch government participated proportionately.
226. Employees were allowed to buy shares at a 10% discount.
227. Dual class limits foreign ownership because only New Zealand nationals can own class A.
228. The government must consent before the company changes its name, relocates its office, or disposes of its principal business.
229. Approximately 54% of the company was sold to Bell Atlantic and Ameritech in 1990, and this issue represents 49.9% of the two company's holding.
230. 62,000 Norwegian citizens, including employees (6 of 10 participated), took advantage of cash rebate and bonus share incentive.
231. The institutional share offer price was set at a 17.6% premium to the price at which they were offered to retail investors.
232. Domestic demand was very high due to promotion, but domestic tranche cut in half to meet high international demand. Within two weeks government forced to sell part of the remaining 5% stake to domestic investors who were underallocated in the initial round.
233. Shares were allocated to domestic and international institutions.
234. Only a small number of managers and employees were actually able to trade on the first day and earn this return.
235. Shares were sold to EBRD. Share sales to employees to come later.
236. 36.8% stake sold, but levels not determined.
237. This issue was to be followed shortly by a GDR issue.
238. Employees receive their shares free, conditional on holding them for two years.

(continued)

239. By law, employees own 15% of privatized Polish SOEs.
240. Individual investors offered a 10% discount.
241. One quarter of the issue was reserved for employees and small shareholders at an 18.4% discount.
242. Issue split into four tranches, with allocations for employees (at a 6.5% discount), small investors, expatriates, and a large bloc that was put up for auction.
243. Shares allocated to employees and small savers, and were purchased at 10.3% and 6.9% discounts, respectively.
244. Employees and small investors will receive a 10% discount to the offer price.
245. Retail offering increased from 63 to 70% at international tranche's expense. All shares were sold at a discount to market price (2% for institutions, larger for small investors).
246. Shares sold to small domestic investors, and were offered at an 8.5% price discount.
247. Offer included direct sale of shareholdings to strategic international telecom companies.
248. Retail investors receive a 5% price discount and one bonus share for every 25 purchased and held for one year.
249. Excess demand statistic based on retail investor demand only. The institutional tranche was 25 times subscribed. About 10% of Portugal's adult population requested share allocations.
250. This includes a direct sale of 2.25% of the company to a Spanish utility.
251. Shares sold to domestic and foreign institutions. Their share was cut from 40 to 35% to satisfy domestic retail demand. An over-allotment option of an additional 10% virtually certain to be exercised. Retail investors required to hold shares three months to quality for 3% discount on price. Over 10% of Portuguese population requested shares.
252. The Portuguese government retains a golden share enabling it to veto strategic decisions.
253. Retail investors receive a 3% price discount.
254. Offering restricted to investors from the Gulf region.
255. This was the first 1.15% tranche of a planned 9% of Gazprom stock to be sold to international investors.
256. Held by Sistema, a holding company linked to the city of Moscow.
257. Maximum limit on foreign shareholdings changed to 25% shortly afterwards.
258. Offering sold by direct sales to domestic and foreign institutions in three tranches.
259. Offer was failing until EBRD purchased over half of the offering.
260. ADR issue offered only in the United States.
261. Shares allocated to domestic and international institutions. The issue was so popular with domestic retail investors that after divestment was complete roughly one in eight Spanish household owned Telefonica shares.
262. This is technically not an SIP, since the state no longer owns any Telefonica shares. It is included here as a share offering by a former SOE.
263. Parliament had to approve sale of shares dropping the state's ownership below 50%.
264. Demand by domestic investors bolstered by unusual price guarantee scheme (for 10% price decline) by Spanish governments.
265. Share sales to small domestic investors priced 4.3% below institutional price.
266. Under a new privatization law, the government will retain a golden share even as its stake is reduced to and below 10%.
267. Employees and retail investors offered shares at a 4% discount to institutional price.

268. This is technically not an SIP, since the state no longer owns any Repsol shares. Offer made to finance Repsol's acquisition of Argentina's YPF.
269. Employees offered shares at a 10% discount from institutional price.
270. Domestic small investors were allowed to purchase shares at 4% discount, and government guarantees to reimburse investors who hold stock for 12 months should share value fall by 10%.
271. Shares sold to domestic and international institutions. Retail investors were given a 3% price discount.
272. This excess demand statistic represented a weighted average of retail and institutional tranches. After this issue, one in three Spanish households now owns stock.
273. The 73.3% domestic allocation was a record high for a Spanish privatization.
274. The original international allocation was 36.7%, but was cut to favor domestic investors.
275. International actually failed in that underwriters were saddled with loses of $17.5 million.
276. Although offer price was set at 13% discount to market price at start of offer period, the share price fell 16.5% during the one-week offering period.
277. These were sold as units of "risk-free" bonds and warrant to purchase 100 shares at offering price.
278. Before the sale the government had 60% of the voting rights.
279. Cannot compute initial stock returns, since this is a unit offering of warrants and bonds.
280. Approximately 1 million Swedes, 11 percent of the population, purchased shares.
281. Most (50 of 55%) of this held by the canton of Zurich, with the city of Zurich holding the remaining 5%. The stake being sold was offered by the canton.
282. U.S. tranche was a Rule 144 private placement.
283. Failed offer; government had planned to sell a 16% stake, but only able to find buyers for 2.8% due to high offer price.
284. Return over first two weeks.
285. The government's stake must remain above 70% for the state to guarantee the firm's loans.
286. The excess demand statistic is based on the international tranche only.
287. Bell Company became a 39% equity investor in December 1984.
288. Government has the right to block transfer of control, if this would affect the strategic policies of the Turkish government.
289. After the issue, private investors hold 27% of the bank, while the staff holds 45%, and a political party holds 28%.
290. The excess demand statistic is based on the international tranche only. Retail investors were offered a 10% price discount.
291. Preferential share allocations were given to employees and U.K. pension funds, but cannot determine exact amount.
292. The government retained the right to appoint two directors, either of whom may veto any resolution of the board of directors or a committee thereof. This right was later terminated.
293. Each employee received 33 shares free of charge, and the government matched purchases by employees one-for-one up to 600 shares. Similar terms were included in almost all subsequent British privatizations and thus are not separately detailed in this table. Interested readers are referred to Price Waterhouse (1989a, 1989b, 1990).
294. The special share gave the government the right to appoint a director. It also mandated that foreign ownership be capped at 15 percent and that all directors be British citizens. Comparable terms were embodied in virtually all of the special shares included in subsequent British privatizations and thus are not separately detailed here. Interested readers are referred to Price Waterhouse (1989a, 1989b, 1990).
295. Employees were given 53 shares free of charge, and the government matched purchases by employees one-for-one. Preferential consideration was given to employee applications.
296. Each employee received 52 shares free and the government matched purchases by employees 2 for 1, up to a maximum purchase of 111 shares.
297. The sale of the ten water holding companies in December 1989 was the first multiple-firm offering in the British privatization program. It was followed almost exactly one year later by divestment of the twelve electricity companies.
298. The employees received free shares based on years of service. The company gave employees 2 shares for each share they purchased, and employees purchased at a 20% discount.
299. The employees received free shares based on years of service. The company gave employees 2 shares for each share they purchased, and employees purchased at a 20% discount.

(continued)

Appendix 1 (*continued*)

300. Underwriters had to support the after-market price, and the government was unable to dispose of the over-allotment share amount.
301. Domestic investors were allowed to buy shares at a 5% discount to international investors.
302. This was the worst first day performance by a British privatization since the October 1987 British Petroleum offering.
303. Employees already own 15% of the stock of Conrail.

Appendix 2: Contact Information for National Privatization Commissions

This table presents contact information for national privatization agencies around the world. This is a comprehensive listing of all national agencies that could be identified through an Internet search performed in May 2003, and the information provided is based on the agencies' Web sites at that time.

ALBANIA
National Agency for Privatisation
Blvd. "Deshmoret e Kombit"
Tirane—Shqiperi, Albania
Tel.: (355) 4 257457; (355) 4 228123
Fax: (355) 4 227933
xhillari@krn_dap.tirana.al
http://www.akp.gov.al

ALGERIA
Ministry of Participation and Promotion of
    Investment
1, rue Ibn Badis El Mouiz
El Biar, Algeria
Tel.: (213) 021 92 98 85; (213) 021 92 98 86
Fax: (213) 021 92 98 90
ministere@mpcr-dz.com
www.mpcr-dz.com/qualif/mpcrang/index.htm

ARMENIA
Ministry of State Property Management
Government House 2
Republic Square
375010 Yerevan
Tel.: (374 1) 506 172, 521 877
Fax: (374 1) 506 172
tender@arminco.com
http://www.privatization.am

AZERBAIJAN
Ministry of Economic Development
Department of Privatization of State Property
20, Yusif Safarov Street
Baku 370025, Azerbaijan
Tel.: (99412) 902408 (switchboard)
Fax: (99412) 903359
office@economy.gov.az,
privat@economy.gov.az
http://economy.gov.az

BANGLADESH
Privatization Commission
Jibon Bima Tower 10 Dilkusha C/A
Dhaka, Bangladesh
Tel.: (880)-2-9551986
Fax: (880)-2-9556433
pb@bdonline.com
http://www.bangladeshonline.com/pb/

BELARUS
Ministry of Economy, Belarus
220050 Minsk, 14, Bersona Str./Institute for
    Privatization and Management, 76,
    Zakharova St., Minsk, 220088
Republic of Belarus
Tel: (IPM) (375-17) 210 01 05
Fax: (IPM) (375-17) 285 37 71
gen@plan.minsk.by;
ipm@ipm.by
http://www.mfa.gov.by
http://www.ipm.by

BENIN
Decommissioning Committee
02 Boîte Postale 8140
Cotonou 02, Benin
Tel.: (229) 31 59 18
Fax: (229) 30 16 60

BOSNIA AND HERZEGOVINA
Agency for Privatization
Sarajevo, 71000
Alipasina 41, Bosnia and Herzegovina
Tel.: (387) 71/ 212 884; 212 885; 212 886
Fax: (387) 71/212 883
apftbiro@bih.net.ba,
apfbih@bih.net.ba
http://www.apf.com.ba

BRAZIL
Main office/BNDES, Privatization Area
Av. República do Chile, 100—19° andar
20139-900, Rio de Janeiro—RJ
Tel: (21) 2277-8061/8062; 3088-8061/8062
Fax: (21) 2240-3890
contact@bndes.gov.br
http://www.bndes.gov.br/english

BULGARIA
Privatization Agency
Aksakov 29 Str.
Sofia 1000, Bulgaria
Tel: (359) 2 987 32 94; 980 42 50; 987 99 80
Fax: (359) 2 980 98 27
press@priv.government.bg
http://www.priv.government.bg

BURKINA FASO
Decommissioning Office
Avenue K. N'Krumah
01 BP 6451 Ouagadougou 01
Tel.: (226) 33 58 93
Fax: (226) 30 77 41
privatisation@fasonet.bf
http://www.privatisation-bf.com

CAMEROON
Technical Commission for Privatization and
    Liquidation; SNI Building (9th Floor)
P.O.Box 1452
Yaounde, Cameroon
Tel.: (237) 23 97 50
Fax: (237) 23 51 08

CAPE VERDE
Cape Verde, Praia
P.O. Box 323
Tel.: (238) 61 47 48
Fax: (238) 61 23 34
cvprivatization@mail.cvtelecom.cv
http://www.cvprivatization.org/english.html

CHILE
Foreign Investment Committee
Teatinos 120, 10th Floor
Santiago, Chile
Tel.: (562) 698 4254
Fax: (562) 698 9476
investment@cinver.cl
http://www.foreigninvestment.cl

CONGO
Privatization Committee of Congo
Tel.: (242) 81 46 21
Fax: (242) 41 22 73

COSTA RICA
Ministry of National Planning and Economic
    Politics, MIDEPLAN
Apartado postal 10127-1000
San Jose, Costa Rica
Tel.: (506) 281-2700
Fax: (506) 281-2717
webedit@ns.mideplan.go.cr
http://www.mideplan.go.cr/index.html

CROATIA
Croatian Privatization Fund
Ivana Lucica 6
10 000 Zagreb, Croatia
Tel.: (385) 1 4569 111
Fax: (385) 1 6115 568
hfp@hfp.hr,investcroatia@hfp.hr
http://www.hfp.hr

CZECH REPUBLIC
National Property Fund of the Czech Republic
FNM CR, Rasinovo nabrezi 42
128 00 Prague 2
Tel.: (420) 2 24991111, 24 991 285, 24 991
    403
Fax: (420) 2 24991241, 2 24 991 379
info@fnm.cz
http://www.fnm.cz/fnm/web.nsf/IndexAN

DOMINICAN REPUBLIC
Commission for the Reform of the Public
  Enterprises
Gustavo Mejía Ricart No. 73
Esq. Agustín Lara, Edif. Latinoamericana de
  Seguros
6to. Piso. Ens. Serrallés
Santo Domingo, D. N. República Dominicana
Tel.: (809) 683-3591
Fax: (809) 683-3888, 683-3964
crepdom@codetel.net.do
http://www.crepdom.gov.do

EGYPT
Ministry of Public Enterprise
2 Latin America Street
Garden City, Cairo, Egypt
Tel.: (20)-2-795-9287
Fax: (20)-2-355-9233
mfayad@idsc.gov.eg
http://www.mpe-egypt.com

ECUADOR
Council for the Modernization of the State
  (CONAM)
Tel.: 04 568 882
Fax: 04 560 170
info@conam.cov.ec
http://www.conam.gov.ec

ERITREA
The National Agency for the Supervision and
  Privatization of Public Enterprises
  Government of Eritrea
Asmara, P.O. Box 4887
Tel.: (291) 1 119383
Fax: (291) 1 127922
http://www.eriemb.se/economy.htm#inv

ETHIOPIA
Ethiopian Privatization Agency
P.O. Box 11835
Addis Ababa, Ethiopia
Tel.: (251)-01-505139
Fax: (251)-01-513955
epa@telecom.net.et
http://www.telecom.net.et/~epa/

GABON
yvesconstant@finances.gouv.ga
www.finances.gouv.ga

GEORGIA
Ministry of State Property Management
#64 Chavchavadze Avenue
Tbilisi, 380062, Georgia
Tel.: (99532) 25 17 42; 25 17 44; 25 19 01
Fax: (99532) 23 59 12
leigh@access.sanet.ge
http://web.sanet.ge/mospm

GHANA
Ghana Investment Promotion Centre
P.O. Box M193, Accra, Ghana
Tel.: (233)-(21)-66 5125–9
Fax: (233)-(21)-66 3801
info@gipc.org.gh
http://www.gipc.org.gh

GREECE
Hellenic Center for Investment
Investors Network
3 Mitropoleos
Athens, Attica 10557, Greece
Tel.: (30) 210 33 55 700
Fax: (30) 210 32 42 079
synergasia@elke.gr
www.elke.gr/elkeweb/static/introduction.htm

HUNGARY
Hungarian Privatization and State Holding
  Company
H-1399 Budapest
P.O.Box 708
Tel.: (36 1) 237 4400
Fax: (36 1) 237 4100
apvrt@apvrt.hu
http://www.apvrt.hu

INDONESIA
Indonesian Ministry of State Owned
  Enterprises
Restructuring and Privatization Division
Gedung Keuangan 16 Lantai
10, Jl.DR. Wahidin Raya Str
2, Jakarta 10710, Indonesia
Tel.: 021-34831746 / 0816-964717
Fax: 021-34831752
sekretariat@bumn-ri.com
http://www.bumn-ri.com

INDIA
Ministry of Divestment
132 Yojana Bhawan
New Delhi—110001, India
Tel.: 3096557
Fax: 3096560
ashourie@nic.in
http://divest.nic.in

IRAN
Iranian Privatization Organization
No.75, Zarafshan Street
Evanak St., faze 4th
Ghods village, POB 516–14665
Tel.: 8083380
Fax: 8087882
www.privatization.org.ir

ISRAEL
Government Companies Authority
Tel.: 972 (2) 6707179, 2-6707150
pniot@mof.gov.il
http://www.gca.gov.il

JAMAICA
National Investment Bank of Jamaica
11 Oxford Road, Kingston 5
P.O. Box 889
Tel.: (876) 960-9690-8
Fax: (876) 9200379
nibj@infochan.com
http://www.nibj.com/about.html

JORDAN
Executive Privatization Commission
P.O. Box 941536
Amman 11194, The Hashemite Kingdom of
    Jordan
Tel.: (962)-6-5670556 / 5678451
Fax: (962)-6-4626254
epu@nol.com.jo
http://epc.gov.jo

KAZAKHSTAN
Ministry of Finance
Committee of the State Property and
    Privatization
36 Auezov Street
473024 Astana, Republic of Kazakhstan
Tel.: 7-3172-33 43 97
Fax: 7-3172-32 09 37
webmaster@minfin.kz
www.mf.minfin.kz

KENYA
Investment Promotion Centre
8th Floor, National Bank of Kenya Building
Harambee Avenue
P.O. Box 55704
City Square, 00200, Nairobi, Kenya.
Tel.: (254) (2) 221401–4
Fax: (254) (2) 336663
info@ipckenya.org
http://www.ipckenya.org

KOREA
Ministry of Planning and Budget
Republic of Korea 520-3 Banpo-dong Seocho-
    Gu Seoul (137-756)
Tel.: (82)-2-3496-5121
Fax: (82)-2-3480-7615
nara@mpb.go.kr
http://www.mpb.go.kr

KOSOVO
Regional Co-ordinator
UN Interim Administration in Kosovo (UNIAK)
Tel. (cell): 377 44 151842
citti@un.org
www.un.org/peace/kosovo/pages/kosovo1
    .htm

KUWAIT
Kuwait Investment Authority
P.O. Box 64
13001 Safat, Kuwait
webmaster@kia.gov.kw
http://www.kia.gov.kw

KYRGYZ REPUBLIC
Investment Promotion Center
57, Erkindik Av.
Bishkek, 720874, Kyrgyz Republic
Tel.: (996-312) 226644
Fax: (996-312) 661075
ipc@infotel.kg
http://www.spf.gov.kg/indexE.html

LATVIA
Latvian Privatization Agency
Valdemara 31, Riga, LV-1887
Tel.: (371)-7021358
Fax: (371)-7830363
info@mail.lpa.bkc.lv
http://www.lpa.bkc.lv

LEBANON
Higher Council for Privatization
Grand Serail- Beirut Central District
Beirut, Lebanon
Tel.: (961)-1-987500
Fax: (961)-1-983061
hcp-gs@pcm.gov.lb
http://www.hcp.gov.lb

LESOTHO
Privatisation Project
Ministry of Finance
2nd Floor, Lesotho Bank Mortgage Division
 Building
Kingsway, Private Bag A249
Maseru 100, Lesotho- Southern Africa
Tel.: (266) 22-317 902
Fax: (266) 22-317 551
mntsasa@privatisation.gov.ls
http://www.privatisation.gov.ls

LITHUANIA
State Property Fund
Vilnius St. 16
2600 Vilnius, Lithuania
Tel.: (370 2) 684999
Fax: (370 2) 684997
info@vtf.lt
http://www.vtf.lt/english/index.html

MACEDONIA
Privatization Agency of the Republic of
 Macedonia
Nikola Vapcarov 7
Box 410, 1000 Skopje, Macedonia
Tel.: (389) 2 117-564
Fax: (389) 2 126-022
agency@mpa.org.mk
http://www.mpa.org.mk

MALAWI
The Privatization Commission of Malawi
CDL House, 5 Independence Drive
P. O. Box 937, Blantyre, Malawi
Tel.: (265) 1 623655
Fax: (265) 1 621248
info@privatisationmalawi.org
http://www.privatisationmalawi.org

MALAYSIA
Economic Planning Unit
Prime Minister's Department, Block B5 & B6
Federal Government Administrative Centre
62502 Putrajaya, Malaysia
Tel.: (603) 8888 3333
Fax: (603) 8888 3755
info@epu.jpm.my
http://www.epu.jpm.my

MALTA
Privatisation Unit, Ministry of Finance
Trade Center, San Gwann Industrial Estate
San Gwann SGN 09, Malta
Fax: (356) 21 448 952
victoria-mary.wilson@gov.mt

MEXICO
Ministry of Finance and Public Credit
Tel.: (52)—55 91 580950
ori@shcp.gob.mx
http://www.shcp.gob.mx/english/index.html

MOLDOVA
State Department for Privatization of the
 Republic of Moldova
26 Puskin str.
MD 2012, Chisinau, Moldova
Tel.: (3732) 23 43 50
Fax: (3732) 23 43 36
dep.priv@moldtelecom.md
http://www.privatization.md

MONGOLIA
State Property Committee
Government Building IV
Ulaanbaatar, Mongolia
Tel.: (976)-11-312460
Fax: (976)-11-312798
spc@mongol.net
http://www.spc.gov.mn

MONTENEGRO
Privatization Council
Terazije 23, YU—11000 Belgrad
Tel.: (381 11) 3 24 82 2
Fax: (381 11) 3 24 87 54
savjet@cg.yu
http://www.savjet.org/en/council/default.htm

MONTSERRAT (to consider privatization)
Economic Development Unit
Government of Montserrat
P.O. Box 292, Montserrat
Tel.: (664) 491-2066/2557
Fax: (664) 491-4632
devunit@candw.ag
http://www.mninet.com/devunit

MOROCCO
Ministry of Public Sector and Privatization
1, Angle Avenue Ibn Sina et Oued Al
   Makhazine Agdal
Rabat, Morocco
Tel.: (212) 37-68-96-14
Fax: (212) 37-67-32-99
minpriv@mtds.com
http://www.minpriv.gov.ma
http://www.finances.gov.ma

MOZAMBIQUE
Ministry of Planning and Finance
Mr. Jose Martins, Consulting Economist
Rua da Imprensa, No 256
Predio\22 Andares—7, Andar, 708/710
CP No 4350, Maputo, Mozambique
Tel: (258)-1-426-515/6
Fax: (258)-1-421-541
utre@teledata.cprm.net
dnpo@dnpo.uem.mz
http://www.mozambique.mz/governo/mpf/
   dnpo

NEPAL
Privatization Cell, Ministry of Finance
Bagh Durbar, Kathmandu, Nepal
Tel.: (977 1) 259 820
Fax: (977 1) 257 854
asimof@mos.com.np
http://www.privat.gov.np

NEW ZEALAND
New Zealand Treasury
P.O. Box 3724
Wellington, New Zealand
Tel.: (64) 4 472 2733
Fax: (64) 4 473 0982
information@treasury.govt.nz
http://www.treasury.govt.nz

NIGER
Ministry of Privatization and Business
   Restructuring
B.P.: 862, Immeuble Sonibank, 5th Floor
Niamey, Niger
Tel.: (227) 73.29.10—73.29.58
Fax: (227) 73.59.91
ccpp@intnet.ne
http://www.nigerprivatisation.com

NIGERIA
The Bureau of Public Enterprises
The Presidency
1 Osun Crescent
Maitama, Abuja, Nigeria
Tel.: (234) 9 4134636–46
Fax: (234) 9 4134657; (234) 9 4134671
info@bpeng.org,
askbpe@bpeng.org
http://www.bpeng.org

PAKISTAN
Privatisation Commission
Government of Pakistan
5-A Constitution Avenue
Islamabad, Pakistan
Tel.: (92) 51 9205146
Fax: (92) 51 9203076
Info@Privatisation.gov.pk
http://www.privatisation.gov.pk

PERU
Comission for the Promotion of Private
   Investment (COPRI)
Paseo de la República 3361—Piso 9
Lima 27—Perú
Tel.: (511) 612-1200
Fax: (511) 221-2941/42
info@copri.org
www.copri.gob.pe

POLAND
Ministry of the Treasury
ul. Krucza 36/Wspolna 6, 00-522 Warszawa
Tel.: (48 22) 695-80-00
Fax: (48 22) 628-08-72   .
minister@msp.gov.pl
http://www.mst.gov.pl/starte.php

REPUBLIC OF THE PHILIPPINES
Committee on Privatization
Tel.: (02) 524-16-33
vencajucom@dof.gov.ph
http://www.dof.gov.ph/htm/privatization.htm

ROMANIA
The Authority for Privatization and
   Management of State Ownership
Cpt. Av. Alexandru Serbanescu Street, 50
sector 1, cod 715151, Bucharest
Tel.: (4021) 303.63.01
Fax: (4021) 310.16.87
info@apaps.ro
http://www.apaps.ro/eng/index.html

RUSSIA
Russian Federal Property Fund
119049 Moscow
Blvd. Leninskii 9
Tel.: (095) 236-71-15
Fax: (095) 956-27-80
rffi@dol.ru
http://www.fpf.ru

RWANDA
Privatisation Secretariat
P.O. Box 4731
Kigali, Rwanda
Tel.: (250) 75383
Fax: (250) 75384
pvs@rwanda1.com
www.minecofin.gov.rw/agencies/privatization/
    index.htm

SAUDI ARABIA
Ministry of Finance and National Economy
Supreme Economic Council
Airport Road
Riyadh 11177
Tel.: 405 0000/405 0080
Fax: 405 9202
info@mof.gov.sa
http://www.mof.gov.sa,
www.saudinf.com

SERBIA
Ministry of Economy and Privatisation of the
    Republic of Serbia
16 Srpskih Vladara St
11000 Belgrade
Tel.: (381) 11 3617-599
Fax: (381) 11 3617-640
officempriv@mpriv.sr.gov.yu
http://www.mpriv.sr.gov.yu

SINGAPORE
Temasek Holdings (Pte) Ltd
60B Orchard Road
#06-18 Tower 2
The Atriu@Orchard, Singapore 238891
Tel.: (65) 6828-6828
Fax: (65) 6821-1188
enquire@temasek.com.sg
http://www.temasekholdings.com.sg

SLOVAK REPUBLIC
National Property Fund of the Slovak Republic
Drieňova 27, 821 01 Bratislava
Tel.: (421-7) 4827-1111
Fax: (421-7) 4827-1289
fnm@natfund.gov.sk
http://www.natfund.gov.sk

SLOVENIA
Agency of the Republic of Slovenia for
    Reconstructing and Privatisation
Kotnikova 28
1101 Ljubljana, Slovenia
Tel.: (061) 13 16 030, (061) 13 16 027
Fax: (061) 13 16 011
webmaster@arspip.si
http://www.arspip.si/ang

SOUTH AFRICA
Department of Public Enterprises
4th Floor, Infotech Building
1090 Arcadia Street
Hatfield, Pretoria 0083
Tel.: (012) 431 1133, 1000, 1098
Fax: (012) 431 1039, 2142
info@dpe.gov.za
http://www.dpe.gov.za

SRI LANKA
Public Enterprises Reform Commision of
    Sri Lanka
11th Floor, West Tower
World Trade Center
Colombo 1, Sri Lanka.
Tel.: 94-1-346831, 338756
Fax: 94-1-326116, 342544
info@perc.gov.lk
http://www.perc.gov.lk

TANZANIA
The Presidential Parastatal Sector Reform
    Commission
2nd Floor Sukari House
Ohio Str/Sokoine Drive
P.O. Box 9252
Dar es Salaam, Tanzania
Tel.: (255)-22-211-5482, 211-7988/9
Fax: (255)-22-211-3065/6
info@psrctz.com
http://www.psrctz.com

TAJIKISTAN
State Property Committee of the Republic of
   Tajikistan
Tel.: (7 3772) 21-86-59
privatization@tajikistan.com
http://privatization.tajikistan.com

THAILAND
Office of State Enterprise and Government
   Securities
Ministry of Finance, Bangkok, Thailand
Rama VI Road
Bangkok, 10400, Thailand
Tel.: (66) 2 278 0936
Fax: (66) 2 278 0923
trev995@vayu.mof.go.th
http://www.privatisation.go.th/content1.html

TONGA
Government Investment Unit
Ministry of Finance
P.O. Box 87
Vuna Road
Nuku'alofa, Tonga
Tel.: (676) 23-925
Fax:: (676) 26-011
tlaume@finance.gov.to

TURKEY
Privatization Administration
Huseyin Rahmi Gurpinar Sokak No 2
Ankara, Turkey
Tel.: (0312) 441 15 00
Fax: (0312) 438 06 52
info@oib.gov.tr
http://www.oib.gov.tr

TURKMENISTAN
Department of Privatization
Ministry of Economy and finance of
   Turkmenistan
Tel.: (993 12) 512 360, 510 257, 510 119

UGANDA
Privatization Unit
Plot 1, Colville Street
P.O. Box 10944
Kampala, Uganda
Tel.: (256) 41 256467 / 256392 / 230300
Fax: (256) 41 342403/259997
info@perds.go.ug
http://www.perds.go.ug

UKRAINE
State Property Fund of Ukraine
18/9 Kutuzov str
Kyiv, 01133, Ukraine
Tel.: (38 044) 2951274
Fax: (38 044) 2966984
marketing@spfu.gov.ua
http://www.spfu.gov.ua

UZBEKISTAN
State Property Committee of the Republic of
   Uzbekistan
Tel.: (99871) 139 2132
Fax: (99871) 139 2133
akbarov@spc.gov.uz
http://www.spc.gov.uz/index.html

VENEZUELA
Venezuelan Investment Fund
Av. Francisco de Miranda
Centro Empresarial Parque del Este Piso 12
La Carlota, Caracas 1071, Venezuela
Tel.: (58)-212-237-5486/ 5726/ 5995/ 5895
Fax: (58)-212-237-6028/ 6109
conapri@conapri.org
http://www.conapri.or

ZAMBIA
Zambia Privatisation Agency
Privatisation House
Nasser Road
P.O. Box 30819
Lusaka, Zambia
Tel.: (260)-1-223859
Fax: (260)-1-225270
zpa@zpa.org.zm
http://www.zpa.org.zm

ZIMBABWE
Privatisation Agency of Zimbabwe
Private Bag 7728
Causeway, 9th Floor
Nelson Mandela/Third Street
Harare
Tel.: (263)-4-251620-4
Fax: (263)-4-253723
humbani@paz.icon.co.zw
http://www.paz.co.zw

Notes

Chapter 1

1. Interestingly, the United States did follow the global model of government ownership of the nation's airports, though it has been slow to follow the subsequent global trend toward airport privatization. In fact, the United States is today a significant laggard in privatizing airports, largely because of the way they are financed with tax-exempt municipal bonds [see Enright and Ng (2001)].

2. The seven largest international oil companies were given the memorable title of "the Seven Sisters" during the 1960s by Enrico Mattei, the head of the Italian state oil company, ENI [Sampson (1975)]. It was never quite clear whether Mattei admired or resented the Sisters (probably both), but he became the very embodiment of the entrepreneurial SOE manager, pushing ENI into the global big leagues by striking oil purchase agreements with the new Libyan government of Muammar Kaddafi. Ironically, the modern foundation named in his honor, Fondazione ENI-Enrico Mattei (FEEM), is a leading proponent of privatization in Europe.

3. It is always tempting to look at a watershed historical event and perceive that both the event and the effects that flowed from it were foreordained. To grasp just how incorrect this is with respect to privatization, I would recommend that any scholar wishing to conduct research in this field take the same step that I did in order to see how privatization evolved as a policy. Go to an academic library and find the shelves where the older issues of the *Economist* are kept. Begin leafing through the magazines from the late 1950s or early 1960s, and read (or copy) those articles dealing with government policies regarding state-owned enterprises. Continue reading these articles, in chronological order, at least through the mid-1980s. This brings home just how revolutionary the early attempts at privatization really were perceived to be. The exercise also gave me tremendous respect for the moral courage of the early privatization pioneers.

4. Using a broader definition of privatization—one that encompassed reactively changing the policies of an immediate predecessor government—the Churchill government's denationalization of the British steel industry during the early 1950s could well be labeled the first "privatization." I thank David Parker for pointing this out to me.

5. Yarrow (1986), Vickers and Yarrow (1991), Menyah, Paudyal, and Inganyete (1995),

Menyah and Paudyal (1996), and Florio (2002) have more detailed discussions of the (stated and unstated) goals of the British privatization program.

6. The desire to promote wider share ownership has both a financial and a political component. Financially, increasing the number of investors willing to purchase corporate equities increases the absorptive capacity of a nation's capital market, thereby either lowering the cost of capital for firms or increasing the number of companies able to raise capital at prevailing rates, or both. Politically, broadening share ownership is perceived to increase public willingness to back market-oriented economic policies and also tends to make it very difficult for subsequent governments to attempt to renationalize divested companies. Most governments actively stress both the political and economic virtues of "people's capitalism" when promoting privatization plans, and several governments have achieved great success at increasing share ownership. The Thatcher privatizations, for example, increased the fraction of the U.K. adult population holding shares from 7 percent in 1979 to 24 percent in 1990.

7. Anyone working in this area will soon notice that the last three syllables of "privatization" are sometimes spelled with an "s" and sometimes with a "z," with the former generally being used by British writers and the latter by most everyone else. Although equity perhaps suggests that the nation that popularized the policy should get the honor of mandating its spelling, empirical evidence suggests the z-spelling is winning out. Of the 96 articles in the reference list of my survey paper with Jeff Netter (2001) with either *privatization* or *privatisation* in their titles, 86 use "z" while 10 use "s."

8. The price-earnings ratio implied by these valuations was an astonishing 162 using prospective-year earnings, and over 200 using current-year earnings. Each share sold in the immediate aftermarket at approximately $12,000 (dollars, not yen), and this price was to rise to $18,000 after the issue was completed. At its peak market valuation in late 1987, NTT had a market value of about $350 billion—by far the highest of any company in the world.

9. As we will discuss in greater detail in chapter 5, it is very hard to predict just how large a privatization program China will ultimately be able to launch. Although the government reaffirmed its commitment to privatizing all but the very largest state enterprises in 1999, the fact that Chinese SOEs are burdened with so many social welfare responsibilities suggests that it will be extraordinarily difficult to implement a privatization program large enough to seriously undermine the state's economic role [Lin (2000), Lin, Cai, and Li (1998), and Bai, Li, and Wang (1997)]. If these difficulties can be overcome, however, the complete sale of Chinese state-owned enterprises would represent the single largest privatization program in history, in terms of both total amount raised and impact on the structure of ownership of business assets.

10. We should point out that this figure includes funds raised by France Telecom, rather than by the French state itself, through FT's $2.33 billion IPO of a 10.5 percent stake in its Wanadoo subsidiary and its $6.69 billion IPO of a similar stake in Orange. Throughout this book, we will count such sales as privatization proceeds because they do in fact reduce government ownership in a commercial enterprise, even though the funds raised flow to the enterprise rather than the Treasury. On the other hand, we do not count France Telecom's record $15.8 billion rights issue in March 2003 as a privatization sale because the French government fully participated in the offering by purchasing a 56 percent share of the issue—proportional to its existing holdings—and thus the offering did not reduce state ownership at all.

Chapter 2

1. The stated goals of the Thatcher government's program, as described in Price Waterhouse (1989a,b), are to (1) raise revenue for the state, (2) promote economic efficiency, (3) reduce government interference in the economy, (4) promote wider share ownership, (5) provide the opportunity to introduce competition, and (6) subject SOEs to market discipline. Vickers and Yarrow's (1991) listing includes these objectives, but adds two more: weakening public-sector unions, thereby easing the problems of public-sector pay determination, and gaining political advantage.

2. Gough (1989) notes Briggs's claim that Archbishop Temple first used the "welfare state" term in wartime Britain to differentiate Britain from the "warfare" state of Nazi Germany.

3. Several other articles discuss the theory of privatization and review the empirical literature, including Boardman and Vining (1989), Vickers and Yarrow (1991), Laffont and Tirole (1991), Shleifer (1998), Havrylyshyn and McGettigan (1999), Nellis (1999, 2001), Sheshinski and Lopez-Calva (1999), and Djankov and Murrell (2002). All of these papers are cited individually either in this chapter or in chapters 4 or 5.

4. Interestingly, in a more recent evaluation of privatization in developing countries, Cook and Kirkpatrick (2003) offer a more balanced overall assessment though they still note the same problems with institutional weaknesses. They state (page 217) that "privatization can be an effective instrument for bringing about significant economic and development gains, but, besides ownership, it involves a set of interlinking issues which include corporate governance, institutional capacity, market competition and political economy."

5. That governments feel a strong temptation to bail out important failing firms was demonstrated yet again in August 2003, when the French government announced its intention to rescue Alcatel from bankruptcy and possible liquidation. This step was announced by a "conservative" government seemingly intent on reducing the state's role in France's economic life, and was especially ironic given the fact that Alcatel was a private firm. The company's role as "national champion" in engineering, coupled with the large number of jobs at stake, forced the government to act—even in the face of strong opposition from the European Union.

6. Although for descriptive purposes we present the viewpoints of the economists discussed above as being diametrically opposed, the degree of actual disagreement among mainstream economists is certainly less than this construct suggests. The opinions of policy makers throughout the world have in fact been moving closer to those expressed by Ronald Coase in his classic 1960 article, "The Theory of Social Cost." In analyzing market failure, Coase says, "All solutions have costs, and there is no reason to suppose that governmental regulation is called for simply because the problem is not handled well by the market or the firm." Substitute "government ownership" for "governmental regulation" and the relevance of Coase's insight to our discussion becomes obvious. Brickley, Smith, and Zimmerman (1997, page 49), in a more recent analysis of the benefits and costs of free markets versus central planning, say markets have worked better because, "First, the price system motivates better use of knowledge and information in economic decisions. Second, it provides stronger incentives for individuals to make productive decisions." Those seeking a more benevolent recent assessment of the benefits of state ownership should refer to Willner (2003).

7. A related literature that we do not review analyzes the relative performance of nonprofit firms and for-profit firms. Brickley and Van Horn (2002), in an analysis of large hospitals, argue that the evidence suggests there is little distinction between the behavior

of nonprofit and for-profit hospitals. Their results suggest the similarities in behavior are due to the effects of competition and not identical objective functions of the managers.

8. Depressingly, Akram (2000) shows that the problem of soft budget constraints is not solved by privatization of Bangladeshi SOEs. Instead, the "entrepreneurs" who purchase these companies continue to demand and receive cheap credit from state banks and other subsidies from the government after "privatization."

9. Two other interesting and unusual examples of how ownership impacts organizational performance are provided by Olds (1994) and Clarke and Xu (2003). Olds uses data from the 1800s to show that after the privatization of the tax-supported Congregationalist churches in New England demand for preachers and church membership rose dramatically. Clarke and Xu use enterprise-level data on bribes paid to utilities in 21 transition countries to examine how the characteristics of the utilities' taking bribes and the firms' paying bribes affect the equilibrium levels of corruption in the sector. After adjusting for other factors, they find that employees of state-owned utilities are more likely to take bribes than are workers in privately owned utilities.

10. This paper has advantages over much of the other work in the area owing to the high-quality data, as well as guidance from a well-developed literature in estimating the determinants of productivity. The authors perform some of the more sophisticated econometric analyses of papers in this area. For example, they replicate their results with a subset of firms that did not experience any within-firm changes in ownership, enabling the authors to be sure that their time-ownership interaction term captures only between-firm variations in ownership. Ehrlich, Gallais-Hamonno, Liu, and Lutter also perform various other robustness checks using different specifications and subsamples as well as controlling for the special characteristics of their sample period (oil price shocks and deregulation in the United States), and find that their results are robust. Finally, they consider the potential for simultaneity effects between ownership and productivity and find that causality goes from ownership to productivity, and not vice versa. The weakness in the work is that it is based on one industry with relatively old data. The authors also note that they make the implicit assumption that all firms are cost minimizing, but if state-owned enterprises have other objectives, it is difficult to interpret the meaning of differences in costs.

Chapter 3

1. In an intriguing empirical study, Chun (2000) studies whether the Hungarian restitution vouchers trade in an efficient market and whether the trading in these instruments is interrelated (integrated) with stock trading on the Budapest Stock Exchange (BSE). He finds that the prices of restitution vouchers do follow a random walk, and thus the market is weak-form efficient. Additionally, Chun shows that this market and the BSE are independent and separately efficient, unlike the stock markets of the other major central European economies.

2. There are many other methods besides the four described above that governments can use to increase private-sector participation. For example, the term "privatization" in the United States means something different from any of these strategies. As López-de-Silanes, Shleifer, and Vishny (1997) show, the privatization debate in the United States refers to the choice between in-house provision of goods and services by (state and local) government employees and the contracting out of that production to private firms. Their empirical study finds that the more binding are state fiscal constraints and the less powerful are public-sector unions, the greater the likelihood of privatization.

3. Longer descriptions of the issues that governments in central and eastern Europe

have confronted when designing voucher privatization programs are provided in Bornstein (1994, 1999), Alexandrowicz (1994), Drum (1994), and Shafik (1995).

4. At a recent OECD conference, Vittorio Grilli, then the director of Italy's privatization program, pointed out an additional political problem with exercising a golden share. When a government uses its share to veto a takeover bid, this is equivalent to publicly stating it does not approve of the bidder. Such a statement is awkward at best and can cause an international incident if the bidder is a foreign company.

Chapter 4

1. Many of the difficulties are similar to those discussed in Temple (1999), who surveys cross-country research on the determinants of growth. Temple discusses the substantial problems that arise in estimating and interpreting cross-country regressions. Tybout (2000) also discusses the difficulties with data in attempting to assess the performance of manufacturing firms in developing countries.

2. Megginson, Nash, Netter, and Poulsen (forthcoming) find that governments selling SOEs tend to sell the more profitable SOEs in the public capital markets and the less profitable ones in the more opaque private markets. Those sold in the public capital markets are the firms that appear in studies of performance. Dewenter and Malatesta (2000) also show performance improvements before privatization in firms that are being privatized.

3. Consistent with the result that state connections matter in bank operations, Hersch, Kemme, and Netter (1997) find that in Hungary the banks made it much easier for firms headed by former members of the *nomenklatura* to get loans than other firms. La Porta, López-de-Silanes, and Shleifer (2002) also clearly document that privately owned banks are more efficient, more profitable, and more supportive of productive enterprise than are state-owned banks.

4. Although all three studies compute most of the performance ratios using a variety of different measures, whenever possible the authors focus on ratios of current-dollar flow measures (i.e., net income ÷ sales), rather than balance-sheet stock measures (property, plant and equipment ÷ total assets) in order to minimize inflation-induced valuation errors and to finesse the impact of different national accounting standards. The other measures generally yield qualitatively similar results.

5. The privatization and liberalization of the British electricity industry is also discussed at length in Newberry (1997) and Vickers and Yarrow (1991), while the regulatory regime adopted for earlier utility privatizations is described in Beesley and Littlechild (1989). None of these works showers the Thatcher government with praise for its policy decisions, though Beesley and Littlechild do find the RPI-X price regulation system adopted in the United Kingdom is superior to the U.S. rate of return regulatory regime.

6. Note that this study is actually summarized in table 7.5 instead of table 7.4, since it uses stock price data as its primary empirical tool. We discuss it here because of the topic covered rather than because of the methodology employed. Eckel, Eckel, and Singal (1997) also examine the two-stage privatization of Air Canada (from 100 percent state ownership to 57 percent, then to zero). Unlike BA, Air Canada does not compete with U.S. carriers on many routes, so there is no significant competitor stock price effect resulting from its divestiture. Air Canada's fares do not fall after the first, partial privatization, but fall a significant 13.7 percent after the final, complete divestiture of state ownership.

7. Ramamurti (1997) details the intense political maneuvering that accompanied the attempt to restructure and slim down FA. The generous severance payments awarded to displaced workers were instrumental in winning union acquiescence in the restructuring

plan, while the presence of effective road-transport competition for rail traffic reduced the threat of a potentially crippling strike weapon.

8. Though they do not quite fit into our empirical classification scheme, six related studies deserve mention here. Smith and Wellenius (1999) and Wellenius (2000) present normative analyses of telecom regulation in developing countries, while Wasserfallen and Müller (1998) discuss the privatization and deregulation of western Europe's telecom industry. Pollitt (1997) analyzes the impact of liberalization on the performance of the international electric supply industry, and Bortolotti, Fantini and Siniscalso (1999) document that effective regulation is a crucial institutional variable in electric utility privatization. Establishing such a regulatory regime allows governments to increase the pace of privatization, sell higher stakes, and maximize offering proceeds. Finally, Wallsten (2001b) shows that exclusivity periods, which are usually granted to telecom monopolies as they are being privatized, are economically harmful to consumers and do not achieve the efficiency objectives assigned to them at the time of divestment. Exclusivity periods do, however, raise the price that investors are willing to pay for privatized telecoms, which largely explains why they are employed.

Chapter 5

1. Djankov and Murrell use the categorization CIS, or Commonwealth of Independent States, rather than FSU to refer to the countries of the former Soviet Union. For consistency, however, we continue using FSU throughout, since the same nations are covered either way.

2. In his analysis of the reasons that Hungary's privatization program has proved to be so much more successful than those in most other central and eastern European countries, Mihályi (2000) emphasizes the importance of selling SOEs directly to Western transnational companies, and thus plugging them into the global trading system. Other countries stressed domestic over foreign ownership, and thus missed out on the opportunity of using privatization as a way of attracting foreign direct investment.

3. The Czech Republic's market collapse of 1997, described in Coffee (1999), and the Lithuanian government's tortuous privatization of the Mazheikiu Nafta refiner in early 2000, described by Samonis (2000), are also examples of what can go wrong in privatization programs.

4. Lau, Qian, and Roland (2000) show theoretically and empirically the Chinese have successfully followed a dual-track approach to market liberalization, as a method of implementing an efficient Pareto-improving reform. The idea was to continue enforcing the existing plan, while liberalizing the market to make implicit transfers to compensate losers under reform.

5. I thank Cyril Lin, Samuel Huang, and George Tian for helping me understand Chinese listing procedures. See http://www.csrc.gov.cn/CSRCsite/eng/elaws/elaws.htm for an English-language summary of Chinese securities laws.

Chapter 6

1. The fifth largest share issue in history is the March 2003 rights offering by France Telecom, which raised $15.8 billion for the company, and is not a true SIP because the government purchased its proportionate stake in the offering.

2. One should note, however, that many of the Chinese SOEs offered for sale have been of dodgy quality, and the government has shown a marked tendency to demand top prices for the "Red Chip" shares offered to foreigners. China may become investment

banker heaven over the next decade, but few Western banks have made any serious money off Chinese SIPs yet.

3. Ljungqvist, Jenkinson, and Wilhelm (2003) report that the average (median) size of non-U.S. IPOs during the 1990s was much larger, $157.1 million ($33.0 million), but this figure includes SIPs (they account for 10.1 percent of the sample, by number) so does not truly represent the average size of private-sector IPOs.

4. Baake and Oechssler (2001) present a similar theoretical model of deliberate government underpricing in privatization IPOs. In their model, governments underprice SIPs and then allocate shares broadly across the population in order to increase their chances of re-election.

5. Early long-run return studies, using both U.S. and international data, are summarized in Loughran, Ritter, and Rydqvist (1994). Later studies employing U.S. data, and finding negative long-run returns, include Loughran and Ritter (1995, 1997), Spiess and Affleck-Graves (1995), and Carter, Dark, and Singh (1998). Only a few U.S. studies, including Brav and Gompers (1997) find (insignificantly) positive long-term returns.

6. For example, Mitchell and Stafford (2000) argue that most corporate actions are not random events. They contend that after controlling for cross-correlation of abnormal returns, most statistical evidence of abnormal performance disappears. Lyon, Barber, and Tsai (1999), drawing on the work of Kothari and Warner (1997), and Barber and Lyon (1997), note five reasons for misspecification in test statistics designed to detect long-run returns. There are three sources of bias—a new listing bias, a re-balancing bias, and a skewness bias—as well as cross-sectional dependence in sample observations and a poorly specified asset-pricing model. Lyon, Barber, and Tsai, among others, suggest several methods to control for misspecification, but there is no one correct method. They conclude that the "analysis of long-run returns is treacherous." Canina, Michaely, Thaler, and Womack (1998) present another approach to dealing with long-run returns and Fama (1998) argues bad model problems are "unavoidable . . . and more serious in tests on long-term returns." Two other papers that do an excellent job of analyzing the problems with estimating long run returns are Brav, Geczy, and Gompers (2000) and Eckbo, Masulis, and Norli (2000).

7. MNNS also use the wealth relative methodology developed by Ritter (1991) as a measure of long-run excess performance. This involves computing how much wealth must be invested in the stock being studied to yield the same terminal wealth as one dollar invested in the reference portfolio or matching firm. Since the JMNN wealth relative measures yield qualitatively identical results to the holding period return and cumulative abnormal return measures, this discussion concentrates on the more traditional measures.

8. All comparisons to dollar-based investments are calculated using currency-adjusted values. The adjustments are made using daily exchange rate data provided by *Datastream*.

Chapter 7

1. The industrial and geographic distribution of syndicated lending during this period is detailed in Kleimeier and Megginson (2000), while Esty and Megginson (2003) discuss the role of loan syndicate structure in managing the political risk of project finance lending.

2. While the two databases used for tables 7.1 and 7.2 do not permit direct comparison, it seems likely that the rising value of bank credit as a percent of American GDP between 1990 and 2000 documented in Panel A is a direct result of the rise of the syndicated loan market as a funding source for mergers and acquisitions. As we will show later, merger and acquisition activity surged in the United States during the 1990s, and most of the M&A loans in the *Loanware* file were in fact arranged for U.S. borrowers.

3. Field (1997) documents that U.S. institutional investors do indeed seem to provide

economically valuable monitoring, in that IPOs with higher institutional ownership levels significantly outperform comparable IPOs with low levels of institutional ownership.

4. The updated version of this listing of SIPs is included as an appendix to this book.

5. Most countries weighing the adoption of international accounting standards should adopt the International Financial Reporting Standards (IFRS), rather than U.S. GAAP standards. The European Union has mandated that all member countries adopt IFRS for companies domiciled there by 2005, and China recently decided in favor of IFRS as well. Even the United States may ultimately be forced to opt for IFRS over GAAP within the next few years. The "principles based" IFRS are increasingly favored over the "rules based" GAAP by companies and investors around the world, and the scandals that engulfed American accounting and management in 2001 and 2002 seriously weakened the prestige of U.S. accounting and reporting practices. On the other hand, a massive scandal involving Italy's Parmalat broke out in early 2004, showing clearly that no accounting system can detect willful fraud by insiders.

Chapter 8

1. The ITU defines a main line as "a telephone line connecting the subscriber's terminal equipment to the public switched network and which has a dedicated port in the telephone exchange equipment" (Wallsten, 2001a, page 6). This means that "main lines per 100 inhabitants" is the same measure as "telephone lines per 100 inhabitants," but we retain the verbiage of the various source articles in our discussion.

2. In the interest of space, we do not delve deeply into the technical aspects of telecom system operation or regulation in this chapter. However, the interested reader can find an excellent description of the technology of modern service provision—and the associated regulatory issues these give rise to within the U.S. context—in Hazlett and Bittlingmayer (2001). Telecommunications markets in industrialized countries are described in Boylaud and Nicoletti [(2000) OECD countries] and Wasserfallen and Müller [(1998), western Europe], while developing country telecommunications markets and regulations are described in Noll (2000), McNary (2001), and other papers discussed later in this chapter.

3. This is documented for telecoms by Wallsten (2002) and for electric utility privatizations by Bortolotti, Fantini, and Siniscalco (1999).

4. The theory of building commitment through noninterference is developed in Perotti (1995) and especially Biais and Perotti (2002). Empirical evidence supporting this theory is presented in Jones, Megginson, Nash, and Netter (1999) and Perotti and van Oijen (2001).

5. The regulatory regime adopted for BT had two key features. First was adoption of the RPI-X pricing formula, whereby BT would be allowed to raise prices on the entire basket of its services according to the formula of the annual change in the retail price index (RPI) minus X percent. The X was originally set at 3 percent, but reached 7.5 percent by the time BT was fully privatized in July 1993. The U.S. rate of return regulatory system was explicitly rejected as both inefficient and needlessly bureaucratic. Along these lines, the second major regulatory change was the establishment of the Office of Telecommunications (OFTEL) as regulator of a private BT. Although the *Economist* originally referred to OFTEL as the "watchpoodle" of BT because of its small staff and limited regulatory powers, later assessments were more favorable and the RPI-X pricing regime was subsequently adopted for other British infrastructure privatizations as well as for Japan's NTT.

6. The price-to-earnings (P/E) ratio implied by these valuations was an astounding 162 using prospective year earnings, and over 200 using current year earnings. Each share sold in the immediate aftermarket for approximately $12,000 (dollars, not yen) and this was to

rise to $18,000 per share at its peak in late 1987, giving NTT a market capitalization of almost $350 billion. Not bad for a phone company!

7. Though the fourth and final offering of the Spanish government's shares in Telefonica was not especially large ($2.84 billion) in an absolute or relative sense, it represented a real watershed for the Spanish privatization program. After this offering, roughly one Spanish household in eight owned shares in this one company, and share ownership had become widespread in a country with little history of equity investing.

8. The FT1 offering was also 17 times oversubscribed and created a record 3.9 million individual shareholders—in a country with a population of 59 million!

Chapter 9

1. In particular, Majumdar (1996) shows that Indian SOEs are vastly less efficient than private firms of comparable size. Using industry-level survey data, he evaluates the performance differences between SOEs, mixed enterprises (MEs), and privately owned Indian companies for the period 1973–1989. SOEs and MEs account for 37% of employment and 66% of capital investment in India in 1989. Majumdar documents efficiency scores averaging 0.975 for privately owned firms, which are significantly higher than the average 0.912 for MEs and 0.638 for SOEs. State sector efficiency improves during concerted "efficiency drives" but declines afterwards.

2. Chapter 7 presents a much more in-depth discussion of the role of financial markets in facilitating economic growth. We reproduce a summary of that discussion here so that this chapter can be used as a "stand-alone" text.

Chapter 10

1. The interested and open-minded reader seeking to understand how citizens of oil-exporting nations view the world petroleum market should visit OPEC's Web site (www.opec.org) and read their editorial and historical statements. This Web site also provides detailed current and historical information about oil production, exports, consumption, and prices. The two best Western sources of information and data about global energy markets are the International Energy Agency (www.iea.org) and the U.S. Department of Energy's Energy Information Administration (www.eia.doe.gov). Most of the data employed in constructing the tables for this chapter are obtained from these two sources, and from data collected by Marie-Cecille Vermelle, whose assistance is gratefully acknowledged. The International Energy Agency (1999, 2001) and Ocana (2003) articles obtained from the IEA Web site, and the EIA (1996) paper entitled "Privatization and the Globalization of Energy Markets" proved especially informative. A useful, if now somewhat dated, analysis of the challenges faced by managers of large NOCs and multinational oil companies is presented in Treat (1994).

2. Russia has not been the only developing country to fully or partially privatize its oil industry, just the only *major* oil exporter to do so. The Argentine national government sold its entire stake in Yacimientos Petroliferos Fiscales (YPF) in a $2.66 billion SIP in June 1993. The company was subsequently acquired by Spain's Repsol. Several other countries—including Brazil—divested pieces of their oil and gas industries during the 1990s. China also began selling minority stakes in three of its NOCs in 2000, and these sales have raised almost $10 billion thus far. However, none of these countries accounts for a meaningful fraction of global petroleum production, either individually or collectively.

3. Professor Stephen Littlechild, who was one of the principal architects of Britain's utility deregulation program, and who also served as the chief regulator of the electricity

industry from 1990 to 1998, describes Britain's ESI privatization and regulatory reform program in Littlechild (2001). Perhaps not surprisingly, he provides a generally favorable assessment of this program, especially when compared to California's disastrous electricity deregulation experience. Assessments of Britain's electric power reforms by Newberry and Pollitt (1997) and Price and Weyman-Jones (1996) are more critical. Both of these studies find that privatization and deregulation improved the operating efficiency of Britain's ESI and lowered prices to consumers, but both stress that more competition could and should have been injected into the industry during this process. The empirical evidence on electricity privatization, presented and discussed in depth in chapter 4, includes the works cited above and studies by Bortolotti, Fantini, and Siniscalco (1999), Steiner (2000), Pombo and Ramirez (2001), Estache (2002), and Zhang, Parker, and Kirkpatrick (2002). Most of these studies find that privatization and implementing new regulation, adopted as stand-alone policies, have small but statistically significant positive impacts on the performance of ESI companies, whereas injecting competition has a much larger and more positive effect. Not surprisingly, implementing all three policies simultaneously yields the largest performance improvement.

4. Japan also relies very heavily on nuclear power to generate its electricity, though Japanese utilities are mostly privately owned. Both Japan and France have encouraged nuclear power for strategic and security reasons, though both countries are now encountering increasingly severe operational, safety, and financial liability difficulties as a result of this support. In most countries, natural gas has become the fuel of choice for new generating plants for both cost and environmental reasons, and the market share of gas as a fuel for electricity production seems likely to continue rising.

5. In an ironic twist on European ESI "privatization," both Italy and Spain enacted "anti-EdF" laws aimed at preventing the French company from exercising operating control over utilities it had purchased in the two countries during the late 1990s. The Italian and Spanish parliaments enacted these laws out of frustration over France's refusal to open its own electricity market to foreign competition. The EU quickly challenged both anti-EdF laws and since France has at last promised to open its market, both will likely be repealed in the near future.

6. In addition to Green and Vogelsang (1994), three other studies empirically evaluate the impact that private ownership has on airline performance. Davies (1971), Ehrlich, Gallais-Hamonno, Liu, and Lutter (1994), and Eckel, Eckel, and Singal (1997) all document superior performance for privately owned airlines versus comparable state-owned carriers or, in Air Canada's case, compared to itself prior to full divestment [Eckel, Eckel, and Singal (1997)]. These studies are evaluated in depth in chapter 4.

7. We are actually able to obtain market capitalization and sales levels for one additional national carrier, China Eastern Airlines, but decide not to use it in computing our P/S multiple. We choose this course both because China Eastern is so much smaller than the other eight airlines and because its P/S value of 1.304 seemed abnormally high—higher in fact than Singapore Airlines, which is usually ranked as the world's best and most profitable international carrier. Including this company in our average P/S multiple would increase the average from 0.36 to 0.46, with a commensurate impact on the valuations presented in column 8 of table 10.9. Since we argue that these values are probably unrealistically high already, we choose not to include China Eastern in our P/S estimation.

8. Perhaps surprisingly, the prospects for privatizing *airports*—rather than airlines—are much more positive. Extensive airport privatizations have already occurred in western Europe and, to a lesser extent, in certain Asian and Latin American countries. Parker (1997) empirically examines British Airport Authority's performance since its divestment in July

1987, while Enright and Ng (2001) present an excellent overview of the history and prospects of airport privatizations. Ironically, the United States has by far the world's largest and most valuable state-owned airport sector, which is a direct result of the industry's reliance on municipal bond and other specialized financing available only to public-sector entities.

References

Chapter 1

The following texts are suggested for further reading: Florio (2002), Megginson and Netter (2001), Nellis (2003), Reviglio (2002), and Wallsten (2002). See also Andrei Shleifer (1998), "State versus Private Ownership," *Journal of Economic Perspectives* 12, pp. 133–150. Full chapter references are given below.

Akram, Tanweer. 1999. "Bangladesh's Privatization Policy." *Journal of Emerging Markets* 4, pp. 65–76.

Anderson, James H., Georges Korsun, and Peter Murrell. 1999. "Ownership, Exit, and Voice after Mass Privatization: Evidence from Mongolia." *Economics of Transition* 7, pp. 215–243.

Appiah-Kubi, K. 2001. "State-Owned Enterprises and Privatization in Ghana." *Journal of Modern African Studies* 39.

Arocena, Pablo. 2003. "The Privatisation Programme of the Public Enterprise Sector in Spain." CESifo working paper, Universidad Pública de Navarra, Pamplona, Spain.

Baer, Werner. 2003. "The Privatization Experience of Brazil." In David Parker and David Saal, eds., *International Handbook on Privatization*. Cheltenham, UK: Edward Elgar, pp. 220–234.

Bai, Chong-en, David D. Li, and Yijiang Wang. 1997. "Enterprise Productivity and Efficiency: When Is Up Really Down?" *Journal of Comparative Economics* 24, pp. 265–280.

Baldwin, Carliss Y., and Sugato Bhattacharyya. 1991. "Choosing the Method of Sale: A Clinical Study of Conrail." *Journal of Financial Economics* 30, pp. 69–98.

Barja, Gover, and Miguel Urquiola. 2003. "Capitalization and Privatization in Bolivia." Working paper, Cornell University, Ithaca, NY.

Barrett, Sean. 2003. "Privatisation in Ireland." CESifo working paper, Trinity College, Dublin, Ireland.

Bemporad, Simone, and Edoardo Reviglio. 2002. "Privatization in Italy and the Role of IRI." Working paper, Italian Ministry of Economics and Finance, Rome.

Bennell, Paul. 1997. "Privatization in Sub-Saharan Africa: Progress and Prospects During the 1990s." *World Development* 25, pp. 1785–1803.

469

Bennell, Paul. 2003. "Privatization in Sub-Saharan Africa." In David Parker and David Saal, eds., *International Handbook on Privatization*. Cheltenham, UK: Edward Elgar, pp. 310–320.

Black, Bernard, Reinier Kraakman, and Anna Tarassova. 2000. "Russian Privatization and Corporate Governance: What Went Wrong?" *Stanford Law Review* 56, pp. 1731–1808.

Boardman, Anthony E., Claude Laurin, and Aidan R. Vining. 2003. "Privatization in North America." In David Parker and David Saal, eds., *International Handbook on Privatization*. Cheltenham, UK: Edward Elgar, pp. 129–160.

Bornstein, Morris. 1999. "Framework Issues in the Privatization Strategies of the Czech Republic, Hungary and Poland." *Post-Communist Economies* 11, pp. 47–77.

Bortolotti, Bernardo, Marcella Fantini, and Domenico Siniscalco. 1999. "Privatisation: Politics, Institutions and Financial Markets." Working paper, Fondazione ENI-Enrico Mattei (FEEM), Milan, Italy.

Bortolotti, Bernardo, Marcella Fantini, and Domenico Siniscalco. Forthcoming. "Privatization around the World: New Evidence from Panel Data." *Journal of Public Economics*.

Chai, Joseph C. H. 2003. "Privatization in China." In David Parker and David Saal, eds., *International Handbook on Privatization*, Cheltenham, UK: Edward Elgar, pp. 235–261.

Chirwa, Ephraim W. 2001. "Industry and Firm Effects of Privatization in Malawian Oligopolistic Manufacturing." Working paper, University of Malawi, Zomba, Malawi.

Christoffersen, Henrk, and Martin Paldam. 2003. "Privatization in Denmark, 1980–2002." CESifo working paper, Aarhus University, Aarhus, Denmark.

Claessens, Stijn, Simeon Djankov, and Gerhard Pohl. 1997. *Ownership and Corporate Governance: Evidence from the Czech Republic.* Washington, DC: World Bank Policy Research Paper No. 1737.

Cook, Paul, and Colin Kirkpatrick. 2003. "Assessing the Impact of Privatization in Developing Countries." In David Parker and David Saal, eds., *International Handbook on Privatization*. Cheltenham, UK: Edward Elgar, pp. 209–219.

Davis, Jeffrey, Rolando Ossowski, Thomas Richardson, and Steven Barnett. 2000. *Fiscal and Macroeconomic Impact of Privatization*. Washington, DC: IMF Occasional Paper 194.

Dumontier, Pascal, and Claude Laurin. 2002. "The Financial Impacts of the French Government Nationalization-Privatization Strategy." Working paper, University of Geneva, Switzerland.

Dyck, I. J. Alexander. 1997. "Privatization in Eastern Germany: Management Selection and Economic Transition." *American Economic Review* 87, pp. 565–597.

Earle, John, and Almos Telgedy. 2001. "Productivity and Ownership Structure in Romania: Does Privatization Matter?" Working paper, Central European University, Budapest, Hungary.

Earle, John S. 1998. "Privatization, Competition and Budget Constraints: Disciplining Enterprises in Russia." SITE working paper no. 128, Stockholm School of Economics, Sweden.

Enright, Michael J., and Flash Ng. 2001. "Airport Privatisation." University of Hong Kong Case HKU149, Hong Kong PRC/SAR.

Estrin, Saul, and Adam Rosevear. 2003. "Privatization in Ukraine." In David Parker and David Saal, eds., *International Handbook on Privatization*. Cheltenham, UK: Edward Elgar, pp. 454–474.

Filatotchev, Igor. 2003. "Privatization and Corporate Governance in Transition Economies." In David Parker and David Saal, eds., *International Handbook on Privatization*. Cheltenham, UK: Edward Elgar, pp. 323–346.

Florio, Massimo. 2002. "A State without Ownership: The Welfare Impact of British Privatisations, 1979–1997." Working paper, University of Milan, Italy.

Gibbon, Henry. 1998. "Worldwide Economic Orthodoxy." *Privatisation International* 123, pp. 4–5.

Gibbon, Henry. 2000. "Editor's Letter." *Privatisation Yearbook.* London: Thomson Financial, p. 1.

Glennerster, Rachel. 2000. "Evaluating Privatization in the Former Yugoslav Republic of Macedonia." Working paper, Kennedy School, Harvard University, Cambridge, MA.

Goldstein, Andrea, and Giuseppe Nicoletti. 2003. "Privatization in Italy 1993–2002: Goals, Institutions, Outcomes, and Outstanding Issues." CESifo working paper, OECD, Paris.

Grigorian, David. 2000. "Ownership and Performance of Lithuanian Enterprises." Policy Research working paper 2343, World Bank Group, Washington, DC.

Hailemariam, Stifanos, Henk von Eije, and Jos van der Werf. 2001. "Is There a 'Privatization Trap'? The Case of Manufacturing Industries in Eritrea." Working paper, University of Groningen, Groningen, The Netherlands.

Hare, Paul, and Alexander Murayev. 2003. "Privatization in Russia." In David Parker and David Saal, eds., *International Handbook on Privatization.* Cheltenham, UK: Edward Elgar, pp. 347–374.

Hodge, Graeme A. 2003. "Privatization: The Australian Experience." In David Parker and David Saal, eds., *International Handbook on Privatization.* Cheltenham, UK: Edward Elgar, pp. 161–186.

Jelic, Ranko, and Richard Briston. 1999. "Hungarian Privatisation Strategy and Financial Performance of Privatised Companies." *Journal of Business Finance and Accounting* 26, 1319–1357.

Jenkinson, Timothy, and Colin Mayer. 1988. "The Privatisation Process in France and the U.K." *European Economic Review* 32, pp. 482–490.

Jones, Derek, and Niels Mygind. 2001. "Ownership and Productive Efficiency: Evidence from Estonia." Working paper, Hamilton College, Clinton, NY.

Jones, Leroy P., Yahya Jammal, and Nilgun Gokgur. 1998. *Impact of Privatization in Côte d'Ivoire: Draft Final Report.* Boston Institute for Developing Economies, Boston University, Boston, MA.

Jones, Steven L., William L. Megginson, Robert C. Nash, and Jeffry M. Netter. 1999. "Share Issue Privatizations as Financial Means to Political and Economic Ends." *Journal of Financial Economics* 53, pp. 217–253.

Keynes, John Maynard. 1935. *The General Theory of Employment, Interest and Money.* New York: Harcourt Brace.

La Porta, Rafael, and Florencio López-de-Silanes. 1999. "Benefits of Privatization—Evidence from Mexico." *Quarterly Journal of Economics* 114:4, pp. 1193–1242.

La Porta, Rafael, Florencio López-de-Silanes, and Andrei Shleifer. 2002. "Government Ownership of Banks." *Journal of Finance* 57, pp. 265–301.

Lin, Cyril. 2000. "Corporate Governance of State-Owned Enterprises in China." Working paper, Asian Development Bank, Manila, Philippines.

Lin, Justin Yifu, Fang Cai, and Zhou Li. 1998. "Competition, Policy Burdens, and State-Owned Enterprise Reform." *American Economic Review* 88, pp. 422–427.

López-de-Silanes, Florencio, Andrei Shleifer, and Robert W. Vishny. 1997. "Privatization in the United States." *RAND Journal of Economics* 28, pp. 447–471.

Macedo, Roberto. 2000. "Privatization and the Distribution of Assets and Income in Brazil." Working paper, Carnegie Endowment for International Peace, Washington, DC.

Mahboobi, Ladan. 2002. *Recent Privatisation Trends in OECD Countries.* Washington, DC: OECD.

Major, Iván. 2003. "Privatization in Hungary and its Aftermath." In David Parker and David

Saal, eds., *International Handbook on Privatization*. Cheltenham, UK: Edward Elgar, pp. 427–453.

Majumdar, Sumit K. 1996. "Assessing Comparative Efficiency of the State-Owned, Mixed, and Private Sectors in Indian Industry." *Public Choice* 96, pp. 1–24.

Majumdar, Sumit K. 1998. "Slack in the State-Owned Enterprise: An Evaluation of the Impact of Soft-Budget Constraints." *International Journal of Industrial Organization* 16, pp. 377–394.

McKenzie, David, and Dilip Mookherjee. 2003. "The Distributive Impact of Privatization in Latin America: Evidence from Four Countries." Working paper, Stanford University, Palo Alto, CA.

Means, H. 2001. *Money and Power*. New York: John Wiley.

Megginson, William L., and Jeffry M. Netter. 2001. "From State to Market: A Survey of Empirical Studies on Privatization." *Journal of Economic Literature* 39, pp. 321–389.

Mejstrík, Michal. 2003. "Privatization and Corporate Governance in the Czech Republic." In David Parker and David Saal, eds., *International Handbook on Privatization*. Cheltenham, UK: Edward Elgar, pp. 375–401.

Menyah, Kojo, and Krishna Paudyal. 1996. "Share Issue Privatisations: The UK Experience." In Mario Levis, ed., *Empirical Issues in Raising Equity Capital*. Amsterdam: Elsevier Science, pp. 17–48.

Menyah, Kojo, Krishna Paudyal, and Charles G. Inyangete. 1995. "Subscriber Return, Underpricing, and Long-Term Performance of U.K. Privatization Initial Public Offers." *Journal of Economics and Business* 47, pp. 473–495.

Mickiewicz, Tomasz, and Maciej Baltowski. 2003. "All Roads Lead to Outside Ownership: Polish Piecemeal Privatization." In David Parker and David Saal, eds., *International Handbook on Privatization*. Cheltenham, UK: Edward Elgar, pp. 402–426.

Nellis, John. 1996. "Finding Real Owners: Lessons from Estonia's Privatization Program." *World Bank Public Policy for the Private Sector Note 66*. Washington, DC: World Bank.

Nellis, John. 2003. "Privatization in Africa: What Has Happened? What Is to Be Done?" Working paper, Center for Global Development, Washington, DC.

Noll, Roger. 2000. "Telecommunications Reform in Developing Countries." In Anne O. Kreuger, ed., *Economic Policy Reform: The Second Stage*. Chicago: University of Chicago Press.

Okten, Cagla, and K. Peren Arin. 2001. "How Does Privatization Affect the Firm's Efficiency and Technology Choice? Evidence from Turkey." Working paper, Louisiana State University, Baton Rouge.

Omran, Mohammed. 2001. "The Performance of State-Owned Enterprises and Newly Privatized Firms: Empirical Evidence from Egypt." Working paper, Arab Academy for Science and Technology, Alexandria, Egypt.

Parker, David. 1999. "Policy Transfer and Policy Inertia: Privatization in Taiwan." *Asia Pacific Business Review* 6, pp. 1–20.

Parker, David. 2003. "Privatization in the European Union." In David Parker and David Saal, eds., *International Handbook on Privatization*. Cheltenham, UK: Edward Elgar, pp. 105–128.

Pivovarsky, Alexander. 2001. "How Does Privatization Work? Ownership Concentration and Enterprise Performance in Ukraine." Working paper WP/01/42, International Monetary Fund, Washington, DC.

Pombo, Carlos, and Manuel Ramirez. 2001. "Privatization in Colombia: A Plant Performance Analysis." Working paper, Universidad del Rosario, Bogota, Colombia.

Price Waterhouse. 1989a. *Privatization: Learning the Lessons from the U.K. Experience*. Author: London.

Price Waterhouse. 1989b. *Privatization: The Facts.* Author: London.

Ramirez, Miguel D. 2003. "Privatization in Mexico and Chile." In David Parker and David Saal, eds., *International Handbook on Privatization.*, Cheltenham, UK: Edward Elgar, pp. 262–290.

Reviglio, Edoardo. 2002. "Strong Markets, Weak States?" Working paper, Italian Ministry of Economics and Finance, Rome.

Roland, Gérard. 2002. "Ten Years After . . . Transition and Economics." *IMF Staff Papers* 48, pp. 29–52.

Rondinelli, Dennis, and Max Iacono. 1996. *Policies and Institutions for Managing Privatization.* Turin, Italy: International Training Centre, International Labor Office.

Ruiz-Mier, Fernando, Mauricio Garron, Carlos Gustavo Machicado, and Katherina Capra. 2002. "Privatization in Bolivia: The Impact on Firm Performance." Working paper, Unidad de Analisis de Políticas Sociales y Económicas (UDAPE), Bolivia.

Sampson, Anthony. 1975. *The Seven Sisters: The Great Oil Companies and the World They Made.* New York: Bantam Books.

Schmitz, James A., Jr.1996. "The Role of Public Enterprises: How Much Does It Differ across Countries?" Federal Reserve Bank of Minneapolis *Quarterly Review* 20, pp. 2–15.

Schwella, Erwin. 2003. "Privatization in South Africa." In David Parker and David Saal, eds., *International Handbook on Privatization.* Cheltenham, UK: Edward Elgar, pp. 291–309.

Shafik, Nemat. 1995. "Making a Market: Mass Privatization in the Czech and Slovak Republics." *World Development* 23, pp. 1143–1156.

Sheshinski, Eytan, and Luis Lopez-Calva. 1999. "Privatization and its Benefits: Theory and Evidence." HIID Development Discussion Paper 698, Harvard University, Cambridge, MA.

Smith, Adam. 1776. *The Wealth of Nations.* (New paperback edition.) New York: Bantam Books.

Smith, Stephen C., Beon-Cheol Cin, and Milan Vodopivec. 1997. "Privatization Incidence, Ownership Forms, and Firm Performance: Evidence from Slovenia." *Journal of Comparative Economics* 25, pp. 158–179.

Sobel, Robert. 1999. *The Pursuit of Wealth.* New York: McGraw-Hill.

Sun, Qian, and Wilson H. S. Tong. 2002. "Malaysian Privatization: A Comprehensive Study." *Financial Management* 31, pp. 5–31.

Sun, Qian, and Wilson H. S. Tong. 2003. "China's Share Issue Privatization: The Extent of Its Success." *Journal of Financial Economics* 70, pp. 183–222.

Suejnar, Jan. 2002. "Transition Economies: Performance and Challenges." *Journal of Economic Perspectives* 16, pp. 3–28.

Temu, Andrew, and Jean M. Due. 1998. "The Success of Newly Privatized Companies: New Evidence from Tanzania." *Canadian Journal of Development Studies* 19, pp. 315–341.

Vickers, John, and George Yarrow. 1991. "Economic Perspectives on Privatization." *Journal of Economic Perspectives* 5, pp. 111–132.

Wallsten, Scott. September 2002. "Returning to Victorian Competition, Ownership, and Regulation: An Empirical Study of European Telecommunications at the Turn of the 20th Century." Working paper, World Bank Group, Washington, DC.

Willner, Johann. 2002. "Public Ownership and Privatisation in Finland." CESifo working paper, Åbo Akademi University, Finland.

Yarrow, George. 1986. "Privatization in Theory and Practice." *Economic Policy* 2, pp. 324–364.

Yergin, Daniel, and Joseph Stanislaw. 1998. *The Commanding Heights: The Battle between Government and the Marketplace that Is Remaking the Modern World.* New York: Simon & Schuster.

Yotopoulos, Pan A. 1989. "The (Rip)tide of Privatization: Lessons from Chile." *World Development* 17, pp. 683–702.

Chapter 2

The following texts are recommended for further reading: Boardman and Vining (1989); Davis, Ossowski, Richardson, and Barnett (2000); Dewenter and Malatesta (2000); Ehrlich, Gallais-Hamonno, Liu, and Lutter (1994); Jones (1985); Karpoff (2001); Laffont and Tirole (1991); Shirley and Walsh (2000); and Shirley and Xu (2001). Full chapter references are given below.

Ahuja, Gautam, and Sumit K. Majumdar. 1998. "An Assessment of Indian State-Owned Enterprises." *Journal of Productivity Analysis* 9, pp. 113–132.

Akram, Tanweer. 1999. "Bangladesh's Privatization Policy." *Journal of Emerging Markets* 4, pp. 65–76.

Akram, Tanweer. 2000. "Publicly Subsidized Privatization: A Simple Model of Dysfunctional Privatization." *Applied Economics* 32, pp. 1689–1699.

Akram, Tanweer. 2001. "The Dismal Performance of Public Sector Corporations in Bangladesh." Working paper, Columbia University, New York.

Alchian, Armen. 1965. "Some Economics of Property Rights." *Politico* 30, pp. 816–829.

Allen, Franklin, and Douglas Gale. 1999. "Corporate Governance and Competition." Working paper, Wharton School, The University of Pennsylvania, Philadelphia, PA.

Angelucci, Mauella, Saul Estrin, Jozef Konings, and Zbigniew Zoliewski. 2001. "The Effect of Ownership and Competitive Pressure on Firm Performance in Transition Countries: Micro Evidence from Bulgaria, Romania and Poland." Discussion paper 2985, CEPR, London.

Atkinson, Scott E., and Robert Halvorsen. 1986. "The Relative Efficiency of Public and Private Firms in a Regulated Environment." *Journal of Public Economics* 29, pp. 281–294.

Bartel, Ann P., and Ann E. Harrison. 2002. "Ownership versus Environment; Disentangling the Sources of Public Sector Inefficiency." Working paper, Columbia Business School, Columbia University, New York.

Berglof, Eric, and Gérard Roland. 1998. "Soft Budget Constraints and Banking in Transition Economies." *Journal of Comparative Economics* 26, pp. 18–40.

Bertero, Elisabetta, and Laura Rondi. 2000. "Financial Pressure and the Behavior of Public Enterprises Under Soft and Hard Budget Constraints: Evidence from Italian Panel Data." *Journal of Public Economics* 75, pp. 73–98.

Bishop, Matthew R., and John A. Kay. 1989. "Privatization in the United Kingdom: Lessons from Experience." *World Development* 17, pp. 643–657.

Boardman, Anthony, Ruth Freedman, and Catherine Eckel. 1986. "The Price of Government Ownership: A Study of the Domtar Takeover." *Journal of Public Economics* 31, pp. 269–285.

Boardman, Anthony, and Aidan R. Vining. 1989. "Ownership and Performance in Competitive Environments: A Comparison of the Performance of Private, Mixed, and State-Owned Enterprises." *Journal of Law and Economics* 32, pp. 1–33.

Bottasso, Anna, and Alessandro Sembenelli. 2002. "Does Ownership Affect Firms' Efficiency? Panel Data Evidence on Italy." Working paper, Universitá di Genova, Italy.

Boycko, Maxim, Andrei Shleifer, and Robert W. Vishny. 1994. "Voucher Privatization." *Journal of Financial Economics* 35, pp. 249–266.

Boycko, Maxim, Andrei Shleifer, and Robert W. Vishny. 1996a. "Second-Best Economic Policy for a Divided Government." *European Economic Review* 40, pp. 767–774.

Boycko, Maxim, Andrei Shleifer, and Robert W. Vishny. 1996b. "A Theory of Privatisation." *Economic Journal* 106, pp. 309–319.

Brada, Josef C. 1996. "Privatization Is Transition—or Is It?" *Journal of Economic Perspectives* 10, pp. 67–86.

Brickley, James A., Clifford Smith, and Jerold Zimmerman. 1997. *Managerial Economics and Organizational Architecture.* Second edition. New York: Richard D. Irwin.

Brickley, James A., and Larry Van Horn. 2002. "Managerial Incentives in Nonprofit Organizations: Evidence from Hospitals." *Journal of Law and Economics* 45, pp. 227–249.

Briggs, A. 1961. "The Welfare State in Historical Perspective." *Archives Europennes de Sociologie* 2:2, pp. 221–259.

Carlin, Wendy, Steven Fries, Marc Schaffer, and Paul Seabright. 2001. "Competition and Enterprise Performance in Transition Economies: Evidence from a Cross-Country Survey." Discussion paper 2840, CEPR, London.

Caves, Douglas W., and Laurits R. Christensen. 1980. "The Relative Efficiency of Public and Private Firms in a Competitive Environment: The Case of Canadian Railroads." *Journal of Political Economy* 88, pp. 958–976.

Caves, Richard E. 1990. "Lessons from Privatization in Britain: State Enterprise Behavior, Public Choice, and Corporate Governance" *Journal of Economic Behavior and Organization* 13, pp. 145–169.

Clarke, George R. G., and Lixin X. 2003. "Privatization, Competition, and Corruption: How Characteristics of Bribe Takers and Payers Affects Bribe to Utilities." Working paper, World Bank Group, Washington, DC.

Coase, Ronald. 1960. "The Theory of Social Cost." *Journal of Law and Economics* 1, pp. 1–44.

Cook, Paul, and Colin Kirkpatrick. 1988. *Privatisation in Less Developed Countries.* New York: St. Martin's Press.

Cook, Paul, and Colin Kirkpatrick. 2003. "Assessing the Impact of Privatization in Developing Countries." In David Parker and David Saal, eds., *International Handbook on Privatization.* Cheltenham, UK: Edward Elgar, pp. 209–219.

Davies, David G. 1971. "The Efficiency of Public versus Private Firms: The Case of Australia's Two Airlines." *Journal of Law and Economics* 14:1, pp. 149–165.

Davis, Jeffrey, Rolando Ossowski, Thomas Richardson, and Steven Barnett. 2000. *Fiscal and Macroeconomic Impact of Privatization.* Washington, DC: IMF Occasional Paper 194.

Denis, Diane K., and John J. McConnell. 2003. "International Corporate Governance." *Journal of Financial and Quantitative Analysis* 38, pp. 1–36.

Dewenter, Kathryn, and Paul H. Malatesta. 2000. "State-Owned and Privately-Owned Firms: An Empirical Analysis of Profitability, Leverage, and Labour Intensity." *American Economic Review* 91, pp. 320–334.

Dixit, Avinash. 1997. "Power of Incentives in Private vs. Public Organizations." *American Economic Review* 87, pp. 378–382.

Djankov, Simeon, and Peter Murrell. 2002. "Enterprise Restructuring in Transition: A Quantitative Survey." *Journal of Economic Literature* 40, 739–792.

Ehrlich, Isaac, Georges Gallais-Hamonno, Zhiqiang Liu, and Randall Lutter. 1994. "Productivity Growth and Firm Ownership: An Empirical Investigation." *Journal of Political Economy* 102, pp. 1006–1038.

Esfahani, Hadi Salehi, and Ali Toosi Arkadani. 2002. "What Determines the Extent of Public Ownership?" Working paper, University of Illinois, Urbana-Champaign.

Färe, R., S. Grosskopf, and J. Logan. 1985. "The Relative Performance of Publicly Owned and Privately Owned Utilities." *Journal of Public Economics* 26, pp. 89–106.

Florio, Massimo. 2002. "A State without Ownership: The Welfare Impact of British Privatisations, 1979–1997." Working paper, University of Milan, Italy.

Frydman, Roman, Cheryl W. Gray, Marek Hessel, and Andrzej Rapaczynski. 2000. "The Limits of Discipline: Ownership and Hard Budget Constraints in the Transition Economies." C. V. Starr Center for Applied Economics working paper, New York University, New York.

Frydman, Roman, Marek Hessel, and Andrzej Rapaczynski. 2000. "Why Ownership Matters? Entrepreneurship and the Restructuring of Enterprises in Central Europe." C. V. Starr Center for Applied Economics working paper, New York University, New York.

Gough, I. 1989. "The Welfare State." In *The New Palgrave Social Economics*. New York: W.W. Norton, pp. 276–281.

Groves, Theodore, Yongmiao Hong, John McMillan, and Barry Naughton. 1994. "Autonomy and Incentives in Chinese State Enterprises." *Quarterly Journal of Economics* 109, pp. 183–209.

Hart, Oliver, Andrei Shleifer, and Robert W. Vishny. 1997. "The Proper Scope of Government: Theory and an Application to Prisons." *Quarterly Journal of Economics* 112, pp. 1127–1161.

Havrylyshyn, Oleh, and Donal McGettigan. 1999. "Privatization in Transition Countries: A Sampling of the Literature." IMF working paper 99/6, Washington, DC.

Hayek, F. A. 1944. *The Road to Serfdom*. Chicago: University of Chicago Press.

Jensen, Michael C., and William H. Meckling. 1979. "Rights and Production Functions: An Application to Labor-Managed Firms and Codetermination." *Journal of Business* 52, pp. 469–506.

Jeronimo, Venilde, José A. Pagán, and Gökçe Soydemir. 2000. "Privatization and European Economic and Monetary Union." *Eastern Economic Journal* 26, pp. 321–333.

Jones, Leroy P. 1985. "Public Enterprise for Whom? Perverse Distributional Consequences of Public Operational Decisions." *Economic Development and Cultural Change* 33, pp. 333–347.

Karpoff, Jonathan M. 2001. "Public versus Private Initiative in Arctic Exploration: The Effects of Incentives and Organizational Structure." *Journal of Political Economy* 109, pp. 38–78.

Katsoulakos, Yannis, and Elissavet Likoyanni. 2002. "Fiscal and Macroeconomic Effects of Privatization." Working paper, Athens University of Economics and Business, Athens, Greece.

Kay, J. A., and D. J. Thompson. 1986. "Privatisation: A Policy in Search of a Rationale." *Economic Journal* 96, pp. 18–32.

Kole, Stacey R., and J. Harold Mulherin. 1997. "The Government as a Shareholder: A Case from the United States." *Journal of Law and Economics* 40, pp. 1–22.

Kornai, Janos. 1988. "Individual Freedom and Reform of the Socialist Economy." *European Economic Review* 32, pp. 233–267.

Kornai, Janos. 1993. "The Evolution of Financial Discipline Under the Postsocialist System." *Kyklos* 46, pp. 315–336.

Kornai, Janos. 1998. "The Place of the Soft Budget Constraint Syndrome in Economic Theory." *Journal of Comparative Economics* 26, pp. 11–17.

Kwoka, John E., Jr. 2002. "The Comparative Advantage of Public Ownership: Evidence from Public Utilities." Working paper, Northeastern University, Boston, MA.

Laffont, Jean-Jacques, and Jean Tirole. 1991. "Privatization and Incentives." *Journal of Law, Economics, & Organization* 7, pp. 84–105.

La Porta, Rafael, Florencio López-de-Silanes, and Andrei Shleifer. 2002. "Government Ownership of Banks." *Journal of Finance* 57, pp. 265–301.

Laurin, Claude, and Yves Bozec. 2000. "Privatization and Productivity Improvement: The Case of Canadian National (CN)." Working paper, Ecoles de HEC, Montreal.

Li, Wei. 1997. "The Impact of Economic Reform on the Performance of Chinese State Enterprises, 1980–1989." *Journal of Political Economy* 105, pp. 1080–1106.

Lin, Justin Yifu, Fang Cai, and Zhou Li. 1998. "Competition, Policy Burdens, and State-Owned Enterprise Reform." *American Economic Review* 88, pp. 422–427.

López-de-Silanes, Florencio. 1997. "Determinants of Privatization Prices." *Quarterly Journal of Economics* 112, pp. 965–1025.

Lülfesmann, Christoph. In press. "On the Virtues of Privatization When Government Is Benevolent." *Journal of Economic Behavior and Organization.*

Macedo, Roberto. 2000. "Privatization and the Distribution of Assets and Income in Brazil." Working paper, Carnegie Endowment for International Peace, Washington, DC.

Majumdar, Sumit K. 1996. "Assessing Comparative Efficiency of the State-Owned, Mixed, and Private Sectors in Indian Industry." *Public Choice* 96, pp. 1–24.

Majumdar, Sumit K. 1998. "Slack in the State-Owned Enterprise: An Evaluation of the Impact of Soft-Budget Constraints." *International Journal of Industrial Organization* 16, pp. 377–394.

Majumdar, Sumit K. 1999. "Comparative Organizational Characteristics of Indian State-Owned Enterprises." *Review of Industrial Organization* 15, pp. 165–182.

Nellis, John. 1994. "Is Privatization Necessary?" *World Bank Viewpoint* Note 17, World Bank Group, Washington, DC.

Nellis, John. 1999. "Time to Rethink Privatization in Transition Economies?" IFC Discussion paper no. 38, World Bank Group, Washington, DC.

Nellis, John. 2001. *The World Bank, Privatization and Enterprise Reform in Transition Economies: A Retrospective Analysis.* Washington, DC: Center for Global Development.

Nickell, Stephen J. 1996. "Competition and Corporate Efficiency." *Journal of Political Economy* 104, pp. 724–746.

Niskanen, William A. 1975. "Bureaucrats and Politicians." *Journal of Law and Economics* 18, pp. 617–643.

Olds, Kelly. 1994. "Privatizing the Church: Disestablishment in Connecticut and Massachusetts." *Journal of Political Economy* 102, pp. 277–297.

Peltzman, Sam. 1971. "Pricing in Public and Private Enterprises: Electric Utilities in the United States." *Journal of Law and Economics* 14, pp. 109–147.

Pinto, Brian, Merek Belka, and Stefan Krajewski. 1993. "Transforming State Enterprises in Poland: Evidence on Adjustment by Manufacturing Firms." *Brookings Papers on Economic Activity*, pp. 213–261.

Price Waterhouse. 1989a. *Privatization: Learning the Lessons from the U.K. Experience.* Author: London.

Price Waterhouse. 1989b. *Privatization: The Facts.* Author: London.

Ros, Augustin J. 1999. "Does Ownership or Competition Matter? The Effects of Telecommunications Reform on Network Expansion and Efficiency." *Journal of Regulatory Economics* 15, pp. 65–92.

Sappington, David E. M., and J. Gregory Sidak. 1999. "Incentives for Anticompetitive Behavior by Public Enterprises," Joint AEI-Brookings Center for Regulatory Studies working paper, Washington, DC.

Sappington, David E. M., and Joseph E. Stiglitz. 1987. "Privatization, Information and Incentives." *Journal of Policy Analysis and Management* 6, pp. 567–582.

Schmidt, Klaus M. 1996. "The Costs and Benefits of Privatization: An Incomplete Contracts Approach." *Journal of Law, Economics, & Organization* 12, pp. 1–24.

Schmitz, Patrick W. 2000. "Partial Privatization and Incomplete Contracts: The Proper Scope of Government Reconsidered." *FinanzArchiv* 57, pp. 394–411.

Shapiro, C., and R. Willig. 1990. "Economic Rationales for the Scope of Privatization." In B. N. Suleiman and J. Waterbury, eds., *The Political Economy of Public Sector and Privatization*. London: Westview Press, pp. 55–87.

Sheshinski, Eytan, and Luis Lopez-Calva. 1999. "Privatization and Its Benefits: Theory and Evidence." HIID Development Discussion Paper 698, Harvard University, Cambridge, MA.

Shirley, Mary M. 1999. "Bureaucrats in Business: The Role of Privatization in State Owned Enterprise Reform." *World Development* 27, pp. 115–136.

Shirley, Mary M., and Patrick Walsh. 2000. "Public vs. Private Ownership: The Current State of the Debate." Working paper, World Bank Group, Washington, DC.

Shirley, Mary M., and Lixin Colin Xu. 1998. "Information, Incentives, and Commitment: An Empirical Analysis of Contracts between Government and State Enterprises." *Journal of Law, Economics, & Organization* 14, pp. 358–378.

Shirley, Mary M., and Lixin Colin Xu. 2001. "Empirical Effects of Performance Contracts: Evidence from China." *Journal of Law, Economics, & Organization* 17, pp. 168–200.

Shleifer, Andrei. 1998. "State versus Private Ownership." *Journal of Economic Perspectives* 12, pp. 133–150.

Shleifer, Andrei, and Robert W. Vishny. 1994. "Politicians and Firms." *Quarterly Journal of Economics* 109, pp. 995–1025.

Stigliz, Joseph. 1993. "Some Theoretical Aspects of Privatization: Applications to Eastern Europe." In Mario Baldassarri, Luigi Paganetto, and Edmund S. Phelps, eds., *Privatization Processes in Eastern Europe*. New York: St. Martin's Press.

Tian, George Lihui. 2003. "Government Shareholding and the Value of China's Modern Firms." Working paper, Peking University, Beijing, People's Republic of China.

Vickers, John, and George Yarrow. 1988. "Regulation of Privatized Firms in Britain." *European Economic Review* 32, pp. 456–472.

Vickers, John, and George Yarrow. 1991. "Economic Perspectives on Privatization." *Journal of Economic Perspectives* 5, pp. 111–132.

Vining, Aidan R., and Anthony E. Boardman. 1992. "Ownership versus Competition: Efficiency in Public Enterprise." *Public Choice* 73, pp. 205–239.

Wallsten, Scott J. 2001. "An Econometric Analysis of Telecom Competition, Privatization, and Regulation in Africa and Latin America." *Journal of Industrial Economics* 49, pp. 1–19.

Wallsten, Scott. September 2002. "Returning to Victorian Competition, Ownership, and Regulation: An Empirical Study of European Telecommunications at the Turn of the 20th Century." Working paper, World Bank Group, Washington, DC.

Willner, Johann. 2003. "Privatization: A Skeptical Analysis." In David Parker and David Saal, eds., *International Handbook on Privatization*. Cheltenham, UK: Edward Elgar, pp. 60–86.

Yarrow, George. 1986. "Privatization in Theory and Practice." *Economic Policy* 2, pp. 324–364.

Zhang, Yin-Fang, David Parker, and Colin Kirkpatrick. 2002. "Electricity Sector Reform in Developing Countries: An Econometric Assessment of the Effects of Privatisation, Competition and Regulation." Working paper, University of Manchester, UK.

Chapter 3

The following texts are recommended for further reading: Bornstein (1999); Bortolotti, Fantini, and Scarpa (2000); Hingorani, Lehn, and Makhija (1997); Klemperer (2002); López-de-Silanes (1997); and Megginson, Nash, Netter, and Poulsen (forthcoming). Full chapter references are given below.

Alexandrowicz, Melinda Roth. 1994. "Mass Privatization Programs." *FPD Note No. 4.* Washington, DC: World Bank.

Baldwin, Carliss Y., and Sugato Bhattacharya. 1991. "Choosing the Method of Sale: A Clinical Study of Conrail." *Journal of Financial Economics* 30, pp. 69–98.

Berglof, Erik, and Patrick Bolton. 2002. "The Great Divide and Beyond: Financial Architecture in Transition." *Journal of Economic Perspectives* 16, pp. 77–100.

Biais, Bruno, and Enrico Perotti. 2002. "Machiavellian Privatization." *American Economic Review* 92, pp. 240–258.

Bornstein, Morris. 1994. "Russia's Mass Privatization Program." *Communist Economies and Economic Transformation* 6:4, pp. 419–457.

Bornstein, Morris. 1999. "Framework Issues in the Privatization Strategies of the Czech Republic, Hungary and Poland." *Post-Communist Economies* 11, pp. 47–77.

Bortolotti, Bernardo, Marcella Fantini, and Carla Scarpa. 2000. "Why Do Governments Privatize Abroad?" *FEEM Note di Lavoro* 23.

Bortolotti, Bernardo, Marcella Fantini, and Domenico Siniscalco. 1999. "Privatisation: Politics, Institutions and Financial Markets." Working paper, Fondazione ENI-Enrico Mattei (FEEM), Milan, Italy.

Bortolotti, Bernardo, Marcella Fantini, and Domenico Siniscalco. Forthcoming. "Privatization around the World: New Evidence from Panel Data." *Journal of Public Economics.*

Boycko, Maxim, Andrei Shleifer, and Robert W. Vishny. 1994. "Voucher Privatization." *Journal of Financial Economics* 35, pp. 249–266.

Boycko, Maxim, Andrei Shleifer, and Robert W. Vishny. 1996a. "Second-Best Economic Policy for a Divided Government." *European Economic Review* 40, pp. 767–774.

Boycko, Maxim, Andrei Shleifer, and Robert W. Vishny. 1996b. "A Theory of Privatisation." *Economic Journal* 106, pp. 309–319.

Brada, Josef C. 1996. "Privatization Is Transition — or Is It?" *Journal of Economic Perspectives* 10, pp. 67–86.

Bulow, Jeremy, and Paul Klemperer. 1996. "Auctions versus Negotiations." *American Economic Review* 86, pp. 180–194.

Chong, Alberto, and Virgilio Galdo. 2002. "Streamlining and Privatization Prices in the Telecommunications Industry." Working paper, Inter-American Development Bank, Washington, DC.

Chong, Alberto, and Florencio López-de-Silanes. November 2002. "Privatization and Labor Force Restructuring around the World." Working paper, Yale University, New Haven, CT.

Chun, Rodney. 2000. "Compensation Vouchers and Equity markets: Evidence from Hungary." *Journal of Banking and Finance* 24, pp. 1155–1178.

Claessens, Stijn. 1997. "Corporate Governance and Equity Prices: Evidence from the Czech and Slovak Republics." *Journal of Finance* 52, pp. 1641–1658.

Cornelli, Francesca, and David D. Li. 1997. "Large Shareholders, Private Benefits of Control, and Optimal Schemes of Privatization." *RAND Journal of Economics* 28, pp. 585–604.

Dewenter, Kathryn, and Paul H. Malatesta. 1997. "Public Offerings of State-Owned and Privately-Owned Enterprises: An International Comparison." *Journal of Finance* 52, pp. 1659–1679.

Drum, Bernard. 1994. "Mass Privatization in Ukraine." *FPD Note No. 8*. Washington, DC: World Bank.

Dyck, I. J. Alexander. 1997. "Privatization in Eastern Germany: Management Selection and Economic Transition." *American Economic Review* 87, pp. 565–597.

European Bank for Reconstruction and Development. 1999. *Transition Report 1999*. London.

Frydman, Roman, Katharina Pistor, and Andrzej Rapaczynski. 1996. "Exit and Voice After Mass Privatization: The Case of Russia." *European Economic Review* 40, pp. 581–588.

Gibbon, Henry. 1997. "A Seller's Manual: Guidelines for Selling State-Owned Enterprises." *Privatisation Yearbook*. London: Privatisation International, pp. 16–26.

Glaeser, Edward L., and José A. Scheinkman. 1996. "The Transition to Free Markets: Where to Begin Privatization." *Journal of Comparative Economics* 22, pp. 23–42.

Gupta, Nandini, John C. Ham, and Jan Svejnar. 2001. "Priorities and Sequencing in Privatization: Theory and Evidence from the Czech Republic." Working paper, William Davidson Institute, University of Michigan, Ann Arbor.

Gupta, Sanjeev, Christian Schiller, Henry Ma, and Erwin Thompson. 2001. "Privatization, Labor and Social Safety Nets." *Journal of Economic Surveys* 15:5, pp. 589–700.

Havrylyshyn, Oleh, and Donal McGettigan. 1999. "Privatization in Transition Countries: A Sampling of the Literature." IMF working paper 99/6, Washington, DC.

Hingorani, Archana, Kenneth Lehn, and Anil Makhija. 1997. "Investor Behavior in Mass Privatization: The Case of the Czech Voucher Scheme." *Journal of Financial Economics* 44, pp. 349–396.

Huang, Qi, and Richard M. Levich. 1998. "Underpricing of New Equity Offerings by Privatized Firms: An International Test." Working paper, New York University, New York.

Husain, Aasim, and Ratna Sahay. 1992. "Does Sequencing of Privatization Matter in Reforming Planned Economies." *International Monetary Fund Staff Papers* 39, pp. 801–824.

Jack, Andrew. 2002. "Sale of Russian Oil Group Leaves Questions over Fairness." *Financial Times* (December 19), p. 4.

Johnson, Simon, Rafael LaPorta, Florencio López-de-Silanes, and Andrei Shleifer. 2000. "Tunneling." *American Economic Review Papers and Proceedings* 90, pp. 22–27.

Jones, Steven L., William L. Megginson, Robert C. Nash, and Jeffry M. Netter. 1999. "Share Issue Privatizations as Financial Means to Political and Economic Ends." *Journal of Financial Economics* 53, pp. 217–253.

Katz, Barbara G., and Joel Owen. 1993. "Privatization: Choosing the Optimal Time Path." *Journal of Comparative Economics* 17, pp. 715–736.

Katz, Barbara G., and Joel Owen. 1995. "Designing the Optimal Privatization Plan for Restructuring Firms and Industries in Transition." *Journal of Comparative Economics* 21, pp. 1–28.

Kikeri, Sunita, John Nellis, and Mary Shirley. 1992. *Privatization: The Lessons of Experience*, Washington, DC: World Bank Group.

Klemperer, Paul. 2002. "What Really Matters in Auction Design." *Journal of Economic Perspectives* 16, pp. 169–189.

López-de-Silanes, Florencio. 1997. "Determinants of Privatization Prices." *Quarterly Journal of Economics* 112, pp. 965–1025.

López-de-Silanes, Florencio, Andrei Shleifer, and Robert W. Vishny. 1997. "Privatization in the United States." *RAND Journal of Economics* 28, pp. 447–471.

Mahboobi, Ladan. 2002. *Recent Privatisation Trends in OECD Countries.* Washington, DC: OECD.

McCurry, Patrick. 2000. "Golden Shares Fail to Shine." *Privatisation International* 136, pp. 41–43.

Megginson, William L., Robert C. Nash, Jeffry M. Netter, and Annette B. Poulsen. Forthcoming. "The Choice between Private and Public Markets: Evidence from Privatization." *Journal of Finance.*

Menyah, Kojo, and Krishna Paudyal. 1996. "Share Issue Privatizations: The UK Experience." In Mario Levis, ed., *Empirical Issues in Raising Equity Capital.* Amsterdam: Elsevier Science, pp. 17–48.

Menyah, Kojo, Krishna Paudyal, and Charles G. Inyangete. 1995. "Subscriber Return, Underpricing, and Long-Term Performance of U.K. Privatization Initial Public Offers." *Journal of Economics and Business* 47, pp. 473–495.

Nellis, John. 2001. *The World Bank, Privatization and Enterprise Reform in Transition Economies: A Retrospective Analysis.* Washington, DC: Center for Global Development.

Nellis, John. 2002. "External Advisors and Privatization in Transition Economies." Center for Global Development working paper #3 (February), Washington, DC.

Nellis, John, and Sunita Kikeri. 1989. "Public Enterprise Reform: Privatization and the World Bank." *World Development* 17, pp. 659–672.

Perotti, Enrico. 1995. "Credible Privatization." *American Economic Review* 85, pp. 847–859.

Perotti, Enrico, and Serhat E. Guney. 1993. "Successful Privatization Plans: Enhanced Credibility Through Timing and Pricing of Sales." *Financial Management* 22, pp. 84–98.

Pistor, Katharina, and Andrew Spicer. 1996. "Investment Funds in Mass Privatization and Beyond: Evidence from the Czech Republic and Russia." *Private Sector*, pp. 33–36.

Rondinelli, Dennis, and Max Iacono. 1996. *Policies and Institutions for Managing Privatization.* Turin, Italy: International Training Centre, International Labor Office.

Schmidt, Klaus M. 1996. "The Costs and Benefits of Privatization: An Incomplete Contracts Approach." *Journal of Law, Economics, & Organization* 12, pp. 1–24.

Seven, Bulent. 2001. "Legal Aspects of Privatisation: A Comparative Study of European Implementations" Doctoral dissertation, University of Essex, Colchester, UK.

Shafik, Nemat. 1995. "Making a Market: Mass Privatization in the Czech and Slovak Republics." *World Development* 23, pp. 1143–1156.

Shafik, Nemat. 1996. "Selling Privatization Politically." *Columbia Journal of World Business* 31, pp. 20–29.

Chapter 4

The following texts are recommended for further reading: Boubakri and Cosset (1998); Boubakri, Cosset, and Guedhami (2002); Galal, Jones, Tandon, and Vogelsang (1992); Galiani, Gerlet, and Schargrodsky (2001); La Porta and López-de-Silanes (1999); Li and Xu (2003); McKenzie and Mookherjee (2003); Megginson, Nash, and van Randenborgh (1994); and Saal and Parker (2003). See also Eytan Sheshinski and Luis Lopez-Calva (1999), "Privatization and Its Benefits: Theory and Evidence," HIID Development Discussion Paper 698, Harvard University, Cambridge, MA. Full chapter references are given below.

Akram, Tanweer. 1999. "Bangladesh's Privatization Policy." *Journal of Emerging Markets* 4, pp. 65–76.

Akram, Tanweer. 2000. "Publicly Subsidized Privatization: A Simple Model of Dysfunctional Privatization." *Applied Economics* 32, pp. 1689–1699.

Andreasson, Bo. 1998. "Privatization in Sub-Saharan Africa: Has It Worked and What Lessons Can Be Learnt?" Gothenburg, Sweden: Swedish Development Advisers.

Appiah-Kubi, K. 2001. "State-Owned Enterprises and Privatization in Guinea." *Journal of Modern African Studies* 39:2, pp. 197–229.

Arin, Kerim Peren, and Cagla Okten. 2002. "The Determinants of Privatization Prices: Evidence from Turkey." Working paper, Louisiana State University, Baton Rouge.

Barber, Brad M., and John D. Lyon. 1997. "Detecting Long-Run Abnormal Stock Returns: The Empirical Power and Specification of Test Statistics." *Journal of Financial Economics* 43, pp. 341–372.

Barja, Gover, and Miguel Urquiola. 2002. "Capitalization and Privatization in Bolivia." Working paper, Cornell University, Ithaca, NY.

Beesley, M. E., and S. C. Littlechild. 1989. "The Regulation of Privatized Monopolies in the United Kingdom." *RAND Journal of Economics* 20, pp. 454–473.

Bhaskar, V., and M. Khan. 1995. "Privatization and Employment: A Study of the Jute Industry in Bangladesh." *American Economic Review* 85, pp. 267–273.

Birdsall, Nancy, and John Nellis. 2002. *Winners and Losers: Assessing the Distributional Impact of Privatization.* Washington, DC: Center for Global Development working paper No. 6.

Boardman, Anthony E., Claude Laurin, and Aidan R. Vining. 2003. "Privatization in North America." In David Parker and David Saal, eds., *International Handbook on Privatization.* Cheltenham, UK: Edward Elgar, pp. 129–160.

Boles de Boer, David, and Lewis Evans. 1996. "The Economic Efficiency of Telecommunications in a Deregulated Market: The Case of New Zealand." *Economic Record,* 72, pp. 24–35.

Bortolotti, Bernardo, Juliet D'Souza, Marcella Fantini, and William L. Megginson. 2002. "Privatization and the Sources of Performance Improvement in the Global Telecommunications Industry." *Telecommunications Policy* 26, pp. 243–268.

Bortolotti, Bernardo, Marcella Fantini, and Domenico Siniscalco. 1999. "Regulation and Privatisation: The Case of Electricity." Working paper, Fondazione ENI-Enrico Mattei (FEEM), Milan, Italy.

Boubakri, Narjess, and Jean-Claude Cosset. 1998. "The Financial and Operating Performance of Newly-Privatized Firms: Evidence from Developing Countries." *Journal of Finance* 53, pp. 1081–1110.

Boubakri, Narjess, and Jean-Claude Cosset. 2003. "Does Privatization Meet the Expectations? Evidence from African Countries." *Journal of African Economics,* pp. 111–140.

Boubakri, Narjess, Jean-Claude Cosset, and Omrane Guedhami. 2002. "Liberalization, Corporate Governance and the Performance of Newly Privatized Firms." Working paper, University of Laval, Quebec.

Boutchkova, Maria K., and William L. Megginson. 2000. "Privatization and the Rise of Global Capital Markets." *Financial Management* 29, pp. 31–76.

Boyland, O., and G. Nicoletti. 2000. "Regulation, Market Structure and Performance in Telecommunications." Paris: Organization for Economic Cooperation and Development.

Brau, Rinaldo and Massimo Florio. 2002. "Privatisations as Price Reforms: Evaluating Consumers' Welfare Changes in the UK." Working paper, University of Milan, Italy.

Cabanda, Emilyn, and M. Ariff. 2002. "Privatisation of Telecommunications Firms: Financial and Production Efficiency." Working paper, Monash University, Australia.

Chirwa, Ephraim W. 2001. "Industry and Firm Effects of Privatization in Malawian Oligopolistic Manufacturing." Working paper, University of Malawi, Zomba, Malawi.

Cragg, Michael I., and I. J. Alexander Dyck. 1999a. "Management Control and Privatization in the United Kingdom." *RAND Journal of Economics* 30, pp. 475–497.

Cragg, Michael I., and I. J. Alexander Dyck. 1999b. "Privatization, Compensation and Management Incentives: Evidence from the United Kingdom." Working paper, Harvard Business School Boston, MA.

Dewenter, Kathryn, and Paul H. Malatesta. 2001. "State-Owned and Privately-Owned Firms: An Empirical Analysis of Profitability, Leverage, and Labour Intensity." *American Economic Review* 91, pp. 320–334.

D'Souza, Juliet, and William L. Megginson. 1999. "The Financial and Operating Performance of Newly Privatized Firms in the 1990s." *Journal of Finance* 54, pp. 1397–1438.

D'Souza, Juliet, and William L. Megginson. 2000. "Sources of Performance Improvement in Privatized Firms: A Clinical Study of the Global Telecommunications Industry." Working paper, University of Oklahoma, Norman, OK.

D'Souza, Juliet, Robert Nash, and William L. Megginson. 2000. "Determinants of Performance Improvement in Newly-Privatized Firms: Does Restructuring and Corporate Governance Matter?" Working paper, University of Oklahoma, Norman, OK.

Dumontier, Pascal, and Claude Laurin. 2002. "The Financial Impacts of the French Government Nationalization–Privatization Strategy," Working paper, University of Geneva, Switzerland.

Eckel, Catherine, Doug Eckel, and Vijay Singal. 1997. "Privatization and Efficiency: Industry Effects of the Sale of British Airways." *Journal of Financial Economics* 43, pp. 275–298.

Ennis, Huberto, and Santiago Pinto. 2002. "Privatization and Income Distribution in Argentina." Working paper, West Virginia University, Morgantown.

Estache, Antonio. 2002. "Argentina's 1990's Utilities Privatization: A Cure or Disease?" Working paper, Free University of Brussels, Brussels, Belgium.

Feng, Fang, Qian Sun, and Wilson Tong. 2002. "Do Government-Linked Companies Necessarily Underperform?" Working paper, Nanyang University, Singapore.

Fink, Carsten, Aaditya Matto, and Randeep Rathindran. 2002. "An Assessment of Telecommunications Reform in Developing Countries." Washington, DC: World Bank working paper 2909.

Florio, Massimo. 2001. "The Welfare Impact of a Privatisation: The British Telecom Case-History." Working paper, University of Milan, Milan, Italy.

Freije, Samuel, and Luis Rivas. 2002. "Privatization, Inequality, and Welfare: Evidence from Nicaragua." Working paper, Instituto de Estudios Superiores de Administración, Caracas, Venezuela.

Frydman, Roman, Cheryl W. Gray, Marek Hessel, and Andrzej Rapaczynski. 1999. "When Does Privatization Work? The Impact of Private Ownership on Corporate Performance in Transition Economies." *Quarterly Journal of Economics* 114, pp. 1153–1191.

Galal, Ahmed, Leroy Jones, Pankaj Tandon, and Ingo Vogelsang. 1992. *Welfare Consequences of Selling Public Enterprises.* Washington, DC: World Bank.

Galiani, Sebastián, Paul Gertler, and Ernesto Schargrodsky. 2001. "Water for Life: The Impact of the Privatization of Water Services on Child Mortality." Working paper, University of California, Berkeley, CA.

Green, Richard, and Ingo Vogelsang. 1994. "British Airways: A Turn-Around Anticipating

Privatization." Chapter 4 in Matthew Bishop, John Kay, and Colin Mayer, eds., *Privatization and Economic Performance*. Oxford: Oxford University Press, pp. 89–111.

Gupta, Nandini. Forthcoming. "Partial Privatization and Firm Performance." *Journal of Finance*.

Gutierrez, Luis H., and Sanford Berg. 2000. "Telecommunications Liberalization and Regulatory Governance: Lessons from Latin America." *Telecommunications Policy* 24, pp. 865–884.

Hersch, Philip, David Kemme, and Jeffry Netter. 1997. "Access to Bank Loans in a Transition Economy: The Case of Hungary." *Journal of Comparative Economics* 24, pp. 79–89.

Jones, Leroy P., Yahya Jammal, and Nilgun Gokgur. 1998. *Impact of Privatization in Côte d'Ivoire: Draft Final Report*. Boston Institute for Developing Economies, Boston University, MA.

Jones, Steven L., William L. Megginson, Robert C. Nash, and Jeffry M. Netter. 1999. "Share Issue Privatizations as Financial Means to Political and Economic Ends." *Journal of Financial Economics* 53, pp. 217–253.

Kikeri, Sunita, and John Nellis. 2002. "Privatization in Competitive Sectors: The Record to Date." World Bank Policy Research working paper 2860, Washington, DC.

Kubota, Keiko. 2000. "The Effects of Market Conditions and Policies on Performance in Telecommunications Sector: Some Evidence." Working paper, World Bank Group, Washington, DC.

La Porta, Rafael, and Florencio López-de-Silanes. 1999. "Benefits of Privatization—Evidence from Mexico." *Quarterly Journal of Economics* 114, pp. 1193–1242.

La Porta, Rafael, Florencio López-de-Silanes, and Andrei Shleifer. 2002. "Government Ownership of Banks." *Journal of Finance* 57, pp. 265–301.

Laurin, Claude, and Yves Bozec. 2000. "Privatization and Productivity Improvement: The Case of Canadian National (CN)." Working paper, Ecoles de HEC, Montreal.

Li, Wei, and Lixin Colin Xu. 2002. "The Political Economy of Privatization and Competition: Cross-Country Evidence from the Telecommunications Sector." *Journal of Comparative Economics* 30, pp. 439–462.

Li, Wei, and Lixin Colin Xu. 2003. "The Impact of Privatization and Competition in the Telecommunications Sector around the World." Working paper, University of Virginia, Charlottesville.

López-Calva, Luis Felipe, and Juan Rosellón. 2002. "Privatization and Inequality: The Mexican Case." Working paper, Universidad de las Américas, Puebla, Mexico.

Macquieira, Carlos, and Salvador Zurita. 1996. "Privatizaciones en Chile: Eficiencia y Politicas Financieras." *Estudios de Administracion* 3, pp. 1–36.

Martin, Stephen, and David Parker. 1995. "Privatization and Economic Performance throughout the UK Business Cycle." *Managerial and Decision Economics* 16, pp. 225–237.

McKenzie, David, and Dilip Mookherjee. 2003. "The Distributive Impact of Privatization in Latin America: Evidence from Four Countries." *Economia* 3, pp. 161–218.

McNary, Robert. 2001. "The Network Penetration Effects of Telecommunications Privatization and Competition." Honors thesis, Stanford University, Palo Alto, CA.

Megginson, William L., Robert C. Nash, Jeffry M. Netter, and Annette B. Poulsen. Forthcoming. "The Choice between Private and Public Markets: Evidence from Privatization." *Journal of Finance*.

Megginson, William L., Robert C. Nash, and Matthias van Randenborgh. 1994. "The Financial and Operating Performance of Newly Privatized Firms: An International Empirical Analysis." *Journal of Finance* 49, pp. 403–452.

Munari, Federico, and Raffaele Oriani. 2002. "Privatization and R&D Performance: An Empirical Analysis Based on Tobin's q." Working paper, Fondazione Eni Enrico Mattei, Milan, Italy.

Nellis, John. 2003. "Privatization in Africa: What Has Happened? What Is to Be Done?" Working paper, Center for Global Development, Washington, DC.

Newbery, David. 1997. "Privatization and Liberalisation of Network Utilities." *European Economic Review* 41, pp. 357–383.

Newbery, David, and Michael G. Pollitt. 1997. "The Restructuring and Privatization of Britain's CEGB—Was It Worth It?" *Journal of Industrial Economics* 45, pp. 269–303.

Noll, Roger. 2000. "Telecommunications Reform in Developing Countries." In Anne O. Kreuger, ed., *Economic Policy Reform: The Second Stage*. Chicago: University of Chicago Press.

Okten, Cagla, and K. Peren Arin. 2001. "How Does Privatization Affect the Firm's Efficiency and Technology Choice? Evidence from Turkey." Working paper, Louisiana State University, Baton Rouge.

Omran, Mohammed. 2001a. "Detecting the Performance Change in the Newly Privatized Egyptian Companies: Does Type of Privatization Really Matter?" Working paper, Arab Academy for Science and Technology, Alexandria, Egypt.

Omran, Mohammed. 2001b. "The Performance of State-Owned Enterprises and Newly Privatized Firms: Empirical Evidence from Egypt." Working paper, Arab Academy for Science and Technology, Alexandria, Egypt.

Omran, Mohammed. 2002. "Initial and Aftermarket Performance of Egyptian Share Issue Privatization." Working paper, Arab Monetary Fund—Economic Policy Institute, Abu Dhabi, UAE.

Otchere, Isaac. 2002. "Intra-Industry Effects of Privatization Announcement: Evidence from Developed and Developing Countries." Working paper, University of Melbourne, Australia.

Parker, David. 1994. "A Decade of Privatisation: The Effect of Ownership Change and Competition on British Telecom." *British Review of Economic Issues* 16, pp. 87–113.

Parker, David. 1997. "The Economic and Financial Performance of BAA: A Study of Privatisation and Regulation." Working paper, Aston University, Birmingham, UK.

Petrazzini, Ben A., and Theodore H. Clark. 1996. "Costs and Benefits of Telecommunications Liberalization in Developing Countries." Working paper, Hong Kong University of Science and Technology, Hong Kong.

Pollitt, Michael G. 1997. "The Impact of Liberalization on the Performance of the Electric Supply Industry: An International Survey." *Journal of Energy Literature* 3:2, pp. 3–39.

Pollitt, Michael G. 1997. "Privatisation and Liberalization on Network Utilities." *European Economic Review* 41, pp. 357–383.

Pombo, Carlos, and Manuel Ramirez. 2001. "Privatization in Colombia: A Plant Performance Analysis." Working paper, Universidad del Rosario, Bogota, Colombia.

Price, Catherine Waddams, and Thomas Weyman-Jones. 1996. "Malmquist Indices of Productivity Change in the UK Gas Industry Before and After Privatization." *Applied Economics* 28, 29–39.

Ramamurti, Ravi. 1996. "The New Frontier of Privatization." In Ravi Ramamurti, ed., *Privatizing Monopolies: Lessons from the Telecommunications and Transport Sectors in Latin America*. Baltimore: John Hopkins University Press, pp. 1–45.

Ramamurti, Ravi. 1997. "Testing the Limits of Privatization: Argentine Railroads." *World Development* 25, pp. 1973–1993.

Röller, L., and L. Waverman. 2001. "Telecommunications Infrastructure and Economic

Development: A Simultaneous Approach." *American Economic Review* 91, pp. 909–923.

Ros, Augustin J. 1999. "Does Ownership or Competition Matter? The Effects of Telecommunications Reform on Network Expansion and Efficiency." *Journal of Regulatory Economics* 15, pp. 65–92.

Saal, David S., and David Parker. 2001. "Productivity and Price Performance in the Privatized Water and Sewerage Companies of England and Wales." *Journal of Regulatory Economics* 20, pp. 61–90.

Saal, David S., and David Parker. 2003. "The Impact of Privatization and Regulation on the Water and Sewerage Industry in England and Wales." Working paper, Aston University, Birmingham, UK.

Smith, Peter L., and Björn Wellenius. 1999. "Mitigating Regulatory Risk in Telecommunications." *Private Sector* (July), pp. 33–44.

Sun, Qian, Jin Jia, and Wilson H. S. Tong. 2002. "Malaysian Privatization: A Comprehensive Study." *Financial Management* 31, pp. 5–31.

Temple, Jonathan. 1999. "The New Growth Evidence." *Journal of Economic Literature* 37, pp. 112–156.

Temu, Andrew, and Jean M. Due. 1998. "The Success of Newly Privatized Companies: New Evidence from Tanzania." *Canadian Journal of Development Studies* 19, pp. 315–341.

Tybout, James. 2000. "Manufacturing Firms in Developing Countries: How Well Do They Do and Why." *Journal of Economic Literature* 38, pp. 11–44.

Verbrugge, James A., William L. Megginson, and Wanda Lee Owens. 1999. "The Financial Performance of Privatized Banks: An Empirical Analysis." Working paper, University of Georgia, Athens.

Vickers, John, and George Yarrow. 1991. "Economic Perspectives on Privatization." *Journal of Economic Perspectives* 5, pp. 111–132.

Villalonga, B. 2000. "Privatization and Efficiency: Differentiating Ownership Effects from Political, Organizational and Dynamic Effects." *Journal of Economic Behavior and Organization* 42, pp. 43–74.

Wallsten, Scott J. 2001a. "An Econometric Analysis of Telecom Competition, Privatization, and Regulation in Africa and Latin America." *Journal of Industrial Economics* 49, pp. 1–19.

Wallsten, Scott J. 2001b. "Telecommunications Privatization in Developing Countries: The Real Effects of Exclusivity Periods." Working paper, Stanford University, Palo Alto, CA.

Wallsten, Scott. 2002. "Does Sequencing Matter? Regulation and Privatization in Telecommunications Reform." Working paper, World Bank Group, Washington, DC.

Wasserfallen, Walter, and Stefan Müller. 1998. "Deregulation and Privatization: Evidence from the Telecommunications Industry in Europe and Implications for Switzerland." Working paper, Studienzentrum Gerzensee, Switzerland.

Wellenius, Björn. 2000. "Extending Telecommunications Beyond the Market: Towards Universal Service in Competitive Environments." *Private Sector* (June), pp. 5–18.

Wolfram, Catherine D. 1998. "Increases in Executive Pay Following Privatization." *Journal of Economic and Management Strategy* 7, pp. 327–361.

Zhang, Yin-Fang, David Parker, and Colin Kirkpatrick. 2002. "Electricity Sector Reform in Developing Countries: An Econometric Assessment of the Effects of Privatisation, Competition and Regulation." Working paper, University of Manchester, UK.

Chapter 5

The following texts are recommended for further reading: Blank, Kraakman, and Tarassova (2000); Cull, Matesova, and Shirley (2002); Djankov and Murrell (2002); Dyck (1997); Frydman, Gray, Hessel, and Rapaczymski (1999); Lin (2000); Roland (2002); Stiglitz (1999); Sun and Tong (2003); Svejnar (2002); and Zinnes, Eilat, and Sachs (2001). Full chapter references are given below.

Anderson, James H., Young Lee, and Peter Murrell. 2000. "Competition and Privatization Amidst Weak Institutions; Evidence from Mongolia." *Economic Inquiry* 38, pp. 527–549.

Andreyeva, Tatiana. 2001. "Company Performance in Ukraine: What Governs its Success." Working paper, RAND Graduate School of Policy Analysis, Los Angeles.

Angelucci, Mauella, Saul Estrin, Jozef Konings, and Zbigniew Zoliewski. 2001. "The Effect of Ownership and Competitive Pressure on firm Performance in Transition Countries: Micro Evidence from Bulgaria, Romania and Poland." Discussion paper 2985. London: CEPR.

Bai, Chong-en, David D. Li, and Yijiaiang Wang. 1997. "Enterprise Productivity and Efficiency: When Is Up Really Down?" *Journal of Comparative Economics* 24, pp. 265–280.

Berg, Andrew, Eduardo Borensztein, Ratna Sahay, and Jeromin Zettelmeyer. 1999. "The Evolution of Output in Transition Economies: Explaining the Differences." IMF working paper, Washington, DC.

Black, Bernard, Reinier Kraakman, and Anna Tarassova. 2000. "Russian Privatization and Corporate Governance: What Went Wrong?" *Stanford Law Review* 56, pp. 1731–1808.

Blanchard, Olivier. 1997. *The Economics of Post-Communist Transition*. Oxford, UK: Clarendon Press.

Broadman, Harry. 2001. "The Business(es) of the Chinese State." *World Economy* 24:7, pp. 849–875.

Brown, David, and John Earle. 2000. "Privatization and Enterprise Restructuring in Russia: New Evidence from Panel Data on Industrial Enterprises." Working paper, RECEP, Moscow.

Cao, Yuanzheng, Yingyi Qian, and Barry R. Weingast. 1999. "From Federalism, Chinese Style to Privatization, Chinese Style." *Economics of Transition* 7, pp. 103–131.

Carlin, Wendy, Steven Fries, Marc Schaffer, and Paul Seabright. 2001. "Competition and Enterprise Performance in Transition Economies: Evidence from a Cross-Country Survey." Discussion paper 2840. London: CEPR.

Claessens, Stijn, and Simeon Djankov. 1999a. "Enterprise Performance and Management Turnover in the Czech Republic." *European Economic Review* 43, pp. 1115–1124.

Claessens, Stijn, and Simeon Djankov. 1999b. "Ownership Concentration and Corporate Performance in the Czech Republic." *Journal of Comparative Economics* 27, pp. 498–513.

Claessens, Stijn, and Simeon Djankov. 2000. "Government Regulation and Privatization Benefits in Eastern Europe." Working paper, World Bank Group, Washington, DC.

Claessens, Stijn, and Simeon Djankov. 2002. "Privatization Benefits in Eastern Europe." *Journal of Public Economics* 83, pp. 307–324.

Claessens, Stijn, Simeon Djankov, and Gerhard Pohl. 1997. *Ownership and Corporate Governance: Evidence from the Czech Republic*. Washington, DC: World Bank Policy Research Paper No. 1737.

Coffee, Jack C., Jr. 1999. "Privatization and Corporate Governance: The Lessons from Securities Market Failure." *Journal of Corporation Law* 25, pp. 1–39.

Coricelli, Fabrizio, and Simeon Djankov. 2001. "Hardened Budgets and Enterprise Restructuring: Theory and an Application to Romania." *Journal of Comparative Economics* 29, pp. 749–763.

Cull, Robert, Jana Matesova, and Mary Shirley. 2002. "Ownership and the Temptation to Loot: Evidence from Privatized Firms in the Czech Republic." *Journal of Comparative Economics* 30, pp. 1–25.

Djankov, Simeon. 1999a. "Ownership Structure and Enterprise Restructuring in Six Newly Independent States." *Comparative Economic Studies* 41, pp. 75–95.

Djankov, Simeon. 1999b. "The Restructuring of Insider-Dominated Firms: A Comparative Analysis." *Economics of Transition* 7, pp. 467–479.

Djankov, Simeon, and Peter Murrell. 2002. "Enterprise Restructuring in Transition: A Quantitative Survey." *Journal of Economic Literature* 40, 739–792.

Djankov, Simeon, and Tatiana Nenova. 2000. "Why Did Privatization Fail in Kazakhstan?" World Bank working paper, Washington, DC.

Dyck, I. J. Alexander. 1997. "Privatization in Eastern Germany: Management Selection and Economic Transition." *American Economic Review* 87, pp. 565–597.

Earle, John S. 1998a. "Post-Privatization Ownership Structure and Productivity in Russian Industrial Enterprises." SITE working paper, Stockholm School of Economics, Sweden.

Earle, John S. 1998b. "Privatization, Competition and Budget Constraints: Disciplining Enterprises in Russia." SITE working paper no. 128, Stockholm School of Economics, Sweden.

Earle, John, and Saul Estrin. 1998. "Privatization, Competition and Budget Constraints: Disciplining Enterprises in Russia." SITE working paper no. 128, Stockholm School of Economics, Sweden.

Earle, John, and Almos Telgedy. 2001. "Productivity and Ownership Structure in Romania: Does Privatization Matter?" Working paper, Central European University, Budapest, Hungary.

Estrin, Saul, and A. Rosevear. 1999. "Enterprise Restructuring and Ownership: The Case of Ukraine." *European Economic Review* 43, pp. 1125–1136.

Fidrmuc, Jana P., and Jan Fidrmuc. 2001. "Firm Performance, CEO Turnover and Managerial Labor Market in the Czech Republic." Working paper, Tilburg University, The Netherlands.

Fischer, Stanley. 2001. "Ten Years of Transition: Looking Back and Looking Forward." *IMF Staff Papers* 48, pp. 1–8.

Frydman, Roman, Cheryl W. Gray, Marek Hessel, and Andrzej Rapaczynski. 1999. "When Does Privatization Work? The Impact of Private Ownership on Corporate Performance in Transition Economies." *Quarterly Journal of Economics* 114, pp. 1153–1191.

Frydman, Roman, Cheryl W. Gray, Marek Hessel, and Andrzej Rapaczynski. 2000. "The Limits of Discipline: Ownership and Hard Budget Constraints in the Transition Economies." C. V. Starr Center for Applied Economics working paper, New York University, New York.

Frydman, Roman, Marek Hessel, and Andrzej Rapaczynski. 2000. "Why Ownership Matters? Entrepreneurship and the Restructuring of Enterprises in Central Europe." C. V. Starr Center for Applied Economics working paper, New York University, New York.

Glennerster, Rachel. 2003. "Evaluating Privatization in the Former Yugoslav Republic of Macedonia." Working paper, Kennedy School, Harvard University, Cambridge, MA.

Grigorian, David. 2000. "Ownership and Performance of Lithuanian Enterprises." Policy Research working paper 2343, World Bank Group, Washington, DC.

Grosfeld, Irena, and Jean François Nivet. 1999. "Insider Power and Wage Setting in Transition: New Evidence from a Panel of Large Polish Firms." *European Economic Review* 43, pp. 1137–1147.

Grosfeld, Irena, and Thierry Tressel. 2001. "Competition and Corporate Governence: Substitutes or Complements? Evidence from the Warsaw Stock Exchange." Working paper, Delta Center, Paris.

Groves, Theodore, Yongmiao Hong, John McMillan, and Barry Naughton. 1994. "Autonomy and Incentives in Chinese State Enterprises." *Quarterly Journal of Economics* 109, pp. 183–209.

Groves, Theodore, Yongmiao Hong, John McMillan, and Barry Naughton. 1995. "China's Evolving Managerial Labor Market." *Journal of Political Economy* 103:4, pp. 873–892.

Harper, Joel T. 2001. "Short-Term Effects of Privatization on Operating Performance in the Czech Republic." *Journal of Financial Research* 24, pp. 119–131.

Havrylyshyn, Oleh. 2001. "Recovery and Growth in Transition: A Decade of Evidence." *IMF Staff Papers* 48, pp. 53–87.

Havrylyshyn, Oleh, and Donal McGettigan. 1999. "Privatization in Transition Countries: A Sampling of the Literature." IMF working paper 99/6, Washington, DC.

Jia, Jin, Qian Sun, and Wilson H. S. Tong. 2002. "Privatization via Overseas Listing: Evidence from China's H-Share Firms." Working paper, Nanyang Technological University, Singapore.

Johnson, Simon, Rafael LaPorta, Florencio López-de-Silanes, and Andrei Shleifer. 2000. "Tunneling." *American Economic Review Papers and Proceedings* 90, pp. 22–27.

Jones, Derek. 1998. "The Economic Effects of Privatization: Evidence from a Russian Panel." *Comparative Economic Studies* 42, pp. 75–102.

Jones, Derek, and Niels Mygind. 2000. "The Effects of Privatization upon Productive Efficiency: Evidence from the Baltic Republics." *Annals of Public and Cooperative Economics* 71, pp. 415–439.

Jones, Derek, and Niels Mygind. 2002. "Ownership and Productive Efficiency: Evidence from Estonian Panel Data." *Review of Development Economics* 6, pp. 284–301.

Kocenda, Evzen, and Jan Svejnar. 2002. "Ownership and Firm Performance after Large-Scale Privatization." Working paper, University of Michigan, Ann Arbor.

Kornai, Janos. 1993. "The Evolution of Financial Discipline under the Postsocialist System." *Kyklos* 46:3, pp. 315–336.

Lau, Lawrence J., Yingyi Qian, and Gerard Roland. 2000. "Reform without Losers: An Interpretation of China's Dual-Track Approach to Transition." *Journal of Political Economy* 108, pp. 120–143.

Li, Wei. 1997. "The Impact of Economic Reform on the Performance of Chinese State Enterprises, 1980–1989." *Journal of Political Economy* 105, pp. 1080–1106.

Lin, Cyril. 2000. "Corporate Governance of State-Owned Enterprises in China." Working paper, Asian Development Bank, Manila, Philippines.

Lin, Justin Yifu, Fang Cai, and Zhou Li. 1998. "Competition, Policy Burdens, and State-Owned Enterprise Reform." *American Economic Review* 88, pp. 422–427.

Lizal, Lubomir, Miroslav Singer, and Jan Svejnar. 2001. "Enterprise Breakups and Performance during the Transition from Plan to Market." *Review of Economics and Statistics* 83, pp. 92–99.

Lizal, Lubomir, and Jan Svejnar. 2001 "Investment, Credit Rationing and the Soft Budget Constraint: Evidence from Czech Panel Data." *Review of Economics and Statistics* 84, pp. 353–370.

Lizal, Lubomir, and Jan Svejnar. 2002. "Privatization Revisited: The Effects of Foreign and Domestic Owners on Corporate Performance." Working paper, University of Michigan, Ann Arbor.

Megginson, William L., Robert C. Nash, and Matthias van Randenborgh. 1994. "The Financial and Operating Performance of Newly Privatized Firms: An International Empirical Analysis." *Journal of Finance* 49, pp. 403–452.

Mihályi, Peter. 2000. "FDI through Cross-Border M&A—The Post-Communist Privatization Story Re-considered." Working paper, New York: UNCTAD.

Nellis, John. 1999. "Time to Rethink Privatization in Transition Economies?" IFC Discussion paper no. 38, World Bank Group Washington, DC.

Perevalov, Yuri, Ilya Gimadi, and Vladimir Dobrodeg. 2000. "Analysis of the Impact of Privatization on the Performance of Medium- and Large-Size Industrial Enterprises in Russia." Working paper ZK, Economic Education and Research Consortium, Moscow.

Pivovarsky, Alexander. 2001. "How Does Privatization Work? Ownership Concentration and Enterprise Performance in Ukraine." Working paper WP/01/42, International Monetary Fund, Washington, DC.

Pohl, Gerhard, Robert E. Anderson, Stijn Claessens, and Simeon Djankov. 1997. *Privatization and Restructuring in Central and Eastern Europe: Evidence and Policy Options.* Working paper, World Bank Technical Paper No. 368, Washington, DC.

Roberts, Bryan, Yevgeny Gorkov, and Jay Madigan. 1999. "Is Privatization a Free Lunch? New Evidence on Ownership Status and Firm Performance." Working paper, University of Miami, FL.

Roland, Gérard. 1994. "On the Speed and Sequencing of Privatization and Restructuring." *Economic Journal* 104, pp. 1158–1168.

Roland, Gérard. 2001. "Ten Years After . . . Transition and Economics." *IMF Staff Papers* 48, pp. 29–52.

Roland, Gérard. 2002. "The Political Economy of Transition." *Journal of Economic Perspectives* 16, pp. 29–50.

Roland, Gérard, and Khalid Sekkat. 2000. "Managerial Career Concerns, Privatization and Restructuring in Transition Economies." *European Economic Review* 44, pp. 1857–1172.

Samonis, Val. 2000. "Mergers and Acquisitions in Transition Economies: "Williams" Lithuania Deal Decomposed." Working paper, Center for European Integration Studies, Bonn, Germany.

Shleifer, Andrei. 1997. "Government in Transition." *European Economic Review* 41, pp. 385–410.

Shleifer, Andrei. 1998. "State versus Private Ownership." *Journal of Economic Perspectives* 12, pp. 133–150.

Smith, Stephen C., Beon-Cheol Cin, and Milan Vodopivec. 1997. "Privatization Incidence, Ownership Forms, and Firm Performance: Evidence from Slovenia." *Journal of Comparative Economics* 25, pp. 158–179.

Stiglitz, Joseph. 1999. "Whither Reform?" Keynote address, Annual World Bank Conference on Development Economics, Washington, DC.

Sun, Qian, and Wilson H. S. Tong. 2003. "China's Share Issue Privatization: The Extent of Its Success." *Journal of Financial Economics* 70, pp. 183–222.

Svejnar, Jan. 2002. "Transition Economies: Performance and Challenges." *Journal of Economic Perspectives* 16, pp. 3–28.

Tian, George Lihui. 2003. "Government Shareholding and the Value of China's Modern Firms." Working paper, London Business School, UK.

Wei, Zuobao, Oscar Varela, Juliet D'Souza, and M. Kabir Hassan. 2003. "The Financial and Operating Performance of China's Newly Privatized Firms." *Financial Management.* 32, pp. 107–126.

Weiss, Andrew, and Georgiy Nikitin. 1998. "Effects of Ownership by Investment Funds on the Performance of Czech Firms." Working paper, Boston University, Boston, MA.

Xu, Xiaonian, and Yan Wang. 1999. "Ownership Structure and Corporate Governance in Chinese Stock Companies." *Chinese Economic Review* 10, pp. 75–98.

Zinnes, Clifford, Yair Eilat, and Jeffrey Sachs. 2001. "The Gains from Privatization in Transition Economies: Is 'Change of Ownership' Enough?" *IMF Staff Papers* 48, pp. 146–170.

Chapter 6

The following texts are recommended for further reading: Biais and Perott (2002); Degeorge, Jenter, Moel, and Tufano (2004); Jones, Megginson, Nash, and Netter (1999); Megginson, Nash, Netter, and Schwartz (2000); and Menyah and Paudyal (1996). See also Nandini Gupta (2002), "Partial Privatization and Firm Performance," working paper, University of Michigan, Ann Arbor; and Avanidhar Subrahmanyam and Sheridan Titman (1998), "The Going Decision and the Development of Financial Markets," *Journal of Finance* 54, pp. 1045–1082. Full chapter references are given below.

Aggarwal, Reena, Ricardo Leal, and Leonardo Hernandez. 1993. "The Aftermarket Performance of Initial Public Offerings in Latin America." *Financial Management* 22, pp. 43–53.

Aussenegg, Wolfgang. 2000. "Privatization versus Private Sector Initial Public Offerings in Poland." Working paper, Vienna University of Technology, Austria.

Aybar, C. Bulent. 2002. "Performance of Privatization ADR Issues: An Empirical Analysis." Working paper, Southern New Hampshire University, Manchester, NH.

Baake, Pio, and Jörg Oechssler. 2001. "Divide et Impera: Strategic Underpricing in Privatizations." *Public Choice* 108, pp. 207–222.

Barber, Brad M., and John D. Lyon. 1997. "Detecting Long-Run Abnormal Stock Returns: The Empirical Power and Specification of Test Statistics." *Journal of Financial Economics* 43, pp. 341–372.

Beatty, Randolph P., and Ivo Welch. 1996. "Issuer Expenses and Legal Liability in Initial Public Offerings." *Journal of Law and Economics* 39, pp. 545–602.

Benveniste, M. Lawrence, and William J. Wilhelm. 1997. "Initial Public Offerings: Going by the Book." *Journal of Applied Corporate Finance* 10, pp. 98–108.

Biais, Bruno, and Enrico Perotti. 2002. "Machiavellian Privatization." *American Economic Review* 92, pp. 240–258.

Boardman, Anthony E., and Claude Laurin. 2000. "Factors Affecting the Stock Price Performance of Share Issued Privatizations." *Applied Economics* 32:11, pp. 1451–1464.

Boubakri, Narjess, and Jean-Claude Cosset. 2000. "The Aftermarket Performance of Privatization Offerings in Developing Countries." Working paper, Ecoles des HEC, Montreal.

Brav, Alon, Christopher Geczy, and Paul Gompers. 2000. "Is the Abnormal Return Following Equity Issuances Abnormal?" *Journal of Financial Economics* 56, pp. 209–249.

Brav, Alon, and Paul A. Gompers. 1997. "Myth or Reality? The Long-Run Underperformance of Initial Public Offerings: Evidence from Venture and Non-Venture Capital-Backed Companies." *Journal of Finance* 52, pp. 1791–1821.

Canina, Linda, Roni Michaely, Richard Thaler, and Kent Womack. 1998. "Caveat Compounder: A Warning About Using the Daily CRSP Equal-Weighted Index to Compute Long-Run Excess Returns." *Journal of Finance* 53, pp. 403–416.

Carter, Richard B., Frederick H. Dark, and Ajai K. Singh. 1998. "Underwriter Reputation, Initial Returns, and the Long-Run Performance of IPO Stocks." *Journal of Finance* 53, pp. 285–311.

Choi, Seung-Doo, and Sang-Koo Nam. 1998. "The Short-Run Performance of IPOs of

Privately- and Publicly-Owned Firms: International Evidence." *Multinational Finance Journal* 2, pp. 225–244.

Choi, Seung-Doo, Sang-Koo Nam, and Gui-Youl Ryu. 2000. "Do Privatization IPOs Outperform the Market? International Evidence." Working paper, Korea University, Seoul.

Davidson, Richard. 1998. "Market Analysis: Underperformance Over?" *Privatisation International Yearbook*. London: IFR Publishing.

Degeorge, François, Dirk Jenter, Alberto Moel, and Peter Tufano. 2004. "Selling Company Shares to Reluctant Employees: France Telecom's Experience." *Journal of Financial Economics* 71, pp. 169–202.

Dewenter, Kathryn, and Paul H. Malatesta. 1997. "Public Offerings of State-Owned and Privately-Owned Enterprises: An International Comparison." *Journal of Finance* 52, pp. 1659–1679.

Dewenter, Kathryn, and Paul H. Malatesta. 2000. "State-Owned and Privately-Owned Firms: An Empirical Analysis of Profitability, Leverage, and Labour Intensity." *American Economic Review* 91, pp. 320–334.

Eckbo, B. Espen, Ronald A. Masulis, and Øyvind Norli. 2000. "Seasoned Public Offerings: Resolution of the 'New Issues Puzzle.'" *Journal of Financial Economics* 56, pp. 251–291.

The Economist. (April 12, 1997). "Fragile, Handle with Care: A Survey of Banking in Emerging Markets." (n.p.).

The Economist. (April 17, 1999). "On a Wing and a Prayer: A Survey of International Banking." (n.p.).

Fama, Eugene F. 1998. "Market Efficiency, Long-Term Returns, and Behavioral Finance." *Journal of Financial Economics* 49, pp. 283–306.

Florio, Massimo, and Katiuscia Manzoni. 2002. "The Abnormal Returns of UK Privatisations: From Underpricing to Outperformance." Working paper, University of Milan, Italy.

Foerster, Stephen R., and G. Andrew Karolyi. 2000. "The Long-Run Performance of Global Equity Offerings" *Journal of Financial and Quantitative Analysis* 35, pp. 3499–3528.

Holbertson, Simon. 1996. "Power Behind the Golden Shares." *Financial Times* (May 4), p. 8.

Huang, Qi, and Richard M. Levich. 1998. "Underpricing of New Equity Offerings by Privatized Firms: An International Test." Working paper, New York University, New York.

Ibbotson, Roger G., Jody Sindelar, and Jay Ritter. 1994. "The Market's Problem with the Pricing of Initial Public Offerings." *Journal of Applied Corporate Finance* 7, pp. 66–74.

Jelic, Ranko, and Richard Briston. 1999. "Hungarian Privatisation Strategy and Financial Performance of Privatised Companies." *Journal of Business Finance and Accounting* 26, 1319–1357.

Jelic, Ranko, and Richard Briston. 2000. "Privatisation Initial Public Offerings: The Polish Experience." Working paper, University of Birmingham, UK.

Jelic, Ranko, Richard Briston, and Wolfgang Aussenegg. 2003. "The Choice of Privatization Method and the Financial Performance of Newly Privatised Firms in Transition Economies." *Journal of Business Finance and Accounting* 30:7/8, pp. 905–940.

Jones, Steven L., William L. Megginson, Robert C. Nash, and Jeffry M. Netter. 1999. "Share Issue Privatizations as Financial Means to Political and Economic Ends." *Journal of Financial Economics* 53, pp. 217–253.

Kerr, Jarrod, and Lawrence C. Rose. 2002. "Privatisation in the New Zealand Stock Market: An Empirical Analysis." Working paper, Massey University, Auckland, New Zealand.

Kothari, S. P., and Jerold B. Warner. 1997. "Measuring Long-Horizon Security Price Performance." *Journal of Financial Economics* 43, pp. 301–340.

Lee, Inmoo, Scott Lochhead, Jay Ritter, and Quanshui Zhao. 1996. "The Costs of Raising Capital." *Journal of Financial Research* 19, pp. 59–74.

Levis, Mario. 1993. "The Long-Run Performance of Initial Public Offerings: The U.K. Experience 1980–88." *Financial Management* 22, pp. 28–41.

Ljungqvist, Alexander P., Tim Jenkinson, and William J. Wilhelm, Jr. 2003. "Global Integration in Primary Equity Markets: The Role of U.S. Banks and U.S. Investors." *Review of Financial Studies* 16:1, pp. 63–99.

López-de-Silanes, Florencio. 1997. "Determinants of Privatization Prices." *Quarterly Journal of Economics* 112, pp. 965–1025.

Loughran, Tim, and Jay R. Ritter. 1995. "The New Issues Puzzle." *Journal of Finance* 50, pp. 23–51.

Loughran, Tim, and Jay R. Ritter. 1997. "The Operating Performance of Firms Conducting Seasoned Equity Offerings." *Journal of Finance* 52, pp. 1823–1850.

Loughran, Tim, Jay Ritter, and Kristian Rydqvist. 1994. "Initial Public Offerings: International Insight." *Pacific-Basin Finance Journal* 2, pp. 165–199.

Lyon, John D., Brad M. Barber, and Chih-Ling Tsai. 1999. "Improved Methods for Tests of Long-Run Abnormal Stock Returns." *Journal of Finance* 54, pp. 165–201.

Masulis, Ronald W., and Ashok N. Korwar. 1986. "Seasoned Equity Offerings: An Empirical Investigation." *Journal of Financial Economics* 15, pp. 91–118.

Megginson, William L., Robert C. Nash, Jeffry M. Netter, and Annette B. Poulsen. Forthcoming. "The Choice between Private and Public Markets: Evidence from Privatization." *Journal of Finance*.

Megginson, William L., Robert C. Nash, Jeffry M. Netter, and Adam L. Schwartz. 2000. "The Long Term Return to Investors in Share Issue Privatizations." *Financial Management* 29, pp. 67–77.

Megginson, William L. and Jeffry M. Netter. 2001. "From State to Market: A Survey of Empirical Studies on Privatization," *Journal of Economic Literature* 39, pp. 321–389.

Menyah, Kojo, and Krishna Paudyal. 1996. "Share Issue Privatisations: The UK Experience." In Mario Levis, ed., *Empirical Issues in Raising Equity Capital*. Amsterdam: Elsevier Science, pp. 17–48.

Menyah, Kojo, Krishna Paudyal, and Charles G. Inyangete. 1995. "Subscriber Return, Underpricing, and Long-Term Performance of U.K. Privatization Initial Public Offers." *Journal of Economics and Business* 47, pp. 473–495.

Mikkelson, Wayne H., and M. Megan Partch. 1986. "Valuation Effects of Security Offerings and he Issuance Process." *Journal of Financial Economics* 15, pp. 31–60.

Mitchell, Mark, and Erik Stafford. 2000. "Managerial Decisions and Long-Term Price Performance." *Journal of Business* 73:3, pp. 287–329.

Omran, Mohammed. 2002. "Initial and Aftermarket Performance of Egyptian Share Issue Privatization." Working paper, Arab Monetary Fund, Economic Policy Institute, Abu Dhabi, UAE.

Paudyal, K., B. Saadouni, and R. J. Briston. 1998. "Privatization Initial Public Offerings in Malaysia: Initial Premium and Long-Term Performance."*Pacific-Basin Finance Journal* 6, pp. 427–451.

Perotti, Enrico. 1995. "Credible Privatization." *American Economic Review* 85, pp. 847–859.

Perotti, Enrico, and Pieter van Oijen. 2001. "Privatization, Political Risk and Stock Market Development in Emerging Economies." *Journal of International Money and Finance* 20: 1, pp. 43–69.

Ritter, Jay R. 1991. "The Long-Run Performance of Initial Public Offerings." *Journal of Finance* 46, pp. 3–27.

Spiess, D. Katherine, and John Affleck-Graves. 1995. "Underperformance in Long-run Stock Returns Following Seasoned Equity Offerings." *Journal of Financial Economics* 38, pp. 243–267.

Su, Dongwei, and Belton M. Fleisher. 1999. "An Empirical Investigation of Underpricing in Chinese IPOs." *Pacific Basin Finance Journal* 7, pp. 173–202.

Welch, Ivo. 1989. "Seasoned Offerings, Imitation Costs, and the Underpricing of Initial Public Offerings." *Journal of Finance* 44, pp. 421–449.

Westerman, Matthew, and Alex Casbolt. 1998. "The Evolving Role of Retail Investors in Privatisation Equity Offers." *Privatisation International* 123 (December), pp. 13–15.

Chapter 7

The following texts are recommended for further reading: Boutchkova and Megginson (2000); Denis and McConnell (2003); La Porta, López-de-Silanes, Shleifer, and Vishny (1998); La Porta, López-de-Silanes, Shleifer, and Vishny (2002); Levine (1997); and Perotti and van Oijen (2001). See also Organization of Economic Cooperation and Development (1999), *OECD Principles of Corporate Governance*, Paris. Full chapter references are given below.

Beck, Thorsten, Ross Levine, and Norman Loayza. 2000. "Finance and the Sources of Growth." *Journal of Financial Economics* 58, pp. 261–300.

Bekaert, Geert, and Campbell Harvey. 2000. "Foreign Speculators and Emerging Equity Markets." *Journal of Finance* 55, pp. 565–613.

Black, Bernard, Reinier Kraakman, and Anna Tarassova. 2000. "Russian Privatization and Corporate Governance: What Went Wrong?" *Stanford Law Review* 56, pp. 1731–1808.

Bortolotti, Bernardo, Marcella Fantini, and Carla Scarpa. 2000. "Why Do Governments Privatize Abroad?" *FEEM Note di Lavoro* 23, Fondazione Eni Enrico Mattei, Milan.

Boutchkova, Maria K., and William L. Megginson. 2000. "Privatization and the Rise of Global Capital Markets." *Financial Management* 29, pp. 31–76.

Boyd, John H., and Mark Gertler. 1994. "Are Banks Dead? Or Are the Reports Greatly Exaggerated?" Federal Reserve Bank of Minneapolis *Quarterly Review* (Summer), pp. 2–23.

Coffee, Jack C., Jr. 1999. "Privatization and Corporate Governance: The Lessons from Securities Market Failure." *Journal of Corporation Law* 25, pp. 1–39.

Demirgüç-Kunt, Asli, and Vojislav Maksimovic. 1998. "Law, Finance, and Firm Growth." *Journal of Finance* 53, pp. 2107–2139.

Denis, Diane K., and John J. McConnell. 2003. "International Corporate Governance." *Journal of Financial and Quantitative Analysis* 38, pp. 1–36.

Domowitz, Ian, Jack Glen, and Ananth Madhavan. 2000. "Growth, Structure, and Corporate Primary Issuance Activity across Countries and over Time." Working paper, Pennsylvania State University, University Park.

Esty, Benjamin C., and William L. Megginson. 2003. "Creditor Rights, Enforcement, and Debt Ownership Structure: Evidence from the Global Syndicated Loan Market." *Journal of Financial and Quantitative Analysis* 38, pp. 37–59.

Field, Laura C. 1997. "Is Institutional Investment in Initial Public Offerings Related to the Long-Run Performance of These Firms?" Working paper, Pennsylvania State University, University Park.

Gibbon, Henry. 1998. "Worldwide Economic Orthodoxy." *Privatisation International* 123, pp. 4–5.

Gibbon, Henry. 2000. "Editor's Letter." *Privatisation Yearbook*. London: Thomson Financial, p. 1.

Henry, Peter Blair. 2000. "Do Stock Market Liberalizations Cause Investment Booms?" *Journal of Financial Economics* 58:1–2, pp. 301–334.

James, Christopher, and Joel Houston. 1996. "Evolution or Extinction? Where Are Banks Headed?" *Journal of Applied Corporate Finance* 9, pp. 8–23.

James, Christopher, and David C. Smith. 2000. "Are Banks Still Special? New Evidence in the Corporate Capital-Raising Process." *Journal of Applied Corporate Finance* 13, pp. 395–422.

Jones, Steven L., William L. Megginson, Robert C. Nash, and Jeffry M. Netter. 1999. "Share Issue Privatizations as Financial Means to Political and Economic Ends." *Journal of Financial Economics* 53, pp. 217–253.

Kaufman, George G., and Larry R. Mote. 1994. "Is Banking a Declining Industry?" Federal Reserve Bank of Chicago *Economic Perspectives* (May/June), pp. 2–21.

Kester, W. Carl. 1992. "Governance, Contracting and Investment Horizons." *Journal of Applied Corporate Finance* 5, pp. 83–98.

Kleimeier, Stefanie, and William L. Megginson. 2000. "Are Project Finance Loans Different from Other Syndicated Credits?" *Journal of Applied Corporate Finance* 12, pp. 75–87.

La Porta, Rafael, Florencio López-de-Silanes, and Andrei Shleifer. 1999. "Corporate Ownership around the World." *Journal of Finance* 54, pp. 471–517.

La Porta, Rafael, Florencio López-de-Silanes, Andrei Shleifer, and Robert W. Vishny. 1997. "Legal Determinants of External Finance." *Journal of Finance* 52, pp. 1131–1150.

La Porta, Rafael, Florencio López-de-Silanes, Andrei Shleifer, and Robert W. Vishny. 1998. "Law and Finance." *Journal of Political Economy* 106, 1113–1150.

La Porta, Rafael, Florencio López-de-Silanes, Andrei Shleifer, and Robert W. Vishny. 1999. "The Quality of Government." *Journal of Law, Economics, & Organization* 15, pp. 222–279.

La Porta, Rafael, Florencio López-de-Silanes, Andrei Shleifer, and Robert W. Vishny. 2000. "Agency Problems and Dividend Policies around the World." *Journal of Finance* 55, 1–33.

La Porta, Rafael, Florencio López-de-Silanes, Andrei Shleifer, and Robert W. Vishny. 2002. "Investor Protection and Corporate Valuation." *Journal of Finance* 57, 1147–1170.

Levine, Ross. 1997. "Financial Development and Economic Growth: Views and Agenda." *Journal of Economic Literature* 35, pp. 688–726.

Levine, Ross, and Sara Zervos. 1998. "Stock Markets, Banks, and Economic Growth." *American Economic Review* 88, pp. 537–558.

Lin, Cyril. 2000. "Corporate Governance of State-Owned Enterprises in China." Working paper, Asian Development Bank, Manila, Philippines.

Maher, Maria, and Thomas Andersson. 1999. "Corporate Performance: Effects on Firm Performance and Economic Growth." Working paper, Organization for Economic Cooperation and Development, Paris.

Megginson, William L., Robert C. Nash, Jeffry M. Netter, and Annette B. Poulsen. Forthcoming. "The Choice between Private and Public Markets: Evidence from Privatization." *Journal of Finance*.

Megginson, William L., and Jeffry M. Netter. 2001. "From State to Market: A Survey of Empirical Studies on Privatization." *Journal of Economic Literature* 39, pp. 321–389.

Menyah, Kojo, and Krishna Paudyal. 1996. "Share Issue Privatisations: The UK Experience." In Mario Levis, ed., *Empirical Issues in Raising Equity Capital.* Amsterdam: Elsevier Science, pp. 17–48.

Morgan Stanley Capital International. 2003. "The Business Week Global 1000." *Business Week* (July 14).

Perotti, Enrico, and Pieter van Oijen. 2001. "Privatization, Stock Market Development, and Political Risk." *Journal of International Money and Finance* 20, 43–69.

Porter, Michael E. 1992. "Capital Choices: Changing the Way America Invests in Industry." *Journal of Applied Corporate Finance* 5, pp. 4–16.

Prowse, Stephen. 1992. "The Structure of Corporate Ownership in Japan." *Journal of Finance* 47, pp. 1121–1140.

Rajan, Raghuram G., and Luigi Zingales. 1998. "Financial Dependence and Growth." *American Economic Review* 88, pp. 559–586.

Shleifer, Andrei, and Robert W. Vishny. 1997. "A Survey of Corporate Governance." *Journal of Finance* 52, pp. 737–783.

Smart, Scott B., William L. Megginson, and Larry J. Gitman. 2004. *Corporate Finance.* Cincinnati, OH: South-Western Publishing.

Subrahmanyam, Avanidhar, and Sheridan Titman. 1998. "The Going Public Decision and the Development of Financial Markets." *Journal of Finance* 54, pp. 1045–1082.

World Bank Group. 2002. *World Development Indicators.* Washington, DC.

Wurgler, J. 2000. "Financial Markets and the Allocation of Capital." *Journal of Financial Economics* 58, 187–214.

Chapter 8

The following texts are recommended for further reading: Bortolotti, D'Souza, Fantini, and Megginson (2002); Boyland and Nicoletti (2000); Chong and Galdo (2002); Gutierrez and Berg (2000); Hazlett and Bittlingmayer (2001); Li and Xu (2002); Noll (2000); Wallsten (2001b); and Wallsten (2002a). Full chapter references are given below.

Biais, Bruno, and Enrico Perotti. 2002. "Machiavellian Privatization." *American Economic Review* 92, pp. 240–258.

Boles de Boer, David, and Lewis Evans. 1996. "The Economic Efficiency of Telecommunications in a Deregulated Market: The Case of New Zealand." *Economic Record* 72, pp. 24–35.

Bortolotti, Bernardo, Juliet D'Souza, Marcella Fantini, and William L. Megginson. 2002. "Privatization and the Sources of Performance Improvement in the Global Telecommunications Industry." *Telecommunications Policy* 26, pp. 243–268.

Bortolotti, Bernardo, Marcella Fantini, and Domenico Siniscalco. 1999. "Regulation and Privatisation: The Case of Electricity." Working paper, Fondazione ENI-Enrico Mattei (FEEM), Milan, Italy.

Boyland, O., and G. Nicoletti. 2000. "Regulation, Market Structure and Performance in Telecommunications." Organization for Economic Cooperation and Development, Paris.

Cabanda, Emilyn, and M. Ariff. 2002. "Privatisation of Telecommunications Firms: Financial and Production Efficiency." Working paper, Monash University, Australia.

Chong, Alberto, and Virgilio Galdo. 2002. "Streamlining and Privatization Prices in the Telecommunications Industry." Working paper, Inter-American Development Bank, Washington, DC.

Fink, Carsten, Aaditya Matto, and Randeep Rathindran. 2002. "An Assessment of Telecommunications Reform in Developing Countries." World Bank working paper 2909, Washington, DC.

Gutierrez, Luis H., and Sanford Berg. 2000. "Telecommunications Liberalization and Regulatory Governance: Lessons from Latin America." *Telecommunications Policy* 24, pp. 865–884.

Hazlett, Thomas W., and George Bittlingmayer. 2001. "The Political Economy of Cable 'Open Access.'" Working paper, American Enterprise Institute, Washington, DC.

Jones, Steven L., William L. Megginson, Robert C. Nash, and Jeffry M. Netter. 1999. "Share Issue Privatizations as Financial Means to Political and Economic Ends." *Journal of Financial Economics* 53, pp. 217–253.

Kubota, Keiko. 2000. "The Effects of Market Conditions and Policies on Performance in Telecommunications Sector: Some Evidence." Working paper, World Bank Group, Washington, DC.

Li, Wei, and Lixin Colin Xu. 2002. "The Political Economy of Privatization and Competition: Cross-Country Evidence from the Telecommunications Sector." *Journal of Comparative Economics* 30, pp. 439–462.

Li, Wei, and Lixin Colin Xu. 2003. "The Impact of Privatization and Competition in the Telecommunications Sector around the World." Working paper, University of Virginia, Charlottesville.

McNary, Robert. 2001. "The Network Penetration Effects of Telecommunications Privatization and Competition." Honors thesis, Stanford University, Palo Alto, CA.

Megginson, William L., Robert C. Nash, and Matthias van Randenborgh. 1994. "The Financial and Operating Performance of Newly Privatized Firms: An International Empirical Analysis." *Journal of Finance* 49, pp. 403–452.

Noll, Roger. 2000. "Telecommunications Reform in Developing Countries." In Anne O. Kreuger, ed., *Economic Policy Reform: The Second Stage*. Chicago: University of Chicago Press.

Parker, David. 1994. "A Decade of Privatisation: The Effect of Ownership Change and Competition on British Telecom." *British Review of Economic Issues* 16, pp. 87–113.

Perotti, Enrico. 1995. "Credible Privatization." *American Economic Review* 85, pp. 847–859.

Perotti, Enrico, and Pieter van Oijen. 2001. "Privatization, Political Risk and Stock Market Development in Emerging Economies." *Journal of International Money and Finance* 20:1, pp. 43–69.

Petrazzini, Ben A., and Theodore H. Clark. 1996. "Costs and Benefits of Telecommunications Liberalization in Developing Countries." Working paper, Hong Kong University of Science and Technology, Hong Kong.

Ros, Augustin J. 1999. "Does Ownership or Competition Matter? The Effects of Telecommunications Reform on Network Expansion and Efficiency." *Journal of Regulatory Economics* 15, pp. 65–92.

Wallsten, Scott J. 2001a. "An Econometric Analysis of Telecom Competition, Privatization, and Regulation in Africa and Latin America." *Journal of Industrial Economics* 49, pp. 1–19.

Wallsten, Scott J. 2001b. "Telecommunications Privatization in Developing Countries: The Real Effects of Exclusivity Periods." Working paper, Stanford University, Palo Alto, CA.

Wallsten, Scott. 2002a. "Does Sequencing Matter? Regulation and Privatization in Telecommunications Reform." Working paper, World Bank Group, Washington, DC.

Wallsten, Scott. 2002b. "Returning to Victorian Competition, Ownership, and Regulation: An Empirical Study of European Telecommunications at the Turn of the 20th Century." Working paper, World Bank Group, Washington, DC.

Wasserfallen, Walter, and Stefan Müller. 1998. "Deregulation and Privatization: Evidence from the Telecommunications Industry in Europe and Implications for Switzerland." Working paper, Studienzentrum Gerzensee, Switzerland.

Chapter 9

The following texts are recommended for further reading: Barth, Caprio, and Levine (2003); Berger (2003); Boehmer, Nash, and Netter (2003); Bonin, Hasan, and Wachtel (2003); Boubakri, Cosset, Fischer, and Guedhami (2003); Clarke, Cull, and Shirley (2003); Jaffee and Levonian (2001); La Porta, López-de-Silanes, and Shleifer (2002); and Sapienza (2003). Full chapter references are given below.

Abarbanell, Jeffrey S., and John P. Bonin. 1997. "Bank Privatization in Poland: The Case of Bank Slaski." *Journal of Comparative Economics* 25, pp. 31–61.

Abarbanell, Jeffrey S., and Anna Meyendorff. 1997. "Bank Privatization in Post-Communist Russia: The Case of Zhilsotsbank." *Journal of Comparative Economics* 25, pp. 62–96.

Baer, Werner, and Nader Nazmi. 2000. "Privatization and Restructuring of Banks in Brazil." *Quarterly Review of Economics and Finance* 40, pp. 3–24.

Barth, James R., Gerald Caprio, and Ross Levine. 2001. "The Regulation and Supervision of Banks around the World." In Robert E. Litan and Richard Herring, eds, *Integrating Emerging Market Countries Into the Global Financial System.* Brooking-Wharton Papers on Financial Services. Washington, DC: Brookings Institution Press, pp. 183–240.

Barth, James R., Gerald Caprio, and Ross Levine. 2004. "Bank Regulation and Supervision: What Works Best?" *Journal of Financial Intermediation* 13, pp. 205–248.

Beck, Thorsten, Juan Miguel Crivelli, and William Summerhill. 2003. "State Bank Transformation in Brazil—Choices and Consequences." Working paper, World Bank Group, Washington, DC.

Beck, Thorsten, Robert Cull, and Afeikhena Jerome. 2003. "Bank Privatization in Nigeria." Working paper, World Bank Group, Washington, DC.

Beck, Thorsten, Asli Demirgüç-Kunt, and Ross Levine. 2003. "Law, Endowments, and Finance." *Journal of Financial Economics* 70, pp. 137–181.

Berger, Allen N. 2003. "International Comparisons of Banking Efficiency." Working paper, Board of Governors, Federal Reserve System, Washington, DC.

Berglof, Eric, and Gérard Roland. 1998. "Soft Budget Constraints and Banking in Transition Economies." *Journal of Comparative Economics* 26, pp. 18–40.

Bhattacharya, A., C.A.K. Lovell, and P. Sahay. 1997. "The Impact of Liberalization on the Productive Efficiency of Indian Commercial Banks." *European Journal of Operations Research* 98, 332–345.

Boehmer, Ekkehart, Robert C. Nash, and Jeffry M. Netter. 2003. "Bank Privatization in Developing and Developed Countries: Cross-Sectional Evidence on the Impact of Economic and Political Factors." Working paper, Wake Forest University, Winston-Salem, NC.

Bonaccorsi di Patti, Emilia, and Daniel C. Hardy. 2003. "The Effects of Banking System Reforms in Pakistan." Working paper, Banca d'Italia, Rome.

Bonin, John, Iftekhar Hasan, and Paul Wachtel. 2002. "Ownership Structure and Bank Performance in the Transition Economies of Central and Eastern Europe: A Preliminary Report." Working paper, New York University, New York.

Bonin, John, Iftekhar Hasan, and Paul Wachtel. 2003. "Privatization Matters: Bank Performance in Transition Economies." Working paper, New York University, New York.

Bonin, John, and Paul Wachtel. 2000. "Lessons from Bank Privatization in Central Europe." In Harvey Rosenblum, ed., *Bank Privatization: Conference Proceedings of a Policy Research Workshop.* Dallas: Federal Reserve Bank of Dallas, pp. 35–51.

Bonin, John, and Paul Wachtel. 2002. "Short Histories of Bank Privatization in Six Transition Economies: A Preliminary Report." Working paper, New York University, New York.

Boubakri, Narjess, Jean-Claude Cosset, Klaus Fischer, and Omrane Guedhami. 2003. "Ownership Structure, Privatization, Bank Performance and Risk Taking." Working paper, Université Laval, Quebec.

Boycko, Maxim, Adrei Shleifer, and Robert W. Vishny. 1996. "A Theory of Privatisation." *Economic Journal* 106, 309–319.

Braz, José. 1999. "Bank (Re)privatization in Portugal." Paper presented at World Bank/Federal Reserve Bank of Dallas Conference on Bank Privatization, Washington, DC, March.

Brock, Philip. 1999. "Emerging from Crisis: Bank Privatization and Recapitalization in Chile." Paper presented at World Bank/Federal Reserve Bank of Dallas Conference on Bank Privatization, Washington, DC, March.

Cetorelli, Nicola, and Michele Gambera. 2001. "Banking Market Structure, Financial Dependence and Growth: International Evidence from Industry Data." *Journal of Finance* 56, pp. 617–648.

Claessens, Stijn, Asli Demirgüç-Kunt, and H. Huizinga. 2001. "How Does Foreign Entry Affect Domestic Banking Markets?" *Journal of Banking and Finance* 25, pp. 891–911.

Clarke, George, and Robert Cull. 2002. "Political and Economic Determinants of the Likelihood of Privatizing Argentine Public Banks." *Journal of Law and Economics* 45, pp. 165–197.

Clarke, George, and Robert Cull. 2003. "Bank Privatization in Argentina: A Model of Political Constraints and Differential Outcomes." Working paper, World Bank Group, Washington, DC.

Clarke, George, Robert Cull, and M. S. Martinez Peria. 2001. "Does Foreign Bank Penetration Reduce Access to Credit in Developing Countries?" Working paper, World Bank Group, Washington, DC.

Clarke, George, Robert Cull, M. S. Martinez Peria, and S. M. Sanchez. 2003. "Foreign Bank Entry: Experience, Implications for Developing Countries, and Agenda for Further Research" *The World Bank Research Observer* 18, pp. 25–59.

Clarke, George R. G., Robert Cull, and Mary Shirley. 2003. "Empirical Studies of Bank Privatization: An Overview." Working paper, World Bank Group, Washington, DC.

Commander, Simon, Mark Dutz, and Nicholas Stern. 1999. "Restructuring in Transition Economies: Ownership, Competition, and Regulation." Working paper, World Bank Group, Washington, DC.

Cornett, Marcia Millon, Lin Guo, Shahriar Khaksari, and Hassan Tehranian. 2003. "The Impact of Corporate Governance on Performance Differences in Privately-Owned versus State-Owned Banks: An International Comparison." Working paper, Boston College, Boston, MA.

Demirgüç-Kunt, Asli, and H. Huizinga. 1998. "Determinants of Commercial Bank Interest Margins and Profitability: Some International Evidence." *The World Bank Economic Review* 13, pp. 379–408.

Demirgüç-Kunt, Asli, and Vojislav Maksimovic. 1998. "Law, Finance, and Firm Growth." *Journal of Finance* 53, pp. 2107–2139.

Dewentei, Kathryn, and Paul H. Malatesta. 2000. "State-Owned and Privately-Owned Firms: An Empirical Analysis of Profitability, Leverage, and Labour Intensity." *American Economic Review* 91, pp. 320–334.

Djankov, Simeon, and Peter Murrell. 2002. "Enterprise Restructuring in Transition: A Quantitative Survey." *Journal of Economic Literature* 40, pp. 739–792.

Gleason, Kimberly, James E. McNulty, and Anita K. Pennathur. 2003. "Returns to Bidders of Privatizing Financial Services Firms: An International Examination." Working paper, Florida Atlantic University, Boca Raton, FL.

Gruben, William C., and Robert McComb. 2003. "Privatization, Competition, and Supercompetivity in the Mexican Banking System." *Journal of Banking and Finance* 27, pp. 229–249.

Haber, Stephen, and Shawn Kantor. 2003. "Getting Privatization Wrong: The Mexican Banking System, 1991–2002." Working paper, Stanford University, Palo Alto, CA.

Jaffee, Dwight, and Mark Levonian. 2001. "The Structure of Banking Systems in Developed and Transition Economies." *European Financial Management* 7, pp. 161–181.

Jones, Leroy P. 1985. "Public Enterprise for Whom? Perverse Distributional Consequences of Public Operational Decisions." *Economic Development and Cultural Change* 33, pp. 333–347.

La Porta, Rafael, and Florencio López-de-Silanes. 1999. "Benefits of Privatization—Evidence from Mexico." *Quarterly Journal of Economics* 114, pp. 1193–1242.

La Porta, Rafael, Florencio López-de-Silanes, and Andrei Shleifer. 2002. "Government Ownership of Banks." *Journal of Finance* 57, pp. 265–301.

La Porta, Rafael, Florencio López-de-Silanes, Andrei Shleifer, and Robert W. Vishny. 1997. "Legal Determinants of External Finance." *Journal of Finance* 52, pp. 1131–1150.

La Porta, Rafael, Florencio López-de-Silanes, Andrei Shleifer, and Robert W. Vishny. 1998. "Law and Finance." *Journal of Political Economy* 106, pp. 1113–1150.

La Porta, Rafael, Florencio López-de-Silanes, Andrei Shleifer, and Robert W. Vishny. 2002. "Investor Protection and Corporate Valuation." *Journal of Finance* 57, pp. 1147–1170.

Levine, Ross. 1997. "Financial Development and Economic Growth: Views and Agenda." *Journal of Economic Literature* 35, pp. 688–726.

Levine, Ross and Sara Zervos. 1998. "Stock Markets, Banks, and Economic Growth." *American Economic Review* 88, pp. 537–558.

López-de-Silanes, Florencio, and Guillermo Zamarripa. 1995. "Deregulation and Privatization of Commercial Banking." *Revista de Análisis Económico* 10, pp. 113–164.

Majnoni, Giovanni, Rashmi Shankar, and Éva Várhegyi. 2003. "The Dynamics of Foreign Bank Ownership: Evidence from Hungary." World Bank Policy Research Paper 3114, World Bank Group, Washington, DC.

Makler, Harry M. 2000. "Bank Transformation and Privatization in Brazil: Financial Federalism and Some Lessons about Bank Privatization." *Quarterly Review of Economics and Finance* 40, pp. 45–69.

Megginson, William L., Robert C. Nash, and Matthias van Randenborgh. 1994. "The Financial and Operating Performance of Newly Privatized Firms: An International Empirical Analysis." *Journal of Finance* 49, pp. 403–452.

Megginson, William L., and Jeffry M. Netter. 2001. "From State to Market: A Survey of Empirical Studies on Privatization." *Journal of Economic Literature* 39, pp. 321–389.

Meyendorff, Anna, and Edward A. Snyder. 1997. "Transactional Structure of Bank Privatizations in Central Europe and Russia." *Journal of Comparative Economics* 25, pp. 5–30.

Moshirian, Fairborz, Zhian Chan, and Donghui Li. 2003. "China's Financial Services

Industry: The Effects of Privatization of the Bank of China Hong Kong." Working paper, University of New South Wales, Sydney, Australia.

Nellis, John. 1994. "Is Privatization Necessary?" *World Bank Viewpoint* Note 17, World Bank Group, Washington, DC.

Ness, Walter L., Jr. 2000. "Reducing Government Bank Presence in the Brazilian Financial System." *Quarterly Review of Economics and Finance* 40, pp. 71–84.

Omran, Mohammed. 2003. "Privatization, State Ownership, and the Performance of Egyptian Banks." Working paper, Arab Monetary Fund, Abu Dhabi, UAE.

Otchere, Isaac. 2003. "Do Privatized Banks in Middle- and Low-Income Countries Perform Better than Rival Banks? An Intra-Industry Analysis of Bank Privatization." Working paper, University of Melbourne, Australia.

Otchere, Isaac, and J. Chan. 2003. "Intra-Industry Effects of Bank Privatization: A Clinical Analysis of the Privatization of the Commonwealth Bank of Australia." *Journal of Banking and Finance* 27, pp. 949–975.

Perotti, Enrico. 1993. "Bank Lending in Transition Economies." *Journal of Banking and Finance* 17, pp. 1021–1032.

Rajan, Raghuram G., and Luigi Zingales. 1998. "Financial Dependence and Growth." *American Economic Review* 88, pp. 559–586.

Sapienza, Paola. 2004. "The Effects of Government Ownership on Bank Lending." *Journal of Financial Economics* 72, pp. 357–384.

Sappington, David E. M., and Gregory Sidak. 1999. "Incentives for Anticompetitive Behavior by Public Enterprises." Joint AEI–Brookings Center for Regulatory Studies working paper, Washington, DC.

Shirley, Mary, and Patrick Walsh. 2000. "Public vs. Private Ownership: The Current State of the Debate." Working paper, World Bank Group, Washington, DC.

Shleifer, Andrei. 1998. "State versus Private Ownership." *Journal of Economic Perspectives* 12, pp. 133–150.

Shleifer, Andrei, and Robert W. Vishny. 1994. "Politicians and Firms." *Quarterly Journal of Economics* 109, pp. 995–1025.

Snyder, Edward A., and Roger C. Kormendi. 1997. "Privatization and Performance of the Czech Republic's Komercdni Banka." *Journal of Comparative Economics* 25, pp. 97–127.

Stiglitz, Joseph. 1993. "Some Theoretical Aspects of Privatization: Applications to Eastern Europe." In Mario Baldassari, Luigi Paganetto, and Edmund S. Phelps, eds., *Privatization Processes in Eastern Europe.* New York: St. Martin's Press.

Unal, Haluk, and M. Navarro. 1999. "The Technical Process of Bank Privatization in Mexico." *Journal of Financial Services Research* 16, pp. 61–83.

Verbrugge, James A., William L. Megginson, and Wanda L. Owens. 1999. "State Ownership and the Financial Performance of Privatized Banks: An Empirical Analysis." Paper presented at World Bank/Federal Reserve Bank of Dallas Conference on Bank Privatization, Washington, DC, March.

Vickers, John, and George Yarrow. 1988. "Regulation of Privatized Firms in Britain." *European Economic Review* 32, pp. 456–472.

Vickers, John, and George Yarrow. 1991. "Economic Perspectives on Privatization." *Journal of Economic Perspectives* 5, pp. 111–132.

Weintraub, Daniela Baumohl, and Márcio I. Nakane. 2003. "Bank Privatization and Productivity: Evidence for Brazil." Working paper, University of Sao Paulo, Brazil.

Wurgler, Jeffrey. 2000. "Financial Markets and the Allocation of Capital." *Journal of Financial Economics* 58, pp. 187–214.

Chapter 10

The following texts are recommended for further reading: Bortolotti, Fantini, and Siniscalco (1999); Eckel, Eckel, and Singal (1997); Ehrlich, Gallais-Hamonno, Liu, and Lutter (1994); Energy Information Administration (1996); Enright and Ng (2001); International Energy Administration and Organization of Economic Cooperation and Development (2001); Ocana (2003); and Zhang, Parker, and Krikpatrick (2002). Full chapter references are given below.

Arocena, Pablo. 2003. "The Privatisation Programme of the Public Enterprise Sector in Spain." CESifo working paper, Universidad Pública de Navarra, Pamplona, Spain.

Bates, Sally. 1999. "Italy's Treasury Flush with Cash Thanks to Enel." *Privatisation International* (December), pp. 9–12.

Bortolotti, Bernardo, Marcella Fantini, and Domenico Siniscalco. 1999. "Regulation and Privatisation: The Case of Electricity." Working paper, Fondazione ENI-Enrico Mattei (FEEM), Milan, Italy.

Davies, David G. 1971. "The Efficiency of Public versus Private Firms: The Case of Australia's Two Airlines." *Journal of Law and Economics* 14:1, pp. 149–165.

Eckel, Catherine, Doug Eckel, and Vijay Singal. 1997. "Privatization and Efficiency: Industry Effects of the Sale of British Airways." *Journal of Financial Economics* 43, pp. 275–298.

Ehrlich, Isaac, Georges Gallais-Hamonno, Zhiqiang Liu, and Randall Lutter. 1994. "Productivity Growth and Firm Ownership: An Empirical Investigation." *Journal of Political Economy* 102, pp. 1006–1038.

Energy Information Administration. 1996. "Privatization and the Globalization of Energy Markets." U.S. Department of Energy, Washington, DC.

Enright, Michael J., and Flash Ng. 2001. "Airport Privatisation." University of Hong Kong Case HKU149, Hong Kong PRC/SAR.

Estache, Antonio. 2002. "Argentina's 1990s Utilities Privatization: A Cure or a Disease?" Working paper, Free University of Brussels, Belgium.

Green, Richard, and Ingo Vogelsang. 1994. "British Airways: A Turn-Around Anticipating Privatization." Chapter 4 in Matthew Bishop, John Kay, and Colin Mayer, eds., *Privatization and Economic Performance*. Oxford: Oxford University Press, pp. 89–111.

International Energy Administration and Organization of Economic Cooperation and Development. 1999. "Electricity Market Reform: An IEA Handbook." Paris.

International Energy Administration and Organization of Economic Cooperation and Development. 2001. "Electricity Market Reform: Competition in Electricity Markets." Paris.

Jack, Andrew. 2002. "Sale of Russian Oil Group Leaves Questions over Fairness." *Financial Times* (December 19), p. 4.

Lane, David. 1999. "World Record Enel IPO." *Privatisation International* (December), pp. 6–8.

Littlechild, Stephen C. 2001. "Competition and Regulation in the U.K. Electricity Industry (with a Brief Look at California)." *Journal of Applied Corporate Finance* 13, pp. 21–38.

Newbery, David, and Michael G. Pollitt. 1997. "The Restructuring and Privatization of Britain's CEGB—Was It Worth It?" *Journal of Industrial Economics* 45, pp. 269–303.

Ocana, Carlos. 2003. "Regulatory Reform in the Electricity Supply Industry: An Overview." Working paper, International Energy Administration, Paris.

Pombo, Carlos, and Manuel Ramirez. 2001. "Privatization in Colombia: A Plant Performance Analysis." Working paper, Universidad del Rosario, Bogota, Colombia.

Price, Catherine Waddams, and Thomas Weyman-Jones. 1996. "Malmquist Indices of Productivity Change in the UK Gas Industry Before and After Privatization." *Applied Economics* 28, pp. 29–39.

Steiner, F. 2000. "Regulation, Industry Structure and Performance in the Electricity Supply Industry." Working paper, Economics Department, OECD, Paris.

Treat, John Elting, ed. 1994. *Creating High Performance International Petroleum Companies: Dinosaurs Can Fly.* Tulsa, OK: PennWell Publishing.

Zhang, Yin-Fang, David Parker, and Colin Kirkpatrick. 2002. "Electricity Sector Reform in Developing Countries: An Econometric Assessment of the Effects of Privatisation, Competition and Regulation." Working paper, University of Manchester, UK.

Chapter 11

Bennell, Paul. 2003. "Privatization in Sub-Saharan Africa." In David Parker and David Saal, eds., *International Handbook on Privatization.* Cheltenham, UK: Edward Elgar, pp. 310–320.

Birdsall, Nancy, and John Nellis. 2003. "Winners and Losers: Assessing the Distributional Impact of Privatization." *World Development* 31, pp. 1617–1633.

Boardman, Anthony E., Claude Laurin, and Aidan R. Vining. 2003. "Privatization in North America." In David Parker and David Saal, eds., *International Handbook on Privatization.* Cheltenham, UK: Edward Elgar, pp. 129–160.

Chong, Alberto, and Florencio López-de-Silanes. 2002. "Privatization and Labor Force Restructuring around the World." Working paper, Yale University, New Haven, CT.

Galiani, Sebastián, Paul Gertler, and Ernesto Schargrodsky. 2001. "Water for Life: The Impact of the Privatization of Water Services on Child Mortality." Working paper, University of California, Berkeley.

Gupta, Nandin. Forthcoming. "Partial Privatization and Firm Performance." *Journal of Finance.*

Lin, Cyril. 2000. "Corporate Governance of State-Owned Enterprises in China." Working paper, Asian Development Bank, Manila, Philippines.

López-de-Silanes, Florencio, Andrei Shleifer, and Robert W. Vishny. 1997. "Privatization in the United States." *RAND Journal of Economics* 28, pp. 447–471.

Megginson, William L. 2003 "The Economics of Bank Privatization." Working paper, University of Oklahoma, Norman.

Saal, David S., and David Parker. 2003. "The Impact of Privatization and Regulation on the Water and Sewerage Industry in England and Wales." Working paper, Aston University, Birmingham, UK.

Sun, Qian, and Wilson H. S. Tong. 2003. "China's Share Issue Privatization: The Extent of Its Success." *Journal of Financial Economics* 70, pp. 183–222.

United Nations. 2002. *Arab Human Development Report 2002.* New York: Author.

Index